Chicago Public Library

REFERENCE

Form 178 rev. 11-00

encyclopedia of
GENOCIDE *and* CRIMES AGAINST HUMANITY

editorial board

encyclopedia of
GENOCIDE *and* CRIMES AGAINST HUMANITY

Dinah L. Shelton [EDITOR IN CHIEF]

[T–Z • INDEX]

MACMILLAN REFERENCE USA
An imprint of Thomson Gale, a part of The Thomson Corporation

THOMSON

GALE

Detroit • New York • San Francisco • San Diego • New Haven, Conn. • Waterville, Maine • London • Munich

Encyclopedia of Genocide and Crimes Against Humanity
Dinah L. Shelton

Library of Congress Cataloging-in-Publication Data

Encyclopedia of genocide and crimes against humanity
Dinah L. Shelton, editor in chief.
    p. cm.
        Includes bibliographical references and index.
        ISBN 0-02-865847-7 (set hardcover : alk. paper)—
        ISBN 0-02-865848-5 (v. 1 : alk. paper)—ISBN 0-02-865849-3
        (v. 2 : alk. paper)—ISBN 0-02-865850-7 (v. 3 : alk. paper)—
        ISBN 0-02-865992-9 (ebook) 1. Genocide—History—
        Encyclopedias. I. Shelton, Dinah.
HV6322.7.E532 2004
304.66303—dc22   2004006587

This title is also available as an ebook.
ISBN 0-02-865992-9
Contact your Gale sales representative for ordering information.

Printed in the United States of America
10 9 8 7 6 5 4 3

Taino (Arawak) Indians

The Taino, also known as the Arawaks, migrated from the Caribbean coast of South America, moving northward along the island chain of the lesser Antilles to the greater Antilles, around 1200 CE. They were agriculturalists whose basic food crops—corn, manioc, and beans—were supplemented by hunting and fishing. By the time the Europeans first encountered the Taino in 1492, they dominated the islands of Hispaniola, Puerto Rico, most of Cuba, and the Bahamas, but they were coming under pressure from the more warlike Caribs of South America as they too moved northward through the lesser Antilles.

The first expedition of Christopher Columbus brought an initial wave of Old World peoples to the Caribbean. Columbus was impressed by the beauty, peaceful nature, and agricultural techniques of the Taino, and often wrote about the richness and productivity of the land. Chieftains, assisted by elders, ruled the land, and groups were linked loosely by confederations. Columbus frequently boasted of large populations that seemed well off and, surprisingly for the Europeans, to have no money. The Taino were more than willing to exchange their small gold objects or cotton for broken mirrors, knives, or copper bells.

Modern scholars do not know for certain the total population of the Taino when the Europeans arrived, and there is heated debate about these numbers. Nonetheless, it can be said that the population was substantial, with villages containing up to five thousand people, and that almost immediately such numbers began to decline. Within half a century after 1492 the Aborigi-nal population of many of the islands was approaching extinction. According to Miguel de Pasamonte, the Taino of Hispaniola numbered 60,000 in 1508. According to Diego Columbus, there were 33,523 in 1510; four years later the population was reported to be 26,334. The total fell to about 18,000 in 1518 and 1519, and only 2,000 Tainos remained on the island in 1542.

What were the causes of this demographic collapse? Those making a case for genocide cite the vivid descriptions of Dominican friar Bartolomé de las Casas who arrived in the islands in 1502, a decade after Columbus's first voyage. In his *Brevissima Relación* and other writings, he characterizes the Spanish settlers, gold seekers, and warlike conquerors as villains. He, too, had shared in the exploitation of the Taino until his conversion, thanks to a compelling sermon by friar Antonio de Montesinos on Whitsunday of 1512. It influenced him to give up his Indians and dedicate his life to their protection. As an eyewitness, he reported the Spanish to be rapacious, burning captives to secure the source of treasure, and forcing them to travel long distances to work in mines or on settler's estates. They raped the native women and took pleasure in maiming and brutalizing Amerindians with war dogs and instruments of torture. His compelling descriptions were supported by the writings of others, such as the Italian traveler Girolamo Benzoni. These accounts, reinforced by the gory illustrations of Theodore de Bry later in the century, led to the Black Legend, which depicted the Spanish as the scourge of whomever they encountered. But the account of Las Casas was intentionally and successfully exaggerated in order to secure legal protections for Native-American peoples from the Spanish Crown.

In fact, several factors coincided and led to the destruction of Taino society. It is impossible to deny the role of the shock of violent conquest. Columbus's first expedition of three small ships engaged in reconnaissance and trade; within months a large-scale expedition of 17 vessels and 1,500 men—and a handful of women—followed. Some of the men had fought in the wars in Italy and the recent conquest of the kingdom of Granada. They brought warhorses, war dogs, and ample military equipment. The group had been influenced by Columbus's pronouncements on the wealth of the islands, the ease of communication with the Natives, the seemingly friendly nature of the Taino women, and the backward technology of the military.

The Spaniards arrived expecting to find wealth, and they were ready to take it by force if necessary, especially as the Spaniards discovered that no one remained of a handful of men left behind by Columbus; all had fallen to the Taino. If one accepts the statistic that the Taino population of Hispaniola at the time of the Europeans' arrival was approximately a half-million, then the ratio of Spanish males to Taino males was 1:167. The superior military technology of the Europeans more than made up for the difference in numbers. Further, the Spanish utilized brutality in the early stages of conquest to subdue the enemy as quickly as possible. Some of Las Casas's descriptions of brutality during the early months of the encounter were likely accurate. Shock led to submission. But mortality for the Europeans was also very high; more than half did not survive their first year on Hispaniola.

Taino were soon distributed to the settlers in the form of an *encomienda,* an Iberian institution that had been used during the reconquest of the peninsula. Simply put, the settler was given a grant of natives, mostly adult married males, who provided tribute (a head tax) to the *encomendero,* who was then responsible for their conversion and civilization. The Spanish Crown frowned on the direct enslavement of the Indians; Queen Isabella had freed Indians enslaved by Columbus to help defray the costs of his second expedition, arguing that the Indians were her free subjects. The Laws of Burgos (1518) restated the policy against Indian slavery, although exceptions were made for Indians who rebelled, killed missionaries or rejected their efforts, or were cannibals. Although technically not slavery, the early *encomienda* in the Caribbean permitted the Spaniard to use Indian labor, either in mining or the creation of plantations for exports to Europe, especially sugar. The institution led to the abuse and death of tributary workers. Migration, either forced or voluntary,

also contributed to the high rate of mortality, as normal subsistence patterns were disrupted.

The impact of culture shock as a technologically more advanced society comes into contact with a less developed one is hard to measure, but evidence exists that this phenomenon did play a role in the collapse of Taino social groups. Las Casas mentions infanticide, which he claimed mothers committed in order to free their infants from the exploitation of the Spanish. Crops were torn up and burned, with starvation as the consequence, but the destruction of crops may have been intentional, carried out by the local population on purpose to deprive the Spaniards of food. Villages became deserted as their residents fled to the countryside. Men and women, too worn out by forced labor, failed to procreate.

Until recently it was believed that the disappearance of the Taino did not involve Old World disease, so important to the collapse of the Amerindian population elsewhere. But there is new evidence that disease did play a role in the Taino disaster. A wave of disease broke out simultaneously with the arrival of the second Spanish expedition in late 1494. Several observers have suggested the loss of a third to a half of the population within that short period of time. There has been much debate among scholars on which disease triggered the huge loss of life; likely candidates have been typhus, which was present with the fall of Granada and the Italian campaigns, or swine flu, similar to the epidemic that occurred at the end of World War I. More recently smallpox has been suggested. Certainly, the smallpox pandemic of 1518 killed most of the remaining Taino on the islands before it spread to the mainland.

Slaving expeditions during the early years of the colony were undertaken to resupply the island's labor force as the Taino population declined. The brunt of slaving fell early on nearby islands, especially the Bahamas. Mortality for enslaved Indians seems exceptionally high. Slaves purchased in the Old World, largely of African origin and transported to the Carribean, ultimately solved the labor problem for European settlers in the lands of the Taino. The legality of slavery was not questioned because it had been practiced in the Mediterranean region for centuries. The long-term demographic consequence for the Caribbean islands was a population of largely European or African origin, or a mixture thereof, with little remnants of the original Aboriginal population, although the significant cultural legacies of the Taino persist.

SEE ALSO Indigenous Peoples; Native Americans

BIBLIOGRAPHY

Alchon, Susan Austin (2003). *A Pest in the Land: New World Epidemics in a Global Perspective*. Albuquerque: University of New Mexico Press.

Cook, Noble David (1998). *Born to Die: Disease and New World Conquest, 1492–1650*. Cambridge: Cambridge University Press.

Rouse, Irving (1992). *The Tainos, Rise and Decline of the People Who Greeted Columbus*. New Haven, Conn.: Yale University Press.

Watts, David (1987). *The West Indies: Patterns of Development, Culture and Environmental Change since 1492*. Cambridge: Cambridge University Press.

Noble David Cook

Talaat

[SEPTEMBER 1874–MARCH 15, 1921]
Turkish political leader

As its principal author, Turkish leader Mehmet Talaat played a decisive role in the decision-making, organization, and implementation of the World War I Armenian genocide. His authority and power to act derived from a dual-track position: He was minister of the interior and, perhaps more importantly, he was the supreme boss of the ruling Committee of Union and Progress Party (CUP). In July 1908 the leaders of this revolutionary Young Turk movement successfully overthrew the despotic reign of Sultan Abdulhamit (1876–1908) in the name of a new constitutional regime. The spokespersons of this movement claimed to be guided by the ideals of the French Revolution—namely, freedom, equality, and brotherhood. Except for a brief six-month period in 1912, CUP remained in near-total control of a succession of Ottoman Turkish governments in the years between 1908 and 1918.

Such control was made possible, however, through Talaat's exceptional skills in political organization and party formation. Due to his innate qualities of leadership, CUP quickly gained inordinate strength not only in Istanbul, then the Ottoman capital, but, more importantly, in the empire's Asiatic provinces, where the bulk of the empire's Armenian population lived as an indigenous population. Parallel to this growing strength, CUP increasingly became dictatorial and monolithic in pursuit of a xenophobic nationalism. This ideological push aimed at rescuing and preserving the tottering empire by way of discarding a languishing ideology of a multiethnic and hence inclusive Ottomanism and replacing it by an exclusive Turkism. The targeting and forcible elimination of the Armenians had thus become a byproduct of this new militant ideology.

To accomplish this task, Talaat decided to rely on CUP's clandestine and highly secretive mechanisms that he himself had created and fostered. As Talaat's principal biographer, Tevfik Çavdar noted, CUP had a two-tiered structure "just like an iceberg" (Çavdar, 1984, p. 190). Talaat used the submerged invisible parts for "illegal" acts in order to carry out CUP's covert and lethal objectives, which included mass murder. World War I afforded an invaluable opportunity in this respect. Accordingly, as revealed by Talaat himself, Parliament was temporarily suspended, martial law was declared, and certain constitutional rights were deferred. As a prelude to the impending genocide, the targeted Armenians were thereby stripped of their most basic human rights.

Alerted to the situation, on May 24, 1915, when the Armenian genocide was being initiated, the Allies publicly and formally pledged to hold "personally responsible" all the Turkish officials who were implicated in these "new crimes against humanity" (Dadrian, 1989, p. 962). Similar references to crimes of Turkey against humanity in the postwar period were made in the Ottoman Parliament and in some of the verdicts issued by the Turkish Military Tribunal. Prosecuting the authors of the Armenian genocide, that tribunal condemned Talaat, along with some other top CUP leaders, including Ismail Enver (Turkish Minister of War in the Ottoman Empire during World War I), to death in absentia.

Talaat's paramount role in the organization of the Armenian genocide was confirmed during the trial of a young Armenian who had assassinated him in Berlin, where Talaat had taken refuge under the fictitious name Sai. A German jury acquitted the assassin on grounds of temporary insanity brought on by a vision of his murdered mother. Given Germany's wartime military and political alliance with Turkey, this verdict was as surprising as it was educational. The general public learned with horror the gruesome details of a centrally organized mass murder orchestrated by Talaat himself, whose image was transformed from victim to arch villain.

SEE ALSO Armenians in Ottoman Turkey and the Armenian Genocide; Atatürk, Mustafa Kemal Pasha; Enver, Ismail

BIBLIOGRAPHY

Çavdar, Tevfik (1984). *Talât Paşa: Bir Örgüt Ustasinin Yaşam Öyküsü* (Talât Pasha: The Life Story of a Master Organizer). Ankara, Turkey: Dost Publishers.

Dadrian, Vahakn (1986). "The Naim-Andonian Documents on the World War I Destruction of Ottoman Armenians: The Anatomy of a Genocide." *International Journal of Middle East Studies* 18:326–328.

Dadrian, Vahakn (1989). "Genocide as a Problem of National and International Law: The World War I

Armenian Case and its Contemporary Legal Ramifications." *Yale Journal of International Law* 14:221–334.

Montgomery, R. G. (1921). "Why Talaat's Assassin Was Acquitted." *Current History Magazine* (July 5):551–555.

Vahakn N. Dadrian

Television

Limited news coverage of major genocides and crimes against humanity prior to the second half of the twentieth century allowed those events to continue outside the glare of public scrutiny that has become possible. The advent of modern television news networks allows for rapid, even instantaneous visual reporting of international crises. Television news coverage of genocide and crimes against humanity can thus inform and shape world opinion, eliciting responses to such atrocities.

The CNN Effect

Television news coverage plays a critical role in ensuring that the global public is informed about international events. It is, in fact, the preferred means by which the majority of the Western public receives its news. The existence of Cable News Network (CNN) and other global television news networks dedicated to instantaneous coverage means that concerned nongovernmental groups and the public at large are often exposed to international news events at the same time as governments. This exposure to international news allows the public to formulate opinions and influence government policy. The broad international reach and the speed of modern television news coverage thereby create pressure on governments to respond quickly to international crises. This phenomenon whereby aggressive television news coverage of live events indirectly shapes the course of those events is known as the CNN Effect or the CNN Factor.

Television news coverage of genocide and crimes against humanity has the potential to limit the extent and severity of those incidents by motivating timely action and resource allocation by governments and nongovernmental groups like relief agencies. Such coverage may even help to prevent future occurrences; an informed public can encourage governments to monitor potential international crises and take preventative action when necessary.

Factors in Television Reporting

The television news media is also a business, and as such is limited by practical considerations. News stories themselves are limited in scope; in a given news segment, each story tends to last no more than one to three minutes. Likewise, the news media's attention to any one event is limited in duration, with sustained coverage rarely lasting longer than a period of a few weeks. The television news media generally only cover one such major event at a time, meaning that while one important international crisis may get the attention it deserves, other crises may go under- or unreported. Moreover, the complicated logistics of reporting from remote, undeveloped locations make certain events of humanitarian concern inaccessible to the media and therefore unavailable to the public.

Profit considerations similarly influence news coverage. The television news media tend to seek out sensational stories—which are most often highly negative—because those stories gather viewers. The global public has demonstrated a tendency toward voyeurism; that is, the public is more interested in seeing exceptional, negative news than in seeing ordinary and/or positive news.

Distortion and Manipulation

The television news media's proclivity to report the sensational can lead the public in developed countries to harbor incomplete and erroneous opinions about the developing world. These misconceptions can lead to frustration and a belief that the situations in the developing world are hopeless and beyond the reach of international aid or intervention. Thus, just as the television media may promote action by news coverage of international crises, the prolonged focus on such negative events may eventually lead to a decline in timely response—or any response—to similar occurrences. This phenomenon is commonly known as "compassion fatigue."

In addition to the editorial and practical decisions made at the studio and executive news media levels, decisions made by reporters in the field may also influence the global public's knowledge of humanitarian crises. For example, the television news media may often provide the global public with unintentional but ignorant misinformation. Coverage of crisis events may be based primarily upon secondary rather than primary accounts of the situation, and the coverage may lack a basic foundation or recognition of the history and context of the situation, thus likely misinforming the public about those events.

Similarly, television reporting of international crises can distort the public's perception of the crises through the camera eye itself. That is, the way a camera shot is framed or angled, in addition to the editing of shots after they are taken, can misrepresent reality. For example, a camera may portray a shot of a well-armed soldier looming in the foreground over the dead body

[JOURNALISTS AND NEWS REPORTS IN THE INTERNATIONAL CRIMINAL PROCESS]

Journalists are often some of the few nonparticipant, neutral observers in situations of genocide and crimes against humanity and are, therefore, in a unique position to impartially record and report those events. Reporters are by nature, though, also witnesses to events they observe. National and international criminal systems have come to recognize this second nature of journalists; journalists are allowed to present to courts information about what they have observed, and may even be compelled by the courts to testify if their knowledge is of critical importance.

Article 15 of the Rome Statute of the International Criminal Court (ICC) allows the prosecutor of the Court to initiate investigations based on information about "crimes within the jurisdiction of the Court"—which include genocide and crimes against humanity—and to pursue "reliable sources" of information about those crimes during the investigations. At the International Criminal Tribunal for the Former Yugoslavia (ICTY), where the prosecutor's investigative powers are essentially the same, journalists have played a significant role in providing information about genocide and crimes against humanity at both the initiation and investigation stages of the criminal process. Furthermore, numerous journalists who reported on the crisis in the former Yugoslavia have voluntarily testified at trials of accused perpetrators.

The ICTY has held that reporters with vital information about genocide or crimes against humanity may even be compelled under certain narrow circumstances to testify regarding their knowledge of those criminal acts. That decision is highly unpopular, however, as journalists and news organizations argue that compelling such testimony harms the perception of those reporters as impartial, and may even endanger them. Should the issue arise in the ICC, however, that court is likely to follow the ICTY's precedent, which engages journalists in the international criminal process beyond their voluntary participation.

Under the Statutes and Rules of the ICC and ICTY, the prosecutor can presumably initiate an investigation based solely on news reports of genocide or crimes against humanity. News reports can be used as information during investigations as well. There is no rule or precedent determining whether reports about genocide and crimes against humanity are admissible as trial evidence standing alone (i.e., without testimony from the journalist who made the report that it is a truthful account of events). The trial courts at the ICTY and ICC must decide news report admissibility on a case-by-case basis under their respective rules of evidence.

In sum, television reports and reporters help record evidence of criminal offenses like genocide and crimes against humanity. That evidence can be used to help bring perpetrators of such atrocities to justice.

---

of a child. What the camera eye may not show is that in reality the soldier is standing fearful, surrounded by a large and angry mob of armed youths. The reaction of the public to crisis situations can thus be significantly affected by the distorted picture of reality that the media may intentionally or unintentionally present.

Furthermore, television can also be manipulated in closed societies to intentionally misinform the public. Governments can use the television news media to disseminate propaganda, encourage stereotypes, and incite hatred and violence against certain religious, ethnic, or political groups (just as radio was used during the genocide in Rwanda in 1994).

Television news coverage of genocide and crimes against humanity may also affect victims of the events. If journalists are not sensitive to the trauma of victims, and are instead imprudent in their investigation and reporting, victims may easily be re-traumatized. On the other hand, thoughtful inquiry and reporting may be quite valuable: Victims often welcome a chance to tell their stories and explain what happened to them; in doing so, the public learns more about the effects of genocide and crimes against humanity on individuals and groups directly affected by those events.

The television news media can be a powerful force in informing and shaping world opinion, and in eliciting responses to international humanitarian crises. While the importance of the CNN effect cannot be understated, the global public should be aware of the limitations that do exist in television news media coverage. By recognizing the practical and editorial decisions behind the images on the TV screen—and by seeking knowledge of international crisis situations through additional sources—the global public will have a fuller, more accurate opinion of world events. Such a better informed public will be more capable of encouraging appropriate and timely responses to threats of genocide or crimes against humanity.

SEE ALSO Film as Propaganda; Films, Dramatizations in; Films, Holocaust

Documentary; Photography of Victims; Propaganda; Radio

BIBLIOGRAPHY

Adelman, Howard, and Astri Suhrke, eds. (1999). *The Path of a Genocide: The Rwanda Crisis from Uganda to Zaire.* Rutgers, N.J.: Transaction Books.

Gradney, Jeff (2000). "Focusing on the Humanity." In *Covering Violence: A Guide to Ethical Reporting about Victims and Trauma,* ed. William E. Coté and Roger Simpson. New York: Columbia University Press.

McLaughlin, Greg (2002). *War Correspondent.* London: Pluto Press.

Minear, Larry, Colin Scott, and Thomas G. Weiss (1996). *The News Media, Civil War, and Humanitarian Action.* Boulder, Colo.: L. Rienner.

Newman, Edward (1995). "Realpolitk and the CNN Factor of Humanitarian Intervention." In *The United Nations in the New World Order: The World Organization at Fifty,* ed. Dimitris Bourantonis and Jarrod Weiner. New York: St. Martin's Press.

"*Prosecutor v. Radoslav Brdjanin and Momir Talic*: Decision on Motion to Set Aside Confidential Subpoena to Give Evidence." June 7, 2002. In the International Criminal Tribunal for the Former Yugoslavia website. Available from http://www.un.org/icty/brdjanin/trialc/decision-e/t020612.htm.

"Rome Statute of the International Criminal Court." International Criminal Court website. Available from http://www.icc-cpi.int/library/basicdocuments/rome_statute(e).pdf.

Rotberg, Robert I., and Thomas G. Weiss, eds. (1996). *From Massacres to Genocide: The Media, Public Policy, and Humanitarian Crises.* Cambridge, Mass.: The World Peace Foundation.

Seib, Philip (2002). *The Global Journalist: News and Conscience in a World of Conflict.* Oxford, U.K.: Rowman & Littlefield.

Shaw, Martin (1996). *Civil Society and Media in Global Crises: Representing Distant Violence.* New York: Pinter.

Kelly Helen Fry

Terrorism, Psychology behind

Research concerning the psychology of terrorism has focused primarily in two directions. First, psychology has examined the impact of terrorism on survivors and victims as well as the population under threat. Second, it has studied the psychology behind perpetrators of terrorism. In other words, psychologists have examined the question of what enables an individual or group to commit acts of large scale property destruction and/or mass murder that may even result in the terrorist's own death for political ends.

Perpetrators

Terrorists often are portrayed as the personification of evil, or as possessing some underlying measure of ex-treme psychopathology. Such a characterization may enable individuals to feel safer, for they may believe that if the targeted perpetrator is eliminated, the threat of terrorism will disappear. Unfortunately, this is not an accurate perception.

There are a myriad of reasons behind the motivations of terrorists, ranging from self-interest and fanaticism to group social influences. Leaders, while unlikely to commit acts of terrorism themselves, are most often motivated by self-interest or fanatical belief systems. Self-interested leaders may be motivated by a desire for power, recognition, money, land, or other self-directed goal. Thus, the use of terrorism may serve as more of a means to these self-serving ends than as an effort to achieve the espoused goal for their people or group. Ironically, many such leaders will work to create barriers to the expressed goal for their people, as the attainment of the goal would lead to an end of their leadership role within the terrorist organization. Thus, for example, terrorist attacks may increase prior to any movement towards resolution of a conflict or peace, because such a resolution would not be in the self-interest of the terrorist group's leadership.

Fanatics or true believers are particularly dangerous, in that they may perceive their terrorist actions as a means for achieving a greater good. This results in a reversal of morality, whereby the taking of innocent lives may come to be viewed as righteous action to be rewarded both in the present and after one's death. Certainly, the pairing of religion and hate is an extremely destructive combination. Religious validation of hate and social inequity only serves to fuel enmity. One of the most effective ways to maintain hate and social inequities is to cite religious doctrine. In fact, leaders may selectively use religious doctrine or scripture to dictate that other religious groups be held as inferior, thereby promoting the formation of intra-religious hatred and the potential for terrorism.

While leaders are necessary for the coordinated survival of a terrorist organization, the continuation of such a group may depend less on the specific, idiosyncratic leader than on the simple presence of someone in a leadership position who has learned basic group dynamics. The most effective terrorist leaders are in tune to the needs and abilities of their followers and can therefore maximize their manipulation of the group towards the overall goals of the terrorist organization. Most terrorist attacks are committed by followers who are otherwise very ordinary people. Unfortunately, they have been made to feel needed, valued, and efficacious by their involvement in the terrorist organization, and this leads them to develop a high level of loyalty to both the leader and the group.

encyclopedia of GENOCIDE *and* CRIMES AGAINST HUMANITY

Robert Lifton argues that one of the features of highly destructive groups is totalism, which extends beyond an "us-them" dichotomy to an "us against them" philosophy. This belief system, taken to the extreme in terrorist and other destructive groups, pushes individuals to separate from all who are not associated with the group. This isolation of group members from those not associated with the group leads to Lifton's second feature of highly destructive groups— environmental control. Through environmental control, leaders can manipulate the majority of what is seen, heard, or experienced by the group and the "purity" of the information to which the group is exposed.

Group dynamics within a terrorist organization can further entrench individual hatred and greatly increase the likelihood of violence. For example, the organizational structure of most terrorist groups is quasimilitary and necessitates conformity to the group ideal. There are often very severe penalties for not conforming, ranging from ostracism and verbal aggression to physical violence. Thus, group members may initially feel pressure to engage in hatred and violence, knowing only too well the ramifications of nonconformance. Later, after engaging in such acts, cognitive dissonance—the internal pressure to achieve consistency between our thoughts and actions—necessitates that members either internalize a rationale for their hatred of the "other" or leave the terrorist organization. The pressure to internalize the group's ideology becomes even more salient upon the introduction of a powerful authority figure or leader. Eventually, the adage of "in for a penny, in for a pound" applies, as terrorist recruits are subjected to increasing levels of commitment, are pressured to conform, and are driven to obey their leaders. In an attempt to avoid cognitive dissonance, recruits become increasing committed to the terrorist organization's ideology and activities, increasingly identify themselves solely as a terrorist group member, and become increasingly loyal to those in positions of authority.

Terrorist organizations also tend to foster a sense of anonymity or de-individuation among members. By stripping individuals of their identities through increased anonymity, de-individuation causes people to become less self-aware, feel less responsible for their actions, and become more likely to engage in violence if placed in a provocative situation. The quasi-military structure of many terrorist organizations, with their uniforms and clearly identifiable proscribed rules for behavior, facilitates the processes of de-individuation, conformity, diffusion of responsibility, and ultimately violence if the terrorist group leadership dictates such behavior.

March 11, 2004: A series of coordinated terrorist bombings rocked Madrid's commuter train system days before Spain's national election. On their way to work that morning, more than 1,800 people were wounded; 191 died. [GUILLERMO NAVARRO/ COVER/CORBIS]

Finally, to facilitate movement along a path of escalating enmity and potential violence, terrorist group leaders promote increasing levels of dehumanization. The process of dehumanization begins with the increased promotion of stereotypes and negative images of the target of their enmity. This is often a necessary tool, used to reduce the cognitive dissonance that may occur when individuals behave negatively towards other human beings. Propaganda is another vital tool used by the terrorist group leadership to stigmatize and dehumanize the "other," as well as to present the target of hate as an imminent threat. Therefore, the terrorist group members may come to believe that their family, friends, and communities existence is dependent on the destruction of the "other."

Concomitant with dehumanization is the process of moral exclusion. Over time, terrorist group members begin to view the "other" as a threat and begin to morally disengage. In other words, certain moral principles that exist within the terrorist's own group no longer pertain to those outside of the group. Thus, terrorist acts, including the killing of other human beings, become morally acceptable, as the "enemy" no longer is included in the terrorist's sphere of morality.

Survivors, Victims, and Restorative Justice

Survivors and victims of terrorism face a myriad of psychological reactions in response to a terrorist attack. These reactions can range from an acute stress reaction to a long-term cluster of symptoms associated with post-traumatic stress disorder and possible accompanying depression. The closer an individual is to a terrorist attack, the greater the likelihood they will experience either short- or long-term psychological effects. The greatest psychological trauma will occur in those individuals who personally experience a direct threat of death or serious injury, or who witnessed the death or serious injury of another and who also felt horror, fear, and intense helplessness in response to the situation.

It is normal for individuals who experience a terrorist attack either directly or indirectly to respond with emotions such as intense grief, anger, detachment, confusion, numbing, and disorientation. Individuals who continue to have such strong emotional and cognitive reactions for more than two days with accompanying recurrent thoughts, flashbacks, and nightmares about the event may be experiencing acute stress disorder. A diagnosis of acute stress disorder is most likely if the individual's functioning on a day-to-day basis is significantly impaired and there is marked evidence of anxiety symptoms.

Most individuals will recover from the trauma associated with terrorism within a relatively short period of time. However for some individuals, particularly those most directly impacted by the event, the symptoms associated with acute stress may extend beyond three months. If the symptoms persist and continue to impair daily functioning, cognitive processing, or relationships, then the person may be experiencing post-traumatic stress disorder and need additional treatment. Symptoms of post-traumatic stress disorder typically include emotional numbing, detachment from others, hypervigilance, anxiety, depression, and intrusion of memories related to the terrorist attack into the individual's daily life or dreams. Additionally, the individual will work to avoid cues reminiscent of the attack and may experience extreme panic, fear, or aggression if confronted directly with sudden reminders or recollections of the terrorist attack.

On a broader societal level, terrorist attacks create an immediate crisis for individuals, groups, and communities directly impacted by the attack. Crisis can be very destabilizing and often results in threats to the individual, such as loss of group pride, an escalation of fear, frustration of needs and wants, and confusion regarding personal identity. In addition, crisis usually leads to an increase in prejudice. Following the terrorist attacks of September 11, 2001, a time experienced by most in the United States as crisis, prejudice and hate crimes spiked. For example, anti-Arab hate crimes increased, attacks on Asian-Americans, particularly immigrants, increased dramatically, and anti-Semitism spiked from 12 to 17 percent. Crisis can also draw individuals to a wide variety of organizations such as religious groups, political groups, and cults, as well as hate groups. Unfortunately, groups with destructive agendas and ideologies built on hate may provide the shortest route to an individual's sense of perceived stability through mechanisms such as scapegoating, just-world-thinking (the belief that people get what they deserve), ingroup-outgroup polarization, hedonic balancing (denigration of the "other" as a means to one's self-esteem), and other processes. It is also important to remember that there may be incredible pressure on leaders to acquiesce to demands of terrorism, as crisis and the constant threat of additional terrorist attacks further destabilizes a culture. It is therefore imperative that leaders and constructive organizations within a culture impacted by terrorism work constructively to bring an end to terrorism, work together to heal the trauma associated with terrorism, and work towards restorative justice.

From a psychological perspective, there are three predominant responses towards ending terrorism: reform, deterrence, and backlash. Reform means addressing the concerns of those who are in situations that may lead them to perceive that desperate measures are the only possible solution to their problems. If their problems are realistically addressed, the urge to take terrorist action may be reduced. Second is backlash. Terrorists often hope that these desperate measures will raise awareness of their concerns and support for their cause. In this instance, terrorism and the media operate within the context of a symbiotic relationship. Backlash occurs when the target audience is appalled, offended, and outraged by the terrorist act as opposed to being drawn in and sympathetic. And, finally, there is deterrence. Essentially, deterrence involves the threat of retaliatory action in response to attacks. Such retaliation can range from sanctions to targeted military attacks. Of all the methods discussed above, deterrence in the absence of the other methods is the least effective.

Both deterrence and restorative justice are difficult to achieve, due to the differences in psychological perceptions between victims and perpetrators of any form

The South Tower of the World Trade Center explodes into flames after being hit by hijacked United Airlines Flight 175. The North Tower smolders following a similar attack some 17 minutes earlier. When both buildings, symbols of U.S. corporate might, collapsed to the ground on September 11, more than 2,000 people had perished. [REUTERS/CORBIS]

of harm or attack. First, a difference in perception of harm exists between victims and perpetrators. Victims perceive the extent of the harm as greater than the perpetrator does, and victims tend to view all actions on the part of the perpetrator, including those resulting in accidental outcomes, as being intentional. In addition, victims feel the reverberations of the harm extending over a much longer period of time, including intergenerationally. Ironically, perpetrators tend to perceive themselves as victims in a reversal of morality. Because of these differences in perception, victims' retaliatory responses tend to be viewed as out of proportion by the original perpetrators, thus enhancing the perpetrators perception that they are in fact being victimized. This may result in further aggression, including terrorist attacks directed towards the original victims, and may unfortunately escalate the cycle of violence. For groups to move beyond this pattern or achieve at least a cessation of violence, each group must come together to understand the partisan perceptions of the "other." This, of course, does not excuse the actions taken by terrorists, but rather explains psychologically why retaliatory responses to terrorism may in fact serve to escalate the danger of future terrorist attacks. Ultimately, each group must work to understand the perceptions of the other and acknowledge the harm caused by all involved so as to move towards restorative justice.

SEE ALSO Perpetrators; Victims

BIBLIOGRAPHY

De Jong, Joop, ed. (2002). *Trauma, War, and Violence: Public Mental Health In Socio-Cultural Context*. New York: Kluwer Academic.

Lifton, Robert J. (1989). *Thought Reform and the Psychology of Totalism*. Chapel Hill: University of North Carolina Press.

Pyszczynski, Thomas A., Sheldon Solomon, and Jeff Greenberg (2002). *In The Wake of 9/11: The Psychology of Terror*. Washington, D.C.: American Psychological Association.

Staub, Ervin (1989). *The Roots of Evil: The Origins of Genocide and Other Group Violence*. New York: Cambridge University Press.

Stout, Chris E., ed. (2002). *The Psychology Of Terrorism*. Westport, Conn.: Praeger.

Woolf, Linda M., and Michael R. Hulsizer (2002/2003). "Intra- and Inter- Religious Hate and Violence: A Psychosocial Model." *Journal of Hate Studies* 2:5–26.

Linda M. Woolf

Tibet

Tibet has been an independent country throughout the historical period and since time immemorial according to Tibetans' own myth-based sense of national identity. That independence is supported by the country's geography, history, language, culture, religion, and race.

Tibet's Rich Culture
Geographically, the Tibetan high plateau is a distinctively demarcated region, with boundaries starting at approximately the 10,000-feet altitude line. It can be clearly perceived on any relief map.

Historically, Tibetan dynasties often conflicted with Chinese dynasties. The Tibetan Yarlung dynasty (which ruled during the sixth through ninth centuries) conquered the Chinese T'ang dynasty (seventh through tenth centuries) for most of the eighth century. No indigenous Chinese dynasty ever conquered Tibet, though the Mongol Empire (thirteenth through fourteenth centuries) and the Manchu Empire (seventeenth through twentieth centuries) incorporated both China and Tibet under their imperial hegemony. The British Empire invaded Tibet and imposed a trade treaty on it, doing the same with China. However, none of these three empires made any attempt to homogenize China and Tibet into a single national entity, or to colonize Tibet with Mongolian, Manchu, British, or surrogate subject Chinese settlers. Except for a few border regions in the Far East, there was almost no Chinese population in high plateau Tibet until the People's Republic of China (PRC) invasion between 1949 and 1951.

Linguistically, the Tibetan language differs from the Chinese. Tibetan is written in an alphabetic system with noun declension and verb conjugation inflections based on Indic languages, as opposed to an ideographic character system. Formerly, Tibetan was considered a member of the "Tibeto-Burman" language group, a subgroup assimilated into a "Sino-Tibetan" language family. Chinese speakers cannot understand spoken Tibetan, and Tibetan speakers cannot understand Chinese, nor can they read each other's street signs, newspapers, or other texts.

Culturally, Chinese people tend not to know the myths, religious symbols, or history of Tibet, nor do Tibetans tend to know those of the Chinese. For example, few Tibetans know the name of any of the Chinese dynasties, nor have they heard of philosophers Confucius or Lao-tzu, and fewer Chinese know of the Yarlung dynasty, or have ever heard of Songzen Gampo (emperor who first imported Buddhism, seventh century), Padma Sambhava (eighth century religious leader), or Tsong Khapa (philosopher 1357–1419). Tibetan and Chinese clothing styles, food habits, family customs, household rituals, and folk beliefs are utterly distinct. The Chinese people traditionally did not herd animals and did not include milk or other dairy products in their diets; in fact, the Chinese people are the only large civilization on the earth that was not based on a symbiosis of upland herding people and lowland agriculturalists. Hence they were the only culture to create a defensive structure, the "Great Wall" in order to keep themselves separate from upland herding peoples such as Tibetans, Turks, and Mongolians.

Religiously, Buddhism is common to both Tibetan and Chinese cultures, being the main religion in Tibet and one of the three main religions in China. However, the main Chinese forms of Buddhism are quite different from the Tibetan forms (widely considered by Chinese Buddhists as an outlandish form of Buddhism they call "Lamaism," or *Lama jiao* in Chinese). Only in the twentieth century, among overseas Chinese and underground on the mainland, has interest arisen among Chinese in the spiritual leader known as the Dalai Lama and Tibetan Buddhist teachings and rituals.

Racially or ethnically, while there is some resemblance in facial features and other physical characteristics among some eastern Tibetan and Chinese individuals, most Chinese and Tibetans are easily distinguishable on sight, and generally do not perceive each other upon meeting as racially or ethnically the same. The Tibetan acclimatization over many centuries to an altitude of two miles or higher has created a pronounced internal physical difference, as Chinese individuals do not acclimatize easily to Tibet, and long years of exposure to the altitude tends to produce various lung disabilities among Chinese settlers. Chinese mothers in wealthy families that settle in Tibet prefer to give birth to their babies in hospitals in neighboring, low-altitude cities such as Hsining or Chengdu.

Chinese Invasion and Dominance
In 1949 the People's Republic of China began invading, occupying, and colonizing Tibet. China entered into

Buddhist monks await the recitation of the Kalachakra Readings by the 14th Dalai Lama, Tenzin Gyatso, in Sarnath, India. Gyatso fled Tibet in 1959 when China's mounting oppression of indigenous groups threatened his safety; he was awarded the Nobel Peace Prize in 1989 for his nonviolent efforts to end Chinese rule there. [ALISON WRIGHT/CORBIS]

Tibet immediately after the communist victory over the Chinese Nationalists, imposed a treaty of "liberation" on the Tibetans, militarily occupied Tibet's territory, and divided that territory into twelve administrative units. It forcibly repressed Tibetan resistance between 1956 and 1959 and annexed Tibet in 1965. Since then it has engaged in massive colonization of all parts of Tibet. For its part, China claims that Tibet has always been a part of China, that a Tibetan person is a type of Chinese person, and that, therefore, all of the above is an internal affair of the Chinese people. The Chinese government has thus sought to overcome the geographical difference with industrial technology, erase and rewrite Tibet's history, destroy Tibet's language, suppress the culture, eradicate the religion (a priority of communist ideology in general), and replace the Tibetan people with Chinese people.

In China itself, communist leader Mao Zedong's policies caused the death of as many as 60 million Chinese people by war, famine, class struggle, and forced labor in thought-reform labor camps. As many as 1.2 million deaths in Tibet resulted from the same policies,

as well as lethal agricultural mismanagement, collectivization, class struggle, cultural destruction, and forced sterilization. However, in the case of Tibet, the special long-term imperative of attempting to remove evidence against and provide justification for the Chinese claim of long-term ownership of the land, its resources, and its people gave these policies an additional edge.

The process of the Chinese takeover since 1949 unfolded in several stages. The first phase of invasion by military force, from 1949 to 1951, led to the imposition of a seventeen-point agreement for the liberation of Tibet and the military takeover of Lhasa. Second, the Chinese military rulers pretended to show support for the existing "local" Tibetan government and culture, from 1951 through 1959, but with gradual infiltration of greater numbers of troops and communist cadres into Tibet. A third phase from 1959 involved violent suppression of government and culture, mass arrests, and formation of a vast network of labor camps, with outright annexation of the whole country from 1959 through 1966. Fourth, violent cultural revolution, from 1966 through 1976, destroyed the remaining monasteries and monuments, killed those resisting the destruction of the "four olds," and sought to eradicate all traces of Tibetan Buddhist culture. A fifth phase of temporary liberalization under Hu Yao Bang was quickly reversed by Chinese leader Deng Xiaoping and led to a mass influx of settlers beginning in the early 1980s. Martial law and renewed suppression took place between 1987 and 1993, with intensified population transfer of Chinese settlers. Finally, from 1993, direct orders of the aging Chinese leadership placed Tibet under the control of an aggressive administrator named Chen Kuei Yuan. Chen proclaimed that the Tibetan identity had to be eradicated in order for remaining Tibetans to develop a Chinese identity. Since Tibetan identity was tied up with Tibetan Buddhism, Tibetan Buddhist culture was in itself seditious, or "splittist," as the Chinese call it.

Chen also was able to use China's growing economic power to invest heavily in internal projects in Tibet, bring in millions more colonists, and he extracted unprecedented amounts of timber, herbs, and minerals from the land. He also toughened up the policies of the People's Liberation Army and the Public Security Bureau.

In 1960 the nongovernmental International Commission of Jurists (ICJ) gave a report titled *Tibet and the Chinese People's Republic* to the United Nations. The report was prepared by the ICJ's Legal Inquiry Committee, composed of eleven international lawyers from around the world. This report accused the Chinese of the crime of genocide in Tibet, after nine years of full occupation, six years before the devastation of the cultural revolution began. The Commission was careful to state that the "genocide" was directed against the Tibetans as a religious group, rather than a racial, "ethnical," or national group.

The report's conclusions reflect the uncertainty felt at that time about Tibetans being a distinct race, ethnicity, or nation. The Commission did state that it considered Tibet a de facto independent state at least from 1913 until 1950. However, the Chinese themselves perceive the Tibetans in terms of race, ethnicity, and even nation. In the Chinese constitution, "national minorities" have certain protections on paper, and smaller minorities living in areas where ethnic Chinese constitute the vast majority of the population receive some of these protections.

In the 2000s, many view the Chinese genocide in Tibet as the result of the territorial ambitions of the PRC leadership. It is seen as stemming from their systematic attempt to expand the traditional territory of China by annexing permanently the vast, approximately 900,000-square-mile territory of traditional Tibet. Tibet represents about 30 percent of China's land surface, while the Tibetans represent .004 percent of China's population. Tibetans were not a minority but an absolute majority in their own historical environment. Chinese government efforts can be seen as aiming at securing permanent control of the Tibetans' land. For this reason, some observers see genocide in Tibet as not merely referring to the matter of religion, that is, of destroying Tibetan Buddhism. Chinese policies have involved the extermination of more than 1 million Tibetans, the forced relocation of millions of Tibetan villagers and nomads, the population transfer of millions of Chinese settlers, and systematic assimilation.

The Dalai Lama

A Tibetan government in exile exists under the leadership of the Dalai Lama in India and Nepal. During the cold war years, the Dalai Lama avoided politics, but tried to work with the Chinese occupiers from 1951 until 1959. He left Tibet to bring the Tibetan genocide to the world's attention. In the early 1980s, he tried to negotiate with Deng Xiaoping and succeeded in sending several fact-finding missions to Tibet. In the meantime, the exile government has worked to preserve the seeds of Tibetan culture and society.

In 1989 the Dalai Lama received the Nobel Peace Prize for his travels around the world to spread the Buddhist message of peace and reconciliation. He has informed the general public of many countries about the Tibetan struggle. His overall policy of nonviolence has been followed by most Tibetans. Despite the historical record, the Dalai Lama calls for dialogue and reconciliation. He has publicly offered to Beijing to lead a plebiscite and campaign to persuade his people to join the Chinese union in a voluntary and legal manner, under a "one country, two systems" formula, as in the cases of Hong Kong and Macao under the following circumstances: (1) all the high-plateau provinces are reunited in a natural Tibet Autonomous Region; (2) Tibet is allowed to govern itself democratically with true autonomy over internal matters; (3) Tibet is demilitarized except for essential border garrisons; and (4) the environment is respected and economic development controlled by the Tibetans themselves.

There were renewed discussions over Tibet starting in 2002 and several delegations made visits to the region.

SEE ALSO China; Mao Zedong; Religion

BIBLIOGRAPHY

Avedon, John (1986). *In Exile from the Land of Snows*. New York: Vintage Books.

International Commission of Jurists (1960). *Tibet and the Chinese People's Republic: A Report to the International*

Commission of Jurists by its Legal Inquiry Committee on Tibet. Geneva: Author.

International Commission of Jurists (1997). *Tibet: Human Rights and the Rule of Law.* Geneva: Author.

Shakabpa, W. D. (1984). *Tibet: A Political History.* New York: Potala Publications.

Smith, Warren W. (1996). *Tibetan Nation: A History of Tibetan Nationalism and Sino-Tibetan Relations.* Boulder, Colo.: Westview Press.

Snellgrove, David, and Hugh Richardson (1968). *A Cultural History of Tibet.* Boston: Shambhala, 1995.

Van Walt, Michael C. (1987). *The Status of Tibet.* Boulder, Colo.: Westview Press.

Robert A. F. Thurman

Tokyo Trial

The International Military Tribunal for the Far East (IMTFE), commonly known as the Tokyo War Crimes Trial, or simply the Tokyo Trial, lasted three times longer than the Trial of the Major German War Criminals, commonly called the Nuremberg Trial. At one point the president of the IMTFE was informed that the trial was utilizing about one-quarter of all the paper consumed by the Allied occupation forces in Japan. The transcripts of the proceedings in open session and in chambers, taken together with the separate opinions, consist of approximately 57,000 pages and, with the even longer full text of the Trial Exhibits and other documentation assembled for use during the trial, the English-language text represents by far the largest collection of material that exists in any European language on Japan and on Japanese relations with the outside world during the critical period between 1927 and 1945.

The IMTFE Charter

The charter of the IMTFE was issued as an order together with a Special Proclamation by General Douglas MacArthur on January 19, 1946, in accordance with orders sent to him in October 1945 by the Joint Chiefs of Staff of the United States, afterward circulated to the Far Eastern Advisory Commission consisting of representatives of the Allied powers.

MacArthur's Special Proclamation said that he established an international military tribunal for the Far East, approved its constitution, jurisdiction, and functions as set out in its charter, and indicated that these steps were without prejudice to any other proceedings that might be established in Japan or within the domains of the countries with which Japan had been at war. He stated that he did this by powers the Allies entrusted to him as supreme commander with responsibility "to carry into effect the general surrender of the

Japanese armed forces," and with the authority bestowed upon him by the governments of the United States, Great Britain, and the Soviet Union at the Moscow Conference of December 1945 and with China's concurrence.

The Charter was strongly influenced by its Nuremberg counterpart but redrafted in compliance with the guidelines given to General MacArthur by the American Joint Chiefs of Staff to suit the different conditions that prevailed in occupied Japan. The Charter established that the supreme commander would select members of the tribunal from names submitted to him by any of the signatories of the Instrument of Surrender. The supreme commander would appoint one of the members to serve as president of the tribunal. The supreme commander would also appoint a general secretary of the tribunal and provide for clerical services and other duties required by the tribunal.

The charter set out the jurisdiction of the tribunal and established the individual responsibility of the accused for acts of state and for acts taken in compliance with superior orders. The supreme commander would designate the chief of counsel. Any of the United Nations engaged in the recent war against Japan might appoint an associate counsel to assist the chief of counsel. Proceedings of the tribunal would be conducted in English and in Japanese. The use of other languages in court later became a contentious matter. It was clear to the Allied powers that the supreme commander and the United States government were determined to go ahead with the tribunal on American terms. Accordingly the Allied powers moved quickly to select their own associate counsel.

The Americans assembled a huge team of more than one thousand lawyers and support staff. In Tokyo as at Nuremberg, the manpower and financial resources committed by the Americans made a huge impact on the collection and processing of documentary evidence collected from German and Japanese archives, offices, and private individuals. At Nuremberg that impact was felt immediately and was continuous throughout the proceedings. At Tokyo, the Americans faced far greater difficulties in extracting documentary evidence from the Japanese government, which continued to function and frequently obstructed them, and so the Americans were less successful in controlling the flow of information to the other national delegations and to the tribunal.

The Indictment

The indictment, mainly the work of the British associate prosecutor, Arthur S. Comyns-Carr, was lodged with the Court during a brief preliminary hearing on

April 29, 1946. Two weeks before, the indictment had been recast following the arrival of the Soviet prosecution team in Tokyo. Other delegations took even longer to arrive (several of the judges did not arrive until the trial had already begun).

Each contingent had its own agenda and priorities. Last-minute changes meant that the basic law of the tribunal and its remit were transformed only days before the accused were arraigned. In addition, many of the accused had been subjected to lengthy pre-trial Allied interrogations by teams deployed by the United States Strategic Bombing Survey, by military, naval and air, intelligence, by Civil Affairs analysts, by prosecutors, and by Japanese government investigators (who, with initial encouragement from the Americans, began and soon ended a series of their own war crimes trials in the months before the IMTFE took shape). These interviews were conducted without the protection of any legal counsel.

The Proceedings Begin

For all these reasons, the proceedings began inauspiciously for both sides but were particularly detrimental to the accused who were dependent upon a defense panel that was seriously weak in the provisions made for qualified legal advisers, translators, clerical staff, and financial resources. The defense was also handicapped by express provisions in the charter that obliged the accused to make written applications in advance before seeking to produce any witness or document in evidence. The prosecution section at Tokyo labored under no such impediments regarding prior disclosure.

The court consisted of eleven members, each representing one of the eleven nations involved in the prosecution. The countries taking part in the prosecution and judgment were: five member states of the British Commonwealth and Empire (Australia, Canada, New Zealand, Great Britain, and India), who, together with the United States and its former Commonwealth of the Philippines, constituted a built-in majority for the Anglo-American common law legal system; China; the Soviet Union; and two Continental European imperial powers, France and the Netherlands. Evidence relating to Korea, Manchuria, the People's Republic of Mongolia, Thailand, Cambodia, Burma, and Portuguese possessions in East Asia was also received by the tribunal, but for legal as well as for political ones those countries or territories were not formally joined in the proceedings.

The legitimacy of the Tokyo Trial depended upon the number and variety of the states that took part in the trial, but more crucially upon the express consent of the Japanese state to submit to its jurisdiction, relinquishing or at least sharing some sovereignty in the process. This is a more modern conception of legality than was applied at Nuremberg. The difference arose because Japan did not, strictly speaking, surrender unconditionally. The Special Proclamation that brought the IMTFE into existence claimed that by the Instrument of Surrender "the authority of the Emperor and the Japanese Government to rule the state of Japan is made subject to the Supreme Commander for the Allied Powers," but in fact those provisions were restricted to measures intended to implement "the unconditional surrender . . . of the Japanese Imperial General Headquarters and of all Japanese Armed forces and all armed forces under Japanese control wherever situated." Thus, Japan surrendered in words that protected the Japanese emperor. On a number of occasions the thrust of questions put to witnesses came perilously close to implicating Emperor Hirohito personally, but the trial also provided powerful support for the viewpoint that he was a benign constitutional monarch who wanted a durable peace and prosperity for his people.

It was a matter of pivotal importance during the trial that the Japanese "sovereignty" was not extinguished with the end of hostilities. The defense made much of the limited nature of the Japanese surrender in framing successive challenges to the powers of the supreme commander, to his promulgation of the tribunal, to the charter, to the nomination of its members and of its president, and to the jurisdiction of the tribunal. These arguments created consternation in court.

The Tokyo Trial indictment did mimic elements that were present in the Nuremberg indictment, but on an altogether grander scale. The same ideas of conspiracy, crimes against peace (the planning, preparation, initiating and waging of wars of aggression), individual criminal responsibility for conventional war crimes, and crimes against humanity appeared in the indictments at Tokyo and at Nuremberg. Thus the conceptual framework was quite similar. But the ways these crimes were dealt with inevitably differed, and there were fifty-five counts on the indictment at Tokyo compared to four at Nuremberg.

The Tokyo Trial looked at events as far back as 1927, because the prosecution argued that a document prepared that year and known as the Tanaka Memorial showed that a "Common Plan or Conspiracy" to commit "Crimes against Peace" bound the accused together. The conspiracy thus began in 1927 and continued through to the end of the Asia and Pacific War in 1945. The Tanaka Memorial was, in fact, a skillful Chinese forgery, but it was not regarded as such by most observers at the time and it was consistent with the private

The International Military Tribunal of the Far East, April 1947. Presiding over the tribunal for the prosecution of Japanese war criminals was a panel of eleven judges—one from each of the Allied powers. [AP/WORLD WIDE PHOTOS]

thinking of key individuals within the Japanese government of its time.

The breadth of the supposed conspiracy took in virtually every facet of Japan's domestic and foreign affairs over a period of nearly two decades, half again longer than the period covered by the Nuremberg Major War Crimes Trial. At the time of the Tokyo Trial, the concept of criminal conspiracy was frequently employed in the battle against organized crime in the United States. It was held in far less esteem as a weapon in the arsenal of public prosecutors elsewhere. The U.S. Department of Justice gave this matter a great deal of thought and produced a treatise on the subject for the benefit of Allied prosecutors in Tokyo. Later, copies of this brief were handed out to individual members of the tribunal.

The prosecution's conspiracy case was summed up later by an American assistant prosecutor at the trial, "The Prosecution Case is a sturdy structure built upon a deep and firm and solid foundation of fact. To its destruction the Defense have brought as tools a microscope and a toothpick." What generally was at issue were not the facts, but the different constructions which the two sides placed on those facts, and this, by its very nature, meant that a great deal of detailed evidence was required to buttress the positions taken by the two opposing sides.

The defense in Tokyo retraced much of the ground covered by the prosecution and went on to explore virtually the whole history of Japan's twentieth-century constitutional, social, political, and international history up to the end of World War II. Evidence directly linking the individual defendants to what is a far broader historical record of domestic and world history became hard to see and, for most of the trial, comparatively little attention was paid to any indisputably criminal activity on the part of the accused. Defense counsel tried in vain to force the prosecution to define the essential elements and to present a Bill of Particulars indicating details of the specific crimes that their individual clients were supposed to have committed. To some extent the emphasis on criminal masked the fact that the charges on the indictment at Tokyo were framed before the prosecution determined who was to be tried. As a result the prosecution experienced real difficulties in finding a sufficiency of evidence to make a truly convincing case against most of the accused.

The twenty-eight defendants charged at the Tokyo Trial were selected following international deliberations and the final decisions were taken by an executive committee of the International Prosecution Section, chaired by Sir Arthur Comyns Carr, K.C. Pretrial briefs were prepared following investigations and interviews with individual suspects, most of whom had been arrested and held in Sugamo Prison because their names appeared on the UN War Crimes Commission's lists of major war crimes suspects. Others were still free when questioned.

The defendants were by and large "establishment" figures who had achieved prominence in the leadership of Japan and had won the confidence and approbation of their fellow citizens through their own administrative competence, intellectual excellence, or distinguished military service. Baron Hiranuma Kiichirô, for instance, had become a judge as far back as 1890, rose by virtue of his talent to become vice-minister of justice in 1911, chief justice of the Supreme Court of Japan in 1921, minister of justice in 1923, vice-president of the Privy Council for a period of twelve years and afterward its president in a career interspersed posts as minister for home affairs and prime minister of Japan. The Tribunal ignored Hiranuma's prewar reputation as a strong admirer of the Western democracies and as a man who held the European totalitarian states in low regard.

Others among the defendants, in their own ways were equally distinguished, and the voices which are heard in their affidavits, testimony, and the documentary records introduced on their behalf show them generally to have been thoughtful, well-meaning, and deeply conscious of their duty to uphold the honor and integrity of Japan. The Japanese public, Western opinion, and a majority of the court, however, were of a different mind.

The Court began hearing the prosecution's case on May 4, 1946. The prosecution presented its evidence in fifteen phases, and the presentation of its Evidence-in-Chief closed on January 24, 1947.

The Tokyo Trial, like the Nuremberg Trial, refused to admit evidence favorable to the defense that might appear to bring the wartime conduct of the Allied powers into disrepute: The Court simply ruled that its jurisdiction was strictly confined to an examination of the conduct of the Japanese side. The court's powers were limited strictly by the terms of the charter and rules of procedure of the Tokyo Trial. There was, arguably, no legal basis on which the tribunal could have gone beyond the intentions of those who had convened the trial and given it authority. This was fully acknowledged in its judgment.

The Defense Panel

As early as February 21, 1946, the Judge Advocate General's (JAG) Department in Washington, D.C., was asked to obtain fifteen or twenty suitable American attorneys to form a defense panel "from which might be drawn by selection or by Court appointment counsel for Defendants charged." On March 19, 1946, General MacArthur informed Justice Northcroft of these developments and indicated that he had that day asked the JAG to increase the number of American defense lawyers from fifteen to twenty-five and to take care that they had the proper experience and qualifications that would allow the Japanese defendants a fair trial and adequate defense.

For each defendant a Japanese defense counsel was found to take charge of his particular case and an American co-counsel assumed what was nominally a junior role. The working relationships between individual American attorneys and their Japanese counterparts were not always easy. At first, not all of the defendants welcomed the Americans who were offered to them, but eventually all came to the conclusion that it was advisable to engage one or other of them. The defense counsel of both nationalities varied enormously in talent, energy, age, and experience.

The Japanese defense counsel labored under immense handicaps. As George Ware revealed years later, when the defense case opened, the chief of defense counsel, Uzawa Sômei, broadcast a nationwide radio appeal for "funds, communications, lodgings and food" (Ware, 1979, p. 145). The outcome was exceedingly disappointing. The attorneys hired by the accused finally had to resort to the expedient of donating $1,000 per head and each of the defendants paid $10,000 into a central pool to provide for translators, clerical staff, and witness expenses. Some of those difficulties were surmounted with the arrival of American associate counsel provided to bolster the defense.

Defense motions to dismiss the charges against the accused were denied, following which the defense presentation of its case began on February 3, 1947, and continued until January 12, 1948. The defense did not attempt to match the structure imposed by the prosecution's case and instead offered its case in six divisions.

In due course, the prosecution and then the defense presented further evidence in rebuttal until February 10, 1948, at which time the defense filed further motions to dismiss, which were rejected. The summations and other closing arguments continued from February 11 to April 16, 1948, when the proceedings were adjourned while the court considered its findings.

By the close of evidence, the court had met in 818 public sessions and heard from 416 witnesses in court, in addition to reading unsubstantiated affidavits and depositions from some 779 others whose evidence the court accepted for whatever probative value they might have had. The deeds recounted in the latter papers had so weakened many of these potential witnesses that it lay beyond their physical or mental capacity to travel to the Japanese capital in order to submit to a cross-examination. In other instances, individual Allied governments put obstacles in the way of potential witnesses for the defense who were prepared to testify on behalf of one or more of the accused or in the general divisions of the defense case. In a number of cases these potential witnesses had been diplomats, senior civil servants, or government ministers before or during the war. The Allied powers also refused to permit the defense counsel any access to its own official documents (other than published records). All of this was prejudicial to the fairness of the proceedings.

Judgment and Sentencing
The 1,781-page judgment of the tribunal took months to prepare. The court president, Sir William Webb of Australia, required nine days to read it in court (November 4–12, 1948). Before the judgment, Admiral Nagano Osami and the former diplomat-cum-railway administrator Matsuoka Yōsuke died of natural causes (a heart attack and pneumonia) brought about or exacerbated by the strain of their circumstances and the poor conditions in which they were kept at Sugamo Prison. Another of the accused, Ōkawa Shūmei, had been found unfit to stand trial after a theatrical episode lasting only a few minutes before he so much as entered a plea of "not guilty," and after protracted inquiries his case had been adjourned *sine die*. All twenty-five of the surviving defendants at the Tokyo Major War Crimes Trial were convicted, and all but two of them were found guilty on at least two charges.

Seven were condemned to death by hanging. Six of the condemned men had been leading military and naval figures. The seventh was a former prime minister, foreign minister, and professional diplomat, Hirota Kôki. All but two of the remaining defendants were sentenced to life imprisonment. The two exceptions, both professional diplomats who served successive terms as foreign ministers in Tōjō Hideki's wartime cabinet, were sentenced to twenty years (Tōgō Shigenori) and seven years Shigemitsu Mamoru).

The Tribunal did not convict any organizations, but General MacArthur's occupying forces were carrying out sweeping political purges of individuals and groups within Japan, blacklisting some 210,288 people, mostly on account of their previous membership in banned organizations.

The judgment and sentences of the tribunal were confirmed by General MacArthur on November 24, 1948, two days after a perfunctory meeting at his office with members of the Allied Control Commission for Japan, who acted as the local representatives of the nations of the Far Eastern Commission set up by their governments. Six of those representatives made no recommendations for clemency. Australia, Canada, India, and the Netherlands were willing to see the general make some reductions in sentences. He chose not to do so. The issue of clemency was thereafter to disturb Japanese relations with the Allied powers until the late 1950s when a majority of the Allied powers agreed to release the last of the convicted major war criminals from captivity.

In neither the Tokyo nor the Nuremberg Trials was it deemed sufficient for the defense to show that the acts of responsible officers or of government ministers and officials were protected as "acts of state." The twin principles of individual criminal responsibility and of universal jurisdiction in the prosecution and punishment of war criminals were firmly established.

Both courts ruled decisively that international law is superior to national law, and added that nothing that national courts or administrations might say could overturn that basic principle, which in times to come should be regarded as binding upon the victor as well as the vanquished. These judgments, by themselves, were not binding upon the domestic practices of states; yet, as all of the great powers and most of the lesser ones of the world at the time did sign the San Francisco Peace Treaty (which provided for all parties to accept the judgment of the Tokyo Tribunal in its entirety), there is a valid line of argument that it does indeed impose obligations upon each of those states (subject to any differences that may exist within their respective constitutions).

To its credit the IMTFE exercised a cathartic function of surpassing importance for the people of Japan and for their former enemies and, to the extent that its judgment was accepted and formally endorsed under the terms of the San Francisco Peace Treaty, it relegitimated, as intended, the Allied occupation of Japan itself.

On March 7, 1950, the supreme commander issued a directive that reduced the sentences by one-third for good behavior and authorized the parole of those who had received life sentences after fifteen years. Several of those who were imprisoned were released earlier on parole due to ill-health.

Hashimoto Kingorô, Hata Shunroku, Minami Jirô, and Oka Takazumi were all released on parole in 1954. Araki Sadao, Hiranuma Kiichirô, Hoshino Naoki, Kaya Okinori, Kido Kôichi, Ôshima Hiroshi, Shimada Shigetarô, and Suzuki Teiichi were released on parole in 1955. Satô Kenryô, whom many, including Judge B. V. A. Röling regarded as one of the convicted war criminals least deserving of imprisonment, was not granted parole until March 1956, the last of the Class A Japanese war criminals to be released. On April 7, 1957, the Japanese government announced that, with the concurrence of a majority of the powers represented on the tribunal, the last ten parolee major Japanese war criminals were granted clemency and were to be regarded henceforth as unconditionally free from the terms of their parole.

The Aftermath
The initial intention of the Allied powers was to hold further international military tribunals in both Germany and Japan once the first major war crimes trials concluded. The defendants selected for the first trials were not regarded as the only major war criminals but as clearly representative members of the groups held responsible for the outbreak of World War II. A large number of persons were held in custody with the intention of bringing them to justice as Class A war criminals. The British and Americans, however, soon lost their appetite for such proceedings (and their expense), and by December 1946 it was clear that no further major international war crimes trials would take place. In the end, however, it was not until Christmas Eve, 1948, that a formal announcement was issued that the last of the nineteen individuals who might have been expected to figure in further proceedings before the IMTFE were to be released rather than face trial.

The decision to release these men was taken as a purely political act and had nothing much to do with the merits of their individual cases. However, it is worth noting that most of these potential accused gave evidence during the Tokyo Major War Crimes Trial and, even when they did not, the nature of their involvement in events described in that trial is evident in the transcripts and other documentation of its proceedings.

An imperial rescript granting an amnesty by general pardon for war crimes committed by members of the Japanese Armed Forces during World War II was issued on November 3, 1946. It had no effect upon the Allied trials, and the news of it attracted little if any interest abroad at the time. However, one can say with a degree of certainty that no Japanese war criminal will ever again be tried on indictment in a Japanese court for crimes related to the period before and during World War II. Foreign governments have long since ceased to reveal any interest in continuing to pursue Japanese war criminals through national courts, and without regard to the dwindling number of people still interested in the apprehension and prosecution of such perpetrators through international institutions, the new permanent International Criminal Court has been denied any jurisdiction at all over crimes committed prior to its own creation.

In discussing the Tokyo trial, matters that have not been explored sufficiently include the political context of the Tokyo Trial proceedings, its charter and limited jurisdiction, the evidence presented in court, the disturbance in the power balance between the two opposing sides, the tables of legal authorities on which the respective sides relied, the one-sided exclusion of evidence to the detriment of the defense, the forensic skills or inadequacies of counsel or members of the tribunal, the differing structures of the prosecution and defense cases, the soundness or otherwise of rulings made by the tribunal during the course of the Tokyo Trial, and the closing arguments found in the summations, rebuttal and sur-rebuttal stages of the proceedings. The judgments of the international tribunals at Nuremberg and Tokyo, arguably the least satisfactory parts of all of the postwar proceedings, are read more frequently but seldom examined by scholars within the historical context of their trial processes.

SEE ALSO Japan; Nuremberg Trials; War Crimes

BIBLIOGRAPHY
Appleman, John Alan (1954). *Military Tribunals and International Crimes.* Indianapolis, Ind: Bobbs-Merrill.
Asahi Shinbun-sha Chôsa Kenkyûshitsu (*Asahi Shinbun Company Research Office*) (1953). *Kyokutô Kokusai Gunji Saiban Mokuroku oyobi Sakuin* (Records of the international military tribunal for the Far East: Catalogue with index). Tokyo: Asahi Shinbun-sha Chôsa Kenkyûshitsu.
Asahi Shinbun Tôkyô Saiban Kishadan (*Asahi Shinbun Tokyo Trial Press Corps*) (1983). *Benron-Hanketsu Hen* (The Oral Proceedings and the Judgment), 2 volumes. Tokyo: Kodansha.
Blewett, George F. (1950). "Victor's Injustice: The Tokyo War Crimes Trial." *American Perspective* 4(3):282–292.
Brackman, Arnold C. (1987). *The Other Nuremberg: The Untold Story of the Tokyo War Crimes Trials.* New York: William Morrow.

Brown, Allan Robert (1957). "The Role of the Emperor in Japan's Decision to Go to War: The Record of the International Military Tribunal for the Far East." Master's thesis. Palo Alto, Calif.: Stanford University.

Chaen, Yoshio (1984–1993). *BC-Kyû Senpan Saiban Kankei Shiryô Shûsei* (Collected materials on BC-Class war crimes proceedings), 10 volumes. Tokyo: Fuji Shuppan.

Dower, John (1999). *Embracing Defeat: Japan in the Wake of World War II.* New York: Norton.

Far Eastern Commission (1947). *Activities of the Far Eastern Commission.* Washington, D.C.: USGPO.

Ginn, John L. (1992). *Sugamo Prison, Tokyo: An Account of the Trial and Sentencing of Japanese War Criminals in 1948, by a U.S. Participant.* Jefferson, N.C.: McFarland.

Hankey, Lord (1950). *Politics, Trials, and Errors.* Oxford: Pen-in-Hand.

Harries, Meirion, and Suzie Meirion (1987). *Sheathing the Sword: The Demilitarisation of Japan.* London: Hamish Hamilton.

Horwitz, Solis (1950). "The Tokyo Trial." *International Conciliation* 465:473–584. New York: Carnegie Endowment for International Peace.

Hosoya, Chihiro, Andô Nisuke, Ônuma Yasuaki, and Richard Minear, eds. (1983). *The Tokyo War Crimes Trial: An International Symposium.* Tokyo: Kodansha International.

Ienaga, Saburô (1977). "Bias in the Guise of Objectivity." *Japan Interpreter* 11(3)271–288.

Ireland, Gordon (1950). "Uncommon Law in Martial Tokyo." *Year Book of World Affairs.* London: Times Books.

Japan Judicial Affairs Board (1952). *Jissô no Saiban Senpan* (The Facts of the War Crimes Trials). Tokyo: Sugamo Homuiin-kai.

Johnson, Galen Irvin (1998). "Defending the Japanese Warlords: American Attorneys at the Tokyo War Crimes Trial, 1946–1948 (International Military Tribunal for the Far East)." Ph.D. diss. Lawrence: University of Kansas.

Keenan, Joseph B., and Brendan F. Brown (1950). *Crimes against International Law.* Washington, D.C: Public Affairs Press.

Kobayashi, Masaki (1983). *Tokyo Saiban.* Feature film. Tokyo: Kodansha International.

Kôjima, Noboru (1971). *Tôkyô Saiban,* 2 volumes. Tokyo: Chuo Koron.

Lewis, John R. (1979). *Uncertain Judgment: A Bibliography of War Crimes Trials.* Santa Barbara, Calif: ABC-Clio.

Minear, Richard H. (1977). "In Defense of Radabinod Pal." *Japan Interpreter* 11(3):263–271.

Minear, Richard H. (1972). *Victors' Justice: The Tokyo War Crimes Trial.* Ann Arbor: Center for Japanese Studies, University of Michigan Press, 2001.

Nandy, Ashis (1995). *The Savage Freud and Other Essays on Possible and Retrievable Selves.* Princeton, N.J.: Princeton University Press.

Nitta Mitsuo, ed. (1968). *Kyokutô Kokusai Gunji Saiban Hôhan Sokkiroku* (Stenographic report of the record of the proceedings of the international military tribunal for the Far East), 10 volumes. Tokyo: O-matsu-dô Shoten.

Parks, William H. (1973). "Command Responsibility for War Crimes." *Military Law Review* 62:1–104.

Piccigallo, Philip R. (1979). *The Japanese on Trial: Allied War Crimes Operations in the East, 1945–1951.* Austin: University of Texas Press.

Poelgeest, Bart van (1989). *Nederland en het Tribunaal van Tokio.* Arnheim, Netherlands: Gouda Quint.

Pritchard, R. John (1996). "The Gift of Clemency following British War Crimes Trials in the Far East, 1946–1948." *Criminal Law Forum* 7(1):15–50.

Pritchard, R. John (1998). "International Military Tribunal for the Far East and the Allied National War Crimes Trials in Asia." In *International Criminal Law,* vol. 3: *Enforcement,* ed. M. Cherif Bassiouni. Ardsley, N.Y.: Transnational Publishers.

Pritchard, R. John, and Sonia M. Zaide, eds. (1981–1987). *The Tokyo War Crimes Trial: The Complete Transcripts of the Proceedings of the International Military Tribunal,* 22 vols. New York: Garland Publishing in association with the London School of Economics and Political Science.

Pritchard, R. John, and Sonia M. Zaide, eds. (1981–1987). *The Tokyo War Crimes Trial: The Comprehensive Index and Guide,* 5 vols. New York: Garland Publishing in association with the London School of Economics and Political Science.

Reel, A. Frank (1949). *The Case of General Yamashita.* Chicago: University of Chicago Press.

Tanaka Toshiyuki (1996). *Hidden Horrors: Japanese War Crimes in World War II.* Boulder, Colo: Westview Press.

Taylor, Lawrence (1981). *A Trial of Generals: Homma, Yamashita, MacArthur.* South Bend, Ind.: Icarus.

Trotter, Ann (1989). "New Zealanders and the International Military Tribunal for the Far East." *New Zealand Journal of History* 23(2):142–156.

United Nations War Crimes Commission (1948). *History of the United Nations War Crimes Commission and the Development of the Laws of War,* ed. George Brand. London: Her Majesty's Stationery Office.

United Nations War Crimes Commission (1947–1949). *Law Reports of Trials of War Criminals,* 15 volumes. London: Her Majesty's Stationery Office.

Ushimura, Kei (2003). *Beyond the "Judgment of Civilization": The Intellectual Legacy of the Japanese War Crimes Trials, 1946–1949,* trans. Steven J. Ericson. Tokyo: LTCB International Library Trust/International House of Japan.

Whitney, Courtney (1950). *The Case of General Yamashita: A Memorandum.* Tokyo: Supreme Commander for the Allied Powers.

R. John Pritchard

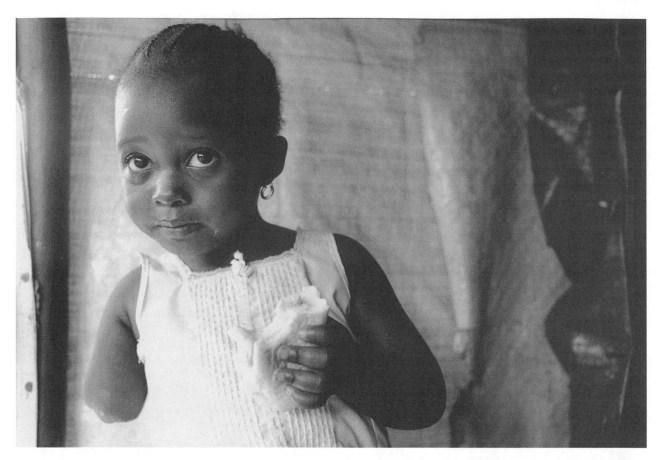

In Sierra Leone, rebels of the Revolutionary United Front frequently amputated the limbs of their victims, including the very young, like this three-year-old girl. [TEUN VOETEN]

Torture

Torture—the infliction of severe physical or mental suffering—is frequently a component of systematic policies and attacks against individuals or groups, in peacetime or in time of war. Torture is used variously as a weapon of war, as a means of soliciting information or confession, as a technique to humiliate or punish, as a tool of repression or intimidation, and as a form of sexual violence. Its typical victims include political opponents; particular national, racial, ethnic, religious or other groups; women; prisoners of war; detainees; and ordinary criminal suspects.

In response, international law has prohibited torture and other cruel, inhuman or degrading treatment in absolute terms. The prohibition of torture and other forms of ill treatment ranks among the most firmly entrenched principles of international law regarding human rights and of international humanitarian law. The right not to be tortured is based on the principles of human dignity and integrity of the person that underlie these bodies of law.

Torture is also considered a crime under international law. It is one of a small number of acts considered so heinous that all countries must play their part in pursuing the perpetrators. As a U.S. court ruled in the landmark case of *Filartiga v. Peña-Irala*, "the torturer has become—like the pirate and slave trader before him—*hostis humani generic*, an enemy of all mankind."

International and National Norms Prohibiting Torture and Other Ill-Treatment

International legal norms prohibiting torture and other forms of ill-treatment have developed, largely since 1945, as central components of the international law of human rights, international humanitarian law, and international criminal law. The Universal Declaration on Human Rights (UDHR) of 1948 includes freedom from torture as one of the fundamental rights belonging to all human beings. Article 5 of the declaration provides that "No one shall be subjected to torture or to cruel, inhuman, or degrading treatment or punishment." Subsequently, identical or similarly worded prohibitions were included in human rights treaties adopted at international and regional levels, and these set legal standards for individual governments to follow. These include Article 7 of the International Covenant on Civil and Political Rights (ICCPR) of 1966, Article 3 of the European Convention on Human Rights of 1950, Article 5 of the American Convention on Human Rights of 1969, and Article 5 of the African Charter on Human and Peoples' Rights of 1981.

These treaties oblige states to refrain from torture or other prohibited treatment, and establish mechanisms for making states accountable if their officials commit such abuses. The prohibition on torture is absolute, and allows for no exceptions. In human rights treaties, torture is invariably listed as a "non-derogable" right. States must never deviate from the prohibition on torture, even, according to Article 4 of the ICCPR, "in time of public emergency which threatens the life of the nation."

A major landmark was the 1984 conclusion of a treaty aimed specifically at stamping out torture: the Convention against Torture and Other Cruel, Inhuman or Degrading Treatment or Punishment (otherwise known as the Torture Convention). By March 2004, this convention had 134 state signatories. The Torture Convention set out specific measures that governments must take to prevent and punish torture, and established its Committee Against Torture to monitor states' compliance and to receive individual complaints.

Regional torture-specific instruments followed. In 1985, the Inter-American Convention to Prevent and Punish Torture came into effect. The European Convention for the Prevention of Torture and Inhuman or Degrading Treatment or Punishment passed into law in 1987, followed by the Robben Island Guidelines on the prevention of torture and ill treatment in Africa in 2002. Under UN auspices, sets of guidelines were developed that aimed at preventing torture. Among these were the UN Code of Conduct for Law Enforcement Officials of 1979 and the UN Body of Principles for the Protection of All Persons under Any Form of Detention or Imprisonment of 1988.

In parallel to these developments in the sphere of human rights, norms prohibiting torture and other ill-treatment also developed in the spheres of international humanitarian law, and the laws of war. The four Geneva Conventions of 1949 list torture and inhuman treatment committed during international armed conflict that are considered grave breaches of the Geneva Conventions (war crimes). Article 3, common to all four of the Geneva Conventions, as well as the second Additional Protocol II to those conventions hold torture and cruel, humiliating. and degrading treatment as prohibited by the law applying to internal armed conflicts.

As the concept of crimes against humanity developed in the wake of World War II atrocities, torture was considered to be covered, although not listed explicitly, in early definitions. The Nuremberg and Tokyo Charters of 1945 and 1946, on which trials of German and Japanese World War II leaders were based, included within their definitions of prosecutable crimes against humanity "other inhuman acts committed against any civilian population." The Control Council Law No. 10 of 1945, used as the basis for prosecuting second-tier Nazis, specifically listed torture as one of the inhumane acts constituting a crime against humanity.

When the International Criminal Tribunal for Former Yugoslavia (ICTY) was established by the UN in 1993, its statute listed torture as among the crimes against humanity that the tribunal could prosecute. The 1994 statute of the International Criminal Tribunal for Rwanda (ICTR) followed suit. The Rome Statute for the International Criminal Court (ICC), which was concluded in 1998, codified crimes against humanity in greater detail. Article 7 of that statute includes the widespread or systematic practice of torture as a crime against humanity, when such practices are committed as part of an attack directed against a civilian population. Also listed are "[o]ther inhumane acts of a similar character internationally causing great suffering or serious injury to body or to mental or physical health."

Torture is also one of the acts that can constitute the crime of genocide. The definition adopted in the Genocide Convention of 1948 included, at Article II(b), "causing serious bodily or mental harm." This definition was intended to cover a range of acts of physical violence falling short of actual killing, as well as acts causing serious mental harm. The ICTR helped to clarify the meaning of this phrase in 1998 in the *Akayesu* case, finding that the definition of serious bodily or mental harm, includes acts of torture, be they bodily or mental, and inhumane or degrading treatment and persecution, and could include rape and other acts of sexual violence or death threats. The Rome Statute included a document that set out the physical and mental elements of each crime that needed to be proved in any given case brought before the ICC. This document, titled "Elements of Crimes" contains the following footnote to the crime of genocide by causing serious bodily or mental harm: "This conduct may include, but is not necessarily restricted to, acts of torture, rape, sexual violence or inhuman or degrading treatment."

The absolute prohibition on torture is has been generally accepted as a part of customary international law, and is therefore binding on all states, not only those that become party to treaties prohibiting torture. This view has been upheld by international courts and tribunals, as well as by national courts. The prohibition has also been recognized as a norm of *jus cogens*, which is an overriding or superior principle of international law.

Torture and other ill-treatment are also specifically prohibited in many national constitutions. Even where a prohibition on torture is not specifically included in the constitution, it has been made into other provisions. For instance, by giving a wide interpretation to the right to life and personal liberty, the Indian Supreme Court has incorporated freedom from torture among its schedule of constitutionally protected rights. Many states have made torture a specific criminal offence under their penal codes. Torture is also commonly criminalized in military codes and through legislation incorporating the war crimes provisions of the Geneva Conventions. After becoming party to the Rome Statute for the ICC, states have also incorporated torture as a crime against humanity, as genocide, and as a war crime in their domestic law.

The international norms in this array of treaties and customary international law impose a range of obligations on states. For instance, states must not only refrain from using torture, they must also take strong positive measures to prevent and punish torture. Article 2.1 of the Torture Convention obliges states to "take effective legislative, administrative, judicial or other measures to prevent acts of torture in any territory under its jurisdiction." Such measures include training law enforcement personnel and other public officials and reviewing rules and practices relating to the interrogation and custody of prisoners and detainees. States must also ensure that statements taken as a result of torture may not be used in court as evidence, except against a person accused of torture as evidence that the statement was made.

States also have an obligation to investigate and prosecute individuals responsible for torture. Under Article 4 of the Torture Convention, states are obliged to ensure that all acts of torture are criminal offences under domestic criminal law, and to impose penalties that reflect their grave nature. States are obliged to carry out a prompt and impartial investigation whenever torture or ill-treatment is alleged, to identify those responsible, and to impose an appropriate punishment, as illustrated in the case of *Velasquez Rodriguez v. Honduras*, tried before the Inter American Court of Human Rights in 1988.

The duty of states to ensure that torturers are brought to justice is not limited to policing what happens within their own borders, since torture is also a crime under international law. According to Articles 5.2 and 7 of the Torture Convention, when an alleged torturer is present within its jurisdiction, regardless of where the torture was committed, a state must either prosecute the person, or extradite them elsewhere to face trial. This exceptional jurisdiction—based only on the nature of the crime itself, regardless of where the crime was committed or by whom—is recognized in international law and is known as universal jurisdiction. The "extradite or prosecute" formula exists also in the Geneva Conventions in relation to grave breaches, thus applying to those who commit torture in the course of an international armed conflict. Even outside the scope of these treaties, states have the right, and may be obliged, under international law to prosecute torture on the basis of universal jurisdiction. There is increasing authority for the proposition that customary international law requires states to prosecute all crimes against humanity, genocide, and war crimes, and that this extends to war crimes committed in internal armed conflict, to individual acts of official torture, and possibly also to cruel or inhuman treatment.

The duty to prosecute torture, and its status as a crime under international law, has a number of important implications. There is increasing consensus that amnesties should not be granted for torture, nor should the normal rules on statutes of limitations or immunities be applied in cases of torture. For instance, the British House of Lords ruled in March 1999 that Augusto Pinochet was not entitled to head-of-state immunity for torture from the time that the Torture Convention applied.

According to Article 13 of the Torture Convention, states must provide access to adequate remedies for victims when torture occurs. Any individual who alleges they have been tortured must have the right to complain to competent authorities, and to have the allegation promptly and impartially examined. Further, victims have a right to reparation, including compensation, restitution, rehabilitation, "satisfaction" (which may include bringing to account those responsible and symbolic measures such as commemorations), and guarantees that torture will not recur. These victim's rights are laid out in a UN draft document regarding the basic principles and guidelines on the right to a remedy and reparation for victims of violations of international human rights law and violations of international humanitarian law, as revised October 2003. Finally, the duty to protect people from torture and other ill treatment extends to the duty not to hand them over to be tortured elsewhere. Article 3 of the Torture Convention prohibits states from expelling, returning, or extraditing a person to another state where there are substantial grounds for believing they could be subjected to torture or other prohibited treatment there.

Definitions of Torture

Torture is absolutely prohibited in all circumstances. But what is it? A common element that appears consistently in definitions is that torture is the intentional infliction of severe pain or suffering, whether physical or mental, on a person. Decisions of international human rights courts and monitoring bodies have been very influential in establishing the basic elements of the definition. International criminal tribunals have relied heavily on these decisions to interpret what constitutes torture when it is being prosecuted as a crime against humanity or as a genocidal act, although they have also departed from the international human rights law interpretations in significant aspects.

The severity or intensity of pain or suffering caused is one factor that will determine whether behavior amounts to torture. An act has to cause "very serious and cruel suffering" to constitute torture, as the European Court of Human Rights decided when called upon to consider whether certain techniques used by U.K. security forces while interrogating IRA suspects in Northern Ireland were lawful (*Ireland v. U.K.*). The court concluded, in its judgment of 1978, that the techniques (hooding; being made to stand against a wall for many hours; subjection to constant noise; and deprivation of sleep, food and drink) were not severe enough to constitute torture, but did constitute inhuman treatment, which is also prohibited under the Torture Convention. The ICTY also followed this approach, finding that the severity of pain or suffering is what sets torture apart from other crimes. Subjective as well as objective factors may be considered in assessing severity. The European Court of Human Rights takes into account all the circumstances, including the duration of the treatment; its physical and mental effects; and the sex, age, and state of health of the victim. The ICTY has also said that subjective as well as objective criteria may be relevant in assessing the gravity of the harm.

As for the definition of mental torture, once again international cases have helped to clarify how to assess whether mental suffering caused by a certain act is severe enough to amount to torture. In the case of *Estrella v. Uruguay*, in 1980, the Human Rights Committee found that mock amputation of the hands of a well-known guitarist was psychological torture.

Another factor that distinguishes torture from other ill-treatment in the international law of human rights is the purpose for which the particular suffering is inflicted. In human rights law, exemplified in Article 1 of the Torture Convention, in order for conduct to amount to torture, it must be inflicted for specific purposes such as obtaining information or a confession, punishment, intimidation, coercion, or discrimination. The European Commission of Human Rights had already established the need for such a purpose in its 1969 decision in a case concerning the conduct of Greek security forces following the military coup. This legal decision, following what came to be known as the "Greek case," confirmed that without such a purpose, the same act would be classified as ill treatment but not torture. The European Court of Human Rights has continued to look for specific purposes before it will categorize an act as torture, for example, in the 1996 case of *Aksoy v. Turkey*. The Israeli Supreme Court, when considering methods used by Israeli security services in interrogating Palestinian suspects in 1999, distinguished between a situation in which sleep deprivation is a side effect inherent in interrogation, which would not be unlawful, and a situation where prolonged sleep deprivation is used as an end in itself, for the purpose of tiring or breaking the prisoner, in which case it would not be lawful.

In international criminal law, however, the requirement of a particular purpose appears to be losing ground. In cases concerning torture as a crime against humanity, although the ICTY and ICTR have held that the act or omission must aim at purposes such as those outlined in Article 1 of the Torture Convention, (e.g., the ICTR in the *Akayesu* case, 1998), they have also said that this is not to be viewed as an exhaustive list, and that the prohibited purpose need not be the predominating or sole purpose. In a further departure, in the Rome Statute's "Elements of Crimes," a footnote to the elements of the crime against humanity of torture states that: "It is understood that no specific purpose need be proved for this crime."

Another difference has opened up between human rights law and international criminal law as regards the state-actor requirement. The Torture Convention requires an act of torture to have been "inflicted by or at the instigation of or with the consent or acquiescence of a public official or other person acting in an official capacity." The rule reflects the traditional purpose of human rights protection, which is to place limits on abuses by states rather than to regulate behavior between private individuals. This approach has shown signs of breaking down in some respects, however. For instance, states are increasingly required to regulate private individuals' behavior in order to protect vulnerable people from ill treatment. In the sphere of international criminal law, non-state actors can be held responsible for torture. The ICTY decided that the definition of torture in the context of crimes against humanity is not identical to the definition in the Torture Convention, and that outside the framework of the Torture Convention, customary international law does not impose a public official requirement in relation to criminal responsibility for torture.

Special elements are added to the crime of torture if it is prosecuted as a crime against humanity, an act of genocide, or a war crime. For example, as a crime against humanity under the Rome Statute, torture must be carried out as part of a widespread or systematic attack against a civilian population, accompanied by the knowledge or intention to further such an attack, and it must be inflicted upon a person in the custody or under the control of the accused. When prosecuted as an act of genocide, the serious bodily or mental harm must be caused to persons belonging to a particular national, ethnical, racial or religious group, and the perpetrator must have intended to destroy that group, in whole or in part. The conduct must either be part of a "manifest pattern of similar conduct" against such a group, or be itself capable of causing such destruction of the group.

The international criminal tribunals have been instrumental in expanding understandings of the definition of torture, for instance, by prosecuting rape and other forms of sexual violence under the heading of torture as a crime against humanity. The ICTY Appeals Chamber has said that, since sexual violence necessarily gives rise to severe pain or suffering, the crime of torture has been established once rape has been proved.

Definitions of Inhuman and Degrading Treatment or Punishment

Again, interpretations of these terms have developed in the law of human rights. Treatment causing less severe suffering, or not for one of the requisite purposes, may nonetheless constitute inhuman or degrading treatment. Solitary confinement, incommunicado detention, and poor prison conditions are examples of behavior that may amount to inhuman treatment, depending on the circumstances. For example, in Öcalan v. Turkey, the European Court of Human Rights found in 2003 that complete sensory isolation, coupled with total social isolation, can destroy the personality and would constitute inhuman treatment. On the other hand, it held that merely prohibiting contact with other prisoners for legitimate reasons such as security does not in itself amount to a violation. In the Greek case, treatment was found to be degrading if it grossly humiliates a person before others, or if it drives a person to act against his or her will or conscience. International criminal tribunals have generally followed these interpretations. In the ICTY and ICTR, using persons as human shields is an example of behavior that has been found to constitute inhuman or cruel treatment.

The definitions of torture and other forms of prohibited treatment, and the boundaries between such various forms of treatment, tend to be somewhat fluid and to change over time. According to the European Court of Human Rights, in its findings in Ireland v. U.K., the distinction between torture and other forms of prohibited treatment was embodied in the Torture Convention in order to allow the special stigma of torture to attach only to deliberate inhuman treatment causing very serious and cruel suffering. The European Court has also consciously amended its standards over the years, classifying as torture acts which it had previously viewed as inhuman treatment in the past. An example of this shift in classification can be seen in the 1999 case of Selmouni v. France.

Sanctions

How does the prohibition on torture and other ill-treatment affect what forms of punishment states may impose, given that the Torture Convention says that torture "does not include pain or suffering arising only from, inherent in, or incidental to lawful sanctions"? The same exclusion appears as part of the definition of torture as a crime against humanity applying in the ICTY, ICTR, and ICC. The main reason for the exclusion is to make clear that punishments such as imprisonment, which might otherwise be challenged on the basis they cause severe suffering, do not constitute torture. The question is to what extent this leaves open the door for other punishments that would otherwise fall foul of the definition but are permitted under national law. Some argue that the phrase rightly leaves what constitutes cruel, inhuman, or degrading treatment or punishment to be determined by the moral and legal standards in each society. Under Islamic shari'a law, theft is punishable by amputation of the right hand, and in certain countries, corporal punishments are administered by the courts. Some national courts have ruled that corporal punishments such as whipping and flogging violate the prohibition on torture or ill-treatment. Examples are Botswana, Zimbabwe, Namibia, South Africa, and St. Vincent and the Grenadines. In Tyrer v. U.K., the European Court of Human Rights found that the punishment of birching (a type of flogging) ordered by a juvenile court was a degrading punishment. The UN Special Rapporteur on Torture reported to the Commission on Human Rights in 1997 that, in his view, corporal punishment violates the prohibition on torture or cruel, inhuman, or degrading treatment or punishment. Further, punishments are subject to scrutiny according to international standards. Subsequently, the commission adopted a Resolution 1997/38, which stated that corporal punishment can amount to cruel, inhuman, or degrading punishment or even to torture. Corporal punishment is prohibited in the Geneva Conventions in relation to prisoners of war or protected civilians in international armed conflict.

The courts of several countries, including Tanzania, Canada, Hungary, and South Africa, have held that the death penalty violates constitutional prohibitions on torture and other forms of ill-treatment. In the Öcalan case, the European Court of Human Rights in 2003 declined to reach a firm conclusion on whether the death penalty was inhuman and degrading in all circumstances, but found that its imposition following an unfair trial did amount to inhuman treatment. The prohibition on torture also places limitations on how the death penalty is implemented. In 1994, the Judicial Committee of the Privy Council, the highest court of appeal for Jamaica, ruled that to carry out executions after 14 years of delay would violate the Jamaican constitution, and that after five years on death row, a prisoner would have suffered inhuman punishment (*Pratt and Morgan v. Attorney General for Jamaica*).

Psychological Impact of Torture

Both physical and mental torture can have lasting psychological effects. In serious cases, post-traumatic stress disorder (PTSD) can be diagnosed. Criteria for PTSD include re-experiencing aspects of a traumatic event in nightmares or flashbacks, avoidance of reminders of the event, sleep problems, memory and concentration problems, anger, and low mood. However, the concept of PTSD is somewhat controversial among mental health experts, and some (such as Derek Summerfield) do not accept that there is a psychiatric illness that is specific of trauma or torture. Such dissenting experts view the reframing of distress as a psychological disturbance to be a distortion, and prefer to look for solutions in a broader social recovery.

Because of the widespread use of torture and the particular needs of those who survive it, specialized torture rehabilitation centers have sprung up all around the world that provide physical and psychological treatment for survivors of torture. Some of these are in the countries where torture is taking place, and others cater primarily for refugee communities. The UN in 1981 established the UN Voluntary Fund for Victims of Torture to provide humanitarian assistance through medical, legal, and other forms of support to torture victims and their families.

International law has increasingly recognized that the psychological impact of torture calls for particular legal remedies. In international standards that are developing on the right to reparation, rehabilitation—including medical and psychological care as well as legal and social services—is specifically identified as one of the forms of reparation to which victims of violations will be entitled. This perspective is explicitly embodied in the UN Draft Basic Principles and Guidelines on the Right to a Remedy and Reparation.

Action of International Institutions and International Jurisdictions against Torture

Monitoring states' records on torture and holding them accountable is the function of international human rights treaty bodies. Among these bodies is the UN Committee Against Torture, established under the Torture Convention, which requires member states to submit regular reports on what they are doing to comply with the treaty, and issues observations and recommendations in response. Although the Committee Against Torture lacks enforcement powers and is frequently frustrated by states' late reporting, most states that are party to the Torture Convention do submit reports and appear before the committee to defend their records. The UN Commission on Human Rights has also taken steps specifically targeting torture. Its Special Rapporteur on Torture takes up cases of alleged torture with governments, carries out country visits, and reports annually to the Human Rights Commission. These mechanisms are designed to respond both to individual or isolated acts and to systematic torture.

Procedures have also been developed specifically to address situations where torture is committed as part of a widespread or systematic pattern of violations. Under Article 20 of the Torture Convention, there is established a confidential inquiry mechanism that allows the committee to look into information that torture is being systematically practiced in a member state. The UN Commission on Human Rights also has a confidential procedure (known as the 1503 Procedure) for considering information pointing toward a consistent pattern of gross and systematic violations. If, after examining the situation, a special working group believes further steps are needed, it can turn the matter over for more public consideration by the commission. This procedure was revised following a review in 2000, in response to the widely held view that it was ineffective.

Individual complaint mechanisms established at regional and international levels have been important in revealing places where systematic torture is taking place, as well as in providing redress for individual victims. United Nations' treaty bodies, including the Committee Against Torture, receive complaints from individuals, but only against states that have agreed to such complaints being referred. The treaty bodies also issue non-binding decisions on whether a violation has taken place. Regional human rights courts, such as the European and Inter-American Courts of Human Rights, have played a leading role in defining torture and other forms of ill-treatment, and have issued many judgments declaring that a violation has occurred and ordering compensation to individual torture victims. However since the remedies they order are directed at the individuals whose cases are before them, these courts have not been able to deal directly with the underlying causes of widespread or systematic torture. Nevertheless, their findings can help to reveal the problem, and may help bring about international pressure for change.

International inspection mechanisms have been established that aim to prevent torture by addressing the conditions it which it occurs. The European Committee for the Protection of Torture and Inhuman or Degrading Treatment or Punishment (the ECPT) operates within Europe and is designed to bring about improvements in conditions in which prisoners and detainees are held. This committee conducts regular inspections of places of detention within its member states, and also makes ad hoc, unscheduled visits in response to specific concerns. After a visit, the committee reports its findings to the state in which the detentions are occurring, and gives that state an opportunity to respond. Normally, the state allows the report to be made public. In 2002, a new Optional Protocol to the UN Convention against Torture was adopted by the UN General Assembly, establishing a similar system of international inspection of places of detention for states that are party to the Convention and that have signed up for participation in the inspection program.

The international community has also taken collective action to hold individuals criminally accountable for torture, along with other crimes under international law. Since the Nuremberg trials, international law has recognized torture in its occurrence as a crime against humanity, but there have been relatively few prosecutions either at the international or national level until the establishment of the ICTY and the ICTR in the 1990s. Torture and ill treatment were prosecuted in some of the post–World War II trials. One example was the "High Command Case" brought by the U.S. against fourteen Nazi defendants in Germany in the 1940s. Torture was singled out by the international commissions of experts that convinced the UN Security Council to establish the ICTY, the ICTR, and, in 2000, the Special Panels in East Timor. It was also one of the violations that spurred the UN to agree to work together with the government of Sierra Leone to establish the

Special Court there in 2002. Numerous indictments for torture have been handed down by these judicial institutions.

There are also examples of countries prosecuting torture as part of an attempt to deal with atrocities in their own past. Klaus Barbie, head of the Gestapo in Paris during the Nazi occupation of France in World War II, was tried in a French criminal court in 1987 for crimes against humanity committed in France during the war, in which acts of torture featured prominently. He was sentenced to life imprisonment. Truth-seeking mechanisms, such as national truth commissions, have also investigated widespread torture. In its report of 2003, the Peruvian Truth Commission concluded that during the period 1983 to 1997 there was a widespread practice of torture by state officials that amounted to crimes against humanity, and recommended that criminal charges be brought against those responsible.

The 1990s saw a significant increase in action by individual states to pursue alleged torturers for acts committed outside their territory, relying either on universal jurisdiction or other permissible bases of jurisdiction, such as the nationality of the victim. The number of states that had amended their law to provide a jurisdictional basis for their courts to prosecute torture committed elsewhere, and the number of actual prosecutions, steadily increased. In 1994 a Danish court convicted Refik Saric under the Geneva Conventions for torturing detainees in a Croat-run prison camp in Bosnia in 1993, and sentenced him to eight years imprisonment. A Spanish court charged former Chilean President Augusto Pinochet with committing torture in Chile, and sought his extradition from the U.K. in 1998. That process was stopped, not due to any jurisdictional impediment, but because Pinochet was found to be unfit to stand trial. Complaints including torture have also been pursued in the courts of several European countries, including Belgium, France, the Netherlands, and Senegal, involving alleged torture in Chad, Mauritania, Rwanda, Algeria, Tunisia, Suriname, Chile, and Argentina.

SEE ALSO Conventions Against Torture and Other Cruel, Inhuman, and Degrading Treatment; Prosecution; Psychology of Perpetrators; Psychology of Victims; Reparations

BIBLIOGRAPHY

Amnesty International (2003). *Combating Torture: A Manual for Action.* Amnesty International

Burgers, J. H., and H. Danelius (1988). *The United Nations Convention against Torture.* Dordrecht, Netherlands: Martinus Nijhoff Publishers.

Burnett, A. (2002). *Guide to Health Workers Providing Care for Asylum Seekers and Refugees*. London: Medical Foundation for the Care of Victims of Torture.

Convention against Torture and Other Cruel, Inhuman or Degrading Treatment or Punishment. GA res. 39/46, Annex, December 10, 1984.

Elements of Crimes of the Rome Statute, Official Record of the First Session of the Assembly of States Parties to the Rome Statute of the International Criminal Court, doc. ICC-ASP/1/3.

Evans, M., and R. Morgan (1998). *Preventing Torture*. Oxford: Oxford University Press.

Harris, D. J., M. O'Boyle, and C. Warbrick (1995). *Law of the European Convention on Human Rights*. London: Butterworths.

Rodley, Nigel S. (1999). *The Treatment of Prisoners under International Law*, 2nd edition. Oxford: Oxford University Press.

Schabas, William A. (2000). *Genocide in International Law*. Cambridge: Cambridge University Press.

United Nations Commission on Human Rights (2003). *Basic Principles and Guidelines on the Right to a Remedy and Reparation for Victims of [Gross] Violations of International Human Rights Law and [Serious] Violations of International Humanitarian Law. Revised Draft of October 2003*. UN Commission on Human Rights document E/CN.4/2004/57. New York: United Nations Commission on Human Rights.

Fiona McKay

Trail of Tears

At the time of European entry into North America, the Cherokee Nation included a large portion of the southern United States. Over the years, however, treaties and military actions reduced the Cherokee lands to an area comprised of western North Carolina, southeastern Tennessee, northern Georgia, and northeastern Alabama. Even here, the Cherokee, a number of whom were educated and literate, lived under the legislative control of whites without recourse to personal legal protection.

As early as 1810 a group known as the Western Cherokee had migrated to Arkansas Territory. Over the years others followed, including the illustrious Sequoyah, inventor of the world-famous Cherokee Syllabary (or Cherokee alphabet). During 1828 these Cherokee traded their Arkansas lands for others in Indian Territory (now Oklahoma).

Two events in 1828 exacerbated the situation for the Cherokee Nation: the election of Andrew Jackson as president of the United States and the discovery of gold on the Cherokee lands of northern Georgia, spawning state laws that annexed the lands for gold-mining and stripped the Cherokee of legal redress from whites. Despite the determined opposition of Cherokee chief John Ross, in 1830 Jackson was able to push through Congress an Indian Removal Bill that would remove, on a so-called voluntary basis, all Eastern Indian tribes to west of the Mississippi River. His administration further supported the power of the states, in defiance of the U.S. Supreme Court, to usurp solemn treaties made with the Cherokee and other tribes. During the winter of 1831–1832 Chief Justice John Marshall ruled that U.S. treaties overrode the laws of the state of Georgia. Jackson supposedly replied, "John Marshall has rendered his decision; now let him enforce it" (Woodward, 1963, p. 171).

When Ross, backed by the Cherokee full-blood majority, stubbornly refused to accede to Jackson's demands, Jackson subverted the accepted Cherokee form of governance and conspired with a group of Cherokee intellectuals who were amenable to removal. Through his representative, the Reverend John F. Schermerhorn, Jackson was able to negotiate the 1835 Treaty of New Echota with the ad hoc group. By this treaty the Cherokee Nation ceded all its lands east of the Mississippi to the United States for a sum of $3.25 million and agreed to relocate to new lands in Indian Territory. A U.S. officer who witnessed the treaty signing opined that if placed before the Cherokee people, the treaty would have been rejected by nine-tenths of them. Former president John Quincy Adams called the treaty "an eternal disgrace upon the country" (Eaton, 1914, p. 55).

Once the Treaty of New Echota was ratified by Congress, Jackson issued a proclamation decreeing that the United States no longer recognized the existing Cherokee governance. U.S. troops commenced rounding up Cherokee and herding them to collection camps at U.S. military posts during 1837 and 1838. Without prior notice terrified families were forced from their homes and driven off their lands, leaving behind all they owned. At times wives, husbands, and children were separated from one another. Often they were abused and degraded by the troops (Jones, 1838, p. 236).

During 1837 and the spring of 1838 over two thousand Cherokee were rounded up by the army and removed forcibly to the West. Traveling both by river and overland, some of these parties suffered cholera and other illnesses, many dying en route. Another twenty-three hundred of the Pro-Treaty Party departed voluntarily, taking an overland wagon route by way of Memphis. A number of Cherokee escaped troops by hiding out in the mountains of western North Carolina.

With a severe drought delaying removal through the summer and fall of 1838, some twelve thousand

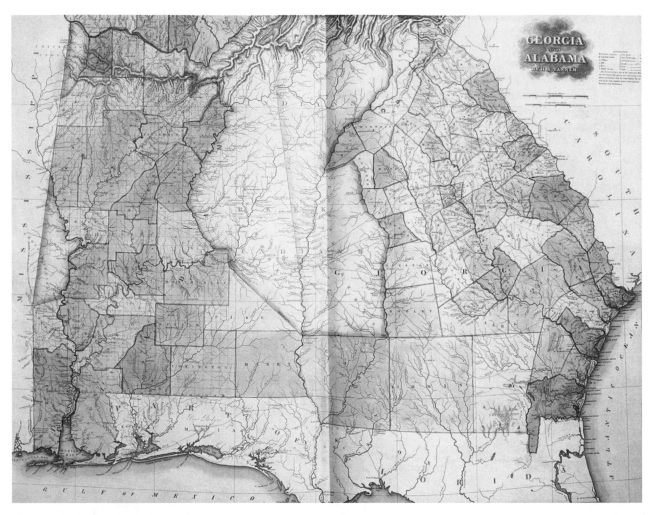

A map of Georgia and Alabama, 1823. As part of its Indian removal policy, the U.S. government forcibly moved Native Americans, during the 1830s, from their homelands in the southeastern United States to lands far west of the Mississippi River. [CORBIS]

Cherokee remained imprisoned in the cramped, disease-ridden stockade pens without bedding, cooking utensils, spare clothing, sanitation facilities, fresh drinking water, adequate food, medical attention, or shelter from the blazing sun. Official records indicate that 353 Cherokee died in the camps, but most historians believe the number was much larger.

Eventually, the surviving Cherokee were moved to collection points for their forced march to Indian Territory. Fort Payne, Alabama, served as one point of debarkation for a party that, lacking tents, blankets, and even shoes, took a middle route through northern Arkansas. Another group was formed at Ross's Landing near Chattanooga. By far the greatest number of Cherokee were herded into camps at Calhoun Agency's Rattlesnake Springs near present-day Charleston, Tennessee.

Here, principally, began the infamous Cherokee Trail of Tears, which followed a winter-imperiled, 800-mile route through Kentucky, Illinois, and Missouri. Detachments of overland wagon caravans organized and departed through October and November 1838 on their fateful three-month journey. Each of these was under the control of Cherokee Nation captains and light-horse police, Ross having convinced General Winfield Scott that the Cherokee themselves could best manage their own removal.

As the first dazed contingent pushed off from Rattlesnake Springs on October 1, the mixed-blood scholar William Shorey Coodey expressed his deep pathos. "Pangs of parting," he observed, "are tearing the hearts of our bravest men at this forced abandonment of their dear lov'd country" (Hoig, 1996, p. 3).

Even at the start of the foreboding three months on the trail, there were problems. Children, the elderly, and those weak with illnesses contracted in the camps were loaded into the few wagons available. Many others were forced to walk and carry whatever goods they possessed. Once on the move, they suffered from billowing trail dust or, when the rains came, wheel-clogging mud that once dried, left deep, travel-impeding ruts. But worse problems developed when severe weather arrived. By the time the lead caravans reached Kentucky, an early blizzard struck, bringing punishing temperatures along with blowing snow and icy roads that made travel even more difficult. Canvas wagon covers provided scant protection at night.

Members of the caravan had already begun to die, among them proud elderly Chief White Path, who in 1827 led a rebellion against white influence on his people. He was buried along the trail near Hopkinsville, Kentucky; his grave is marked by a long pole and linen flag.

A traveler from Maine, who encountered the Cherokee exodus in early December, observed the wagons loaded with the sick, feeble, and dying as the majority of the Cherokee struggled forth against the flesh-numbing winds. One young Cherokee mother "could only carry her dying child a few miles further, and then she must stop in a stranger land and consign her much loved babe to the cold ground and pass on with the multitude" (New York Observer, 1839).

The Cherokee agony grew even worse upon reaching the ice-clogged Ohio River and beyond. Blasts of snow and freezing rain plagued the march; dysentery, whooping cough, and other diseases decimated the doctorless caravans. Funerals were conducted at almost every camping place, leaving a pathetic line of gravesites to mark the route across southern Illinois and Missouri. "For what crime," missionary David Butrick moaned, "was this whole nation doomed?" (Kutsche, 1986).

The death toll for the Cherokee removal and Trail of Tears has been estimated to be as high as four thousand. This does not include fatalities that occurred during the tribe's painful resettlement in the wilds of Indian Territory. Nor was even the loss of homes and property in their former Nation as disastrous as the intense rancor and divisiveness that the removal had caused among the Cherokee themselves. It would wrench their Nation apart and lead to years of factional bloodshed.

SEE ALSO Forcible Transfer; Indigenous Peoples; Native Americans

BIBLIOGRAPHY

Eaton, Rachel Caroline (1914). *John Ross and the Cherokee Indians.* Menasha, Wis.: George Banta Publishing.

Hoig, Stanley W. (1998). *The Cherokees and Their Chiefs: In the Wake of Empire.* Fayetteville: University of Arkansas Press.

Hoig, Stan (1996). *Night of the Cruel Moon: Cherokee Removal and the Trail of Tears.* New York: Facts on File.

Jones, Evans (1838). *Baptist Missionary Magazine* (September)18:236.

Kutsche, Paul (1986). "Butrick Journal." In *ABC Documents* 4519, 18.3.3, vol. 4, dating to October 1838.

New York Observer, January 26, 1839.

Woodward, Grace Steele (1963). *The Cherokees.* Norman: University of Oklahoma Press

Stan Hoig

Transitional Justice

Transitional justice refers to a field of activity and inquiry focused on how societies address legacies of past human rights abuses, mass atrocity, or other forms of severe social trauma, including genocide or civil war, in order to build a more democratic, just, or peaceful future.

The concept is commonly understood as a framework for confronting past abuse as a component of a major political transformation. This generally involves a combination of complementary judicial and nonjudicial strategies, such as prosecuting perpetrators; establishing truth commissions and other forms of investigation about the past; forging efforts toward reconciliation in fractured societies; developing reparations packages for those most affected by the violence or abuse; memorializing and remembering victims; and reforming a wide spectrum of abusive state institutions (such as security services, police, or military) in an attempt to prevent future violations.

Transitional justice draws on two primary sources to make a normative argument in favor of confronting the past (if one assumes that local conditions support doing so). First, the human rights movement has strongly influenced the development of the field, making it self-consciously victim-centric. Transitional justice practitioners tend to pursue strategies that they believe are consistent with the rights and concerns of victims, survivors, and victims' families.

An additional source of legitimacy derives from international human rights and humanitarian law. Transitional justice relies on international law to make the case that states undergoing transitions are faced with certain legal obligations, including halting ongoing human rights abuses, investigating past crimes, identifying those responsible for human rights violations, imposing sanctions on those responsible, providing reparations to victims, preventing future abuses, preserving and enhancing peace, and fostering individual and national reconciliation.

Defining Transitional Justice

At its core, transitional justice is a link between the two concepts of transition and justice. The etymology of the phrase is unclear, but it had already become a term by the 1992 publication of the three-part volume *Transitional Justice: How Emerging Democracies Reckon with Former Regimes* edited by Neil Kritz, which brings together the early and significant texts of the field. The term itself is misleading, as it more commonly refers to "justice during transition" than to any form of modified or altered justice.

Transitional justice has certain defining characteristics. First, it includes the concept of justice. Although the field depends on international legal principles that require the prosecution of perpetrators, this context also includes broader forms of justice, such as reparations programs and truth-seeking mechanisms.

The second key concept is transitional, which refers to a major political transformation, such as regime change from authoritarian or repressive rule to democratic or electoral rule or a transition from conflict to peace or stability. Although transitions are understood as long processes, there is also an emphasis on key historical moments such as those that occurred in Chile (1990), East Timor (2001), Guatemala (1994), Poland (1997), Sierra Leone (1999), and South Africa (1994). When a society "turns over a new leaf" or "gets a fresh start," mechanisms of transitional justice can help strengthen this process.

The transitional justice framework recognizes that transitions are complex and often characterized by both impediments and opportunities for new and creative democratic strategies. For example, the transition might be a negotiated settlement resulting in a tenuous peace or fragile democracy. The existing judicial system might be weak, corrupt, or ineffective. Justice during a transition may be limited by barriers such as a large number of perpetrators that is far beyond the capacity of the legal system to prosecute. Similarly, there might be an abundance of victims and survivors, many of whom would like the opportunity to tell their stories or receive financial compensation. Legal or constitutional limitations to accountability, such as amnesties for perpetrators associated with the former regime, may result from negotiations, thereby limiting prosecutorial capabilities. Nascent democratic institutions might suffer from authoritarian enclaves or the lasting influence of former power brokers. In these contexts transitional justice requires an awareness of multiple imperatives during a political transition, suggesting that comprehensive justice must be sought in a context in which other values are also important, including democracy, stability, equity, and fairness to victims and their families.

Development of a Field

The origins of the field can be traced back to the post–World War II setting in Europe (e.g., the International Military Tribunal at Nuremberg and denazification programs in Germany). However, the transitional justice framework gained coherence in the last two-and-a-half decades of the twentieth century, especially beginning with the trials of the former members of the military juntas in Greece (1975) and Argentina (1983), in which domestic judicial systems successfully tried the intellectual authors of past abuses for their crimes.

The truth-seeking efforts in Latin America's Southern Cone—such as the Argentine National Commission on the Disappearance of People (1983), the Uruguayan nongovernmental effort that resulted in a best-selling report entitled *Uruguay: Never Again, and the Chilean Truth and Reconciliation Commission* (1990)—further expanded the possibilities of comprehensive justice during transition, relying on the idea of truth as an "absolute, unrenounceable value" (Zalaquett, 1993, p. xxxi). Argentina's and Chile's additional efforts to provide different forms of reparation to victims also made important contributions to establishing justice for victims of human rights abuses.

These developments emerged because democratic activists and their allies in government sought to find new and creative ways to address the past. To accomplish this, they began to develop the nascent transitional justice framework as a way to strengthen new democracies and comply with the moral and legal obligations that the human rights movement was articulating, both domestically and internationally.

Eastern European endeavors to deal with past violations by opening up the files of former security agencies (e.g., the Stasi Records Act in Germany in 1991) or banning past human rights offenders from positions of power through disqualification (e.g., what occurred in Czechoslovakia in 1991) also contributed to debates on how to achieve justice during transition.

In 1995, drawing on experiences from Latin America and Eastern Europe (Boraine, Levy, and Scheffer, 1997), South Africa established a Truth and Reconciliation Commission to address past human rights crimes. Since then truth commissions have become widely recognized instruments of transitional justice, and commissions have been formed in many parts of the world, including East Timor, Ghana, Peru, and Sierra Leone. All differ from previous models, and many demonstrate important innovations.

The creation of ad hoc tribunals for the former Yugoslavia and Rwanda, while not specifically designed to strengthen democratic transitions, have enhanced jurisprudence in transitional justice and achieved some visible victories for accountability. The ratification of the International Criminal Court (ICC) also represents an extremely important moment in the history of transitional justice.

Efforts to prosecute perpetrators of human rights abuses in Chile and Guatemala in the late 1990s and early 2000s have arguably strengthened movements for criminal accountability on the national level and been influential on an international scale in demonstrating the potential of this approach.

Comprehensive Approach to Past Abuse

By the first decade of the twenty-first century there was increasing consensus among scholars and practitioners about the basic contents of the transitional justice framework, which accepts the general premise that national strategies to confront past human rights abuses, depending on the specifics of the local context, can contribute to accountability, an end to impunity, the reconstruction of state-citizen relationships, and the creation of democratic institutions. It then proposes that such a national strategy consider the following complementary approaches in an effort to contribute to comprehensive justice at a critical political juncture. These include:

- Prosecution of perpetrators, whether on the domestic level, in a hybrid internationalized court (i.e., the Special Court for Sierra Leone), or in an international court, such as the ICC.

- Establishing the truth about the past through the creation of truth commissions or other national efforts, such as engaging in major historical research, compiling victims' testimonials or oral histories, supporting the work of forensic anthropologists in determining the exact nature of victims' deaths, or exhuming the bodies of those killed.

- Establishing reparations policies that take into account the requirements of, or moral obligations to, the victims. These policies can include economic compensation as well as a variety of health (physical and mental) and education benefits, and symbolic measures, such as a state apology.

- Remembering and honoring victims through a series of measures, including consulting with victims to develop memorials and museums of memory, converting public spaces such as former detention camps into memorial parks and interpretive sites, and catalyzing constructive social dialogue about the past.

- Developing reconciliation initiatives, such as working with victims to determine what they require in order to experience healing and closure, and forging peaceful coexistence among former adversaries without sacrificing justice and accountability for perpetrators.

- Reforming institutions that have a history of abusive behavior, including, for example, security forces or the police, in order to prevent future patterns of abuse and establish state-society relationships based on functioning and fair institutions.

SEE ALSO Chile; East Timor; El Salvador; International Criminal Tribunal for the Former Yugoslavia; Reparations; Sierra Leone; Truth Commissions

BIBLIOGRAPHY

Bassiouni, M. Cherif, ed. (2002). *Post-Conflict Justice*. New York: Transnational Publishers.

Boraine, Alex, Janet Levy, and Ronel Scheffer, eds. (1997). *Dealing with the Past*. Cape Town, South Africa: Institute for Democracy in South Africa.

Crocker, D. A. (1999). "Reckoning with Past Wrongs: A Normative Framework." *Ethics & International Affairs* 13:43–61.

Hayner, Priscilla (2002). *Unspeakable Truths: Facing the Challenge of Truth Commissions*. New York: Routledge.

Kritz, Neil, ed. (1995). *Transitional Justice: How Emerging Democracies Reckon with Former Regimes*, Vols. I–III. Washington, D.C.: U.S. Institute of Peace Press.

Mendez, Juan E. (1997). "Accountability for Past Abuses." *Human Rights Quarterly* 19:255.

Nino, Carlos S. (1996). *Radical Evil on Trial*. New Haven, Conn.: Yale University Press.

Zalaquett, Jose (1993). "Introduction to the English Edition." In *Chilean National Commission on Truth and Reconciliation: Report of the Chilean National Commission on Truth and Reconciliation*, trans. Phillip E. Berryman. South Bend, Ind.: University of Notre Dame Press.

Louis Bickford

Truth Commissions

A truth commission is an official, temporary body set up to investigate a period of past human rights violations or violations of human rights law. After taking statements from victims, witnesses, and others, a truth commission produces a final report that is usually made public and serves as an official acknowledgment of what was often before either widely denied or little understood.

The 1990s showed a sharp increase in the global interest in such unofficial truth-seeking for countries emerging from repressive rule or armed conflict, and this interest has continued in the decade of the 2000s. By 2004 there were over thirty examples of truth commissions that had existed in all regions of the world.

The initial meeting of South Africa's Truth and Reconciliation Commission, in East London, South Africa, April 15, 1996. The commission hears the first-hand accounts of victims of the apartheid regime. [AP/WORLD WIDE PHOTOS]

A truth commission is officially sanctioned, either by the government or the armed opposition, where relevant, sometimes also with the backing of the international community such as the United Nations. A truth commission can thus be distinguished from the efforts undertaken by nongovernmental organizations to document abuses, as important as those also may be, as such official commissions generally have better access to information and will receive much greater attention to their work.

Goals of Truth Commissions

A truth commission may be established with a number of aims. In addition to discovering or more publicly revealing the extent of past abuses, such a commission can look into the causes as well as the consequences of what took place, identifying patterns of wrongdoing and broader institutional responsibility, that cannot always be done through the courts. In addition, a truth commission is usually focused primarily on victims' experiences, providing victims and survivors with a supportive context in which to recount their story. Some

victims find the process of telling their story to an official and credible body an important part of their healing process, although many still find it painful to remember and describe such traumatic memories in great detail. Another important aim of a truth commission is to learn from the past in order to put forward recommended reforms that will help prevent such abuses in the future.

Truth commissions are understood to be part of the broader field of transitional justice, and are best instituted when done in a manner that complements other initiatives to obtain accountability. While truth commissions themselves do not have the power to put someone in jail for their past deeds, they may still make publicly known that certain named individuals were responsible for past crimes, which can have other subsequent effects. Indeed, the late twentieth century has shown that the relationship between truth commissions and other forms of accountability, especially that of prosecution and vetting, can be quite positive. Often there is a clear interrelationship between truth commissions and other measures that address victims, as well as broader societal needs, such as reparations programs and institutional reform.

Truth commissions are usually set up through national legislation, or sometimes by way of presidential decree. In some cases, such as in El Salvador and Sierra Leone, a truth commission was first agreed to in a national peace accord. Their terms of reference can be quite broad, typically covering more than a decade of violence or abuses, sometimes going back even as far as thirty-five or forty years. The founding legislation or decree may leave some flexibility for the commission to determine its precise scope, but generally a truth commission is directed to try to determine the causes as well as consequences of the abuses that took place, through speaking with victims, undertaking research and investigations, holding public hearings, if appropriate, and completing a final report with recommendations.

The first truth commissions were established in the 1970s, but the first well-known truth commission was established in Argentina in 1983, at the end of a seven-year period of military rule. This National Commission on the Disappeared found that close to eight thousand persons had been forcibly "disappeared" by government forces during the period of military rule. Years later, the findings from this commission were used to implement a reparations program for families of the victims. Since then, prominent truth commissions have been established throughout Latin America, Africa, and Asia, and there has been at least one example in eastern Europe. For example, the early- to mid-1990s saw such commissions established in Chile, El Salvador, Haiti, Guatemala, and South Africa, and by the early 2000s, such bodies were created in Peru, East Timor, Ghana, and Sierra Leone. By that time, it was widely accepted in the international community that transitions from authoritarianism or armed conflict were likely to at least consider establishing an official, nonjudicial truth-seeking mechanism as part of a transitional accountability package.

Despite the increasing support for and understanding of these investigative bodies on the international level, it remains important that the decision to establish a truth commission—including the precise form that it might take and powers and mandate that it is given—remain a national one. One of the primary purposes of a truth commission, that of assisting a process of national reflecting and acknowledgment of the wrongs committed in the past, is unlikely to result from an internationally imposed or internationally determined process.

However, there may be an important role for the international community in providing funding and technical assistance, and in some cases some of the members of a truth commission have been internationals.

How Truth Commissions Operate

Typically operating for one to two years, a truth commission generally takes statements from thousands of victims, its staff traveling throughout the country and perhaps even overseas to collect information from survivors of the past violence. A few of the truth commissions that have existed have been given quite strong investigatory powers, including powers to subpoena and the powers of search and seizure, allowing them to enter into premises without prior notice. These powers have been used to obtain documents and other information from prisons and government offices, for example.

The South African Truth and Reconciliation Commission received a great amount of international attention, in part because it was given unique powers to grant amnesty to individuals who confessed and fully described their crimes, if those individuals could demonstrate that the crimes were committed for political rather than personal motivation. This arrangement set out in the Commissions founding legislation, contributed to hundreds of perpetrators describing the details of their crimes in public hearings, aired live on radio and broadcast on television, making it impossible for the public to deny the level of abuse that had taken place under apartheid. The South African commission is the only truth commission that has been given amnesty-granting powers. Others can either request or subpoena perpetrators to come forward, but without offering an amnesty in exchange.

The question of how these nonjudicial investigatory bodies relate to or have an impact on prosecutions of human rights abusers in the courts has been of great interest over the years. Initially, especially in the early to mid-1990s, there was fear that the creation of truth commissions would somehow displace or reduce the possibility of prosecutions taking place for the crimes covered by the commission. In some cases, an existing amnesty, or a new agreement to grant amnesty in the context of a peace accord, has spurred the establishment of a truth commission. But there is rarely an explicit link between the two. There often is an overlap in the substantive focus of a truth commission and any domestic or international investigations that may be underway for the purposes of prosecuting accused perpetrators. However, time has shown that these commissions can in fact strengthen the possibility of successful prosecutions, by sharing information with the courts during or after the commission's investigations are completed. The Truth and Reconciliation Commission in Peru, for example, established a judicialization unit within the commission and prepared cases that it recommended for prosecution by the appropriate authorities.

Some truth commissions also contribute to individual accountability by naming the names of persons that they find to be responsible for abuses in the past. The El Salvador Commission on the Truth, for example, named over forty persons, identifying their direct involvement in planning or carrying out some of the most egregious acts that took place during the country's civil war from 1980 to 1991. The minister of defense was named for his direct involvement in major atrocities committed years earlier, for example, and the president of the Supreme Court was named for prejudicial and politically motivated attempts to block investigations into a 1981 massacre. Some persons named by the Salvadoran commission were removed from their posts, but the government quickly passed a broad amnesty that prevented prosecutions.

Truth commissions are generally established where widespread abuses took place and where they were unaccounted for or officially denied at the time. However, some countries that have suffered some of the more infamous histories of genocide or intense violence in the decades of the late twentieth century, such as Rwanda or Cambodia, have chosen not to put a truth commission in place. This may be due to a lack of popular interest in delving into the past, or perhaps insufficient political interest in investigating and revealing the full nature, extent, and institutional or personal involvement in past crimes. There can be political and personal risks as well as traumas associated with digging into such a fraught and painful period, and thus some countries choose not to institute such an inquiry during a political transition.

While all truth commissions as of the early 2000s have found and reported on unspeakable violence, few have concluded that the violence constituted genocide, per se. The truth commission in Guatemala, called the Commission for Historical Clarification, was under pressure from victims and survivor groups to include such an explicit finding it its final report, in recognition of the tens of thousands of indigenous Mayan people who were targeted and killed in the course of the war. After close legal analysis of the nature and extent of the violence, the commission did conclude that government forces committed "acts of genocide" as part of its counterinsurgency strategy early in the civil war. This finding, along with the commission's other strong conclusions, received an emotional response from a population whose suffering had very rarely been acknowledged by the state.

Over time, new truth commissions have been formed with more creative and far-reaching mandates. Some have been designed to work very closely with indigenous or nationally rooted and community-based mechanisms. In East Timor, for example, a truth commission facilitated perpetrator confessions and negotiated agreement for low-level perpetrators to undertake community service or provide a symbolic payment, thus allowing the perpetrator to be reintegrated fully into his or her community. In Sierra Leone, some truth commission hearings ended with indigenously based cleansing ceremonies, with Sierra Leonean paramount chiefs overseeing a process of accepting back into the community those wrongdoers who had confessed. More of these kinds of creative approaches may well be incorporated into new truth commissions in the future.

Because truth commissions are generally instituted after a period of repression or violence has come to an end, their main focus is to learn from that past and to make specific recommendations to help prevent the reoccurrence of such abuses in the future. These recommendations often include institutional reforms, such as strengthening the judicial system or legal framework so that proper and independent oversight of the actions of government and armed forces will take place when complaints are made. In some contexts, recommendations also address social, educational, and even cultural aspects of society and the need to make changes, addressed not only to the government but sometimes to society at large.

In addition to reforms that may take place on an official level, advocates hope that an honest understanding and recognition of the extent of past abuses will help to strengthen societal resistance to allowing such events to take place again.

But few truth commissions have had the power to adopt conclusions that are mandatory. Such conclusions are often considered as recommendations, and some well-formulated proposals have not been followed up by the government and implemented as policy. The commission itself generally ceases to exist with the submission of its report, leaving the lobbying around policy implementation to civil society organizations. A few truth commissions, however—in El Salvador and Sierra Leone—have been given the power to address resolutions to the government that are agreed in advance to be obligatory. In addition, the legislation that set up the Sierra Leone commission allows for the creation of a follow-up committee at end of the commission's work. The goal of that commission is to track and publicly report on the progress of implementation of the original commission's recommendations. These and other examples show society's increasing concern to strengthen the long-term impact of truth commissions.

SEE ALSO Argentina; Chile; El Salvador; Guatemala; South Africa

BIBLIOGRAPHY

Chapman, Audrey R., and Patrick Ball (2001). "The Truth of Truth Commissions: Comparative Lessons from Haiti, South Africa, and Guatemala." *Human Rights Quarterly* 23:1.

Chilean National Commission on Truth and Reconciliation (1993). *Report of the Chilean National Commission on Truth and Reconciliation,* trans. Phillip E. Berryman. Notre Dame, Ind.: Notre Dame University Press.

Goldstone, Richard J. (1996). "Justice as a Tool for Peace-Keeping: Truth Commissions and International Criminal Tribunals." *New York University Journal of International Law and Politics* 28:485.

Hayner, Priscilla B. (2001). *Unspeakable Truths: Confronting State Terror and Atrocity.* New York: Routledge.

Parleviet, Michelle (1998). "Considering Truth: Dealing with a Legacy of Gross Human Rights Violations." *Netherlands Quarterly of Human Rights* 16:141.

Posel, Deborah, and Graeme Simpson, eds. (2002). *Commissioning the Past: Understanding South Africa's Truth and Reconciliation Commission.* Johannesburg, South Africa: Witwatersrand University Press.

Rotberg, Robert I., and Dennis Thompson, eds. (2000). *Truth v. Justice: The Morality of Truth Commissions.* Princeton, N.J.: Princeton University Press.

Truth and Reconciliation Commission of South Africa (1999). *Truth and Reconciliation Commission of South Africa Report.* New York: Grove's Dictionaries.

Villa-Vicencio, Charles, and Wilhelm Verwoerd, eds. (2000). *Looking Back, Reaching Forward: Reflections on the Truth and Reconciliation Commission of South Africa.* London: Zed Books.

Priscilla B. Hayner

Tudjman, Franjo
[MAY 14, 1922–DECEMBER 10, 1999]
First Croatian president

Franjo Tudjman was born in Veliko Trgovisce, a village in the Hrvatsko Zagorje region in northern Croatia. He was the first president of Croatia, following its creation as an independent state in 1991.

During World War II Tudjman fought alongside his father and brothers as an officer in the partisan forces of communist leader Joseph Broz Tito (Marshal Tito) against Croatia's pro-Nazi Ustache regime, founded on April 10, 1941, as the so-called Independent State of Croatia (Nezavisna Drzava Hrvatska, NDH). After the war Tudjman served in the Ministry of Defense and was a member of the general staff of the Yugoslav National Army (JNA) in Belgrade, attaining the rank of major general. In 1961 Tudjman left the JNA to pursue an academic career in Croatia. From 1961 to 1967 he was the director of the Institute for the History of the Workers Movement located in Zagreb. In 1967 Tudjman resigned from the institute after Croatian communist authorities sharply criticized the Declaration on the Croatian Language that he had signed. The same year Tudjman was expelled from the Croatian Communist Party and thus began a new period in his life as a dissident and nationalist. In 1972 he was jailed for two years as a result of his activities in support of the "Croatian Spring" (the Croatian movement which advocated greater political autonomy in former Yugoslavia); he was jailed again in 1981 for three years for his writings on Yugoslav history. As a historian, Tudjman was accused of being a Holocaust revisionist because of his controversial 1989 book, *Bespuca povijesne zbiljnosti* (Wastelands: Historical Truth, translated also as The Horrors of War), in which he attempted to minimize the number of Jews who had perished in the Holocaust.

In 1989 Tudjman established a political party called the Croatian Democratic Union (HDZ) and became its chairman. The HDZ won the first free elections in Croatia in 1990. As its presidential candidate, Tudjman declared that NDH, the puppet state of Nazi Germany, "had not simply been a quisling creation, but was also an expression of the historical aspirations of the Croatian people to have their own state." During the same campaign he also declared, "Thank God, my wife is neither a Serb nor a Jew."

In 1990 Tudjman became the first democratically elected president of the newly proclaimed state of Croatia. In the elections of 1992 and 1997, he was re-elected as president.

After the declaration of Croatia's independence in 1991, which coincided with open aggression by Serbia and the federal army against the newly founded state, Tudjman's policy, which combined military and diplomatic means, secured the existence of Croatia as a sovereign state. In 1995 Croatia's military forces in their Operations Flash and Storm liberated about 25 percent of the territory that had been occupied by Serbian paramilitary forces since 1990. These military operations resulted in the mass exodus of the Serbian population as approximately 200,000 fled to Serbia and Bosnia and Herzegovina, or more precisely the Serb Republic (Republika Srpska).

In regard to Bosnia and Herzegovina, Tudjman's policy was both ambiguous and controversial. He engaged in secret negotiations with the Serbian leader Slobodan Milosevic to partition this state.

Following Operation Storm, Tudjman became the subject of an investigation by the International Criminal Tribunal for the Former Yugoslavia (ICTY) but he was never formally charged for the war crimes that occurred during and after this campaign in August 1995. Tudjman's name, however, appeared in the ICTY's indictment of the Croatian General, Ante Gotovina, for war crimes. In it the Chief Prosecutor of the ICTY, Carla del Ponte, accused Gotovina and President Tudjman of participating "in a joint criminal enterprise, the common purpose of which was the forcible and permanent removal of the Serb population from the Krajina region."

SEE ALSO Croatia, Independent State of; Karadzic, Radovan; Mladic, Ratko

BIBLIOGRAPHY

"Franjo Tudjman, Ex-Communist General Who Led Croatia's Secession, Is Dead at 77" (1999). *The New York Times.* (December 11).

International Criminal Tribunal for the Former Yugoslavia. "Amended Indictment of Ante Gotovina." Available from http://www.un.org/icty/indictment/english/got-ai040224e.htm.

Lukic, Reneo (2003). *L'agonie yougoslave, 1986–2003. Les États-Unis et l'Europe face aux guerres balkaniques* (The Agony of Yugoslavia: The United States, Europe and the Wars in the Balkans, 1986–2003). Quebec, Canada: Les Presses de l'Université Laval.

Lukic, Reneo, and Allen Lynch (1996). *Europe from the Balkans to the Urals, the Disintegration of Yugoslavia and the Soviet Union.* Oxford University Press: Oxford.

Reneo Lukic

Tuzla see Yugoslavia.

Uganda

Since 1962, Ugandans have suffered gross violation of human rights, including genocide, government-sponsored violence, acts of elimination of elites, forced exiles and expulsions, imprisonment without trial, and denial of the other basic human rights. More than 2 million people have been killed, maimed, imprisoned, or forced into exile. Various political elites have sought power to control and to distribute resources at the expense of human rights. Ugandans have not yet developed mechanisms to change government leaders by peaceful means. Political change has been effected through violence, and this has invariably led to other forms of violence. The distribution of resources along ethnic and racial lines was a legacy of British colonialism. During the colonial period, the Europeans and Asians received the highest incomes because they controlled the state and business, respectively. Among the African population, the Baganda were the richest because they produced cash crops—cotton and coffee—and played the role of colonial subimperialists. Western Uganda became a reservoir of labor for the colonial state as well as the managers of the cash crop economy in Buganda. The armed forces of the colonial era were recruited mainly from the Luo and Sudanic speakers of the northern region. This specialization along racial and ethnic lines became the source of instability and violence in postcolonial Uganda. Unsophisticated leaders like Obote and Amin exploited the politics of ethnicity and historical imbalances to entrench themselves. They branded whole populations guilty for the inequities of British colonialism and imposed collective punishment regardless of class or political association and sympathies.

Genocide

Thousands of Ugandans have suffered from acts of genocidal massacre. Since independence in 1962, Uganda has witnessed massacres directed against certain ethnic and consolidated social groups. Between 1966 and 1971, the first Obote regime targeted the Baganda, and 400 to 1,000 people were reported to have been killed. The Amin Regime (1971–1979) targeted the Acholi and Langi, particularly those in the armed forces, and thousands were eliminated. During the Tanzania-led war to oust Amin, groups of people suspected of supporting or sympathizing with Amin or even those who only came from the ethnic groups in his home region were killed. These included Muslims in the Ankole–Masaka areas, the people of West Nile, and Nubians scattered in the urban centers. In the second Obote administration (1980–1985), the Baganda were again targets for killings. The activities of both the government and the guerrilla armies in the Luwero Triangle caused the deaths of more than 300,000 people and the flight of many more from the area. From 1986 to 2003, the people of the Acholi region in northern Uganda were indiscriminately terrorized. More than 100,000 people were killed and more than 20,000 children abducted. These killings were managed by individuals trying to destabilize the political machinery of the Uganda state.

The fall of Kampala on April 11, 1979. A Tanzanian soldier uncovers mutilated bodies at the State Research Bureau, headquarters of Idi Amin's dreaded secret police. [BETTMANN/ CORBIS]

The Elimination of Political and Commercial Elites

The violent struggle to control the state has led those in power to eliminate their political rivals. In the period from 1962 to 1971, many political opponents of the first Obote regime were either imprisoned (including Grace Ibingira, George Magezi, Balaki Kirya, Lumu, Ben Kiwanuka, and some members of the Buganda royal family, such as Prince Badru Kakungulu) or forced into exile (Sir Edward Mutesa II). When Amin came to power, he eliminated political and commercial elites who seemed to be a threat to his grip on Uganda. Those killed in the Amin period have been listed elsewhere, but they included prominent individuals such as Chief Justice Ben Kiwanuka, the Anglican Archbishop Janan Luwum, writers such as Byron Kawaddwa, Father Clement Kigggundu, and prominent business people. The elimination of prominent individuals continued throughout the Uganda National Liberation Front (UNLF) governments (1979–1980), the second Obote administration (1980–1985), the Okello junta years (1985–1986), and the early part of the National Resistance Movement (NRM) government. The impact of these eliminations has been the reduction of the number of individuals capable of offering alternative leadership to this unfortunate country.

Exiles and Expulsions

Since 1969, Uganda has lost thousands of people through exile and expulsions. During the Amin regime, more than 80,000 people were forced to leave Uganda. By 1984, about a quarter of a million Ugandans were living in exile as refugees. In the period from 1980 to 1983, almost the whole of the West Nile district population was forced into exile by the atrocities committed by the Uganda National Liberation Army.

Whole ethnic and social groups have been expelled from Uganda. In October and November 1969, Obote's government expelled about 30,000 Kenyan workers, most of them Luos. Their brutal expulsion did not make headlines in the international news because no strong international economic interests were involved. In 1972, Idi Amin expelled some 75,000 Asians of Indo-Pakistani origin and appropriated their properties. Although they have been compensated and some have returned, the action was a brutal one. In 1982–1983, functionaries of the official ruling party, the Uganda People's Congress (UPC), caused the expulsion of some 75,000 Banyarwanda who had over the years settled in western Uganda (Ankole, Rakai, and parts of Masaka). In the same period, the UPC government fanned primordial forces within Karamoja that led to internal conflicts in that region. Some 20,000 to 40,000 Karamajog were killed, and many were displaced in the same period.

Denial of Basic Human Rights

Between 1966 and 1986, Ugandans were denied basic human rights. The right to freedom of opinion was denied, as was the right of association. The media was state controlled, and political parties, trade unions, student organizations, and later, some religious organizations were proscribed. There was, particularly in the period after 1971 to 1985, complete absence of the rule of law. Court verdicts were not respected by the security forces. The security forces could arrest people without warrant and detain them for as long as they wished. But these forces were immune from prosecution. When the Museveni government came to power in 1986, it instituted a commission of inquiry into past human rights abuses and the creation of the Human Rights Commission. The situation dramatically changed for the better.

Conclusion

The 1995 Constitution put in place mechanisms facilitating conflict resolution, including separation of powers among the executive, legislative, and judicial branches of government. However, permanent peace and security can only be viable when Ugandans accept, in word and deed, the mechanisms for changing the guard without violence as embedded in the 1995 Constitution. Any rash action to change the Constitution to suit personal arrangements could cast Uganda back twenty years. The positive achievements of the last seventeen years would be thrown into the dust bin.

SEE ALSO Death Squads

BIBLIOGRAPHY

Amnesty International. (1978). *Human Rights in Uganda: Report.* London: Author.

Clay, Jason (1984). *The Eviction of the Banyarwanda: The Story behind the Refugee Crisis in Western Uganda.* Cambridge, Mass.: Cultural Survival.

Harrell-Bond, B. E. (1986). *Imposing Aid: Emergency Assistance to Refugees.* New York: Oxford University Press.

Human Rights Watch/Africa (1997). The Scars of Death: Children Abducted by the Lord's Resistance Army in Uganda. Washington, D.C.: Human Rights Watch.

International Commission of Jurists (1977). *Uganda and Human Rights: Report of the UN Commission on Human Rights.* Geneva: Author.

Kasozi, A. B. K. (1994). *The Social Origins of Violence in Uganda, 1964-1985.* Montreal: McGill-Queen's University Press.

Mamdani, Mahmood (1973). *From Citizen to Refugee: Uganda Asians Come to Britain.* London: Frances Printer.

Mamdani, Mahmood (1976). *Politics and Class Formation in Uganda.* New York: Monthly Review Press.

Melvern, Linda (2000). *A People Betrayed: The Role of the West in Rwanda's Genocide.* London: Zed.

Ryan, S. D. (1971). "Uganda: A Balance Sheet of the Revolution." *Mawazo* 3:37–64.

A. B. Kasozi

Ukraine (Famine)

In the Ukrainian language, the famine of 1932 and 1933 famine is called "holodomor," which means extermination by starvation. It is also referred to as the "artificial famine," "terror famine," and "terror-genocide." Until the end of the 1980s, however, the Soviet Union dismissed all references to the famine as anti-Soviet propaganda. Denial of the famine declined after the Communist Party lost power and the Soviet empire disintegrated. With the declassification and publication of Western and Soviet historical documents, it became impossible to continue to deny the occurrence of the now well-attested catastrophe. The con-

troversy did not abate, however, despite newly uncovered evidence. Instead, new disputes arose over whether the famine was Ukrainian or Soviet, whether its victims should be regarded primarily as Ukrainians or as peasants, and if it was appropriate to call the famine genocidal.

The Surge of Recurrent Famines

During the first three decades of communist rule, Ukraine experienced a series of food crises. The first widespread famine began in the summer of 1921, and lasted two years. It affected one-third of the Ukrainian population, and killed approximately one million people. Possibly three or four times more people died in Russia, which also suffered a famine during that time. Little information and no mortality data are available for the shorter starvation periods, which occurred from 1924 to 1925 and from 1928 to 1929. The most costly in human lives was the great famine of 1932 and 1933. It is also this famine for which the classification of genocide is claimed.

Later, fatal food shortages were experienced during World War II, but they occurred mainly in the cities and thus form a separate category. After the war, Ukrainians again faced famine conditions in 1946 and 1947, notably in the central and southern regions of the country. Victims numbered in the hundreds of thousands. In each instance, food shortages were not exclusive to Ukraine. Concomitant famines took place in Russia and other parts of the sprawling Soviet empire.

Peasants constituted the majority of victims in all the famines, except during the war. The common features of all the famines were adverse climatic conditions, poor crop yields, mismanagement, corruption, and waste. The main cause of starvation, however, was excessive grain procurements ordered by the government. The state extracted exorbitant amounts of foodstuffs from the peasants, with the full knowledge that it was condemning them to annihilation.

The readiness of the allegedly proletarian state to sacrifice the interests of the peasantry, which comprised three-quarters of its population, was evident throughout the whole of the Soviet Union, but the origin and handling of food shortages in Ukraine had specific features that distinguished them from the situation elsewhere in the USSR. This is because the Russo-centric government was mistrustful of Ukrainians, many of who resented the loss of their bid for national independence after the Revolution.

Moscow responded to the 1921 drought and ensuing famine that swept the Volga valley and Northern Caucasus in Russia and the southern steppe lands of Ukraine with two very different policies. Food taxation was suspended in the famished provinces of Russia, famine relief was organized, and requests were sent for Western aid. Meanwhile, however, Ukraine's dire situation was ignored; in fact, the country was obliged to send some of its own meager crop to help Russia. Western aid began arriving in September 1921, and by the end of the year the American Relief Administration (ARA) was providing meals for one million people. The Ukrainian famine was finally acknowledged and the country opened to foreign aid only at the beginning of 1922. Even that only occurred after the ARA put pressure on Moscow at the behest of the American Jewish Joint Distribution Committee (JDC), which had received alarming news about Jews starving in southern Ukraine.

At the height of its operations in 1922, the ARA fed over eight million people in Russia, with funds provided by the U.S. Congress, and nearly one million people in Ukraine, with the aid of funds supplied mainly by the JDC. Both famines received wide publicity in the Western media, and photographs and films were made for the purpose of raising funds. Even after recognition of the famine situation in Ukraine, starving Ukrainian provinces continued to be taxed and food trains continued to be sent not only from northern Ukraine, which were blessed with a reasonably good harvest, but also from the starving southern provinces. As late as May 1922, Western observers were baffled and scandalized to see southern Ukraine sending foodstuffs to Russia. In addition, Ukraine was obliged to give refuge to hundreds of thousands of Russian refugees, and to numerous Red Army units.

Drought and poor harvests occurred again in 1922, but this time Moscow decided to export grain rather than retain its crop to feed its own people. Shocked, Western relief organizations protested, but to no avail. To counter bad publicity, on October 15, 1922, Moscow declared that the famine had ended. Trapped by their own humanitarian convictions, Western relief agencies kept their soup kitchens open for another year, even though the Soviet government continued to export grain. Strikes by port workers and even the burning of grain elevators in the Ukrainian port of Mykolaiv had no effect on Soviet export policy. The Soviet authorities did not engineer mass starvation in 1921, but once the famine broke out, the government quickly recognized its utility as a tool of state policy. In Ukraine, in other words, the famine was seen as an effective way to physically weaken nationalist and anarchist elements, which had challenged Moscow's rule over Ukraine until the autumn of 1921.

After the famine, while Party leaders fought over Lenin's mantle in Moscow, Ukraine acquired a certain amount of autonomy. To make their rule more palatable, and to placate Ukrainian national feelings, the victorious Bolsheviks began their rule by promoting policies of "indigenization" and "Ukrainization." The party and the state recruited native Ukrainians, even former members of defunct Ukrainian national parties. The use of Ukrainian language was promoted in the republic's schools and administration. The main beneficiaries of these new policies were Ukrainian intellectuals and farmers. The former began to create nationally conscious socio-economic and political elites, whereas the latter took advantage of the liberal "New Economic Policy" (NEP) to recover from the famines of previous years. An influx of rural populations into the urban centers helped to Ukrainianize the previously Russified towns and cities. The country was undergoing a wide-ranging national renaissance. Such a national revival rekindled old fears in the Kremlin, however, and Ukraine was once again perceived as presenting a challenge to the hegemony of the government and a threat to the integrity of the multinational empire.

Stalin's Revolution from Above

Ten years after the Bolshevik seizure of power, Stalin's ascendancy over the USSR was complete. As the party's chief theoretician and decision maker, Stalin could now take up Lenin's unfinished job of eliminating the last vestiges of capitalism and pursue his personal ambition of transforming the rich but backward empire into a powerful socialist state. In order to become a fatherland for the world proletariat and a vanguard of world revolution, the USSR had to undergo an industrial revolution, for which agriculture was the only available source of capital. The party's left wing had long advocated agricultural collectivization as a way of bringing socialism to the countryside and giving the state direct control over farm production. Stalin took the leftist platform and pushed it to the extreme.

The collectivization of agriculture was approved in December 1927, and was made part of the latest Five Year Plan, the cornerstone of the NEP. Five months later, Stalin rationalized his abandoning the NEP. He argued that, with almost equal yields, Russia nonetheless produced twice as much market grain in 1913 as the Soviet Union did in 1926. Large-scale farming, run by rich landlords in 1913, and by *sovkhozes* (state farms employing agricultural workers) and *kolkhozes* (collective farms organized as cooperatives) in 1926, sent 47 percent of their produce to the market, while *kulaks* (rich farmers) sold 34 percent of theirs before the revolution and only 20 percent after it. But while the first two categories of farm enterprises accounted for half of all grain production in 1916, their share in 1926 was only 15 percent. The *seredniaks* ("middle," or subsistence farmers) and the *bedniaks* (poor farmers) increased their share of crop production from 50 to 85 percent, but reduced their sales from 15 to 11 percent in 1926. The problem was clear: the middle and poor peasants had become the main grain producers, but they consumed most of their crop. The solution to grain shortages, Stalin argued, lay in the "transition from individual peasant farming to collective farming." Large-scale farming was also supposed to increase production by taking advantage of "modern machinery and scientific knowledge," but above all, Stalin insisted, it was a system that was "capable of producing a maximum of grain for the market."

Collectivization was expected to meet with stiff opposition from the kulaks—because they had the most to lose—and Ukrainian peasants, who were not familiar with the Russian tradition of *obshchina* (commune). Stalin launched his struggle against these hostile elements with the call to "liquidate the kulaks as a class." The drive for "dekulakization" was launched in December 1929, and, like collectivization, was subordinated to state planning. The most intense period of dekulakization was from January to March 1930, and coincided with the main push for collectivization. As a result of dekulakization, deportation, and other upheavals connected with collectivization, 282,000 peasant households disappeared in Ukraine between 1930 and 1931. By the end of that period there were no real kulaks left in the region.

In theory, kolkhozes were voluntary organizations. Many bedniaks and *batraks* (landless farm workers) freely signed up, expecting a better life. Most peasants, however, preferred to stick to individual farming. The scope and tempo of collectivization were regulated. To meet their monthly quotas, peasants were coerced to join collectives by the levy of exorbitant taxes on individual farm incomes, false accusations, administrative intimidation, and physical violence. The peasants resisted, however, and by June 1929 only 5.6 percent of households had joined kolkhozes in the Ukraine.

Grain producing regions in Ukraine and the Northern Caucasus, especially the rich and predominantly Ukrainian Kuban' region, were specially targeted for rapid collectivization. In October, 10.6 percent of Ukrainian peasant households were in kolkhozes. In the steppe region, the figure was 16 percent. Mismanagement, insufficient farm machinery and draught power (horses and tractors), and other woes continued to undermine the institution. Peasants fled and the kolkhozes collapsed. Undaunted, on November 7, 1929, Stalin declared the collectivization movement a great success and bolstered his claim by ordering 25,000 specially selected industrial workers to be sent to the countryside to continue to help with the organization and management of kolkhozes. Additional cadres were periodically dispatched, and by the spring of 1930, the Ukraine had 50,000 activists with special powers to organize, punish and intimidate, and terrorize the peasants.

Reinforced state violence produced the desired results. By the end of February 1930, more than half of all individual households in the USSR had been collectivized, and in Ukraine the number reached 68.5 percent. The government's success was achieved with unbridled violence and at the cost of many peasant lives. Terror reigned in the villages. To protect their men, women often took over their role in opposing the formation of kolkhozes and in their dismantling. Resistance peaked in the early spring of 1930, when the OGPU (state police) recorded 6,528 mass peasant uprisings, with 2,945, or 45 percent, taking place in Ukraine.

As kolkhozes collapsed in Ukraine and the North Caucasus, Stalin was forced to sound a temporary retreat. On March 2, 1930, the newspaper *Pravda* published Stalin's essay "Dizzy with Success," in which collectivization was once again declared a success, with certain excesses being blamed on overzealous activists. Stalin once more reaffirmed the principle of voluntary adhesion to the kolkhozes. The peasants took him at his word and began to leave the collectives. By September, only 21 percent of peasant households remained collectivized in the USSR; 34 percent in Ukraine. If this was a new NEP, as some had hoped or feared, it was of short duration. Renewed collectivization began in October 1930. By August 1931 the Ukrainian steppe was wholly collectivized, and by the following year, three-quarters of Ukrainian peasants were working in kolkhozes.

Collectivization was at the heart of a revolution aimed at solving several other problems besides economic ones. In ideological terms, the termination of the NEP meant the triumph of socialism, although the *kolkhozniks* called it the return of serfdom. Politically, it meant the extension of party control over the countryside by means of reliable personnel in newly established Machine and Tractor Stations that were created to service the kolkhozes with machinery and to supervise them politically. The principal loser was to be the peasant, demoted from independent producer to agricultural worker, akin to the city worker but bound to the more primitive conditions of country life.

The Ukrainian Famine of 1932–1933

Dekulakization and deportation deprived Soviet agriculture of its ablest and most conscientious farmers.

In Kiev, Ukrainian Orthodox priests hold a commemorative service in 2003 to mark the seventieth anniversary of the Soviet-imposed Ukrainian famine/genocide (1932–1933). The death toll from the famine has been estimated at between six and seven million. [AP/ **WORLD WIDE PHOTOS**]

Productivity declined while wastage increased. It has been claimed that three million tons of grain were lost in Ukraine during the 1931 harvest. This is probably an exaggeration, but together with unfavorable weather conditions, it helps to explain why Ukrainian harvests of 1931 and 1932 were lower than the official figures used by Moscow to set its procurement plans. The Kremlin, insisting on high quotas, had great success. It took in 7.5 million tons of grain in 1930 and more than 7 million tons in 1931, and planned to match the latter figure in 1932. State procurement claimed a very high proportion of Ukrainian production: 30 percent in 1930 and 41 percent in 1931.

By the summer of 1932, however, Ukrainian leadership realized that it would not be able to deliver the exorbitant amount it had originally agreed to provide. Ukrainian party leaders pleaded with Stalin for a reduction in the quota. In June 1932 Vlas Chubar and Hryhorii Petrovsky, members of the Ukrainian party's Central Committee, wrote the Kremlin about the menace of wide-scale starvation. In the fall of 1932, the boss of the Kharkiv region, informed Stalin of the famine in his province, only to be ridiculed for telling "fairy-tales." The original plan for grain procurement for the 1932 harvest was ultimately reduced three times, but the state still managed to extract 4,270,000 tons of grain, enough to feed at least 12 million people for an entire year. Workers and other citizens of Ukraine, whose food needs at that time were supposed to be met by the government, numbered about eight million.

It was not only the confiscation of foodstuffs, but also the way the confiscation was carried out that created hardships for Ukrainian peasants. In theory, the land worked by the kolkhoz belonged to the state, whereas the harvest belonged to the kolkhoz. But the kolkhoz could divide the crops among its members only after the state took its share and reserves were set aside for the next sowing. In the meantime, kolkhozniks were supposed to fend for themselves. Many tried to take an "advance" for their work by cutting a few sheaves of unripened wheat or competing with mice for the gleanings that the harvesters left behind. On August 7, 1932, however, Stalin imposed a new law that made the "plunder of state property" a crime punishable by death or, in extenuating circumstances, ten years' imprisonment.

Fifty-five thousand people were soon arrested for pilfering grain that they themselves had cultivated, and 2,000 individuals were condemned to death. In November, a blacklist was introduced to punish kolkhozes that failed to meet their monthly grain deliveries. A blacklisted collective lost the right to all commercial transactions, including the sale of such basic necessities as salt, matches, and kerosene, and the kolkhoz administration that harbored such criminals was usually purged. In early 1933, 200,000 kolkhoz employees were inspected, and one-fourth of them were dismissed or otherwise purged. Included in these numbers were 11,420 kolkhoz chairmen, of whom 6,089 were purged.

Individual peasants who were in arrears in meeting their quotas were subjected to food fines and confiscations, which often meant the confiscation of everything edible, including the bread or vegetables found on their kitchen tables. Groups of activists, comprised of city workers or members of local "committees of poor peasants," went from house to house, prodding the earthen floors with metallic spikes to uncover hidden food reserves. To prevent peasants from fleeing the village or even merely seeking provisions outside their village, a passport system was introduced on December 27, 1932. Only city dwellers were entitled to passports. The peasants were thus confined to the village. As they had been in the days of serfdom, the peasants were once more bound to the soil. Peasants wandering in the cities were rounded up: the luckier ones were sent home, while others were punished for the crime of speculation.

Left with insufficient food, the peasant population starved. Famine broke out in the winter of 1931 and 1932, and reached a high point that spring. Hundreds of thousands of people died before the new harvest brought some relief. A new phase of food shortages began in the fall of 1932 and peaked the following spring. Foreign eyewitnesses and native survivors, who either escaped or outlived the Soviet regime, have described the horrors of this famine in contemporary accounts. Starving peasants consumed domestic animals, including dogs and cats, together with various food surrogates like tree buds, weeds, and herbs. Some resorted to cannibalism, and dug up human corpses and the carcasses of dead animals. A nearby forest or river saved many an amateur hunter or fisherman. People died by the hundreds and thousands. Just how many died from starvation in Ukraine will never be known.

Deaths due to malnutrition were not recorded. Deductions made from the official censuses of 1926 and 1939, and the suppressed census of 1937, have given rise to various interpretations and conclusions. Estimates for Ukraine vary from four to ten million. Six million was the figure a Kharkiv official gave an American newspaper editor in 1933—it still seems the most plausible.

Was the Ukrainian Famine Genocide?

By the end of the 1980s, British, Italian, and German diplomatic archives provided the definitive evidence necessary to establish the historicity of the great Ukrainian famine. It is more complex to resolve the question of the genocidal nature of the catastrophe. Scholars have had reservations in judging Stalin's intent, as required by the United Nations Convention on Genocide. A conclusive assessment of the Soviet leader's motivations had to await the opening of Soviet archives. Over time, however, four approaches to the problem were developed. Some scholars flatly rejected the notion that the famine was genocide, others avoided the problem of classification by using descriptive terms such as "great famine," "artificial famine," or "man-made famine." Still others accepted the idea of genocide, but saw its victims primarily as the kulaks, or peasants; and, finally, some scholars recognized the famine as a genocide that was specifically directed against the Ukrainian nation. Russian and Ukrainian scholars use the term *holod* (*golod* in Russian, meaning hunger, starvation, or famine) or *holodomor* (*golodomor*), which is emotionally close to the notion of genocide, but without the legalistic overtone.

Stalin was not only well informed about the famine, he was its chief architect and overseer. He sent Molotov and Kaganovich to the Ukraine and the Northern Caucasus to organize and enforce the grain procurement that made the tragedy inevitable. The word *famine* was banned from the media and official documents, but it was used openly in high party circles. The Secretary-General himself used the word in a letter to Molotov, sent in June 1932, in which he blamed local mismanagement for a "state of ruin and famine" in a number of Ukrainian regions. If the party leadership had made a mistake in planning the grain procurement, it could have corrected its errors once it realized the magnitude of the famine. There were more than three million tons of grain reserves in the USSR in January 1933, enough to feed well over ten million people. The government could have organized famine relief and accepted help from outside, as it did in 1921. Instead Moscow rejected foreign aid, denounced those who offered it, and exported its own foodstuffs abroad. More than a million and a half tons of grain were sold abroad in 1932 and again in 1933, enough to feed five million people during both years. Such behavior is more than callous; it shows a direct intent on the part of the perpetrators to destroy a part of the population by starvation.

The "peasantist" interpretation of the Ukrainian famine either accepts or rejects the idea of genocide, but emphasizes that the victims were peasants, rejecting the association of victimhood with Ukrainian ethnicity. In his *Black Book of Communism,* Stephane Courtois insists on the similarity between the Stalin regime's deliberate starvation of a child of a Ukrainian kulak, and the Nazi regime's starvation of a Jewish child. In this literary construct, there is no clash between the Ukrainian peasant's two identities, even if the reference to his kulak class gives the false impression of the victims of the famine, for by that time there were no kulaks left in Ukraine. Nicolas Werth, whose long study of the Soviet Union is included in Courtois's *Black Book,* openly poses this question, but after presenting arguments for the "ethnicist" and "peasantist" interpretations, Werth settles on an explanation that embraces the ethnicist approach, blaming the deaths on an ethnically oriented policy of, if not genocide, than certainly willful extermination. For Mark Tauger, this ethnic orientation is unacceptable. He argues that there was no Ukrainian famine, only a Soviet famine in which peasants in Ukraine were also victims.

Of Georgian background, Stalin had a keen awareness of the "nationality question" in the multiethnic Russian and then Soviet empire. On August 11, 1932, he intimated to an associate that, unless proper measures were taken, Ukraine could be lost. The half-million-strong Communist Party of Ukraine, he complained, was full of "conscious and unwitting Petliurists," "agents of Pilsudski," and other "rotten elements." Stalin argued that the Polish dictator, Pilsudski, was not dozing.

His associate, Kaganovich, concurred, adding that local Ukrainian activists had become convinced that their grain procurement quota could not be met, and that Ukrainians were being punished unjustly. Kaganovich detected a sense of "solidarity and rotten mutual guarantee," not only in the middle echelons but even in the top levels of the administration. Stalin was also irritated that, when Chubar and Petrovsky had pleaded to have Ukraine's quotas lowered, Kossior did not react. This exchange between Stalin and Kaganovich suggests that they were aware that the imposition of unreasonably high procurement targets was creating a dangerous situation in Ukraine, where peasant and national factors intermingled. The Polish dictator, Pilsudski, could become a threat only if he could find allies in the disgruntled Ukrainian political apparatus and a disaffected Ukrainian peasantry. Political purges

could eliminate the first danger, and just as in 1921 and 1923, food could be used to transform revolting peasants into an obedient rural proletariat.

Despite the passport system, Ukrainian peasants left their villages and went to Belarus and Russia, where the food situation was much better than in Ukraine. On January 22, 1933, Molotov and Stalin signed a secret directive to stop this practice. Railways were forbidden to sell tickets to Ukrainian peasants, and the OGPU was ordered to be more vigilant. The directive referred to a mass movement to undermine the Soviet state by the agents of Pilsudski and other enemies. The ban on travel also applied to the Kuban *okrug* in the North Caucasus. A primary grain producing region, Kuban had also been ruthlessly dekulakized and exorbitantly taxed, and had fallen behind the procurement schedule. With 61 percent of its 1.5 million population Ukrainian, Kuban became a prime target of Skrypnyk's efforts to Ukrainianize the 3 million Ukrainians living in North Caucasus. Individuals promoting Ukrainization were called counterrevolutionary agents and directly blamed for the local sabotage of grain deliveries. Ukrainization in the North Caucasus was brought to an end.

The vast majority of famine victims during 1932 and 1933 were Ukrainians, primarily living in the Ukrainian SSR, but also in adjacent regions of Russia. The high number of Ukrainian deaths stands in sharp contrast to the low number of Russian deaths, both in absolute terms and in relation to their populations. The correlation between the ethnic and social identities of the group forming the vast majority of famine victims is inescapable. The peasantry had been the raison d'être of the Ukrainization policy and the mainstay of the Ukrainian national revival. Now both were linked by the authorities to peasant sabotage, and they were attacked. Ukrainian cultural elites were decimated, and by 1933 Ukrainization ground to a halt and was replaced by a new policy of Russification.

SEE ALSO Kulaks; Lenin, Vladimir; Stalin, Joseph; Union of Soviet Socialist Republics

BIBLIOGRAPHY

Ammende, Ewald (1936). *Human Life in Russia.* Cleveland: John T. Zubal, 1984.

Bilinsky, Yaroslav (1999). "Was the Ukrainian Famine of 1932–1933 Genocide?" *Journal of Genocide Research* vol. 37(2):147–156.

Conquest, Robert (1986). *The Harvest of Sorrow: Soviet Collectivization and the Terror-Famine.* London: Hutchinson.

Courtois, Stéphane, et al. (1999). *The Black Book of Communism: Crimes, Terror, Repression.* Cambridge, Mass.: Harvard University Press.

Dolot, Miron (1985). *Execution by Hunger: The Hidden Holocaust*. New York: W.W. Norton.

Englerman, David C. (2003). *Modernization from the Other Shore. American Intellectuals and the Romance of the Russian Development*. Cambridge, Mass.: Harvard University Press.

Graziosi, Andrea (1997). *The Great Soviet Peasant War: Bolsheviks and Peasants, 1917–1933*. Cambridge, Mass.: Ukrainian Research of Institute Harvard University.

Green, Barbara (1996). "Stalinist Terror and the Question of Genocide: The Great Famine." In *Is the Holocaust Unique: Perspectives on Comparative Genocide*, ed. Israel W. Charny. Boulder, Colo.: Westview Press.

Hryshko, Wasyl (1983). *The Ukrainian Holocaust of 1933*, ed. and tran. Marco Carynnyk. Toronto: Bahrianyy Foundation.

Isajiw, Wsevolod W., ed. (2003). *Famine-Genocide in Ukraine, 1932–1933: Western Archives, Testimonies and New Research*. Toronto: Ukrainian Research and Documentation Center.

Luciuk, Lubomyr, ed. (2004). *Not Worthy: Walter Duranty's Pulitzer Prize and The New York Times*. Kingston, Ont.: Kashtan Press.

Madden, Cheryl, ed. (2003). *Holodomor: The Ukrainian Genocide 1932–1933*. Special issue of *Canadian American Slavic Studies* 37, no. 3.

Martin, Terry (2001). *The Affirmative Action Empire. Nations and Nationalism in the Soviet Union, 1923-1939*. Ithaca, N.Y.: Cornell University Press.

Serbyn, Roman, and Gohdan Krawchenko, eds. (1986). *Famine in Ukraine: 1932–1933*. Edmonton: Canadian Institute of Ukrainian Studies.

Sysyn, Frank (1999). "The Ukrainian Famine of 1932–1933: The Role of the Ukrainian Diaspora in Research and Public Discussion." In *Studies in Comparative Genocide*, ed. Levon Chorbajan and George Shirinian. New York: St.Martin's Press.

Tauger, Mark B. (2001). *Natural Disaster and Human Action in the Soviet Famine of 1931–1933*. The Carl Beck Papers in Russian & East European Studies, Number 1506, June.

Tauger, Mark B. (1955). *The Black Deeds of the Kremlin: A White Book. Vol. 2: The Great Famine in Ukraine in 1932–1933*. Detroit, Mich.: Dobrus.

Roman Serbyn

Union of Soviet Socialist Republics

The Union of Soviet Socialist Republics (USSR) was the official name of communist Russia from December 1922 until its collapse in late 1991. This self-proclaimed Marxist state was created out of the ruins of the Tszarist Empire following the Bolshevik Revolution of October 1917 and the ensuing civil war in Rus-sia. In the view of many scholars, the USSR under Vladimir Lenin (1870–1924) and Joseph Stalin (1878–1953) evolved into a totalitarian dictatorship directly responsible for the deaths of millions of Soviet citizens. Here the nature and scale of the crimes against humanity perpetrated by the Soviet state from the October Revolution to the death of Stalin will be examined, along with differing perspectives on Leninist and Stalinist terror.

Historical Context

Before World War I the Russian Empire had been an autocratic monarchy presided over by Tsar Nicholas II, who formally claimed the divine right to rule single-handedly. Russian political culture lacked liberal or democratic roots and institutions, and for many centuries the state had dominated society, often using repressive methods carried out by a prototype secret police force. As a consequence of this police state and emergent modernization during the course of the late nineteenth century, social tensions ran deep in tsarist Russia. For various political and socioeconomic reasons, these tensions between peasants and landlords, urban industrial workers and their bosses, and alienated middle-class intellectuals and the anachronistic tsarist state grew in the decades before 1914. Indeed, in 1905 and 1906 a full-scale, but ultimately abortive, revolution had occurred that threatened to overthrow monarchical rule. The nail in tsarism's coffin came during World War I. Russia's largely unsuccessful efforts to conduct the war against Germany and Austria added significantly to internal discontent. The result was the February Revolution of 1917, which forced Nicholas II to abdicate in favor of a centrist provisional government.

Despite meaningful democratic reforms the provisional government was unable to win mass support and it was, in turn, removed from power by the 1917 Bolshevik October Revolution. The Bolsheviks, led by Lenin, were a small urbanized Marxist party whose political mentality and revolutionary goals are critical for an understanding of the later communist crimes against humanity. It would not be an exaggeration to argue that the Bolsheviks were utopian revolutionaries (some might say megalomaniac fanatics) who were utterly convinced that capitalism, liberalism, and parliamentarianism were dead, that socialism, and ultimately communism, represented the inevitable wave of the future, and that human society and individuals were perfectible by state engineering. They were deeply contemptuous of dissenting views and, more than any other Russian political movement, were prepared to countenance class-based violence in a society that was itself highly prone to violent confrontation. In short, the Bolsheviks' revolutionary "ends"—the destruction

Lubyanka Prison and a portion of Revolution Square (Moscow) in the 1940s. Revolution Square (*Ploshchad Revolutsii*) gets its name from the bitter fighting that occurred at this spot in October 1917. The notorious Lubyanka Prison is still a government building, but no longer a prison. [HULTON-DEUTSCH COLLECTION/CORBIS]

of capitalist exploitation, the emancipation of the working class, the transformation of "bourgeois" values, and the creation of a socialist state and society—justified any means of achieving these ends, including class discrimination, illegal arrest and incarceration, even mass executions. The origins of Leninist and Stalinist terror can thus be traced to this intransigent ideological orthodoxy.

After the Bolsheviks seized power, their many opponents rallied to contest the Marxist vision of Russia's future. A truly bitter and tragic civil war ensued, one that pitted the so-called Reds, the Bolsheviks and their extreme left-wing socialist allies, against the Whites, mainly ex-tsarist forces backed, half-heartedly, by several foreign states, the United States and Great Britain among them. The barbarity of the Russian Civil War, the class and ethnic hatreds exacerbated by the conflict, the arbitrary nature of both Red and White terror, and

the sheer scale of violence must surely have brutalized Russian political culture, coming as they did on top of four years of world war and revolutionary upheaval. The civil war certainly engendered a siege mentality among the Bolshevik victors, who from that point on tended to see enemies everywhere, at home and abroad; a veritable "capitalist encirclement." Red terror under Lenin has thus been rationalized as a desperate last-ditch method of survival foisted onto an isolated and inward-looking band of revolutionaries in conditions of profound social, economic, and military turmoil.

Taking a position less sympathetic to the Bolsheviks, one may argue that state-sponsored class repression was inherent in Leninist ideology, predated the civil war, and was therefore not a consequence of the objective circumstances of the time. Indeed, Lenin almost welcomed the prospect of civil war as a means of purifying Russian society, purging it of "class enemies" and "traitors"—the landed gentry, capitalists, Orthodox priests, tsarist officials, bourgeois intellectuals, even kulaks (better-off peasants). The Bolsheviks' total belief in Marxism, which they regarded as scientific, assured them that they alone were right and everyone else was wrong, and their penchant for class discrimination transformed minor acts of nonconformity into "counterrevolutionary sabotage." Accordingly, the use of state terror became a conscious and deliberate instrument of governance under Lenin, arguably the principal method of maintaining and consolidating Bolshevik rule. Hence, it was Lenin who established the basis for later Stalinist atrocities.

Leninist Crimes
One of the first decrees of the Bolshevik regime in December 1917 was the creation of the Cheka, the original Soviet secret police force and forerunner of the much-vaunted KGB. The job of the Cheka was to root out all counterrevolutionary and antistate activities to bolster the fragile Leninist government. By June 1918 as the civil war got under way, reports of Cheka "excesses" began to reach Moscow. According to official statistics, the Cheka killed 12,733 prisoners between 1918 and 1920; unofficial calculations suggest a figure closer to 300,000. Lenin himself actively contributed to the wave of Red Terror. On August 11, 1918, shortly before an attempt was made to assassinate him, Lenin sent a now infamous telegram to local Bolsheviks, insisting that they "hang (hang without fail, so that the people see) no fewer than one hundred known kulaks, rich men, bloodsuckers. . . . Do it in such a way that for hundreds of versts [kilometres] around, the people will see, tremble, know, shout: they are strangling and will strangle . . . the bloodsucker kulaks" (Pipes, 1996, p. 50). One month earlier the tsar and his family had been murdered by local Bolsheviks in Ekaterinburg. The spiral of terror and counterterror was growing.

The arrest of large numbers of alleged counterrevolutionaries meant that they had to be detained somewhere. Decrees in September 1918 and April 1919 sanctioned the establishment of the first concentration and labor camps, the latter originally conceived as sites for rehabilitating petty criminals through physical work. The most notorious of these early Soviet camps was the prison on the Solovetskii Islands in the White Sea in the far north of Russia. The camp population there grew from 3,000 in 1923 to approximately 50,000 in 1930. Between 1931 and 1933 around 25,000 convicts perished building the White Sea Canal, one of Stalin's pet schemes involving forced labor. From these relatively humble origins emerged the vast system of Soviet labor camps, widely known as the Gulag Archipelago (*Gulag* being, in Russian, the acronym for Main

Administration of Camps). These camps housed not only political prisoners, but also ordinary criminals. Generally, they lived in appalling conditions, often in the most remote and inhospitable locations of the USSR. Inmates were in essence slave labor, whose contribution to the Soviet economy, especially from the 1930s, should not be overlooked.

The communist state also launched attacks on organized religion in the USSR. In March 1922, for instance, Lenin ordered the confiscation "with the most savage and merciless energy" of valuables belonging to the Orthodox Church. According to Richard Pipes, the aim was twofold: to secure vital assets for the cash-strapped Soviet government and to smash the power of the Orthodox Church and its hold over the peasantry. Even at a time of relative liberalization under the New Economic Policy (1921–1929), Lenin advocated the execution of large numbers of "reactionary clergy . . . so that they will not dare even to think of any resistance for several decades" (Pipes, 1996, p. 153–54). Lenin, also in 1922, insisted on the death penalty for the arrested leaders of the Socialist Revolutionary Party, but he was overruled and finally relented, with the leaders instead given lengthy prison terms. Nevertheless, Lenin's implacable attitude toward political and ideological adversaries undoubtedly contributed to the formation of a one-party state in Soviet Russia, a major step on the road to which was the forcible dissolution of the Constituent Assembly (the multiparty national parliament) as early as January 1918.

Lenin may have been the initiator of many of the repressive measures undertaken between 1918 and 1923, but all leading Bolsheviks, to a greater or lesser degree, shared his intolerance of opposition and fundamental belief in a state-sponsored transformation of human society. Lev Trotsky, Grigorii Zinoviev, Nikolai Bukharin, and Stalin all supported harsh policies against real and perceived opponents of the regime. However, serious disagreements emerged among the Bolshevik hierarchy, especially as Lenin's failing health from 1922 on led to an internal party power struggle. Lenin was acutely aware of the dangers of internal party disunity and attempted, rather ineffectually, to paper over the cracks in leadership. A year before his death in January 1924 he dictated a document that became known as "Lenin's Testament," in which he evaluated the strengths and weaknesses of six top Bolsheviks. The most notable comments, given subsequent developments, related to Stalin. In April 1922 Stalin had been appointed General Secretary of the Communist Party (the Bolshevik Party had been renamed the Communist Party in 1918) partly as a result of his close cooperation with Lenin, who valued the Georgian as a tough, practical activist who got things done. However, relations between the two men soured in 1922 and 1923, and in his testament Lenin warned that Stalin was "too crude" to serve as General Secretary. He advised the Party to find a way of removing Stalin from his post.

Portentously, Lenin's strictures were ignored. In the course of the ugly internecine power struggles that transformed the Party during the 1920s, Stalin was able to build up majority support in his position as General Secretary. His successive rivals, first Trotsky, then Zinoviev and Lev Kamenev, and finally Bukharin, were all out-voted and out-manuevered; by 1929 Stalin had emerged as the clear leader of the Communist Party. His reliance on behind-the-scenes machinations, outright slander, and administrative measures against his opponents concealed another of his characteristics: He was a workaholic who intervened in, and had practical solutions for, all the major and often secondary problems that confronted the Soviet state. What is more, he appeared to be a true Marxist dedicated to the construction of socialism in the USSR. Stalin was thus a very capable, not unintelligent, leader who commanded the respect of his followers. He was also, or at least became by the 1930s, a morbidly suspicious, capricious, and volatile man, who was possibly driven by an insatiable lust for power.

Stalinist Crimes

Stalin's regime was arguably the most repressive in modern history. As a result of his so-called revolution launched in 1928 and 1929—the forced collectivization and "dekulakization" of the countryside and the intensely rapid tempos of industrialization—millions of Soviet citizens, particularly peasants, endured dire living conditions and often direct persecution at the hands of Stalinist leaders whose overriding priority was to make the USSR economically and militarily secure. As many as eight million peasants, the majority Ukrainian, starved to death in the Great Famine of 1932 and 1933, which Robert Conquest has insisted was a manmade catastrophe deliberately engineered by Stalin in order to smash Ukrainian nationalism. Whether this controversial interpretation is correct or not, the scale of human suffering endured in the early 1930s beggars belief. There was hope that the relatively moderate policies of the years 1934 to 1936 would curtail the suffering, but by 1937 mass arrests and executions became the norm. Archival figures made public shortly before the demise of Soviet communism indicate that approximately 800,000 people were shot between 1921 and 1953, a staggering 681,692 of whom were executed during the Great Terror of 1937 and 1938. Official statistics suggest that around 3.5 million people were detained in labor camps and internal exile during the Ter-

ror, the number rising to 5.5 million at the time of Stalin's death in 1953. On both counts many scholars have speculated that the actual totals were significantly higher. In the absence of definitive data, however, it seems prudent to accept the archival figures as essentially accurate.

Horrendous as they are, the bald statistics cited above obscure the unimaginable depths of human misery, the families ripped apart, the countless orphaned children, the mental and physical torture of prisoners, the uprooting of entire peoples from their homelands, the trampling on human integrity and dignity. How can all this be explained? Was the Terror simply a product of the deranged mind of a power-hungry tyrant? Or was there a larger purpose behind the seemingly arbitrary mass arrests and executions? Scholars have debated these and related issues for many decades. Research conducted in the 1990s and early 2000s demonstrates that rather than being a unitary phenomenon possessing a single aim, the Great Terror was a multifaceted process composed of separate but related political, social, and "national" (ethnic) dimensions, the origins and goals of which were different, but which coalesced during the events of 1937 and 1938.

There is no doubt that Stalin was the prime perpetrator of the Terror, even if historians disagree on whether he had a long-term blueprint to eliminate his opponents. It is generally accepted, however, that the process of mass repression was set in motion by the December 1934 assassination of Sergei Kirov, the popular Leningrad Communist Party chief and, so it was rumored at the time, rival to Stalin. Although the jury is still out on Stalin's precise role in this assassination, it is clear that he used Kirov's murder to attack various opponents of the regime, including former Party leaders Zinoviev and Kamenev who were placed under arrest. Beginning in the summer of 1936, and more conclusively during the spring of 1937, Stalin extended these repressive measures, seeking, it appears, to eliminate any real or potential political opposition to his rule. In so doing, he broke an unwritten Leninist principle: never arrest Communist Party members and officials.

The list of actions to which Stalin provided direct input is long: The Soviet leader initiated and orchestrated the three great Show Trials of August 1936, January 1937, and March 1938, as a result of which his former Bolshevik rivals Zinoviev, Kamenev, and Bukharin, among others, were executed. In September 1936 Stalin appointed Nikolai Ezhov, a known hardline adversary of "anti-Party elements," as head of the NKVD (secret police). He oversaw the decimation of the Red Army command from May through June 1937. He signed numerous death warrants and ratified numerous executions, thousands of the condemned being loyal Party and state officials; he even ordered the arrest of several members of his own extended family and close relatives of his colleagues, presumably in an attempt to test the latter's loyalty. Together with his propagandists, he set the overall tone and atmosphere of the Terror: the xenophobic suspicion of foreign spies and agents; the all-pervasive fear of wreckers, saboteurs, and double-dealers; and the endless exhortations to uphold Bolshevik vigilance in the face of these "enemies of the people." In short, as one expert has written, Stalin's "name is all over the horrible documents authorizing the terror" (Getty and Naumov, 1999, p. 451).

Aside from these politically motivated aspects, another fundamental characteristic of the Great Terror was the social component. Studies conducted in the late 1990s document the interrelationship between, on the one hand, social disorder and evolving secret police strategies to contain it in the early to mid-1930s and, on the other, the onset of mass arrests in the summer of 1937. According to one historian, the Great Terror represented "the culmination of a decade-long radicalization of policing practice against 'recidivist' criminals, social marginals, and all manner of lower-class individuals" (Hagenloh, 2000, p. 286). The threat of social instability posed by criminals, hooligans, other "socially harmful elements," and even armed gangs of bandits was taken seriously by secret police chiefs. By 1937 the lethal triumvirate of political opposition, social disorder, and ethnic subversion had raised fears among the increasingly xenophobic Stalinist elite of a broadly based anti-Soviet "fifth column" linked to foreign agents and spies. In response, on July 31, 1937, Stalin and his co-leaders sanctioned the notorious NKVD Order No. 00447, which specified by region the number of people to be sentenced either to death (approximately 73,000) or eight to ten years in the Gulag camps (approximately 186,500).

The decree remained in force until November 1938. The intent of this massive purge of socially harmful elements was to destroy what appeared to the Stalinists to be the social base for an armed overthrow of the Soviet government. Thus, one of the most interesting conclusions of new research is that, contrary to conventional wisdom about the elite status of the Great Terror's victims, in strictly numerical terms the bulk of those repressed were ordinary noncommunist citizens, kulaks, workers, and various "social marginals": recidivist criminals, the homeless, the unemployed, all those suspected of deviating from the social norms of the emerging Stalinist system.

It is also now recognized that beginning in the summer of 1937 the NKVD launched national sweeps of specific categories of foreigners and Soviet citizens of foreign extraction. Central and East Europeans were particularly targeted, but so were Koreans, Chinese, Afghans, and many other minorities who were deported from their homelands or arrested en masse. The so-called Polish Operation, ratified by the Politburo on August 7, 1937, resulted in the arrest of approximately 140,000 people, a staggering 111,000 of whom were executed. Similar campaigns were directed against Germans, Finns, Balts, and numerous others who were perceived to be real or potential spies and agents of foreign anti-Soviet intelligence agencies, although the percentages of those killed were generally lower than in the Polish Operation. A significant proportion of the victims were Jews and members of national communist parties. Whether the former were targeted specifically because of their ethnic origin is unclear. Stalin's anti-Semitic tendencies appear to have been far more pronounced in the postwar period. Such was the scale of the "national operations" that from about February 1938 on they became the prime function of secret police activity, more pervasive than the campaigns associated with Order 00447. Indeed, ethnically based repression did not end in the late 1930s. Although the number of arrests and executions decreased significantly after November 1938, during World War II entire populations (Volga Germans, Chechens, Ingushi, Kalmyks, Crimean Tartars, and others) were deported from their homelands to Central Asia and Siberia, accused of subversive tactics, espionage, and collaboration with the occupying Nazi forces.

Inevitably, these examples of Soviet ethnic cleansing have compelled some scholars to compare Stalinist and Nazi policies of extermination. The term *Stalinist genocide* employed by several specialists suggests a close relationship and moral equivalence between Nazi and Soviet terror. If one views the latter in an intentional versus functional framework, it appears that both elements of motivation were applicable: The intended victims were the traditional suspects (peasants, political opponents, and supporters of the tsarist regime) and the functional victims were those invented within the specific context of developments in the late 1930s, consisting of replaceable elites and alien nationals. Although it is important to recognize the enormity of Stalinist repression, it is critical, as many historians do, to emphasize the uniqueness of the Holocaust "the only example which history offers to date of a deliberate policy aimed at the total physical destruction of every member of an ethnic group. There was no equivalent of this under Stalinism" (Kershaw and Lewin, 1997, p. 8).

Union of Soviet Socialist Republics

The key issue of motive remains. Why did Stalin order the mass arrest of loyal Party and state bureaucrats? Why was the terror extended to include socially harmful elements? Why did the vicious assault on ethnic minorities escalate in late 1937 and continue well into 1938? Traditional explanations for the strictly political aspects of the Great Terror stress Stalin's lust for power and his determination to liquidate all real and perceived rivals in a paranoiac drive for autocratic rule. Large numbers of "Old Bolsheviks," former opponents, and a host of unreliable double dealers, wreckers, and saboteurs were targeted in what became an arbitrary frenzy of bloodletting. By eliminating these undesirables and replacing them with devoted "yes men," Stalin's power base was mightily strengthened. However, beginning in the 1980s so-called revisionist historians challenged this Stalin-oriented approach, arguing that one man could not, and did not, decide everything. Moreover, to these historians a certain systemic rationale existed for the apparently irrational waves of repression, one linked to center-periphery conflicts, interelite rivalries, and the chaotic and dysfunctional elements of the highly bureaucratized regime.

Although Stalin's motives remain, and will continue to remain, obscure, it appears that the decision to launch the mass operations in the summer of 1937 was related to reverses in the European and Asian arenas. In particular, the lessons of the Spanish Civil War induced an atmosphere of panic in the Kremlin and incited the Stalinists to seek "enemies" at home and abroad. The Soviet leadership's fears of a fifth column among Party, state, and military elites, who in the event of war could rely on broad support from socially harmful elements and hostile national minorities in the USSR, seem to account for the dramatic rise in arrests and executions. To this extent the threat of war and a potential fifth column represent the crucial link between the three dimensions of the Great Terror: political, social, and national. Only in the context of the Stalinists' grave fears for the security and integrity of the Soviet state can the mass repressions of 1937 and 1938 be understood.

Although mass arrests and executions abated after November 1938, repression continued in the USSR throughout World War II. Portrayed in the Soviet media as a heroic war of patriotism, there were many grim sides to this life-and-death struggle between the two totalitarian giants. Internally, Stalin used the conflict to target and deport entire peoples accused of collaborating with the Nazis. The number of Gulag inmates may have decreased in these years as many were released to fight the Germans, but the living and working conditions of those who remained were nothing

short of atrocious. Famine, epidemics, overcrowding, summary shootings, and inhuman exploitation for the war effort were commonplace. For instance, in 1942 the Gulag Administration registered 249,000 deaths (18 % of the camp population) and in 1943 it registered 167,000 deaths (17%). The "myth" of the Battle of Stalingrad and the euphoria of total victory in May 1945 have tended to obscure the horrendous suffering perpetrated by the regime on millions of Soviet citizens during World War II. It was not about to end.

One of the more reprehensible features of Stalin's rule after World War II was his increasing anti-Semitism. Indeed, at the time of his death in March 1953 it appears that he was planning another vast general purge of Soviet society based on the fictitious anti-Jewish Doctors' Plot that broke in January of the same year. Already in 1948 and 1949 hundreds of Jewish intellectuals had been arrested, at least one of whom, the world-renowned actor and theater director Solomon Mikhoels, was murdered. As a leading scholar has written: "Jews were systematically removed from all positions of authority in the arts and the media, in journalism and publishing, and in medicine and many other professions" (Werth, 1999, p. 245). The campaign reached a peak in the summer of 1952 with the secret trial of the members of the Jewish Anti-Fascist Committee, thirteen of whom were executed. There is some evidence that the aging and ill Stalin was at this time preparing to expose a wide-scale "Judeo-Zionist conspiracy," which was to conclude with the mass deportation of Soviet Jews to Birobidzhan, a barren region in Eastern Siberia. A major part of this final Stalinist plot was the arrest of several high-ranking Jewish doctors accused, among other things, of complicity in the deaths of two Soviet luminaries. Their trial, it seems, was set for mid-March 1953. Stalin's timely demise on March 5 put an end to their suffering and brought to a close the era of mass repression in the USSR. His successors, notably Nikita Khrushchev, renounced terror, released large numbers of Gulag prisoners, and attempted, not altogether successfully, to "de-Stalinize" Soviet politics and society.

The historical legacy of Stalin has often been framed in the following way: he was a cruel, but necessary, leader who after 1928 industrialized and modernized the USSR and thus established the economic, social, and military basis for victory over the Nazis in World War II. Given Soviet Russia's "backwardness," this could only have been accomplished rapidly by means of state coercion and pressure. Few, if any, contemporary scholars would subscribe to such an apologist interpretation of the Stalinist regime. There can be no justification—political, economic, military, and certainly not moral—for the crimes against humanity perpetrated from 1928 to 1953. However, this does not mean no connection exists between Stalin's revolution from above and the mass repressions. Indeed, a convincing consensus is emerging that stresses the interrelatedness of the two phenomena. The terror, it is argued, was inextricably linked to the massive campaigns of industrialization and the forced collectivization and dekulakization of Soviet agriculture from 1928 and 1929 on. The intense social flux and dislocation, the rising crime levels, the peasant resistance to collectivization, the urban tensions resulting from rapid industrialization, the limited success of the initiatives on the "nationality question," and the contradictory pressures on the bureaucracies and other elites, which engendered insubordination, deceit, and local and regional cliques and networks, all these outcomes of Stalin's revolution from above created conditions that were propitious for the hunt for "enemies". Add to this equation Stalin's considerable goals for personal power and his paranoias, and the built-in need for scapegoats to explain the dire state of Soviet material consumption, and the origins of mass repression become more explicable.

Conclusion

Leninist and Stalinist crimes against humanity are not easily elucidated. A multiplicity of factors—internal and external, ideological and practical, personal and systemic—must be carefully weighed. It is not enough to simply point the finger at two "evil," power-hungry men, highly relevant though they are to the entire process of Soviet mass repression. What motivated them? What were their fears? In what concrete political, economic, and military contexts did they make their decisions? What role did other actors play in fanning the flames of state violence? To what extent did elite attitudes reflect and magnify broader social mentalities, such as anti-Semitism and chauvinism? Here it is suggested that the roots of Soviet terror lay not only in the personal ambitions and whims of Lenin and Stalin, but also equally in the ideologically driven utopian mission of creating the perfect communist society purged of the politically and socially unfit in circumstances of international isolation and perceived foreign threats.

SEE ALSO Chechens; Cossacks; Gulag; Kalmyks; Katyn; Lenin, Vladimir; Memory; Stalin, Joseph; Statistical Analysis; Ukraine (Famine); Utopian Ideologies as Motives for Genocide

BIBLIOGRAPHY

Applebaum, Anne (2003). *Gulag. A History of the Soviet Camps.* London: Allen Lane.

Conquest, Robert (1971). *The Great Terror: A Reassessment.* London: Pimlico Press, revised edition of *The Great Terror: Stalin's Purge of the Thirties.* Harmondsworth, U.K.: Penguin, 1990.

Getty, J. Arch, and Oleg V. Naumov, eds. (1999). *The Road to Terror: Stalin and the Self-Destruction of the Bolsheviks, 1932–1939.* New Haven, Conn.: Yale University Press.

Hagenloh, Paul (2000). "'Socially Harmful Elements' and the Great Terror." In *Stalinism: New Directions,* ed. S. Fitzpatrick. London: Routledge.

Holquist, Peter (2003). "State Violence as Technique: The Logic of Violence in Soviet Totalitarianism." In *Stalinism: The Essential Readings,* ed. D. L. Hoffmann. Oxford: Blackwell Publishing.

Kershaw, Ian, and Moshe Lewin, eds. (1997). *Stalinism and Nazism: Dictatorships in Comparison.* Cambridge: Cambridge University Press.

McLoughlin, Barry, and Kevin McDermott, eds. (2003). *Stalin's Terror: High Politics and Mass Repression in the Soviet Union.* Basingstoke, U.K.: Palgrave Macmillan.

Pipes, Richard, ed. (1996). *The Unknown Lenin. From the Secret Archive.* New Haven, Conn.: Yale University Press.

Sebag Montefiore, Simon (2003). *Stalin. The Court of the Red Tsar.* London: Weidenfeld and Nicolson.

Service, Robert (2003). *A History of Russia from Nicholas II to Putin.* Harmondsworth, U.K.: Penguin.

Solzhenitsyn, Alexander (1974–1978). *The Gulag Archipelago, 1918–1956.* 3 volumes. London: Collins/Harvill Press.

Suny, Ronald G. (1998). *The Soviet Experiment: Russia, the Soviet Union and the Successor States.* New York: Oxford University Press.

Tucker, Robert C. (1990). *Stalin in Power: The Revolution from Above, 1928–1941.* New York: Norton.

Werth, Nicolas (1999). "A State Against Its People: Violence, Repression, and Terror in the Soviet Union." In *The Black Book of Communism. Crimes, Terror, Repression,* ed. S. Courtois et al. Cambridge, Mass.: Harvard University Press.

Yakovlev, Alexander N. (2002). *A Century of Violence in Soviet Russia.* New Haven, Conn.: Yale University Press.

Kevin McDermott

United Nations

The United Nations was created during and in the wake of World War II, which was a global cataclysm that brought death to millions of civilians. Most of those civilians were primary targets, and often not even enemy targets. The genocide of the Jews, Gypsies, Slavs and others by Nazi Germany, and the brutal repression and discrimination that preceded it, lent weight to the argument that peace and justice were inseparable, the other side of the coin from war and oppression. As stated in September 1944 by the Commission to Study the Organization of Peace, an influential United States non-governmental organization: "it has become clear that a regime of violence and repression within any nation of the civilized world is a matter of concern for all the rest."

Human Rights in the Charter of the United Nations

On August 14, 1941, the Atlantic Charter was agreed to by U.S. president Franklin D. Roosevelt and U.K. prime minister Winston S. Churchill, along with forty-seven other nations. These charter signatories envisaged a world that would enjoy "freedom from want and fear." Some five months later, the Declaration of the United Nations of January 1, 1942, advocated complete victory over the enemies of the Allied powers, declaring that this was "essential to defend life, liberty, independence, and religious freedom, and to preserve human rights and justice in their own lands as well as in other lands." This declaration was signed by twenty-six nations, which were later joined by twenty-one others.

The eloquent language of the documents to which these nations had pledged themselves doubtless played an important role in mobilizing the Allies' total commitment to victory over the Axis powers, but it was not a guarantee that the values espoused in the document would be seriously embraced in the postwar world. By the time of the second phase of the Dumbarton Oaks Conversations between the United States, the Soviet Union, Great Britain, and China (September 29 through October 7, 1944), divisions among these nations were already apparent. The Chinese delegation fought to insert a condemnation of racism into the draft UN Charter and to prevent human rights being given only the most minimal acknowledgment in the text. The United States, Great Britain, and the Soviet Union were opposed. The Dumbarton Oaks Conversations ultimately yielded proposals that included only one somewhat marginal provision on human rights. In the words of the proposals, the new organization would "facilitate solutions of international economic, social, and other humanitarian problems and promote respect for human rights and fundamental freedoms."

The politics of the Dumbarton Oaks negotiations made it unlikely that any more forceful statement could ever achieve acceptance. The Soviet Union under Stalin was no defender of human rights, Churchill wanted nothing that would threaten Great Britain's colonial empire, and the United States had to cater to its substantial constituencies favoring isolationism and its strict notion of state sovereignty. The United States was also concerned about the human rights implications of legal racial segregation that still held sway in its south-

ern states. The shock and disappointment of less powerful allies, especially Latin American and British Commonwealth states (Canada, Australia and New Zealand), and of American nongovernmental organizations, led to a confrontation on these issues at the San Francisco Conference which ultimately adopted the United Nations Charter. The accumulating evidence of the scope and depravity of the crimes against humanity perpetrated by Nazi Germany lent weight to the cause of those states who wished greater attention be paid to human rights issues. In the words of Paul Gordon Lauren,

> as more and more details about the shocking extent of the Holocaust began to seep their way out from under the earth of unmarked mass graves in occupied territories, and from under the barbed wire enclosures of the extermination camps into the world, it became nearly impossible to ignore the connection between racial and religious discrimination, especially as revealed by the recent extremes of Nazi philosophy, on the one hand, and genocidal war on the other (Lauren, 1998, p. 183).

As a result of these currents, several references to human rights were inserted into the UN Charter's preamble, and six articles (Articles 1, 13, 55, 62, 68, and 76) were added. Of special note is Article 1, paragraph 3, which includes among the purposes of the United Nations: "To achieve international cooperation in promoting and encouraging respect for human rights and fundamental freedoms for all, without distinction as to race, sex, language or religion." The establishment of a Commission on human rights was also explicitly envisaged, in Article 68. On the other hand, traditional notions of sovereignty were acknowledged in Article 2, paragraph 7: "Nothing contained in the present Charter shall authorize the UN to intervene in matters which are essentially within the domestic jurisdiction of any State." Much of the subsequent history of the UN's involvement in the field of human rights has been devoted to resolving the tension between protecting the sovereignty and jurisdictional discretion of individual states and creating an international body that could play a credible role in preventing or punishing human-rights violations.

Studies of Human Rights Topics

The UN's member states put up no real resistance to allowing the UN to sponsor studies of human rights problems in general, as long as they did not involve passing judgment on the behavior of individual states. The UN Sub-Commission on Prevention of Discrimination and Protection of Minorities (now the Sub-Commission on Promotion and Protection of Human

Under UN guard, Tutsis, carrying little more than food and a change of clothing, flee the Rwandan capital of Kigali. [TEUN VOETEN]

Rights), a group of individual experts elected by the Commission on Human Rights, has over decades produced many such studies on a variety of topics. These reports are frequently published under the imprimature of the United Nations. Two of the Sub-Commission's studies dealt with the subject of genocide, one by Nicodème Ruhashyankiko (1978), and one by Benjamin Whitaker (1983). Even in the case of these studies, political issues could cause problems. For example, the Ruhashyankiko study was published by the UN, but the Whitaker report was not, because it included as an example of genocide the Turkish massacre of Armenians in the second decade of the twentieth century. This massacre was denied by the Turkish government, which lobbied successfully to block the publication of Whitaker's work.

Human Rights Standard-Setting and Treaties

Another area of UN human-rights activity involved the setting of legal standards and definitions. This endeavor was generally not controversial. The first major text adopted outside of the bodies specifically concerned with human rights issues was the Convention on the Prevention and Punishment of the Crime of Genocide, adopted by the UN General Assembly December 9,

1948. This was an instrument that criminalized the type of human rights violation that the Nazi government had committed against millions of its citizens and conquered subjects. On the following day, December 10, 1948, the General Assembly adopted the Universal Declaration of Human Rights. Although the declaration had only the force of a recommendation, it quickly became the standard of the international human rights movement. It had been drafted by the UN's intergovernmental Commission on Human Rights, which had its foundation in UN Charter Article 68.

The Declaration became the first element of an International Bill of Human Rights that would eventually be completed by a series of binding treaties, including the International Covenant on Economic, Social and Cultural Rights (ICESCR) and the International Covenant on Civil and Political Rights (ICCPR), both of which were adopted on December 16, 1966, and came into force in 1976. Specialized treaties have also been adopted on racial discrimination, torture, discrimination against women, children's rights, and migrant workers' rights. In addition, numerous soft-law instruments (that is, documents containing normative standards that may reflect but do not of themselves constitute legally binding texts) have been adopted by the

United Nations Headquarters in New York City, framed by the flags of its 191 member nations. Founded in 1945, the United Nations is an international organization committed to maintaining peace and promoting economic development worldwide. [JOSEPH SOHM; CHROMOSOHM INC./CORBIS]

General Assembly, the Economic and Social Council (ECOSOC: an intergovernmental body, described in the Charter as a principal organ of the UN but reporting and effectively subordinate to the General Assembly), and other UN bodies that codify best practice in such fields as the treatment of prisoners. Many of these instruments have been invoked by UN treaty bodies and regional human rights courts, as guidance to the interpretation of rules of international human-rights law.

Monitoring Human Rights Norms by Treaty Bodies

The principal mode of resolving the tension between the UN Charter's human rights clauses and the domestic jurisdiction clause during the first two decades of the organization's existence was to favor domestic jurisdiction, or at least to give preference to a narrow view of what amounted to improper intervention. The UN's human rights bodies adopted a hands-off approach to allegations of human rights violations. These simply could not be discussed, much less become the subject of resolutions that involved making judgments about a state's human rights behavior.

Instead, the UN relied upon so-called treaty bodies, that is, special committees tasked with the responsibility of supervising the extent of states' compliance with the human rights treaties. By definition, states can waive their sovereign rights of immunity from scrutiny if they accepted a treaty obligation explicitly permitting scrutiny. Even then, however, the main form of supervision consists of a review of periodic reports submitted by the states themselves—a system of supervision whose intrusiveness was perceived to be minimal. Five of the treaties now have provisions whereby states may

officially accept that the committee in question may consider complaints from individuals within their jurisdiction: the ICCPR, Race Convention, Torture Convention, Women's Convention, and Migrant Workers' Convention. Four of these also provide for the consideration of possible interstate disputes (ICCPR, Race Convention, Torture Convention, and Migrant Workers' Convention), although this faculty has yet to be employed. Two envisage the possibility of the committee studying a practice of violation (Torture Convention, automatically, under Article 20; and Women's Convention, on the basis of its Optional Protocol). The Torture, Women's, and Migrant Workers' Conventions envisage the compulsory adjudication of disputes between states that are party to the treaties. This procedure has not yet been used.

The review of periodic reports proved to be a more effective process than might have been expected. While the states' reports (often self-serving) were the only official basis for such reviews, committee members found that nongovernmental organizations would brief them informally, so that they were in a position to ask probing questions of the delegations. During the cold war, the opposition of the Soviet Union and its allies to any kind of outside judgment of their domestic practices meant that the committees would refrain from formulating conclusions resulting from the review. However, the early 1990s saw a relaxation of this inhibition, with the committees' adopting findings on the extent of state compliance and making recommendations on measures that could address the problems they found. These amounted to judgments, even though they were not formally binding.

The early inability of the committees to make country-specific observations led them to develop statements by way of what was called General Comments. General Comments serve as an authoritative aid to interpretating of the nature and scope of the obligations contained in the treaties, as the normative language is often couched in very general terms. The practice continued even after the country-specific comments began to be produced.

Another basis of guidance to the appropriate interpretation of treaties lies in the consideration of individual cases by the committees entrusted with that function. The most evolved jurisprudence is that of the Human Rights Committee under the ICCPR. Nevertheless, the committees' conclusions on individual cases are not legally binding on the state concerned. Unlike the European and inter-American regions, the broader, global community has not yet been willing to accept an international human rights court.

Monitoring Human Rights Norms
by Special Procedures

The last three decades of the twentieth century saw a radical evolution in the attitude of the UN, especially of the Commission on Human Rights. The Commission, building on two resolutions of ECOSOC (Resolutions 1235 [XLII], 1967; and 1503 [XLVII], 1970), developed what came to be called its special procedures. These were designed to address member-states' unwillingness to deal with individual violations, but were primarily concerned with violations of extreme gravity, or on a massive scale, such as would be associated with crimes against humanity. In the words of ECOSOC Resolution 1503, what was to be studied or investigated were "situations appearing to reveal a consistent patterns of gross . . . violations of human rights."

The effect of ECOSOC Resolution 1235 was to pave the way for the Sub-Commission or the Commission to decide that a specific country situation could be discussed, made the subject of a resolution and even, if agreed by the Commission, put under investigation by an ad hoc group or a special rapporteur. To achieve this, the situation had to be introduced by a member of the Sub-Commission or the Commission, and a vote had to be taken to authorize the drafting of a resolution.

By Resolution 1503, information submitted by nongovernmental organizations or individuals was to be treated confidentially in a protracted procedure involving both the Sub-Commission and the Commission. The (expert) Sub-Commission tended to unearth situations for consideration by the Commission, whereas the (intergovernmental) Commission tended either to drop consideration of the situations or, at best, keep them under review. Only rarely did they become the object of sustained study. For historical reasons, the names of countries whose situations are kept under consideration are announced by the chair of the Commission, although such announcements were not originally contemplated by Resolution 1503. It is generally thought that some situations have been dealt with under Resolution 1503 when there would not have been the political will to deal with them in public session, and that the procedure, including the public announcement of reviewed situations, provided at least some pressure on the states whose practices were impugned.

Yet some situations are so appalling that even being taken up under Resolution 1503 would be an inadequate response. This was the case with Argentina in the latter half of the 1970s, where the alleged violations consisted, notoriously, of thousands of enforced disappearances of perceived political opponents of the military regime. There was insufficient political will in the UN to adopt a resolution that would permit a formal, public investigation of the situation. Frustrated with this inability to act, some member states began to a search for an alternative approach to the existing country-specific special procedures.

What emerged was the first of the thematic special procedures. In 1980, the Commission established the Working Group on Enforced or Involuntary Disappearances. The notion was that the group would consider the problem not just in one country, but in all countries. The basic mandate seemed anodyne enough—it was to study the general phenomenon of enforced disappearance. But the working group was also intended to take effective action. On this basis, the group, composed of five individual delegation members (one from each of the UN's five regions), began transmitting allegations of enforced disappearances to the member state in which the disappearances occurred. The allegations came overwhelmingly from nongovernmental sources. The working group would then report to the Commission, country by county, on the allegations received during the previous year, and on any responses received from the governments in question. Thus, although the group dealt with the general phenomenon of enforced disappearance, the procedure was also country-specific. Furthermore, individual cases were taken up with a view to seeking clarification of the fate of alleged victims. Indeed, when individuals were detained in circumstances suggesting that they might "disappear," the group developed the technique of making urgent appeals to the governments responsible for such detentions. These appeals were telexed (later faxed) messages addressed directly to the foreign minister of the state in question. Meanwhile, in countries where there appeared to be a problem of enforced disappearance involving more than just isolated cases, the group sought permission from the state to visit and explore the matter on the spot.

Slowly other themes or categories of human rights violation were accepted as deserving similar attention. In 1982, the Commission created the position of special rapporteur on summary or arbitrary executions, and in 1985 it established a special rapporteur on torture, a development long sought by nongovernmental organizations campaigning against torture, such as Amnesty International. By 2004 there were more than twenty special rapporteurs on a broad range of human rights issues, including such civil and political rights as religious intolerance, the independence of judges and lawyers, and human rights defenders. The creation in 1991 of the Working Group on Arbitrary Detention is of special interest. Given a mandate not just to study the phenomenon, but to investigate cases of alleged arbitrary detention, the group not only comments on country-specific alleged violations, it also has a specific function of assessing whether or not, in its view, a particular detention should be characterized as arbitrary. On the other hand, more recently the Commission has created special rapporteurs to deal with issues in the area of economic and social rights, such as the right to education, to adequate housing and to health, which do not so readily lend themselves to taking action on individual cases.

Human Rights and International Criminal Law

The evolution of machinery to scrutinize states' performance in the field of human rights has far exceeded what might have been expected of international law and organizations by earlier generations, or even at the founding of the UN. Nevertheless, it has still failed to stop repressions that amount to crimes against humanity or even genocide. Nor is it likely that the establishment of an international human rights court could have provided a bulwark against outbreaks of mass atrocity.

In the 1990s, increasing awareness of the problem of impunity for the individual perpetrators of criminal human rights violations gave impetus to almost dormant early UN concern with international criminal law. After the General Assembly's early endorsement of the International Law Commission's draft of the Principles of Nuremberg, it took that Commission till the mid-1990s to complete decades of work on the Code of Crimes against the Peace and Security of Mankind (1996) and to draft a statute for an international criminal court (1994). Meanwhile, having failed to act effectively to prevent atrocities—including acts of genocide in the former Yugoslavia in the early 1990s, and the wholesale genocide in Rwanda in 1994—the Security Council established the first ad hoc courts (the International Criminal Tribunal for the Former Yugoslavia and the International Criminal Tribunal for Rwanda) to bring the perpetrators and organizers of those atrocities to justice, regardless of rank or political status. This development can be seen as a political expedient as much as a means for the imposition of justice. Nonetheless, it gave new impetus to the movement toward establishing a standing international criminal court. The time was ripe to embark on the project, and the UN's 1998 diplomatic conference in Rome adopted the Rome Statute of the International Criminal Court.

SEE ALSO United Nations Commission on Human Rights; United Nations General Assembly; United Nations Security Council; United Nations Sub-Commission on Human Rights

BIBLIOGRAPHY

Alston, Philip, ed. (1992). *The United Nations and Human Rights: A Critical Appraisal.* Oxford: Oxford University Press.

Alston, Philip, and James Crawford, eds. (2000). *The Future of UN Human Rights Treaty Monitoring.* Cambridge: Cambridge University Press.

Bassiouni, M. Cherif (1998). *The Statute of the International Criminal Court: A Documentary History.* Ardsley, N.Y.: Transnational Publishers.

Cassese, Antonio, Paola Gaeta, and John R.W.D. Jones (2002). *The Rome Statute of the International Criminal Court: A Commentary.* Oxford: Oxford University Press.

Dormenval, Agnes (1991). *Procedures onusiennes de mise en oeuvre des droits de l'homme: Limites ou defauts?* Paris: Presses Universitaires de France.

Kuper, Leo (1985). *The Prevention of Genocide.* New Haven, Conn.: Yale University Press.

Lauren, Paul Gordon (1998). *The Evolution of International Human Rights: Visions Seen.* Philadelphia: University of Pennsylvania Press.

Lee, Roy S., ed. (1999). *The International Criminal Court: The Making of the Rome Statute: Issues, Negotiations, Results.* The Hague: Kluwer.

Lempinen, Miko (2001). *Challenges Facing the System of Special Procedures of the United Nations Commission on Human Rights.* Turku/Abo: Institute for Human Rights, Abo Akademi University.

Russell, Ruth B., and Jeannette E. Muther (1958). *A History of the United Nations Charter: The Role of the United States 1940–1945.* Washington, D.C.: The Brookings Institution.

Schabas, William A. (2000). *Genocide in International Law.* Cambridge: Cambridge University Press.

Schabas, William A. (2003). *An Introduction to the International Criminal Court.* Cambridge: Cambridge University Press.

Tolley, Howard (1987). *The U.N. Commission on Human Rights.* Boulder, Colo.: Westview Press.

Nigel S. Rodley

United Nations Commission on Human Rights

The United Nations Commission on Human Rights is the first, and remains the only, body operating within the framework of an international organization that is devoted exclusively to promoting universal respect for human rights throughout the world.

The Commission was envisaged as part of the United Nations (UN) when it was founded after World War II. The first words of the UN Charter state:

We the peoples of the United Nations are determined to save succeeding generations from the

As chair of the United Nations Commission on Human Rights (shown here in its 1947 composition in Geneva, Switzerland), Eleanor Roosevelt spearheaded the drive to draft the Universal Declaration of Human Rights. [BETTMANN/CORBIS]

scourge of war, which twice in our lifetime has brought untold sorrow to mankind, and to reaffirm faith in fundamental human rights, in the dignity and worth of the human person. . . (Preamble, Sect. 1 and 2)

It was within this context, following the atrocities of a war that dramatically illustrated what would come to be known as crimes of genocide and crimes against humanity, that the UN Commission on Human Rights was created. It was a time when reaffirming the fundamental values of dignity and respect for human life was vital.

Origin and Creation

The Commission on Human Rights benefits from the fact that it is the only "technical commission" mandated by the UN Charter (Article 68), signed in San Francisco on June 26, 1945. It is thus a statutory body of the UN and had been planned for from the organization's inception. It was formally created on February

16, 1946, by the Economic and Social Council (ECOSOC), one of the principal bodies of the UN. Inclusion of the Commission in the UN Charter did not occur without considerable discussion at the San Francisco conference, which was responsible for drafting the Charter.

In fact, the four "sponsoring powers" at the San Francisco conference (China, the United States, the United Kingdom, and the former Soviet Union), whose role was essential in preparing the Charter, viewed the creation of a human rights commission with apprehension. They recognized the risk of its limiting or interfering with national sovereignty in a highly sensitive area, one where the state was traditionally tied to its prerogatives. It was only at the eleventh hour, just prior to the expiration of the allotted deadline (May 4, 1945), that the four countries filed joint amendments, one of which provided for a commission for "the development of human rights." The principal terms of its creation may be found in Article 68 of the UN Charter. It is important to note, however, that the efforts of nongovernmental organizations (NGOs) alone ensured the commission's creation at the San Francisco conference. In particular, it was the representatives of private organizations recognized by the U.S. States delegation who, through their perseverance, succeeded in influencing member states to include in the UN's projected amendments a provision for a special commission on human rights, even though it was initially agreed that the Charter itself would not specifically mention a technical commission.

This episode illustrates the essential role that NGOs and civil society can play in advancing human rights and promoting their respect throughout the world, by their intervention on an international scale. Such activist groups have grown in strength and diversity throughout the decades of the Commission's existence, but the Commission itself has been inconsistent in its recognition of these participants, and often it has attempted to limit their involvement.

Status and Functions
Prior to the final establishment of the Commission (in 1946), debate turned to the subject of its composition, namely, whether it would be made up of independent experts or representatives of the member states. The latter proposal was eventually adopted, with the Commission officially composed of representatives from eighteen member states. Its composition has been expanded several times over the years and as of 2004 there are fifty-three members, designated by the ECOSOC on the basis of regional geographic representation. Some believe a Commission of independent experts known for their competence and impartiality would ensure a more objective approach to human rights and, in particular, the question of violations; others see the direct involvement of national governments in the Commission's work as increasing the effectiveness of its proposals and ensuring the application of its recommendations. The risk of the first approach, a truly independent Commission, is that it would become isolated, without any grasp of the realities and changes that primarily stem from existing governments. In the second approach, that adopted by the UN, states serve as both judges and parties (since they are the principal entities implicated in any violations), and the Commission risks finding its work impeded whenever the interests of a powerful state or group of states are involved.

In hindsight one may posit that in its actions to the present, the Commission might have been better able to fulfill its human rights mission if its activities had been based on the work of independent bodies and ex-

perts, such as its Sub-Commission on the Promotion and Protection of Human Rights and working groups, or its special rapporteurs (individuals responsible for examining specific violations or human rights situations within a country). This would not, of course, eliminate the specter of negative pressure from some states, especially when the Commission is being pressured from within for various reasons associated with an international situation. It remains the case, however, that arrangements could be made to limit such negative effects and prevent states that demonstrate little respect for human rights from sitting on the Commission or presiding during a session. To achieve this end, certain criteria have been proposed, such as a state's ratification of the major human rights conventions or a state's permanent agreement to allow special rapporteurs on its territory.

The Commission's mandate and responsibilities as originally defined in its statutes (ECOSOC Resolution 5(I) of February 16, 1946, and Resolution 9(II) of June 21, 1946, both of which are still applicable) are extensive and highly diverse. The Commission, which meets in an annual session, is responsible for presenting proposals, recommendations, and reports related to an international declaration of human rights and other declarations and conventions in this area; the protection of minorities; and the abolition of distinctions based on race, sex, language, or religion. It is also responsible for research activities and formulates recommendations when requested by ECOSOC. In addition, the Commission can look into "any other problem involving human rights" that is not otherwise stipulated, which opens up a nearly unlimited field of activity. In short, one may view the Commission as a specialized body within the UN responsible for implementing the fundamental terms of the UN Charter designed to promote "universal respect for, and observance of, human rights and fundamental freedoms for all without distinction" (Article 55), and basing its activities on commitments formally made by member states for that purpose (Article 56). In the decades following its somewhat tentative initial phase, the Commission made increasingly greater use of the mechanisms granted at its inception, primarily for investigating human rights violations around the world. The Commission has evolved through three successive phases: a standard-setting phase, a promotional phase, and a protectionist phase. Here the first and last of those phases will be addressed.

Standard-Setting Phase: Development of the Fundamental Instruments of Human Rights
Although the Charter clearly indicates that one of the principal objectives of the UN is to encourage respect for human rights, it does not define the substance of

those rights or the specific steps for ensuring their application. During the first years of its existence (1947–1954), the Commission overcame this void by devoting itself almost exclusively to drafting the instruments that would define those rights and ensure their international adoption: the Universal Declaration of Human Rights (adopted December 10, 1948), and the two international covenants, one on civil and political rights, the other on economic, social, and cultural rights (both were adopted in 1966).

The Universal Declaration is the "foundational" instrument; it establishes basic principles and defines rights by specifying their scope. Although the crime of genocide and crimes against humanity are not expressly mentioned in the text, the Declaration contains terms that can be directly related to such crimes. In its preamble the Declaration states that "disregard and contempt for human rights have resulted in barbarous acts which have outraged the conscience of mankind," and the Declaration itself is advanced as "a common standard of achievement for all peoples and all nations to the end that every individual and every organ of society shall strive to promote respect for these rights." As for the recognition of those principles and rights, the Declaration incorporates the following: the principle of equality in dignity and rights (Article 1); the prohibition of any discrimination, especially through race, color, sex, language, religion, political or any other opinion, national or social origin, property, birth, or any other status (Article 2); the right to life, liberty, and personal security (Article 3); and the prohibition of slavery and torture (Articles 4 and 5).

Corresponding clauses have been included in the International Covenant on Civil and Political Rights later drafted by the Commission, which identifies a specific mechanism for inspection and is legally binding on the states that have ratified it.

Coincident with the Universal Declaration, the UN General Assembly adopted the Convention on the Prevention and Punishment of the Crime of Genocide on December 9, 1948. This marked an important step in the definition and identification of genocide and the pursuit and punishment of its perpetrators. The Commission on Human Rights, preoccupied with the preparation of the Universal Declaration, did not participate significantly in drafting the Genocide Convention. This task was entrusted to a special committee—the Ad Hoc Committee on Genocide—created by ECOSOC.

The Commission did however contribute some twenty years later to the preparation of the draft Convention on the Non-Applicability of Statutory Limitations to War Crimes and Crimes Against Humanity. In 1965, in light of the requirement for legal action sched-

uled to begin at that time, as mandated by the laws of certain states, the Commission began studying the legal procedures that could be used to establish the nonapplicability of statutory limitations for such crimes. It proposed that a specific convention be formulated after the study ended; the General Assembly finally adopted such a convention in 1968. The Convention on the Non-Applicability of Statutory Limitations to War Crimes and Crimes Against Humanity stipulates the crimes that are not subject to statutory limitations, identifies the individuals responsible for those crimes (in particular, any government officials), and indicates the commitments and steps states must make and follow in matters of extradition and statutory limitations. In the years subsequent to the Convention's adoption, the Commission regularly studied the "question of punishing war criminals and individuals guilty of crimes against humanity" and the necessity of international cooperation for such purposes. Concerning this last point, the Commission examined a set of draft principles adopted by the General Assembly in 1973 entitled Principles of International Co-operation in the Detection, Arrest, and Punishment of Persons Guilty of War Crimes and Crimes Against Humanity.

The Commission's work on standard-setting continued beyond this initial period as it drafted other special instruments (declarations and conventions): primarily the International Convention on the Elimination of All Forms of Racial Discrimination (1965), the Convention on the Elimination of All Forms of Discrimination Against Women (1979), the Convention Against Torture and Other Cruel, Inhuman, or Degrading Treatment or Punishment (1984), and the Convention on the Rights of the Child (1989). The Convention Against Torture, in particular, should be considered in light of acts that may be classified as crimes against humanity, for it contains a precise definition of the term *torture* and also institutes a specific control mechanism through its Committee Against Torture (composed of experts and empowered to examine documents or complaints related to violations of the Convention).

Protectionist Phase: Examination of Human Rights Violations

During the first two decades of its existence, the Commission did not follow up on the many complaints of human rights violations it had received since the UN's founding, claiming a lack of jurisdiction even though its mandate in no way prohibited investigation. Its primary focus was standard-setting, studies on specific rights, and promotional efforts with various states (e.g., technical cooperation, consulting services, a system of periodic reports).

Beginning in the late 1960s, under pressure from countries newly admitted to the UN following their independence, the Commission began to concretely address violations. It instituted procedures for examining documents and attempted to identify "situations of flagrant and systematic human rights violations" (on the basis of ECOSOC Resolution 1235 (XLII) of June 6, 1967, and Resolution 1503 (XLVIII) of May 27, 1970). Simultaneously, the Commission created special groups of experts responsible for investigating a region or country. The first, formed in 1967, was the ad hoc group of experts to investigate human rights in South Africa; it initially investigated torture and the improper treatment of prisoners arrested by the police in the Republic of South Africa. New ad hoc groups of experts were later created to investigate alleged human rights violations in other countries or territories, but since the 1980s the Commission has frequently assigned the study of a human rights situation in a specific country to a single expert known as a "special rapporteur."

In the same period the Commission also regularly appointed special rapporteurs with so called thematic mandates (in other words, mandates not restricted to a specific country), who became responsible for examining a specific type of violation that could be found throughout the world (such as extrajudicial, summary, or arbitrary execution; forced or involuntary disappearance; torture). In their publicly available reports submitted annually to the Commission, special rapporteurs identify, and establish the facts of, various cases and situations, which in certain circumstances involve crimes against humanity and/or genocide.

During the past few decades, based on reports and other sources of information at its disposal, the Commission has examined and identified situations that revealed the existence of such crimes. It has adopted resolutions condemning those acts, demanding that the responsible parties be judged and that all available steps be taken to eliminate such actions and prevent their reoccurrence in the future.

Situations That Constitute Crimes of Genocide and Crimes Against Humanity

During a single ten-year period, from 1990 through 2000, the Commission examined two large-scale occurrences of human rights violations involving the crime of genocide and crimes against humanity in the former Yugoslavia and in Rwanda. This led to protective actions in both situations. The extreme gravity of the events that transpired and the urgency of confronting them prompted the Commission to convene special sessions, the first held since its inception.

Former Yugoslavia

Serious human rights violations in Bosnia and Herzegovina, Croatia, and the Federal Republic of Yugoslavia (Serbia and Montenegro) resulted in the first of the Commission's responses. In 1992 it held its first two special sessions to discuss these issues (August 13–14 and November 30–December 1), organized at the request of the required majority of its members. During the first session a special rapporteur was appointed and a new special session convened to examine the rapporteur's reports. On this basis, in its Resolution 1992/S-2/1 of December 1, 1992, the Commission categorically condemned the ethnic cleansing ongoing in Bosnia and Herzegovina, acknowledging that Serbian leaders in the territories under their control in Bosnia and Herzegovina, the Yugoslav army, and the political leaders of the Serb Republic bore primary responsibility for the practice. The Commission demanded that ethnic cleansing be discontinued immediately. The Resolution also forcefully restated the following: Anyone perpetrating or authorizing such crimes against humanity is individually responsible for those violations and the international community will spare no effort to bring them to justice.

Additionally, all states were invited to examine the extent to which the acts committed in Bosnia and Herzegovina and Croatia constituted genocide as defined by the Convention on the Prevention and Punishment of the Crime of Genocide. On this point, on December 18, 1992, the General Assembly itself declared that "the abhorrent policy of ethnic cleansing was a form of genocide" (General Assembly Resolution 47/121); the Commission would reaffirm the term *genocide* in its later resolutions.

During the years that followed the special rapporteur—whose mandate was regularly renewed—submitted new reports to the Commission, which, in response, adopted resolutions at each of its sessions, denouncing and condemning the substantiated crimes, and demanding that any violations be discontinued and those responsible be brought to justice. After 1993 the situation in Kosovo also deteriorated, especially in terms of ethnic cleansing, and this led to grave concerns on the Commission's part. Simultaneously, the systematic use of rape as a weapon of war and an instrument of ethnic cleansing, particularly in Bosnia and Herzegovina, was forcefully denounced and qualified as a "war crime" by the Commission. On May 25, 1993, the Security Council, in its Resolution 827, created the International Criminal Tribunal for the Former Yugoslavia (ICTY). The Commission requested that all the states cooperate and support this body.

In line with the general agreement for peace in Bosnia and Herzegovina (the Dayton Accord of November

21, 1995, signed in Paris on December 14), the Commission demanded an end to human rights violations in the Federal Republic of Yugoslavia (Serbia and Montenegro), in Bosnia and Herzegovina, and in Croatia. It also recommended that steps be taken to assist in the return of refugees and displaced persons, that the states involved provide information on the fate of those who had disappeared, and that an effort be made to promote democratic institutions. The special rapporteur, with an extended mandate, was asked to carry out these missions in the three states, especially in Kosovo. At each of its following sessions, the Commission reviewed the findings of the rapporteur and adopted resolutions concerning the human rights situation in those countries. On April 13, 1999, in the face of continued violations and the massacres carried out against the Kosovars after Serb authorities had revoked their autonomy, the Commission adopted a special resolution devoted exclusively to the human rights situation in Kosovo (Resolution 1999/2). This resolution strongly condemned the widespread and systematic practice of ethnic cleansing, demanded the immediate discontinuation of all repressive actions that might worsen the situation, and asked the international community and the ICTY "to bring to justice the perpetrators of international war crimes and crimes against humanity, in particular those responsible for acts of ethnic cleansing and identity elimination in Kosovo."

Following the retreat of Serb forces from Kosovo on June 10, 1999, new developments in the region (primarily the establishment of the UN Interim Administration Mission and the International Security Force in Kosovo) led to the Commission's modifying its approach. However, it continued to regularly examine, at each of its sessions, the human rights situation in the countries in question on the basis of reports prepared by the special rapporteur and by the "special representative" of the Commission who was appointed in 2001.

Rwanda

During the 1990s the Commission also examined the situation in Rwanda, and its investigation revealed that acts of genocide had been committed there, with serious and extensive human rights violations occurring after April 1994. This led to the Commission's convening a third special session on May 24 and 25. In its Resolution (S-3/1), the Commission "believing that genocidal acts may have occurred in Rwanda," condemned all violations of international humanitarian law and human rights committed in the country and asked all parties to put an end to the situation at once. It further affirmed that any individual who commits or authorizes violations of human rights or international humanitarian law is personally responsible and must ac-

count for his or her actions in a court of law. To further its inquiry, the Commission appointed a special rapporteur to investigate the human rights situation in Rwanda by traveling there. It also asked that given the urgency of the situation, all existing mechanisms available to the Commission be utilized: primarily the special rapporteur on extrajudicial, summary, or arbitrary executions; the special rapporteur on torture; the Secretary General's special representative on internally displaced persons; the working group on forced or involuntary disappearances; and the working group on arbitrary detention; as well as the monitoring organizations instituted by international human rights conventions. In particular, the special rapporteur becames responsible for gathering information on "acts which may constitute breaches of international humanitarian law and crimes against humanity, including acts of genocide in Rwanda."

In his report dated June 28, 1994, the special rapporteur issued the following findings: "The charges are threefold: genocide through the massacre of the Tutsi, political assassinations of a number of Hutu and various violations of human rights." On the basis of information appearing in this report and another prepared by an expert commission created on July 1, 1994, by the Security Council, the Human Rights Commission, during its next regular session held in the spring of 1995, strongly condemned the acts of genocide, the violations of international humanitarian law, and all human rights violations committed during the conflict in Rwanda following the tragic events of April 6, 1994 (attacks on the aircraft which cost the lives of the president of Rwanda and the president of Burundi). After reaffirming the personal responsibility of all individuals who commit such crimes and other serious violations, and the need to bring them to justice, the Commission asked that all states cooperate fully with the International Criminal Tribunal for Rwanda (ICTR), which the Security Council created through Resolution 955 on November 8, 1994.

During the sessions that followed, the Commission continued to examine the human rights situation in Rwanda, paying particular attention to the information supplied by the special rapporteur, whose mandate was regularly renewed. In its successive resolutions, the commission repeatedly condemned the crime of genocide, crimes against humanity, and all other human rights violations in Rwanda, insisting on the individual responsibility and prosecution of all their perpetrators, and the full cooperation of all member states with the ICTR.

The Commission has also begun to address the situation of survivors of genocide and massacres, in particular the large number of traumatized children and female victims of rape and sexual abuse. In this context it has emphasized the importance of human rights observers and the Human Rights Field Operation in Rwanda, initiated by the UN High Commissioner on Human Rights in cooperation with the Rwandan government. The field operation is responsible for investigating violations of human rights and humanitarian law, including acts of genocide and crimes against humanity, and monitoring the evolving human rights situation by preventing the occurrence of new violations. In 1997 the special rapporteur was succeeded by a "special representative," authorized by the Commission to recommend ways to improve the human rights situation and provide technical assistance. The special representative's mandate ended in 2001, concluding the Commission's specific examination of the human rights situation in Rwanda.

Commission Response

In the face of two serious situations involving massive and systematic violations of human rights, in the former Yugoslavia and Rwanda, the Commission responded decisively and quickly: convening for the first time in special session and utilizing special rapporteurs who were able to investigate violations already committed or in progress, and whose mandate lasted for several years. The Commission also made use of monitoring committees to track the application of human rights conventions and the existing "resources" available to special rapporteurs and working groups responsible for examining such issues as extrajudicial or summary executions, torture, arbitrary detention, and involuntary disappearances. The Commission's activities and decisions have also been coordinated with those of other competent UN agencies, especially the Security Council and the two international ad hoc tribunals that were created to bring those responsible for the acts in question to trial.

In this context the Commission has contributed to fact-finding and been particularly helpful inidentifying the acts that constitute crimes of genocide or crimes against humanity. Nonetheless, it is unfortunate that the Commission was unable to intervene earlier to prevent such situations or, at least, to limit the violations, whether in Rwanda or the former Yugoslavia. However, "early warning" procedures are now in effect that will allow the Commission to remain better informed about potentially serious human rights violations, although its ability to respond in concrete ways is still too limited. The prevention of violations remains a critical issue; it can be strengthened by the presence of human rights observers in the field before a situation deteriorates significantly and becomes totally uncontrollable.

Struggle against Impunity

Starting in the 1990s, the Commission began to regularly examine the issue of impunity, which, while intended to ensure that those guilty of violations do not escape justice, is also part of a system of prevention and dissuasion. In 1993 it formed a subcommission to study the impunity of human rights violators. Previously, several special rapporteurs and working groups of the Commission had raised the question within the context of their respective mandates (e.g., extrajudicial execution, torture, involuntary disappearance). Determining that the practice was increasingly widespread and that it encouraged violations and served as a fundamental obstacle to the respect of human rights, the Commission, through various resolutions, insisted the phenomenon be countered. It asked member states to take the steps necessary to prevent impunity while supplying possibly relevant information on it. For the Commission, denouncing the violations, holding perpetrators individually responsible for their acts, and obtaining justice for the victims are essential to promoting human rights and preventing future violations. Similarly, releasing information about the suffering of the victims and establishing the truth about the perpetrators of human rights violations are vital for the rehabilitation of victims and any subsequent reconciliation.

As part of its study, the subcommission drafted a document entitled, "Set of Principles for the Protection and Promotion of Human Rights Through Action to Combat Impunity" (divided into three sections: the right to know, the right to justice, and the right to reparation). It was sent to the Commission in 1998 and then distributed to various states. While emphasizing the importance of the ICTY and ICTR, the Commission also strongly insisted on the need to establish a permanent criminal court as an important component of the struggle against impunity. When the Rome Statute of the International Criminal Court (ICC) was adopted on July 17, 1998, the Commission encouraged member states to join and collaborate. Similarly, in its resolutions, it has regularly stressed the importance of the Convention on the Preparation and Punishment of the Crime of Genocide by asking those states that have not yet ratified it to do so.

In its resolutions the Commission has also incorporated the mechanisms established by certain states in which serious violations have occurred, primarily investigative commissions and truth and reconciliation commissions, and it has additionally encouraged other states in a similar situation to institute their own mechanisms for redress. In its 2003 session the Commission asked that an independent study be prepared and recommendations provided on the most effective practices to help states combat all aspects of impunity.

The role of the United Nations Commission on Human Rights in preventing genocide and crimes against humanity falls within the scope of its overall activities and is one of the many functions it has developed since its creation: the drafting of norms and principles, the use of special studies and technical assistance to promote human rights, the use of special procedures and field missions to help provide protection. The complementary nature of, and interaction among, these different approaches and methods highlight the specific contributions of the Commission and its huge potential. It is this potential that should be further explored to encourage prevention and, in particular, those activities that will discourage the most serious human rights violations, namely genocide and crimes against humanity.

SEE ALSO Impunity; Roosevelt, Eleanor; Rwanda; United Nations; United Nations General Assembly; United Nations Security Council; United Nations Sub-Commission on Human Rights; Yugoslavia

BIBLIOGRAPHY

Alston, Philip (1992). "The Commission on Human Rights." In *The United Nations and Human Rights*, ed. Philip Alston. Oxford: Clarendon Press.

Degni-Ségui, René, Special Rapporteur of the Commission on Human Rights (1994). *Reports on the Situation of Human Rights in Rwanda*. UN documents E/CN.4/1995/7 and E/CN.4 1995/12.

First Special Session: Situation of Human Rights in the Territories of the Former Yugoslavia, August 13–14, 1992. UN document E/CN.4/1992/84/Add.1/Rev.1.

Human Rights Monitor, International Service for Human Rights. "Geneva: Quarterly Analytical Review of UN Human Rights Meetings Including Sessions of the UN Commission on Human Rights (since 1988)." Available from http://www.ishr.ch.

Lempinen, Miko (2001). *Challenges Facing the System of Special Procedures of the United Nations Commission on Human Rights*. Turku/Abo: Institute for Human Rights, Abo Akademi University.

Marie, Jean-Bernard (1975). *La Commission des droits de l'homme de l'ONU*. Paris: Editions Pedone.

Second Special Session: Situation of Human Rights in the Territories of the Former Yugoslavia, November 30–December 1,1992. UN document E/CN.4/1992/S-2/6.

Tolley, Howard (1987). *The UN Commission on Human Rights*. Boulder, Colo.: Westview Press.

Third Special Session: Situation of Human Rights in Rwanda, May 24–25, 1994. UN document ECN.4/S-3/4.

Jean-Bernard Marie

United Nations General Assembly

To achieve the declared purposes of the United Nations (UN), the UN Charter of 1945 provided for the establishment of a number of organs, including the General Assembly and Security Council. The Assembly is empowered to discuss any question or matters within the scope of the Charter. For this reason it can be described as the world's most important forum for political discussion. Also, owing to its various functions under the Charter, it holds a prominent position among the organs of the UN. Committees and other bodies established by the Assembly to study and report on specific issues carry out much of its work.

The Assembly is the only principal organ of the UN in which all member states are represented; it was conceived to closely resemble, in both function and structure, a representative legislative assembly. President Franklin D. Roosevelt often referred to the Security Council as the body with the power, while the Assembly was the place for small countries to "let off steam."

Composition
The Assembly's composition and role under the Charter give it a legitimacy that few other international organs possess. It is made up of representatives of the member states of the UN. These individuals act on the instructions of their governments. In this way the Assembly is a conference of states, not a world parliament of representatives for all peoples of the world. Nearly every state in the world is a member of the UN and represented in the Assembly.

An issue that arises from time to time is that of representation at the Assembly. Each member state has one vote in the Assembly. However, only one delegation is entitled to be admitted from each member state. This may seem straightforward at first, but the Assembly sometimes must deal with rival claimants from the same state. Such a scenario arises as a result of armed conflicts and civil wars around the globe. The Assembly has the right and responsibility to decide between rival claimants, but in so doing, it can be described as determining which faction is the rightful government of a particular state. A number of important controversies developed over representation, most notably those involving China between 1949 and 1971, the Congo in 1960, Yemen in 1962, and Kampuchea (Cambodia) from 1970 to 1991.

Several political and legal issues surface in deciding between rival claimants, but it is difficult to discern any definite criteria for recognition apart from a general leaning toward the principle of effectiveness. This means that a government will be regarded as the legitimate representative of a state as long as it has not been replaced by a rival claimant independent of the support of a foreign power. This can be seen in the Assembly's decision in 1971 to recognize the government in Beijing, and not that in Taiwan, as the legitimate representative of China.

More significant was the policy regarding the Pol Pot regime in Kampuchea (Cambodia) after it lost power to the Heng Samrin government in 1979. Many states believed that the new government owed its position to the support of foreign powers, in particular Vietnam. The regime thus lacked legitimacy in the eyes of the international community, despite the fact that it had replaced one of the most despotic governments of the twentieth century. The Assembly continued to recognize the representatives of Pol Pot, in spite of the appalling human rights record of that government. The UN decision was very controversial, especially because the scale and extent of the killings, and persecution of Cambodians by the regime, were well known at the time. Many historians referred to these events as genocide. However, owing to the fact that the perpetrators and victims belonged to the same national group, they were not accepted as constituting genocide according to the narrow definition of the crime under international law. The issue posed the serious question of whether a regime that perpetrated such crimes against its own people should remain its legitimate state representative in the Assembly. There are no easy answers.

The UN is dedicated primarily to the maintenance of international peace and security by protecting the territorial integrity, political independence, and national sovereignty of its members. But the overwhelming majority of today's conflicts are internal, not interstate. Moreover, the proportion of civilians killed in such conflicts has dramatically increased from about one in ten at the start of the twentieth century to around nine out of ten at its close. This has forced the Assembly and other organs to seek to reconcile the foundational principle of member states' sovereignty and the mandate to maintain international peace and security with the equally compelling mission to promote human rights and the general welfare of people within those states.

The Secretary-General has addressed the dilemma within the conceptual framework of two notions of sovereignty: one vested in the state, the second in peoples and individuals. This is reflected in the 2001 *Report of the International Commission on Intervention and State Sovereignty*, which advances the argument that state sovereignty implies responsibility, and the primary responsibility for the protection of its people lies with the state. However, when a population begins to suffer serious harm, as a result of internal war, insurgency, repression, or state failure, and the state in question is unwilling or unable to halt or avert it, the principle of nonintervention yields to the international responsibility to protect.

Functions and Powers of the General Assembly

Under the UN Charter, the functions and powers of the Assembly are wide-ranging but ill-defined. This stands in direct contrast to the unambiguous primacy given to the Security Council in relation to the maintenance of international peace and security. It is important to bear in mind that the UN by its very nature does not infringe on the independence and sovereign powers of member states. Article 2(7) of the Charter expressly prohibits interference in matters that essentially fall within the domestic jurisdiction of states. The nonintervention clause is a fundamental principle of the organization. In practice, deciding whether a matter is within the domestic jurisdiction of a state or not is more a political than legal question. Furthermore, human rights and related issues may be deemed matters of concern to the international community if they pose a threat to international peace and security.

The Assembly's powers are described in Chapter IV of the Charter. Although Articles 10 and 14 grant generous powers to the Assembly, Articles 11 and 12 appear to restrict these. Decisions on important questions (peace and security, new members, budgetary issues) require a two-thirds majority. A simple majority may reach decisions on other issues. The powers of the Assembly may be summarized as follows:

- To make recommendations on cooperation in the maintenance of international peace and security

- To discuss any question relating to international peace and security, and to make recommendations, except when a dispute or situation is under discussion by the Security Council

- To discuss and, with the same exception as above, make recommendations on any question within the scope of the Charter or affecting the powers and functions of any organ of the UN

- To initiate studies and make recommendations to promote international political cooperation; the development and codification of international law; the recognition of human rights and fundamental freedoms for all; and international collaboration in economic, social, cultural, educational, and health fields

- To make recommendations for the peaceful settlement of any situation, regardless of origin, that might impair friendly relations among nations

- To consider reports from the Security Council and other UN organs

- To approve the UN budget and divide contributions among members

- To elect the nonpermanent members of the Security Council, the members of the Economic and Social Council, and those members of the Trusteeship Council that are elected

- To elect, jointly with the Security Council, the Judges of the International Court of Justice (ICJ)

- To appoint on the recommendation of the Security Council, the Secretary-General

Procedures and Voting

According to Article 18 of the Charter, each member of the Assembly shall have one vote, allowing equal participation in decisions. This is intended to reflect the sovereign equality of member states.

The Assembly is required to meet in regular sessions, and these usually begin each year in September. At the start of each regular session, the Assembly elects a new president, twenty-one vice-presidents, and the chairpersons of the Assembly's six main committees. To ensure equitable geographical representation, the presidency of the Assembly rotates each year among five groups of states: African, Asian, Eastern European, Latin American and Caribbean, and Western European and other states. In addition to its regular sessions, the Assembly may meet in special sessions at the request of the Security Council, a majority of member states, or one member if the majority of members concurs. At the beginning of each regular session, the Assembly holds a general debate, with heads of state and government often addressing the body, and member states express their views on issues of international concern.

Most questions are discussed in the Assembly's six main committees, where voting occurs by simple majority:

1. First Committee: Disarmament and International Security Committee

2. Second Committee: Economic and Financial Committee

3. Third Committee: Social, Humanitarian and Cultural Committee

4. Fourth Committee: Special Political and Decolonisation Committee

5. Fifth Committee: Administrative and Budgetary Committee

6. Sixth Committee: Legal Committee

The majority of the Assembly's decisions are made through the affirmative vote of two-thirds or more of its members. Proposals representing a decision of the Assembly have frequently been adopted without a formal vote taken in plenary meetings. Resolutions may be adopted by acclamation, without objection or without a vote, or the vote may be recorded or taken by roll call. This consensus approach has played a significant role in the practice of the Assembly. Although the decisions of the Assembly are not legally binding on governments, they carry significant moral and persuasive authority. No proposals have been made to change the voting system at the Assembly. However, the large number of smaller states admitted as members does raise legitimate questions given the disparity in size, population, and other characteristics of member states.

Expansion of Powers through Practice

Article 10 of the Charter is its most significant; it defines the Assembly's powers of discussion and recommendation in their broadest form:

> The General Assembly may discuss any questions or any matters within the scope of the present Charter or relating to the powers and functions of any organs provided for in the present Charter, and, except as provided in Article 12 may make recommendations to the Members of the United Nations or to the Security Council or to both on any such questions or matters.

It is evident from this Article, and the practice of the Assembly, that the range of questions or matters which the Assembly is authorized to discuss is as wide as the scope of the Charter itself. Since adoption, its broad terms have been the principal basis for an expansion of its role beyond that envisaged by the Charter's drafters. When this Article was being drafted, it provoked a serious crisis that was resolved only after high-level consultation between the former Soviet Union and the United States. The original proposal put forward would have given the Assembly no real power in the political field. Although most of the differences of opinion concerned the issue of the maintenance of international peace and security in relation to those of the Security Council, the matter of the Assembly's freedom of discussion was also crucial.

The general scope of this Article and the breadth of powers it confers have been referred to many times in plenary and committee meetings by representatives who wished to stress the overall responsibility of the Assembly as a world forum for considering international problems. However, the vagueness and sweeping extent of Article 10 also reflect the Assembly's lack of power to make a binding decision. Although such decisions or recommendations may carry significant weight and authority, it is because they are not binding that they too often are imprecise and general in nature.

Articles 11 and 12 circumscribe the role of the Assembly. However, it is clear from these and other articles that while the Security Council has primary responsibility for the maintenance of international peace and security, it does not have exclusive competence, especially as far as the Assembly is concerned. The smaller and middle power states were opposed to any restriction on the jurisdiction of the Assembly, whereas the major powers stressed the need to avoid disputes between the Assembly and Security Council on vital matters. Nevertheless, the extent of the limitation imposed on the Assembly should not be exaggerated. It applies only to the Assembly's recommendatory, not deliberative, powers. The right of the Assembly to discuss, consider, and debate any issues, including those relating to the maintenance of international peace, remains. The reason for such a rule arises from the different role and functions of the Assembly. An international crisis does not automatically guarantee an agreed upon response, and the differences in the composition of the Security Council and Assembly could lead to conflicting responses from both.

A major step in the development of the Assembly's role was the adoption of the Uniting for Peace resolution on November 3, 1950 (passed in connection with the crisis in Korea). Under this resolution the Assembly may take action if the Security Council, because of a lack of unanimity among its permanent members, fails to act in a case where there appears to be a threat to peace, breach of peace, or act of aggression. The Assembly is empowered to consider the matter immediately and make recommendations to members for collective measures. This includes, in the case of a breach of peace or act of aggression, the use of armed force when necessary to maintain or restore international peace and security.

Acting under Uniting for Peace Resolution 377(V) of November 5, 1950, the Assembly established the United Nations Emergency Force to secure and supervise the cessation of hostilities between Egypt and Israel. The resolution has been utilized additional times, most notably in 1956, after Egypt nationalized the Suez Canal and, in response, Britain, France, and Israel attacked Egypt. Both Britain and France vetoed ceasefire resolutions in the Security Council. The United States appealed to the General Assembly, calling for a ceasefire and withdrawal of forces. An emergency session was called under the Uniting for Peace resolution. In this case the Assembly's intervention did facilitate the resolution of the crisis. However, the willingness of the states concerned to comply with the Assembly's demands was due to a complex set of circumstances surrounding the military intervention.

Uniting for Peace was next used by the United States to pressure the Soviet Union into ceasing its intervention in Hungary in 1956. Again, an emergency session of the General Assembly was held and the Soviet Union was ordered to end its intervention. No visible evidence exists that the action influenced Soviet policy to any significant extent at the time. However, two years later the procedure was used to facilitate the resolution of another crisis, that existing in Lebanon.

The cold war and activities of the Asian-African group of states, in particular the support given to various independence movements, led to a new role, not earlier envisaged, for the Assembly. The repeated use of the veto on the Security Council meant that the Assembly was being called on to perform functions originally regarded as the special province of the Security Council. Thus in 1950, when it became apparent that the Security Council could no longer effectively address the mounting hostilities in Korea, the Assembly, on the initiative of the United States, assumed residual responsibility for taking measures necessary to maintain international peace in case of a threat or breach of peace. Often during the cold war all sides used the Assembly as a forum to pursue a war of words. The smaller and middle powers did not oppose the incremental growth in the influence of the Assembly; they now possessed equal say. In this way, political developments combined with a liberal interpretation of the provisions of the Charter to permit the Assembly to assume significant responsibilities for the maintenance of international peace and security.

It is important to note that the Assembly does not possess any formal mandatory powers along the lines of the Security Council. It can only make recommendations on matters of international peace and security. However, the resolutions it adopts may have a binding effect if they reflect established principles of international law. There is a clear difference between declaring that an existing law calls for a certain response and creating new law.

Convention on the Prevention and Punishment of the Crime of Genocide

As the International Military Tribunal (IMT) at Nuremberg (established to try Nazi war criminals in the aftermath of World War II) drew to a close, the first session of the Assembly was getting underway. The judgment handed down at the Nuremberg Tribunal was controversial in several respects. The limited scope given to "crimes against humanity" at the time was one of the main reasons why it was considered necessary to draft a convention that specifically addressed the crime of genocide.

A crime against humanity referred to a rather wide range of atrocities, but it also had a narrow aspect, in that the prevailing view was that crimes against humanity could only be committed in association with an international armed conflict or war. The Allies had insisted at Nuremberg that crimes against humanity could only be committed if they were associated with one of the other crimes within the IMT's jurisdiction, that is, war crimes and crimes against peace. In effect, they imposed a connection or "nexus," as it became known, between crimes against humanity and international armed conflict. The Assembly wanted to bridge the gap which many perceived to exist in international law as a result by recognizing that one atrocity, namely genocide, would constitute an international crime even if it were committed in time of peace. The price to pay for this, according to William Schabas, was an exceedingly narrow definition of the mental and material elements of the crime. The distinction between genocide and crimes against humanity is less significant today, because the recognized definition of crimes against humanity has evolved and now unquestionably refers to atrocities committed against civilians in both peacetime and wartime.

After the IMT handed down its judgment between September 30, and October 1, 1946, Cuba, India, and Panama asked that the subject of genocide be put on the agenda of the General Assembly's first session. These states were concerned that international law did not seem to govern atrocities committed in peacetime (as opposed to those perpetrated during a time of armed conflict or war). The draft resolution submitted referred to the fact that the punishment of the very serious crime of genocide when committed in time of peace lies within the exclusive territorial jurisdiction of individual states concerned, while crimes of relatively lesser importance are declared as international crimes and have been made matters of international concern. In requesting a report on the possibilities of declaring genocide an international crime and ensuring international cooperation for its prevention and punishment, the Assembly acknowledged that it was not a legislative body and therefore could not make law as such. Nonetheless, any measure it took was vested with incontestable authority.

The final version of Resolution 96(I), adopted by the Assembly on December 11, 1946, called for the preparation of a draft convention. It also affirmed that genocide was a crime under international law. Even though Resolution 96(I) was adopted unanimously and without debate, it is not legally binding. However, the ICJ has acknowledged that such resolutions may have normative value. They can provide evidence of the existence of a customary rule, and the emergence of a legally binding provision.

The Convention on the Prevention and Punishment of the Crime of Genocide was adopted by the Assembly on December 9, 1948, and entered into force two years later on January 11, 1951, after ratification by twenty member states. During the drafting process, significant disagreement arose among states regarding the nature and extent of the crime of genocide. Article I creates an obligation on states to prevent and punish genocide. This was added by the Legal Committee based on proposals from Belgium and Iran. However, there was nothing in the related debates that clarified what the scope and implications of the obligation were. This stood in marked contrast to the provisions in the Convention dealing with punishment. The Legal Committee completed its review of the draft convention on December 2, 1948. The draft resolution and convention were adopted by thirty votes to none, with eight abstentions. The interventions by states provide some insights into their concerns at the Committee stage. The United Kingdom abstained, as it believed governments, not individuals, should be the focus of the Convention. Poland and Yugoslavia were critical of the Convention's failure to prohibit hate propaganda and measures aimed against a nation's art and culture. Czechoslovakia felt the Convention as adopted would do little to prevent genocide.

Article II of the Convention defines genocide as:

> any of the following acts committed with intent to destroy, in whole or in part, a national, ethnical, racial or religious group, as such: killing members of the group; causing serious mental or bodily harm to members of the group; deliberately inflicting on the group conditions of life calculated to bring about its physical destruction in whole or in part; imposing measure intended to prevent births within the group; forcibly transferring children of the group to another group.

Under the Convention, the crime of genocide has both a physical element (certain actions, such as killing members of a racial group) and a mental element (the acts must be committed with intent to destroy, in whole or in part, a national, ethnic, racial, or religious group "as such"). Although earlier drafts had included "political groups," this wording was dropped during the final drafting stages. Also excluded was the concept of cultural genocide—destroying a group by forcible assimilation into a dominant culture. The drafting history makes clear that the Convention was intended to cover the physical destruction of a people and that some governments feared they could become vulnerable to a charge of genocide for certain actions.

When the Convention was adopted, two associated resolutions were passed. The first raised the issue of trying individuals charged with genocide before a competent international tribunal. It invited the International Law Commission to study the desirability of establishing an international criminal court. A second resolution concerned the application of the Convention to dependent territories.

The International Law Commission, a subsidiary body of the Assembly, is a body of experts responsible for the codification and progressive development of international law. The Commission has examined the issue of genocide on a number of occasions during the course of its work on draft codes and statutes. In 1954 it concluded that the definition of genocide set forth in the Convention should be modified, but later decided that the original text ought to be retained as this definition was widely accepted by the international community. Hence, the original definition of genocide in the Convention is essentially repeated in Article 6 of the Rome Statute of the International Criminal Court (ICC), which was agreed to in 1998, and in the relevant statues of the ad hoc International Criminal Tribunals for the Former Yugoslavia (ICTY) and Rwanda (ICTR).

Sabra and Shatila Refugee Camps in Lebanon

The Assembly formally addressed the issue of genocide for the first time in 1982, when it debated the massacre of Palestinians at the Sabra and Shatila refugee camps in Beirut, Lebanon. Although the term had been mentioned in previous debates, on this occasion the Assembly qualified the massacre as genocide, while the Security Council, following the lead of the Secretary-General's report, condemned the "criminal massacre of Palestinian civilians in Beirut." Cuba proposed a resolution declaring the massacres to be an "act of genocide."

In the ensuing debate little attention was paid to the actual scope and meaning of genocide under international law. The Singapore delegation accused the Assembly of using "loose and casual language when referring to issues with a precise legal definition." Such sentiments were echoed by a number of other delegations. Finland probably best reflected the view of those states not supporting the use of the term *genocide*, in declaring that its use had prevented the Assembly from giving unanimous expression "to the universal outrage and condemnation" with regard to the massacre. In spite of the heated debate, the Assembly adopted Resolution 37/123(D) on December 16, 1982, paragraph 2 of which resolved that "the massacre was an act of genocide."

It is by no means clear under the 1948 Convention on Genocide that the Assembly, in fact, had the authority to make such a determination. However, it is inevitable that a body of this nature will be dominated by political rather than legal arguments, especially when considering the tragic fate of Palestinian civilians left behind in Beirut after the agreed upon departure of Palestinian fighters.

The Former Yugoslavia and Rwanda

In December 1992 the General Assembly adopted Resolution A/RES/47/147 on the general situation in the former Yugoslavia and cited the Genocide Convention in its preamble. It also endorsed a resolution of the Commission on Human Rights adopted at that body's special session in August 1992, "in particular its call for all States to consider the extent to which the acts committed in Bosnia and Herzegovina and in Croatia constitute genocide." On December 20, 1993, the Assembly reaffirmed in Resolution A/RES/48/88 its determination to prevent acts of genocide and crimes against humanity and noted that the ICJ in its order of September 13, 1993, in the case *Bosnia and Herzegovina v. Yugoslavia (Serbia and Montenegro)*, had called on the government of Yugoslavia to immediately take all measures within its power to prevent the commission of the crime of genocide. Another resolution, A/RES/47/121, described ethnic cleansing as "a form of genocide," but this finding was not consistent with later resolutions on ethnic cleansing that made no reference to genocide. Resolutions equating ethnic cleansing with genocide are problematic. Although there is no generally recognized text defining ethnic cleansing, there is a consensus among scholars and others that it is aimed at displacing a population, whereas genocide is intended to destroy it. Such descriptions ultimately do not serve the best interests of victims of either crime, or further the credibility of the Assembly.

Since 1992 the Assembly has referred to genocide on a number of occasions when adopting resolutions in relation to the crisis. In December 1995 the Assembly elaborated on the issue of genocide in Bosnia and declared that rape, in certain circumstances, could constitute an act of genocide (Resolution A/RES/50/192). The 1999 Report of the Secretary-General on the fall of Srebrenica (made pursuant to Assembly Resolution 53/35) was very critical of the Security Council's failure to take decisive action and referred to the attempted genocide in Bosnia.

Given the event's scale, it is surprising that just one of the Assembly's resolutions on the crisis in Rwanda referred to genocide. On December 23, 1994, Resolution 49/206 expressed deep concern at the reports issued by the Special Rapporteur and Commission of Experts indicating that genocide and crimes against humanity were committed, and condemned the acts of genocide that had taken place in Rwanda.

Apartheid and Forced Disappearances
The Assembly has also adopted resolutions dealing with various other crimes against humanity, including apartheid and forced disappearances. One of the best illustrations of the limitations of the Assembly and UN, as well as their potential, is the policy with regard to apartheid. On June 22, 1946, India requested that the treatment of Indians in the Union of South Africa be included in the agenda of the Assembly's first session. The General Committee did not support South Africa's request that the Indian matter be removed from the agenda on the grounds that it was essentially within the domestic jurisdiction of South Africa. Following a debate in the Assembly, Resolution 44(I) was adopted on December 8, 1946, which declared that the treatment of Indians in South Africa should conform with the international obligations under the agreements concluded between the two governments and the corresponding provisions of the UN Charter. A year later, in November 1947, the Assembly was unable to adopt any resolution on the Indian complaint for lack of a two-thirds majority.

The Assembly did adopt numerous resolutions on the issue over the next five decades, but a turning point was Resolution 1761 of November 6, 1962. The resolution, sponsored by a number of African states, urged member states to impose economic and other sanctions against South Africa and established a Special Committee (which later became the Committee on Apartheid) to monitor the situation. The debates increasingly focused on demands that the situation in South Africa be recognized as a threat to international peace and security and that universal sanctions be imposed against South Africa. During the cold war Western nations believed that the Security Council alone should make the determination that a denial of human rights posed a threat to international peace. In this context there was bound to be natural antagonism between the Assembly and the Council.

On November 30, 1973, the Assembly adopted the International Convention on the Suppression and Punishment of the Crime of Apartheid. It declared, among other things, that apartheid is a crime against humanity. Furthermore, apartheid was found to include the "[d]eliberate imposition on a racial group or groups of living conditions calculated to cause its or their physical destruction in whole or in part." It is noteworthy that the South African government was excluded from the Assembly in 1974 when its delegation's credentials were rejected. At the same time UN bodies granted the liberation movements of South Africa Observer status and the Assembly recognized them in 1975 as the authentic representatives of the overwhelming majority of people in that country.

On December 18, 2002, the Assembly adopted by consensus two resolutions related to disappearances and missing persons. Resolution A/RES/57/215 on enforced or involuntary disappearances expressed concern at the growing number of enforced disappearances in various regions of the world. It affirmed that any act of enforced disappearance is an offense to human dignity and a flagrant violation of human rights. It urged governments to take steps to prevent and suppress the practice. It encouraged all states to abide by the principles outlined in the Declaration on the Protection of All Persons from Enforced Disappearance, adopted by the Assembly on December 18, 1992 (Resolution A/RES/47/133).

Resolution A/RES/57/207 on missing persons noted the issue of persons reported missing in connection with international conflicts and urged states to respect international humanitarian law. In both cases the Assembly used language such as "urges," "requests," "calls upon," or "appeals" to exhort members to comply, reflecting the fact that an Assembly resolution or declaration alone cannot impose legal obligations on states.

Conclusion
There have been many instances in which the Assembly has acted within its area of competence when addressing issues of international peace. If a conflict is characterized by questions of fundamental human rights, then it is arguable that the Assembly should assume the primary role in protecting those rights. When the grave risk of genocide or some other serious violation of human rights exists, then it is best that the consideration of any military intervention be first brought before the Security Council. However, if the Security Council rejects a proposal for intervention when significant humanitarian or human rights issues are at stake, or the Council fails to decide on such a proposal within a reasonable period of time, then responsibility falls to the Assembly to take appropriate action. Although the Assembly lacks the authority to take direct action, a decision in favor of action, if supported by a large majority of states, would largely legitimize any subsequent intervention.

The ability to achieve the overall two-thirds majority within the Assembly to invoke the Uniting for Peace process is very unlikely when political realities are taken into account. Political realities play an even larger role when the Security Council fails to act because of the threat of veto. As a result, vital time can be lost before decisive action is taken to remedy a situation on the ground. In the case of genocide and crimes against humanity, such action will often be too late for victims.

When a resolution targets a specific violation or country, it is difficult to evaluate its effectiveness over time. It seems that formal resolutions may send important signals, but these too are almost impossible to measure. Political matters still tend to dominate debates, but these should not overshadow the accomplishments in the promotion of human rights across the full spectrum of UN activities.

SEE ALSO Convention on the Prevention and Punishment of Genocide; United Nations; United Nations Commission on Human Rights; United Nations Security Council; United Nations Sub-Commission on Human Rights; United Nations War Crimes Commission

BIBLIOGRAPHY

Chesterman, Simon, ed. (2001). *Civilians in War*. London: Lynne Rienner.

Claude, Inis, Jr. (1956). *Swords into Plowshares*. New York: Random House.

Commission of Inquiry into the Events at the Refugee Camps in Beirut (February 9, 1983). Final Report (authorized translation). *The Jerusalem Post*.

Goodrich, Leyland M. (1960). *The United Nations*. London: Stevens.

Goodrich, Leyland M., Edward Hambro, and Ann P. Simons (1969). *Charter of the United Nations*, 3rd edition. New York: Columbia University Press.

Gutman, Roy, and David Rieff (1999). *Crimes of War*. New York: Norton.

Holzgrefe, J. L., and Robert O. Keohane, eds. (2003). *Humanitarian Intervention—Ethical, Legal and Political Dilemmas*. Cambridge, U.K.: Cambridge University Press.

Report of the International Commission on Intervention and State Sovereignty: The Responsibility to Protect (2001). Ottawa: International Development Research Centre.

Report of the Independent Inquiry into the Actions of the United Nations During the 1994 Genocide in Rwanda (1999). UN Document S/99/1257.

Report of the Secretary General Pursuant to General Assembly Resolution 53/3: The Fall of Srebrenica (1999). UN Document A/54/549.

Schabas, William A. (2000). *Genocide in International Law*. Cambridge, U.K.: Cambridge University Press.

Schabas, William A. (2001). *An Introduction to the International Criminal Court*. Cambridge, U.K.: Cambridge University Press.

Simma, Bruno (2002). *The Charter of the United Nations—A Commentary*, 2nd edition. Oxford: Oxford University Press.

White, Nigel D. (1997). *Keeping the Peace*, 2nd edition. Manchester, U.K.: Manchester University Press.

Ray Murphy

United Nations Security Council

The United Nations was created at the end of World War II. That war cost the lives of millions of people, some in battle, many others as a result of systematic and organized annihilation. When it was over, people everywhere longed for the creation of a better world and an end to all war.

Out of this desire, the United Nations came into being. Fifty-one governments agreed to sign the UN Charter, an international treaty that bound its signatories to a commitment to eliminate war and promote peace. The UN Charter begins with a promise to prevent the "untold sorrow" of war, after which it lists the rights and duties of each member government. Since its creation in 1945 the UN has grown to include 192 member nations. While the UN has not, so far, come close to fulfilling all the hopes and dreams of its founders, it remains the world's principal organization for the promotion of international peace and security.

The most powerful division of the UN is the Security Council, which all member states are bound by the UN Charter to obey. The Council comprises the representatives of fifteen member governments. Five of these are permanent members: China, the United States, the United Kingdom, France, and Russia. Each of these five states has a veto in the Council, which means any one of them can stop any decision they do not like. Ten other states, elected by the General Assembly, sit in the Council for a period of two years, after which ten different states are chosen. When disagreements between states occur, it is the job of the Security Council to mediate between them before disputes escalate to war.

The United Nations and Human Rights
Since the UN was created, its members have tried to set basic standards of behavior for the world to follow. In 1948 the UN General Assembly, which comprises every UN member, agreed to a document called the Universal Declaration of Human Rights. This outlined the rights that the members believed belonged to everyone in the world. The declaration recognized that the most fundamental of all human rights is the right to life. The Universal Declaration of Human Rights determines that people have the right to freedom and security, that they should be free from slavery, they should have the right to a fair trial, to marry, to own property, and to believe in whatever religion they choose.

The UN tries to monitor any country which is breaking these rules through a special organization called the UN Commission on Human Rights. Through such monitoring, the UN makes sure that the rest of the world is aware of each country's human rights record. This was the beginning of an historic effort to build an edifice of treaty law on behalf of human rights. The UN set itself the task of defining human rights standards and measuring the performance of individual states against the principles embodied in the UN Charter. In these early years, the organization recognized human rights violations vary both in degree and in nature, and therefore needed to be carefully categorized.

The 1948 Genocide Convention

Although the crime of genocide has been perpetrated throughout human history, little was done to prevent or punish it until the end of World War II. That war was the occasion during which the most comprehensive genocide of the twentieth century was committed: the systematic extermination of the Jews. To address this terrible crime, the UN drafted the 1948 Convention on the Prevention and Punishment of Genocide—the world's first truly universal, comprehensive, and codified protection of human rights. The Genocide Convention, which preceded the Universal Declaration of Human Rights by twenty-four hours, confirmed one of the great ideals of the UN Charter: a respect for human rights and fundamental freedoms for all.

The Genocide Convention stood for a fundamental and important principle; that whatever evil may befall any group, nation, or people, it was a matter of concern not just for that group but for the entire human family. The crime of genocide is the denial of the right of existence of entire human groups, just as homicide is the denial of the right to live of individual human beings. The Genocide Convention defines genocide to mean certain acts, enumerated in Article II, committed with the intent to destroy, in whole or in part, a national, ethnical, racial or religious group. The Genocide Convention provides that conspiracy, direct and public incitement to commit genocide, and complicity in genocide shall be punishable by international law, and that there can be no defense of sovereign immunity.

In dealing with the crime of genocide on a multinational basis, the world governments, through the United Nations, appreciated that genocide was a matter of concern to all states. Before 1945, efforts to legislate internationally were very limited. Since 1945, however, multinational treaties have become the prime legal mechanism by which states entered into mutual commitments for common purposes. Under such treaties, states agree to act in accordance with rules agreed upon among their fellow nations.

At the heart of the Genocide Convention is the recognition of the principle that preventing and punishing

United Nations peacekeepers from Bangladesh arrive in Liberia in October of 2003. [AP/WIDE WORLD PHOTOS]

of genocide requires international cooperation. The convention relies on the procedures and institutions of the United Nations to prevent genocide. It clearly recognized that the commission of certain extraordinary crimes anywhere in the world had an effect on the peace and security of all nations, and that it was usually associated with breaches of international peace and security. It noted that the most flagrant examples of genocide had historically occurred during major wars, and steps to curb genocide were thus considered part of the attempt to preserve peace.

The first recognition of genocide as a crime under international law was officially agreed unanimously by the United Nations General Assembly on December 11, 1946. After two years of consideration by committees at the United Nations, on December 9, 1948, the General Assembly adopted the Genocide Convention to outlaw genocide. The UN Security Council assumed a central role in the application of the Genocide Convention—it provides the measure of international enforcement outlined in the treaty.

Article VIII of the convention recognizes that "any contracting party may call upon the competent organs of the UN to take such action under the Charter of the UN as they consider appropriate for the prevention and suppression of acts of genocide or any other acts enumerated in Article III." This article, although it adds nothing new to the UN Charter, is important in that it states explicitly the right of states to call upon the UN with a view to preventing and suppressing genocide. It is the only article in the Genocide Convention that deals with prevention. For the most part, however, the Genocide Convention emphasizes punishment. It was intended as a warning that those who supported or executed a policy of genocide would not be tolerated or excused. Rather, they would have to answer for their sins to the world community of states. The Genocide Convention, despite its title, concentrates almost exclusively on the punishment of the offender rather than prevention of the offense.

Since the enactment of the Genocide Convention there have been major international disputes justified by claims of ethnic, racial, and religious hatreds. The use of genocide during conflict seems to have increased over the years, some experts have said that genocide occurs so often in some regions that it has come to be considered normal. It is estimated that genocide and politicide—state sponsored massacres—have claimed more than twice as many victims as war and natural disasters since 1945. Yet the Genocide Convention is a weak instrument with which to deal with the modern occurrence of genocide. It has become important only for its symbolic value because there has been no Security Council action taken to punish any of the numerous genocides that have taken place since 1945.

Complaints of genocide have been brought to the United Nations since the end of World War II, but even so, the UN has never formally applied the Genocide Convention to any of them. The complaints have not been wholly ignored. Too often, however, they have been redefined as disasters requiring humanitarian assistance. In the absence of internationally sanctioned intervention, such humanitarian aid is often all that is available for genocide victims. Recurring debates on the Genocide Convention have taken place in the Sub-Commission for the Prevention of Discrimination and Protection of Minorities, a part of the Commission on Human Rights, but there does not yet exist a committee charged with ensuring that the Genocide Convention is implemented.

The Genocide Convention is only as effective if the UN member states are willing and determined to employ their power and influence to implement it. It is up to the Security Council to decide when force should be deployed to prevent and suppress it. In the last years, however, the Security Council has allowed a respect for state sovereignty and territorial integrity to take precedence over the concern for protection against genocide. Without stern and timely action by the Security Council, the Genocide Convention has been mostly meaningless in deterring this and other gross violations of human rights. It was not until the creation of two tribu-nals—the International Criminal Tribunals for the Former Yugoslavia in May 1993, and the International Criminal Tribunal For Rwanda in November 1994—that redress was provided for the crime of genocide. These represent the first legal mechanisms created to punish the crime of genocide. In July 1998, the international legal venue for the punishment of such crimes, promised by the 1948 Genocide Convention, was finally created, with the UN adoption of the Rome Statute and the formation of the International Criminal Court.

Peacekeeping

During the cold war, the UN was unable to do the job for which it was created and international co-operation proved to be a difficult goal to attain. During these years, a more modest and realistic role for the UN was devised. As a neutral organization, it could help mediate conflict, monitor ceasefires, and aid in the separation of hostile armed forces. Two novel missions were undertaken through the Security Council at this time. In 1947 a mission of unarmed military observers—the UN Truce Supervision Organization (UNTSO)—was created, first used in the Balkans and then in Palestine. In 1956 an armed peacekeeping force was established in the Sinai to monitor a buffer zone between Egypt and Israel. Both these missions continue today.

Over the years there have been a total of fifty-two peacekeeping missions. UN peacekeepers rely on minimal force to defuse tension and prevent fighting. The soldiers for UN missions are provided by member governments, who loan troops from their national armies. With the effective use of the peacekeeping forces, the UN has contributed to the containment or resolution of conflicts. The achievements of UN peacekeeping were recognized in 1988 with a Nobel Peace Prize.

A New World Order

It was widely accepted during the cold war that the unilateral use of force to save victims of gross human rights abuses was a violation of the UN Charter, which restricted the right to use force on the part of individual states to purposes of self-defense. The Security Council is empowered under Chapter VII of the UN Charter to authorize the use of force to maintain international peace and security. However, there has always been controversy about how far this allows the council to authorize intervention to stop gross human rights violations that occur inside state borders. To enforce the global humanitarian norms that evolved in the wake of the Holocaust challenges, however, the Security Council must confront a very strongly held principle—that of non-intervention in the domestic affairs of states.

In 1990, with the end of the cold war, it suddenly seemed possible to aspire to the creation of a New

World Order—an international community based on the rule of law and collective security. At the first summit meeting of the Security Council in January 1992, the UN was given ambitious new goals of nation building and peacemaking. It was a hope that the close of the twentieth century would witness the civilized evolution of the global community and the gradual eradication of endless, regional bloodletting throughout the world.

As cold war tensions eased, there was enhanced cooperation in the Security Council. Opportunities were provided to resolve long-standing conflicts, but the end of the cold war also saw new conflicts erupt into violence, many couched in nationalist terms, with hostilities based on ethnic, religious, cultural, and linguistic differences. Responding to this new world disorder the Council turned to the UN Security Council's peacekeeping force, which grew rapidly in size and scope. The complexity of the situations facing the peacekeepers increased, as well.

The end of the cold war led to the hope that the UN could move beyond peacekeeping and into peace enforcement. Unfortunately, the financial, organizational, and operational resources that such a change required were never provided by the Security Council or other UN members. The demand for peacekeeping outstripped the supply of troops and political will. There was a failure by member nations to recognize that the UN could only do as much or as little as its members were willing to agree and pay for.

The last decade of the twentieth century saw a series of tragedies, in Rwanda, Somalia, Liberia, and the former Yugoslavia. Crimes against humanity were committed and documented, including genocide, mass killings, and massive refugee flows. Civilians in these countries were the main targets of armies and militia. The UN missions sent to cope with these disasters were as much engaged in nation building as in performing their military function, and they required civilian experts and relief specialists to work in parallel with soldiers. In Mozambique and El Salvador, the UN peacekeeping missions helped to demobilize combatants, destroy weapons, coordinate massive humanitarian assistance programs, and monitor human rights. Missions in Haiti, Somalia, and Cambodia were tasked with rebuilding state infrastructures, creating or reinstating judicial systems and organizing and observing elections. In these years, maintaining neutrality proved difficult. Many UN peacekeepers had to confront situations in which civilians were victimized, or when they themselves were attacked or killed. Where governmental authority broke down, there was a limit to the effectiveness of UN actions.

Security Council Resolution 688

In 1991 the debate in the Security Council focused on the question of whether the Council could legitimately address humanitarian concerns raised by Iraq's repression of the Kurdish people without violating the ban on UN Charter's ban on intervention in the domestic jurisdiction of sovereign states. At first, the Western nations argued that force was not an option. Soon, however, a flood of press coverage showed the suffering of the people of northern Iraq who had been forced to flee into the mountains and were now dying from hypothermia, exhaustion, and disease. These images went a long way to reverse the noninterventionist policy. On April 5, 1991, Security Council Resolution 688 was passed, authorizing the use of force against Iraq to protect the Kurdish minority from atrocities. In the Council, the United States argued that Iraq's treatment of its civilian population threatened regional stability. Great Britain and France were the only two countries to argue that the domestic jurisdiction did not apply to human rights because such rights were not essentially domestic. After all, it was argued, the Council had invoked Chapter VII, the enforcement powers of the UN Charter, to enforce a mandatory arms embargo against the apartheid state, South Africa. It should therefore be possible to do so again in this new context.

Although Resolution 688 did not authorize military action to enforce human rights, it was only the second time that the Security Council had collectively demanded an improvement the protection of human rights as a contribution to the promotion of international security. (The first time was when the Security Council imposed a mandatory embargo on apartheid South Africa.) Resolution 688 enumerated the consequences of Iraq's repression as a threat to international security, and is believed to provide a justification for military action aimed at enforcing human rights for Iraq's Kurds. This argument was later deemed flimsy, but the Western powers that relied upon it as legal cover for taking military action nonetheless used it to publicly justified their intervention in humanitarian terms.

The operation to save the Kurds in northern Iraq in 1991 depended upon meeting three objectives. First, humanitarian aid had to be brought to the refugees who were dying on the mountains. Second, the people had to be rescued and provided with safe haven. Third, a secure political environment had to be created in order for the Kurds to return to their homes. There is no doubt that thousands of people were saved by the intervention of Western-led forces, but the underlying political reasons for the distress of the Kurds remained to be addressed. It had been the Iraqi government's oppression of the Kurds that had caused the humanitarian crisis, and that government did not restrict its oppression to the Kurds. Western humanitarian intervention in northern Iraq did nothing to assist the equally persecuted Shi'ite people in the south of the country.

The intervention on behalf of Iraq's Kurds was, nonetheless, an example of the reconfigured role adopted by the UN Security Council of the post–cold war era. In the latter part of the twentieth century, the Security Council played a decisive role in legitimizing the threat or use of force in defense of humanitarian values. How much of a change in international behavior could be attributed to the Security Council's new stance is still debated.

Somalia

In the case of Somalia, the Security Council broke new ground by authorizing armed intervention on humanitarian grounds. Council Resolution 794, which authorized U.S. intervention in Somalia in December 1992, suggested that humanitarian intervention was securing a significant status in a new world order. The intervention was given milestone status, because it seemed as though Western armies would now be used for greater protective effect throughout the world. It was the first time that the UN Security Council invoked the enforcement powers of the UN Charter against sovereign government without seeking that government's consent and for a purely humanitarian reason. Somalia would also mark a turning point of a different sort, however, for it was a military failure that reduced the UN peacekeeping force to chaos.

In 1991 Somalia had been gripped by famine due to the collapse of the state, a civil war, and the failure of humanitarian agencies to supply assistance. Within a year, there were hundreds of thousands of people dying of malnutrition. A humanitarian disaster of catastrophic proportions developed. On December 3, 1992, the UN Security Council passed Resolution 794 to allow the U.S. military to enter Somalia to protect the food and medical supplies that were being shipped to the starving but were being looted by armed gangs. The resolution determined that the humanitarian crisis in Somalia was a threat to international peace and security, but what was most extraordinary was that it permitted intervention even though the sovereign power (the Somalian government) was incapable of giving its consent, having collapsed with the onset of the civil war.

In March 1993 the U.S. operation was transferred to the UN, and the mission immediately became more ambitious. Now the goal was to restore law and order and compel the Somali militia to disarm. UN Security Council Resolution 814, another landmark document, gave the UN troops a mandate to restore law and order. The new mission, called the United Nations Operation in Somalia (UNOSOM II) got under way, but by this time the security situation in Somalia had deteriorated badly. Warlords vied for power, particularly around the capital city of Mogadishu, and they tested the Security Council's resolve. It was in Mogadishu that the pitfalls of combining force with peacekeeping were tragically exposed. In June 1993, twenty-three Pakistani peacekeepers were murdered by rampaging mobs while trying to inspect weapons that were under UN supervision. After that, the Security Council passed Resolution, 837, mandating its troops to arrest the warlord deemed responsible for the murders. Meanwhile, elite U.S. forces also mounted a series of raids in an effort to capture the warlord, and an untold number of Somalians were killed in consequence of these raids. Although these U.S. operations were outside the command and control of the UN Security Council, the UN was widely blamed for the violence. There were objections from other troop-contributing countries about the United States' insistence on working outside the control of UN mission's command and control structure. On October 3, 1993, a total of eighteen U.S. servicemen lost their lives in a badly bungled arrest attempt. To the jubilation of the Somalian warlords, the United States immediately announced that it was pulling out its troops and urged all western nations to do likewise.

The Security Council commissioned a report on what had happened in Somalia. It recommended that the UN return to peacekeeping, to the principles of consent, neutrality, and impartiality. The report recommended that the UN should never again try to mount an enforcement action. Another result of failure in Somalia was quickly evident in Washington, D.C., where both the U.S. administration and Congress evinced a sudden and dramatic reduction in support for UN endeavors. It was an ignominious end to the United Nation's first attempt at rebuilding a failed state, resulting in a dramatic loss of UN credibility and prestige.

Bosnia

The question of humanitarian intervention in former Yugoslavia was another Security Council preoccupation during the 1990s. In spring 1992 Serbia, having laid waste to parts of Croatia, turned its attention to Bosnia and Herzegovina. Witnesses provided graphic, indisputable evidence of the ethnic cleansing of whole regions, the demolition of entire villages and murder of their inhabitants, the bombardment of civilian populations, and the creation of camps where thousands of men were starved and tortured and women were systematically raped.

The Council passed numerous resolutions condemning Serb aggression and authorizing the use of "all necessary measures" to halt it. However, none of the UN member nations were willing to provide the means to enforce the measures, so the resolutions remained moribund. The UN Protection Force, (UNPROFOR), as a strictly peacekeeping mission, provided armed escorts for relief convoys, but there was a general failure to defend and demilitarize the UN-established "safe-havens," for which an estimated thirty thousand peacekeeping troops were considered necessary. The failure of states to volunteer adequate numbers of troops led to these supposedly safe areas being over run. UN peacekeepers were forced to stand by as helpless observers of the massacres in Bosnia. International respect for the United Nations as a credible presence sank to the lowest point in its history. The UN mission for former Yugoslavia, the largest and most expensive in UN history, turned out to be barely capable of protecting itself.

In 1995, the North Atlantic Treaty Organization (NATO), with authorization from the Security Council, initiated widespread air strikes against the Bosnian Serbs. Some observers believe that this action persuaded Slobodan Milosevic, then President of the rump Yugoslavian state, to enter peace negotiations. The NATO action was the first time a group of states justified force against another on humanitarian grounds without an explicit Security Council resolution to provide legitimacy for the action.

The success of the 1995 NATO air strikes led some nations to believe that the threat and use of bombing could achieve quick results. This meant that in March 1999, when evidence of Serbian ethnic cleansing in Kosovo led to a new intervention by Western states. The Western states were not prepared to bear the burden of potentially negative public opinion should there be troops casualties, which would be inevitable in a ground-based war. Through a combination of bombing and the threat of a ground force, Milosevic was forced to accede to demands that Kosovar refugees be allowed to return to their homes and for a UN civil administration to help build a multiethnic society based on the rule of law.

Rwanda

The genocide in Rwanda in 1994 is one of the most blatant examples of the ineffectiveness of the Genocide Convention. The genocide began in April 1994, when the war in Bosnia and Herzegovina had been under way for more than two years, and little had been done by the UN Security Council to stop it. The lack of action in Bosnia and Herzegovina is thought to have encour-

aged the Rwandan perpetrators that they could act with impunity. For three months, between April and July 1994, genocide was central to the task of Hutu rebels who had seized power and claimed to constitute an interim government. Up to one million people were killed.

The genocide in Rwanda was a planned political campaign that made effective use of racist propaganda to incite hatred and violence against a minority. The widespread participation in genocide and the brutality of the killings have no parallels in modern history. Making the situation worse was the brazenness of the perpetrators, who made no attempt to conceal what was happening. The killings took place in broad daylight, in full view of the international media.

There was ample evidence of the extensive preparation and planning for the genocide went on for months in advance of the first killings. Nonetheless, the UN Security Council did not make any move to implement the Genocide Convention, either to prevent its occurrence or to stop it once it began. This raises the fundamental question: Why?

In October 1993, the UN Security Council decided to create the UN Assistance Mission for Rwanda (UN-AMIR), comprising a small force of peacekeepers. The UNAMIR force was duly shipped to Rwanda, and was kept there even as the environment grew increasingly hostile. The mission had a weak mandate and minimal force capacity. Some have argued that this feeble effort actually encouraged the Hutu genocide conspirators, signaling they could continue with their plans without fear of intervention.

The failed Somalia intervention was still fresh in the Security Council's memory. When it came to Rwanda, the most important consideration was to devise a mission that was as small and as cheap as possible and that would avoid any effort at peace enforcement, even after the genocidal killings were ended. In order to comply with these considerations the Council altered the terms of Rwanda's peace agreement. Under the terms of the agreement, a neutral force was to ensure security throughout Rwanda but the Security Council decided instead that the peacekeepers should only assist in ensuring the security of the capital city of Kigali. Although the original peace accords called for peacekeepers to confiscate arms and neutralize the armed gangs throughout the country, the UN Security Council refused. There would be no "peace enforcement" and no "mission creep," whereby increasingly difficult mandates might be given to the UN mission.

Instead, the UN Security Council devised a peacekeeping mission that was extremely limited in its engagement within Rwanda. No attention seems to have been focussed on Rwanda's serious human rights abuses, even though they had been clearly outlined in the publication of two landmark human rights reports to the UN Commission on Human Rights. The author of one of these reports, Bacre Waly Ndiaye, was the Special Rapporteur for the Commission on Human Rights for Extrajudicial Summary, or Arbitrary Executions. He provided evidence that, in Rwanda, the Hutu political leadership was desperate to cling to power and was fueling ethnic hatred with a well-orchestrated propaganda campaign. The massacre of Rwanda's Tutsis was intentional and well organized. Ndiaye recommended that the militia should be disbanded, the distribution of arms should cease, and anti-Tutsi propaganda silenced. There could be no impunity for the killers. Finally, Ndiaye called for communal policing and immediate and effective measures to protect civilians at risk. In spite of this report, the ten nonpermanent members of the Security Council insisted on viewing the Rwanda debacle as a small civil war.

From the very beginning of the Rwanda disaster, in December 1993, it was clear that the UNAMIR mission confronted enormous problems. In the weeks immediately preceding the genocide, it received detailed information about militia training, arms dumps, political murders, hate propaganda, and death lists. The rising level of ethnic extremism in Rwanda was also of great concern to the Belgian government, which provided the troops for the Rwanda mission. In February 1994 the Belgian ambassador to the UN, Paul Noterdaeme, attempted to warn everyone that the peacekeepers of UNAMIR were in grave danger and in need of immediate reinforcements and a stronger mandate—no one listened.

When the genocide began, two permanent Security Council member states—the United States and the United Kingdom—insisted on referring to the Rwandan violence as a civil war, and focused Security Council discussion on obtaining a ceasefire. In the first weeks of genocide, no one paid attention to civilian mass killings, even though the massacres were taking place nowhere near the actual fighting. Another permanent member of the Security Council, France, was intimate with the affairs of Rwanda, but kept silent about the realities of what was happening, even during council meetings.

Some of the non-permanent members of the council, notably New Zealand, Spain, Nigeria, and the Czech Republic tried to convince the United States and the Great Britain to pay attention to the daily murder of thousands upon thousands of civilians. However, none of the permanent members were willing to discuss sta-

bilizing, reinforcing, or even re-supplying the UNAMIR peacekeepers, who were still trying to carry out rescue missions in Kigali. At the end of April 1994, the United States, Great Britain, and France refused to publish a Presidential Statement, drafted on the initiative of New Zealand Ambassador Colin Keating, that officially acknowledged the genocide that was now in full swing in Rwanda.

The Force Commander of UNAMIR, Major-General Dallaire, was later openly critical of the permanent member states in the Security Council who had the means to help, but refused. He bemoaned the lack of political will in Great Britain, and the United States that permitted the spread of the genocide and the slaughter of thousands of people trapped inside schools, churches, and clinics.

SEE ALSO Convention on the Prevention and Punishment of Genocide; Humanitarian Intervention; International Criminal Tribunal for Rwanda; International Criminal Tribunal for the Former Yugoslavia; Peacekeeping; Rwanda; United Nations; United Nations Commission on Human Rights; United Nations General Assembly

BIBLIOGRAPHY
Bellamy, Alex J., Paul Williams, and Stuart Griffin (2004). *Understanding Peacekeeping*. Cambridge, U.K.: Polity Press.

Carnegie Commission on Preventing Deadly Conflict (1997). *Preventing Deadly Conflict: Final Report*. Washington, D.C.: Carnegie Commission on Preventing Deadly Conflict.

Dallaire, Romeo A. (1996). "The Changing Role of UN Peacekeeping Forces: The Relationship between UN Peacekeepers and NGOs in Rwanda." In *After Rwanda: The Co-Ordination of United Nations Humanitarian Assistance*, ed. Jim Whitman and David Pocock. London: Macmillan Press.

Durch, William, ed. (1996). *UN Peacekeeping, American Politics, and the Uncivil Wars of the 1990s*. New York: St. Martin's Press.

Fein, Helen (1993). "Accounting for Genocide after 1945: Theories and Some Findings." *International Journal on Group Rights* 1:79–106.

Joint Evaluation of Emergency Assistance to Rwanda (1996). *The International Response to Conflict and Genocide: Lessons from the Rwanda Experience: Synthesis Report*. Copenhagen: DANIDA.

Prunier, Gérard. (1995). *The Rwandan Crisis: History of a Genocide*. New York: Columbia University Press.

Wheeler, Nicholas J. (2000). *Saving Strangers: Humanitarian Intervention in International Society*. Oxford: Oxford University Press.

Linda Melvern

United Nations Sub-Commission on Human Rights

The United Nations Sub-Commission on the Promotion and Protection of Human Rights was created by the Economic and Social Council (ECOSOC) in 1947 as the main expert body to advise the Commission on Human Rights. It has become a permanent advisory body for the Commission on all human rights issues, better described as a scientific advisory body or "think tank" for the Commission. In contrast to the Commission, which is comprised of state representatives, the Sub-Commission consists of twenty-six independent experts. Its annual three-week sessions in Geneva are attended by its members and alternates, government observers, United Nations bodies and specialized agencies, other intergovernmental organizations, and nongovernmental organizations in consultative status with the Economic and Social Council. Indeed, the Sub-Commission has become an important link between intergovernmental institutions and the public through representation by nongovernmental organizations. Consequently, its relations with its parent bodies have not always been harmonious.

The Sub-Commission has achieved many notable results, including the elaboration of draft conventions, declarations, and general principles on subjects as diverse as racial discrimination, the death penalty, the rights of indigenous peoples, the rights of minorities, the independence of the judiciary, and the human rights responsibilities of transnational corporations. Its in-depth studies have resulted in the creation of new special rapporteurs and working groups of the Commission on Human Rights addressing topics such as the independence of the judiciary, freedom of opinion, arbitrary detention, religious intolerance, toxic waste, the right to food, the right to adequate housing, human rights, and terrorism. Its debates, resolutions, and studies dealing with the issue of genocide have served to refine the definition and understanding of genocide contained in the 1948 Convention on the Prevention and Punishment of the Crime of Genocide, to review the historical development and legal implications of the convention's provisions, to apply its template to various historical events, and to recommend ways in which the international community can improve its response to genocide.

The original functions of the Sub-Commission on the Prevention of Discrimination and the Protection of Minorities (as it was known from 1947 to 1999) were to undertake studies, particularly in the light of the Universal Declaration of Human Rights, and to make recommendations to the larger Commission on Human Rights concerning the prevention of discrimination of any kind relating to human rights and fundamental freedoms and the protection of racial, national, religious and linguistic minorities. In addition, the Sub-Commission was charged with the duty to perform any other functions, which may be entrusted to it by the council or the Commission. The Sub-Commission's mandate and activities have substantially evolved over the last half century to include considering specific questions in public and private, examining petitions from alleged victims and NGOs, sending communications to governments, and adopting resolutions on particular situations.

Consideration of Country Situations

When the Commission on Human Rights requested in 1966 to be empowered by the Economic and Social Council to make recommendations about specific human rights violations brought to its attention, ECOSOC Resolution 1235 (XLII) of 1967 was adopted authorizing both the Commission and the Sub-Commission "to examine information relevant to gross violations of human rights and fundamental freedoms." Three years later, ECOSOC Resolution 1503 (XLVII) provided for a confidential procedure to handle communications revealing a consistent pattern of gross and reliably attested violations of human rights.

In practice, Resolution 1235 has served as the basis for annual public debate in the Commission and Sub-Commission on human rights violations in various countries. Allegations ranging from disappearances to torture to genocide have been discussed during these debates, on the basis of which both the Commission and Sub-Commission began the practice of adopting resolutions expressing concern about the situation in specific countries. Through resolutions and the Sub-Commission chairman's statements, as well as the strategic withdrawal of draft resolutions on certain conditions, the Sub-Commission has been able to achieve dialogue with governments and furthered the adoption of measures to improve human rights. Further, the Sub-Commission has played an important role regarding countries not dealt with by the Commission by originating resolutions and initiatives that were later adopted by the Commission.

Several of the Sub-Commission's resolutions have called attention to situations involving genocide. With regard to the former Yuglosavia, the Sub-Commission noted in Resolution 1993/17 that the "abhorrent policy of ethnic cleansing was a form of genocide." Its resolution on the same subject one year later went further, declaring that the Sub-Commission was

> appalled by the acts of genocide carried out by the rebel Pale Serbs in Bosnia and Herzegovina,

including the evidence indicating that large-scale massacres of the Muslim population have taken place after the occupation of the safe areas of Zepa and Srebrenica.

The resolution emphasized that any peace plan should not contain provision for impunity for acts of genocide, ethnic cleansing, or other serious war crimes. In a 1995 resolution expressing solidarity with the special rapporteur on the former Yugoslavia for his decision to resign from his position following the Srebrenica massacres, the Sub-Commission noted, "a veritable genocide is being committed massively and in a systematic manner against the civilian population in Bosnia and Herzegovina, often in the presence of United Nations forces."

With regard to the situation in Rwanda, a Sub-Commission resolution of August 1994 expressed deep concern "at the convincing and appalling evidence of the genocide resulting from the massacres of the Tutsis, the political assassinations of the Hutus and the various attacks on human rights in Rwanda." It further deplored the tardy and insufficiently effective intervention of the international community (including the UN and the OAU), making it impossible to prevent the genocide. It recommended effective follow-up to the report of the special rapporteur on the situation of human rights in Rwanda, giving an account of political assassinations and genocide. At the same session, the Sub-Commission adopted a thematic resolution on the strengthening and punishment of the crime of genocide, in which it claimed that the atrocities being committed in Rwanda and the former Yugoslavia highlighted the deficiencies of the Genocide Convention. It recommended improving the convention by adding a clause concerning universal jurisdiction and considering extending its application to political genocide.

Again in 1995, the Sub-Commission expressed concern at the "convincing and appalling evidence of the genocide resulting from the massacres of the Tutsis, the political assassinations of the Hutus and the various attacks on human rights in Rwanda." That same year, the Sub-Commission adopted a resolution on the prevention of incitement to hatred and genocide, particularly by the media. This resolution referred to the situations in Rwanda, the former Yugoslavia, Zaire, and Burundi, categorically condemning the role played with increasing frequency by printed or audiovisual media in inciting genocidal hatred. Finally, the Sub-Commission's 1996 resolution on Rwanda noted with dismay that more than two years after genocide on an enormous scale, no judgment condemning those guilty had been delivered either by the International Criminal Tribunal for Rwanda (ICTR) or by national or foreign

courts. The Sub-Commission expressed further concern that "persons responsible for acts of genocide were infiltrating Rwanda with the purpose of eliminating the witnesses of the genocide."

With regard to the situation in Burundi, the Sub-Commission adopted Resolution 1996/4 drawing attention to the findings of the special rapporteur on the situation of human rights in Burundi regarding "genocide by attrition." Further, it appealed to the Burundian authorities to spare no effort in "banishing the specter of genocide." It called upon them or the authorities to create mutual trust among ethnic groups, encourage peaceful coexistence, and return quickly to the rule of law.

Although it held discussions on the situation in Cambodia, the Sub-Commission was unable to pass a resolution on the country. In 1991 the Sub-Commission considered and dropped from its agenda a draft resolution that referred to "the atrocities reaching the level of genocide committed in particular during the period of Khmer Rouge rule." In 1978 the governments of Canada, Norway, and the U.K. had submitted statements concerning the continuation of violations of human rights in Democratic Kampuchea, along with voluminous evidence containing the factual basis for a charge of genocide. Democratic Kampuchea rejected the Sub-Commission's decision to appoint a member to analyze the materials submitted "as an impudent interference in internal affairs" and denied all allegations in the years hence.

Indeed, it was the political sensitivities inherent in country resolutions that gradually eroded the Sub-Commission's role in condemning human rights violations in particular countries. In 1990, to protect the independence of its members, the Sub-Commission introduced secret voting on any resolution relating to an individual country. In 1999 the Commission on Human Rights decided through its inter-sessional Working Group on Enhancing the Effectiveness of the Commission on Human Rights that the Sub-Commission should not make any pronouncements on the human rights situation in any country already under consideration by the Commission (it also reduced its session time from four to three weeks). Most drastically of all, in its decision 2000/109, the Commission withdrew the Sub-Commission's right to adopt country-specific resolutions or even to refer to country-specific situations in thematic resolutions. Three years later, in Resolution 2003/59, the Commission prohibited the Sub-Commission chairpersons from issuing country-specific statements.

Nongovernmental organizations (NGOs) have been highly critical of this fundamental role change.

Despite the fact that the Sub-Commission may still consider country situations during its debates, NGOs point to a decline in the quality and quantity of such debates and poor or nonexistent reporting. For example, revisiting the issue of the Rwandan genocide at its 2002 session, Sub-Commission member El-Hadji Guissé criticized the UN for failing to intervene during the genocide and suggested it might have done otherwise had the victims been of another race. Nothing further was stated for the record and no action was taken. Such scant consideration of an issue that had received considerable attention in earlier sessions would seem to support the contention coming from within the Sub-Commission itself that the experts increasingly saw little point in addressing the protection of human rights in individual countries.

Confidential Procedure

The 1503 (Confidential) Procedure arose out of the Economic and Social Council Resolution 1503 (XLVIII) of 1970. It authorized the Commission on Human Rights to establish a process for the examination of communications (a UN euphemism for complaints) pertaining to "situations which appear to reveal a consistent pattern of gross and reliably attested violations of human rights requiring consideration by the Commission." It constitutes the oldest human rights complaint mechanism in the United Nations. NGOs and others hailed its establishment as a significant success because it opened up new ways for complaints to receive a formal examination, even when they involved states that had not ratified the relevant human rights treaties. Previous to the adoption of this procedure, the Commission had employed communications only as a means of identifying general trends, without responding to the violations at issue.

The resolution, and the confidential procedure it established, originated in the dramatic change in the composition of the major UN organs that had occurred by the mid-1960s. This was a time when the many newly independent African and Asian states gained membership in the UN, and total membership of the Commission on Human Rights went from 18 in 1960 to 21 in 1967. Developing countries were eager to press for additional means by which to pursue the struggle against racist and colonialist policies.

The Confidential Procedure involves a process by which complaints are examined in order to identify the existence of a consistent pattern of gross violations of human rights. First, the Sub-Commission would undertake a review of thousands of complaints received by the United Nations Secretariat. (After the year 2000, a Working Group on Communications, rather than the entire Sub-Commission, was tasked with this responsibility.) Those cases considered that appeared to indicate "a consistent pattern of gross and reliably attested violations of human rights and fundamental freedoms" are passed along to the Commission on Human Rights. A separate Working Group on Situations would then undertake a pre-examination of the evidence and, finally, the full Commission would meet in private session to discuss each situation.

Resolution 2000/3 provided the Commission with a repertoire of responses to these situations, including appointing an independent expert to make direct contacts with the government and the people concerned, keeping the case under consideration, transferring the case to the public procedures, or dismissing the situation. Perhaps the most effective of these, in terms of applying pressure on states against which complaints have been lodged, is the possibility that the situation will be transferred to a public procedure. When the Commission returns to public session, the chairperson announces the list of countries that have been examined under the 1503 process, the violations at issue, and any action taken to date.

More than 80 states have been examined by the Commission under the 1503 Procedure since 1972. The majority of these countries were responsible for a large number of human rights violations, including torture, arbitrary detention, summary or arbitrary executions, and disappearances. The 1503 procedure has never been formally employed to deal with specific allegations of genocide. On the other hand, complaints against several countries have alleged situations of gross violations of human rights that might have amounted to genocide. These include Rwanda (considered from 1993 to 1995), Burundi (considered from 1974 to 1975) and Cambodia (considered in 1979).

The 1503 Confidential Procedure has been criticized for its secrecy, slowness, complexity, and vulnerability to political influence. Reform was initiated in July 2000 by ECOSOC Resolution 2000/3 to streamline the process, but the procedure's importance has nevertheless diminished, due to the rapid development over the years of the public procedures and the system of individual complaints before treaty bodies. At the same time, the procedure provides a useful, incremental technique for placing increasing pressure on offending governments, while encouraging them to engage in a constructive exchange of views to improve the situation. At the minimum, the 1503 procedure affords a mechanism for complaints to be received through official UN channels and for governments to respond.

Studies

The loss of its ability to respond to human rights violations within particular countries has increased the relative importance of the Sub-Commission's studies program, which was established in 1952. Studies are in-depth reports on particular human rights issues carried out by Sub-Commission members who are designated as special rapporteurs for the preparation of a report on a particular issue. Upon completion, studies are submitted to the Sub-Commission for discussion. The level of interest in any given report varies; the experts may take a keen interest, or they may make only general, noncommittal remarks. Unless the Sub-Commission members have significant concerns about the report, it will usually be submitted to the Commission for broad dissemination.

With the proliferation of studies over the years, the Sub-Commission established criteria in 1997 for selecting new subjects for study. It determined that priority should be given to subjects for study recommended by the Commission on Human Rights. After these, priority should be given to subjects suggested by the working groups of the Sub-Commission. Special attention should be given to subjects proposed by treaty bodies, and economic, social, and cultural rights should be considered as a priority area in the selection of new studies. Finally, the Sub-Commission determined that proposals for isolated studies that lacked the necessary background and framework should be discouraged.

The Sub-Commission has made key contributions to the definition and understanding of genocide through its studies. The two most notable in this regard are those of Nicomède Ruhashyankiko and Benjamin Whitaker, both entitled "Study on the Question of the Prevention and Punishment of the Crime of Genocide." The Ruhashyankiko report originated in a 1967 decision of the Sub-Commission to undertake a study of the question. Ruhashyankiko was a member of the Sub-Commission and a Rwandan national. He presented a preliminary report and three progress reports to the Sub-Commission before the presentation of his final study in 1978.

The Ruhashyankiko study was largely devoted to a history of the adoption of various articles of the 1948 Genocide Convention and an examination of controversies concerning the interpretation, value, and scope of those provisions. The report concluded that the 1948 convention should only be considered a "point of departure" in the adoption of effective international measures to prevent and punish genocide; but argued against interpreting the convention in broader terms than those envisaged by the signatories. According to Ruhashyankiko, it was preferable to adhere to the con-

vention's spirit and letter, and then prepare new instruments whenever appropriate. The report acknowledged that a number of allegations of genocide had been made since the adoption of the convention, but noted that these allegations were not promptly investigated by an impartial body, making it impossible to determine whether they were well-founded. Ruhashyankiko recommended the establishment of an ad hoc committee to inquire into all allegations of genocide brought to the attention of the Commission on Human Rights. He also recommended that serious consideration be given to the establishment of an international criminal court to try allegations of genocide.

Ruhashyankiko's report was generally well-received, although some argued with the exception of his omission of the Armenian massacres that occurred in the Ottoman Empire from 1915 to 1918. While reference to the Armenian genocide had been included in the preliminary study, Ruhashyankiko removed it from the final report. This deletion prompted impassioned critiques by Sub-Commission members and by NGOs who felt that the event deserved mention. They cited the significant size of the genocide, its comparatively recent occurrence, the ample documentary evidence establishing its existence (including a predetermined plan to exterminate the Armenian nation), the disturbing growth of movements challenging the veracity of the Holocaust, the need to analyze causation in past cases to contribute to future prevention, and perhaps most importantly, the overall moral obligation of the United Nations to adhere to historical truth and objectivity. In an attempt to address the political pressures that influenced Ruhashyankiko's decision to delete the reference, several members drew attention to the fact that the international law of state succession absolved the modern Republic of Turkey of responsibility for crimes committed by the Ottoman Empire. This did not prevent the observer from the Turkish government from taking the floor on several occasions to strongly deny the occurrence of the Armenian genocide.

Partially in an attempt to resolve this issue, the Sub-Commission and the Economic and Social Council requested a revision and updating of the Ruhashyankiko report. Benjamin Whitaker was appointed to undertake this task. During the Sub-Commission's discussions of the scope of the report, Whitaker observed that the first study was excellent, but there were "some omissions due to political pressure exerted on the Special Rapporteur who had prepared it . . . [that] resulted in the flagrant omission of the genocide of the Armenians." According to Whitaker, "rectifying such omissions was a matter of integrity and independence for the Sub-Commission."

Whitaker's final report cited nine instances of genocide in the twentieth century, including the Ottoman massacre of Armenians, that he claimed resulted in the killing or death-marching of "at least one million, and possibly well over half the Armenian population." The Turkish government intervened to advocate deletion of the mention of genocide. These debates resulted in a resolution that simply took note of Whitaker's report, but stopped short of endorsing it.

Another important study with regard to genocide was prepared in 1998 by Gay J. McDougall, entitled "Systematic Rape, Sexual Slavery and Slavery-like Practices during Armed Conflict." Commissioned in response to revelations concerning the more than 200,000 women enslaved by the Japanese military in so-called comfort stations during World War II, the report was cited by the International Criminal Tribunal for the former Yugoslavia (ICTY) as an authoritative statement of international criminal law in a landmark sexual violence case involving the detention, torture, and killing of civilians in a prison camp in Bosnia and Herzegovina.

McDougall's study provided a description of the legal framework for crimes against humanity, slavery, genocide, torture, and war crimes, and it outlined individual criminal liability for both perpetrators and those complicit in such crimes. It called for an effective response to sexual violence committed during armed conflict; emphasized that rape and other forms of sexual abuse are crimes of violence which may constitute slavery, crimes against humanity, genocide, grave breaches of the Geneva Conventions, war crimes, and torture; and reinforced the existing legal framework for the prosecution of these crimes, with a view to achieving a more consistent and gender-responsive application of human rights and humanitarian and international criminal law. The report concluded that systematic rape, sexual slavery and slavery-like practices during armed conflict constitute violations of human rights, and of humanitarian and international criminal law, and as such must be properly documented, the perpetrators brought to justice, and the victims provided with full criminal and civil redress. McDougall claimed that even in the absence of armed conflict, sexual slavery and other forms of sexual violence, including rape, may be prosecuted under existing legal norms as slavery, crimes against humanity, genocide, or torture. While women per se are not listed as a protected group under the Genocide Convention, the report argued that targeting a protected group "through attacks against its female members is sufficient to establish the crime of genocide." McDougall further contended that the prosecution need not establish intent to destroy the entire group on a national or an international basis, but "the intent to destroy a substantial portion or an important subsection of a protected group or the existence of a protected group within a limited region of a country is sufficient grounds for prosecution for genocide."

This report received important endorsement and follow-up by both the Sub-Commission and the Commission. In Decision 1999/105, the Commission on Human Rights approved the request of the Sub-Commission to extend the mandate of the special rapporteur for a year, to enable her to submit an update on developments to the next Sub-Commission session. Her updated report considered developments and actions at the international and national levels to end the cycle of impunity for sexual violence committed during armed conflict. The Sub-Commission also asked the High Commissioner for Human Rights to prepare a report on the subject, which built upon McDougall's conclusions and recommendations. High Commissioner Mary Robinson's report noted not only that the statutes of the international criminal tribunals restated the definition of genocide found in the 1948 convention, but that genocide had been interpreted and developed in international case law—including ICTR's first judicial interpretation of the Genocide Convention in the *Akayesu* case, where the trial chamber adopted a broad interpretation of genocide, including rape and sexual violence when committed with the intent to destroy, in whole or in part, a protected group.

Following the first McDougall report, the Sub-Commission began the annual adoption of resolutions on systematic rape, sexual slavery, and slavery-like practices. In Resolution 2003/26, the Sub-Commission underlined as significant the latest verdicts of the ICTY, the ICTR, and the Special Court for Sierra Leone, which acknowledged that rape and sexual enslavement are crimes against humanity. It also noted with approval the Rome Statute of the International Criminal Court's special recognition that sexual violence and sexual slavery committed in the context of either an internal or an international armed conflict may constitute crimes against humanity, war crimes, and genocide, thus falling within the jurisdiction of the Court.

Another issue with clear relevance to genocide that became the subject of a Sub-Commission study is that of population transfers. The first report on the human rights dimensions of population transfer, including the implantation of settlers and settlements, was submitted in 1993 by Awn Shawkat Al-Khasawneh and Ribot Hatano. It found that population transfer is, prima facie, unlawful and violates a number of rights affirmed in human rights and humanitarian law for both transferred and receiving populations. In Resolution 1993/34, the Sub-Commission endorsed the conclusions and recommendations of the preliminary report and requested Al-Khasawneh to continue the study on the human rights dimensions of population transfer and to submit a progress report on the question to next Sub-Commission session. It also recommended that a multidisciplinary expert seminar provide input for the final report.

Al-Khasawneh's final report, submitted in 1997, recommended that the Sub-Commission consider the possibility of preparing an international instrument to codify international standards regarding population transfer and the implantation of settlers. Such an instrument would expressly reaffirm the unlawfulness of population transfer and the implantation of settlers and define national responsibility in the matter of unlawful population transfer, including the implantation of settlers. It would also establish the criminal responsibility of individuals involved in population transfer, whether such individuals be private or officials of the state and provide a means for adjudicating claims presented by the individuals or populations involved. The report also recommended that the Commission on Human Rights adopt an instrument that embodied the principles of international law recognized by states as being applicable to population transfer and the implantation of settlers. To this end, it included in its annex a Draft Declaration on Population Transfer and the Implantation of Settlers.

Working Groups

Since the 1970s, substantial parts of the Sub-Commission's deliberations have focused on the work of its inter- or pre-sessional working groups: the Working Group on Contemporary Forms of Slavery (established in 1974); the Working Group on Indigenous Populations (created in 1982) and the Working Group on Minorities (established in 1995). Composed of five members each, working groups devote their attention to the in-depth analysis of specific issues, the study of cases, and the drafting of new international standards. Working groups have constituted a unique platform for witnesses and victims, since they permit oral and written statements by NGOs who need not have ECOSOC consultative status or be recognized by their respective governments (they need only be directly concerned with the subject at hand). Year after year, the working groups have provided an opportunity to receive and publicly discuss allegations of specific human rights violations.

The Sub-Commission also establishes sessional working groups, which meet during its annual sessions to consider particular agenda items. Examples include the Working Group on Transnational Corporations, the Working Group on the Administration of Justice, and the Working Group on the Encouragement of Universal Acceptance of Human Rights Instruments. Each working group submits its reports to the Sub-Commission for consideration. On some questions, the Sub-Commission adopts its own resolutions and decisions. On others, it formulates draft resolutions and decisions for consideration by the Commission on Human Rights and the Economic and Social Council.

The Working Group on Indigenous Populations has dealt with the issue of genocide by examining the effectiveness of the standards contained in national, regional, and international instruments in providing adequate protection to indigenous persons. On several occasions, its discussions included alleged genocide or ethnocide in countries such as Guatemala, El Salvador, and Bangladesh. The Permanent Forum on Indigenous Issues, a body created in 2000 to advise the Economic and Social Council, recommended in 2003 that the Working Group on Indigenous Populations "undertake a study on genocidal and ethnocidal practices perpetrated on indigenous peoples, including programs for sterilization of indigenous women and girls, the use of indigenous communities as subjects for nuclear testing or storage of radioactive waste, and the testing of unapproved drugs on indigenous children and peoples."

The Working Group on the Administration of Justice dealt in depth with genocide through a working paper prepared by Louis Joinet on measures to be taken to give full effect to the Convention on the Prevention and Punishment of the Crime of Genocide. Indeed, the events in Rwanda and the former Yugoslavia prompted this working group's inclusion of an agenda item on genocide. This, in turn, led to Joinet's paper, which was intended more as a pragmatic study than an update of the Ruhashyankiko or Whitaker studies.

Joinet noted that, although the convention was the first such instrument in the history of the United Nations, it had never been implemented. In order to remedy the convention's deficiencies, he proposed a number of measures. Chief among these was the inclusion of a quantitative criterion in the definition of genocide and the extension of the scope of the convention to cover various categories of genocide. At the criminal level, Joinet believed it was desirable to encourage proposals concerning genocide by omission or by complicity and rejection of the doctrine of owed obedience. He believed that states should be made responsible for instituting a juridical basis and establishing an obligation of compensation. Joinet further recommended that technical assistance be provided to states that had not yet ratified the convention or had not yet taken the legislative steps necessary for its implementation.

Joinet recommended giving priority to measures for encouraging prevention of the crime of genocide. In his view, this could be accomplished by defining two methodological approaches: repressive measures and incentives designed to combat incitement to and provocation of genocide; and the establishment of a working group on prevention of genocide. Such a body would be distinct from any international criminal court and would have both a preventive and a repressive role to play. The purpose would be to facilitate the task of future international jurisdiction.

In discussing Joinet's proposals, some Sub-Commission members advocated a more cautious approach. They argued that a clear enforcement mechanism already existed within Article 9 of the Genocide Convention, which outlined the compulsory jurisdiction of the International Court of Justice over cases of genocide. They suggested that this mechanism would not necessarily need revising, but an additional protocol to the convention could be used to expand the definition of the crime of genocide.

Other members argued that it was necessary to expand the definition of genocide by including in it the concepts of cultural, political, and economic genocide. Although genocide was considered a crime against humanity not subject to prescription, that definition had never been given effect. Joinet countered that making too many changes to improve the convention might hamper progress in combating genocide. The pragmatic approach would be to avoid any reform of the convention and to consider only one or two specific proposals that were based on existing initiatives. Unfortunately, none of the suggestions made by Joinet were taken up by bodies in a position to implement such measures.

SEE ALSO Geneva Conventions on the Protection of Victims of War; Impunity; United Nations; United Nations General Assembly; United Nations Security Council; United Nations War Crimes Commission; Whitaker, Benjamin

BIBLIOGRAPHY

Alfredsson, Gudmundur, Jonas Grimheden, Bertrand G. Ramcharan, and Alfred de Zayas, eds. (2001). *International Human Rights Monitoring Mechanisms.* The Hague: Martinus Hijhoff Publishers.

Al-Khasawneh, Awn Shawkat (1997). *Human Rights and Population Transfer. Sub-Commission on the Promotion and Protection of Human Rights.* UN Docs (E/CN.4/Sub.2/1993/17 and Corr.1, E/CN.4/Sub.2/1994/18 and Corr. 1, E/CN.4/Sub.2/1997/23; E/CN.4/Sub.2/1997/23.

Alston, Philip, and Henry J. Steiner (2000). *International Human Rights in Context: Law, Politics, Morals, Second Edition.* Oxford: Oxford University Press.

Bossuyt, Marc (1985). "The Development of Special Procedures of the United Nations Commission on Human Rights." *Human Rights Law Journal* 6:19–47.

Brownlie, Ian, ed. (2002). *Basic Documents in International Law,* 5th edition New York: Oxford University Press.

Eide, Asbjorn (1992). "The Sub-Commission on Prevention of Discrimination and Protection of Minorities." In *The United Nations and Human Rights: A Critical Appraisal,* Philip Alston, ed. Oxford: Clarendon Press.

Kleine-Ahlbrandt, William Laird (2001). *Bitter Prerequisites: A Faculty For Survival From Nazi Terror.* W. Lafayette, Ind.: Purdue University Press.

McDougall, Gay (1998, 2000). "Systematic Rape, Sexual Slavery and Slavery-like Practices during Armed Conflict." Geneva: UN Sub-Commission on the Promotion and Protection of Human, Rights: Doc. E/CN.4/Sub.2/1998/13, Doc. E/CN.4/Sub.2/2000/21.

Newmann, Frank, and David Weissbrodt (2001). *International Human Rights: Law, Policy and Process,* Ottawa: Anderson Publishing.

Nowack, Manfred (1991). "Country-Oriented Human Rights Protection by the UN Commission on Human Rights and its Sub-Commission." *Netherlands Yearbook of International Law* 22:39–90.

Nowack, Manfred, ed. (2003). *Introduction to the International Human Rights Regime.* The Hague: Marinus Nijhoff Publishers.

Rodley, Nigel S. (2003). "United Nations Human Rights Treaty Bodies and Special Procedures of the Commission on Human Rights: Complementarity or Competition?" *Human Rights Quarterly,* 25, no. 4:882–908.

Ruhashyankiko, Nicomède, "Study on the Question of the Prevention and Punishment of the Crime of Genocide." Sub-Commission on the Promotion and Protection of Human Rights. Doc E/CN.4/Sub.2/416 of 1978.

Tolley, Howard (1984). "The Concealed Crack in the Citadel: The United Nations Commission on Human Rights Response to Confidential Communications." *Human Rights Quarterly* 6(4):420–462.

Tolley, Howard (1987). *The UN Commission on Human Rights.* Boulder, Colo: Westview Press.

Whitaker, Benjamin (1985). "Study on the Question of the Prevention and Punishment of the Crime of Genocide." Sub-Commission on the Promotion and Protection of Human Rights: Doc E/CN.4/Sub.2/1985/6.

United Nations Economic and Social Council (1967). "ECOSOC Resolution 1235 (XLII)." U.N. Doc. E/4393.

United Nations Economic and Social Council (1970). "Procedure for Dealing with Communications Relating to Violations of Human Rights and Fundamental Freedoms." ECOSOC Resolution 1503(XLVIII) of 27 May 1970.

Stephanie Kleine-Ahlbrandt
The views expressed herein are those of the author alone and do not necessarily reflect the views of the United Nations.

John Allsebrook Simon, the first Viscount Simon, was Churchill's Lord Chancellor and the Chair of the British Cabinet Committee on the Treatment of War Criminals. In 1942 he introduced to the House of Lords the British government's proposal of a multinational committee to investigate war crimes. [HULTON-DEUTSCH COLLECTION/CORBIS]

United Nations War Crimes Commission

The United Nations War Crimes Commission (UNWCC) was inaugurated on October 20, 1943, by representatives of the seventeen Allied nations. It was the only international framework that dealt with the issue of war crimes and war criminals during World War II. The commission continued to operate until March 31, 1948, and in the course of its four-and-a-half years of existence had created a total of 8,178 files (representing 36,810 individuals and groups). Significantly, some of the most important notions elaborated by the UNWCC found their way into the Nuremberg Charter.

The idea of establishing a United Nations (UN) "commission on atrocities" was first advanced by British prime minister Winston S. Churchill in June 1942 during his visit to the United States. Churchill was in part responding to intense pressure coming from the exiled Polish and Czech governments in London, who envisioned the threat of reprisals against Germany by the Allied nations as a deterrent against further atrocities by the Nazis. However, both Britain and the United States ascribed low priority to the war crimes problem at the time and wanted to postpone dealing with the issue of punishing war criminals for as long as possible.

On September 7, 1942, John Viscount Simon, the Lord Chancellor and Chair of the British Cabinet Committee on the Treatment of War Criminals (CCTWC) introduced to the House of Lords the British government's proposal to set up a UN Commission for the Investigation of War Crimes. Its task would be "to collect material, supported wherever possible by depositions or by other documents, to establish such crimes, especially where they are systematically perpetrated, and to name and identify those responsible for their perpetration." Simon asserted that the proposal had the support of the United States and of the European allies, though he acknowledged that replies from the Soviet Union, China, the British Dominions, and India were still forthcoming.

The Soviet Union put up the greatest obstacles to the establishment of the UNWCC. Moscow had been piqued by the fact that London had ignored the Soviet Union during the preliminary stages of the establishment of the Commission and had appealed to the Soviet Union for support only at the last moment. In January 1943 Moscow responded in a positive manner, but then prompted further delay by opposing London's intention to include participation by the Dominions in the work of the Commission. On July 27, 1943, Moscow announced that it was prepared to meet British wishes regarding the participation of the Dominions, India, and Burma on the condition that the Federated Republics of the USSR—Ukraine, Belorussia, Moldavia, Lithuania, Latvia, Estonia, and Karelo-Finska—would also be allowed to participate. This move by the Soviet Union was clearly designed to gain political capital: recognition of its annexation of the Baltic States, would set a precedent that would help the Soviet Union claim the right to enlarge its representation in future international organizations. When London declined, Moscow decided not to respond to Britain's invitation to the Allied meeting to establish the UNWCC, scheduled for October 20, 1943.

The meeting was chaired by Viscount Simon, who set out the two principal aims of the Commission: first, to investigate allegations of war crimes and, where possible, to record evidence of the crimes and identify the individuals responsible; and second, to report those cases in which it appeared that adequate evidence of such crimes might be forthcoming to the appropriate governments. A clear distinction was made between investigation, which would be the work of the Commission, and the task of trying war criminals. The latter, Simon told the delegations, would represent a later stage requiring decisions by the relevant governments, not the Commission. Finally, according to Simon, British policy held that the fates of those judged to be major war criminals was a political question that remained to be answered. The participants agreed to locate the UNWCC's headquarters in London, and appointed Mackinon Wood, a British citizen, secretary-general. In part because the Soviets were absent, the appointment of a chairman was left to the Commission's plenum.

British officials did not assign a high priority to the UNWCC, despite the fact that Britain had been the driving force behind its establishment. One reason was fear of acts of revenge by Germans against British pris-

oners of war. Another was trepidation over the possibility that the Commission, under pressure from the various governments-in-exile in London, might act in ways that were not consonant with British interests. In fact, officials of the British Foreign Office succeeded in limiting the Commission's mandate to investigating war crimes committed against Allied nationals. For them the Commission was largely a means to neutralize the insistent calls for acts of retribution against the Germans that were being made by the governments-in-exile, and to create an impression that the war criminals issue was being handled. There had also been foot-dragging in the U.S. State Department. The United States wanted to maintain as low a profile as possible vis-à-vis the punishment of war criminals out of fear for the fates of its own captives in German hands, and until the final months of the war, never delved deeply into this complex question.

Almost as soon as the UNWCC had begun to function, the fears of both the British Foreign Office and the U.S. State Department materialized. Although British and U.S. officials expected the UNWCC to confine itself to the investigation of alleged war crimes and criminals, leading members of the Commission refused to accept this narrow mandate and urged the UNWCC to come up with a comprehensive plan for trying war criminals, and to devise ways and means to track and apprehend individuals charged with war crimes. The chairman of the Commission, Sir Cecil Hurst, and, to an even greater extent, Herbert C. Pell, the U.S. representative, failed to be faithful to the Foreign Office's and State Department's objectives, but prompted the Commission to formulate its own proposals for policy and action. Hurst had served as the Foreign Office's Legal Adviser (1928–1929), and subsequently became a panel judge for the Permanent Court of International Justice (and was its president from 1934 to 1936). Pell, a former U.S. congressman from New York and a friend of U.S. president Franklin D. Roosevelt, had served as U.S. minister to Portugal from May 1937 to 1941 when he was posted to Hungary, where he stayed throughout most of the year.

Many of the UNWCC representatives (who were legal scholars of sterling reputation), agreed that the work of the Commission should not be limited to an examination of dossiers and the compilation of lists of criminals, and decided that the Commission should tackle arguments of a legal nature, as well. The Commission's activities developed along three lines: the investigation of allegations and evidence in relation to war crimes; law enforcement and the punishment of war crimes; and the formulation of legal principles having to do with war crimes and the liability of perpetrators. Accordingly, the Commission appointed three committees.

Committees

The Committee on Facts and Evidence (Committee I) was charged with the review of complaints (to be submitted by the various governments), the compilation of lists of alleged war criminals for consideration by the Commission, and the formulation of recommendations with respect to the investigation of war crimes. The Belgian representative, General Marcel de Baer, a lawyer and judge in the city of Antwerp, was elected its chairman.

It was the responsibility of Committee I to determine whether material that had been submitted to the Commission was legally sufficient to establish a case. As the UNWCC possessed no detective or investigative powers, it had to wait until charges were submitted by the various governments, and then had to hope for the best with regard to the accuracy of the information it received, and the diligence and good faith of the providers of this information. A name was entered on a list, not in the aftermath of judicial proceedings, but consequent to the statement of a single party. The person charged was not summoned to answer questions, and evidence was obtained, not from persons under oath, but from written statements. In addition to its designation of persons as "accused," the Commission introduced lists of "suspects," and "witnesses."

The Committee on Means and Methods of Enforcement (Committee II) would recommend to the Commission the methods and policies it should adopt in regard to the apprehension, surrender, detention, investigation, and prosecution of alleged war criminals. The recommendations, if adopted by the Commission's plenum, were then to be transmitted to the member governments for their consideration. The chief efforts of Committee II were to be directed toward the incorporation of clauses providing for the apprehension of war criminals into the anticipated armistice with Germany; the composition of draft conventions that would provide for the establishment of courts to prosecute the war criminals who could not be tried or were not likely to be tried before national courts; and the creation of war crimes offices or agencies in defeated enemy countries that would carry out the identification and arrest of war criminals. Pell was chairman of Committee II.

The Committee on Legal Questions (Committee III), chaired by Professor of Criminal Law Stephan Glaser of Poland, was the advisory board of the Commission. It strove to articulate the more theoretical aspects of the arguments that centered on: the concept of war crimes, the putative criminal nature of aggressive war,

collective responsibility, individual responsibility vis-à-vis orders by superiors, gaps in national legislation, and the putative criminal nature of specific acts resembling (but technically not classifiable as such) the notion of war crimes. At the same time the committee was called on to make determinations on the criminal nature of alleged criminal acts or the liability of accused persons in cases in which there were multiple sources of ambiguity. The committee's counsel was also sought in regard to what should be, in the context of changing international laws and customs of war, the scope of the retributive actions of the UN.

On November 29, 1944, the UNWCC established a branch in Chungking, China (at the time the provisional capital of China), which it named the Far Eastern Sub-Commission. Its mission was to undertake a study of the alleged criminal acts perpetrated by the Japanese. Wang Chung Hui, Secretary-General of the Supreme National Defense Council of China was elected its first chairman. Until March 1947 (when it was dissolved), the Far Eastern Sub-Commission held thirty-eight meetings—each of them attended by UNWCC representatives from the United States, Britain, China, and the Netherlands. About 90 percent of the allegations of crimes presented to the Sub-Commission came out of the Chinese National Office. In addition, the UNWCC created a small subcommittee of in London, under the chair of Wellington Koo, the Chinese UNWCC representative.

Commission Proceedings

Guidelines for the operation of the UNWCC took shape during its initial meetings. Fears for the safety of persons who participated in any way in the work of the Commission led to a press ban and a ban on the taking of photographs of UNWCC members. It was also agreed that the Commission needed to work in closed sessions; only those Commission proceedings that centered on select matters of special interest would make their way into written communiqués. To encourage members of the Commission to express their views, it was decided that debates that were part of Commission proceedings would not be recorded. The Commission was scheduled to meet every week, but much of its actual work was conducted within the three committees.

Not surprisingly, the Commission was furnished with limited resources and inadequate facilities. Its secretariat consisted of only a secretary-general, a liaison officer, and three clerks. The Commission was given no lawyers, investigators, technical assistants, or other specialists. Except for clerical tasks, all work was performed by the representatives and their deputies. Furthermore, Commission representatives, with the exception of those from the United States and the United Kingdom, held other positions and could devote only part of their time to Commission affairs.

Legal Issues

The first question on which the Commission had to determinations was: What is a war crime? No agreed-upon definition existed, nor did there exist a binding list of war crimes. In early December 1943 the UNWCC, instead of compiling an extensive and binding list of war crimes, decided to adopt the list of war crimes that had been prepared by the 1919 Commission on the Responsibility of the Authors of the War and on the Enforcement of Penalties established by the preliminary peace conference of Paris in January 1919. Not only did this measure reduce the risk of being criticized for inventing new war crimes after the acts had been perpetrated, but Italy and Japan had been parties to the preparation of the 1919 document and Germany had never objected to it. Commission members recognized, however, that this list could be neither final nor definitive, and saw it as a starting point and a practical foundation for their work. Accordingly, there was no steadfast definition of the term *war crime* until the end of the war.

Another point of debate that the Commission failed to reach agreement on until the end of the war was the question of whether a war of aggression amounted to a war crime. There were two competing schools of thought. One school of thought held that acts committed by individuals for the purpose of launching an aggressive war were, strictly speaking, *lega lata,* not war crimes; the other maintained that international law had developed in such a way as to almost guarantee that aggressive war amounted to a war crime that entailed individual liability. All agreed, however, that the launching and waging of a war of aggression was illegal. Only after the London Conference (June 26, 1945–August 8, 1945), where delegates of the United States, Great Britain, the Soviet Union, and France negotiated the guiding principles for prosecuting war criminals at the insistance of the United States, had incorporated the notion of aggressive war into the Charter of the International Military Tribunal and identified aggressive war as a war crime did the War Crimes Commission include this high crime as being within its purview.

International law did not recognize war crimes as any offenses committed by an enemy nation against its own nationals or those of other enemy countries. The initiative to limit the War Crimes Commission's jurisdiction to investigating crimes committed against nationals of the Allied nations came from the British. Ac-

cording to this notion, German atrocities perpetrated against, for example, Polish citizens were considered war crimes, whereas atrocities perpetrated against Hungarian, Romanian, or, of course, German nationals were not. The latter were deemed to appertain to the domestic policy of sovereign states, and were therefore to be prosecuted by the successor governments of former enemy countries, Germany included. This reasoning would of course have bearing on Hitler's principal victims—European Jews, but also on populations such as the nationals of neutral countries, stateless persons, and non-Jewish nationals of the Axis.

Several UNWCC members, however, objected to such an asymmetrical interpretation of the term *war crime,* and the ensuing discord developed into a severe crisis of confidence between, on the one hand, the American and British representatives on the Commission and, on the other, their respective foreign ministries. Shortly after the UNWCC began its work, Pell raised the question of crimes perpetrated by Germans against citizens of the Third Reich and insisted on allowing the Commission to investigate such offenses. He wanted all such atrocities committed after January 30, 1933—the day Hitler became Germany's Chancellor—to be classified as war crimes. In addition, he recommended that the term *crimes against humanity* (which was hardly common at that time) should refer to, among other things, crimes committed against stateless persons or against any persons by reason of their ethnicity or religion.

The members of Committee III, having been appointed to make determinations on the kinds of crimes that would make up the Commission's scope of work, proposed as one category of crime: ". . . crimes committed against any person without regard to nationality, stateless persons included, [as well as crimes committed] because of race, nationality, religious, or political belief, irrespective of where they have been committed." Accordingly, Hurst notified the British government of the Commission's readiness to investigate atrocities that had been committed on racist, political, or religious grounds. Any decision in this regard, however, depended on the concurrence of the British and U.S. governments. As late as mid-November 1944 (after the United States had been consulted), Hurst was notified by officials of the British government that the crimes that Committee III was putting forward were not to be considered war crimes. He was also notified that the Commission could collect evidence with respect to the German campaign of mass murder—though the British government thought that it would be a mistake for the Commission to undertake this additional and heavy burden.

Pell was no more successful with U.S. government officials, who continued to endow the term *war crime* with a narrow interpretation. But through his repeated appeals (some made directly to Roosevelt), Pell prevented the U.S. administration from pushing the issue asside. The United States reversed its position when it realized that the American public would not accept distinctions made among the victims of Axis nation atrocities according to whether they were Allied or Axis nationals—particularly after the massacre of European Jewry had been publicly revealed. The altered U.S. position led to the incorporation of the notion of crimes against humanity into the Nuremberg Charter of August 8, 1945 (admittedly in its narrow form), and so into international law. When Pell was discharged from the Commission in January 1945, it would take until January 1946 for the Commission to agree that crimes against humanity as described in the London Charter were war crimes within its jurisdiction.

Evidence and Cases

The Commission's prime task was, as stated previously, to investigate allegations of war crimes, and (where possible) to record evidence of the crimes and identify the perpetrators. In December 1943 each of the member governments of the UNWCC was asked to establish its own National War Crimes Office for the purpose of investigating war crimes that had caused detriment to it or its nationals, preparing charges against the alleged war criminals, and transmitting the charges, along with the relevant information and material, to the Commission for examination. The National War Crimes Offices were also encouraged to transmit to other governments information pertaining to war crimes that might be of value to those governments. In other words, the responsibility for field investigations and the preparation and transmission of charges fell to the individual National Offices. The War Crimes Commission had to examine the charges in the presence of representatives of the National Office that had made the allegations. Whenever the Commission then determined that there appeared to be sufficient evidence that a war crime had been committed, it placed the names of the alleged war criminals on its list.

Until the end of the war the number of charges that had been transmitted to the Commission by the National Offices remained small, relative to the enormous number of crimes that had been perpetrated. In an effort to overcome this difficulty, Committee I adopted the practice of listing the names of persons belonging to an entire military unit when it appeared that war crimes had been committed on such a scale that all members of that unit could be presumed to have taken part in them. The Commission also wanted the govern-ments of enemy-occupied countries to submit to the Commission lists of all enemy personnel in authority, military and civilian, in each occupied district since 1939. Moreover, the Commission suggested that all members and former members of the SS and the Gestapo be apprehended and interned. It was anticipated that there would be difficulties with regard to identifying, investigating, and convicting members of these notorious organizations, and the arrest of these persons was meant to assure that they would be available on request. The Commission, in fact, had adopted the view that these organizations were, by definition, criminal, and that membership in them, by itself, was sufficient evidence against to warrant the accused for the purpose of both his being listed by the Commission and put on trial. In this instance also, the Commission made a final decision only after the Americans had incorporated the concept of criminal organizations into their memorandum, "The Trial and Punishment of Nazi War Criminals," which would become the core of the Nuremberg Charter.

The UNWCC completed its first list of German and Italian war criminals in December 1944. It contained 712 names, all of them submitted by European governments. Among those named were forty-nine high-ranking Nazi officials. In addition to Adolf Hitler, Hermann Göring, Joseph Goebbels, Heinrich Himmler, and Hans Frank, the group of forty-nine consisted of generals, administrators of occupied regions, and political appointees such as Joachim von Ribbentrop, Konstantin von Neurath, Hjalmar Schacht, and Arthur Seyss-Inquart. The Commission was of the opinion that the proper course for bringing these high-ranking war criminals to justice was to try them in a court of law—not to impose penalties by political fiat. Furthermore it rejected as irrelevant the doctrine of the immunity of heads of state or members of government.

An International Court

Still another complex issue, one that had preoccupied the UNWCC from its earliest meetings, centered on the type of court that should be used to try persons accused of war crimes. Although legal proceedings were beyond the Commission's jurisdiction, its members insisted on examining the issue. On February 25, 1944, Committee II, under Pell's chairmanship, began to examine prospects for the creation of an international court. No consensus was reached as to whether such a court would be a body composed exclusively of jurists or some sort of military tribunal. Most Committee members seemed to prefer a combination of the two. For his part, Pell preferred a judicial body that would be composed of jurists, military officers, and lay persons. He wanted the prospective court's trial judges to recognize that a major part of their endeavor would be to make the outbreak of future wars less probable.

The creation of an international court quickly became a focal point of discord between the UNWCC and the British government. The increasing disposition of the Commission members to delve into questions such as the type of court or code of law to be used greatly troubled the British Foreign Office, which objected to the creation of a court or any other judicial machinery. The Foreign Office wanted persons accused of war crimes to be tried by military courts or, in some countries, civil courts that would apply existing laws and principles. Each Allied government was to be entrusted with trying all cases that arose from allegations of offenses that had been committed on its own territory or against its own nationals.

Nevertheless, in September 1944, the Commission approved a final draft of the Convention for the Establishment of a UN Joint Court. It contained twenty-nine Articles, but did not include a detailed list of war crimes. Instead, the court would handle allegations of offenses committed against the laws and customs of war. The Commission wished to endow the Court with the latitude of action to carry out the intentions of the Allied governments—such as they had been expressed in numerous public statements and in general international treaties or conventions pertaining to the laws of war. Although it proposed that the court be given the power to impose the death penalty, the draft convention made sure to protect the rights of defendants.

Yet members of the Commission realized that setting up such a court would be a long process, and that therefore interim courts would be needed. Moreover, Pell, who was aware that both the President and the U.S. State Department of favored military courts, had put much effort into convincing Commission members to support the idea of interim military courts. According to the draft convention, "mixed military tribunals" would have the jurisdiction to try nationals of enemy countries accused of having committed war crimes. The judges were to be nationals of Allied countries, and each tribunal would consist of no less than five members. The rules of procedure were to be consistent with practices that were habitual in the Allied nations and to be framed by the tribunals' appointing authorities. Prosecution was to be left to the relevant nation, and the tribunals would have the power to subpoena persons and documents. Trial in a mixed military tribunal would not bar proceedings before an international tribunal. The Commission regarded both types of courts—an eventual UN Court (to be created by treaty) and mixed military tribunals to be appointed by military commanders—as complementary, not as competitors.

Strongly opposed to the UNWCC proposal of a treaty court, the British government tried to enlist Washington's support in its effort to have the proposal withdrawn, and meanwhile held back its response to the UNWCC. Frustrated, Hurst reached the conclusion that the Foreign Office was once again disregarding Commission proposals. Similarly, Pell was extremely disappointed when he found that neither the President nor Secretary of State of the United States had reacted in a positive way to what he regarded as his major achievement—convincing the Commission to propose the establishment of a military court. When the two governments finally adopted the military tribunal proposal, both Pell and Hurst were no longer the respective American and British representatives to the UNWCC.

Hurst felt he had been put in an impossible position being unable to decipher the views of the British government, and therefore unable to relay them to Commission members. As chairman, he found it increasingly difficult to contend with the repeated complaints within the Commission about the scarcity of attention or guidance coming from London, and he resigned in early January 1945—ostensibly for medical reasons. The British government quickly appointed William Viscount Finlay to replace him, who had been a judge in England since 1924 and during World War II served as Chairman of the Blockade Committee at the Ministry of Economic Warfare. It was calculated that the appointment of this prominent figure was done to dispel accusations of Britain's indifference to the Commission. When Finlay died a few months later, on July 4, 1945, Sir Robert Craigie replaced him.

The British government was extremely fearful that Pell would become UNWCC chairman. In the end, Lord Robert Alderson Wright, a senior British judge who was the Commission's nominal Australian representative, was elected chairman, on January 17, 1945. The British were not alone in opposing Pell. Relations between Pell and the U.S. State Department, tense from the outset, had grown worse. The State Department, motivated in part by animosity toward Pell, had worked to constrain whatever actions he wished to take, to reject most of his initiatives, and to undermine his position in the eyes of the British. State Department officials could not abide Pell's independence of judgment and action. Perhaps the best explanation for the clash between Pell and the U.S. government lay in the U.S. government's lack of an established policy or even principles vis-à-vis the treatment of suspected war criminals, and in the State Department's predilection for postponing decisions on the issue. Pell, who regarded himself as a statesman and not a bureaucrat, had believed (erroneously) that he could influence overall U.S. policy toward Germany. His limited legal knowledge had naturally prompted him to focus on policy matters. When, shortly after his appointment, Pell realized that the State Department did not regard the question of the treatment of suspected war criminals as a serious matter and that no one in the State Department actually cared much about the UNWCC, he decided that he had better act on his own initiative to further the development of a policy toward war criminals. Taking advantage of the fact that he had been Roosevelt's appointee, Pell did not hesitate to bypass the State Department and attempt to enlist Roosevelt's support for his proposals directly. Inevitably, the poor relations between the State Department and Pell influenced the State Department's overall attitude toward the UNWCC. In the end, the State Department maneuvered to have Pell replaced (as the Commission's U.S. representative) by his deputy, Colonel Joseph V. Hodgson.

With the conclusion of the war, Wright was determined to prevent the Commission from being pushed to the sidelines. He even sought to have the scope of the Commission's mandate expanded and to have the Commission play an active part in the gathering of evidence on war crimes. However, when he proposed to set up a War Crimes Investigation Team at the Supreme Headquarters of the Allied Expeditionary Force (SHAEF, the command headquarters of the commander of Allied forces in Europe), the British government ruled out the possibility because of its longstanding low appreciation of the UNWCC and its interest in transferring responsibility for dealing with war criminals to the individual countries. Wright had more success in furthering the goals of the Commission when he convened a conference of representatives of the various National War Crimes Offices, which took place in London on May 31, 1945. At the conference he spoke about the importance that the UNWCC had ascribed to the work of the National War Crimes Offices, and explained that the Commission's primary function had been to act as a sort of central clearing house for the written statements in which war crimes were alleged. The Commission had promulgated its conviction that justice and not revenge should be the aim of those working to prosecute alleged war criminals. With this in mind, Wright wanted the Commission to act as a central advisory bureau and liaison that could coordinate the activities of the National War Crimes Offices and military authorities in Germany and Austria.

The Commission's wish to cooperate with military authorities was partially fulfilled when the Allied the-

ater commanders in Germany and Austria were authorized to accept lists of war criminals directly from the Commission, and to apprehend and detain those listed in the absence of further proof of their having committed war crimes. An officer of SHAEF, furthermore, had been attending the Commission's meetings regularly, starting in May 1945. Wright also succeeded in coming to an agreement with U.S. Supreme Court Justice Robert J. Jackson, who had been appointed Chief of Counsel for the Prosecution of Axis Criminality by president Harry S. Truman on May 2. Jackson regarded the Commission as a supporting body, and expected it to provide him with evidence that would help him to acquire an overview of the war crimes that had been perpetrated by the highest-ranking Axis authorities. Following Jackson's appointment, there were close contacts between the Commission and the staffs of the Chief Prosecutors of the United States, Great Britain, and France, prior to and during the trial of the major war criminals at Nuremberg—as well as between the Commission and the attorneys preparing the subsequent proceedings. The UNWCC furnished the prosecution with first-hand information and evidence of crimes committed in the occupied countries.

In the final analysis, despite the obstacles put up mainly by the British Foreign Office and U.S. State Department, the UNWCC was successful in its undertaking to formulate a policy on the handling of war criminals, and had prompted individual governments to grapple with the question of which policies they would adopt. The most important of the UNWCC proposals that made their way into the U.S. ground plan for punishing war criminals and, thereafter, into the Charter of the International Military Tribunal, were the concepts of aggressive war, criminal organizations, mixed military courts, and crimes committed by an enemy against its own nationals. Summing up the importance of the Commission's activities for the year 1944 and the beginning of 1945, Wright would declare, in the official history of the UNWCC, that "[T]he United Nations had ready to their hands when the time came, a more or less practical scheme for the prosecution and punishment of war criminals, which was capable of being completed and put into effect when the Nazi resistance collapsed." The UNWCC ultimately presented 80 lists that contained the names of 36,529 suspected war criminals (of whom 34,270, were German and 1,286 Italian).

SEE ALSO Jackson, Robert; London Charter; Morgenthau, Henry; Nuremberg Trials; War Crimes

BIBLIOGRAPHY

Blayney, Michael S. (1976). "Herbert C. Pell, War Crimes and the Jews." *American Jewish Historical Quarterly* 65 (June):335–352.

Bloxham, Donald (2001). *Genocide on Trial: War Crimes Trials and the Formation of Holocaust History and Memory*. Oxford, U.K.: Oxford University Press.

Ginsburgs, George, and V.N. Kudriavtsev, eds. (1990). *The Nuremberg Trial and International Law*. Dordrecht, Netherlands: Martinus Nijhoff Publishers.

Jones, Priscillia Dale (1991). "British Policy towards German Crimes against the Jews, 1939–1945." *Leo Baeck Institute Year Book* 36:339–366.

Kochavi, Arieh J. (1998). *Prelude to Nuremberg: Allied War Crimes Policy and the Question of Punishment*. Chapel Hill: University of North Carolina Press.

Overy, Richard (2001). *Interrogators: The Nazi Elite in Allied Hands, 1945*. London: Allen Lane/The Penguin Press.

Smith, Bradley F. (1981). *The Road to Nuremberg*. New York: Basic Books.

United Nations War Crimes Commission, ed. (1948). *History of the United Nations War Crimes Commission and the Development of the Laws of War*. London: His Majesty's Stationary Office.

Arieh J. Kochavi

United States Foreign Policies Toward Genocide and Crimes Against Humanity

Since World War II, many instances of genocide have been alleged to have occurred in all regions of the world. They have presented serious challenges to foreign policymakers in many countries including the United States. The United States has, historically, projected itself as a democratic state that champions respect for human rights and fundamental freedoms. American officials and diplomats have repeatedly reaffirmed these principles at international conferences and forums. Presidents have enshrined them in doctrines that underpin the course of United States foreign policy at different times in American history. Given the heinous nature of the crime of genocide, it is unsurprising that the United States would at least take action, if not exercise leadership, in dealing with the crime whenever it occurs.

In principle, there are at least two ways in which the United States could react to genocide, or allegations of genocide. One is at the level of norms and principles. In other words, the United States could work to promote the development and acceptance of international norms and rules regarding genocide. In this connection, playing an active role in drafting, and vigorously

supporting the application of, a treaty like the Genocide Convention comes to mind. The United States could also actively support the creation of international bodies such as courts to conduct trials of people accused of committing genocide. Alternatively, and perhaps in conjunction with the development of norms and rules, the United States could take concrete measures in cases of genocide, or when allegations of genocide are made. These could involve taking timely measures to prevent genocide before it occurs, especially in cases where there is advance warning. Or, they could involve proposing and supporting the application of sanctions—political, economic, and military—in order to bring an end to the atrocities and to bring the perpetrators to justice.

The United States' experience in dealing with the issue of genocide involves its participation in the development and advancement of international norms and rules on genocide and its official reaction to various instances of genocide. It is possible to assess how and how well United States foreign policymakers have taken concrete measures to deal with the atrocities that were committed in those cases.

The United States and the Development of Norms and Rules on Genocide

United States policymakers had their first opportunity to contribute to the elaboration of international norms and rules regarding the crime of genocide in the period immediately following World War II. The genocide of World War II was on the agenda of the first session of the United Nations General Assembly in 1946. Diplomats as well as activists, including Raphael Lemkin, had lobbied the General Assembly to take the issue up and to consider what measures could be taken to deal with any future cases of genocide. With U.S. support, the General Assembly adopted a resolution that branded genocide a crime under international law and called for the adoption of an international treaty on the subject. The treaty, the Genocide Convention, was completed two years later, in December 1948.

The most important negotiations on the Genocide Convention took place in the Sixth (Legal) Committee of the General Assembly, although at various stages during the negotiation process, the United Nations Secretariat and the Economic and Social Council (ECOSOC) made proposals that influenced the final product. United States diplomats were actively involved, making constructive contributions throughout the drafting process, especially in the ECOSOC and the Sixth Committee. They negotiated significant compromises on contentious issues related to the definition of the crime of genocide. They also advanced and successfully de-

First Lady Eleanor Roosevelt addresses a meeting of the American Red Cross on April 11, 1934, in Washington, D.C. She had joined the American Red Cross as a private citizen in 1912. [AP/WORLD WIDE PHOTOS]

fended the inclusion of an article in the Convention that contemplated the creation of a permanent international court to try those accused of committing genocide; and defended a role for the International Court of Justice in dealing with issues of state responsibility for genocide.

The compromises that the United States delegates worked out on these issues were not easy to reach. The issues were important to many states, some of which, especially the Soviet Union and its supporters, were determined to preserve maximum discretion for individual states in dealing with the genocide of the recent past as well as any future cases that may occur. In brief, the Soviet Union and its supporters were concerned about the impact that the Convention could have on their freedom of action and their exercise of national sovereignty. In the end, however, the United States representatives carried the day on all the issues that were important to them.

When the work on the Genocide Convention was completed, one would have expected that the United States would have moved quickly to ratify it, accepting it as the cornerstone international legal document on genocide. After all, the United States was the major ally during World War II in the defeat the Nazi regime, whose practices had led to the adoption of the Convention in the first place. The United States had also championed the creation of the Nuremberg Tribunal, and been a major participant in it. And it had been successful in the negotiations on the convention itself. Thus, one might have expected that the United States Senate, the only chamber of the Congress that must give advice and consent to the ratification of treaties, would have quickly given its approval to the convention. However, this was not to be. In June 1949 president Harry Truman formally requested the Senate's advice and consent to ratification; but it was not until almost forty years later, in February 1986, that the Senate actually did so, and even then it imposed a number of conditions that seriously undermined the main object and purpose of the Convention. Further, it was not until October 1988 that the Congress adopted the legislation needed to implement the Convention, finally opening the way for president Reagan to deposit the United States instrument of ratification at the United Nations. The Convention formally became binding on the United States in February 1989.

During the intervening forty years, between the time when president Truman requested advice and consent to ratification and the time when the Senate agreed to do so, the Senate Committee on Foreign Relations held several hearings on the Convention. During the 1970s, the committee at times seemed poised to recommend ratification to the Senate as a whole, but every time, the hopes of the Convention's most ardent supporters were dashed.

The arguments that were advanced against ratification of the convention by its most vociferous critics changed very little over those forty years. They criticized specific aspects of the definition of the crime, quibbling over the groups that were the object of protection of the convention (Article II) and over the specific acts that could be considered genocidal (Article III). They also expressed grave concern about the creation of an international criminal court to try anyone accused of committing genocide (Article VI), fearing that Americans, especially members of the U.S. armed forces, would be dragged into such a court on trumped up charges of genocide. In addition, they opposed the role of the International Court of Justice (in Article IX) in resolving disputes among states regarding the interpretation or application of the Convention. The critics of the convention in the United States used essentially the same arguments as those used by the Soviet Union's representatives during the negotiations on the Convention: they were concerned about the possible negative impact that the Convention could have on the freedom of action of the United States and its exercise of national sovereignty.

The executive branch was generally supportive of ratification through all the years the Genocide Convention was under consideration in the Senate. Presidents Truman, Nixon, and Carter were especially supportive. President Reagan endorsed ratification shortly before his re-election bid in 1984, although he had not supported ratification earlier in his first term. Diplomats and other government officials were also often supportive, and testified before Senate committees. In general, the Convention's supporters argued that ratification was important from the standpoint of the image of the United States as a champion of freedom and human rights throughout the world. Indeed, some supporters, especially diplomats, made a point of noting that the United States was often taken to task in international forums for not having ratified the Convention, and that its failure to do so had undermined its effort to exercise leadership in dealing with genocide and other serious human rights abuses.

Most of the opposition to ratification came from extremely conservative members of the Senate, mainly Republicans, who were supported by extreme right-wing nongovernmental organizations like the Liberty Lobby. However, representatives of the prestigious American Bar Association also criticized the convention relentlessly at the 1950 Senate hearings. The association changed its position to support the ratification effort in the 1970s, but many of its earlier criticisms continued to haunt the debate, undermining efforts to secure ratification. In the end, while those who favored ratification won the battle—after all, the Senate eventually gave its advice and consent to ratification—the opponents of ratification effectively won the war. They were able to impose conditions on the ratification—a package of understandings and reservations collectively known as the Lugar-Helms-Hatch Sovereignty Package—that effectively gutted the main object and purpose of the treaty. The Sovereignty Package rejects the authority of the International Court of Justice to deal with disputes regarding the interpretation and application of the Convention that might involve the United States, except with the specific consent of the United States. It also affirms the supremacy of the U.S. Constitution over the Convention and expresses reservations about the creation of a permanent international criminal court to try perpetrators of genocide. Several West European allies of the United States expressed objections to the terms of the Sovereignty Package, but in the end the United States became a party to the treaty in accordance with the terms of the package.

The terms of the Sovereignty Package has undermined the moral position of the United States in dealing with cases of genocide, and they have had serious practical implications as well. For example, the reservation to the authority of the International Court of Justice to deal with disputes regarding the interpretation and application of the Convention effectively insulated the United States from any challenges to its exercise of discretion in interpreting and applying the convention. At the same time, however, it made it impossible for the United States to take any other country to task for its practices, however heinous, because that country could, under the doctrine of reciprocity in international law, invoke the United States' reservation in self-defense. Indeed, the purpose of the Sovereignty Package was to reduce the U.S. ratification of the Convention to a merely symbolic gesture, and in that, it succeeded.

Recent events suggest that the situation has not changed much, and may even have worsened. The United States' reaction to the recently created International Criminal Court provides a case in point. The U.S. negotiators on the Genocide Convention secured the adoption of an article (Article VI) that contemplated the creation of a permanent international criminal court to try anyone accused of committing genocide. The General Assembly followed up on this article and charged the International Law Commission with studying the possibility of creating such a court. However, the discussion in the commission in the late 1940s was rapidly brought to a close by the political tensions brought on by the emerging cold war between the United States and the Soviet Union. Profound disagreements among various parties involved in the project as to the nature and functioning of such a court also contributed to the problem.

Although some scholars and diplomats tried to keep the issue of creating a court alive during the post-World War II period, it was not until the 1990s that concrete achievements were made. The UN Security Council, with United States support, created two ad hoc international criminal tribunals to deal with cases arising from the Bosnian and Rwandan genocides in the early 1990s. Although these courts will cease to exist when they have fulfilled their mandates, the genocides they were created to deal with stimulated renewed and serious discussion about the need to create a permanent international criminal tribunal to deal with genocide as well as other significant crimes, such as war crimes and crimes against humanity.

The discussions, which took place through the mid-1990s, concluded in a major conference in Rome in July 1998, attended by representatives of 160 countries, including the United States. The vast majority of countries that attended the conference voted to adopt the statute for the court (the Rome Statute) that emerged from it, but seven countries, including the United States, voted against it. The statute was quickly and broadly accepted, however, and the International Criminal Court (ICC) came into existence in July 2002.

The ICC could try individual persons charged with committing genocide, war crimes, and crimes against humanity. Cases could be referred to it in various ways, including the Security Council, the states that are parties to the statute, and the court's prosecutor. The United States had voted against the statute because of disagreements over several issues, including circumstances under which the court could exercise jurisdiction, especially the possibility that the court would exercise jurisdiction over persons from countries that are not a party to the statute. The statute became the subject of lively debate within the United States, with many distinguished professionals in international law arguing that the United States' fears and concerns were exaggerated, if not unfounded. The court's supporters urged president Clinton to reconsider the U.S. position and to at least sign the statute. The president's signature would indicate that the United States approved the creation of the court in principle, although it would not be legally bound by the court's statute until it ratified it. In December 2000, shortly before leaving office, president Clinton signed the statute, but not with unreserved enthusiasm. He believed that his signature would reaffirm the United States' support for international accountability for grave crimes such as genocide, and would make it possible for the United States to remain engaged in making the court an instrument of impartial justice in the years ahead. However, he remained concerned about flaws in the statute, in particular that the court might exercise jurisdiction over persons from countries that had not ratified the statute, and he indicated that he would recommend to his successor that the statute be withheld from the Senate, postponing any request for advice and consent to ratification until these concerns were addressed.

Although president Clinton was persuaded to sign the statute, even with misgivings, some members of Congress expressed outrage, stating that they would never approve a resolution of ratification. Moreover, the Clinton's successor went substantially beyond his recommendation. Unlike the controversy over the Genocide Convention, where the executive branch was usually supportive—and never vocally opposed—to ratification, incoming President George W. Bush joined the opposition to the court. In fact, president Bush took the unprecedented step of the statute, delivering notice to the United Nations that the United States had no intention of becoming a party to it. Among other things, the administration claimed to want to protect American servicemen from being arbitrarily accused of committing genocide (or war crimes or crimes against humanity) and dragged before the ICC to stand trial. This was the same argument that had been made repeatedly in the Genocide Convention debates in the Senate. The Bush administration did not stop with unsigning the statute. It demanded that individual countries sign agreements stating that they would not hand over to the court any U.S. nationals who might be accused of genocide, war crimes, or crimes against humanity, and it threatened to terminate military assistance to countries that refused to sign such agreements. It also demanded that the United Nations Security Council agree to immunities for U.S. military personnel involved in UN peacekeeping operations, a move that provoked dismay among diplomats and high-ranking civil servants, such as Secretary-General Kofi Annan.

Clearly, the United States has experienced difficulty in dealing with the elaboration and acceptance of international norms and rules on genocide and related crimes. On the one hand, policymakers at the highest levels have repeatedly condemned genocide, war crimes, and crimes against humanity, and they have affirmed the United States' commitment to freedom, respect for human rights, and a stable international order based on respect for law. Nonetheless, there have been serious disagreements on how best to realize those commitments. Although U.S. negotiators have been active in framing norms and rules, strong opposition to accepting legal obligations in this field has been expressed in various quarters, especially among the most conservative members of Congress. The result—in the case of the Genocide Convention a symbolic acceptance; in the case of the ICC, outright hostility—has led many to conclude that the United States may say that it wants a stable international order based on law, but is not willing to be held accountable to the same rules that it expects everyone else to accept.

The United States' Reaction to Instances of Genocide

Genocide has occurred on numerous occasions, both before and after World War II. The most prominent cases occurred in Cambodia in the mid-1970s, Bosnia in the early 1990s, and Rwanda in 1994. Some say that genocide occurred in other instances as well. One example that predates World War II was the slaughter of ethnic Armenians in Ottoman Turkey during the years 1915 and 1916. Others took place in the postwar years—in Indonesia, for example, in the slaughter of hundreds of thousands of communists in the mid-

1960s, and in the invasion and occupation of East Timor, beginning in the mid-1970s; in Paraguay against the Ache Indians, in the early 1970s; in Burundi in sporadic strife between Hutus and Tutsis from the early 1970s to the 1990s; in Iraq in the late 1980s in what came to known as the Anfal campaign against the Kurds and at the time of the first Gulf War against the Marsh Arabs; and in Kosovo in the late 1990s.

All of these instances of alleged genocide, each occurring under their own specific historical and political conditions, challenged U.S. policymakers to develop appropriate responses. At the time of the Armenian genocide, the United States had not yet emerged as the major world power that it became in the post World War II period. In some cases, the genocide occurred under conditions that might be called a civil war, in other cases, not. Even the magnitude of the genocides, in terms of victims and the length of time over which they occurred, differed. Nonetheless, research has shown that the United States' reaction to the genocides has varied relatively little over time. Numerous obstacles have usually stood in the way of taking concrete action, and such measures as have been taken have usually been taken late, aimed more at dealing with post-genocide issues than at saving lives.

The Armenian genocide provides a good starting point for understanding how genocides can occur with impunity because those who might be in a position to prevent or mitigate the effects of the crime have failed to take effective measures. U.S. government officials and foreign dignitaries at various levels took an interest in the plight of the Armenians. The United States Ambassador in Constantinople at the time, Henry Morgenthau, Sr., labored strenuously to try to protect the Armenians, meeting with Ottoman officials to protest their treatment, sending numerous cables to State Department officials urging action, and even raising funds to try to assist survivors and to relocate hundreds of thousands of them to the United States. After almost two years of fruitless work, he returned to the United States, frustrated that he had been unable to stop the bloodshed. It is estimated that one million Armenians were either killed outright or died as a result of the conditions of life imposed on them between 1915 and 1916.

Despite the pleas of Morgenthau and others, and reports of the atrocities in some of the mass media, the United States refused to take the side of its allies, Great Britain and France, who condemned the slaughter, or to approach Germany, which was allied to the Ottoman Empire, because it did not want to abandon its neutral stance at that time. Top-level policymakers even advised Ambassador Morgenthau not to protest too

strongly to the Ottoman officials about the genocide. He was counseled to be respectful of their claim that their actions were domestic and not of concern to outside powers, and even that there was some validity to their claim that their actions were aimed at dealing with a national security threat. In short, intervention in this case was not deemed wise because it was not perceived as falling within the national interest of the United States.

This pattern of dealing with the Armenian genocide set a precedent, and in later instances of genocide similar arguments were advanced as to why the United States could not take measures on behalf of the victims. Even during World War II, at a time when the Nazi regime in Germany was engaged in the genocide that would eventually take the lives of an estimated six million Jews and members of other groups, reports of the atrocities were greeted in U.S. policymaking circles with incredulity, disbelief, and even lack of interest. What British Prime Minister Winston Churchill called the "crime without a name" was already evident, yet it was greeted by denial or indifference. All efforts were directed at winning the war against Hitler's Germany, which was seen as the only effective way of stopping the atrocities. It was only after the war that statesmen were prepared to come to terms with the truth of what had happened, and they established measures such as the Nuremberg Tribunal to punish the perpetrators, bringing some sense of justice to survivors and relatives of victims.

The Armenian genocide and the genocide of World War II occurred at times when international communications and transportation were slow and cumbersome. Yet reliable information about what was going on in these instances of genocide was abundant and ready at hand. The problem was not really a lack of awareness or information; it was a lack of political will to do anything about the problem under the circumstances. More recent instances have occurred under different circumstances, when communications are virtually instantaneous, and improvements in transportation have reduced the time it would take to get to a trouble spot to hours rather than days and weeks, but still a lack of will has prevailed. The Cambodian, Bosnian, and Rwandan genocides illustrate how, even under a different kind of international system brought about in part by advances in technology the arguments against taking action in clear cases of genocide remain essentially the same.

Cambodia has a long and sometimes tragic history, but it surely entered into its darkest period in April 1975, when the Khmer Rouge, headed by the infamous Pol Pot, triumphantly entered the capital city of Phnom

Penh after having won a five-year civil war. Previous to this momentous event, many foreign observers as well as Cambodians saw the Khmer Rouge fighters as potential liberators of the country, and believed that better times would follow their victory. Instead, the victory of the Khmer Rouge immediately turned into a nightmare of unimaginable proportions. During the three and a half years that the Khmer Rouge was in control, some 1.5 million people out of a total population of about 8 million people died.

In the West in general, and the United States in particular, the initial reaction to the Khmer Rouge's victory and atrocities was muted. In fact, there was a tendency to engage in a form of denial, to believe that the slaughter would stop, that it would not be indiscriminate and was, instead, targeted at a relatively small group of political opponents. This form of denial was sometimes accompanied by a debate over whether or not genocide was actually occurring in Cambodia. It was clear that Cambodians were killing Cambodians, but did this constitute genocide? Or were the Khmer Rouge engaged in what might be called "politicide"; that is, the killing of persons for political reasons.

To say that the Khmer Rouge was engaged in genocide in the sense that the crime is defined in the Genocide Convention would have required that the targeted groups be national, ethnical, racial or religious, not political. Even in the earliest stages, it was clear that certain categories of persons—for example, former military officers, policemen, and government officials—were targeted, and it is known that such persons were executed along with members of their families, including infants and children. Moreover, although most of the victims were, in fact, Cambodians, there seems no doubt that certain specific ethnic groups including Vietnamese, Chinese, and Cham minorities, were targeted for elimination, and that the Khmer Rouge also set out to eliminate Buddhism as a religious force in Cambodian society. They actually succeeded in achieving these objectives to a large extent, and these actions were surely genocidal in nature, consistent with the terms of the Genocide Convention.

Given the magnitude of the crimes, what could or should the United States have done? In retrospect, it is easy to say that concrete actions could have been taken in an effort to stop the atrocities. But it must be borne in mind that, at the time the Khmer Rouge came to power in Cambodia, the Vietnam War was drawing to a close. That war had become so unpopular in the United States and elsewhere that it would have been impossible for anyone to argue in favor of U.S. military intervention, even it if was motivated by a desire to stop the slaughter. In fact, there were some who argued that

U.S. policies during the Vietnam war—the bombing raids on Cambodia, the "incursion" in 1970, and the financial and military support of the Lon Nol government—had all actually contributed to the Khmer Rouge victory.

If military intervention was not in order, what else could the United States have done? President Gerald Ford, and some high-ranking government officials like Secretary of State Henry Kissinger, occasionally addressed the unfolding tragedy, making statements about the "bloodbath" taking place. Apart from that, the United States largely ignored the tragedy. It maintained an economic embargo against Cambodia, but such policies are rarely if ever effective. During the presidential campaign in 1976, then-candidate Jimmy Carter argued in favor of restoring morality to American foreign policy, but when he became president in 1977, he found it difficult to translate these goals into reality. Yet, the reports coming out of Cambodia provided chilling details of the genocidal massacres that were underway, and they were widely discussed in Congress. In April 1978, President Carter denounced the government of Cambodia for its policies and called upon other members of the international community to protest the genocide. In 1978 and 1979, congressional hearings were held on the subject, and investigations were conducted by the United Nations. Both Congress and the UN concluded that there was growing evidence that genocide had occurred in Cambodia. However, it fell to the Vietnamese to do something about the matter. Vietnamese forces invaded Cambodia in January 1979 to overthrow the Pol Pot government and impose a new order.

It can be argued that the Vietnamese invasion of Cambodia was a significant contribution to humanity, but it was not received as such in much of the world. At the time of the invasion, the United States was concerned with improving relations with China, which was the principal backer of the Khmer Rouge, as a way of bringing pressure to bear on the Soviet Union to be more amenable to U.S. interests. Moreover, the United States, along with other states in the region, found it difficult to accept without protest the invasion of one state by another, fearing that a dangerous precedent could be set. Incredible as it may seem, when controversy arose over which delegation to seat in the fall 1979 United Nations General Assembly meeting in New York—the ousted Pol Pot regime or the Vietnamese backed regime then in control of the country—the Association of Southeast Asian Nations (ASEAN) and China argued strongly in favor of the Pol Pot regime. The dispute had to be resolved by committee, in which the United States bowed to Chinese and ASEAN interests and voted to seat the Pol Pot regime. The United Stated did, at least, go on to claim that the issue of seating a delegation was purely technical and legal, and that its support of seating the Pol Pot regime did not imply approval of that regime's policies. The United States maintained this stance during the Reagan administration and beyond, supporting at one time the seating of a coalition delegation that consisted of some Khmer Rouge elements.

Even though statesmen missed opportunities to apply the Genocide Convention for various political reasons, the Cambodian genocide remained a matter of concern to scholars, activists, and politicians in the United States and abroad during the 1980s and 1990s. Some argued in favor of bringing a case against the Khmer Rouge to the International Court of Justice under Article IX of the Genocide Convention, which authorizes the ICJ to deal with the matter of state responsibility for genocide. Cambodia had ratified the convention with no reservation to Article IX, so there was no legal hindrance for another state party to the convention to bring a case relating to state responsibility. However, efforts to persuade another party to the convention to take up the case were to no avail. So far as the United States was concerned, it could not have brought a case to the court after becoming a party to the convention in 1989 because of its reservation to Article IX, as set forth in the Sovereignty Package, which blocks the court from dealing with a case involving the United States without the specific consent of the United States. Under the doctrine of reciprocity in international law, Cambodia could invoke the U.S. reservation in self-defense.

The possibility of bringing the surviving perpetrators of the Cambodian genocide to trial came to the forefront in the 1990s. In 1998, during the administration of President Clinton, the United States expressed interest in putting Pol Pot on trial, but he died in April 1998, escaping, as it were, a judgment day. However, a number of his accomplices were still alive, and the Clinton administration argued in favor of exploring ways of bringing them to trial. Finally, in 2000, the United Nations and the Cambodian government reached preliminary agreement on the creation of a mixed tribunal, consisting of Cambodian as well as international judges. The Cambodian parliament approved the agreement, but subsequent disagreements over issues of Cambodian sovereignty delayed its work. Justice for the victims of the Cambodian genocide therefore remained elusive.

The Cambodian genocide occurred in a remote region of the world at a time when an unpopular war was being brought to a close. In contrast, the Bosnian genocide in the early 1990s occurred in Europe at a time when profound changes for the better were occurring in the international system—namely, the end of the cold war. Under these fundamentally different circumstances, it would seem that a case for the application of the Genocide Convention would have been easy to make. However, no firm action was taken, either in the early stages of the genocide or later, as it unfolded, and such actions as were eventually taken, important though they were, were mainly in the form of post-genocide actions.

United States policymakers failed to take effective measures to put an early stop to the genocide in Bosnia, in part because of a lack of will, and in part because of uncertainty about what the United States' role should be. Analysts and policymakers engaged in a seemingly endless debate over the question of the cause of the conflict. Some argued that the killing simply reflected the reemergence of age-old hatreds that had characterized ethnic relations in Yugoslavia for hundreds of years. Communist oppression had muted these hatreds for several decades, it was argued, but with the end of the cold war and communist rule in Yugoslavia, the hatreds had reappeared with a vengeance. Thus, no outside intervention would be able to stop the conflict. Even Lawrence Eagleburger, an acknowledged expert on Yugoslavia, who became Secretary of State toward the end of president George W. Bush's administration, held this viewpoint.

Those who advocated some form of intervention pointed out that such views ignored the fact that Bosnians of various religious and ethnic backgrounds had intermarried in large numbers, that they lived in ethnically mixed communities, and that strife among the various communities was virtually nonexistent. The administration, however, held firmly to the position that the conflict was not one in which the United States should become involved. In fact, the United States initially disapproved of the secession of Slovenia, Croatia, and Bosnia from the Yugoslav federation, and only reluctantly agreed to recognize their independence in April 1992. The administration also repeatedly stressed that the problem was a European one and had to be settled by the European states, a position that accurately reflected the European viewpoint at the time. Thus, until the end of the Bush administration, the United States concentrated on encouraging humanitarian actions that could be taken by the United Nations to try to relieve hunger and ensure the availability of medical supplies in Bosnia.

The Clinton administration, which came into office in January 1993, at first seemed poised to take concrete action. The president had himself addressed the

UN Secretary General Kofi Annan shakes hands with a survivor of the Rwandan genocide, May 1998. It was during this trip to Rwanda that Annan apologized to the Parliament of Rwanda for the United Nations great failure to intervene. [AP/WORLD WIDE PHOTOS.]

Bosnian genocide during the presidential campaign, and he spoke eloquently of the need for action and of the United States' commitment to respect for human rights. High-ranking officials, including Secretary of State Warren Christopher, addressed the issue in congressional hearings and elsewhere early during the administration. However, there remained opposition in important circles to any intervention by the United States to end the genocide. General Colin Powell, for example, was opposed to intervention. Some of President Clinton's aides were also opposed, expressing concern that entanglement in a controversial international conflict might jeopardize important domestic policy initiatives. Consequently, while the Serbians continued their policy of ethnic cleansing, the administration retreated from its earlier strong position and the president pursued an ineffective policy of engaging in a lot of rhetoric to condemn the genocide but failing to follow up the rhetoric with action.

A combination of measures taken by the United States, the United Nations, and NATO beginning early in 1994 slowly, but finally, brought an end to the genocide. So far as the United States was concerned, the

Clinton administration was moved to act by increasing domestic political pressure in Congress, the media, and public opinion to do something about Serbian atrocities against civilians, which were now widely reported in the media. The United States supported United Nations resolutions calling for the end of the arms embargo, which would allow the Bosnians to fight back against the Serbian forces. NATO involvement began extremely slowly, with air strikes against Serbian military installations. The Serbians remained defiant through most of 1994 and into 1995, carrying on their policy of ethnic cleansing with impunity. Toward the end of 1995, substantial NATO air strikes against Serbian military positions forced Serbia to the negotiating table, and the Dayton Peace Accords were signed in December 1995. One of the key provisions of the accords was that the parties to the agreement were bound to cooperate fully with the International Criminal Tribunal for the former Yugoslavia, which had been set up by the United Nations Security Council, with United States backing, in May 1993.

In contrast to the Cambodian and Bosnian genocides, which occurred over a period of several years, the

Rwandan genocide in 1994 lasted for only about three months, from April to June. Again, the United States—indeed, the entire international community—missed the opportunity to act in a timely manner consistent with the terms of the Genocide Convention to stop the slaughter and save perhaps hundreds of thousands of lives. The actions that were eventually taken, important as they may have been, were more along the lines of post-genocide measures designed to try to bring to justice the perpetrators and to help the victims and their survivors to resume a more or less normal life.

United States policymakers reacted to the outbreak of the Rwandan genocide much as those in other countries did. In response to the immediate outbreak of violence, President Clinton ordered the evacuation of Americans in Rwanda into neighboring Burundi, and U.S. troops were dispatched to provide protection to the evacuees, if necessary. Beyond that, however, the administration tended to view the early stages of the crisis more as a civil war than as a huge humanitarian crisis such as genocide. The administration was not inclined to intervene in a civil war in Africa because of events that had occurred in Somalia in October 1993. At that time, the United States had participated in a United Nations mission in Somalia to provide famine assistance in the wake of devastation arising from feuding among warlords. However, in October 1993, American soldiers were attacked and many were killed. The corpses of some of those soldiers were dragged through the streets of Mogadishu by an angry mob. This episode led to the withdrawal of U.S. forces from Somalia, and a rethinking on the part of the Clinton administration of the conditions under which U.S. forces would be used abroad in support of United Nations actions.

The new US policy, which clearly implied a reduced U.S. participation in UN peacekeeping activities, had a decisive impact on the question of intervening to stop the Rwandan genocide. At the time the genocide began, the United Nations had a small force in Rwanda (the United Nations Assistance Mission in Rwanda, or UNAMIR), which had been sent in to support the implementation of the Arusha Accords of August 1993. The accords had been adopted at the conclusion of negotiations that were held in Arusha, Tanzania, to try to resolve growing tensions between Hutus and Tutsis in Rwanda. Among other things, the accords called for the establishment of a transitional government including representatives of both Hutus and Tutsis. However, the small UNAMIR force was inadequate to halt the growing violence in Rwanda. When UN Secretary-General Boutros Boutros-Ghali urged the drastic expansion of the force, the United States objected and, instead, demanded that the force be withdrawn. Still remembering

the events of Somalia, the United States was prepared to support humanitarian assistance, which became especially important when hundreds of thousands of refugees, Hutus as well as Tutsis, began to flow into neighboring countries, where the genocide continued, but opposed the use of force. Even after the United Nations agreed to expand the size and mandate of UNAMIR in May 1994, the United States quibbled over which countries should provide military personnel, and disputed the kind and quantity of equipment that would be needed. Officials could not even agree on measures short of military force, such as destroying the Hutu-controlled radio and television services, or jamming broadcasts that exhorted Hutu to exterminate Tutsi. The administration even refused to use the word "genocide" to describe the events going on in Rwanda.

Like the Bosnian genocide, the Rwandan genocide led to demands for justice in the wake of the disaster. Here the United States has played a significant role. In November 1994, it supported a UN Security Council resolution to create an international criminal court to try persons accused of committing crimes in Rwanda and in neighboring states. Specifically, the mandate of the International Criminal Tribunal for Rwanda is to try persons accused of committing genocide and other violations of international humanitarian law in the territory of Rwanda between January 1, 1994, and December 31, 1994. It may also try Rwandan citizens for committing genocide or other violations of international human law during the same time period in the territory of neighboring states, which means that the tribunal can exercise jurisdiction over crimes committed in the refugee camps that had been established in neighboring countries as Rwandans fled their own country.

SEE ALSO African Crisis Response Initiative; Armenians in Ottoman Turkey and the Armenian Genocide; Bangladesh/East Pakistan; Cambodia; East Timor; El Salvador; Genocide; Guatemala; Hiroshima; Holocaust; Indonesia; Iran; Iraq; Jackson, Robert; Khmer Rouge; Kosovo; Kurds; Lemkin, Raphael; Morgenthau, Henry; Pinochet, Augusto; Pol Pot; Proxmire, William; Refugees; Rwanda; Somalia, Intervention in; Tibet; United Nations Security Council; Yugoslavia

BIBLIOGRAPHY

Barron, John, and Anthony Paul (1977). *Murder of a Gentle Land: The Untold Story of Communist Genocide in Cambodia.* New York: Reader's Digest Press.

Des Forges, Alison. (1999). *Leave None to Tell the Story: Genocide in Rwanda.* New York: Human Rights Watch.

Etcheson, Craig (1984). *The Rise and Demise of Democratic Kampuchea.* Boulder, Colo.: Westview Press.

Holbrooke, Richard (1998). *To End a War*. New York: Random House.

Kiernan, Ben (1996). *The Pol Pot Regime: Race, Power, and Genocide in Cambodia under the Khmer Rouge, 1975–79.* New Haven, Conn.: Yale University Press.

Kuper, Leo (1977). *The Pity of it All: Polarization of Racial and Ethnic Relations.* Minneapolis: University of Minnesota Press.

Kuper, Leo (1985). *The Prevention of Genocide*. New Haven, Conn.: Yale University Press.

LeBlanc, Lawrence (1991). *The United States and the Genocide Convention.* Durham, N.C.: Duke University Press.

Lemkin, Raphael (1944). *Axis Rule in Occupied Europe*. Washington, D.C.: Carnegie Endowment for International Peace.

Ponchaud, Francois (1978). *Cambodia: Year Zero*. New York: Holt, Reinhart and Winston.

Power, Samantha (2002). *A Problem from Hell: America and the Age of Genocide.* London: Harper Collins Publishers.

Riemer, Neal, ed. (2000). *Protection against Genocide*. Westport, Conn.: Praeger Publishers.

Robinson, Nehemiah (1960). *The Genocide Convention: A Commentary.* New York: The American Jewish Committee.

Ronayne, Peter (2001). *Never Again? The United States and the Prevention and Punishment of Genocide since the Holocaust.* New York: Rowman and Littlefield.

Shawcross, William (1979). *Sideshow: Kissinger, Nixon, and the Destruction of Cambodia.* New York: Simon and Schuster.

Zimmerman, Warren (1996). *Origins of a Catastrophe: Yugoslavia and Its Destroyers.* New York: Times Books.
Lawrence J. LeBlanc

Universal Jurisdiction

Like every concept, *jurisdiction* may have different meanings. The word comes from Latin roots: *jus* or *juris* means "law," and *dicere* means "to say" or "to read." Therefore, "jurisdiction" can be understood to mean; "to say the law" and, as a derivative, "the power to say the law." Presently, jurisdiction is understood as the legislative, adjudicative, and executive power that provides, respectively, the competence to prescribe, adjudicate, or execute the law. In particular, it refers to the territorial competence of courts. Jurisdiction in criminal matters may be considered either as substantial or procedural law.

Prescriptive jurisdiction basically depends upon the enactment of laws by individual states, or by the state's adoption of international conventions. In the case of genocide, most states have become parties to the 1948 Genocide Convention, and the majority of states

have incorporated the convention into their internal legal order. No international convention yet exists on crimes against humanity, except for where they may be found within the conventions that create international criminal tribunals. Executive power, in criminal law, is one of the forces (such as the police) that is permitted to intervene to enforce a search or arrest warrant. In principle, no state is allowed to exercise executive power on the territory in other states. The courts within a particular state exercise adjudicative jurisdiction, which is the authority to render a decision on a case.

Adjudicative Jurisdiction

Adjudicative jurisdiction can be discussed on a material, personal or territorial level. With genocide, the material jurisdiction is given by the crime itself, which has been largely uniformly understood and defined worldwide since the 1948 Genocide Convention. On the personal level, there is an onus in criminal law that every natural person over a certain age can be prosecuted for a crime, which is committed within the boundaries of a state's borders. For personal jurisdiction, therefore, it is more a question of defining the exceptions than of defining the rule. For instance, there are exceptions for some persons under a certain age; persons eligible for or having been granted immunities; or persons of a certain status, such as military persons serving duty in foreign states, when the state they serve has signed specific conventions with the state in which they committed the act.

The most controversial question debated in recent years is the extent the courts of a particular state can adjudicate crimes which have been committed outside the territory of that state. In criminal law there are different means of jurisdiction over an accused; but the means are not recognized equally by all states. The most easily recognizable and applicable basis of jurisdiction is the *territorial principle*, whereby persons may be tried and punished for crimes committed on the territory of the state that seeks to prosecute them. Further, persons may be prosecuted by their state of nationality for a crime no matter on which territory they commit it. This is called the *active personality principle*. In the first means of claiming jurisdiction, the primary interest of a state is to maintain law and order in its territory, which is the most basic duty and prerogative of states. In the second case, states may be interested in maintaining a certain level of morality among their citizens, even when those citizens act abroad. More controversial is the right for states to adjudicate crimes that have been committed abroad by foreigners but against their own citizens. This is the *passive personality principle*. Normally, it should be in fact the duty of the state where the crime has been committed, or even the state of the nationality of the author of the crime, to prosecute the person who has committed the crime. Yet, most states still maintain the prerogative to exercise the passive personality principle, if only to avoid a denial of justice if the territorial or the national states do not proceed against the author of the crime.

Universal Jurisdiction

One even more controversial issue is whether states are allowed to judge foreign persons who have committed crimes abroad against other foreigners. In this case, the state doing the judging has no connecting link with the persons or the crimes, except for the fact that the suspects are possibly present on their territory. This principle is usually known as the *universality principle,* or as *universal jurisdiction.*

One view is that this principle is recognized when states expressly or tacitly allow other states to proceed against their own citizens, or permit another state to prosecute individuals for crimes that have been committed on their own territory. In such cases, jurisdiction may be transferred to another state through ad hoc agreements, bilateral treaties, or through multilateral treaties. Customary law may also allow the application of this principle, as is historically the case with piracy. Universal jurisdiction, therefore, is not new. During the Middle Ages, it was primarily applied by small states in Europe when they were fighting gangs of international thieves.

Among the many multilateral treaties which allow adjudicative jurisdiction to be delegated in such a way, are those intended to fight transnational criminality such as terrorism, narcotics, or in certain fields of international humanitarian law and human rights (torture, for example). Indeed, states consider that serious transnational crimes and criminals can only be dealt with by promoting transnational accountability and mutual assistance in criminal matters, including allowing all the states party to certain treaties to prosecute the criminals where they can catch them.

Of course, this kind of jurisdiction implies that states agree on the definition of the crimes that can be prosecuted, and that they trust each other's respective legal systems. At the very least, the states must agree that the possible evil of the prosecution by dubious foreign judicial systems is matched by the necessity to severely repress certain crimes and criminals. It is a matter of weighing the need for crime control against a possible lack of procedural guarantees.

One other view, more naturalist, and which believes in the existence of a legislative power above the individual states, is that universal jurisdiction applies to crimes that affect the international community and are against international law, and are therefore crimes against mankind. Those who commit such crimes are considered to be enemies of the whole human family (*hostes humani generic*), and should be prosecuted wherever they are. In this view, the international community as a whole delegates to individual states the task of judging certain crimes and some criminals of common concern.

The *Lotus* Case, 1927

The ambit (sphere) of the jurisdiction of states in criminal law has been dealt with by numerous specific international treaties, yet no general treaty provides for a comprehensive solution of the jurisdiction of states in criminal cases. The most comprehensive and authoritative opinion to date was issued by the Permanent International Court of Justice in the *Lotus* Case of 1927.

In this case, the court had to deal with a case of collision between two ships, one French (*Lotus*) and one Turkish (*Boz-Kourt*), in the Mediterranean high seas, which caused loss of life among the Turkish sailors. On the arrival of the *Lotus* in Constantinople, the French lieutenant and officer on the bridge at the time of the collision was arrested and prosecuted by the Turkish authorities on a charge of homicide by negligence. The Turks invoked Article 6 of the Turkish Penal Code, which gave the Turkish courts jurisdiction, on the request of the injured parties, to prosecute foreigners accused of having committed crimes against Turkish nationals. The French government protested against the arrest, and the two states agreed to consult the Permanent Court of International Justice to determine whether Turkey had acted in conflict with the principles of international law by asserting criminal jurisdiction over the French officer. France alleged that Turkey had to find support in international law before asserting its extraterritorial jurisdiction, whereas Turkey alleged that it had jurisdiction unless it was forbidden by international law.

In its judgment, the court decided with the thinnest majority that Turkey had not infringed international law. It ruled, instead, that France had not proven its claim that international law provided a restriction of adjudicative jurisdiction. As president of the court Max Huber clearly stated: "restrictions upon the independence of States cannot be presumed." Where international law does not provide otherwise, states are free to adjudicate cases as long as their executive power is not exercised outside its territory:

> far from laying down a general prohibition to the effect that States may not extend the application of their laws and the jurisdiction of their courts to persons, property, and acts outside their terri-

tory, it leaves them in this respect a wide measure of discretion which is only limited in certain cases by prohibitive rules; as regards other cases, every State remains free to adopt the principles which it regards as best and most suitable.

According to this case, states would be free to adjudicate cases of genocide committed abroad, even by foreigners against foreigners, as long as third-party states cannot prove that this extraterritorial jurisdiction is prohibited. The burden of proof that a state acts in contradiction to international law, at least as far as its jurisdiction is concerned, lies on the plaintiff state. Both treaties and the development of customary law (as evidence of a general practice accepted as law) are, of course, the best sources from which to discover whether individual states use a recognized principle of jurisdiction or if they trespass the limits and interfere with other states' internal and domestic affairs.

The Nuremberg Statute and the Post–WWII Prosecutions

The Nuremberg Statute of 1945, provided the first express prohibition of crimes against humanity. The term genocide has also been used in several indictments by national courts that have judged Nazis after the end of the war.

Yet, the Nuremberg Statute was only applicable to the crimes committed by the Nazis and their allies, although those crimes may have been committed on non-German territory. In addition, it has been argued that the jurisdiction of the Allies to judge the Nazis for the core crimes of aggression, war crimes, and crimes against humanity either stemmed from Germany's surrender to the Allies, and therefore from the jurisdiction of Germany itself to judge its own nationals, or was derived from the fact of Germany's occupation.

The 1948 Genocide Convention

The clearest ambit of the adjudicative jurisdiction of states for crimes of genocide is provided by Article 6 of the 1948 Genocide Convention, which states that:

> Persons charged with genocide or any of the other acts enumerated in article III shall be tried by a competent tribunal of the State in the territory of which the act was committed, or by such international penal tribunal as may have jurisdiction with respect to those Contracting Parties which shall have accepted jurisdiction.

The question to be raised is whether states that are parties to this convention allow themselves to prosecute persons who have committed or participated to a genocide in a third country, whether or not such persons are nationals of the state that wants to prosecute

them. The text of Article 6 does not say whether the term "shall be tried," provides for compulsory territorial jurisdiction or whether a state may, on the basis of customary international law, bring someone accused of genocide before its own courts on the basis of either extraterritorial jurisdiction or universal jurisdiction.

As a matter of fact, the preparatory work of the treaty shows that the authors of the working draft clearly contemplated universal jurisdiction. Yet, an historical analysis of the Convention leads to the conclusion that most states, at the start of the cold war, clearly wanted to avoid such a broad interpretation. The Soviet representative at the conference, for instance, stated "no exception should be made in the case of genocide to the principle of the territorial jurisdiction of states, which alone was compatible with the principle of national sovereignty." According to the Egyptian representative, "it would be very dangerous if statesmen could be tried by the courts of countries with a political ideology different from that of their own country." This opinion was also shared by the American representative, who thought that prosecution for crimes committed outside the territory of a state could only be allowed with the consent of the territorial state. The representatives of some countries, including Burma, Algeria, and Morocco, even made formal declarations according to which no crime of genocide committed on their territory could be judged by state courts other than their own.

The jurisdiction of an international penal tribunal was agreed upon as a compromise between the states that wanted to limit jurisdiction to the territorial principle and those that wanted to broaden its meaning.

The preparatory work of a treaty merely provides a "supplementary means of interpretation," to be used only when ordinary interpretation leaves the meaning ambiguous or obscure, or leads to a result that is manifestly absurd or unreasonable. Besides, the 1948 Genocide Convention is more than fifty years old and the jurisdiction of states to prosecute crimes of genocide must be reviewed according to the evolution undergone by customary law in the time since it was first written. Indeed, the very restrictive approach of Article VI has been criticized by some authorities, who sometimes base their opinion on the specific nature of the crime considered. This can be seen in the work of the International Law Commission (2000); the American Law Institute, in its *Restatement of the Foreign Relations Law of the United States* (1987); and the International Court of Justice (ICJ), in the *Genocide* case (1993). It is similarly apparent in the opinions handed down by individual judges in the *Arrest Warrant* case (2002) as well as in the work of the International Criminal Tribunal of Former Yugoslavia (ICTY), for example in the

Tadic case (1995). This view is also shared by a considerable number of academics and authors, who propose that the crime of genocide, or even crimes against humanity, should be prosecuted on the basis of universal jurisdiction.

For these authorities and authors, Article VI of the 1948 Genocide Convention, by obliging states to prosecute crimes of genocide committed on their territory, does not prevent states from prosecuting them if they are committed in third countries. They also generally insist on the fact that genocide is a crime of concern not only for individual states but for the international community as a whole.

International law is created by states, however, and not by "authorities" or by doctrine. It is therefore necessary to verify whether the evolution of the practice of the states and their *opinio juris* expressed since 1948 can match the evolution of the doctrine. As a matter of fact, it is hard to find many cases of prosecutions for acts of genocide outside the territorial state where the acts have been committed.

The Eichmann and Demjanjuk Cases in Israel
In 1961 Adolf Eichmann was abducted in Argentina by Israeli agents and taken to Israel, where he was prosecuted and condemned for his participation in the genocide committed by the Nazis. Argentina strongly protested the abduction, although its opposition to the judgment itself was less vocal. In any case, the German authorities clearly agreed that Eichmann, a German citizen having committed crimes in Germany, should be prosecuted by Israel. The German authorities probably did not feel that they were acting in accordance with customary law. It is likely, instead, that they approved Eichmann's prosecution in Israel for political reasons and because they did not want to hamper the repression of Nazis.

On the other hand, the Israeli courts did not rely on Germany to assert their competence to judge Eichmann. Instead, they acted on two different grounds. The first was an invocation of the passive personality principle, whereby the state of Israel asserted its legitimacy to judge acts that had been committed against Jews even before the state of Israel existed. The second ground underlying the Israeli courts' claim of jurisdiction was a reference to a mix of international morality and law:

> [T]hese crimes constitute acts which damage vital interests; they impair the foundations and security of the international community; they violate the universal moral values and humanitarian principles that lie hidden in the criminal law systems adopted by civilised nations. The under-

lying principle in international law regarding such crimes is that the individual who has committed any of them and who, when doing so, may be presumed to have fully comprehended the heinous nature of his act, must account for his conduct

The reasoning of the Israeli court was that a crime can be defined by the "international community", and that states are empowered to serve as "executive agents" of that international community, as long as the instruments under international law are not enacted and in force.

What is interesting about the Eichmann case is not the declarations of the Israeli courts, but the fact that most other states did not react negatively against the application of universal jurisdiction by Israel for its prosecution of a case of genocide. Even Argentina, which did protest harshly against the abduction of Eichmann from its territory, did not go so far as to lodge a formal complaint against the judgment of the Israeli courts.

Another case concerning the Nazi genocide occurred in 1986, when a U.S. court agreed to extradite John Demjanjuk, alleged to have been a camp warden in Treblinka. By agreeing to the extradition, the United States recognized the jurisdiction of Israeli courts to judge Demjanjuk, who had become a naturalized U.S. citizen after the end of World War II. Demjanjuk was tried in Israel and acquitted on the merits of the case. However, neither the Eichmann case nor the Demjanjuk case can be considered as setting a precedent for other states.

Other Relevant Examples
The jurisdiction of states to judge acts of genocide that have been committed in other states has been considered in various cases arising out of the genocide in Rwanda, which occurred in 1994. Overall, however, the invocation of universal jurisdiction has been rather heterogeneous and ambiguous.

In 1994, for instance, Austria put the former commander of a Serbian military unit, Dusko Cvjetkovic, on trial for acts of genocide committed in the former Yugoslavia. The defense protested that Austria did not have jurisdiction, but the Appeals Court justified the Austrian court's right to conduct the trial in the following terms:

> Article VI of the Genocide Convention, which provides that persons charged with genocide or any of the acts enumerated in Article III shall be tried by a competent tribunal of the State where the act was committed, or by such international penal tribunal as may have jurisdiction with re-

spect to those Contracting Parties which shall have accepted its jurisdiction, is based on the fundamental assumption that there is a functioning criminal justice system in the locus delicti (which would make the extradition of a suspect legally possible). Otherwise—since at the time of the adoption of the Genocide Convention there was no international criminal court—the outcome would be diametrically opposed to the intention of its drafters, and a person suspected of genocide or any of the acts enumerated in Article III could not be prosecuted because the criminal justice in the locus delicti is not functioning and the international criminal court is not in place (or its jurisdiction has not been accepted by the State concerned) (Reydams, 2003).

Cvjetkovic was tried in Austria, and a jury acquitted him of all charges.

In 1996 in France, the Appeal Court of Nîmes expressly rejected the French assertion of jurisdiction in the case Wanceslas Munyeshyaka, stating that Article VI of the Genocide Convention did not allow the application of universal jurisdiction for cases of genocide. This judgement was overruled by the French Supreme Court, but only on the very technical ground that alternative justifications for claiming jurisdiction were available: France could invoke either the Torture Convention of 1984, or it could base its jurisdictional claim on a specific law, based on UN Security Resolution 955, which had been adopted in France in response to the genocide in Rwanda.

In Switzerland, Fulgence Niyonteze, former mayor of Mushubati, Rwanda, was tried in 1997 by the military courts for his participation in the genocide. Although the prosecutor had indicted Niyonteze for murder, grave breaches of international humanitarian law, genocide, and crimes against humanity, the Swiss court refused to judge him for genocide or for crimes against humanity because Switzerland was not, at the time of the trial, a signatory to the 1948 Genocide Convention and had incorporated no provision for genocide or crimes against humanity in its domestic laws. The court did, however, convict Niyonteze for murder, incitement to murder, and grave breaches of the Geneva Conventions arising from his participation in the internal conflict of Rwanda.

The Military Court of Appeal dismissed the judgement of the Swiss court on indictment of murder and incitement to murder, retaining only the conviction regarding grave breaches of the Geneva Conventions. Unlike the Genocide Convention, the Geneva Conventions expressly provide for the possibility to judge a person on the basis of universal jurisdiction.

In 1998 a German court sentenced a Serb named Nikola Jorgic to life imprisonment for acts of genocide, basing its claim to jurisdiction on the German Criminal Code, which provided for universal jurisdiction in cases of genocide. Interestingly, the Higher Court expressly mentioned "the generally accepted non-exclusive interpretation of Article VI of the 1948 Genocide Convention" to assert that there is no prohibition of universal jurisdiction under international law regarding the prosecution of acts of genocide. The Federal Supreme Court confirmed that a hypothetical norm forbidding the application of universal jurisdiction would be contrary to the rule prohibiting genocide, which is a peremptory (*jus cogens*) norm. In a later case, Maksim Sokolovic (1999), the Federal Supreme Court even dropped the requirement that a special link exist between the accused person and Germany in order to prosecute him for genocide on the basis of universal jurisdiction.

In 2001 four Rwandese were prosecuted in Belgium for having participated in the Rwandan genocide in the Butare province. However, Belgium applied universal jurisdiction in order to judge them for war crimes only. They were not charged with crimes against humanity or genocide, apparently because universal jurisdiction for these crimes had only recently (in 1999) been added to the 1993 Act Concerning the Punishment of Grave Breaches of International Humanitarian Law, 1993. In this case, as in the French and Swiss trials, the Republic of Rwanda never challenged the assertion of universal jurisdiction.

In fact, in many cases where universal jurisdiction has been used to judge suspects of the genocide in Rwanda, the prosecuting states have either indicted and sentenced the accused on the basis of national provisions of humanitarian law, or they have enacted a special law on the implementation of the status of the International Criminal Tribunal for Rwanda. Indeed, the states that applied universal jurisdiction for acts of genocide committed in Rwanda were encouraged to do so by the international community, and especially by the UN Security Council. Therefore, it is difficult to draw definitive conclusions on the general acceptance by states of the universal jurisdiction for the crime of genocide.

Legislative Practice of States

Some states have implemented legislation that allows the prosecution of crimes of genocide and crimes against humanity according to universal jurisdiction. For example, Australia, Belgium, Canada, Germany, The Netherlands, Spain and, to some extent, Argentina, Ethiopia, and Venezuela allow for judging these crimes even if they have been committed abroad. Switzerland, which only became a party to the Genocide Convention in 2000, expressly enacted a law providing for universal jurisdiction for the crime of genocide by including the following passage in the Message of the Council of Ministers:

> with the view of the "jus cogens aspect" of the prohibition of genocide as well as of its effects "erga omnes," there is no doubt that the prosecution of the crime of genocide must be based, in international law, on universal jurisdiction. Therefore, States may—and even must—prosecute or extradite foreign nationals or their own nationals who are suspect of having committed an act of genocide, even if the act has not been committed on their territory. This does not constitute a violation of the principle of non-intervention in other States' internal affairs.

Unfortunately, there has been no instance in which, at the time of becoming party to the Genocide Convention, a state has made a formal declaration on the question of the extent of jurisdiction as provided for by Article VI. The reaction of the international community to such an interpretation would provide good evidence of the state of customary law on this matter.

In all the cases where states adopted universal jurisdiction into their own legislation, customary law was consolidated. The states also put themselves in a situation where they cannot deny other states the right to prosecute one of their nationals for crimes of genocide. On the other hand, the huge majority of states seem neither to have implemented the Genocide Convention into their own legal system, nor to have extended their own jurisdiction for genocide to universality. Most recently, some states have shown a strong opposition against extraterritorial jurisdiction and against states that allow themselves, by law, to exercise such jurisdiction. Others became aware of the excesses universal jurisdiction could trigger and so downplayed its importance. The Belgian legislation on universal jurisdiction and its application by investigating judges and courts was notably the focal point of heated debate in doctrinal and political circles.

Universal Jurisdiction and the International Criminal Court

These developments, which may give the appearance that customary law could have evolved towards a more permissive jurisdiction, at least as far as a crime of genocide is concerned, have to be reconsidered since the Rome Statute of the International Criminal Court (ICC) was adopted in 1999.

The Rome Statute provides for the jurisdiction of the ICC for crimes of genocide and for crimes against humanity, with the definition of genocide being the same as under the 1948 Genocide Convention. Therefore, it is argued, states that are party to both the Genocide Convention and the Rome Statute wished to favor either the territorial or the active personality principle on the one hand, or the jurisdiction of the ICC on the other. With the emergence of the ICC, the first justification of the exercise of universal jurisdiction by a state—the Israeli explanation that the competence of its own courts derived from the fact that there was no international court allowed at that time to prosecute international crimes, in particular genocide—would now be invalidated.

Yet, the ICC only has jurisdiction when a crime has been committed on the territory of a state party to the Rome Statute or by a national of a state party to the Statute. Therefore, it is argued that universal jurisdiction could still be applied by states that are parties to both the 1948 Genocide Convention and to the Rome Statute when the crime which is prosecuted has been committed on the territory of states—and by a national of states—which are not parties to the Rome statute.

Cases Heard before the International Court of Justice

The question of the admissible extension of a state's criminal jurisdiction could have been laid to rest by the International Court of Justice (ICJ) in the case of the Arrest Warrant of April 11, 2000, issued by the Democratic Republic of Congo (DRC) against Belgium. In this case, an investigating judge of Belgium issued an arrest warrant for grave breaches of international humanitarian law against the Minister of Foreign Affairs for DRC President Laurent Desire Kabila. Belgium had no connecting point with the case, except that the plaintiffs were residing in Belgium. The DRC had two main points of contention about the arrest warrant. The first was that Belgium had applied extraterritorial jurisdiction to events that had taken place in the DRC, and therefore had violated its territorial authority and the principle of sovereign equality among all members of the United Nations. The other was that Belgium had violated customary law regarding the diplomatic immunity of Ministers of Foreign Affairs while still holding office.

Unfortunately for the sake of international law, Congo later abandoned its claim that the *in absentia* proceedings against its minister was an exorbitant exercise of Belgium's jurisdiction. Moreover, the court could save its reasoning on universal jurisdiction because it found, by thirteen votes to three, that Congo was right to complain on the basis of the sovereign immunity argument.

In another case, the Republic of the Congo filed an application on December 2002 to the ICJ, instituting proceedings against France. The application sought to annul the investigations and prosecution measures taken by a French investigating judge following a complaint concerning crimes against humanity and torture allegedly committed in the Congo by Congolese officials against individuals of Congolese nationality. Among the individuals targeted by the French measures were the President of the Republic of the Congo, the Congolese Minister of the Interior, and some generals, including the Inspector-General of the Congolese Armed Forces and the Commander of the Presidential Guard. France is a party to the 1984 Torture Convention, and it has implemented a provision in its Criminal Procedure Code expressly allowing for universal jurisdiction in its courts in cases of torture. Congo, however, is not a party to the Torture Convention. It therefore considers that the issuing of the arrest warrant against Congolese authorities is a violation of its sovereignty. In its complaint, the Congo complained that

> by attributing itself universal jurisdiction in criminal matters and by arrogating to itself the power to prosecute and try the Minister of the Interior of a foreign State for crimes allegedly committed by him in connection with the exercise of his powers for the maintenance of public order in his country [France violated] the principle that a State may not, in breach of the principle of sovereign equality among all Members of the United Nations (. . .) exercise its authority on the territory of another State.

In this case, the question of immunity could allow the court to avoid rendering a judgment on the merits of universal jurisdiction, at least as far as the Congolese president and minister of the interior are concerned. It would be difficult, however, to see how the court could avoid making a decision on universal jurisdiction in the case of the generals, who most probably do not qualify for any claim of immunity. Therefore, the question to be decided by the court is whether states are allowed to prosecute a person on the basis of universal jurisdiction when the territorial state or the state of the nationality of the author of the alleged crime is not a party to a convention that provides for universal jurisdiction.

Some Practical Considerations

Even if the ICJ allows France to prosecute actors of crimes against humanity on the basis of universal jurisdiction in the *Congo v. France* case, it is unlikely that national courts will rush to judge cases committed abroad by foreigners against foreigners. Indeed, many obstacles still remain.

One of the most obvious obstacles is the difficulty for states to allocate important human and financial resources to investigate cases, to prosecute, judge, and possibly imprison persons who perhaps disturbed the morale and security of the community of nations, but who did not specifically endanger the public order of the State where the arrest was carried out. For this reason, states more likely will be tempted to deny the entrance onto their territory of persons suspected of having committed acts of genocide, or, if such persons are found on their territory, to extradite them rather than to judge them.

It is also very difficult for states to judge cases of genocide or crimes against humanity committed outside their borders. Such states could face grave political problems. In addition, the difficulty of gathering evidence would force the prosecuting state to rely on assistance from the territorial States, which are not likely to provide assistance if they deny the jurisdiction of the prosecuting state. Finally, cultural and linguistic differences between the state of judgment and the persons to be judged present further obstacles. With all these elements in mind, it would appear to be highly preferable that each state be encouraged to judge the acts of genocide or crimes against humanity, which have been committed on its territory. This could be encouraged through assistance from the international community, or by allowing the International Criminal Court to judge such cases.

SEE ALSO Eichmann Trials; Extradition; Immunity; National Prosecutions; Pinochet, Augusto; War Crimes

BIBLIOGRAPHY

Bassiouni, M. Cherif (2001). "Universal Jurisdiction for International Crimes: Historical Perspectives and Contemporary Practice." *Virginia Journal of International Law* 42:1–100.

Benavides, Luis (2001). "The Universal Jurisdiction Principle: Nature and Scope." *Anuario Mexicano de Derecho Internacional* 1:19–96.

Cassese, Antonio and Myriam Delmas-Marty, eds, (2002). *Juridictions nationales et crimes internationaux.* Paris: Presse Universitaire de France.

Guillaume, Gilbert (2003). "La compétence universelle: du code de Justinien à l'affaire Yerodia." In *La Cour internationale de justice à l'aube du XXIe siècle. Le regard d'un juge,* ed. Gilbert Guillaume. Paris: Pedone.

Henzelin, Marc (2000). *Le Principe de l'universalité en droit pénal international.* Bruxelles: Bruylant.

Henzelin, Marc (2002). "La compétence pénale universelle: une question non résolue par l'arrêt Yerodia." *Revue Générale de Droit International Public* 106:819–854.

Macedo, Steve, ed. (2004). *Universal Jurisdiction.* Philadelphia: University of Pennsylvania Press.

Randall, Kenneth (1988). "Universal Jurisdiction under International Law." *Texas Law Review* 66:785–841.

Reydams. Luc. (2003). "Belgium's First Application of Universal Jurisdiction: the Butare Four Case." *Journal of International Criminal Justice* 1:428–436.

Reydams, Luc. (2003). *Universal Jurisdiction.* Oxford, U.K.: Oxford University Press.

Sassoli, Marco (2002). "Le génocide rwandais, la justice militaire suisse et le droit international." *Revue Suisse de Droit International & Européen* 12:151–178.

Schabas, William (2003). "National Courts Finally Begin to Prosecute Genocide, the Crime of Crimes." *Journal of International Criminal Justice* 1:39–63.

Stern, Brigitte (2003). "Le génocide rwandais face aux autorités françaises." In *La répression internationale du génocide rwandais,* ed. Laurence Burgorgue-Larsen. Bruxelles: Bruylant.

CASE LAW

Arrest Warrant of 11 April 2000 (*Democratic Republic of the Congo v. Belgium*), Judgment, 15 February 2002; reprinted in *International Legal Materials* 41(2003):536.

Application of the Convention on the Prevention and Punishment of the Crime of Genocide (*Bosnia and Herzegovina v. Yugoslavia (Serbia and Montenegro)*, Order on Further Requests for the Indication of Provisional Measures, 13 September 1993, (1993) International Court of Justice Reports: 325; reprinted in *International Legal Materials* 32 (1993):1601–1613.

Lotus (France vs. Turkey), 1927 Permanent Court of International Justice Reports, series A, no. 10, p. 4.

Prosecutor v. Tadic (Case No. IT-94-1-AR72), Decision on the Defence Motion for Interlocutory Appeal on Jurisdiction, 2 October 1995, reprinted in *International Legal Materials* 35(1996):35–73.

Marc Henzelin

Utilitarian Genocide

The pioneer genocide scholar Vahakn Dadrian introduced the concept of "utilitarian genocide" in a landmark 1975 article, "A Typology of Genocide." He identified five "ideal types" of genocide, based mainly on the primary objective of the perpetrator:

- cultural genocide, aiming at assimilation;
- latent genocide, a by-product of war;
- retributive genocide, localized punishment;
- utilitarian genocide, to obtain wealth;
- optimal genocide, aiming at total obliteration;

As examples of utilitarian genocides, Dadrian cited the atrocities committed against Moors and Jews in the course of dispossesing them of businesses during the Spanish Inquisition, the forced removal and "decimation" of the Cherokees in the U.S. southern state of Georgia in 1829, and the ongoing enslavement and killing of Indians in Brazil.

Even though some contemporary scholars use expressions such as "economically motivated" or "devel-opmental genocide" instead of the actual term *utilitarian genocide,* there is broad agreement that (1) these terms basically cover systematic persecution and mass killings in order to obtain and/or monopolize access to land and to resources like gold or lumber; (2) generally, this type of genocide has been committed by European settlers or their descendants, with direct or indirect state authorization, against indigenous peoples in the Americas, Africa, and Australia; and (3), utilitarian motives are often mixed with or bolstered by racism and dehumanizing images.

Most scholars also agree that the destruction of indigenous peoples still continues, especially in Latin America. A case in point is the nearly total extermination of the Aché (Guayaki) Indians in Paraguay during the 1970s.

The subsequent scholars who have adopted either the term *utilitarian genocide* or its basic propositions include Irving Louis Horowitz, who in 1976 noted that "the conduct of classic colonialism was invariably linked with genocide" (pp. 19B20). Helen Fein, in 1984 used the synonym *developmental genocide,* that is, "instrumental acts to rid of peoples outside their [the colonizer's] universe of obligations who stood in the way of economic exploitation" (p. 5), and in 1987, Roger Smith observed that "the basic proposition contained in utilitarian genocide is that some persons must die so that others may live" (p. 25). In 1990 Frank Chalk and Kurt Jonassohn included genocide "to acquire economic wealth" in their typology of four types of genocide based on the primary motive of the perpetrator.

Even though the term *utilitarian genocide* is relatively new, it has long been acknowledged that utilitarian motives have played an important part in the destruction of groups, particularly in the New World. In his classic account of Spanish policy towards the Native population of the Americas, *The Tears of the Indians,* Dominican cleric Bartolomé de Las Casas wrote about two stages of *extirpation*: "the first whereof was a bloody, unjust, and cruel war they made upon them, a second by cutting off all that so much as sought to recover their liberty, as some of the stouter sort did intend. . . . That which led the Spaniards to these unsanctified impieties was the desire of Gold" (pp. 3B4).

SEE ALSO Amazon Region; Genocide; Indigenous Peoples

BIBLIOGRAPHY

Chalk, F. and K. Jonassohn (1995). *The History and Sociology of Genocide.* New Haven, Conn.: Yale University Press.

Dadrian, Vahakn (1975). "A Typology of Genocide." *International Review of Modern Sociology* 5:201B212.

de Las Casas, Bartolomé (1972). *Tears of the Indian.* New York: Oriole Chapbooks.

Fein, Helen (1984). "Scenarios of Genocide: Models of Genocide and Critical Responses." In *Toward the Understanding and Prevention of Genocide,* ed. I. W. Charny. Boulder, Colo.: Westview Press.

Horowitz, Irving Louis (1976). *Genocide, State Power and Mass Murder.* New Brunswick, N.J.: Transaction Books.

Smith, Roger (1987). "Human Destructiveness and Politics: The Twentieth Century as an Age of Genocide." In *Genocide and the Modern Age,* ed. I Wallimann and M. Dobkowski. New York: Greenwood Press.

Eric Markusen
Matthias Bjørnlund

Utopian Ideologies as Motives for Genocide

Genocides have existed for as long as humans have recorded history. There are instances of the intentional destruction of an entire group of people in the Hebrew Bible, and the Romans destroyed Carthage in a manner that sought to make impossible the continued existence of Carthiginians. In the Middle Ages the papacy launched a crusade designed to annihilate physically every follower of the Albigensian heresy. Since the late fifteenth century instances of colonial genocides—in the Caribbean, North America, Australasia—have been entwined with the history of European expansion around the globe.

Some of these acts certainly had an ideological dimension. When the Israelites conquered Canaan and "devoted to destruction by the edge of the sword all in the city, both men and women, young and old" (Joshua 6:21–24), they were, in the Bible's recounting, inspired by God and his promises to them as his chosen people. The medieval church also believed it was acting in God's name and for the cause of Christianity when it stamped out heresies. But more typically, other genocides were acts of revenge and retribution in war, as with the Roman conquest of Carthage, or simply efforts to obtain land and wealth. In the colonial period Europeans conducted brutal attacks on people considered inferior, but the motivation was generally control over resources. In these actions little evidence of a fully articulated political ideology existed.

In the twentieth century, however, genocides became more systematic, more extensive, and more deadly. They also became far more thoroughly imbued with an ideological character, with the claim, by perpetrators, that the utter destruction of an enemy group would pave the way toward a future of unlimited prosperity, uncontested power, and cultural efflorescence for the dominant group. In short, regimes that practiced genocide promised utopia to their followers.

The word *utopia* generally conjures up images of peace and harmony, of a society marked by well-being and cozy comfort. Thomas More's classic sixteenth-century fable *Utopia* (from which the word derives) conveys this vision, although More may well have been writing in an ironic mode. Many religious communities, such as the Anabaptists and Quakers, have seen themselves as the harbingers of the ultimate utopia, God's kingdom on earth. Nineteenth-century liberals and socialists also imagined a utopian world free of hostile conflict, one in which either the natural workings of the market or the social ownership of property would bring prosperity to all and, in the socialist version, social equality as well. Nationalists such as Guiseppe Mazzini believed that once every group had its own state, individual nations would flourish and create a harmonious community of nations.

Utopian goals of these kinds have never been fulfilled, but their advocates struggled mightily and contributed powerfully to many of the democratic and socially progressive advances of the modern era, from universal suffrage to the abolition of slavery to social welfare programs. However, there has also been an underside to utopianism. Invariably, its advocates have imagined a homogeneous society of one sort or another. In religious versions of utopia everyone would follow one god and one set of beliefs. In liberal utopias every country would operate according to the same market principles, and nationalists and socialists imagined each country possessing the same sort of political institutions.

These utopian visions have constantly come up against the sometimes harsh reality of human difference. For all the advocacy of equality many utopians presumed the inferiority of women. Nineteenth-century advocates of political rights and social equality often reserved these advances for men of property and the white race. The rest of the world, including eastern and southeastern Europeans in the view of some, was presumed to be too backward to excercise their rights responsibly, either because the populations had not yet reached the proper stage of development or were constitutionally inferior, usually by virtue of race, of ever reaching that level.

Utopianism became far more dangerous in the twentieth century because it so often was linked to mass-based social movements that seized power, established revolutionary regimes, and venerated the state as the critical agent of social transformation. By no means were all these states practitioners of the worst kinds of violence against civilian populations. At the same time the most prevalent perpetrators of genocides in the twentieth century were revolutionary regimes of either

Під прапором партії більшовиків, під керівництвом Ленінського ЦК і вождя світового пролетаріату тов. Сталіна—
вперед, до вершин радості і щастя людства

An artist has portrayed a rather idealized tableau of the Soviet Union, with Lenin's portrait in the upper left-hand corner. [THOMAS JOHNSON/SYGMA/CORBIS]

fascist or communist commitments (Nazi Germany, the Stalinist Soviet Union, Cambodia under the Khmer Rouge) or states in the throes of some kind of uneasy revolutionary transformation (the late Ottoman Empire under the Young Turks, the former Yugoslavia under Slobodan Milosevic, Rwanda under the Hutu).

The particular utopias these regimes or states advocated varied significantly. Yet every one of them envisioned a homogeneous society of one sort or another, which necessarily meant the expulsion or extermination of particular groups. Indeed, all these regimes claimed that utopia would be created only through the destruction of one or more enemy groups. The historian Saul Friedländer has coined the powerful term *redemptive anti-Semitism* to describe the Nazi hatred of Jews. According to the Nazis, Aryan life would flourish once Jews had been driven completely from the German realm. Similarly, one can see a kind of redemptive vision at work in the Young Turk attack on Armenians, the Khmer Rouge assault on Muslim Chams and Vietnamese, and the murderous actions of the Hutu against Tutsi. Each of these regimes promised their followers a brilliant future once the enemy was destroyed. The redemptive vision, the annihilation of one group as the decisive means for creating the future, marked the road to utopia.

The regimes defined by explicitly national or racial ideologies were most open about the enemy status of the "other." In a Nazi-dominated Europe so-called Aryans would stand astride a continent cleansed of Jews, while Slavs would be reduced to subordinate status. In the Greater Serbia envisioned by Slobodan Milosevic and his supporters, there could be no place whatsoever for Muslims and Croats. Even under some communist regimes, the differences among people would be reduced to mere exotica, whereas the fundamental institutions and life forms would be the same. Those who refused to follow the socialist path (Chechens and Tatars in the Stalinist Soviet Union, Cham and Vietnamese in Cambodia) would either be driven out or killed. All these genocidal regimes expressed in their propaganda and policies the sharp, binary distinction they drew between the goodness of the dominant group and the utterly benighted and dangerous character of the enemy population.

The Bolsheviks took power in Russia in 1917 fully confident that they could create a classless, egalitarian society. By clearing away the rubble of the past, they believed, the path would be opened to the creation of the new society that would permit the ultimate efflorescence of the human spirit. In Marxian terms the "realm of necessity" would finally be surmounted by the "realm of freedom," material prosperity in conditions of social equality would lay to rest all the pathologies of class-riven societies and the nefarious traits of individual human beings. Within the harmonious socialist society human freedom would develop in unimaginable ways, resulting in a society marked by unbounded prosperity and cultural creativity and the emergence of the new Soviet man and woman. However, the creation of that society first required the pursuit of the class opponents who would never be reconciled to the socialist vision.

From the civil war of 1918 and 1920 to the forced collectivization campaign of the late 1920s and early 1930s, the Soviets developed a set of purge practices targeting entire population groups characterized as the enemies of socialism. Then in the 1930s and extending until Stalin's death in 1953, the designated enemies were increasingly defined as members of particular ethnic and national groups, including Koreans, Chechens and Ingush, Crimean Tatars, Germans, Jews, and many others. All of them were viewed as security concerns, but even more important, as somehow constitutionally resistant to the siren song of Soviet socialism. As Stalin elevated the Russian nation to the most heroic and progressive within the Soviet federation, certain other nationalities and ethnicities were assigned the typical Soviet language for outcasts: traitors, vermin, bloodsuckers, parasites. This kind of biological language indicated a racialization of nationality and ethnicity, because virtually every single Korean or Chechen was seen to carry the nefarious traits within his or her body. Soviet socialism could only be saved by the purge of these groups, usually forced deportation in such horrendous conditions that the results were extremely high mortality rates.

The Nazis claimed that only Aryans were a "culture-producing" and economically productive people, who, therefore, were entitled to dominate others. Aryans are the "Prometheus of mankind from whose bright forehead the divine spark of genius has sprung at all times," Adolf Hitler wrote in *Mein Kampf.* In contrast, Jews were a "culture-destroying race" who embodied filth and disease. Through their inherent, biologically driven desire for domination, they threatened to overwhelm Aryans. Hard-fought racial struggle, through which Aryans would demonstrate their mettle, was the path to the utopian future. This would be a war of annihilation in which one side would triumph and the other would be utterly destroyed. Aryan health and prosperi-

ty would be restored and become even greater through the victorious struggle against the Jews. With final victory Germany as a nation would be powerful, its rule uncontested, its domination feared. As a people, Germans would be productive and prosperous, the masters of nature through engineering and science, yet at the same time they would be able to revel in the retreat to a pristine natural order. Everyone would be joined in a racially homogeneous grouping, with healthy members and the elderly well cared for. This was the Nazi ideal of *Volksgemeinschaft,* the organically unified, racially select people's community that would create a new culture that brought together rural and urban, menial and intellectual workers. As Hitler claimed in 1937, "a new feeling of life, a new joy in life" and a "new human type" were emerging, with men and women who would be "healthier and stronger."

The post-World War II genocidal regimes also espoused utopia coupled with the utter castigation of those perceived to stand in the way of its fulfillment. On the second anniversary of the Khmer Rouge victory, President Khieu Samphan depicted in bucolic terms a Democratic Kampuchea with freely flowing water, freshly flowering plants, and smiling people. Radio Phnom Penh described Cambodians of all sorts toiling together happily in the fields, harvesting rice, building dams, and clearing forests as they developed a new, prosperous, and egalitarian society. According to the Khmer Rouge vision, proper politics would enable Cambodians to vastly increase the rice harvest, and all of Cambodia's peasants would benefit from electricity and tractors. This was a developmental vision, but also a deeply utopian one in which efforts of will would surmount existing limits of production. "When a people is awakened by political consciousness, it can do anything," suggested one party slogan. Cambodians were to become "masters of the earth and of water," "masters of the rice fields and plains, of the forests and of all vegetation," "masters of the yearly floods."

With its completely collectivized society, Democratic Kampuchea had even surpassed the fellow communist states of China, Vietnam, and North Korea. But the enemies of the revolution, urban dwellers, peasants who retained "individualistic" views, and, especially, ethnic and religious minorities, were beyond the pale. They were deemed impure and unclean, and therefore threatened the health of the noble Khmer population. Echoing the biological language that both the Nazis and Soviets used, the Khmer Rouge claimed that enemies were microbes, which, if not removed, would burrow their way into the healthy population. Rotten, infected parts of the population had to be removed and eliminated, and this applied especially to the Vietnamese and Cham.

The leaders of Yugoslavia in the late 1980s and 1990s also projected a utopian future based on the exclusive reign of one particular segment of the population, the Serbs. Over and over Slobodan Milosevic and other Serb nationalist leaders invoked the supposedly glorious history of Serbs and their tragic present, in which, it was claimed, Serbs were oppressed by the inferior peoples around them, whether Muslims, Croats, or Westerners of various stripes. Serbian Orthodox clerics associated with the national cause claimed that God looked down with special grace on the Serb people. Others claimed that Serbs were the "historic" people of the South Slav lands, who for hundreds of years had fought heroically against the Turks and in the nineteenth and twentieth centuries had led courageous struggles for democracy and national independence. Places of mixed ethnicity such as Sarajevo and Dubrovnik were thus sites of pestilence and prostitution. Muslims especially were called dogs, even packages or cabbages, particularly dehumanizing terms that perpetrators used to refer to their victims. Only an exclusive nation-state, cleansed of Muslims, Croats, and any non-Serbs, Serb nationalists claimed, would allow the potential of the people to burst forth in torrents of creativity and development.

Cleanliness and purity are terms that, necessarily, signify their binary opposites, the unclean and the impure. In all these instances, and others as well, such as the genocide of Armenians in the late Ottoman Empire, those who were considered unclean were an active source of pollution that threatened to contaminate the clean and the pure. Hence, they had to be at least quarantined and, in the most extreme cases, eradicated altogether. For some of the powerful revolutionary systems of the twentieth century, the dirt that anthropologist Mary Douglas famously described as "matter out of place" was, in fact, human matter, and it had to be eradicated through political action. In excluding "dirt," these systems were reshaping the very composition of their societies.

Such immense, wide-ranging efforts required the mobilization of populations, both as active participants and complicit bystanders. Regular security forces did not suffice for actions that involved the killing of hun-dreds of thousands and even millions of people. The active killers in the armies and internal security units were supplemented by paramilitaries, and also by the citizens who denounced their neighbors to the authorities and seized the property and possessions of those who had been deported and killed. In this manner twentieth-century genocides became social projects.

Utopian ideologies have often generated activism directed at a more humane and peaceful future. But the propensity of utopians to think in homogeneous terms, of creating societies devoid of difference, also lurks behind many of the massive violations of human rights that have occurred in the twentieth century. In so many instances the perpetrators of genocides were those who believed that it was indeed possible to create a future of unlimited prosperity and creativity once the enemies—so often defined in national or racial terms—had been eliminated. Utopian ideologies, alongside the immense organizational capacities of the modern state, helped to make genocides prevalent and the number of their victims staggering in the twentieth century.

SEE ALSO Cambodia; Developmental Genocide; Genocide; Hitler, Adolf; Linguistic Genocide; Milosevic, Slobodan; Pol Pot; Stalin, Joseph; Union of Soviet Socialist Republics; Utilitarian Genocide

BIBLIOGRAPHY

Chandler, David (1991). *Voices from S-21: Terror and History in Pol Pot's Secret Prison.* Berkeley: University of California Press.

Friedländer, Saul (1997). *Nazi Germany and the Jews. Vol. 1: The Years of Persecution, 1933–1939.* New York: HarperCollins.

Kiernan, Ben (1996). *The Pol Pot Regime: Race, Power, and Genocide in Cambodia under the Khmer Rouge, 1975–79.* New Haven, Conn.: Yale University Press.

Popov, Nebojša, ed. (2000). *The Road to War in Serbia: Trauma and Catharsis.* Budapest: Central European University Press.

Weitz, Eric D. (2003). *A Century of Genocide: Utopias of Race and Nation.* Princeton, N.J.: Princeton University Press.

Eric D. Weitz

Victims

Under international law, victims of human rights abuse have a right to a remedy and to reparations for violations committed by or with the acquiescence of the state. Thorny questions arise over who can be considered a victim, the types of damages or reparations available, and the relationship of victims to the prosecution of offenders.

Starting in 1989, the United Nations Sub-Commission on Human Rights developed a set of principles on reparations, now known as the Basic Principles and Guidelines on the Right to a Remedy and Reparation for Victims of Violations of International Human Rights and Humanitarian Law. In addition, the UN human rights treaty bodies and the regional human rights commissions and courts, especially in Latin America and Europe, have considered several aspects related to victims and reparations. National courts and administrative compensation schemes have also contributed to defining issues involving victims.

Who are Victims?

The UN's Basic Principles document, in paragraph 8, defines a victim as follows:

> A person is a "victim" where, as a result of acts or omissions that constitute a violation of international human rights or humanitarian law norms, that person, individually or collectively, suffered harm, including physical or mental injury, emotional suffering, economic loss, or impairment of that person's fundamental legal rights. A "victim" may also be a legal personality,

a dependant, or a member of the immediate family or household of the direct victim, as well as a person who, in intervening to assist a victim or prevent the occurrence of further violations, has suffered physical, mental, or economic harm.

Defining who is a victim in concrete circumstances can often prove difficult and controversial, especially where there are large numbers of potential victims. In the wake of large-scale atrocities, countries have grappled with defining victims for purposes of government-created reparations programs. For example, in Chile the government decided to focus solely on those killed and disappeared by the security forces, leaving aside the vastly larger number of those who were tortured while in detention and survived, and those who were forced into exile. While this decision was justified as a way to spend limited funds on the "worst" violations, the effect was to infuriate survivors. According to a 2002 study by the Chilean human rights group CODEPU, survivors read this as a lack of recognition for the severity of their own suffering and an attempt to paper over the extent of the crimes. In South Africa, the mandate of the post-apartheid Truth and Reconciliation Commission similarly restricted the category of "victim" to those who suffered from the gross violations—killing, torture, abduction—prohibited under South African as well as international law. Critics of the TRC pointed out that this limited mandate excluded the legal pillars of *apartheid*: forced removals, passed laws, residential segregation and other forms of racial discrimination and detention without trial. By doing so, it shifted the focus from the complicity and benefits of *apartheid* to whites as a group to the misdeeds of a

In March 2001 army-backed paramilitary forces increased their raids on Barrancabermeja, Colombia. A victim lies dead on the street while others look on or walk away. [TEUN VOETEN]

smaller group of security force operatives, easily characterized as "bad apples." The definition of "victim" thus acts to limit and frame discussion over reparations.

The definition of *victim* can also raise difficult issues that touch on family and customary law. In both court-generated and administrative reparations schemes, it has been easy to define the persons who have been physically or mentally harmed, and their spouses and children if they are deceased, as victims as a result of that loss. Moreover, courts, including the European Court of Human Rights, have found that the family members of the victim of a forced disappearance are themselves victims, as the product of the anguish and uncertainty of not knowing the fate of their loved one, or, more generally, of a human rights violation and the subsequent impunity of the perpetrators. Administrative compensation schemes have taken one of two routes: either they have compensated the immediate victims, and allowed their heirs and successors (as defined in local law) to receive the compensation if the victims were dead or disappeared, or they have specified the percentage of awards to be paid to each category (spouse, child, etc.) of surviving relatives in cases of death.

Regional human rights courts have also grappled with the definition of *victim* for purposes of assigning compensation. In the case of injuries resulting in death, both the European and Inter-American Courts of Human Rights allow claims for the harm to the victims themselves prior to death, to their families for wrongful death, and for family members' own harms in conjunction with the abuses against the persons killed. Both economic and moral damages are covered. The Inter-American Court, in its extensive jurisprudence on reparations, has developed a particularly expansive definition of family, which includes siblings as well as spouses, parents, and children of the person killed or disappeared. If the victim survives, he or she can of course bring claims on his or her own behalf, but the court has also presumed (in a 1999 case involving Ecuador) that close family members have suffered in cases of detention, torture or unfair trial, and awarded compensation to them. In addition to suffering and health damage, the court has awarded family members compensation for the costs of burial, and for the costs (including lost income) incurred in looking for the victim.

The court has also taken cultural attributes of the victim into account in awarding reparations. Rather than strictly apply national laws on inheritance, the court has defined its own principles, which includes taking into account "local law," including customary law. In the 1994 *Aloeboetoe* case, the court found that customary law among the Saramacas, or Maroons, of Suriname, included multiple marriages. In a case involving the summary execution of a number of Saramaca men, the court allowed reparations for the multiple wives and children of the victims. In a 2002 case involving the disappearance of a Guatemalan Ma'am indigenous leader, the court allowed damages for support of the victim's father and half-sister, based on evidence that Ma'am culture required the elder brother to support parents and younger siblings.

Victims can be collectivities as well as individuals and family members. The clearest example is the destruction of property as part of a campaign of genocide or "ethnic cleansing." The destruction of a mosque, church, temple, or synagogue creates a collective harm to the community that worshiped there, and that community (perhaps represented by the religious authorities) is the victim. More generally, collective reparations may be needed when the destruction of a community has been so thorough that there are few survivors left to file claims or they have been dispersed so widely that the original community has ceased to exist. Compensation may include payment for the loss of community cohesion, community institutions and culture.

Individual reparations fail to capture the collective element of the harm in situations of genocide or crimes against humanity. A major aim of the organizers of atrocities is the destruction of the community fabric. The attempt is not simply to kill, but to isolate, terrorize, and sow distrust. Military forces may seek to make local civilians complicit in atrocities, forcing them to watch or even to participate in the violations of their neighbors' basic human rights. These harms to community life and trust cannot easily be redressed through individual awards.

In addition to individual claims for loss of life or liberty, damage to health, loss of jobs, pensions, and economic prospects, Germany paid collective reparations to Jewish organizations and to the State of Israel after the Holocaust. Survivor organizations argued that collective reparations were necessary to compensate for the property, lives, and suffering of those with no living heirs or dependants, for the loss of institutions and communities, and for the damage to the very fabric of the Jewish people's existence. A total of $3.45 billion deutsch marks were eventually paid to Israel for acts against the Jewish people, in addition to substantial amounts of compensation to other European states and to individual victims and survivors.

Courts have generally been reluctant to design categories of collective reparations. In the above-referenced *Aloeboetoe et al.* case before the Inter-American Court of Human Rights, the court grappled with the issue of collective moral reparations. The court first discussed and ultimately denied the request for monetary compensation, as follows:

> [T]he Court believes that all persons, in addition to being members of their own families and citizens of a State, also generally belong to intermediate communities. In practice, the obligation to pay moral compensation does not extend to such communities, nor to the State in which the victim participated; these are redressed by the enforcement of the system of laws. If in some exceptional case such compensation has been granted, it would have been to a community that suffered direct damage (*Aloeboetoe et al.*, paragraph 83).

However, in the final statement of reparations, the court, in paragraph 95 of its decision, "orders the State of Suriname, as an act of reparation, to reopen the school house located in Gujaba and staff it with teaching and administrative personnel so that it will function on a permanent basis as of 1994, and to make the medical dispensary already in place in that locality operational during that same year." These measures to provide education and health care to the community in effect formed a kind of collective reparations.

A second case in which the Inter-American human rights system grappled with the prospect of collective reparations is *Chanay Pablo v. Guatemala*, more commonly referred to as the *Colotenango* case. Members of a paramilitary civil patrol opened fire on a group of protesters in the town, killing Juan Chanay Pablo and injuring several others. The victims filed a complaint in the courts and subsequently in the Inter-American Commission on Human Rights. Throughout this period, civil patrol members frequently intimidated and attacked the witnesses, the accusers, and an attorney participating in the case. Guatemala and the Commission, were able to reach a friendly settlement in March 1997. Guatamala agreed to provide Q300,000 (some $43,000) to financially compensate the individuals directly affected by the Colotenango attack, and to ensure that justice was done. In addition, "the State of Guatemala shall provide communal assistance to the affected communities of Colotenango, in accordance with a program of projects agreed upon by the parties."

Outside the context of collective victims, courts and administrative schemes have generally not recognized bystanders or witnesses to crimes against humanity as victims for purposes of reparations, at least without a showing of personal harm. One question that has arisen is whether those who are not part of the target ethnic group, but who are killed because they are attempting to defend the target group, can be considered victims of genocide. In a case involving genocide against the Mayan people of Guatemala, brought in Spain, a bare eight-judge majority of the Spanish Supreme Court found in 2003 that Spanish priests who had been killed or disappeared for their work with poor, mostly Mayan communities could not bring genocide charges on their own behalf, as Spanish citizens had not themselves been the target of a genocidal campaign. The seven dissenting judges argued that, as victims targeted because they were defending others from genocide, the priests should be considered equally as victims of genocide.

In situations of genocide or massive crimes against humanity, international tribunals have not to date provided specific help to victims. In Rwanda, the International Criminal Tribunal for Rwanda (ICTR), through the Office of the Registrar, attempted to provide minimal support for witnesses coming before the Tribunal, who were often in desperate financial straits. On its own initiative, in September 2000, the Registrar's office launched an initiative to provide legal advice, psychological counseling, physical therapy, and monetary assistance, and also contributed to a number of projects in Taba township, the locality where the mayor was convicted of genocide and where there were hundreds of survivors, most of them destitute women. But the Tribunal soon found that the needs far exceeded its capacity, that it was ill-equipped to design and administer reparations schemes, and that to do so adequately would require the amendment of the Tribunal's statute and rules. The effort was scaled back, although the judges and prosecutor agreed that the Security Council should amend the ICTR's statute to allow it a greater role in compensation. The statute of the International Criminal Court (ICC) allows the ICC to award reparations, and sets up a trust fund to compensate victims of genocide, crimes against humanity, and war crimes, but as of 2004 it had minimal resources and had not yet made any awards.

What Rights Do Victims Have?
First, and most importantly, victims have a right to a remedy, and to reparations for harm done. The law on reparations arises in part from the requirements of international human rights treaties, and in part evolves from the law of state responsibility, which prescribes the reparations states must pay to other states for international law violations, including harm to the citizens of the aggrieved state. The basic human rights instruments encompass a "right to a remedy." Article 8 of the Universal Declaration of Human Rights holds that "[e]veryone has the right to an effective remedy by the competent national tribunals for acts violating the fundamental rights granted him by the constitution or by law." Article 2 of the International Covenant on Civil and Political Rights, in subsection 3, requires parties to "ensure that any person whose rights or freedoms as herein recognized are violated shall have an effective remedy, notwithstanding that the violation has been committed by persons acting in an official capacity," and article 9, subsection 5 requires compensation for unlawful detention, article 14, subsection 6, specifies compensation for wrongful conviction. Articles 6 and 13 of the European Convention, and articles 8 and 25 of the American Convention on Human Rights have similar provisions, as do the Convention against Torture and the Convention on the Elimination of Racial Discrimination, in Articles 14 and 6, respectively. Other specialized treaties and non-binding human rights instruments also call for compensation to victims. The statute of the International Criminal Court recognizes that individual offenders can also owe reparations, and sets out provisions on reparations in articles 75 and 79.

The UN Draft Principles recognize both material and moral elements to reparations. Material reparations for an individual may include the restitution of access to, and title of, property taken or lost, a job, freedom, or a pension or a person's good name. They may include medical, psychiatric, or occupational therapy aimed at rehabilitation. They may encompass monetary compensation in the form of a lump sum, a pension, or a package of services for the victim and for the survivors of those killed. For collectivities, restitution of cultural or religious property, communal lands, or confiscated public buildings, and compensation for such property as cannot be returned, are options.

Moral reparations are as important—generally more important from the victims' perspective—than material ones. They cover a wide range of measures, most having to do with a felt need for telling the story, for justice, and for measures to avoid the repetition of crimes. They may include disclosure of the facts of a victim's mistreatment or a loved one's death, disclosure of the names and positions of those responsible, and disclosure of the patterns of repression. They may in-

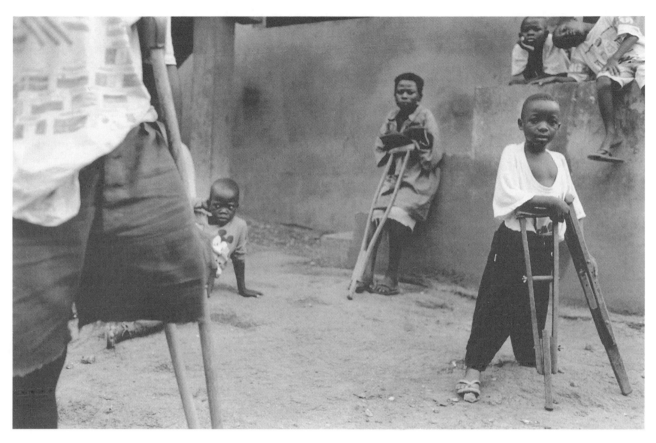

The most brutal violence in Sierra Leone was often perpetrated against children. Several with amputated limbs stay at a shelter in Freetown, 1999. [TEUN VOETEN]

clude official acknowledgement that government agents wronged the victims, and an apology may be officially offered. They may also include the guarantee that those responsible suffer consequences, whether criminal, civil, or administrative will be brought to justice and removed from positions of power.

Moral reparations may also be as basic as the identification and exhumation of the bodies of victims, and assistance in reburials and culturally appropriate mourning ceremonies. Assistance with finding the bodies of the dead or disappeared (that is, those kidnapped and surreptitiously killed, usually by security forces) is particularly key. These moral reparations also have a collective aspect, when entire communities dedicate memorials or markers to their dead. Other collective measures of moral reparation may include days of remembrance, the dedication of parks or other public monuments, renaming of streets or schools, preservation of archives or of repressive sites as museums, or other ways of creating public memory. Educational reform, the rewriting of history texts, and education in human rights and tolerance are all encompassed within the idea of "guarantees of non-repetition." So too, in a broader sense, are the reform of courts, police and mili-

tary forces, and other arms of state authority that may be implicated in the original violations.

The trend in international law, finally, is to open up both civil and criminal court processes to allow increased access and voice to victims. Thus, the Inter-American Court of Human Rights in 1997 changed its procedures to allow victims direct representation before the court, rather than indirect representation through the Inter-American Commission. The European Convention on Human Rights has allowed direct victim representation since its Protocol 11 entered into force in 1998. The Rome Statute of the ICC similarly allows victims to be present, and at certain points to make representations before the court. The Colombian Constitutional Court, in the 2003 *Acevedo Martelo* case, held that in cases of human rights violations (as opposed to common crimes), the rights of victims had to be given considerable weight, and could override the rights of defendants to not have their cases reopened.

The rights of victims to be granted access to a remedy, to reparations, and to some level of participation in criminal processes will, of course, be more complex in situations of genocide or crimes against humanity, given the sheer numbers of victims and the limited resources available. A mixture of individual and collective measures, and of moral and material reparations, will, under the best of circumstances, be the most that can be done, and yet be less than ideal. Creativity and attention to how these issues fit into larger reconstruction and development processes will be needed in such situations, if these rights are to be made a reality.

SEE ALSO Compensation; Psychology of Survivors; Reparations

BIBLIOGRAPHY

Barkan, Elazar (2000). *The Guilt of Nations: Restitution and Negotiating Historical Injustices.* Baltimore, Md.: Johns Hopkins University Press.

Brooks, R. L., ed. (1999). *When Sorry Isn't Enough: The Controversy over Apologies and Reparations for Human Injustice.* New York: New York University Press.

CODEPU/APT (2002) *Truth Commissions: An Uncertain Path?* English executive summary available from http://www.apt.ch/americas/mexico/Executive%20Summary.pdf.

Mani, Rama (2002). *Beyond Retribution.* Cambridge, U.K.: Polity Press.

Pross, Christian (1998). *Paying for the Past.* Baltimore, Md.: Johns Hopkins University Press.

Sancinetti, Marcelo A., and Marcelo Ferrante (1999). *El Derecho Penal en la Proteccion de los Derechos Humanos.* Buenos Aires: Hammurabi.

Shelton, Dinah (1999). *Remedies in International Human Rights Law.* Oxford: Oxford University Press.

Torpey, John, ed. (2003). *Politics and the Past: On Repairing Historical Injustice.* Lanham, Md.: Rowman & Littlefield.

United Nations (2000). "Report to the Secretary-General of the ICTR," U.N. Doc. S/2000/1198, 15 Dec. 2000. The ICTY came to similar conclusions, see U.N. Doc. S/2000/1063, 2 Nov. 2000.

United Nations Sub-Commission on Human Rights (2003). *Basic Principles and Guidelines on the Right to a Remedy and Reparation for Victims of Violations of Internaitonal Human Rights and Humanitarian Law,* Rev. 15 (August). Available from http://www.unhchr.ch/html/menu2/revisedrestitution.doc.

Vandeginste, Stef (2003). "Victims of Genocide, Crimes Against Humanity, and War Crimes in Rwanda: The Legal and Institutional Framework of Their Right to Reparation." In *Politics and the Past: on Repairing Historical Injustice,* ed. John Torpey. Lanham, Md.: Rowman & Littlefield.

Wilson, Richard A. (2001). "Justice and Legitimacy in the South African Transition." In *The Politics of Memory,* ed. Alexandra Barahona de Brito, et al. Oxford, U.K.: Oxford University Press.

Naomi Roht-Arriaza

Videotaped Testimonials

Most survivor narratives of genocidal acts generated in the twentieth century exist in written or audio format. If survivors spoke about their experience in front of a camera, it was either in a war crimes trial setting or for a documentary filmmaker. The development of easy-to-use, affordable video technology in the early 1980s enabled oral history projects not only to record the voice but also the face of the interviewee. Early videotaping projects focused primarily on Holocaust survivors, while others gathered the testimonials of survivors of the Armenian genocide. Aging survivors, the awareness that their stories would soon be lost, and a growing trend toward a visually oriented society generated a multitude of videotaping projects in the 1980s and 1990s. The projects vary in size (amount of testimonies), scope (domestic vs. international), content (types of experiences covered), methodology (interview format and location of interview), and purpose (memorialization, therapy, research, education).

Survivor and remembrance groups as well as research- and education-oriented institutions such as universities, research centers, and museums began to recognize the need for visual history. From large institutions or projects that engage in local and international videotaping of Holocaust survivors (e.g., the Fortunoff Video Archive for Holocaust Testimonies at Yale, United States Holocaust Memorial Museum, Yad Vashem) to smaller, locally oriented groups like memorial sites (e.g., the National Museum at Auschwitz, Ravensbrück Memorial Museum), videotaping survivors while they speak about their experience has become much more common among not only Jewish Holocaust survivors but also other victim groups and witnesses to the Nazi program of mass murder, such as the Sinti and Romani (so-called gypsy) survivors, rescuers, and liberators. By the end of 2003 an extraordinary amount of such survivor and witness accounts—estimated to number around 70,000—had been gathered worldwide. The majority (75%) of this massive data was collected by one project—the Survivors of the Shoah Visual History Foundation. Founded by filmmaker Steven Spielberg, it began to videotape survivors and other witnesses in 1994 and concluded its collection phase by 1999. Unprecedented on many levels, as of 2004, the foundation remains the largest archive of videotaped testimonials of Jewish Holocaust survivors, Sinti and Romani survivors, and other witnesses.

Projects documenting genocidal crimes in places like Bosnia, Cambodia, and Rwanda as well as South Africa have consulted some of the larger Holocaust video archives on issues regarding videotaping survivors. The use of a video camera as a tool to create testimonials also plays a crucial role in a project called WITNESS. Founded in 1992 by the musician Peter Gabriel, the Lawyers Committee for Human Rights, and the Reebok Foundation, WITNESS provides guidance, encouragement, and funding to local grassroots efforts to document human rights abuses with a video camera and to use the resulting video to expose those abuses and stimulate change.

Videotaping techniques and interviewing styles vary widely, and numerous factors determine the most suitable methodology. The projected purpose of the testimonies, the financial resources available, and the intended location of the interviews are just a few elements to consider. Resources may impose limits on the kind of video-recording equipment available and thus influence the visual quality of the testimony. The quality of video may be important because the resulting testimonies could be intended for use in museum exhibits or documentaries, so broadcast-quality video may be required. Or, videotaping in remote geographic areas may limit the options on video equipment. Projects also differ in the choice of a specific setting for taping. There could be a number of different settings in which to conduct interviews: in a studio, interviewee's home, or another location relevant to the interviewee's experience. A studio can create a neutral environment, whereas the interviewee's home can provide a personal environment and degree of comfort that may help the interviewee to recall his or her memories in addition to providing a visual background unique to each interviewee. Videotaping testimonials on location of the former sites of persecution or genocidal acts can provide an additional visual and create a direct link between the past event (interviewee's narrative) and the present (a visual of the interviewee in the actual location) or give "physical evidence such as . . . forensic documentation of corpses or mass graves" (Stephenson, 2000, p. 44).

The size and intent of a project may determine whether the interview will be conducted with a time limit. If no such limitation exists, survivors have the opportunity to tell as much as they can remember and/or even correct previous statements in follow-up sessions. A time restriction is often implemented to enable a greater number of interviewees to tell their stories. The interviewing methodology ranges from a freeflowing approach, in which interviewers only ask questions for follow-up or clarification, to a more structured approach, in which interviewees are guided to tell their story in a more chronological manner, to those conducted in an investigatory manner. Historians interested in specific events and individuals involved in criminal investigations or trials prefer the more directed approach with as many clarifying questions asked as

possible. However, this does not preclude other interviews from yielding equally important information. Ultimately, the "quality"—a very subjective and not easily defined descriptor—of an interview is shaped by the interviewee, not the interviewer. The interview may include descriptions of life before, during, and after the event. Some projects focus exclusively on the actual event and are less concerned with the before and after an approach often taken if the intent is to document the event for legal purposes or if the project's limited resources make a closer focus imperative. It is important to include narration on the life led before the act of genocide occurred if that way of life became extinct as a result. Therefore, allowing survivors to verbally recreate the past adds historical value. Equally important is the discussion of survivors' experiences after the event up to the time of taping, especially if the interview occurs many years after the fact. How does one cope with the experience? How does one go on living? Videotape also allows for the inclusion of additional documentary evidence-showing on camera a prisoner uniform worn in a concentration camp, a number tattooed on one's arm, or photos of family members who perished are just a few examples. A commonality exists among these approaches: allowing the survivors to tell the story in their own words.

First-person accounts have been considered by some as questionable historical resources. Memory is deemed too unreliable, particularly if testimonies are taken many years after the event. In 2000, however, historian Christopher Browning noted about his research on a Jewish forced labor camp, for which he used Holocaust survivor testimonies taken over several decades after World War II ended, that those testimonies were "more stable and less malleable" than he had anticipated (p. 91). The argument that only sources created at the time of the event are reliable should also be questioned. German documents created during the 1940s were often "designed to mislead rather than to inform, to hide rather than to reveal"(Bauer, 2001, p. 23). Videotaped survivor testimonies are especially crucial when historical knowledge has largely been based on perpetrator documentation and, as in the case of the Holocaust, the perpetrators tried to eradicate not only a people but also all documentation of that eradication itself.

Many efforts to collect Holocaust survivor testimonies audiovisually have been initiated to preserve the past and to educate future generations. Video records simultaneously the words, facial expressions, body language, and visual context surrounding survivors while they recount their experience and, as such, makes history not only come alive but also gives it a human dimension.

The videotaped interviews with Holocaust survivors and witnesses to the atrocities of World War II in the 1970s, 1980s, and 1990s present a unique opportunity for future generations of educators, students, and researchers. However, the faces and voices of survivors of other genocides should be included to create comprehensive documentation on genocides in general.

SEE ALSO Evidence; Films, Armenian Documentary; Films, Holocaust Documentary; Memoirs of Survivors; Memorials and Monuments; Television

BIBLIOGRAPHY
Bauer, Yehuda (2001). *Rethinking the Holocaust*. New Haven, Conn.: Yale University Press.

Browning, Christopher (2000). *Nazi Policy, Jewish Workers, German Killers*. Cambridge: Cambridge University Press.

Ringelheim, Joan (1992). *A Catalogue of Audio and Video Collections of Holocaust Testimony*, 2nd edition. New York: Greenwood Press.

Stephenson, Michèle (2000). "Video for Change: A Practical Guide for Activists." Available from http://www.witness.org.

"The Archive". In the Survivors of the Shoah Visual History Foundation website. Available from http://www.vhf.org.

Totten, Samuel, ed. (1991). *First-Person Accounts of Genocidal Acts Committed in the Twentieth Century: An Annotated Bibliography*. Westport, Conn.: Greenwood Publishers.

Karen Jungblut

Wallenberg, Raoul

[AUGUST 4, 1912–JULY 17, 1947]
Swedish diplomat

Raoul Wallenberg has entered history as a humanitarian activist who took considerable personal risks to save men, women, and children from impending genocide. In the summer and fall of 1944, and until his disappearance in January 1945, Wallenberg was affiliated with the Swedish Legation in Budapest, Hungary, where he conducted a special rescue mission to save many thousands of Hungarian Jews from deportation to the Nazi extermination camps. Wallenberg had no kinship to the victims; he was a Lutheran by faith and a neutral Swede by nationality. Yet he accepted a difficult and dangerous assignment in a foreign country—a mission which he carried out with skill, determination, and courage.

Early Life and Humanitarian Appointments

Wallenberg was born in 1912 in Stockholm to an aristocratic family of industrialists and bankers. In 1930 he graduated from secondary school with top grades, in particular in Russian, which would serve him well in his later career. Following compulsory military service, he traveled to the United States to study architecture at the University of Michigan in Ann Arbor, from which he received his B.S. degree in 1935. Following his return to Sweden, he took a position with a Swedish firm in Cape Town, South Africa, engaged in the sale of building materials. In 1936 he was employed at a branch office of a Dutch bank in Haifa, Palestine (present-day Israel). In Palestine he met Jews who had fled from persecution in Germany. Back in Sweden, Wallenberg became the business partner of Kálmán Lauer, a Hungarian Jew based in Stockholm and director of the Central European Trading Company, an import and export firm specializing in fine foods such as *foie gras.* In 1941 Wallenberg became foreign trade representative of the firm and in this capacity traveled to many European countries, including Hungary, Germany, and Nazi-occupied France.

World War II is remembered as the stage for the major genocide of the twentieth century, following the Ottoman extermination of Armenians. Adolf Hitler's "final solution of the Jewish question" first consumed the Polish, Baltic, Ukrainian, Russian, and West European Jews from countries under Nazi occupation. Until 1944 the 700,000 Jews in Hungary had been spared, since Hungary's head of state, Admiral Miklós Horty, was an ally of the Germans, and thus Hitler's henchmen could not freely operate there. This situation changed when Hungary was occupied by the Nazis in March 1944, and the deportation of Hungarian Jews to Auschwitz-Birkenau began. The first victims were the Jews from the countryside, more than 400,000 of whom were deported in the months of May and June 1944.

Faced by grave danger, some of the Jews in Budapest sought protection from the embassies of neutral countries, especially those Jews who could show some links with those countries and thus request special passports. The Swedish Legation in Budapest issued some seven hundred temporary passports; those possessing the passports were exempted from having to wear the Star of David. In view of the magnitude of the

Raoul Wallenberg, Swedish Renaissance man and diplomat, used his diplomatic status to save Hungarian Jews during the Holocaust. He also negotiated with Adolf Eichmann and other Nazi officers for the cancellation of deportations to concentration camps by playing on their fears that the Allies would eventually prosecute those responsible for such war crimes. [USHMM]

problem, Valdemar Langlet, head of the Swedish Red Cross, provided assistance to the Swedish Legation. He rented buildings in the name of the Red Cross and identified these buildings as the "Swedish Library" or "Swedish Research Institute," although they were essentially intended as hiding places for Jews. Furthermore, the Legation turned to the Ministry of Foreign Affairs in Stockholm and requested more staff.

Meanwhile, following the establishment of the American War Refugee Board in 1944, an organization whose task was to save Jews from Nazi persecution, the World Jewish Congress, held a meeting in Stockholm to organize a rescue mission for the Hungarian Jews. The organization considered sending Count Folke Bernadotte, chairperson of the Swedish Red Cross and a relative of King Gustav V. When the Hungarian government did not approve Bernadotte, Lauer proposed that Wallenberg be sent instead.

In late June 1944 Wallenberg was appointed first secretary of the Swedish Embassy in Budapest. The embassy granted him very broad powers of initiative, and he did not have to clear his decisions concerning the rescue mission with Stockholm or with the Swedish Le-

gation in Budapest, which at the time was headed by Minister Carl Ivar Danielsson and assisted by his deputy Legation secretary Per Anger.

Assisting the Jews
When Wallenberg arrived in Budapest on July 9, 1944, about 200,000 Jews were still in the capital. SS-Obersturmbannführer Adolf Eichmann intended to deport all of them within a few days, but King Gustav V addressed a letter to Horty containing a humanitarian appeal to stop the deportation of Jews. Upon Horty's intercession, the deportations were canceled. Historians speculate that the cancelling of deportations was in part due to SS-Chief Heinrich Himmler, who was attempting to negotiate a separate peace agreement with the Western Allies and thus believed he would improve his negotiating position by making certain concessions toward the Jews.

Wallenberg's first task in Budapest was to design a Swedish protective passport (Schutz-Pass), printed in blue and yellow (Sweden's national colors), bearing the Three Crowns heraldry in the center. Although these "protective passports" were not documents customarily recognized in international diplomatic practice, they did appear official enough and impressed the German and Hungarian authorities sufficiently to persuade them to leave the bearers in peace. Initially 1,500 such passports were issued, soon thereafter another 1,000, and eventually the quota was raised to 4,500. Scholars estimate that Wallenberg actually issued three times that amount. Meanwhile his department at the Swedish Legation continued to grow, eventually employing 340 persons and volunteers, and harboring 700 persons who lived on the premises of the Legation.

When on October 15, 1944, Horty announced that he was seeking a separate peace agreement with the Russians, German troops quickly deposed him, and he was replaced by the leader of the Hungarian Nazis, Ferenc Szálasi, the leader of the Arrow Cross movement. Thereupon Wallenberg proceeded to expand the "Swedish houses" to thirty-two buildings, mostly in Budapest, where many of the Jews resided. The number of inhabitants of these houses reached 15,000. Other diplomatic missions in Budapest also started issuing protective passports.

In November 1944 Eichmann forced thousands of Jews to leave Hungary by foot, some 200 kilometers to the Austrian border. Wallenberg distributed protective passports, food, and medicine to many victims of these forced marches, and by threats and bribes persuaded the Nazis to release those who had been given Swedish passports. Then followed the deportations by trainloads, and again Wallenberg personally went to the

A four-meter-high (13-feet-high) bronze monument to Raoul Wallenberg, the Swedish diplomat who saved tens of thousands of Hungarian Jews in World War II, was unveiled Friday May 28 1999, in the Stockholm suburb Lidingo, where he was born. The sculpture symbolizes Wallenberg with hands behind his back, clandestinely giving out Swedish passports. [AP WIDE WORLD PHOTOS]

train stations to save individuals. Reports claim that he climbed on trains and passed bundles of protective passports to the occupants.

Early in January 1945 Wallenberg learned that Eichmann was about to liquidate the Jews in the ghettos. Wallenberg, with the assistance of an Arrow Cross member Pa'l Szalay, whom he had bribed, approached General August Schmidthuber, commander of the German troops in Hungary. Due to this intervention, the massacre was averted. On January 12, 1945, Soviet troops entered Budapest and found some 120,000 Jews still alive in the city. On January 17, Wallenberg and his chauffeur traveled to the Soviet military headquarters in Debrecen, in eastern Hungary. It appears that there he was arrested on suspicion of espionage for the United States and taken to Lubjanka Prison in Moscow, where, according to Soviet sources and the so-called

Smoltsov Report, he died of a heart attack on July 17, 1947. Another version of the story stated that Wallenberg was still alive in the 1970s and 1980s. Following the collapse of the Soviet Union, new efforts were undertaken to clarify his fate, and in confidential talks between Russian and Swedish diplomats, the version emerged that he had been executed in 1947. A Swedish-Russian working group that investigated the matter found no hard evidence to support this theory.

Wallenberg's Legacy

It is not certain exactly how many persons were directly or indirectly saved by Wallenberg's mission. Certain is that his tireless efforts, combined with the initiatives taken by the Swedish Red Cross, the International Committee of the Red Cross, other diplomatic missions in Budapest, and the papal nunciature, saved as many as 100,000 Hungarian Jews from the Holocaust.

There are many parks, monuments, statues, and institutes named after him, notably the Raoul Wallenberg Human Rights Institute at the University of Lund in Sweden.

On June 20, 2000, the United Nations Secretary-General Kofi Annan remarked at a memorial service in Budapest that "Raoul highlighted the vital role of the bystander, of the third party amidst conflict and suffering. It was here, in the face of despair, that his intervention gave hope to victims, encouraged them to fight and resist, to hang on and bear witness."

Wallenberg is an honorary citizen of the United States, Canada, Israel, and the city of Budapest.

SEE ALSO Rescuers, Holocaust

BIBLIOGRAPHY

Anger, Per (1995). *With Raoul Wallenberg in Budapest: Memories of the War Years in Hungary*, trans. David Mel Paul and Margareta Paul. Washington, D.C.: Holocaust Library.

Besymenski, Lew (2000). *Die Wahrheit über Raoul Wallenberg: Geheimdokumente und KGB-Veteranen beschreiben die Mission und die Ermordung des schwedischen Diplomaten, der im Zweiten Weltkrieg Ungarns Juden zu retten versuchte.* Göttingen, Germany: Steidl Verlag.

Derogy, Jacques (1980). *Le Cas Wallenberg.* Paris: Éditions Ramsay.

Gann, Christoph (1999). *So viele Menschen retten wie möglich (Saving as Many Persons as Possible).* Munich: C. H. Beck.

Gilbert, Joseph (1982). *Mission sans retour: l'Affaire Wallenberg.* Paris: Albin Michel.

Handler, Andrew (1996). *A Man for All Connections: Raoul Wallenberg and the Hungarian State Apparatus, 1944–1945.* Westport, Conn.: Praeger.

Larsson, Jan. "Raoul Wallenberg." Available from http://www.raoul-wallenberg.org.

Marton, Kati (1995). *Wallenberg: Missing Hero.* Boston: Arcade Publishing.

Skoglund, Elizabeth (1997). *A Quiet Courage: Per Anger, Wallenberg's Co-Liberator of Hungarian Jews.* Grand Rapids, Mich.: Baker Books.

Swedish Ministry of Foreign Affairs (2000). *Raoul Wallenberg: Report of the Swedish-Russian Working Group.* Stockholm: Swedish Ministry of Foreign Affairs.

Wallenberg, Raoul (1995). *Letters and Dispatches,* tran. Kjersti Board. New York: Arcade.

Werbell, Frederick, and Thurston Clarke (1982). *Lost Hero. The Mystery of Raoul Wallenberg.* New York: McGraw-Hill.

Alfred de Zayas

Wannsee Conference

On January 20, 1942, Reinhard Heydrich, the head of the Nazi Security Police and the SS Security Service, and fourteen other senior SS officers, Nazi Party officials, and civil servants met in a villa in the Berlin suburb of Wannsee to discuss preparations for the Final Solution. When American legal investigators uncovered minutes (the sixteenth copy out of an original thirty) for the meeting among German Foreign Office records in March 1947, the meeting rapidly attained postwar notoriety and became known as the Wannsee Conference.

The conference's impact lay partly in the clarity with which its minutes (or so-called Protocol) revealed Nazi thinking. Consisting largely of an extended presentation by Heydrich, the Protocol offered a sober account of the evolution of Nazi policy on the Jews, culminating in "new possibilities in the East." A table slated 11 million European Jews, divided up by country, for inclusion in the plan. Although murder was not explicitly proposed, one section of the Protocol was unequivocal:

> In large, single-sex labour columns, Jews fit to work will work their way eastwards constructing roads. Doubtless the large majority will be eliminated by natural causes. Any final remnant that survives will doubtless consist of the most resistant elements. They will have to be dealt with appropriately, because otherwise, by natural selection, they would form the germ cell of a new Jewish revival.

None of the participants at the meeting, many coming from long-established ministries—the Ministry of the Interior, the Ministry of Justice, the Foreign Ministry, and the Reich Chancellery—protested. To many postwar observers it seemed incredible that such educated men, eight of them holding doctorates, had gone along with such proposals. As a symbol of the orderly governance of genocide, the protocol remains without parallel.

A more contentious subject among scholars is the meeting's policy significance for the emergence of the Final Solution. Heydrich's invitation and opening remarks suggested that the meeting was of great importance and was needed to clarify fundamental issues. Postwar investigators were also aware that around December, when the meeting was originally scheduled to take place, Hans Frank had alluded in Poland to fundamental discussions taking place in Berlin. For these reasons and coupled with the Protocol's systematic listing of all European Jews, many postwar observers believed it was at the Wannsee Conference that genocide had been decided. What cast doubts on this assertion, however, are the facts that mass killings had begun in Russia six months earlier, preparations for the Belzec camp were well underway, and the Chelmno death camp had been in operation since early December 1941. Moreover, it is not clear that Heydrich or his guests were senior enough to make important decisions about the Final Solution.

Historians have therefore puzzled over a meeting that seemed to be asking questions well after the shooting had started. Their answers have varied according to their broader understanding of how genocidal policy emerged. For those who believe a fundamental command was uttered in July 1941 or indeed earlier, Wannsee's function seems, at best, secondary and may have been almost entirely symbolic—as the historian Eberhard Jäckel argued in a seminal article in 1992. For those historians, by contrast, who believe that a decision to murder all European Jews—as opposed to the Soviet killings—crystallized piecemeal over the second half of 1941, the meeting's timing makes more sense as a response to an emerging consensus among Nazi leadership about the way to go forward. The timing may also have resulted from the negative reaction among some Berlin officials to the rapidly disseminated news that Berlin Jews had been shot on arrival in Riga on November 29 and 30, 1941. One of the first mass executions of German Jews, this had a different psychological significance than the already familiar content of the *Einsatzgruppen* reports from Russia. Wannsee was thus partly convened to ensure that the Reich's ministries were on board.

What is also clear is that Heydrich invited many of the agencies with whom his security police had regularly experienced disputes over lines of authority. Indeed, some agencies, notably representatives of the general government, were added only as an afterthought when new evidence of their resistance to his mandate came to light. Heydrich wanted to assert the SS's and specifically his leadership on the Jewish question. Moreover, to remove potential opposition to the deportation of more German Jews, he wanted to obtain agreement on any special categories to be exempted—highly decorated Jewish veterans from World War I, Jews in mixed marriages, and so forth. Much of the Protocol was taken up with these matters, and it is clear that Heydrich sought to undo most of the protection for half-Jews and also quarter-Jews that the Ministry of the Interior had thus far managed to maintain. This was the one significant area in which the Protocol registered any dissent from Heydrich's proposals, although in advocating the "compromise" of sterilizing all half-Jews, the Interior Ministry's Wilhelm Stuckart went much further in Heydrich's direction than had previously been the case.

The Wannsee Conference's true impact is hard to gauge. It is known that Heydrich was pleased with the outcome, and he conveyed to his subordinates the notion that the Security Police's authority had been enhanced. The deportation of German Jews, and the killing rate, both accelerated in the spring. On the question of the *Mischlinge* (half-Jews), however, followup meetings showed that considerable resistance to their being equated with "full Jews" remained, and in this regard Heydrich did not achieve the breakthrough he had hoped for.

SEE ALSO Germany; Heydrich, Reinhard; Holocaust

BIBLIOGRAPHY

Gerlach, Christian (2000). "The Wannsee Conference, the Fate of German Jews and Hitler's Decision in Principle to Exterminate All European Jews." In *The Holocaust. Origins, Implementation, Aftermath*, ed. Omer Bartov. New York: Routledge.

Huttenbach, Henry R. (1996). "The Wannsee Conference Reconsidered 50 Years After: SS Strategy and Racial Politics in the Third Reich." In *Remembrance and Recollection. Essays on the Centennial Year of Martin Niemöller and Reinhold Niebühr and the 50th Year of the Wannsee Conference*, ed. Hubert Locke and Marcia Littell. Lanham, Md.: University Press of America.

Jäckel, Eberhard (1995). "On the Purpose of the Wannsee Conference." In *Perspectives on the Holocaust. Essays in Honor of Raul Hilberg*, ed. James S. Pacy and Alan P. Wertheimer. Boulder, Colo.: Westview Press.

Roseman, Mark (2002). *The Villa, the Lake, the Meeting. Wannsee and the Final Solution*. London: Penguin.

Mark Roseman

War

For many centuries, western European attitudes toward the legality of war were dominated by the teachings of the Roman Catholic Church. War was regarded as a means of obtaining reparation for a prior illegal act, and was sometimes regarded as being commanded by God. In this way much of the debate centered on the distinction between just and unjust wars, a distinction that began to break down in the late sixteenth century. In time, leaders justified wars if they were undertaken for the defense of certain vital interests, although there were no accepted objective criteria for determining what those vital interests were. In the twenty-first century, international lawyers and states rarely use the term *war*. This is because "war" has a technical and somewhat imprecise meaning under international law, and states engaged in hostilities often deny there is a state of war. The difference between war and hostilities falling short of war may appear very fine, but it can have important consequences especially in regard to the relations between states. Since the adoption of the United Nations Charter in 1945, there is a general prohibition on the use of force by states except in accordance with the provisions of the Charter itself. In this way the question is more about the use of force than the right to declare war. This is reflected in the difficulty government representatives have had in finding an acceptable definition for the crime of aggression under the 1998 Rome Statue of the International Criminal Court.

Laws of War/International Humanitarian Law

Among the equivalent and interchangeable expressions, the "laws of war," the "law of armed conflict," and "international humanitarian law," the first is the oldest. War crimes come under the general umbrella of international humanitarian law, and may be defined as the branch of international law limiting the use of violence in armed conflicts. The expression "laws of war" dates back to when it was customary to make a formal declaration of war before initiating an armed attack on another state.

In the twenty-first century, the term *armed conflict* is used in place of *war,* and while the military tend to prefer the term *law of armed conflict,* the International Committee of the Red Cross and other commentators use the expression "international humanitarian law" to cover the broad range of international treaties and principles applicable to situations of armed conflict. The fundamental aim of international humanitarian law is to establish limits to the means and methods of armed conflict, and to protect noncombatants, whether they are the wounded, sick or captured soldiers, or civilians.

International humanitarian law is comprised of two main branches; the law of the Hague and the law of Geneva. The law of the Hague regulates the means

Refugees forced from their homes as a result of the Spanish Civil War arrive at the French border town of Luchon. [HULTON-DEUTSCH COLLECTION/CORBIS]

and methods of warfare. It is codified primarily in the regulations respecting the Laws and Customs of War on Land ("the Hague Regulations") annexed to the 1907 Hague Convention IV ("the Hague Regulations"). These govern the actual conduct of hostilities and include matters such as the selection of targets and weapons permissible during armed conflict. The law of Geneva is codified primarily in four conventions adopted in 1949, and these are known collectively as the Geneva Conventions for the Protection of War Victims. Their aim is to protect certain categories of persons, including civilians, the wounded, and prisoners of war.

After the piecemeal development of international humanitarian law at the end of the nineteenth century and the beginning of the twentieth century, the experience of World War II exposed the shortcomings in the legal regulation of this field dramatically. This realization led to the adoption of the four Geneva Conventions for the Protection of War Victims in 1949. The adoption of the Conventions, coupled with the earlier well developed body of Hague law governing the conduct of hostilities by armed forces, meant that traditional interstate wars, or "armed conflicts" to use the language of the Conventions, were now well-regulated, in theory at least. The phrase "armed conflict" was em-

ployed to make it clear that the Conventions applied once a conflict between states employing the use of arms had begun, whether or not there had been a formal declaration of war.

As the majority of armed conflicts in the cold war period were not interstate wars of the kind envisaged by traditional international humanitarian law, obvious gaps in the legal regulation governing armed conflicts remained. The adoption of the Geneva Conventions marked a break with the past in that Article 3, which was common to all four Conventions, sought to establish certain minimum standards of behavior "in the case of armed conflict not of an international character." In an attempt to address deficiencies in the 1949 Geneva Conventions, Additional Protocols I and II were adopted in 1977.

Protocol I applies to international armed conflict and brought what was often referred to as "wars of national liberation" within the definition of international conflicts. Protocol II, on the other hand, did not apply to all noninternational armed conflicts, but only to those that met a new and relatively high threshold test. Despite the time and effort that was involved in drafting and agreeing the Protocols, the result was less than satisfactory, especially from the point of view of classifying armed conflicts to determine which Protocol, if any, applies in a given case. The applicability of Protocol II is quite narrow, and this helps explain in part why so many states are party to it.

Codification of War Crimes

The United Nations Commission for the Investigation of War Crimes was established in the aftermath of World War II in order to prepare the groundwork for the prosecution of war criminals arising from atrocities committed during the war. One of the features of the 1945 Charter of the International Military Tribunal at Nuremberg is that the crime of genocide did not appear in its substantive provisions. Consequently, the Tribunal convicted the Nazi war criminals of "crimes against humanity" for the crimes committed against the Jewish people in Europe.

The relationship between war crimes, genocide, and crimes against humanity is somewhat complex due to the historical development of each category of international crime. The most significant practical legal issue to be considered is the necessity for some form of armed conflict before there can be a war crime. In the case of genocide, there is no requirement for such crimes to take place in the context of a war or armed conflict. However, such crimes can often be committed as part of a wider conflict to achieve some of the broader aims of participants. The chaos and breakdown in law and order characteristic of armed conflict provides potential perpetrators with an opportunity to pursue illegitimate objectives and methods.

Historically, it was also probably easier to evade responsibility for such crimes when they were committed in the course of an armed conflict. With the advent of the International Criminal Tribunals for the former Yugoslavia and Rwanda, Special Courts and the International Criminal Court, this situation no longer prevails.

The concept of a war crime is broad and encompasses many different acts committed during an armed conflict. It is synonymous in many people's minds with ethnic cleansing, mass killings, sexual violence, bombardment of cities and towns, concentration camps, and similar atrocities. War crimes may be defined as a grave or serious violation of the rules or principles of international humanitarian law—for which persons may be held individually responsible. The Geneva Conventions oblige states to provide effective penal sanctions for persons committing, or ordering to be committed grave violations of the Conventions. In fact, in such cases all states are required to assume power to prosecute and punish the perpetrators. Such provisions only apply if the violations were committed in the course of an international armed conflict. In reality, it is often difficult to determine if a particular situation amounts to an "international" or a "noninternational armed conflict." However, although legally of some significance, it does not alter the serious nature of the crimes in the first instance.

Furthermore, decisions of the International Criminal Tribunals for the former Yugoslavia and Rwanda have ruled that many principles and rules previously considered applicable only in international armed conflict are now applicable in internal armed conflicts, and serious violations of humanitarian law committed within the context of such internal conflicts constitute war crimes. Such decisions, and the adoption of the Rome Statute of the International Criminal Court, have tended to blur the legal significance of the distinction between international and noninternational armed conflicts.

Genocide and Crimes Against Humanity

The judgment of the International Military Tribunal at Nuremberg was controversial in some respects. One of the main reasons why it was considered necessary to draft a convention that dealt specifically with the crime of genocide was the limited scope given to "crimes against humanity" at the time.

A crime against humanity referred to a wide range of atrocities, but it also had a narrow aspect, and the prevailing view in the aftermath of World War II was that crimes against humanity could only be committed in association with an international armed conflict or war. The Allies had insisted at Nuremberg that crimes against humanity could only be committed if they were associated with one of the other crimes within the Nuremberg Tribunal's jurisdiction, that is, war crimes and crimes against peace. In effect they had imposed a requirement or nexus, as it became known, between crimes against humanity and international armed conflict. For this reason many considered that a gap existed in international law that needed to be addressed. The General Assembly of the United Nations wanted to go a step further recognizing that one atrocity, namely genocide, would constitute an international crime even if it were committed in time of peace. The distinction between genocide and crimes against humanity is less significant today, because the recognized definition of crimes against humanity has evolved and now refers to atrocities committed against civilians in peacetime and in wartime. The Rome Statute of the International Criminal Court provides that crimes against humanity must have been committed as part of a "widespread or systematic attack directed against any civilian population."

Some states were concerned that international law did not seem to govern atrocities committed in peacetime (as opposed to during a time of armed conflict or war) and called for the preparation of a draft convention on the crime of genocide. The Convention on the Prevention and Punishment of the Crime of Genocide was adopted in 1948, and entered into force on January 11, 1951.

Under the Convention, the crime of genocide has both a physical element—certain listed acts such as killing, or causing serious mental or bodily harm to members of a racial group—and a mental element, which upholds the acts must be committed with intent to destroy, in whole of in part, a national, ethnic, racial or religious group "as such." Although earlier drafts had included political groups, this was later dropped during final drafting stages. In this way, the killing of an estimated 1.5 million Cambodians by the Khmer Rouge is not generally considered to have been genocide as defined under the Genocide Convention (both the perpetrators and the majority of the victims were Khmer). However, its widespread and systematic nature qualifies it as one of the twentieth century's most notorious crimes against humanity. The definition in the Convention is essentially repeated in Article 6 of the Rome Statute of the International Criminal Court, and in the relevant statues of the International Criminal Tribunals for the former Yugoslavia and Rwanda.

SEE ALSO International Criminal Court; International Criminal Tribunal for Rwanda; International Criminal Tribunal for the Former Yugoslavia; Nuremberg Trials; United Nations War Crimes Commission; War Crimes

BIBLIOGRAPHY

Chesterman, Simon, ed. (2001). *Civilians in War.* Boulder, Colo.: Lynne Rienner.

Claude, Inis, Jr. (1956). *Swords into Plowshares.* New York: Random House.

Commission of Inquiry into the Events at the Refugee Camps in Beirut (1983). *Final Report of the Commission of Inquiry into the Events at the Refugee Camps in Beirut The Jerusalem Post.* February 9, 1983.

Goodrich, Leyland M. (1960). *The United Nations.*London: Stevens.

Goodrich, Leyland M., Edward Hambro, and Ann P. Simons (1969). *Charter of the United Nations,* 3rd edition. New York: Columbia University Press.

Gutman, Roy, and David Rieff (1999). *Crimes of War.* New York: Norton.

Holzgrefe, J. L., and Robert O. Keohane, eds. (2003). *Humanitarian Intervention: Ethical, Legal, and Political Dilemmas.* Cambridge, Mass.: Cambridge University Press.

International Commission on Intervention and State Sovereignty (2001). *Report of the International Commission on Intervention and State Sovereignty: The Responsibility to Protect.* Ottawa: International Development Research Center.

International Committee of the Red Cross (ICRC). Available from: http://www.icrc.org.

Report of the Independent Inquiry into the Actions of the United Nations During the 1994 Genocide in Rwanda. UN Doc. S/99/1257. Published 1999.

Simma, Bruno (2002). *The Charter of the United Nations: A Commentary,* 2nd edition. New York: Oxford University Press.

Schabas, William A. (2000). *Genocide in International Law.* Cambridge, Mass.: Cambridge University Press.

Schabas, William A. (2004). *An Introduction to the International Criminal Court,* 2nd Edition. Cambridge, Mass.: Cambridge University Press.

United Nations (1999). *Report of the Secretary General Pursuant to General Assembly Resolution 53/35: The Fall of Srebrenica.* UN Doc. A/54/549.

White, Nigel D. (1997). *Keeping the Peace,* 2nd edition. New York: Manchester University Press.

Ray Murphy

War Crimes

Grave offenses against the laws of warfare entailing the penal responsibility of individuals constitute war crimes, long punished according to national laws and procedures. At the international level, war crimes were first clearly defined after World War II by the Charter of the International Military Tribunal. The international experience with prosecuting and punishing war criminals was followed by the codification of rules in the 1949 Geneva Conventions, the 1977 Additional Protocols, the statutes of international criminal tribunals for former Yugoslavia and Rwanda, and most recently, in the Statute of the International Criminal Court.

Much earlier precedents for punishing war crimes can be found in ancient Greece and Rome, the Laws of Manu in India, the code of Bushido in Japan, the Old Testament and the Qur'an. Violations of the laws and customs of war were punished by military commanders or national tribunals. Internationally, the first reported trial against a war criminal took place in Breisach in 1474, and in which Peter of Hagenbach was condemned for "crimes against the laws of man and of God."

The Lieber Code, promulgated by President Lincoln during the U.S. Civil War in 1863, was one of the first attempts to codify laws of war on national level. It provides for the following:

> all wanton violence committed against persons in the invaded country, all destruction of property . . . all robbery, all pillage or sacking, even after taking a place by main force, all rape, wounding, maiming, or killing of such inhabitants, are prohibited under the penalty of death, or such other severe punishment as may seem adequate for the gravity of the offense. A soldier, officer, or private, in the act of committing such violence, and disobeying a superior ordering him to abstain from it, may be lawfully killed on the spot by such superior.

The Oxford Manual on the laws of war on land, adopted in 1880 by the Institute of International Law, provided in Article 84 that "offenders against the laws of war are liable to the punishments specified in the penal law." Article 3 of the 1907 Hague Convention respecting the laws and customs of war on land only required that "a belligerent party which violates the provisions of the . . . Regulations shall, if the case demands, be liable to pay compensation. It shall be responsible for all acts committed by persons forming part of its armed forces." No individual personal responsibility was yet introduced into international law.

World War I

World War I led to a major step forward in the development of the rules concerning war crimes. Offenses against the law of war were prosecuted by national courts of several belligerent countries, and the Treaty of Versailles (1919) proclaimed that the responsibility for these offenses fell to the German emperor. However, an attempt to create an international court was opposed by the United States. The Dutch government granted asylum to the now-deposed emperor, William II of Hohenzollern, who could then not be tried by the special tribunal envisaged by the treaty.

Article 228 of the treaty also stated that "the German Government recognizes the right of the Allied and Associated Powers to bring before military tribunals persons accused of having committed acts in violation of the laws and customs of war." The persons accused of the crimes, however, were not handed over. Instead, Germany tried some of the accused before the Supreme Court of Leipzig, created expressly for this purpose. Of the 896 individuals accused of war crimes, only 45 were tried, and only 9 were convicted. The sentences were light and the convicted prisoners were pardoned a few years later.

Prosecution of War Crimes during and after World War II

Determined not to repeat the problem of allocating war-crimes responsibility after World War I, the Allied powers tried a new approach during World War II. They repeatedly warned the Axis powers of their responsibility for war crimes. The Moscow Declaration of 1943 distinguished between two sorts of war crimes. The first category of crimes were committed by German soldiers and members of the Nazi party who were responsible for, or took a consenting part in atrocities, massacres, and executions. They were sent back to be tried and punished in the countries where their crimes had been committed. The second category of German war criminals constituted those whose offenses had no particular geographical localization. These would be punished by joint decision of the governments of the Allies.

For the first category of war criminals, the first trials were held in Krasnodar (Russia) and Kharkov (Ukraine) in 1943, before the war had ended. Military tribunals for the second category of criminals were set up in Germany's occupation zones and were regulated by Law No. 10, of the Allied Control Council, which was passed on December 20, 1945 and which established a uniform basis of material law and procedure.

International prosecution was based on the London Agreement for the prosecution and punishment of the major war criminals of the European Axis Power, signed on August 8, 1945. This agreement includes the Nuremberg Charter of the International Military Tribunal. Article 6 of the charter established individual re-

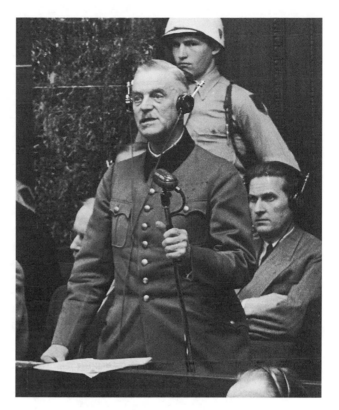

Field Marshal Wilhelm Keitel on trial at Nuremberg. Convicted of war crimes for planning and overseeing Germany's military campaigns during World War II, he was hanged at dawn on October 16, 1946, his final request to be shot by a firing squad, as befits a loyal soldier, having been denied. [HULTON-DEUTSCH COLLECTION/CORBIS]

sponsibility for crimes against peace, war crimes, and crimes against humanity. It was the first time that this terminology appeared in an international treaty. The definitions of each category of crime, as given by the charter, was only exemplary, not exhaustive.

The principles established by the Charter and the judgment of the Nuremberg tribunal were affirmed and recognized by the United Nations General Assembly Resolution 95(I), which was adopted on December 11, 1946. They were not fully formulated until later, however—in 1950, by the International Law Commission. Another tribunal, similar to that of Nuremberg, was established in Tokyo and was based on a Special Proclamation of General Douglas MacArthur as the Supreme Commander in the Far East. MacArthur took this action by virtue of the authority delegated to him by the four Allied Powers at war with Japan.

Non-Applicability of Statutory Limitations
In order to avoid the accused escaping prosecution because of statutory limitations to the crimes committed during the World War II, member states drafted the

Convention on the Non-Applicability of Statutory Limitations to War Crimes and Crimes against Humanity, which was adopted by the United Nations General Assembly on November 26, 1968. At the regional level, the European Convention on the Non-Applicability of Statutory Limitations to Crimes against Humanity and War Crimes was signed at Strasbourg on January 25, 1974. This new convention narrowed the definition of crimes against humanity in comparison with the United Nations Convention.

The 1949 Geneva Conventions and 1977 Additional Protocols

The four Geneva Conventions adopted on August 12, 1949, underlined the importance of domestic legislation and domestic jurisdiction in the prosecution and punishment of war criminals. According to the Conventions, the contracting parties must:

- enact legislation necessary to provide effective penal sanctions for grave breaches;
- search for those who have committed or gave the order to commit grave breaches;
- bring such persons before its courts, regardless of their nationality, or hand over such persons for trial to another contracting party for trial and punishment; and
- take measures necessary to suppress all acts contrary to the provisions of the convention other than the grave breaches.

Grave breaches are defined in common Articles 50/51/130/147 as acts committed against persons and property protected by the conventions, including:

- willful killing;
- torture or inhuman treatment, including biological experiments;
- willfully causing great suffering or serious injury to body or health;
- unlawful deportation or transfer or unlawful confinement of a protected person under the Fourth Convention;
- compelling a protected person to serve in the forces of a hostile Power; willfully depriving a protected person of the rights of fair and regular trial prescribed in the conventions;
- taking of hostages
- extensive destruction and appropriation of property, not justified by military necessity and carried out unlawfully and wantonly.

The First Additional Protocol revisited the definition of war crimes, specifying the conditions that would render such crimes punishable by law. It is important to emphasize that not all war crimes are, in fact, "grave breaches" as listed in the Geneva Conventions and the First Additional Protocol. The broader conceptual category of war crimes covers both grave breaches and other serious violations of the laws and customs of war, but according to the First Additional Protocol, not every violation of the laws of warfare "would of necessity constitute a punishable act."

The First Protocol supplemented, developed, and clarified the "system of repression" stipulated in the 1949 Geneva Conventions by explicitly accepting the same list of "grave breaches" as were defined in the Conventions, and by requiring that the system of repression, whereby war crimes may be prosecuted and punished, be applied to these grave breaches. In addition, the protocol expanded the list of grave breaches to include any willful act or omission that seriously endangers the physical or mental health or integrity of any person who is in the power of an enemy and which violates any in a series of specified prohibitions. The specified prohibited acts include any unjustified act or omission or medical procedure not required by the state of the victim's health; physical mutilation; medical or scientific experiments; or the removal of tissue or organs. For an act to constitute a violation it must have been committed willfully, in violation of relevant provisions of the Protocol, and it must have caused death or serious injury to body or health. The Protocol goes on to list the following acts as criminal under international law

- Making the civilian population or individual civilians the object of attack;
- Launching an indiscriminate attack affecting the civilian population or civilian objects in the knowledge that such attack will cause excessive loss of life, injury to civilians or damage to civilian objects;
- Launching an attack against works or installations containing dangerous forces in the knowledge that such attack will cause excessive loss of life, injury to civilians or damage to civilian objects;
- Making non-defended localities and demilitarized zones the object of attack;
- Making a person the object of attack in the knowledge that he is *hors de combat*;
- The perfidious use of the distinctive emblem of the red cross, red crescent, or red lion and sun, or of other protective signs recognized by the Conventions of this Protocol;
- The transfer by an occupying power of parts of its own civilian population into the territory it occu-

Ofuna prison, a POW camp in Yokohoma, Japan, August 1945. The Japanese interrogation camp was described by American prisoners of war as one of the worst in the area. [AP/WIDE WORLD PHOTOS]

pies, or the deportation or transfer of all or parts of the population of the occupied territory within or outside this territory;

• Unjustifiable delay in the repatriation of prisoners of war or civilians;

• Practices of apartheid or other inhuman and degrading practices involving outrages upon personal dignity, based on racial discrimination;

• Intentionally targeting clearly recognized historic monuments, works of art, or places of worship which constitute the cultural or spiritual heritage of peoples, resulting in the extensive destruction thereto, when such locales or objects have been accorded special protection and when these targets are not located in the immediate proximity of military objectives;

• Depriving a person protected by the Conventions and the Protocol of the rights of fair and regular trial.

In addition to the grave breaches, other serious violations of the laws and customs of war, including those stipulated in Article 23 of the 1907 Hague Regulations, remain war crimes and are punishable within the framework of customary international law.

The Nuremberg principles specified that complicity is also a crime under international law. Therefore, joint offenders and accessory accomplices are also punishable. An individual who commits a war crime is personally liable, regardless of his rank or governmental position. The commander is responsible, as are his subordinates for such violations. Military commanders must prevent or suppress war crimes, report breaches, and ensure that members of armed forces under his command are aware of their obligations.

Treatment of Offenders

An offender who benefits from the status of prisoner of war can be validly sentenced only if the sentence has been pronounced by the same courts and the same procedure as would be used in trying the members of the armed forces of the detaining power. The Convention and the Protocol prescribe judicial guarantees of the fair treatment for all military and civilian offenders. Even if a person does not benefit from the status of protected persons, that person will always benefit from the fundamental guarantees provided by human rights and by Article 75 of the Protocol, which express rules of customary law. The death penalty cannot be imposed if such penalty has been abolished by the detaining power.

Repression of War Crimes after 1945

Several domestic jurisdictions prosecuted and punished war criminals after 1945. One case was the massacre of forty-seven Arabs in Kafr-Kassem in October 29, 1956. Another occurred in 1958, when a military tribunal in Jerusalem condemned two officers and six border guards to seven to seventeen years imprisonment. The sentence was later reduced. In the United States, in 1971, a court martial sentenced U.S. Lieutenant William Calley to life imprisonment for his responsibility in the My Lai massacre of March 16, 1968, in which 347 civilians were killed in a village 510 kilometers outside of Saigon, Vietnam. His sentence was later reduced to 20 years, and he was paroled in 1974. Two other officers received disciplinary sanctions for their involvement in the same incident.

After the invasion of Kuwait in 1990, the United States, the United Kingdom, and the UN Security Council warned Iraqi authorities to respect the rules of war. The Security Council passed Resolution 674 in October 29, 1990, reaffirming the duty of Iraq "to comply fully with all terms" of the Fourth Geneva Convention and proclaiming Iraq's liability, as well the liability of individuals, for grave breaches. The resolution invited the UN member states "to collate substantial information in their possession or submitted to them on the grave breaches by Iraq . . . and to make this information available to the Security Council." In the wake of the second Iraq war, the provisional Iraqi government adopted the statute of a special tribunal in 2003 to try war criminals, including Iraq's former president, Saddam Hussein.

Crimes Committed in Former Yugoslavia and in Rwanda

During the conflicts in Yugoslavia, the UN Security Council required compliance with the rules of international humanitarian law and affirmed individual responsibility for violations. The United Nations created a commission of experts to investigate the crimes committed on the territory of former Yugoslavia. With Resolution 808 (1993), the Security Council established the International Tribunal for the Former Yugoslavia (ICTY). The tribunal deals with grave breaches of the Geneva Convention, violations of the laws and customs of war, genocide, and crimes against humanity (Articles 2 through 5). The definition of war crimes was based on the provisions of the Geneva Conventions and customary rules of international law.

With Resolution 955 (1994), the Security Council established the International Criminal Tribunal for Rwanda (ICTR), which was responsible for prosecuting genocide and other serious violations committed in the territory of Rwanda and its neighboring between January 1 and December 31, 1994. The list of crimes includes genocide, crimes against humanity, and violations of Article 3 of the Geneva Conventions and of the Convention's Additional Protocol II. The crimes were limited to those committed in the course of the internal conflict.

The statutes of both tribunals affirmed the principle of individual responsibility for planning, instigating, ordering, committing, or otherwise aiding and abetting in the planning, preparation, or execution of such acts. The concept of command responsibility was included: the official position of the accused does not relieve the person of responsibility nor mitigate the punishment, nor does the fact that the person ordered the acts but did not commit them personally. The fact that an accused person acted on the orders of a superior does not relieve the person of responsibility, either, but "may be considered in mitigation of the punishment."

By April 2004, the ICTY had tried forty-six individuals accused of genocide, war crimes, and crimes against humanity: Twenty-five of the defendants were judged guilty and began serving their sentences, A further sixteen were found guilty but began the process of filing appeals. Three persons were found not guilty on appeal. Two of the accused were acquitted. By the same date, the ICTR had completed trials for twenty cases.

The tribunals have concurrent jurisdiction with national courts, but in cases of conflict, the international tribunals have primacy over national courts and may formally request national courts to defer to them. Both tribunals made significant contributions to the development of international humanitarian law and to criminal law in general. They also helped to define and explain legal norms and establish the path for the future International Criminal Court (ICC). For instance, the appeals chamber of the ICTY, after hearing the *Tadic* case, came to the conclusion that "customary international law imposes criminal liability for serious violations of common Article 3, as supplemented by other general principles and rules on the protection of victims of internal armed conflict, and for breaching certain fundamental principles and rules regarding means and methods of combat in civil strife."

The Special Court for Sierra Leone

The Special Court for Sierra Leone was established on January 16, 2002, by joint agreement of the government of Sierra Leone and the United Nations. The court was mandated to try those who bear the greatest responsibility for serious violations of international humanitarian law and Sierra Leonean domestic criminal law committed in the territory of Sierra Leone since November 30, 1996. As of November 2003, thirteen persons from all three of the country's former warring factions were indicted by the special court. They were charged with war crimes, crimes against humanity, and other serious violations, including murder, rape, extermination, acts of terror, enslavement, looting and burning, sexual slavery, conscription of children into an armed force, and attacks on UN peacekeepers and humanitarian workers.

International Criminal Court

After several attempts in the past, most notably in 1919 and 1937, the United Nations adopted the Rome Statute of the International Criminal Court on July 17, 1998. The ICC is independent from the United Nations, and its relations with them is governed by an agreement that has been approved by the UN General Assembly. The treaty creating the ICC came into force on July 1, 2002, and by February 19, 2004, ninety-two states had become signatories to the treaty. The ICC's judges and prosecutor were elected in 2003. The court is based in the Hague.

In its founding statute, the ICC enumerates the crimes over which it has jurisdiction. These include genocide, war crimes, crimes against humanity, and crimes of aggression. The ICC accepts the 1948 Genocide Convention's definition of what constitutes the crime of genocide. The Rome Statute also provides a detailed definition of what constitutes a crime against humanity, which is markedly better developed than the definition provided in the Nuremberg Charter. It also defines several other essential terms, including extermination, enslavement, deportation and forcible transfer or torture.

It was only long after the fact that some war crimes became the subject of public scrutiny, including the atrocities committed by the Japanese during its "Rape of Nanking" in December 1937. Here, captors and prisoners party to this massacre watch from above while Japanese soldiers below taunt, and then bayonet, their Chinese victims. [BETTMANN/CORBIS]

The ICC assumes jurisdiction over war crimes that have occurred "as part of a plan or policy or as part of a large-scale commission of such crimes." These are not the only acts against which the ICC can take action however. According to the Rome Statute, the ICC can prosecute

(1) Grave breaches of the Geneva Conventions of August 12, 1949;

(2) Other serious violations of the laws and customs applicable in international armed conflict, within the established framework of international law. The statute then goes on to descript 26 specific prosecutable acts that may be committed in international armed conflicts;

(3) In the case of an armed conflict not of an international character, the ICC may prosecute any violations of the 1949 Geneva Conventions that have been committed against persons taking no active part in the hostilities, including members of armed forces who have laid down their arms and those who are no longer in active combat due to sickness, wounds, detention, or any other cause;

(4) Other serious violations of the laws and customs applicable in armed conflicts not of an international character, within the established framework of international law, referring to the provision of Protocol II and customary rules of international law.

The Statute specifies that its right to prosecute acts perpetrated in "armed conflicts not of an international character" does not apply to situations of internal disturbances and tensions such as riots, isolated and sporadic acts of violence, or other acts of a similar nature. Moreover, it presupposed that prosecutable violations in noninternational armed conflicts must have taken place in the territory of a state when there is protracted armed conflict between governmental authorities and organized armed groups, or a similarly protracted armed conflict between such groups.

The Rome Statute affirms several broadly accepted legal principles such as *nullum crimen sine lege* and *nulla poena sine lege* (there can be no prosecution, nor punishment, for acts that were not prohibited by law at the time). This establishes that, even though an act may today be defined as illegal, that law cannot be applied retroactively to a time when it was not yet a part of the legal code. The statute also affirms the concept of *non bis in idem*, which disallows double jeopardy: an individual cannot be tried twice for the same offense. In addition, it affirms the principle of individual responsibility, denies prosecutorial jurisdiction over persons less than 18 years of age, and establishes that there is no statute of limitation for the crimes under its jurisdiction. Finally, it expressly holds commanders and other superior officers responsible for acts carried out under their orders, and rejects the defense strategy of claiming immunity for individuals who hold (or held, at the time of the violation) head-of-state status.

These provisions constituted a significant step forward in international criminal law, particularly by filling certain gaps that had been left unaddressed in the Geneva Conventions. For instance, neither the Geneva Conventions, nor their Additional Protocols included a provision to address the defense that an accused was innocent by virtue of acting on the orders of a superior. Article 33 of the ICC's Rome Statute states that, a person who commits a prosecutable crime on the orders of another (a government or military superior) cannot escape criminal responsibility except in certain specific circumstances. The defendant, in such a case, must be able to show the law was manifestly lawful, or that he or she was under a legal obligation to obey orders of the Government or the superior in question or did not know that the order was unlawful. By the very definition of genocide or crimes against humanity, however, any orders to commit such crimes are manifestly unlawful, which makes the defense of "acting on superior orders" extraordinarily difficult to sustain.

The creation of the International Criminal Court is due, in large part, to the efforts of non-governmental organizations (NGOs). A coalition of thirty NGOs was created on February 25, 1995, which quickly grew to 800 by the opening of the Rome Conference (at which the ICC was created) in June 1998, of which 236 were in attendance at the meetings. During the conference, attendees focused on substantive issues and sought to establish the broadest possible jurisdiction for the newly created court. They also worked to create a system of complementarity, by which national courts held primary responsibility for prosecutions; an independent prosecutor, and a court that was free from the interference of any political body, including the Security Council. Other issues addressed by the conference included provisions for restitution for victims, the incorporation of gender concerns within the definition of actionable crimes; and a mechanism to assure the court with adequate funding over the long term.

SEE ALSO Geneva Conventions on the Protection of Victims of War; Hague Conventions of 1907; Humanitarian Law; Nongovernmental Organizations

BIBLIOGRAPHY

Askin, Kelly Dawn (1997). *War Crimes Against Women: Prosecution in International War Crimes Tribunals.* The Hague: Martinus Nijhoff.

Ball, H. (1999). *Prosecuting War Crimes and Genocide: The Twentieth-Century Experience.* Lawrence: University Press of Kansas.

Bantekas, Ilias (2002). *Principles of Direct and Superior Responsibility in International Humanitarian Law.* Manchester, U.K.: Manchester University Press.

Bassiouni, M. C., and P. Manikus (1996). *The Law of the International Criminal Court for Former Yugoslavia.* Irvington-on-Hudson, N.Y.: Transnational.

Baxter, R. R. (1951). "The Municipal and International Law Basis of Jurisdiction over War Crimes." *British Yearbook of International Law* 28:382–393.

Beigbeder, Yves (1999). *Judging War Criminals: The Politics of International Justice.* London: Macmillan.

Cassese, A., P. Gaeta, and J. R. W. D. Jones, eds. (2002). *The Rome Statute of the International Criminal Court: A Commentary,* 2 volumes. Oxford: Oxford University Press.

Dinstein Y., and M. Tabory (1996). *War Crimes in International Law.* The Hague: Martinus Nijhoff.

Dörmann K., L. Doswald-Beck, and R. Kolb (2003). *Elements of War Crimes under the Rome Statute of the International Criminal Court: Sources and Commentary.* Geneva: International Committee of the Red Cross.

Green, L. C. (1984). "War Crimes, Extradition and Command Responsibility." *Israel Yearbook on Human Rights* 14:17–53.

Jescheck, Hans-Heinrich (1992). "War Crimes." In *Encyclopedia of Public International Law,* volume 2, ed. R. Bernhardt. Amsterdam: North-Holland Publishing Company.

Kniriem, A. von (1959). *The Nuremberg Trials*. Chicago, Il.: Regnery Co.

Lee, Roy S., ed. (2001). *The International Criminal Court: Elements of Crimes and Rules of Procedure and Evidence*. Ardsley, N.Y.: Transnational Publishers, Inc.

McCormack, Timothy L. H., and Gerry J. Simpson, eds. (1997). *The Law of War Crimes: National and International Approaches*. The Hague: Kluwer Law International.

Pritchard R. John, and Sonia Magbanua Zaide, eds. (1981–1988). *The Tokyo War Crimes Trial*. 22 volumes. New York: Garland.

Röling, B. V. A., and C. F. Rüter eds. (1977). *The Tokyo Judgment: The International Military Tribunal for the Far East*. Amsterdam: APA-University Press Amsterdam.

Smith, Bradley F. (1977). *Reaching Judgment at Nuremberg*. London: Andre Deitch.

State of Israel (1992–1995). *The Trial of Adolf Eichmann: Record of Proceedings in the District Court of Jerusalem*, 8 volumes. Jerusalem: Ministry of Justice.

Tanaka, Y. (1996). *Hidden Horrors: Japanese War Crimes in World War Two*. Boulder, Colo.: Westview Press.

Taylor, Telford (1992). *The Anatomy of the Nuremberg Trials*. New York: Alfred A. Knopf.

United Nations War Crimes Commission (1947–1949). *Law Reports of Trials of War Criminals*, 15 volumes. London: Her Majesty's Stationery Office.

United Nations War Crimes Commission (1949). *History of the United Nations War Crimes Commission*. London: Her Majesty's Stationery Office.

U. S. House of Representatives (July 15, 1970). *Investigation of the My Lai Incident: Report of the Armed Services Investigating Subcommittee of the Committee of Armed Services, House of Representatives, 91st Congress, 2nd session, Under authority of H.Res. 105*. Washington, D.C.: U.S. Government Printing Office.

Weyas, A. M. de (1989). *The Wehrmacht War Crimes Bureau 1939–1945*. Lincoln: University of Nebraska Press.

Jiri Toman

Weapons of Mass Destruction

Genocide and crimes against humanity are "weapons neutral." They can be effected with simple tools like guns and machetes, or with sophisticated ones like atomic bombs or asphyxiating gas. Thus, in addition to proving the use of such weapons, a prosecutor would need to show the necessary intent against a group in the case of genocide, or the knowledge that the use was part of an attack on a civilian population in the case of crimes against humanity. The efforts to make weapons of mass destruction unavailable for genocide, or any other purpose, will be explored here.

Early Usage of the Term

The term *weapons of mass destruction* was apparently coined by the *London Times* in 1937 to describe the bombing and destruction of the Basque town of Guernica by German planes assisting the rebels in the Spanish Civil War. As such, it referred to fairly conventional weaponry, used in massive amounts. It soon came to bear a more restrictive meaning, applying to certain unconventional weapons. Thus, the very first resolution adopted by the United Nations (UN) General Assembly at its initial session in 1946 created an Atomic Energy Commission, whose major task was drawing up proposals "for the elimination from national armaments of atomic weapons and of all other major weapons adaptable to mass destruction." A parallel body, the Assembly's Commission on Conventional Armaments, in 1948 addressed the difference between conventional armaments and weapons of mass destruction. "Weapons of mass destruction," it suggested, "should be defined to include atomic explosive weapons, radioactive material weapons, lethal chemical and biological weapons, and any weapons developed in the future which have characteristics comparable in destructive effect to those of the atomic bomb or other weapons mentioned above." Physicist Albert Einstein and mathematician/philosopher Bertrand Russell had hydrogen bombs particularly in mind when they issued their so-called Pugwash Manifesto in 1955, calling on scientists to "assemble in conference to appraise the perils that have arisen as a result of the development of weapons of mass destruction."

After the terrorist attacks in New York City and Washington, D.C., in September 2001, which some categorized as crimes against humanity, the term seemed again to acquire a broader connotation. Now it included the use of planes being deliberately crashed to wreak death and destruction, and suicide bombers attempting indiscriminate killing. In this respect, weapons of mass destruction came close to the concept of terrorist bombing, criminalized by treaty. The 1998 International Convention for the Suppression of Terrorist Bombings prohibited the use of explosives or other lethal devices in public places. "Explosive or other lethal device" was defined as an explosive or incendiary weapon or device that is designed, or has the capability, to cause death, serious bodily injury, or substantial material damage; or a weapon or device that is designed, or has the capability, to cause death, serious bodily injury, or substantial material damage through the release, dissemination, or impact of toxic chemicals, biological agents or toxins or similar substances, or radiation or radioactive material. The definition, however, in its narrower meaning, referred solely to nuclear, biological, and chemical weapons, the kind that

A bystander examines the rusted remains of Iraqi missile heads at Aziziyah, 90 kilometers south of Baghdad, February 27, 2003. Although the United States believed Saddam Hussein's regime possessed weapons of mass destruction when it invaded Iraq, none were found. [REUTERS/CORBIS]

Iraq's alleged possession of the United States used to justify its invasion of that country in 2003.

As in 1946, the General Assembly is still concerned with the general issue, and the problem may be proliferating. The Assembly's provisional agenda for its sixtieth session in 2005 includes an item on "the development and manufacture of new types of weapons of mass destruction and new systems of such weapons."

Banning Barbaric Weapons in the Law of Armed Conflict

Eliminating specific kinds of barbaric weapons (and certain other tactics of war) has a long history in codes of chivalry and customary international law. Efforts to proscribe weapons of mass destruction (especially through the negotiation of treaties) are thus part of a broader movement that has defined the objects to be banned in various general (and overlapping) categories. Multilateral treaty-making concerning barbaric weapons began with the Declaration of St. Petersburg

in 1868 and has proceeded at two levels of abstract thought that might be described as principles and rules.

At the level of principle are propositions such as "means of injuring the enemy are not unlimited," or "it is forbidden to use weapons of a nature to cause superfluous injury or unnecessary suffering, or which fail to discriminate between soldiers and civilians." The 1972 Convention on the Prohibition of the Development, Production and Stockpiling of Bacteriological (Biological) and Toxin Weapons and on Their Destruction (hereafter referred to as the Biological and Toxin Weapons Convention) describes the use of such weapons as "repugnant to the conscience of mankind." Sometimes, these principles are promulgated as standards to govern broad categories. Other times, they lead to narrow agreement that a particular weapon is illegal, but a very similar practice is perhaps not. So it was that the Declaration of St. Petersburg avowed that the legitimate objective of war, to weaken military forces of the enemy, "would be exceeded by the em-

encyclopedia of GENOCIDE *and* CRIMES AGAINST HUMANITY

ployment of arms which uselessly aggravate the sufferings of disabled men, or render their death inevitable." Notwithstanding this generality, the parties agreed specifically only to "renounce, in case of war among themselves, the employment by their military or naval troops of any projectile of a weight below 400 grams, which is either explosive or charged with fulminating or inflammable substances."

Parties attending the First Hague Peace Conference in 1899 agreed not to use expanding bullets or "projectiles, the sole object of which is the diffusion of asphyxiating or deleterious gases." At the Second Hague Peace Conference in 1907 participants concurred that it was "especially forbidden . . . to employ poison or poisoned weapons." As "especially forbidden," in more general terms, was the employment of "arms, projectiles, or material calculated to cause unnecessary suffering." These became the fundamental principles of the laws of armed conflict, or international humanitarian law.

Although the term *weapons of mass destruction* had not yet been coined, the first treaty that can be regarded, in retrospect, as addressing them is the 1925 Protocol for the Prohibition of the Use in War of Asphyxiating, Poisonous or Other Gases, and of Bacteriological Methods of Warfare (otherwise known as the Geneva Protocol of 1925). The Protocol proclaims, "the use in war of asphyxiating, poisonous or other gases, and of all analogous liquids materials or devices, has been justly condemned by the general opinion of the civilized world." It then adds: "The High Contracting Parties, so far as they are not already Parties to Treaties prohibiting such use, accept this prohibition, agree to extend this prohibition to the use of bacteriological methods of warfare and agree to be bound as between themselves according to the terms of this Declaration." Many member states ratifying the Protocol entered a reservation (or exception) that turned it into a promise not to be the first in a particular conflict use the prohibited weapons, but left retaliatory use open. Implicit was the assumption that it was legal to develop and possess such weapons, although illegal to use them in making the first strike (or at all). Thinking about development and possession leads a state inevitably to contemplating arms control or disarmament, rather than merely forbidding use.

Sophisticated weapons, such as nuclear bombs, require testing (or they did until the recent development of sophisticated computer models significantly obviated that need). Both the 1963 Treaty Banning Nuclear Weapon Tests in the Atmosphere, in Outer Space and Under Water, and the 1968 Treaty on the Non-Proliferation of Nuclear Weapons addressed, albeit weakly, the development and possession of nuclear weapons. The 1963 treaty still permitted underground tests, and the 1968 treaty acknowledged the nuclear status of the five countries that originally possessed the bomb, although this was subject to an as yet unrealized obligation to negotiate disarmament. Nuclear weapons were also addressed in numerous condemning resolutions adopted by the General Assembly that many diplomats and commentators believed represented international customary law in declaring their use illegal against people. A majority of the International Court of Justice (ICJ) took a different view, however, of the status of these resolutions in the 1996 *Advisory Proceedings* on the Legality of the Threat or Use of Nuclear Weapons, saying nuclear weapons were not totally illegal in themselves; each case turned on proving the necessary breach of more general rules. In a 1963 resolution adopted unanimously by acclamation, the General Assembly solemnly called on states "to refrain from placing in orbit around the earth any objects carrying nuclear weapons or any other kinds of weapons of mass destruction, installing such weapons on celestial bodies, or stationing such weapons in outer space in any other manner."

A more comprehensive assault on development and acquisition of certain weapons of mass destruction is the 1972 Biological and Toxin Weapons Convention. It bans a type or quantity of biological agents or toxins that is not justified for prophylactic, protective, or other peaceful purposes, and equipment or means of delivery designed to use them in armed conflict. Parties undertake to destroy or divert to peaceful purposes, not later than nine months after the treaty's entry into force, all agents, toxins, weapons, equipment, and means of delivery in their possession or under their jurisdiction or control. The reference to prophylactic, protective, and other peaceful purposes has created an opportunity for some slippage, as the Convention does not provide for inspections or other means of enforcement. In the early 1990s, when Russia revealed the extent of cheating by the former Soviet Union and the international community became concerned about Iraq's pursuit of weapons of mass destruction, negotiations began for a Protocol (or amendment) to the Convention that might provide for monitoring. These efforts collapsed early in the twenty-first century when the administration of President George W. Bush took a different approach to inspection regimes that could be potentially applied to the United States itself. Instead, the National Strategy to Combat Weapons of Mass Destruction, a policy statement issued by the U.S. government in December 2002, emphatically asserts a right to use overwhelming force, including nuclear weapons, and even preemptively, to counter threats of use of any kind of weapon of mass destruction against the United States or its allies.

Enforcement Mechanisms in Treaties Banning Weapons

The 1993 Convention on the Prohibition of the Development, Production, Stockpiling and Use of Chemical Weapons and on Their Destruction (often referred to as the 1993 Chemical Weapons Convention) contains enforcement mechanisms that could potentially be highly intrusive. It established in the Hague an international organization, the Organization for the Prohibition of Chemical Weapons (OPCW), whose functions include verification of compliance. The Convention's basic obligations are starkly comprehensive:

> 1. Each State Party to this Convention undertakes never under any circumstances: (a) To develop, produce, otherwise acquire, stockpile or retain chemical weapons, or transfer, directly or indirectly chemical weapons to anyone; (b) To use chemical weapons; (c) To engage in military preparations to use chemical weapons; (d) To assist, encourage or induce, in any way, anyone to engage in any activity prohibited to a State Party under this Convention. 2. Each State Party undertakes to destroy chemical weapons it owns or possesses, or that are located in any place under its jurisdiction or control, in accordance with the provisions of this Convention. 3. Each State Party undertakes to destroy all chemical weapons it has abandoned on the territory of another State Party, in accordance with the provisions of this Convention. 4. Each State Party undertakes to destroy any chemical weapons production facilities it owns or possesses, or that are located in any place under its jurisdiction or control, in accordance with the provisions of this Convention. 5. Each State Party undertakes not to use riot control agents as a method of warfare.

Paragraph 5's prohibition of riot control agents in warfare settles an issue much disputed in earlier international practice. The Convention defines riot control agents as chemicals that "can produce rapidly in humans sensory irritation or disabling physical effects which disappear within a short time following termination of exposure." If riot control agents are banned specifically in war, however, by implication they may be legal in domestic law enforcement. At a review conference on the Convention in 2003, the International Committee of the Red Cross (ICRC) expressed concern about increasing interest among police, security, and armed forces in incapacitating chemical agents. The ICRC fears that the development of new incapacitants domestically could undermine both the Convention and its underlying humanitarian norms. If it is "legal"

for a state to use a particular weapon against its own people in situations short of armed conflict, the inhibitions against using it in armed conflict lose some of their power.

A more general problem also exists. Chemicals, like guns and machetes, may have dual uses (good and bad), and some chemicals, benign in themselves, may be precursors to weapons of mass destruction. Thus, the 1993 Convention, like treaties dealing with nuclear and bacteriological weapons (and narcotic drugs, for that matter), must strike a complex balance between licit and illicit uses.

The Convention is enforced through self-reporting, by routine inspections, and in requests for clarification that parties may make to question other parties' compliance. Each party can also request an on-site "challenge inspection" of any facility maintained by another party "for the sole purpose of clarifying and resolving any questions concerning possible non-compliance with the provisions of [the] Convention." OPCW has limited resources but infinite potential for strong enforcement and as a model to be applied to other weapons.

Developments

In spite of their clear illegality under the laws of armed conflict, the use of biological and chemical weapons is not among the war crimes within the jurisdiction of the new International Criminal Court (ICC), formed by the Rome Statute of 1998. Their use, along with that of nuclear weapons, was included in early drafts of this instrument. When it became apparent that states which were nuclear powers would not accept the reference to nuclear weapons, some developing countries insisted that less technologically sophisticated weapons of mass destruction should not be included either. Nonetheless, the absence of these weapons from the ICC's jurisdiction does not affect their illegality under general international law.

At a historic meeting at the level of heads of state and government on January 31, 1992, the Security Council asserted that the "proliferation of nuclear, chemical and biological weapons constitutes a threat to international peace and security." When the Council reexamined the subject in late 2003, it was amid fears that nonstate actors as well as outlaw regimes were seeking to acquire, traffic in, or use weapons of mass destruction. As President Bush told the General Assembly in September 2003: "The deadly combination of outlaw regimes and terror networks and weapons of mass murder is a peril that cannot be ignored or wished away." He also noted the United States had worked with Russia and other former Soviet states to dismantle and destroy or secure weapons and dangerous materials left over from another era. (The nuclear weapons abandoned in Belarus, Kazakhstan, and Ukraine were of particular concern.) He added that eleven nations were cooperating in a "proliferation security initiative," aimed at interdicting lethal materials in transit.

A significant feature of this new landscape is the recognition of weapons of mass destruction not only as an arms control problem, but also as a matter of international criminal law that merits the same kind of legal analysis as efforts to address terror and narcotics. Accordingly, there have been proposals for the Security Council, as well as the General Assembly, to call on states to adopt and enforce laws that would prohibit the involvement of nonstate actors with such weapons or delivery systems for them.

SEE ALSO Gas; Iraq; Nuclear Weapons; War Crimes

BIBLIOGRAPHY

Deller, Nicole and John Burroughs (2003). "Arms Control Abandoned: The Case of Biological Weapons." *World Policy Journal* XX(2). Available from http://www.worldpolicy.org/journal/articles/wpj03-2/deller.html.

"Etymologies & Word Origins: Letter W, Weapon of Mass Destruction." Available from http://www.wordorigins.org/wordow.htm.

Fidler, David P. (2003). "Weapons of Mass Destruction and International Law." American Society of International Law Insights. Available from http://www.asil.org/insights/insigh97.htm.

Goldblat, Jozef (2002). *Arms Control: The New Guide to Negotiations and Agreements*, 2nd edition. New York: Sage Publications.

Graham, Kennedy (2003). "Weapons of Mass Destruction: Restraining the Genie." *New Zealand International Review* xxviii(3):2.

Russell, Bertrand, and Albert Einstein (1955). "The Russell–Einstein [Pugwash] Manifesto." Available from http://www.pugwash.org/about/manifesto.htm.

Stanley Foundation (2003). "Global Disarmament Regimes: A Future or a Failure?" Available from http://reports.stanleyfoundation.org.

"Transcript of Address by President Bush to the United Nations General Assembly." *The New York Times* (September 24, 2003), Section A, page 12, column 1.

United Nations, Weapons of Mass Destruction Branch, Department for Disarmament Affairs, website. Available from http://disarmament.un.org:8080/wmd.

Yepes-Enriquez, Rodrigo, and Lisa Tabassi, eds. (2002). *Treaty Enforcement and International Cooperation in Criminal Matters with Special Reference to the Chemical Weapons Convention*. The Hague: T.M.C. Asser Press.

Roger S. Clark

West Papua, Indonesia (Irian Jaya)

New Guinea, the largest tropical island in the world, is divided roughly in half. To the east is Papua New Guinea (PNG), independent since 1975. To the west is Papua (163,000 square miles), which comprises approximately one-fourth of the total area of the Indonesian archipelago. Papua is often called West Papua (WP) to distinguish it from PNG. The two halves of the island are divided along a 500-mile north–south colonial boundary that, in places, runs directly through the middle of villages. Until 1962, WP was a colonial possession of the Dutch.

In 1961 WP was on the verge of independence, although both Indonesia and the Netherlands made claims of sovereignty to the territory. Cold war tensions had been injected into the WP sovereignty dispute and, in addition, between the Dutch colonial power and the oil companies in WP; rivalry over WP's rich oil and gold deposits further added to the complexity of the situation. UN Secretary-General Dag Hammarskjold was preparing to reject both Indonesian and Dutch claims to sovereignty of Papua in favor of granting independence to the West Papuans themselves. However, Hammarskjold's plan ended abruptly with his death in a midnight plane crash near Ndola, Northern Rhodesia. All matters relating to WP, even under the auspices of the United Nations, subsequently became embroiled in the cold war.

From a Western perspective, the tragic disappearance of Michael Rockefeller in 1961 cast a further pall on the subject of Papuan self-determination. The Rockefeller family had been associated with Standard Oil for most of the previous century, and this company was conducting oil exploration in West Papua when Michael visited in 1961. As Michael and a Dutch anthropologist, Rene Wassing, were crossing the fifteen-mile wide mouth of the Eilanden River on the southern coastline, their boat overturned. It drifted out to sea, the two men clinging to its sides.

The following day, when the boat was twenty miles from shore (according to Wassing, who was interviewed by the author), Michael Rockefeller attempted to swim ashore. "We could see no land anywhere," explained Wassing, who was later rescued. The world media attributed the disappearance of Michael Rockefeller to cannibalism, an intangible influence on the UN reversal of support for Papuan self-determination.

In August 1962, the UN reached the New York Agreement, which abrogated Dutch sovereignty in favor of Indonesian control until 1969. According to the agreement, the Papuan people would then be permitted to decide for themselves whether or not they wanted to remain under Indonesian rule. The quest to control Irian Jaya (as WP was called when it was no longer Netherlands New Guinea) was in the hands of Major-General (later president) Suharto in the early 1960s. This same army under his command was credited by the American Central Intelligence Agency (CIA) with perpetrating one of the worst massacres of the twentieth century in Java and Bali during the years 1965 and 1966.

The task of "ascertaining the freely expressed will of the population" (in the words of the agreement) should not have been done under Indonesian oversight, yet it was, and all Papuan aspirations of independence met with Indonesian rejection. Papuans, who had voted under Dutch rule, were not allowed to do so freely under Indonesia's control. Only a small portion of the population was permitted to vote, and then only under extreme duress.

In the years leading up to the UN-mandated Act of Free Choice in 1969, the Indonesian army engaged in widespread killing to quell Papuan resistance. In the latter half of the 1960s, thousands of Papuans were massacred, such as in the Kebar Valley and the Paniai uprising, showing that Indonesia would stop at nothing to retain the territory. Papuan resistance only intensified, however. Remnants of the 3,000-strong Papuan Battalion, which had been formed by the Dutch, became guerrilla units that were collectively known as the Organisasi Papua Merdeka (Free Papua Movement; OPM). The OPM became the bane of the Indonesian occupation army, attracting a cross-section of the Papuan population. By 1967, the OPM was powerful enough to take over the former Dutch capital, Manokwari. They held it for several days, until the city was bombed and strafed, then retaken by Indonesian paratroopers.

For the historically momentous vote in 1969, the army carefully chose "representatives" who would conform to Indonesian directives. Many who wanted a pro-Papua outcome were massacred. Whole villages—men, women, and children alike—were forced to dig their own burial pits before being killed by the Indonesian army. The 100 or so villagers living in Iapo, on the shore of Lake Sentani, were but one example of this village-wide approach to killing. The smoke from their burning bodies served to warn thirty other nearby villages how the army dealt with independence sympathizers. Similar crimes against humanity were perpetrated in many areas of West Papua before the UN-mandated Act of Free Choice. By a show of 1,025 hands (983 males, 42 females) the "vote" was considered unanimous: all favored Indonesian rule. In Jayapura,

the new capital, the army used tanks and machine-guns to clear the streets of 5,000 Papuans who protested the injustice. None of the handful of UN observers present raised an objection to the gross infringements of human rights that the Indonesian army committed in order to secure an outcome favorable to Indonesia. Officially, the UN "took note" of the outcome, tacitly acknowledging the vote. Anything less would have been tantamount to criticism of President Suharto's "New Order" and its anti-communist credentials which, in the height of the cold war era, were considered overwhelmingly important to Western interests.

Papua became a "military operations area" during Suharto's presidency, and was placed under the control of Indonesian security forces. In addition, the vast territory, with some of the richest gold deposits and the purest oil in the world, was transformed into a multibillion dollar source of revenue for U.S. mining and oil interests.

The Indonesian Army, too, had business interests that extended throughout Indonesia as a corollary of the territorial command structure, reaching from Jakarta to remote villages in WP. Thus, the ousting of Suharto from government in 1998 made no difference locally, for the army remained in place. According to the WP-based human rights group, Elsham, when the Indonesian economy suffered a downturn in the late 1990s, the army intensified its exploitation of WP, particularly through illegal logging schemes. In addition to the army, Indonesian security forces in WP included also police, air force and navy personnel. Among these, a special unit of the police known as mobile brigade (BriMob) is noted for being particularly ready to resort to brutality. The most notorious, however, has been the army special unit known as Kopassus (the Special Forces Command), which also operates as an intelligence service.

In 1977, when Indonesian armed forces moved into the highlands, the most densely populated area of WP, many villages in the mountain valleys were strafed and bombed by Vietnam surplus OV-10 "Bronco" aircraft. According to W. H. Vriend of the Government Hospital, author of the 2003 book *Smoky Fires*, there were American advisers for the Indonesian pilots, deployed on the tarmac at the main airport in the Papuan highlands at Wamena. An estimated 70 percent of the Tagi people of the Western Dani valley were killed in such raids. Papuans themselves say seventeen thousand people died. Kopassus officers directly from Jakarta selected many Papuan leaders and articulate individuals for slaughter. Extrajudicial killings have occurred throughout the decades since WP fell under Indonesian rule.

In 1997, along the southern foothills of the central range, Major-General Prabowo Subianto (Suharto's son-in-law and head of Kopassus) was responsible for bombing and strafing of villages, and causing widespread starvation by laying waste to all gardens and farm-animals.

In the early twenty-first century, the population of PNG was estimated at 5.5 million inhabitants. By contrast, the indigenous population of WP is only 1.8 million, with an additional 1.7 million "transmigrants" mainly from the Indonesian islands of Java and Sulawesi. Had the indigenous population of WP grown at the same rate as PNG, it should have achieved a total of approximately 3.4 million. The explanation for the Papuan population deficit can be found in the policies pursued by the Indonesian army and police stationed in Papua. The deliberacy of their violence, and the intent underlying their actions, predicates the accusation of genocide.

The indigenous peoples of WP have more recently faced a new threat to their survival, according to medical workers in three regions of the territory who allege that the Indonesian army is deliberately using Javanese prostitutes known to be infected with HIV-AIDS. One of these medical officers produced a detailed report, listing not only the names of sixteen prostitutes brought from Surabaya to Papua, but also the names of those who had become infected from those sixteen, and those who had died.

Today, WP has the highest incidence of HIV-AIDS in Indonesia, more than twice that of PNG. Poisoning of water and food supplies by army personnel has also been alleged, such as in the February 2004 case reported in the *Courier-Mail* in which seventeen Papuans died in Ilaga Hospital.

Far from arriving in WP to liberate the indigenous peoples from Dutch colonial rule, the Indonesian military since the 1960s has simply replaced the Dutch as colonial overlords with a prison-guard mentality. To the occupying forces, Papuan ethnicity has been treated as the equivalent of a crime. The activities of the Indonesian army in this once-ignored half-island is steadily attracting more Western attention, yet the Kopassus strategy of dealing with Papuan aspirations for independence remains what it has always been: to eliminate it at the source.

SEE ALSO Indonesia

BIBLIOGRAPHY

Brundige, Elizabeth, Winter King, Priyneha Vahali, Stephen Vladeck, and Xiang Yuan (2003). *Indonesian Human Rights Abuses in West Papua: Application of the Law of Genocide to the History of Indonesian Control.* Available from www.law.yale.edu/outside/html/Public_Affairs/426/westpapuarights.pdf.

Lagerberg, Kees (1979). *West Irian and Jakarta Imperialism.* New York: St. Martin's Press.

Poulgrain, Greg (1984). *West Papua: The Obliteration of a People.* London: Tapol.

Vriend, W. H. (2003). *Smoky Fires: The Merits of Development Co-Operation for Inculturation of Health Improvements.* Amsterdam: Vrije Universteit.

Greg Poulgrain

Whitaker, Benjamin
[SEPTEMBER 15, 1934–]
Advocate for minority rights

Benjamin Whitaker's career has been completely devoted to justice, in particular justice for those in greatest need. He has worked tirelessly for the protection of minorities and recognized the importance of this to the prevention of genocide.

Born in London, Whitaker studied modern history and law at Oxford. He practiced as a barrister from 1959 through 1967. In 1966 he was elected to Parliament, representing Hampstead in London, and was immediately given a role with the Ministry of Housing and Local Government, becoming Junior Minister for Overseas Development in 1969. He left Parliament in 1970.

In 1971 Whitaker became Executive Director of the Minority Rights Group (MRG), a nongovernmental organization (NGO) founded in the late 1960s by a group of academics, lawyers, and journalists. MRG focused on the need to protect the rights of persons belonging to minorities and the collective rights of minorities. It specialized in producing expert reports on minorities or minority issues, to use as a basis for lobbying, often at an international level. MRG's reports were highly regarded throughout the human rights community. Their level of credibility was a tribute to Whitaker's leadership, not least because MRG had a small budget and depended on his ability to identify experts and persuade them to donate their writing.

Under Whitaker's guidance, MRG produced several reports on genocide, most notably those authored by René Lemarchand on Burundi and by Leo Kuper on the international prevention of genocide. MRG attended the annual sessions of the United Nations (UN) Commission on Human Rights and its Sub-Commission on the Prevention of Discrimination and the Protection of Minorities (now the Sub-Commission on the Promotion and Protection of Human Rights). The early 1970s were difficult days for those trying to draw UN attention to human rights violations; Whitaker would later regale students with stories of how NGOs, prohibited from mentioning an offending state's name in a UN forum, would refer to "a long slender State on the other side of the Andes from Argentina." Whitaker had the wisdom to enlist Kuper as a member of MRG's delegation on such occasions, thus informing Kuper's understanding of the international community's approach to the prevention of genocide as well as MRG's advocacy.

In 1975 Whitaker became a member of a UN body of independent experts, the UN Sub-Commission on the Prevention of Discrimination and the Protection of Minorities. From 1976 through 1978 he chaired its working group on slavery, and in 1982 produced its report on contemporary slavery. Following this, Whitaker was assigned the role of special rapporteur on genocide for the Sub-Commission, for which he produced a report in 1985. The Whitaker Report, as it came to be known, assessed the failings of the 1948 UN Convention on the Prevention and Punishment of the Crime of Genocide, and drew on contemporary thinking to come up with recommendations. It is important to note that, when embarking on this work in 1984, Whitaker circulated a questionnaire on genocide to UN members, organizations, and agencies; regional bodies; academics; and NGOs. Thus, a wide range of responses informed his conclusions.

The Whitaker Report called for the establishment of an international criminal court and a system of universal jurisdiction, what was called, "a double system of safeguard," to ensure the punishment of genocide. Whitaker did not, however, view punishment as the first priority in the fight to eradicate genocide, asserting that those who were likely to commit genocide were not easily deterred by the threat of retribution. Rather, he called for a number of preventive measures at the international level designed to reflect stages in the evolution of genocide; anticipate its occurrence; provide early warning of its onset; and determine action to be taken at the outset of or during genocide to stop it. Whitaker recognized that the prevention of genocide required first a database of continuously updated information, to enable the identification of patterns of developing genocides. Armed with such a resource, a permanent body of coordination linked with UN agencies and the International Committee of the Red Cross (ICRC) could, argued Whitaker, help to save thousands of lives.

Whitaker envisaged that such a body would be able to draw on a broad range of responses to the early warning of genocide. Allegations would be investigated. UN organs, related organizations, member states, interregional organizations, and the media could be engaged. When appropriate, local leaders could be asked

to intercede. To defuse tension, UN or ICRC conciliators or mediators could be brought in. A sanctions regime employing such measures as economic boycotts and exclusion from certain international activities could also be introduced.

Whitaker additionally recommended that an impartial and respected UN body be created to deal exclusively with genocide. He argued that ideally a body monitoring adherence to the 1948 UN Genocide Convention should be created, possibly under the "competent organs" article, Article VIII, of the Convention. Modeled on the UN Committee against Torture, such a committee would review allegations of genocide, interview the state concerned, and undertake its own investigations. In addition to reporting annually to the UN General Assembly, the proposed Committee on Genocide would be empowered to bring urgent situations to the immediate attention of the UN Secretary General. This would have the advantages of removing the determination of genocide from the political arena through the use of independent experts and ensuring a timely response at the appropriate level by avoiding the sometimes lengthy cycle of the UN human rights system.

Whitaker recognized that amending the UN Genocide Convention to create a treaty monitoring body might be a difficult process, and suggested that a UN Commission on Human Rights working group on genocide might provide an alternative. He concluded his report by stating, "the reforms recommended will, like most things worthwhile in human progress, not be easy. They would however be the best living memorial to all the past victims of genocide. To do nothing, by contrast, would be to invite responsibility for helping cause future victims" (p. 46). Whitaker departed from the MRG and UN Sub-Commission on the Prevention of Discrimination and the Protection of Minorities in 1988 and went on to work for the Gulbenkian Foundation. Fifteen years after he wrote his 1985 report, he chaired a session of the Raphael Lemkin Centenary Conference in London, where scholars discussed the new International Criminal Court.

SEE ALSO Genocide; United Nations Sub-
Commission on Human Rights

BIBLIOGRAPHY

Kuper, Leo (1984). *International Action against Genocide.* London: Minority Rights Group.

Robinson, N. (1960). *The Genocide Convention.* New York: Institute of Jewish Affairs.

Whitaker, Benjamin (1985). *On the Question of the Prevention and Punishment of the Crime of Genocide. Sub-*

Commission on Prevention of Discrimination and Protection of Minorities. Revised 1986. UN Document E/CN.4/Sub.2/1985/6.

Bernard F. Hamilton

Wiesel, Elie

[SEPTEMBER 30, 1928–]
Romanian-born writer, novelist, Nobel Peace Prize Laureate 1986, spokesman for humanity, and Holocaust survivor.

Elie Wiesel was born on September 30, 1928, in Sighet, Romania. The town of his birth is located in the region of Northern Transylvania annexed by Hungary in September 1940. The Wiesel family remained relatively untouched by the violence of the Holocaust until the German invasion of March 1944. At that time, the methods that the Germans had developed over three years within Poland were imposed immediately in Hungary. Within weeks, Hungarian Jews were ghettoized, and between May 15 and July 8, 1944, 437,402 of them were sent on 147 trains, primarily to Auschwitz II-Birkenau, the death camp. Weisel was but fifteen years old when he deported to Auschwitz. It is through the lens of his religious worldview that Wiesel was later to write of his experience.

Wiesel arrived in Auschwitz with his parents and three sisters. He immediately faced the Nazi selection process: "men to the left, women to the right" is the way he described it. His mother and younger sister were sent to the gas chambers, and his older sisters were sent to work. He and his father, Shlomo Wiesel, were sent to Buna-Monowitz, the slave labor complex known as Auschwitz III. He remained there until the forcible evacuation of Auschwitz on January 18, 1945, after which he and his father set off on foot to Bergen-Belsen, on what became known as a death march. Wiesel and his father arrived in Bergen-Belsen, but within days of their arrival, Shlomo Wiesel died of exhaustion and despair. Wiesel was liberated from Bergen-Belsen on April 11, 1945, and was taken with a children's group to France where he began his recovery and resumed his education. He studied at the Sorbonne, where he worked on but never completed his Ph.D., and earned a meager living writing for Israeli newspapers. Wiesel came to the United States in 1956 as the United Nations correspondent for an Israeli newspaper, *Yediot Acharonot.* He became an American citizen in part because it was easier than dealing with the bureaucracy involved in renewing his French travel documents.

Weisel is the author of more than forty books. In his early books, Wiesel struggled to find meaning for

A survivor of three concentration camps who lost most of his family to the Holocaust, writer Elie Wiesel remains a powerful voice for the victims of war and injustice. [GETTY IMAGES]

his suffering, to endow his destiny and the history of the Jewish people with a transcendent purpose in the wake of what seemed to him to be the collapse of the religious covenantal framework. *Night* (1960), his first book to be published in English (translated from the French), is a memoir, although it is often described as a novel. It is the only book aside from a chapter in his autobiography, *All Rivers Run to the Sea* (1995), in which Wiesel directly deals with the Holocaust. Widely regarded as a classic in Holocaust literature, *Night* is the story of a young boy, reared in the ways of Torah and fascinated by the eternity of Israel. The protagonist is rudely shocked by history when he is transported from his hometown of Sighet to Auschwitz, from a world infused with God's presence to a world without God and humanity. An earlier version of the work, written in Yiddish and entitled *When the World Was Silent,* was first published in Argentina in 1956 after a decade of self-imposed silence. The later, French version of the book is shorter and couched in less overtly angry language, and featured an introduction by Wiesel's mentor, the French writer Francois Mauriac.

Night forms one part of a trilogy. It was followed by the novel *Dawn* (1961), which tells the story of a

Holocaust survivor who is recruited to join a Jewish underground organization in pre-state Palestine. The protagonist of this novel is chosen to execute a British soldier in retaliation for the execution of one of his comrades. The final volume of the trilogy was originally published in English under the title *Accident* (1962; its title in French was *Le Jour*). This is the story of a Holocaust survivor who became a correspondent for an Israeli newspaper. The protagonist is struck by a car (the "accident" of the title) and hovers between life and death. His condition serves as the externalization of the survivor's inner struggle.

Only in Weisel's fourth book, *The Town Beyond the Wall* (1964), does the author succeed in the effort to endow suffering with meaning. The major character is a young Holocaust survivor who has made his way to Paris after the war. His mentor, the man who teaches him the meaning of survival, is not a Jew with memories of Sinai and Auschwitz. Rather, he is a Spaniard who learned his own lessons of death and love during the Spanish Civil War. From this man, Pedro, the young survivor learns two lessons that have shaped Wiesel's writings ever since. Pedro tells the young man:

> You frighten me. . . . You want to eliminate suffering by pushing it to its extreme: to madness. To say "I suffer therefore I am" is to become the enemy of man. What you must say is "I suffer therefore you are." Camus wrote that to protest against a universe of unhappiness you had to create happiness. That's an arrow pointing the way: it leads to another human being. And not via absurdity.

In other words, Pedro teaches the protagonist that the only way to redeem suffering and endow it with meaning is to treat its memory as a source of healing. In his public career and in all the rest of his writings, Wiesel has remained faithful to this insight.

With Martin Buber and Abraham Joshua Herschel, Wiesel came to represent Jewish history and values to Jews and non-Jews outside of Israel. He is particularly revered throughout the American Jewish community, having achieved iconic status. Non-Jews also perceive Wiesel as the non-Israeli embodiment of the Jewish people for this generation, and because he is not an Israeli, Wiesel is untainted by some of the negative aspects of Israel's late twentieth and early twenty-first century policies.

Wiesel neither directs any organization nor heads any movement, he has no institutional base. Unlike Jacob Neusner or the late Gershom Scholem, Wiesel has not defined a field of scholarship. Although employed by a university—Wiesel is the Andrew Mellon University professor of the Humanities at Boston University—he has not built a power base within academia. Widely regarded as a spokesperson for Israel, he deliberately stands apart from partisan Israeli politics. In Israel, for a time, he was regarded by many as *yored,* one who has left Israel and abandoned the quest for a national Jewish renaissance in the ancient homeland. The one institutional base he did enjoy—as chairman of the United States Holocaust Memorial Council—was rather problematic, and Wiesel was uncomfortable with his institutional role. He served in this capacity for eight years, but resigned on the eve of his departure for Oslo to receive the Nobel Peace Prize in December 1986. (The museum's architectural design and the creation of the exhibition's storyline were created after his resignation.) Wiesel is perhaps the only Jewish leader who speaks without the power of office or vast wealth to command the attention and respect of his audience. Seemingly aloof from politics, he stands above the controversies that consume most others within the American Jewish leadership.

Although Wiesel has influenced both Jewish and Christian theologians, he is not a religious figure in any ordinary sense. Rabbis lead their congregations; they speak from their pulpits; they are ordained by tradition. Hasidic masters have a court and a community, disciples and students, followers and supporters. They counsel their community and have authority over their followers. Theologians propose new religious interpretations and gain influence by virtue of their teachings. Wiesel has been called a non-Orthodox *rebbe,* the leader of a diverse group of admirers and followers, yet he does not exercise his authority in any direct way. Wiesel's teachings are open to diverse interpretations depending on the background of the critic. Like a Hasidic master, Wiesel has more admirers and followers than peers or friends.

What Wiesel offers is entry into the experience of the Holocaust and the shadows that remain in its aftermath. The sacred mystery of our time may be the face not of God, but of the anti-God: the evil side of humanity. Through Wiesel's work and persona, the non-survivor is offered a glimpse of what was but is no longer, of unspeakable horror and of the painful but productive process of regeneration after destruction. The non-survivor is offered only a glimpse, for as Wiesel has said: "only those who were there will ever know and those who were there can never tell."

Wiesel always writes as a Jew, but he does not speak only of Jews. He raises his voice on behalf of all who are in pain, all who are in need of refuge. He was a visible and influential spokesman for Soviet Jewry, taking trips to the Soviet Union during the 1960s and telling of his encounters with Soviet Jews in *The Jews of Silence* (1966). He is also an ardent supporter of Israel and refuses to criticize Israel outside of Israel. His attitude toward Israel is primarily one of gratitude for its creation, and in this he has much in common with many other Holocaust survivors. He worked against apartheid in South Africa, and continues to take up the cause of black South Africans and starving Ethiopians, as he did in earlier years for Biafrans. He has asked for refuge for Central Americans and for Iranian Bahais in much the same way as he pleaded for Soviet Jews. He traveled to Thailand to plead for the Cambodian victims of genocide and to Argentina to act of behalf of disappeared persons. Wiesel considers all these events a shadow of the Holocaust, a reflection of an evil unleashed across the planet—one whose mysterious implications are not yet known.

An example of Wiesel's style in influencing others can be seen in his encounter with president Ronald Reagan over the President's proposed 1985 trip to Bitburg to lay a wreathe at the graves of Waffen SS soldiers. Even within the American Jewish community, many were reluctant to confront the President, who had thus far been so supportive of Israel, but Wiesel provoked a confrontation with Reagan, and did so courteously, deliberately, and insistently. Just days before the president's scheduled trip to Germany, Wiesel attended a White House ceremony to receive the U.S. Congressional Gold Medal. While there, he took the opportunity to speak his mind, and said, "I belong to an ancient people that speaks truth to power." Speaking directly to president Reagan he said: "that place is not your place, Mr. President. Your place is with the victims of the SS."

Charles Silberman, a distinguished commentator on American Jewish history, regards this moment as a high point in the assertion of Jewish dignity and Jewish acceptance within America, ranking it with the nomination of senator Joseph I. Lieberman, an observant Jew, as the Democratic candidate for Vice President in 2000. A man of peace, Wiesel nonetheless supported president George W. Bush's invasion of Iraq in 2003. He explained that he opposed all war and the killing it entails, but believed that some evils must be confronted.

Teaching has always been central to Wiesel's very sense of self. He first taught as a Distinguished Professor of Judaic Studies at the City College of New York (1972–1976). Since 1976, he has been the Andrew W. Mellon Professor in the Humanities at Boston University, where he also holds the title of University Professor. He is a member of the faculty in the Department of Religion as well as that of the Department of Philosophy. He was the first Henry Luce Visiting Scholar in Human-

ities and Social Thought at Yale University, a position he held from 1982 to 1983.

Wiesel has received numerous awards. In addition to the Nobel Prize for Peace, which he received in 1986, he was also awarded the Presidential Medal of Freedom, the U.S. Congressional Gold Medal, and the Medal of Liberty. In addition, he was granted the rank of Grand-Croix in the French Legion of Honor. He is married to Marion Wiesel, who often serves as his translator, and they have one son, Elisha.

SEE ALSO Auschwitz; Holocaust; Memoirs of Survivors; Psychology of Survivors

BIBLIOGRAPHY

Abrahamson, Irving, ed. (1985). *Against Silence: The Voice and Vision of Elie Wiesel.* New York: Holocaust Library.

Berenbaum, Michael (1994). *Elie Wiesel, God, The Holocaust and the Children of Israel.* West Orange, N.J.: Berhman House.

Chmiel, Mark (2001). *Elie Wiesel and the Politics of Moral Leadership.* Philadelphia: Temple University Press.

Estess, Ted L. (1980). *Elie Wiesel.* New York: F. Ungar.

McAfee Brown, Robert (1983). *Elie Wiesel, Messenger to all Humanity.* South Bend, Ind.: University of Notre Dame Press.

Rittner, Carol, ed. (1990). *Elie Wiesel: Between Memory and Hope.* New York: New York University Pres.

Roth, John K. (1979). *A Consuming Fire: Encounters with Elie Wiesel and the Holocaust.* Atlanta: John Knox Press.

Roth, John K. (1992). "From Night to Twilight: A Philosopher's Reading of Elie Wiesel." *Religion in Literature* 24(1):59–73.

Sibelman, Simon P. (1995). *Silence in the Novels of Elie Wiesel.* New York: St. Martin's Press.

Wiesel, Elie (1972). *Souls on Fire.* New York: Random House.

Wiesel, Elie (1987). *The Night Trilogy: Night, Dawn, Day.* New York: Harper/Collins.

Wiesel, Elie (1995). *All Rivers Run to the Sea: Memoirs.* New York: Alfred A. Knopf.

Wiesel, Elie (1999). *And the Sea Is Never Full: Memoirs, 1969–.* New York: Alfred A. Knopf.

Michael Berenbaum

Wiesenthal, Simon
[DECEMBER 31, 1908–]
Polish humanitarian

Born in 1908, in Buczacz, Galicia (in the Polish Ukraine), Simon Wiesenthal was raised in a typical *shtetl* (small Jewish town) environment. The family moved to Lvov, Vienna, and finally back to Buczacz.

Simon Wiesenthal, Nazi hunter, ninety years old at the time of this 1999 photo. In April 2003 Wiesenthal announced his retirement, saying that he had found all the mass murderers he had been looking for. According to Wiesenthal, the only Austrian war criminal still alive is Alois Brunner, Adolf Eichmann's right-hand man, believed to be hiding in Syria.[AP/WORLD WIDE PHOTOS]

Wiesenthal continued his education in Prague, where he was trained as an architect. Leaving school in 1932, Wiesenthal returned to Lvov, where he married Cyla Muller in 1936 and, due to anti-Semitism, only received the formal degree of architectural engineer in 1939. In the wake of the nonaggression pact between the Nazis and the communists in 1939, the Russians took over Lvov, and Wiesenthal was no longer allowed to practice his profession.

On June 28, 1941, the Nazis occupied Lvov, and Wiesenthal and his family were swept up in the Nazi occupation. Wiesenthal went through a series of concentration camps, including Gross-Rosen, Janowska, Buchenwald, and finally Mauthausen, in Austria, from which the U.S. Army liberated him on May 5, 1945. Shortly thereafter he was reunited with his wife, who was the only other member of their extended families to survive, and in 1946 their only child, a daughter, was born.

Humanitarian

Wiesenthal began his postwar career by aiding the U.S. war crimes investigators in the immediate aftermath of liberation. In May 1945 he submitted his first extensive list of Nazis perpetrators to the U.S. authorities, and joined their team as an investigator and translator. The onset of the cold war between the Western countries and the Soviet Union caused the United States and the other Western Allies to turn away from the pursuit and judgment of Nazis, by either ignoring them or using them as either scientific or intelligence assets. (This was true of the Soviet Union and other Communist bloc countries as well.) By 1947 the U.S. Army had begun to abandon the effort, but using files that had been collected by the army, Wiesenthal opened the first Jewish Historical Documentation Center in Linz. He maintained this center until 1954, when he closed it down due to the lack of interest and support, sending his files to Yad Vashem, Israel's center for Holocaust study and commemoration. For the next few years Wiesenthal worked as a journalist and with refugee agencies.

The trial of Adolf Eichmann in Israel in 1961 brought both Wiesenthal and the pursuit of Nazis back into the limelight. While many people have claimed full credit for the capture, Wiesenthal's contribution of persistent tracking and important information greatly helped the Israeli operation. The question of credit for the capture has remained one of the major controversies associated with Wiesenthal throughout his career, with Mossad chief Isser Harel claiming sole responsibility and denying Wiesenthal any credit for the capture. Despite Harel's position, historians believe that Wiesenthal did contribute to the effort of tracking and capturing Eichmann, particularly by keeping the effort going until the Israelis became involved.

As a result of this renewed interest, Wiesenthal decided to move to Vienna and to reopen his Documentation Center there. Continuing to work independently, he became famous as the world's leading Nazi-hunter. Over the next decades he investigated and helped bring to justice over one thousand Nazi war criminals. Some of the more prominent cases included Franz Stangl, the commandant of Sobibor and Treblinka, Franz Murer, commandant of the Vilna ghetto, Karl Silberbauer, the policeman who arrested Anne Frank, Hermine Braunsteiner Ryan, the former Majdanek guard who was located in the Unites States, thus publicizing the presence of Nazi war criminals in the United States and Eduard Roschmann, second in command of the Riga ghetto.

From the early stages of his postwar career, Wiesenthal spoke up for other groups, not only Jews. In the 1950s he began to speak about the fate of the

Roma and Sinti under the Nazis, and has continued to draw attention to their persecution in Europe. He also spoke out on behalf of other threatened groups such as the Cambodians under Pol Pot and the Kurds. He championed the Soviet dissident Andrei Sakharov, and helped draw the world's attention to the fate of Raoul Wallenberg, the Swedish diplomat who saved Jews during the Holocaust and vanished after being arrested by the Soviets in 1945.

Prolific Author

Wiesenthal has been a prolific author over the years. Among his most significant works are *The Murderers Among Us* (1967), which interweaves chapters describing Wiesenthal's life and beliefs with those describing his pursuit of specific Nazis; *The Sunflower* (1970, 1998), which is a symposium on forgiveness with responses from major thinkers; *Every Day Remembrance Day* (1987), a calendar of anti-Semitism throughout Jewish history; and a last volume of memoirs, *Justice Not Vengeance* (1989). His other books include *Sails of Hope,* which deals with the theory of Christopher Columbus' supposed Jewish ancestry, as well as other works related to the Holocaust. In 1989 *The Murders Among Us* was made into a major television film starring Ben Kingsley. Johanna Heer and Werner Schmiedel's acclaimed documentary about Wiesenthal, *The Art of Remembrance,* appeared in 1997. Wiesenthal has been the subject of many books, particularly the biography by Hella Pick, *Simon Wiesenthal: A Life in Search of Justice* (1996) and Alan Levy's *The Wiesenthal File* (1993).

Controversy

Wiesenthal's career has been marked by some significant controversies. From 1970 to 1990 there was an ongoing bitter feud with Austrian Chancellor Bruno Kreisky. The feud was connected to Austrian politics, Israel, and Jewish identity. Kreisky, who was an assimilated Jew, accused Wiesenthal of surviving the war by collaborating with the Nazis. After a series of lawsuits, Wiesenthal finally won a judgment of slander against Kreisky, who died shortly after. This controversy was later dwarfed by the Waldheim affair. In 1986 the World Jewish Congress (WJC) launched a public relations campaign aimed at convincing Austrians (and the world) that former United Nations Secretary General Kurt Waldheim was a Nazi war-criminal and unfit to be elected as president of Austria. Wiesenthal reacted cautiously and, while agreeing that Waldheim had lied and covered up his wartime activities, refused to label him a war criminal without specific proof that would hold up in a court of law. The WJC reacted angrily, and viciously attacked Wiesenthal, who refused to back

down. Ultimately Waldheim was elected, Wiesenthal called for his resignation, the United States placed Waldheim on its "watch list" (preventing him from entering the country), and the bitter feelings between Wiesenthal and the WJC lingered.

The Simon Wiesenthal Center

In 1977 the Simon Wiesenthal Center in Los Angeles was founded by Rabbi Marvin Hier to continue Wiesenthal's work. The Center has offices in New York, Miami, Toronto, Jerusalem, Paris, and Buenos Aires. The innovative Museum of Tolerance was opened in Los Angeles in 1993, the New York Tolerance Center in 2004, and the Center for Human Dignity is planned by the Wiesenthal Center for Jerusalem. The Center's agenda mirrors that of Wiesenthal, being involved in campaigns against Nazi war criminals, current anti-Semitic and other extremist activities, particularly on the Internet, and human rights issues in general. Its film division has produced a number of documentaries, including two Academy Award–winning films, (*Genocide* in 1981 and *The Long Way Home* in 1997), and its publications include *Genocide: Critical Issues of the Holocaust* (1983), *The Simon Wiesenthal Center Annual* (1984–1990), and *Dismantling the Big Lie: The Protocols of the Elders of Zion.* While the Center bears Wiesenthal's name and has acted in association with Wiesenthal, both Wiesenthal and the Center maintain the right to act independently of each other.

Wiesenthal's Legacy

Over the course of his long career Wiesenthal has received many honors, including the U.S. Congressional Gold Medal (1980) and Presidential Medal of Freedom (2000), French Legion of Honor (1986), Great Medal of Merit (Germany, 1985), Erasmus Prize (Amsterdam, 1992), and he was named an honorary citizen of Vienna in 1995. In 2004 Wiesenthal was awarded an honorary knighthood (KBE) by Queen Elizabeth of England.

Wiesenthal's accomplishments go beyond the honors he has accumulated. They include being the inspiration of the Simon Wiesenthal Center, which in 2004 had close to a half-million members worldwide, and is one of the leading Jewish human rights organizations in the world. For the first two decades after the Holocaust, his was essentially the only voice that kept the memory of that period alive for the public, particularly in Europe, and especially in the countries where National Socialism and the Holocaust originated. For the survivors and for many Jews who were born after the war he became the symbol of a new Jewish resolve to no longer be passive, thus overcoming the guilt associated with the claim that Jews were led "like sheep to the slaughter." His resolve to avoid revenge and to focus on bringing the Nazis to justice served as an affirmation of the legal process and earned him international respect. Wiesenthal's persistent efforts, against determined opposition, eventually helped lead to the creation of Nazi hunting units in various countries including the United States, and also helped to normalize the concept of governmental action against war criminals. War crimes tribunals, such as those dealing with the genocides of Bosnia and Rwanda, might not have occurred had Wiesenthal not kept the pursuit of Nazi war criminals on the world's agenda for so long. By fighting to keep the memories of the victims alive and to bring justice to their killers, however delayed, he managed to help change the world's reactions to genocide and war crimes.

SEE ALSO Holocaust; Prosecution; Psychology of Victims

BIBLIOGRAPHY

Levy, Alan (1993). *The Wiesenthal File.* London: Constable.

Wiesenthal, Simon (1967). *The Murderers among Us,* ed. Joseph Wechsberg. London: Heinemann.

Wiesenthal, Simon (1970). *The Sunflower,* tran. H. A. Piehler. London: W. H. Allen.

Wiesenthal, Simon (1982). *Max and Helen: A Remarkable True Love Story.* New York: William Morrow.

Wiesenthal, Simon (1987). *Every Day Remembrance Day: A Chronicle of Jewish Martyrdom.* New York: Henry Holt.

Wiesenthal, Simon (1989). *Justice, Not Vengeance.* London: Weidenfeld and Nicolson.

Mark Weitzman

Women, Violence against

The term *violence against women* refers to gender-based aggression, which disproportionately victimizes women and girls. Sexual assault, battering by intimates, sexual abuse of children, sex trafficking, sexual harassment, forced pregnancy, and often prostitution and pornography are considered included, as are dowry burnings, honor killings, female infanticide, and female genital mutilation. When a woman or girl is violated or killed because she is female—due, for instance, to misogyny or sexual stereotypes or gendered roles of masculinity or femininity—she is subjected to violence against women. Such attacks often occur on the basis of sex combined with race, ethnicity, religion, nationality, and age, exacerbated by poverty and economic dependence. Likened to a war on women, violence against women, pervasive if largely invisible outside recognized wars, is surrounded by victim blaming, shaming, denial, and a culture of inevitability. It often explodes during armed conflict and genocide.

Most acts of violence against women are formally illegal but largely ignored by local, national, and international legal systems. Human rights instruments and peremptory norms binding on states guarantee equal protection of the law and prohibit discrimination on the basis of sex. To explicitly combat violence against women and ineffective law enforcement against it, the Organization of American States (OAS) promulgated the Convention on the Prevention, Punishment, and Eradication of Violence Against Women in 1994. The United Nations committees that interpret the Convention on the Elimination of All Forms of Discrimination Against Women (CEDAW) and the International Covenant on Civil and Political Rights (ICCPR) have determined that officially ignoring violence against women violates these conventions. The Beijing Platform for Action calls on states to take strong measures against these acts. Although some action has been taken regionally in Europe and Latin America against official violence against women in the form of rape in custody, little has been done anywhere to stop the widespread pattern of violence against women that is pervasive and officially condoned.

International humanitarian law and the laws of war have long prohibited rape and enforced prostitution in both domestic and international armed conflicts, yet those provisions too have seldom been enforced. Women targeted for genocide were violated in sex-specific ways during the Holocaust, yet the Nuremberg Tribunal did not recognize these atrocities as such. Genocide was defined in the Genocide Convention (1949) that emerged from that experience, specifying abuses inflicted with intent to destroy peoples as such; sexual violence was not specifically listed. Concepts of crimes against humanity emerging from this era also did not include widespread and systematic assaults on the basis of sex, nor did they focus on atrocities committed on the basis of sex combined with race, ethnicity, nationality, or religion. Most violence against women, in war as well as peace, has thus been committed with effective impunity.

In the last decade of the twentieth century, this pattern began to change in the international system. Beginning in 1991, Croatian and Bosnian Muslim women survivors spoke out against the mass rapes systematically inflicted on them as a weapon of the genocidal onslaughts directed by Serbian forces against their communities. By the turn of the century, they had civilly sued Radovan Karadzic, leader of the Bosnian Serbs, for genocidal rape and won under the Alien Tort Claims Act (ACTA) in the United States. Their case established sexual acts of violence against women as legally genocidal under international law for the first time. Also during this period the International Tribunal for Former Yugoslavia (ICTY) indicted perpetrators for rape and other sexual atrocities as war crimes and as crimes against humanity, specifically as slavery. The tribunal eventurally indicted Slobodan Milosevic, the former president of Serbia, for genocide. The International Tribunal for Rwanda (ICTR) made greater strides, convicting Hutu leaders of rape and other sexual atrocities against Tutsi women as genocide in its breakthrough *Akayesu* opinion. As a crime against humanity, rape was there defined internationally for the first time, as "a physical invasion of a sexual nature, committed on a person under conditions which are coercive."

The International Criminal Court (ICC) built on these advances. Under its Rome Statute (1998), the definition of genocide remained the same, permitting interpretation of killing, serious bodily or mental harm, destructive conditions of life, and measures to prevent births to encompass gender-based violence when committed for genocidal purposes. The ICC definition of crimes against humanity expressly included "rape, sexual slavery, enforced prostitution, forced pregnancy, enforced sterilization, or any other form of sexual violence of comparable gravity," when committed as part of a widespread or systematic attack knowingly directed against a civilian population. Gender-based persecution through such acts was also recognized as a crime against humanity. This implementation of international law, emancipated from hostilities recognized as armed conflict, together with doctrines of universal jurisdiction and other devices available in some national courts, offers hope that the legal impunity that has long marked violence against women may be coming to an end.

SEE ALSO Female Infantacide and Fetal Murder; Rape; Reproduction

BIBLIOGRAPHY

Commission on Human Rights (1994). *Preliminary Report Submitted by the Special Rapporteur on Violence against Women, Its Causes and Consequences.* E/CN.4/1995/42. Available from http://www.unhchr.ch/Huridocda/Huridoca.nsf.

Commission on Human Rights (1996). *Report of the Special Rapporteur on Violence against Women, Its Causes and Consequences.* E/CN.4/1996/53. Available from http://www.unhchr.ch/Huridocda/Huridoca.nsf.

Committee on the Elimination of Discrimination Against Women (1992). *General Recommendation 19.* UN Doc. CEDAW/C/1992/L.1/Add.15. Available from http://www.un.org/womenwatch/daw/cedaw/recomm.htm#recom/19.

Inter-American Convention on the Prevention, Punishment, and Eradication of Violence Against Women (Convention of Belem do Para) (1994). 33 I.L.M. 1534.

Kadic v. Karadzic. 70 F3d 232 (1995).

MacKinnon, Catharine A. (2004). "Genocide's Sexuality." In *Political Exclusion and Domination*, ed. Stephen Macedo and Melissa Williams. New York: New York University Press.

Prosecutor v. Akayesu. (1998). ICTR-96-4-T

Russell, Diana E. H., and Nicole Van de Ven, eds. (1976) *Crimes against Women: Proceedings of the International Tribunal.* Millbrae, Calif.: Les Femmes.

Catharine A. MacKinnon

World War I Peace Treaties

After World War I, the Allied and Associated powers concluded a series of peace treaties with the so-called Central powers: Germany (at Versailles, June 28, 1919), Austria/SaintGermain (September 10, 1919), Bulgaria (Neuilly, November 27, 1919), Hungary (Trianon, June 4, 1920), and Turkey, (Sèvres, August 10, 1920). Turkey fought successfully against the implementation of the August 10 treaty, and a new peace agreement was negotiated and signed at Lausanne, July 24, 1923. The United States Senate refused to ratify the treaties, however. Instead, the U.S. government concluded separate peace treaties with the former Central Powers.

None of the peace treaties concluded after World War I contained dispositions concerning the punishment of genocide. Within the context of the overall fighting, there had been many armed conflicts, which led to radical population reductions and even to the total disappearance of some races and nations, but at that time international law did not recognize specific rules on their prohibition and punishment. On the other hand, there were dispositions in the treaties connected with violations of the laws and customs of war.

Article 227 of the 1919 Treaty of Versailles merits special attention, because it called upon the Allied and Associated powers to publicly arraign the defeated German emperor, William II of Hohenzollern, on the charge of having committed a supreme offense against international morality and the sanctity of treaties. It further called for the constitution of a special tribunal to try the accused, and assured the former emperor the guarantees essential to the right of defense. The tribunal was composed of five judges, one each to be appointed by the United States, Great Britain, France, Italy, and Japan.

The former emperor, however, had taken refuge in the Netherlands, whose government refused his extradition, arguing that the crimes alleged in the arraignment—supreme offenses against international morality and the sanctity of treaties—had no counterpart in the articles of the Dutch Penal Code. William II never appeared before an international tribunal, and no judgment was ever rendered on him.

Article 228 of the Treaty of Versailles contained the following disposition:

> The German Government recognizes the right of the Allied and Associated Powers to bring before military tribunals persons accused of having committed acts in violation of the laws and customs of war. Such persons shall, if found guilty, be sentenced to punishments laid down by law. This provision will apply notwithstanding any proceedings or prosecution before a tribunal in Germany or in territory of her allies.

Articles 229 and 230 of the treaty concerned the composition of the tribunals, the accused's right of defense and right to counsel, and the obligation of the German government to cooperate in furnishing evidence of any crimes alleged and brought before tribunals.

The Allied powers suspected that more than 900 German soldiers had violated the laws and customs of war. Among the suspects were some of the top generals in the German High Command. From this great number, however, only twelve individuals stood accused before the Tribunal of Leipzig. Of these, only six were found guilty. They received prison sentences not to exceed four years.

There were identical dispositions in the corresponding articles of the peace treaties concluded with other defeated Central Powers, (Articles 173 to 175 of the treaty of St. Germain, Articles 118 to 120 of the Neuilly treaty, Articles 157 to 159 of the Trianon treaty, and Articles 228 to 230 of the treaty of Sèvres). In the turmoil of the postwar period, however, these provisions were not applied. None of the treaties included rules that might be brought to bear against citizens of a victorious state who might be accused of violating the laws and customs of war.

SEE ALSO Impunity; Minorities

BIBLIOGRAPHY

Appleman, J. A. (1971). *Military tribunals and International Crimes.* Westport, Conn.: Greenwood Press.

Lachs, M. (1945). *War Crimes: An Attempt to Define the Issues.* London: Stevens.

Schwarzenberger, G. (1968). *International Law as Applied by International Courts and Tribunals. Volume 2: The Law of Armed Conflict.* London: Stevens.

G. G. Herczegh

Wounded Knee

The Wounded Knee massacre took place December 29, 1890, on the Pine Ridge Indian Reservation in South Dakota. The massacre was precipitated when the Seventh Cavalry of the U.S. Army tried to disarm a group of about 500 Lakota Sioux under the leadership of Chief Big Foot. During the contentious process of disarming, a shot was fired. After this, the army began a merciless slaughter. Within hours, the Seventh Cavalry killed between 270 and 300 of Big Foot's people. Of these, 170 to 200 were women and children. The army killed a few men who were fighting back, but the large majority of Lakotas were destroyed while trying to flee or hide. In a few instances, soldiers shot Lakotas at point blank range, three or more miles from the place the firing began.

The chain of events that led to Wounded Knee began six weeks earlier, when the United States government decided to use massive military force to suppress the Ghost Dance on Lakota reservations. The Ghost Dance originated in the teachings of Paiute prophet Wovoka, living on the Walker River Indian Reservation in Nevada. In 1889, Wovoka began to forecast the coming of a new world in which non-Indians would be destroyed or removed, game restored, and tribal ancestors returned to life. Portions of several tribes in the western United States adopted Wovoka's teachings, including several Lakota communities.

Although many scholars have argued that the Lakotas fundamentally altered Wovoka's originally "peaceful" teaching into one of hostility toward European Americans, thus justifying military action, recent scholarship has called this view into question. It is doubtful that the Lakotas changed Wovoka's teachings. Rather, the government's decision to suppress the Ghost Dance among the Lakotas, but not among other tribes, resulted from long-standing American perceptions of the Lakota Sioux as particularly treacherous, as well as army officers' perceptions that the situation on the Lakota reservations afforded an opportunity to demonstrate the continued importance of the army's mission in the West.

The army's invasion of Lakota country, the single largest military operation since the Civil War, was designed to overawe the Lakota ghost dancers into giving up the dance. At first, this strategy had some success. In late November and early December several groups of ghost dancers surrendered. On December 15, however, military officials began to lose control of the situation when reservation Indian police killed Sitting Bull at his home on the Standing Rock Reservation. Fearing for their lives, most of Sitting Bull's people fled south,

The United States Seventh Cavalry massacred over 300 Lakota (Sioux) men, women, and children at their encampment beside Wounded Knee Creek in South Dakota, on December 29, 1890. Here, Miniconjou Sioux chief Big Foot lies dead in the snow. He was among the first to die that morning. [NATIONAL ARCHIVES AND RECORDS ADMINISTRATION]

with some joining Big Foot's village on the Cheyenne River. Army officers responded to these events by adopting a punitive attitude toward Big Foot and the ghost dancers among his people. Big Foot was characterized as "defiant and hostile" and the army positioned troops near his village to secure his arrest.

For their part, Big Foot and the other leaders of his community were deeply fearful of the army's intentions. Having received an invitation from Lakota leaders at Pine Ridge to help with their ongoing diplomatic efforts to secure a peaceful conclusion to the army's invasion of their country, Big Foot decided on December 24 to leave Cheyenne River and travel through the rough country of the Badlands to Pine Ridge. Big Foot's evasion of military surveillance increased army officers' frustration. More than ever they desired to punish Big Foot and his people. Hence, officers in charge of the campaign issued orders to all units to try to find Big Foot, and should they succeed, to disarm him, adding: "If he fights, destroy him." On December 28, the Seventh Cavalry intercepted Big Foot and his people about twenty-five miles from Pine Ridge and escorted them

to nearby Wounded Knee Creek. The next morning the Seventh Cavalry began to carry out its orders.

Much of the analysis of Wounded Knee has focused on who fired the first shot. One theory is that army officers planned in advance to open fire, perhaps to avenge the Seventh Cavalry's defeat under George Armstrong Custer at the Little Bighorn fourteen years before. Another theory is that the first shot was fired when a single Indian refused to give up his gun and it discharged accidentally when soldiers tried to take it from him. A third theory, advanced by the army after the massacre, is that a few Lakotas, acting in concert, opened fire.

Wounded Knee qualifies as an instance of genocide most obviously under the first of these theories, as it holds that the destruction of Big Foot's people was intentional. In all likelihood, however, army officers probably did not plan the massacre and instead intended to use the threat of force to secure a bloodless disarmament of Big Foot's people. Nonetheless, even under the second (very likely) theory or the third (very doubtful) theory, the events after the first shot reveal widespread genocidal impulses. Although army officers testified before a court of inquiry that they and their men took great pains to prevent the killing of women and children, their testimony collapses under the weight of the sheer number of casualties and the circumstances of their deaths.

Regardless of who fired the first shot, the killing fields of Wounded Knee must be placed within a long tradition of racist Indian-hating in American culture, reflected in widely held axioms like "nits breed lice" and "the only good Indian is a dead Indian," and manifested in numerous instances in which the army, volunteers, and civilians engaged in acts of indiscriminate slaughter with the intent to kill as many Indians as possible. Neither the army's campaign to suppress the Lakota Ghost Dance nor nineteenth-century U.S. Indian policy explicitly called for the extermination of all Indians. Yet, both were premised on the view that Indian opposition to U.S. authority was illegitimate and deserving of punishment, and that it was therefore legiti-mate to use the threat of extermination to secure policy objectives. In many instances, as at Wounded Knee, the threat of genocide became reality.

SEE ALSO Indigenous Peoples; Massacres; Native Americans; Racism

BIBLIOGRAPHY

Brown, Dee (1971). *Bury My Heart at Wounded Knee: An Indian History of the American West*. New York: Holt, Rinehart, & Winston.

Mooney, James (1896). *The Ghost-Dance Religion and the Sioux Outbreak of 1890*. Fourteenth Annual Report of the Bureau of Ethnology, 1892–1993. Washington, D.C.: Government Printing Office.

Ostler, Jeffrey (2004). *The Plains Sioux and U.S. Colonialism from Lewis and Clark to Wounded Knee*. Cambridge: Cambridge University Press.

Utley, Robert (1963). *The Last Days of the Sioux Nation*. New Haven, Conn.: Yale University Press.

Jeffrey Ostler

Yugoslavia

Between 1991 and 1999, the Socialist Federative Republic of Yugoslavia (population: approximately 23 million) disintegrated amid four successive wars. Although the violent end of federal Yugoslavia was not determined by its bloody origins, those origins should not be omitted from an account of its denouement, in part because they were deliberately evoked to mobilize support for war in 1991 and 1992.

World War II: 1941–1945

After the kingdom of Yugoslavia capitulated to Germany in April 1941, Hitler divided the country among the Axis states. Germany annexed most of Slovenia, occupied Serbia, and administrated eastern Vojvodina. Italy annexed or occupied much of the Croatian coastland, southern Slovenia, western Macedonia and Kosovo, and tried in vain to control Montenegro by means of an autonomous administration. Hungary annexed the remainder of the province of Vojvodina and eastern Slovenia. Bulgaria took Macedonia and a sliver of southeastern Serbia.

The occupiers established puppet regimes. Croatia, Bosnia and Herzegovina were put in the charge of a Croatian nationalist group, the fanatical Ustashas, whose leaders had spent the 1930s as Mussolini's clients and sometimes his prisoners. The *poglavnik* (equivalent to *führer*) of the self-styled Independent State of Croatia (Nezavisna Drzava Hrvatska, NDH) was Ante Pavelic. Its leaders were obsessed with eliminating the Serb Orthodox population, which was seen as the historic obstacle to Croatian sovereignty.

The NDH's population of 6.3 million included only 3.4 million Croats. The remainder were mostly Serb (1.9 million), Muslim (700,000), German (150,000) and Jewish (37,000). In line with Axis policy, the Ustashas deported and killed Jews and Roma. The Serb population was the strategic target, however, owing to its size and to Ustasha ideology. At least 20,000 Serbs were killed in pogroms during summer 1941. By 1945, in line with the *Ustasha* intention to eradicate the Serb Orthodox population by mass conversion, expulsion, and murder, enough death and destruction had been achieved to make the NDH the bloodiest regime in Europe after Germany itself.

In Serbia, the Nazis formed a "government of national salvation" under Milan Nedic, who saw himself as caretaking until the royalist government could return from exile in London. Pavelic's equivalent in Belgrade was Dimitrije Ljotic, who received limited German support for his Serbian fascist movement. Even without an ideology of genocide, Nazi mechanisms functioned efficiently and the situation for Jews and Roma was no better than in Croatia. Serbia was proclaimed *Judenfrei* (Free of Jews) in early 1942.

Some army officers took to the hills and formed a royalist resistance movement, the Chetniks, loyal to the royalist government but also to a Serbian nationalist program. Savage Nazi reprisals in Serbia in 1941 soon quieted this movement's anti-German actions, but it continued to commit atrocities against Croats and Muslims in the NDH. Proportionately, Muslim losses in the war were heavier than Serb or Croat losses.

Croatian and Serbian nationalist crimes strengthened the resistance movement launched in summer 1941 by the Communist Party of Yugoslavia under a shadowy figure called Josip Broz, later known as Tito, who was supported by the USSR. The engorged but Axis-occupied Croatian state became the principal battleground between the partisans and their pro-fascist or anti-communist opponents, with each side's armed forces numbering around 150,000 by 1943.

At least a million Yugoslavs (6% of the pre-war population) were killed between 1941 and 1945, mostly at their compatriots' hands. The killing continued after the war, as Tito's victorious forces took revenge on their real and perceived enemies. British forces in Austria turned back tens of thousands of fleeing Yugoslavs. Estimates range from 30,000 to 55,000 killed between spring and autumn 1945.

Native German and Hungarian communities, seen as complicit with wartime occupation, were brutally treated; tantamount in some cases to ethnic cleansing. The *Volksdeutsch* settlements of Vojvodina and Slavonia largely disappeared. Perhaps 100,000 people—half the ethnic German population in Yugoslavia—fled in 1945, and many who remained were compelled to do forced labor, murdered, or later ransomed by West Germany. Some 20,000 Hungarians of Vojvodina were killed in reprisals. Albanian rebellions in Kosovo were suppressed, with prisoners sent on death marches towards the coast. An estimated 170,000 ethnic Italians fled to Italy in the late 1940s and 1950s. (All of these figures are highly approximate.)

The partisans were not always ruthless to their wartime opponents. By contrast with Germany, however, the postwar order in Yugoslavia did not allow an impartial examination of the war years. Grief was made more bitter by the anger and vengefulness of those whose struggles and sufferings were officially distorted or denied. Tito's regime created an official celebratory myth about the "People's Liberation War," denying partisan atrocities and negotiations with Germans and exaggerating their role in defeating the Axis. While this helped to unify the traumatized nationalities in the wake of fascism's defeat, it could not silence the truths and counter-myths handed down within families throughout Yugoslavia and nursed among Serb and Croat émigrés. In particular, many Croats came to resent what they saw as excessive attention to the Ustasha regime and a corresponding exculpation of Serbian nationalist crimes. By the time Titoist orthodoxy relaxed and the archives yielded their secrets, in the 1980s—confirming that the partisans' black-and-white, epic version had concealed an unsurprising pattern of shifting allegiances and power—plays in which Tito's forces

eventually bested their enemies—it was too late for reconciliation.

The Wars of Yugoslav Succession (1991–1999)

The wars of the 1990s—from Slovenia, to Croatia, then Bosnia and Herzegovina, and finally Kosovo—were the result of four factors:

- the weakness of Yugoslavia's institutions of central government
- the rise of aggressive nationalism in Serbia
- the collapse of one-party communist systems in Europe around 1990—including in Yugoslavia
- the Yugoslav People's Army's embrace of Serbian nationalism.

After Tito's death in 1980, Yugoslavia's federal system proved incapable of providing effective governance. Once each decade, Tito had rebalanced the system, effectively decentralizing power until Yugoslav unity rested on three pillars: Tito's own prestige; the coherence of the League of Communists of Yugoslavia (LCY), as the communist party was called; and the Yugoslav People's Army (*Jugoslovenska narodna armija*, JNA). The first and second of these decayed over the 1980s; the third endured in deepening isolation from democratic change.

Political and economic competencies devolved to the six republics and two autonomous provinces of Kosovo and Vojvodina. The federation became, in a vivid phrase coined by Croatian economist Branko Horvat, an alliance of regional oligarchies. The resultant instability encouraged restiveness among the republics and revived long-standing mutual grievances. In Serbia, one politician turned this situation to his advantage. Slobodan Milosevic (b. 1941) rose in the 1980s to head the Serbian League of Communists. Milosevic played upon the Serbs' bitterness over their status in Yugoslavia.

These feelings centered on the southern province of Kosovo, site of the mythologized 1389 battle against the Ottoman empire, and traditionally celebrated as the cradle of Serbian culture. With more than 20 percent of Serbia's population, Kosovo in the 1980s was more than 80 percent ethnic Albanian. Since the late 1960s, Albanians had ceased to be a second-class nationality in Kosovo. This evolution, formalized by Kosovo's federal status in the 1974 constitution, was felt as unacceptable by many Serbs. In 1986 Serbia's Academy of Sciences and Arts purported to speak for the nation when it alleged—with inflammatory intent—that Serbs in Kosovo were subject to "physical, political, legal, and cultural genocide."

Milosevic was the first senior politician to acknowledge Serbian anger over Kosovo as valid. With the help of media manipulation, staged rallies, and covert agitation, he seized the leadership of the Serbian communists in late 1987, then used the same techniques to abolish the autonomy of Kosovo and Vojvodina. When he succeeded in changing the leadership in Montenegro (population 0.58 million), Milosevic controlled half the federal units.

Although public opinion was orchestrated, these early successes were enabled by an extraordinary groundswell of support. Journalists, intellectuals, and artists echoed the simple message that Serbia and the Serbs—some 36 percent of Yugoslavia's population—must be "united" at any cost. Even those who disliked Milosevic's methods believed that his "antibureaucratic revolution" was necessary. Dissenters were few and, thanks to the machinery of party-state power, easily marginalized.

Milosevic's wider ambition was to intimidate the other republics into letting Yugoslavia be re-centralized under Serbian hegemony. The international community, eager to see Yugoslavia restabilized, was vaguely sympathetic. But Serbia's strongman had not foreseen the collapse of European communism after November 1989. This reduced the strategic significance Yugoslavia had enjoyed during the cold war, poised between the Western and Eastern blocs. It also encouraged nascent pro-democratic groups in Yugoslavia, especially in the western republics of Slovenia and Croatia, where they found common cause with communists who were worried by Serbian revanchism.

Serbia's vaunting ambition had emboldened other republics. The last congress of the LCY, in January 1990, was suspended when the Slovenian delegation walked out after their reform proposals were jeeringly rejected. Slovenia and Croatia scheduled multiparty elections for the spring. Far from backing down at this reversal, Milosevic escalated his threats against other republics. If the political structures were too weak and the JNA was still too indecisive to give him the leverage he needed, he would use demography instead—the 25 percent of Yugoslavia's Serbs who lived outside Serbia.

Slovenia and Croatia

In the late 1980s, Slovenia's challenge to the federal system was as profound as Serbia's, but opposite in method and intention. With under two million inhabitants, abutting Italy and Austria, by 1990 Slovenia was "the most successful and modern economy in Central and Eastern Europe." Some two-fifths of export trade was with western Europe.

Milosevic's recentralizing drive spurred Slovenian nationalism. This took political form, in terms of resistance to the Serbian bloc in federal structures, and the-

oretical and cultural forms, in the unprecedented irreverence toward Titoist myths. With newly elected leaders, Slovenia declared sovereignty in July 1990. In late December, the result of a referendum allowed the leadership to announce that independence would be declared the following June. If Serbia supplied the main leverage to destroy Yugoslavia, the timetable was Slovenia's.

Determined not to be left behind, Croatia (population: 4.78 million) committed itself to secede alongside Slovenia, although Croatia's position vis-à-vis Serbia was incomparably worse. Milosevic was willing to let Slovenia go, but not Croatia. After Croatia's first multiparty elections in spring 1990, the Serbian media had conducted a frenzied campaign to instil fear and hatred of Croatian intentions. Cynically exploiting fears of an Ustasha revival, this campaign targeted Croatia's 580,000 Serbs, especially the compact Serb communities in the central highlands. Agents were sent to stir up discontent. Open rebellion started in autumn, with armed roadblocks around the town of Knin. The Yugoslav army and Serbian ministry of interior supplied the weapons.

Agitation was made easier by the nationalism of Franjo Tudjman (1922–1999). His election platform included two crucial claims: Croatia must have "self-determination in its natural and historic borders," and the NDH (1941–1945) "was not only a formation in the service of the [Nazi German-Fascist Italian] occupier, but also the expression of the historic aspirations of the Croatian people." The former claim disclosed Tudjman's covetous interest in neighbouring Bosnia and Herzegovina, while the latter—playing into the hands of Serbian propaganda—signaled a readiness to rehabilitate aspects of the Ustashas' record.

So pressing was the threat posed by Serbia and its local proxy forces in Knin that most Croatians—like most Serbians, though arguably with better reason—wanted a strong leader, whatever the price. In Tudjman's case, the price was an authoritarian kleptocracy and, less predictably, a habit of conspiring with his Serbian counterpart. Far from sharing his supporters' revulsion at Milosevic, Tudjman saw the other man as his natural partner for achieving a historic concordat that would settle the Serbs' and Croats' differences once and for all. In his vision, this required splitting Bosnia and Herzegovina, which he saw as an artificial construct, much of which belonged by historical right to Croatia, and whose majority Muslim inhabitants were descended from apostate Catholics, that is, Croats.

Tudjman sought opportunities to plot the dismemberment of Bosnia and Herzegovina with Milosevic, most notoriously at Karadjordjevo on March 25, 1991.

At that meeting, he hoped to exploit the other man's vulnerability after the JNA chiefs of staff—aligning themselves ever more closely with Milosevic—had failed to panic the federal presidency into declaring a state of emergency. This was a critical misreading of the situation. Tudjman thought that a chastened Milosevic would cooperate over Bosnia and Herzegovina, whereas his recent setback actually hardened Milosevic's—and the JNA's—resolve to stop Croatia from escaping intact. On March 16, Milosevic met Serbia's district leaders. Proclaiming his readiness to "defend the interests of our republic and also the interests of the Serb people beyond Serbia," he told his audience that "borders, as you know, are always dictated by the strong and never by the weak" (Sell, 2002, p. 137).

Tudjman, however, trusted Milosevic crony Borisav Jovic's private assurances that Milosevic was uninterested in Croatia's Serbs or their ultimate fate. By this time, the Croatian Serb rebels, backed by the JNA, had proclaimed their own state—the Republic of Serb Krajina (RSK)—and controlled key transport routes. Typically, Croatia held its referendum only a month before the date set for secession. When 93 percent of an 84 percent turn-out supported "sovereignty and independence," confrontation became unavoidable.

Independence and War

Slovenia prepared its 20,000-strong armed forces in high secrecy, readying itself to take over border crossings and resist army intervention. Slovenia's showdown with the JNA began on June 25, the day it declared independence. Local and international observers were surprised at the skill and determination of the Territorial Defence forces. JNA confidence—based on poor intelligence and anti-Slovenian prejudice—that the Slovenes would back down after a show of force was quickly dispelled. After ten days, the Slovenian side had suffered 13 dead and 112 wounded, compared with 39 dead and 139 wounded on the JNA side.

The JNA chiefs of staff—after long careers in a bubble of privilege and unaccountability—were angered by their humiliation. Under terms brokered by the European Community, some 22,000 JNA personnel were withdrawn, mostly to bases in Croatia and Bosnia and Herzegovina. The chiefs of staff now shed the residual Yugoslavist loyalty which had deterred them from overthrowing the federal organs in March, and threw in their lot with Serbian nationalism.

The war in Croatia was less clear-cut and vastly more destructive of life and property. After incidents against and involving police forces in spring and early summer, the rebel forces, along with JNA regulars and Serbian paramilitaries, began to target large numbers of civilian Croats in and around the territory claimed by the self-styled RSK, killing many and driving away survivors. By November they controlled almost a third of the country. The worst fighting in this undeclared war was in the east, where Croat forces, unaided by forces from the Croatian capital of Zagreb, valiantly defended Vukovar until the city was rubble. After Serbian forces captured the city, more than 200 Croats were removed from the hospital and shot. This was the first indisputable war crime. By December, half a million people had been displaced in Croatia or fled as refugees. Damage was estimated at some $18.7 billion.

The United Nations Protection Force (UNPROFOR)

The United Nations Security Council's first action in the war was to impose an arms embargo on all parties in September 1991. The fighting continued regardless. The attacks on Vukovar and Dubrovnik showed that real war could not be averted. After twelve cease-fires in Croatia collapsed, UN envoy Cyrus Vance succeeded in making the thirteenth stick: Milosevic compelled the leaders of the RSK to accept. The January 2, 1992, agreement (called the Vance Plan) provided for 10,000 (later 14,000) UN peacekeepers to stabilize the disputed territory while a political settlement was worked out.

Over the next several years, UNPROFOR failed to demilitarize the rebel areas or to create conditions for the return of refugees. Indeed, refugee numbers swelled as Serbs in government-controlled areas were attacked in retaliation for the crimes of the rebels. According to human rights activists, 11,000 Serb-owned homes were destroyed outside rebel areas during the year after the January 1992 cease-fire. Non-Serbs in RSK territory were killed and expelled under the eyes of UN peacekeepers. Illogically, the UN protected Serbs in Serb-controlled territory while it did nothing for those who remained in government-controlled territory, who were at much greater risk.

The so-called Republic of Serb Krajina was now a twilight land ruled by a paramilitary mafia, sustained by plunder, contraband and humanitarian aid. The mafiosi never believed that the Croatians could retake the territory. Their total intransigence played into Tudjman's hands: he appeared reasonable by comparison. As time passed, his barely concealed ambition of recovering the territory minus its Serb population appeared almost pragmatic.

Writing in a special edition of *Globus* news magazine (Zagreb, December 11, 1999) shortly after Tudjman's death, his former chef de cabinet, Hrvoje Sarinic, recalled the eve of Operation Storm in August 1995, when Croatia recaptured most of the Serb rebel-held territory: "All attempts at a peaceful solution (which, to tell the truth, we didn't even want) had failed. The military-police forces got the order to establish the constitutional and legal system." This attitude was obvious at the time, though not publicly acknowledged by the United Nations.

Despite its failures, the UN mission served Croatia's longer-term interests, stabilizing the country while it built up its forces. By late 1994, the Western powers were impatient with the stalemate. The turning point was a U.S.–Croatian memorandum on defense cooperation, signed in November 1994. This led to training and planning assistance which was put to use the following summer.

Bosnia and Herzegovina

Bosnia and Herzegovina (4.12 million) was the only Yugoslav republic without a titular nation, hence the only one that could not become a nation-state. Serb and Croat nationalists traditionally claimed part or all of Bosnia and Herzegovina, as well as authority over the Muslim plurality (44% in 1991).

The first multiparty election in Bosnia and Herzegovina was effectively a national plebiscite, with results reflecting the region's ethnic balance (Serbs were 31% and Croats were 17% of the population). The main Muslim political party was led by Alija Izetbegović (1925–2003), a peaceable if erratic Islamic dissident who had been jailed in the 1980s by the republic's repressive communist structures. He tried to form a unity government with the main Serb and Croat parties. While the Croats were tactically cooperative, the Serbs—led by Radovan Karadzic, a colorful psychiatrist and poet—categorically resisted efforts to strengthen Bosnia and Herzegovina's sovereignty.

In spring and summer 1991, Serb-majority regions in the north and east formed "autonomous regions," which formed the territorial basis for a breakaway Serb entity. JNA garrisons supplied arms to nascent Serb forces and later encircled major cities with heavy weapons. Izetbegović could either capitulate to Serb pressure, tying Bosnia and Herzegovina unconditionally to Serbia and its satellite, Montenegro; or he could follow the path taken successfully by Slovenia and bloodily by Croatia. The first option was unacceptable to most Muslims and all Croats; the second was intolerable to the Serbs.

In mid-October 1991, the Serb delegates boycotted the Bosnia and Herzegovina parliament's vote on sovereignty. Before exiting the chamber to set up their own "Serb Assembly" (which at once appealed to the JNA for protection), Karadzic issued a warning. His words,

and Izetbegović's response, are quoted in the book, *Unfinished Peace*: "Do not think that you will not lead Bosnia into hell, and do not think that you will not perhaps lead the Muslim people into annihilation, because the Muslims cannot defend themselves if there is war." Izetbegović replied: "His words and manner illustrate why others refuse to stay in Yugoslavia. Nobody else wants the kind of Yugoslavia that Mr. Karadzic wants anymore. Nobody except perhaps the Serbs" (Tindemans et al., 1996, p. 34).

Speculating that even war would be better than a future as Milosevic's vassals, the Muslim and Croat leaders sought international recognition for Bosnia and Herzegovina in December 1991. Such recognition had been preempted by a Bosnian Serb "plebiscite" on remaining in Yugoslavia in November. The European Community required a referendum. Held in early March, it was duly boycotted en masse by the Serbs, whose leaders had preemptively proclaimed a "Serb Republic of Bosnia and Herzegovina" in January 1992. The result was treated as valid ground for granting international recognition, but, incredibly, the Bosnia and Herzegovina government's requests for practical defensive aid, or merely for UN peacekeepers, were turned down. The local leaders' irresponsibility was abetted by the irresponsibility shown by the outside powers.

The JNA had prepared for Bosnia and Herzegovina's independence since December 1991 by transferring Bosnian Serb troops into Bosnia and Herzegovina. When international recognition came, on April 6–7, 1992, Bosnia and Herzegovina had only a fractured police force, a nascent, Muslim-led Patriotic League, and a Croat militia to defend it. This lack of readiness was due partly to the difficulty of acquiring weapons. Unlike Slovenia and Croatia, Bosnia and Herzegovina's borders all lay within Yugoslavia. Lack of readiness can also, in part, be attributed to Izetbegović's refusal to accept that the JNA would target Muslims for their faith or national identity.

In May 1992, the JNA ostensibly withdrew some 14,000 JNA forces from Bosnia and Herzegovina, leaving behind some 75,000 who were allegedly Bosnians by origin. This remaining force, along with artillery, tanks, and fighter planes, became the Army of the Serb Republic, which operated in key respects as an extension of the JNA. When the Serb faction occupied a town, Muslim and Croat community leaders and intellectuals were shot or abducted. Thousands of Muslims and Croats were herded into unused industrial facilities, where they were starved, tortured, and even killed. By late summer, the Serb forces controlled 70 percent of Bosnia and Herzegovina, and more than a million people had been displaced from their homes. The rump

Bosnia and Herzegovina government quickly settled on a strategy of endurance, publicizing Serb and later Croat atrocities while clamoring for full-scale international intervention. The rag-tag forces enlisted by the government held some 10 percent of the country in the center and east. Croat forces controlled the remainder. Sarajevo's 400,000 inhabitants were helpless under bombardment.

Croat strategy was divided. Many Croat nationalists were convinced that compact Croat-majority areas in the southwest and northeast of the republic, as well as mixed areas in central Bosnia, should secede and join Croatia proper. A separate Bosnian Croat entity called Herzeg-Bosna was declared unilaterally, with Zagreb's support, in July 1992. On the other hand, an equal or greater number of Croats, living in mixed communities, regarded Bosnia and Herzegovina as their homeland, to be preserved intact.

Tudjman shared the nationalist view. He sent the Croatian Army over the border to fight the Serbs, but then switched in 1993 to attacking their nominal ally, the Army of Bosnia and Herzegovina, with its predominantly Muslim troops. The alliance collapsed in spring 1993 as the Croats, encouraged by international proposals for apportioning territory among the nationalities, made a bid to control their majority areas and parts of central Bosnia. They established concentration camps for Muslims. But early success turned sour when the Bosnia and Herzegovina Army fought back well, and also committed crimes against Croat civilians. The Western mediators' only significant peacemaking success came in early 1994, when they persuaded the Bosnian Croat forces to stop their war. The separatist ambitions of the Bosnian Croats went unchanged, however, and Western hopes that the reconstituted alliance would be able to reverse Serb gains were in vain.

Peace Plans

The first and best peace plan was presented by European mediator Lord Carrington in October 1991. This would have framed new relations between sovereign and independent Republics, with special status for minority areas. When, alone among the republic leaders, Milosevic rejected Carrington's plan with impunity, the chance of a unified solution was lost. For the next three-and-a-half years, the international community drifted.

Western leaders seemed unable to judge the significance of a regional conflict in southern Europe that threatened no vital interest except fundamental principles of international law, human rights, and acceptable interstate conduct. Having recognized the independence of Bosnia and Herzegovina without then letting its government defend itself, these leaders declared that these fundamental principles must be upheld. Envoys were tasked to design settlements that would reverse land grabs and vast refugee movements without any credible external coercion. The Vance-Owen Plan (January 1993) envisaged ten cantons, nominally mixed but each dominated by one nationality, with a weak central government. It was followed by the Owen-Stoltenberg plan (July 1993), which awarded 53 percent of Bosnia and Herzegovina as contiguous territory to the Serbs. The Contact Group plan (July 1994) proposed to split the country between the Serbs (49%) and the Muslim-Croat Federation (51%), which U.S. diplomats brokered in February and March 1994. This was the ratio confirmed at Dayton.

Milosevic's attitude to these plans was pragmatic. He supported them all, but kept his options open by letting men, materiel, and fuel flow from Serbia to the Bosnia Serbs. By late 1994, about half of the territory of Bosnia and Herzegovina was covered by air-to-ground missile systems, which had been imported from Serbia to deter NATO from overflying Bosnia and Herzegovina. No nationalist by conviction, and eager for economic sanctions (which had been imposed in 1992) to be lifted, he felt little loyalty to Serb rebel leaders—his partners in the "joint criminal enterprise." He was ready to bargain away their territory on terms which would not weaken him in Serbia, where his position was less secure than it appeared from outside. At home he faced runaway inflation (running at about 1% *hourly* by late 1993) and staples such as flour and oil were rationed.

By late November 1991, Milosevic wanted a truce in Croatia, which he eventually imposed on a reluctant Serb rebel leadership. A year later, Bosnian Serb conquests became a liability. Politically, however, he needed to make a show of being forced to renounce the concept of a "Greater Serbia," that most Serbian voters embraced, but with which he had only flirted. Intoxicated by their devastating early success, however, the rebel leaders refused realistic compromises. Impunity fed their hubris. Not until 1995 were the Western powers ready to use force on a wide enough scale to reassure Milosevic that he could abandon the rebels (in Croatia) or compel them to compromise (in Bosnia and Herzegovina) without opening himself to weighty charges of betrayal.

The moral nadir of international policy-making in Bosnia and Herzegovina was to be found, however, not so much in these failed plans as in Resolution 836 of the UN Security Council (June 1993). This resolution stated that six places unconquered by Serb forces were to be "safe areas. . .free from armed attacks and from any other hostile act." While seemingly promising to protect civilians in those areas, Britain and France ensured that this resolution only committed the UN to deter attacks on civilians. If deterrence failed, UN troops would use force, but only in self-defense. This diplomatic sleight helped to enable the mass slaughter at Srebrenica two years later.

UN Secretary-General Kofi Annan has since accepted that "the United Nations hierarchy" made "errors of judgment . . . rooted in a philosophy of impartiality and non-violence wholly unsuited to the conflict in Bosnia." In his *Report of the Secretary General Pursuant to General Assembly Resolution 53/35 (1998): The Fall of Srebrenica*, he wrote, "The provision of humanitarian aid" was not "a sufficient response to ethnic cleansing and to an attempted genocide." For, "a Member State of the United Nations, left largely defenseless as a result of an arms embargo imposed upon it *by the United Nations*, was being dismembered by forces committed to its destruction. This was not a problem with a humanitarian solution". Yet, whatever the mission leaders' failings, many staff did excellent practical work, delivering aid that sustained minority pockets in hostile areas.

Endgame

By spring 1995, UNPROFOR had suffered almost 200 casualties. Frustration over these losses, and over the general stalemate led Western governments to allow the new UN commander in Bosnia and Herzegovia, Lt. Gen. (now Sir) Rupert Smith (U.K.), leading 31,000 peacekeeping troops, to be more assertive. When Smith ordered air strikes against unmanned military targets, following the sort of violation of safe areas that had rarely been punished before, the Bosnian Serb military chief, General Ratko Mladic, took more than 300 UN hostages, humiliated French troops in Sarajevo, and tried to capture the eastern "safe area" of Gorazde.

Although no hostages were harmed, Smith argued that UNPROFOR must reduce its vulnerability to allow the mandated use of force against the Serb side. Extra French and British troops were sent to Sarajevo as a rapid reaction force, capable of swift military response. Western commitment to the Muslim safe areas again wavered, but before any decision to extract UN troops from those enclaves could be taken, Mladic took the initiative. Having failed to take Gorazde, his men attacked two other safe areas in eastern Bosnia: Srebrenica and Zepa. As they closed in upon Srebrenica, Smith's civilian and military superiors in UNPROFOR refused to allow air-strikes. Dutch peacekeepers in the enclave yielded quietly to Mladic on July 11. Over 7,000 Muslim men and boys were separated from their families and executed.

This atrocity, the worst crime in Europe since 1945, sparked serious Western efforts to end the war. Smith was given authority to order air strikes in the event of further violations of safe areas. The principle of "proportionality" (counterstrikes calibrated to equal, but not exceed, the damage done by the attack that triggered them) was dropped. Thus, when mortar bombs hit a crowded Sarajevo marketplace on August 28, NATO launched a comprehensive air assault on Bosnian Serb arsenals and communications.

In early August, government forces—enhanced by U.S. technical support—recaptured most of the rebel territory in Croatia, leading to the immediate exodus of up to 150,000 Serbs and the murder over succeeding weeks of hundreds more, mostly elderly civilians who had stayed on in the recaptured areas. In 1991 there were 580,000 Serbs in Croatia. A decade later, the census found 201,600. Although the population has undoubtedly grown since then, the Serb community has probably lost a quarter of a million members as the price of pointless rebellion.

The success of Operation Storm opened the way for Croatian troops to push into Bosnia and Herzegovina from the west, justified by Mladic's effort to conquer the safe area of Bihac, while the Bosnia and Herzegovina Army made gains in central Bosnia. As Serb-held territory fell from 70 to around 50 percent of Bosnia and Herzegovina, U.S. envoy Richard Holbrooke gained broad acceptance of the principles for a settlement negotiated at an air force base in Dayton, Ohio. The "General Framework Agreement for Peace in Bosnia and Herzegovina" (known as the Dayton Accords) divided the country into two distinct "entities," the Serb Republic and the (Muslim-Croat) Federation. The weak "common institutions" (parliament, presidency and constitutional court) had power over foreign policy and trade, customs and monetary policy, inter-entity law, transport, and communications. Everything else—military, police, taxation, justice, education—was controlled by the entities, or by the ten sub-units known as "cantons" within the Federation. Ultimate authority was vested in a Peace Implementation Council, represented in Bosnia and Herzegovina by an international viceroy, the High Representative, and backed up by a NATO-led, multinational Implementation Force. At the outset, this force numbered 60,000 troops; by late 2003 its troop strength had been reduced to 7,000.

Dayton was a skillfully managed exercise in underachievement. Nominally civic but substantially ethnic, the Accords delivered an armed truce that has only slowly moved toward a self-sustaining peace and not yet toward a viable state. The international political and military resources mobilized in 1995 should have yielded a better solution for the peoples of the region. Misunderstanding Milosevic as a blood-and-soil nationalist, the international mediators conceded too much, recognizing the Republika Srpska, an entity forged by ethnic cleansing, and failing to impose a workable governance system.

When they realized what the Dayton Accords meant in practice, the Bosnian Serb leaders switched from being their harshest critics into their stoutest defenders. In effect, The power of the U.S. had been used to obtain a partitionist solution of the sort that Britain and France, with their "realist" (i.e., pro-Serb) policies, had pursued since 1993.

Toward War in Kosovo

After Milosevic's 1989 putsch, Kosovo's Albanians stuck to nonviolent strategies, ignoring Serbian political structures and developing a "parallel system" of basic education and healthcare. By 1996, this system was dilapidated. In the wake of Dayton, nobody believed any longer that nonviolence would win international backing against Serbia. Guerrilla bands calling themselves the Kosovo Liberation Army (KLA) wanted confrontation with the Serbian police, which readily obliged. Fighting escalated in 1998; by August, some 200,000 Kosovars had fled into the hills and another 100,000 had left the province.

Threatened with NATO bombardment, Milosevic accepted an unarmed observer mission and a negotiating process. Predictably, this attempt to avert the worst met with failure. Milosevic had nowhere to fall back to from Kosovo, while the KLA was fighting for Kosovo's independence. With both sides playing for the highest stakes, the conflict duly resumed.

In Kosovo, as in Croatia and Bosnia and Herzegovina, international policy was atrocity-driven. The galvanizing role played earlier by the destruction of Vukovar and the slaughter at Srebrenica was now performed by the murder of 45 Albanians at Racak in January 1999. Milosevic and the Albanian leaders were given an ultimatum: accept an international settlement granting Kosovo the widest measure of autonomy, or face punishment by NATO missiles. The Albanians eventually saw their own interest and signed, isolating Milosevic. For him, defiance held more appeal than capitulation.

NATO leaders found themselves bombing Serbian military targets and civic infrastructure. Serbia responded by killing an estimated 11,000 Albanians and driving almost one million out of the province. This ethnic cleansing fortified the Western leaders' resolve to persevere. After 78 days, Milosevic agreed to pull out of Kosovo. A UN administration was established to oversee reconstruction and nurture self-government, with 42,000 NATO troops providing security.

No sooner had NATO occupied Kosovo and refugees flooded back than a reverse ethnic cleansing commenced. At least half the remaining Serb minority population was terrorized into fleeing northwards into Serbia. Despite its overwhelming troop strength, NATO was unwilling or unable to stop this exodus and, as had happened in Bosnia and Herzegovina, some observers accused the U.S. of prioritizing the protection of its troops over the responsibility to protect civilians. Kosovo's suspended sovereignty gave Albanian extremists a political excuse to cleanse the Serbs from the territory. The wave of violence in March 2004, causing 19 deaths, was a grim reminder that Kosovo could not be stabilized without resolving its final political status.

Having played his last nationalist card, Milosevic could no longer rule by dividing his opponents. Yet he was equally unable to normalize his state without destroying his own party-state powerbase. He lasted until October 2000, eleven years longer than the Berlin Wall—a unique achievement among Europe's communist leaders.

The wars of Yugoslav sucession were fought for power over people and territory. National identities were used as labels for political constituencies. The escalatory logic of the terminal crisis consisted in the readiness of leaders on all sides to discover and pursue maximal goals, in essence daring their opponents to trump them. In this process, fathered by Milosevic and facilitated by Tudjman, legitimacy was pitted against coercive resources in a complex pattern, until trumping meant nothing short of war.

SEE ALSO Bosnia and Herzegovina; Croatia, Independent State of; Ethnic Cleansing; Humanitarian Intervention; Incitement; International Criminal Tribunal for the Former Yugoslavia; Izetbegović, Alija; Karadzic, Radovan; Kosovo; Massacres; Milosevic, Slobodan; Mladic, Ratko; Peacekeeping; Propaganda; Safe Zones; Tudjman, Franjo

BIBLIOGRAPHY

Annan, Kofi. *Report of the Secretary-General Pursuant to General Assembly Resolution 53/35 (1998): The Fall of Srebrenica.* United Nations publication A/54/549, 15 November 1999.

Banac, Ivo (1984). *The National Question in Yugoslavia: Origins, History, Politics.* Ithaca, N.Y.: Cornell University Press.

Carmichael, Cathie (2002). *Ethnic Cleansing in the Balkans: Nationalism and the Destruction of Tradition.* London: Routledge.

Djilas, Milovan (1962). *Conversations with Stalin.* New York: Harcourt, Brace & World.

Djilas, Milovan (1977). *Wartime*. London: Secker & Warburg.

Gow, James (1977). *Triumph of the Lack of Will: International Diplomacy and the Yugoslav War*. London: Hurst.

Gow, James (2003). *The Serbian Project and Its Adversaries: A Strategy of War Crimes*. London: Hurst.

Judah, Tim (2000). *Kosovo: War and Revenge*. New Haven, Conn.: Yale University Press.

Lukic, Reneo, and Allen Lynch (1996). *Europe from the Balkans to the Urals: The Disintegration of Yugoslavia and the Soviet Union*. Oxford: Oxford University Press and the Stockholm International Peace Research Institute.

Ramet, Sabrina (2002). *Balkan Babel: The Disintegration of Yugoslavia from the Death of Tito to the Fall of Milosevic*, 4th edition. Boulder, Colo.: Westview Press.

Ripley, Tim (1999). *Operation Deliberate Force: The UN and NATO Campaign in Bosnia 1995*. Lancaster, Pa.: Centre for Defence and International Security Studies.

Simms, Brendan (2001). *Unfinest Hour: Britain and the Destruction of Bosnia*. London: Allen Lane/The Penguin Press.

Sell, Louis (2002). *Slobodan Milosevic and the Destruction of Yugoslavia*. Durham, N.C.: Duke University Press.

Silber, Laura, and Allan Little (1995). *The Death of Yugoslavia*. London: Penguin Books and BBC Books.

Thompson, Mark (1999). *Forging War: The Media in Serbia, Croatia, Bosnia and Herzegovina*. Luton, U.K.: University of Luton Press.

Tindemans, Leo, et al. (1996). *Unfinished Peace: The Report of the International Commission on the Balkans*. Berlin: Aspen Institute.

Ugresic, Dubravka (1998). *The Culture of Lies*. University Park: Pennsylvania State University Press.

Mark Thompson

Yuki of Northern California

In the first half of the nineteenth century, the Yuki flourished in the rugged Coast Range Mountains of Mendocino County, Northern California. They lived along the middle fork of the Eel River in settlements of approximately 150 people and subsisted by hunting deer, fishing salmon, and gathering acorns and other wild plants. Their population was extremely dense and may have numbered more than 10,000 Indians. The Yuki enjoyed a rich annual round of religious celebrations, social dances, trade expeditions and war raids. Although they were regarded as a fierce and warlike group by their neighbors, their weapons were bows and arrows and mortality in any battle was very low. Life was eventful and satisfying.

The Yukis earliest encounter with whites may have occurred in 1833, when a Hudson's Bay Company fur trading party led by Michael Laframboise passed peacefully through the mountain valley that forms the heart of Yuki territory. They remained only a few days before departing, leaving just memories and a few trade beads. Not until 1854 did whites again venture into the valley, when an American exploration party consisting of the brothers Pierce and Frank Asbill, with their friend Jim Nephus, discovered this isolated, lush, almost perfectly round valley. While riding through the valley on horseback, they encountered a great congregation of Yuki and, in the confusion that followed, the whites killed a number of Indians and escaped unharmed. The following year, this party returned to spend the summer in the beautiful valley, hunting deer and tanning skins. During their stay, the whites befriended young Yuki, but when they departed at the end of the summer, they kidnapped thirty-five girls and young women to sell as wives to Mexican vaqueros in the Sacramento Valley.

Other explorers soon followed the Asbill party and word spread in Northern California of the remote mountain valley named "Round Valley" by Europeans. Settlers were attracted to the area for its cattle ranching potential, whereas the U.S. government identified it as a desirable place to gather Indians from a number of Northern California tribes displaced by settlers, gold miners, and ranchers. The government declared the entire valley an Indian Reservation in June, 1856, but this proclamation came too late as settlers were already entrenched. They continued to arrive and stake large land claims in the southern half of the valley, leaving the government only the northern end for the reservation.

Simmon P. Storms, Indian agent for Round Valley Reservation, erected reservation buildings, surrounding them with a stockade; he also relocated here a group of Maidu from the Sacramento Valley. A farm was begun, but few Yuki were attracted to farming; most continued to pursue their traditional hunting and gathering existence in the valley and surrounding mountains. Some Yuki tried to drive out the reservation personnel shortly after their arrival by killing stock animals and threatening the personnel with bows and arrows. In response, Storms claimed that reservation staff "were forced to kill many of. . .[the Indians]. . . , which stopped their proceedings" (Miller, 1979, p. 49). When settlers tried to prohibit the Yuki from their traditional hunting and gathering activities in the valley, the Indians killed a few cattle, horses, and pigs for food.

The settlers were quick to retaliate and formed expeditions to punish the Yuki. These expeditions were best described in the testimony of a responsible settler under oath to a California State Investigating Committee in 1860:

. . . in one thousand eight hundred and fifty six the first expedition by the whites against the Indians was made, and [the expeditions] have continued ever since; these expeditions were formed by gathering together a few white men whenever the Indians committed depredations on their stock; there were so many of these expeditions that I cannot recollect the number; the result was that we would kill, on an average, fifty or sixty Indians on a trip, and take some prisoners, which we always took to the reserve; frequently we would have to turn out two or three times a week (Miller, 1979, p. 49).

This statement, substantiated by other settlers, implies that at least five thousand Yuki were murdered in and around Round Valley each year, although presumably the numbers decreased as the Yuki population declined.

Hostilities between the Indians and the settlers were not entirely one-sided, but the Yuki killed did not kill any white men until 1857, when, in desperation, they killed two whites, one of whose "favorite amusement[s] is said to have been shooting at the Indians at long range, and he usually brought down his game" (Miller, 1979, p. 50). Citing this killing as an example of the constant danger they were exposed to, the settlers sent word to California Indian Superintendent Thomas J. Henley for troops to protect them. The troops marched through the mountains in the summer of 1858 and caused over two thousand Indians to descend on the reservation for their own protection. When the troops departed, so did the Indians.

The settlers continued to send raiding parties to pursue and kill Yuki and other Natives living in the nearby mountains. The U.S. Department of the Interior dispatched Special Agent J. Ross Browne in 1858 to investigate the Indian Wars in and around Round Valley. Browne reported at the end of September that the situation was a "war of extermination" being waged against the Indians (Miller, 1979, p. 55). Even settlers who were missing no stock launched parties to go into the mountains and hunt Indians; some settlers boldly invaded Round Valley Reservation in broad daylight shooting adult Indians and kidnapping younger ones to sell into virtual slavery outside the valley. Such massacres continued with shocking intensity and frequency so U.S. troops were again transported to Round Valley in January, 1859, with instructions to protect the Indians and whites from each other and generally to maintain the peace. When it became apparent that Lieutenant Edward Dillon, the officer in charge, intended to be fair to both Indians and whites alike, the settlers concluded that the soldiers would not punish the Indians so they continued their own murderous raids. At the same time, they began petitioning California Governor John B. Weller to commission a company of volunteers to hunt down the Yuki more effectively. The settlers did not bother to wait for the commission, but raised a complement of volunteers who selected Walter S. Jarboe as their leader. His company of Eel River Rangers commenced their raids in July, murdering indiscriminately all Indians they could find, regardless of age or sex. This intense pace of raids and killings went on for six months until Jarboe's commission expired in January, 1860. In subsequent testimony one volunteer in Jarboe's unit claimed that "Captain Jarboe told me his company had killed more Indians than any other expedition . . . ever . . . ordered out in this State" (Miller 1979, p. 72).

After Jarboe's company was decommissioned, the settlers continued for several years to raid Yuki and other Indian camps in the area. But by 1860, there were only three hundred Yuki on Round Valley reservation, with perhaps another few hundred in the surrounding mountains. Through an extremely intense campaign of genocide, the flourishing Aboriginal Yuki population had been drastically reduced by more than ten thousand Indians in only five years. The effects on neighboring mountain tribes were equally devastating.

What became of the survivors on Round Valley Reservation? Under the tutelage of Indian agents and missionaries, they became victims of cultural genocide as they were encouraged to exchange their Indian languages, worldview, knowledge, and cultural values for the English language and European values and culture. As tribal elders died, the rich Yuki culture and language disappeared with them. By 1900 there were only about one hundred Yuki. In 2003, fewer than one hundred mixed-blood individuals claim Yuki ancestry.

SEE ALSO Developmental Genocide; Indigenous Peoples; Native Americans

BIBLIOGRAPHY

Miller, Virginia P. (1978). "Yuki, Huchnom, and Coast Yuki." In *Handbook of North American Indians, Vol. 8, California,* ed. Robert F. Heizer. Washington, D.C.: Smithsonian Institution.

Miller, Virginia P. (1979). *Ukomno'm: The Yuki Indians of Northern California.* Socorro, N.M.: Ballena Press.

Miller, Virginia P. (1994). "Yuki." In *Native America in the Twentieth Century,* ed. Mary B. Davis. New York: Garland Publishing.

Patterson, Victoria, DeAnna Barney, Les Lincoln, and Skip Willits, eds. (1990). *The Singing Feather.* Ukiah, Calif.: Mendocino County Library.

Susman, Amelia, and Robert F. Heizer, eds. (1976). "The Round Valley Indians of California." In *Contributions of the University of California Archaeological Research Facility 31.* Berkeley, Calif.: Archaeological Research Facility.

Virginia P. Miller

Zulu Empire

From the 1810s until its destruction by the British in 1879, the Zulu kingdom was the largest in southeastern Africa, occupying most of what is today KwaZulu-Natal province, in South Africa. The Zulu kingdom was rather small and insignificant until King Shaka (ruled c. 1816–1828) conquered many neighboring polities. Shaka is a highly ambiguous figure in popular memory today. For Zulu ethnic nationalists in South Africa, and for many Pan-Africanists throughout the world, he serves as a symbol of African achievement and anti-colonial resistance. For many whites, in contrast, Shaka became a symbol of African barbarism. However, the debates about Shaka do not necessarily follow racial lines: some whites have seen Shaka as a rather heroic figure, while many black South Africans have seen Shaka as an oppressor who indiscriminately slaughtered not only his opponents, but also innocent non-combatants, including women and children.

Already in the 1820s, when Europeans began expanding into the lands of the Zulus and their immediate neighbors, a territory that the Europeans called Natal, Europeans used Shaka's alleged atrocities to justify their own activities. As elsewhere in the colonized world, Europeans portrayed themselves as saving native peoples from the often deadly upheavals fomented by the natives' own leaders. In the Zulu case, however, this rhetoric ultimately became a highly detailed and well-developed complex of stories and historical arguments, all centered around Shaka and the chain of events that he allegedly set in motion, which became known as the *mfecane*.

According to European accounts of the mfecane, Shaka revolutionized African society, politics, and especially warfare. In this version of the events, the entire Zulu kingdom became a permanent standing army, highly centralized, disciplined, and aggressive. Not only did Shaka and his armies attack their immediate neighbors, they also chased refugees for hundreds, even thousands, of miles, sending them as far away as the Great Lakes region of East Africa. In the process, Shaka's forces supposedly killed more than a million Africans, a figure which received the sanction of authority when it was cited by Hannah Arendt in *The Origins of Totalitarianism* (1951). At the same time, most of South Africa was cleared of its inhabitants, becoming "empty land" conveniently awaiting colonization by Boer trekkers and British settlers. During the twentieth century, apartheid ideologues claimed that the thirteen percent of South Africa's land set aside for blacks as "homelands" or "Bantustans" coincided with the small pockets in which the refugees from Shaka's mfecane huddled.

Since the 1960s, research by numerous historians has demonstrated that much of the mfecane was actually a myth created by South African whites. Indeed, the term *mfecane* itself, though seemingly of African origin, was actually coined by whites. The Shakan military system had been developed by numerous people for generations preceding Shaka, and it was not unique to the Zulu kingdom. Shaka's rule did not even effectively extend throughout the whole of present-day KwaZulu-Natal province, let alone the vast territories beyond. Refugees from the Shakan wars did indeed ultimately migrate as far as East Africa, but over decades and of their own accord: The Zulu army was barely able to act just beyond the borders of the Zulu kingdom; it had neither the ability nor the desire to "chase" refugees farther than that.

Those who died during the Shakan wars probably numbered only in the tens of thousands, as the KwaZulu-Natal region itself had only a few hundred thousand inhabitants at the beginning of Shaka's reign. Blacks were largely confined to what became the homelands, not by Shaka's wars, but by decades of land expropriation by white settlers. One historian, Julian Cobbing, has even gone so far as to argue that white slave raiders of the 1810s and 1820s invented the idea of the mfecane as an alibi to cover up their own attacks on Africans. This last argument has received a lot of attention, but has not held up in the face of further research. Nevertheless, the other criticisms of the mfecane, by Cobbing and others, have become accepted by most specialists in the subject.

The debate surrounding Shaka's reign has often had as much to do with the nature of the evidence as with the actual historical events. For example, two of the richest sources on the Shakan era are the diaries of the English adventurers Nathaniel Isaacs and Henry Francis Fynn. Both observers were clearly biased against Shaka, and both accounts were written well after the fact. There is even a letter in which Isaacs urges Fynn to sensationalize his account in order to attract more readers. In the 1920s, the missionary A. T. Bryant published a compendious history of the Zulu kingdom based on oral traditions he had collected, but Bryant never makes it clear what comes from the oral traditions and what stems from his own admitted efforts to "clothe the dry bones" of history.

The most exhaustive and well-documented collection of Zulu oral tradition is that produced by James Stuart, a British colonial official in Natal during the late nineteenth and early twentieth centuries. Though Stuart was also arguably biased against the Zulus in some ways, he seems to have been rather meticulous and even-handed in his recording of the evidence that Africans gave to him. Certainly, although the testimony collected by Stuart contains much that is critical of Shaka and other Zulu kings, there is also much that is positive, and there is no shortage of criticism of European rule. More recently, the Zulu-speaking poet Mazisi Kunene has published a novel-length praise poem on Shaka's life based upon oral traditions, but another black South African, Mbongeni Malaba, has taken Kunene to task for glossing over the negative aspects of Shaka's rule. Black South Africans have never been unanimous in their opinions on Shaka.

Although the numbers and geographical extent of the killings during Shaka's reign have been exaggerated by many white commentators, there is little doubt that Shaka (and his successor, Dingane, who ruled during the period from 1828 to 1840) did order the extermination of large numbers of people, including innocent civilians. Some of this killing was ordered out of personal vindictiveness, but even that done "for reasons of state" could still be considered genocide. Like other perpetrators of genocide, both Shaka and Dingane targeted whole categories of people for elimination, including at various times all the subjects of the Ndwandwe, Mthethwa, Langeni, Thembu, and Qwabe kingdoms. On the other hand, Shaka and Dingane did not always ruthlessly pursue such objectives to their logical conclusions, but rather relented and even incorporated some of their former enemies as full-fledged subjects of the Zulu kingdom. Over time, many of Shaka and Dingane's victims, or at least their descendants, not only forgave and forgot, but even came to identify themselves as Zulus.

SEE ALSO Apartheid; Shaka Zulu; South Africa

BIBLIOGRAPHY

Etherington, Norman (2001). *The Great Treks: The Transformation of Southern Africa, 1815–1854*. London: Longman.

Hamilton, Carolyn, ed. (1995). *The Mfecane Aftermath: Reconstructive Debates in Southern African History*. Johannesburg: Witwatersrand University Press; Pietermaritzburg: University of Natal Press.

Mahoney, Michael R. (2003). "The Zulu Kingdom as a Genocidal and Post-genocidal Society, c. 1810 to the Present." *Journal of Genocide Research* 5:251–268.

Michael R. Mahoney

Zunghars

The Zunghar nation developed in the early seventeenth century from nomadic tribes of Western Mongols who had established a homeland beyond the Altai Mountains, astride the modern China-Kazakhstan border. By 1700, the Zunghars had created an empire that included the oasis towns of Eastern Turkestan, and were sufficiently strong to pose a threat to both their Russian and Chinese neighbors. Following several conflicts with the nomads, the Chinese emperor, Qianlong, grasped an opportunity to conquer Zungharia in 1755. He easily succeeded but, after Chinese forces withdrew, the Zunghars rose in revolt, prompting the Qing ruler to seek a final solution to his Zunghar problem. Acting at the behest of the emperor, Chinese armies intentionally exterminated at least 180,000 people during the ensuing campaign, representing some 30 percent of the Zunghar population. An outbreak of smallpox ravaged the remainder, leaving less than one-third of the Zunghars alive to face either slavery or exile. Having assailed the populace, the Chinese emperor subsequently arranged the eradication of the Zunghar culture. In intentionally destroying part of a national group in these ways, Qianlong was committing genocide, as defined by Article II of the current United Nations Genocide Convention.

The Qing descended from Manchuria during the seventeenth century and established control over the core China by 1681. Although they incorporated cooperative foreigners into their system, the Qing dealt with their more unruly neighbors through a combination of diplomacy, tribute, and force, often setting one group against another. The principal aim of their efforts was to ensure that barbarians never presented a united front against the new dynasty. The Qing established control over Outer Mongolia in 1691 and invaded Tibet in 1720. By the mid-eighteenth century, they ruled over a massively expanded Chinese territory. Meanwhile, a new nation was developing farther west, beyond the Altai Mountains and the ever-expanding reach of Beijing.

In the early seventeenth century, the Choros, Dorbet, and Khoits, tribes of the Western Mongols (also referred to as Oirats), settled in the region of the Irtysh River, near the modern border between China and Kazakhstan, and united to form the embryonic Zunghar nation. From their capital at Kubakserai, on the banks of the Imil River, they developed agriculture and crafts, which brought an air of diversity and sedentary culture to their nomad society. The Zunghars embraced Buddhism, along with the majority of Mongols, established temples and monasteries in their lands, and maintained a body of literature in a modified Mongolian script that suited their phonetic system.

The power and influence of the Zunghars increased throughout the seventeenth century. Under the capable leadership of Galdan Boshughtu (r. 1671–1697), their homeland stretched from Lake Balkhash to the Altai and their empire incorporated the conquered oasis towns of Hami, Turfan, and Kashgar, in East Turkestan. They repeatedly attacked Russian settlements in Siberia and even invaded Outer Mongolia in 1688, forcing its populace to seek Qing protection. After Russia and China, each influenced by the perceived threat of the nomads, settled their differences in the Treaty of Nerchinsk in 1689, the Zunghars became "the last real Inner Asian threat to [the] Qing" (Rossabi, 1975, p. 141). Over the coming decades, they repeatedly clashed with Chinese armies. Galdan Bo-

shughtu fought the Qing in Mongolia during the 1690s and further battles occurred in 1720, when the Chinese ousted Zunghar invaders from Tibet, and in 1731, when the Zunghars again marched on Mongolia. Even though the Zunghars agreed a temporary accord with the Qing in 1739, trade disputes continued to plague relations between the two powers.

The death of Galdan Tsering, in 1745, marked the beginning of the end of the Zunghars, then civil war, tore their nation apart. After losing the power struggle to a rival, Amursana fled to the open arms of the Chinese emperor in 1754. Qianlong (r. 1736–1795) immediately discerned an opportunity to conquer the Zunghars and secure his frontiers from what he perceived as a continuing threat. He formed an alliance with Amursana and dispatched an army of at least fifty thousand troops to Zungharia in the spring of 1755. The soldiers spread propaganda leaflets as they advanced, promising rewards and protection in return for Zunghar compliance. Disunited and weakened by years of civil war and confronted by such a large Chinese force, the Zunghars were unable to mount any effective opposition and their leaders fled. Those who remained readily capitulated and, in the summer of 1755, the Qing army withdrew.

Amursana expected to govern all of Zungharia, but was sadly disappointed. Instead, Qianlong sought to divide and rule, so he split the land into four territories, only one of which was reserved for Amursana. Angry and bitter, Amursana instigated an armed revolt and attacked a Chinese border force. When news reached Beijing, the emperor flew into a rage and immediately began to reassemble his army. In 1756, a Qing force, comprising more than 400,000 mostly Manchu and Mongolian troops, flooded into Zungharia. Amursana had already fled westwards. Encountering no organized resistance, the army "set about the universal destruction of the Oirat population" (Zlatkin, 1983, pp. 450–451).

Qianlong repeatedly called for the extermination of the Zunghars, but was inconsistent when speaking of who should be spared. He ordered, "Show no mercy at all to these rebels. Only the old and weak should be saved" (Qianlong, quoted in Perdue, 2003a, p. 50). In another edict, however, he commanded the massacre of all the followers of any rebel leader who refused to prostrate himself before the Chinese and beg the right to surrender. Later, he demanded the destruction of all able Zunghar males and reserved female survivors as slaves for his troops. Following the repeated issue of such callous yet inconsistent edicts, confusion reigned. Nevertheless, as the emperor continued to reward commanders who carried out massacres and to punish those who captured only territory, it became prudent to err on the side of slaughter: Russian officials in Siberia reported that "Manchu troops massacred men, women, and children, sparing no one" (Perdue, 2003a, p. 52).

Between the summer of 1756 and January 1757, the Khalkha Mongols of Outer Mongolia rose in rebellion against the Qing. In spite of the temporary distraction, which forced Qianlong to withdraw his Mongol troops from Zungharia, the remaining soldiers continued to massacre the Zunghar population. During this period, Amursana returned to his homeland and attempted to organize resistance against the Chinese. However, he was unable to raise more than 10,000 troops and, despite bravely engaging his enemy, was forced to flee in the summer of 1757. Qianlong spared 50,000 soldiers to send in hot pursuit of Amursana, betraying a personal loathing of the Zunghar leader. Nevertheless, the fugitive escaped to Russia, where he died of smallpox in September that same year.

Scholars differ in their opinions as to Qing policy after the flight of Amursana. Fred Bergholz, whose work is based mostly on Russian secondary sources, argues that, until 1759, "Qianlong's armies carried out the killing of every Oirat they could find" (Bergholz, 1993, p. 402). In contrast, Peter C. Perdue, who bases his findings largely on Chinese primary sources, contends that Qing policy became more lenient as the immediate perceived threat had disappeared, and the emperor wished to avoid driving the few remaining Zunghars southward to join an imminent rebellion in Turkestan. Nevertheless, he notes that, in the fall of 1757, Qianlong criticized two of his leading generals as they "shrank back from wholesale slaughter, despite continual prodding" (Perdue, 2003a, p. 53). The overall result of Qing policy, however, was the intentional extermination of a substantial part of the Zunghar population.

The estimated total Zunghar population was 600,000. Of these, Owen Lattimore estimates that 50 percent were exterminated, 20 percent died of smallpox, and 30 percent survived in exile or slavery. Peter C. Perdue, however, suggests that 30 percent were exterminated, 40 percent died of smallpox, and 30 percent survived in exile or slavery. Both Lattimore and Perdue base their estimates on Chinese sources. Ilya Zlatkin, who bases his work mostly on Russian sources, suggests that only 7 percent survived, but makes no distinction between exterminations and smallpox-related deaths.

The academics, Frank Chalk and Kurt Jonassohn, have identified strong, centralized authority and dehumanization as two preconditions that facilitate the majority of genocidal actions. In eighteenth-century China, the emperor wielded absolute power under a heavenly mandate and ruled through his generals and elite Confucian officials, who implemented his designs. As unruly neighbors, the Zunghars were considered barbarians. Moreover, the inscription on a 1758 victory tablet, describing the Zunghars as evil and fierce demons who "made men their food" (Krueger, 1972, p. 68), suggests an attempt by Chinese authorities to place the nomads far outside the bounds of human obligation.

For over half a century, the Zunghars had repeatedly clashed with the Chinese, who perceived the nomads as a constant threat to their frontiers and, when Amursana personally betrayed Qianlong, he embarrassed and infuriated the emperor, who sought a terrible revenge. The Qing had not previously employed massacre in managing nomad relations but, as Qianlong noted, "It was only because they repeatedly submitted and then rebelled that we had to wipe them out" (Ch'ien-lung, quoted in Perdue, 2003a, p. 53). The Son of Heaven needed to send a powerful message throughout his empire to terrorize anyone who might dare question his imperial authority. Such motives translated into intent as the emperor issued a series of edicts that explicitly called for the extermination of at least part of the Zunghar nation, and encouraged the slaughter by rewarding those of his commanders who complied, while punishing those who did not. In the face of overwhelming odds, the Zunghars, weakened and disunited by years of civil war, were effectively defenseless. During the campaign, their ability to resist declined still further when a smallpox epidemic claimed between 20 and 40 percent of their original population.

Not content with destroying the populace, the Chinese emperor subsequently arranged the eradication of the Zunghar culture. Qianlong confiscated the Mongol genealogies, which no longer survive, and commissioned Chinese archivists and historians to record a one-sided history of his actions. Most Zunghar documents were burned during the campaign of extermination. The Qing destroyed the equipment and herds of the Zunghars, erased their settlements, and repopulated Zungharia with nomads from Manchuria and Mongolia. Qianlong's actions were so successful that the Zunghar nation and culture effectively disappeared.

SEE ALSO China

BIBLIOGRAPHY

Barfield, Thomas (1992). *The Perilous Frontier: Nomadic Empires and China.* Cambridge, Mass.: B. Blackwell.

Bergholz, Fred (1993). *The Partition of the Steppe: The Struggle of the Russians, Manchus, and Zunghar Mongols for Empire in Central Asia, 1619–1758.* New York: Peter Lang.

Chalk, Frank, and Kurt Jonassohn (1990). *The History and Sociology of Genocide: Analyses and Case Studies.* New Haven, Conn.: Yale University Press.

Krueger, John (1972). "The Ch'ien-lung Inscriptions of 1755 and 1758 in Oirat-Mongolian." *Central Asiatic Journal* 16:59–69.

Lattimore, Owen (1950). *Pivot of Asia: Sinkiang and the Inner Asian Frontiers of China and Russia.* Boston: Little, Brown.

Millward, James (1998). *Beyond the Pass: Economy, Ethnicity and Empire in Qing Central Asia, 1759–1864.* Stanford, Calif.: Stanford University Press.

Perdue, Peter C. (2003b). "Shanghai, 1903: Erasing the Empire, Reracing the Nation." Paper presented at the University of Chicago Graduate Workshop on "Asia in the World, the World in Asia." Available from http://cas.uchicago.edu/workshops/asiaworld/pdf/ReRacing.pdf.

Rossabi, Morris (1975). *China and Inner Asia: From 1368 to the Present Day.* New York: Pica Press.

Schirokauer, Conrad (1991). *A Brief History of Chinese Civilization.* San Diego: Harcourt Brace Jovanovich.

Zlatkin, I. IA. (1983). *Istoriia Dzhungarskogo Khanstva, 1635–1758,* 2nd edition, tran. Alison Rowley. Moscow.

Richard Pilkington

glossary

Ad Hoc Tribunal: a court created to deal with specific disputes, generally by an international body like the United Nations Security Council; such a court has a geographical, subject-matter, and temporal limits on its jurisdiction.

Anschluss: annexation of Austria by Germany on March 13, 1938.

Anthrax: virus that produces black postules, vomiting, fever, and finally suffocation in two to four days. It can lie dormant for decades and has been used as a biological weapon for the mass destruction of individuals. Anthrax infection can occur in three forms: cutaneous (skin), inhalation, and gastrointestinal. *B. anthracis* spores can live in the soil for many years, and humans can become infected with anthrax by handling products from infected animals or by inhaling anthrax spores from contaminated animal products. Anthrax can also be spread by eating undercooked meat from infected animals.

Assimilation: systematic process of one group taking on the customs, language, or religion of another group. The process often deprives a group of its own language, customs, and tradition based on the presumed inferiority or lack of utility of its culture.

Asylum: refuge and protection in another state that an individual can receive. Under current international refugee law, asylum is based on a well-founded fear of persecution based on race, religion, nationality, political opinion, or membership in a social group.

Blood Diamonds: diamonds from areas controlled by forces or groups opposed to legitimate government. The diamonds are often mined by children, who are frequently killed or mutilated by the forces based on suspicion of theft, lack of productivity, or sport. Rebel forces use the diamonds to finance arms purchases and other illegal activities. Once the diamonds are brought to market, their origin is difficult to trace and once polished, they can no longer be identified.

Blood Libel: widespread belief in parts of Europe that Jews killed Christian children and used their blood for Passover meals.

Capital Punishment: penalty involving loss of life, by shooting, hanging, lethal injection of other means; still imposed in some countries for serious crimes.

Cold War: state of political tension and military competition that stopped short of actual war between communist countries and western democracies. It began shortly after World War II in 1948 and continued until the fall of communism about forty years later.

Collectivization: the act or process of collective control, especially over the production and distribution of property. It was practiced during the Stalin years and in many communist countries. Where it was practiced it was forcibly imposed and the attendant protests were often accompanied by loss of life, torture, imprisonment, and starvation.

Cutaneous: Most (about 95%) anthrax infections occur when the bacterium enters a cut or abrasion on the skin, such as when handling contaminated wool, hides, leather or hair products (especially goat hair) of infected animals. Skin infection begins as a raised itchy bump that resembles an insect bite but within one to two days develops into a vesicle and then a painless ulcer, usually one to three cm in diameter, with a characteristic black necrotic (dying) area in the center. Lymph glands in the adjacent area may swell. About 20 percent of untreated cases of cutaneous anthrax will result in death. Deaths are rare with appropriate antimicrobial therapy.

Dehumanization: "killing" the humanity of another. It is the process of depriving others of human qualities, personality, or spirit.

Democide: the systematic killing of the members of a country's general population, or the murder of any person or people by a government. It includes genocide, politicide, and mass murder.

Denazification: the efforts of Allied powers after World War II to eliminate the influence of Nazism, and to remove Nazis from public life in Germany.

Desaparecidos: Spanish word for "the disappeared." They are people who have been taken into custody by state agents and whose whereabouts, custody and fate are either hidden or denied by the state. Most are eventually murdered by the state.

Detention: the practice of detaining individuals or groups of individuals for the purpose of trial. However individuals are often detained without charge or trial and for long periods of time. Sometimes this results in death, torture, or the disappearance of detained persons.

Displaced Person: persons or groups of persons who have been forced to flee or leave their places of habitual residence as a result of, or in order to avoid, the effects of armed conflict, situations of generalized violence, violations of human rights or natural or human-made disasters and who have not crossed an internationally recognized State border.

Ecocide: massive and organized degradation of the environment in armed conflict.

Ex Post Facto: the retroactive application of a law.

Extermination: a category of crime against humanity involving killing on a large scale.

Extrajudicial Execution: a killing on political or other grounds that is not the consequence of a fair trial, held in accordance with recognized international standards.

Grave Breaches: war crime term established by the 1949 Geneva Conventions. It includes such acts as willful killing, torture or inhuman treatment, will-

fully causing great suffering, extensive destruction and appropriation of property that is not justified by military necessity, unlawful deportation, and taking of hostages.

Indemnification: compensation for damage, loss, or injury suffered.

Inhalation: initial symptoms may resemble a common cold. After several days, the symptoms may progress to severe breathing problems and shock. Inhalation anthrax is usually fatal.

Intestinal: the intestinal disease form of anthrax may follow the consumption of contaminated meat and is characterized by an acute inflammation of the intestinal tract. Initial signs of nausea, loss of appetite, vomiting, and fever are followed by abdominal pain, vomiting of blood, and severe diarrhea. Intestinal anthrax results in death in 25 to 60 percent of cases.

Junta: paramilitary group that seeks governmental or state control through threat or use of armed force.

Just War (*jus ad bellum*): aside from the rhetorical use of such an expression to characterize any war for the side offering a justification, there is a technical use applicable in addition to war justified on the basis of self-defense (just cause). Just war offers a doctrine in which the use of force is justified to punish wrongs and protect the innocent in order to uphold standards of civilized conduct.

Lustration: ritual purification. It was the policy in Eastern and Central European countries of banning individuals who served in former regimes from important governmental posts of the current government. While it was used to insure the success of democratic reforms, it also raised questions of international standards of procedural fairness as individuals were often dismissed solely based on party affiliation or political association.

Mercenary: soldier who fights for a country other than his or her own country, and for remuneration rather than out of loyalty and patriotism.

Miscegenation: the marriage or cohabitation between a white person and a member of another race or racially distinct group.

Paramilitary: armed group not formally part of a state's military, but often informally affiliated with it.

Partisans: irregular troops that are engaged in guerrilla warfare and are often behind enemy lines. During World War II this term was applied to resistance fighters in Nazi-occupied countries.

Politicide: the murder of any person or people by a government because of their politics or for political purposes.

Punitive Damages: damages paid by one state to another state to punish the former state for its actions.

Purge: mass expulsion of political opponents from a political or social movement or political party. Such expulsions sometimes involve the extrajudicial killing of opponents.

Ratification: an official confirmation and acceptance of a previous act, often referred to in international treaties as the means by which the text negotiated by diplomatics is subsequently approved by the various states and becomes legally binding, making the act valid from the moment it was done.

Resettlement: applies to the relocation of a population. Used negatively, the term refers to the policy of forcible removal of people from their homes and relocating them in another area for developmental or political reasons. Used in a positive sense, resettlement also refers to the relocation of refugees from their region of origin to countries that accept them as immigrants.

Scapegoating: process of one group finding another group blameworthy for the troubles the former group is experiencing. The process excuses the former group of self-blame, allowing it to feel better about itself. The Jews were seen as scapegoats by Nazi Germany shortly before and during the Holocaust.

Status Quo ante: the situation in effect (status quo) before a significant event.

filmography

Film is the twenty-first century's lingua franca as visual images of daily events are seen around the globe. The power of film to enlighten and inform the public of genocide and crimes against humanity necessitates its inclusion as a research source. The films selected in this filmography were done so on the basis of availability and recognition by the film and human rights communities. The list includes fictional stories based on real events as well as documentaries and television series.

Marlene Shelton

[AFGHANISTAN]

Kandahar [2001]
d. Mohsen Makhmalbaf
This film—part documentary, part fiction—follows a woman's journey as she searches for her sister in war-torn Afghanistan.

Return to Kandahar [2003]
d. Paul Jay and Nelofer Pazira
The star of the film, *Kandahar,* returns to Afghanistan to find her childhood friend, the inspiration for the original film.

[ALGERIA]

Chronicle of the Years of Embers [1975]
d. Mohamed Lakhdar-Hamina
This film deals with Algeria's struggle for independence from France's colonial rule. This story follows the journey of a peasant from his impoverished village to his involvement with the Algerian resistance prior to the Algerian war for independence.

1975 Winner of the Palm D'Or (Cannes)

Battle of Algiers [1966, 2004 (RE-RELEASE)]
d. Gillo Pontecorvo
This internationally acclaimed film was banned by the French government for its realistic portrayal of the vicious battle for independence fought by the Algerian resistance fighters in the 1950s. This film is considered a classic for its documentary style of storytelling. It contains a prescient scene of Algerian women planting a bomb in a popular cafe.

1966 Winner of the Golden Lion (Berlin)

1968 Academy Award Nominee: Best Director and Screenplay

[AMAZON REGION]

At the Edge of Conquest: The Journey of Chief Wai Wai [1993]
d. Geoffrey O'Connor
This film follows the leader of the Waiapi Indians of the Amazon region and their extraordinary leader, Chief Wai Wai, as he journeys from isolation to Brazil's capital to fight for his people.

1993 Academy Award Nominee

Amazon Journal [1996]
d. Geoffrey O'Connor
This film chronicles events in the Amazon region beginning with the assassination of Chico Mendes in 1988 through 1995 and the impact of the encroaching modern world on the indigenous people of the region.

[ANCIENT WORLD]

The Trojan Women [1971]
d. Michael Cacoyannis
This film, based on the play by Euripides, has an all-star cast led by Katherine Hepburn, Vanessa Redgrave, and

Irene Pappas. Euripides story of the fall of Troy and the fate of the women as the Greek army approaches.

1971 Best Actress Award, National Board of Review (Irene Pappas)

[ANTI-SEMITISM]

Gentlemen's Agreement [1947]

d. Elia Kazan

This film is about a reporter (Gregory Peck) who pretends to be Jewish in order to write a story about anti-Semitism in 1940s New York. This film was controversial and thought provoking for its time.

1948 Academy Award Winner: Best Film, Best Director, Best Supporting Actress (Celeste Holm)

The Garden of the Finzi-Continis [1971]

d. Vittorio de Sica

This beautiful film is set in Italy in 1938. In the town of Ferrara, the Finzi-Contini's are a wealthy Jewish family (Dominique Sanda) living in luxury and seclusion from the gathering clouds of war outside the walls of their estate. Their fate is inevitable as Mussolini's racial laws goose-steps in line with Hitler's.

1971 Academy Award Winner: Best Foreign Language Film

Cabaret [1972]

d. Bob Fosse

Life is a cabaret old chum, until the Nazi's come to town. 1930s Berlin at its most decadent with showgirls and naughty banter and a showgirl (Liza Minnelli) who lives life large and uncensored.

1973 Academy Awards Winner: Best Director, Best Actress (Liza Minnelli), Best Supporting Actor (Joel Grey), Best Art Direction, Best Cinematography, Best Film Editing, Best Music Score, Best Sound

Liberty Heights [1999]

d. Barry Levinson

This coming of age film is about fathers and sons (Adrien Brody), and life in 1954 Baltimore when Jews were not allowed to cross the tracks or swim in the pool.

[APARTHEID-NELSON MANDELA]

Cry Freedom [1987]

d. Sir Richard Attenborough

This is the true story of South African journalist Donald Woods and his friendship with black activist Steve Biko (Denzel Washington). The film covers Woods attempts to get answers to the suspicious death of Biko while in custody and his fleeing the country as a result of his investigation.

1987 Academy Award Nominees: Best Supporting Actor (Denzel Washington), Best Music and Best Song

Cry, the Beloved Country [1995]

d. Darrell Roodt

This film is about apartheid in South Africa through the experiences of an African Cleric, (James Earl Jones) and

a wealthy, white landowner, (Richard Harris) in the 1940s.

Mandela and de Klerk [1997]

d. Joseph Sargent

This made-for-television movie is Nelson Mandela's (Sidney Poitier) story of his crusade against the repressive apartheid government of F.W. de Klerk (Michael Caine).

[ARGENTINA]

The Official Story [1985]

d. Luis Puenzo

This is a fictional account of events during Argentina's Dirty War. High school history teacher Alicia Marnet de Ibanez (Norma Aleandro) lives a comfortable life in Buenos Aires with her husband, Roberto, a lawyer, and their five-year-old adopted daughter. This tranquil life is forever changed when Alicia discovers the truth about her daughter's adoption.

1986 Academy Award Winner: Best Foreign Language Film

La Amiga [1988]

d. Jeanine Meerapfel

This film is the story of two girls growing up during the time of Argentina's Dirty War and the struggles to remain friends as their lives change and go in different directions (Liv Ullmann). The film focuses on the organization of Madres de Plaza de Mayo (Mothers of the Mayo Plaza in Argentina) who marched and demanded the return of their children.

1990 Berlin Film Festival: Peace Film Award—Honorable Mention (Jeanine Meerapfel)

1988 San Sebastian Film Festival: Best Actress Awards (Liv Ullmann and Cipe Lincovsky)

For These Eyes [1998]

d. Gonzalo Arijon and Virginia Martinez

This film is the story of a young girl named Daniela who thought she was the daughter of an agent of the SIDE, the Argentinean Secret Service but she was in fact, Mariana Zaffaronni, the daughter of two Uruguayan activists who disappeared during Argentina's Dirty War from 1976 to 1983. This story follows her grandmother's 16-year search and the legal and emotional outcome of finding her.

[ARMENIANS IN OTTOMAN TURKEY]

Ararat [2002]

d. Atom Egoyan

This film travels between 1915 Turkey and present-day Canada and tells the story of an Armenian-Canadian family and how they come to terms with the history of the 1.5 million Armenians killed during World War I. This film has been criticized by the Turkish government as one-sided and propaganda.

Germany and the Secret Genocide [2003]

d. Michael Hagopian

This film uses archival footage to document the involvement of Germany in the first genocide of the twentieth century when 1.5 million Armenians were killed by the Ottoman government.

[AUSCHWITZ]

Night and Fog [1955]

d. Alain Resnais

This documentary was filmed in postwar Auschwitz and is stark in its image of what took place during the Nazi regime.

Playing for Time [1980]

d. Daniel Mann and Joseph Sargent

This made-for-television film is adapted from Fania Fenelon's autobiography by Arthur Miller. It tells the story of a group of female prisoners (Vanessa Redgrave, Jane Alexander) at Auschwitz whose lives are spared when they perform music for their captors.

1981 Emmy Award Winner: Outstanding Drama Special, Lead Actress (Vanessa Redgrave), Supporting Actress (Jane Alexander), Outstanding Writing (Arthur Miller). Peabody Award

Sophie's Choice [1982]

d. Alan J. Pakula

Polish beauty Sophie (Meryl Streep) falls in love with Nathan (Kevin Kline) in postwar America but is haunted by the memories of a decision she made during internment in Auschwitz.

1983 Academy Award Winner: Best Actress, Meryl Streep

[AUSTRALIA]

Rabbit-Proof Fence [2002]

d. Phillip Noyce

This film set in 1931 is the true story of aborigine Molly Craig who leads her younger sister and cousin over 1,500 miles of the Australian outback to return them safely to their homes after being taken by white settles to become domestic staff. This story deals with the Stolen Generations, a program to civilize the aboriginal population.

2003 Australian Film Institute Winner: Best Film

[BABI YAR]

Holocaust, Part 2: The Road to Babi Yar [1978]

d. Marvin Chomsky

Holocaust is a four-part miniseries that aired in 1978. This miniseries follows the fate of two families—the Weiss family, who are Jewish, and Erik Dorf's (Michael Moriarty), who joins the Nazi party. Part two is set in 1941 and the massacre of Jews at Babi Yar is depicted.

1979 Emmy Award Winner: Best Drama Series, Best Directing (Marvin Chomsky), Best Costumes, Best Film

Editing, Outstanding Lead Actor in a Limited Series (Michael Moriarty), Outstanding Lead Actress in a Limited Series (Meryl Streep)

[KLAUS BARBIE]

Hotel Terminus [1988]

d. Marcel Ophuls

This documentary details the life and times of Klaus Barbie, the Butcher of Lyon, who was Gestapo chief during the Nazi occupation of France.

1989 Academy Award Winner, Best Documentary Film

[BOSNIA and HERZEGOVIA]

Welcome to Sarajevo [1997]

d. Michael Winterbottom

The Bosnian war in Sarajevo is backdrop to a British journalist's attempt to save an orphaned girl from the brutality of war.

Shot through the Heart [1998]

d. David Attwood

Two best friends (Linus Roache and Vincent Perez) end up on opposite sides of the war in Sarajevo with tragic consequences.

1999 Peabody Award

Srebrenica: A Cry From the Grave [1999]

d. Leslie Woodhead

This documentary narrated by Bill Moyers tells the story of the massacre in July 1995 of over 7,000 Muslims in Srebrenica, Bosnia, a city that was supposed to be a safe-zone protected by the UN and NATO.

Harrison's Flowers [2000]

d. Elie Chouraqui

The wife (Andie MacDowell) of a Newsweek reporter missing in 1991 war-torn Yugoslavia risks her life to find him aided by a fellow journalist (Adrien Brody).

[BURMA/MYANMAR]

Inside Burma: Land of Fear [1996]

d. David Munro

Investigative reporter and award-winning filmmaker John Pilger exposes the brutality and repression inside Burma.

Bullfrog Films

[CAMBODIA]

The Killing Fields [1984]

d. Roland Joffe

This film is based on the true story of the friendship between Sydney Schanberg (Sam Waterson), a reporter for the New York Times and Dith Pran (Dr. Haing S. Ngor), a translator and assistant. When Pot Pol conducts his cleaning campaign of Year Zero, Dith Pran's family with Schanberg's help escape to the United States and he remains behind to help cover the story.

1985 Academy Awards: Best Supporting Actor (Dr. Haing S. Ngor), Best Cinematography (Chris Menges), and Best Film Editing (Jim Clark)

Samsara [1989]

d. Ellen Bruno

Documentary on the devastation of the war in Cambodia and the tragic impact it has had on the country.

Sundance Film Festival: Special Jury Award

[CANADA]

Kanehsatake [1994]

d. Alanis Obomsawin

This documentary film by Native American Alanis Obomsawin covers the armed confrontation between the Native American Mohawks and the Canadian government forces during a 1990 standoff in Kanehsatake, a village in the Mohawk nation.

Produced by The National Film Board of Canada

Best Documentary Film, American Indian Film Festival

A Fight Against Time: The Lubicon Cree Land Rights [1995]

d. Ed Bianchi

A documentary focusing on the case made by the five hundred Lubicon Lake Cree Indians that logging, gas, and oil companies are profiting from their lands while they become increasingly impoverished.

No Turning Back: The Royal Commission on Aboriginal Peoples [1996]

d. Greg Coyes

A documentary film on the Royal Canadian Commission that traveled and interviewed more than a thousand aboriginal representatives on their history with the Canadian government.

[CATHOLIC CHURCH]

Amen [2002]

d. Constantin Costa-Gavras

This film focuses on two characters, one an SS officer (Ullrich Tukar) and the other a Jesuit priest (Mathieu Kassovitz), and makes a case that the Catholic Church collaborated with the Nazis during the war.

[CHECHENS]

Immortal Fortress: A Look Inside Chechnya's Warrior Culture [1999]

d. Dodge Billingsley

Dodge Billingsley's film leads him through down dark alleys and secret meetings to film the Chechen perspective on its fight for independence from Russia.

[CHEYENNE]

Little Big Man [1970]

d. Arthur Penn

This film is the story of Jack Crabb looking back on his life from old age and recalling his life spent with the Cheyenne Indians.

New York Film Critics Award for Best Supporting Actor (Chief Dan George)

[CHILDREN]

Forbidden Games [1952]

d. Rene Clement

This film set in 1940 follows five-year-old Paulette as she witnesses the death of her parents and takes refuge with a family in the countryside. There, she and the farmer's son take part in ritual burials in a cemetery they create for themselves.

1952 Academy Award for Best Foreign Language Film

Children of War [2000]

d. Alan and Susan Raymond

This documentary chronicles the effects of war and terrorism on children in four parts of the globe: Bosnia, Israel, Rwanda, and Northern Ireland.

2000 Emmy Award: Outstanding Non-fiction Special

[CHILE]

Missing [1982]

d. Constantin Costa-Gavras

This film is based on the actual experiences of Ed Horman (Jack Lemmon) and his search for his son, missing in Chile during the Pinochet coup.

1983 Academy Award: Best Screenplay Based on Material from Another Medium

Chile: Hasta Cuando? [1987]

d. David Bradbury

The director and film crew captured on film the arrests and murders taking place during the military dictatorship of General Augusto Pinochet.

1987 Academy Award Nominee

Inside Pinochet's Prison [1999]

This documentary was secretly filmed by East German journalists and filmed in the concentration camps of the Pinochet regime.

Journeyman Pictures

Chile: A History in Exile [1999]

This documentary records the journey of Cecilia Aranada as she returns to Chile after escaping the bloody Pinochet regime. Cecilia interviews Chileans who lost family members or survived torture at the hands of the military.

[CHINA]

To Live [1994]

d. Yimou Zhang

This story of a married couple (Li Gong and You Ge) struggling to survive and not lose hope through the dramatic changes occurring in communist China.

1994 Winner of Cannes Grand Jury Prize for director Yimou Zhang

Xiu Xiu, The Sent Down Girl [1998]

d. Joan Chen

A young teenage girl, Xiu Xiu, is sent to a remote area of China to do manual labor.

1999 National Board of Review Freedom of Expression Award for Joan Chen

Morning Sun [2003]

d. Carma Hinton, Richard Gordon, Geremie R. Barme

This two-hour documentary focuses on events during the Cultural Revolution using newsreels combined with first-hand accounts of members of a then high school generation reflecting back on those disturbing times.

[COLLABORATION-RESISTANCE]

Pimpernel Smith [1941]

d. Leslie Howard

The Scarlet Pimpernel theme is revisited once again by Leslie Howard. This time he plays Professor Horatio Smith who takes his students on an archaeological dig in 1939 Germany where his students discover their professor is smuggling enemies of Hitler out of the country. This film angered the Germans for its less-than-flattering depiction of them.

Casablanca [1942]

d. Michael Curtiz

Rick Blaine (Humphrey Bogart), an American nightclub owner in Casablanca during World War II, has his life turned upside down when Ilsa Lund Laszlo (Ingrid Bergman) walks into his.

1942 Academy Award Winner: Best Picture, Best Director (Michael Curtiz), Best Screenplay (Julius and Philip Epstein, Howard Koch)

The Sorrow and the Pity [1969]

d. Marcel Ophuls

This documentary investigates France's Vichy government's collaboration with the Nazis during the occupation.

1972 National Board of Review: Best Foreign Language Film

Julia [1977]

d. Fred Zinnemann

This film, based on Lillian Hellmann's (portrayed by Jane Fonda) novel Pentimento, tells of her relationship with a childhood friend, Julia (Vanessa Redgrave), and the devotion she has to her. Their friendship is put to a test when Julia asks Lillian to smuggle money from Paris into Berlin.

1978 Academy Award Winner for Best Supporting Actors (Jason Robards and Vanessa Redgrave), Best Screenplay Based on other Material

The Last Metro [1980]

d. Francois Truffaut

In occupied Paris in 1942, a theater director's wife (Catherine Deneuve), valiantly struggles to manage the Montmartre Theatre, while her husband, a German Jew, is in hiding.

1981 Winner of 10 Cesar awards

Terrorists in Retirement [1985]

d. Mosco Boucault

This documentary film narrated by Simone Signoret was initially banned by French television. In interviews with the terrorists, the truth is revealed that they were Jewish communists who were resistance fighters during the Nazi occupation of Paris. The film reveals their arrest and torture at the hands of the French police.

Au Revoir Les Enfants [1987]

d. Louis Malle

This film is based on events in the life of director Louis Malle while he was at a boarding school during World War II. In this story two boys become friends at a Catholic boarding school, one is French and the other is being hidden by the friars because he is Jewish.

1987 Winner of the Golden Lion, Venice Film Festival

Europa Europa [1990]

d. Agnieszka Holland

A Jewish boy separated from his family in Germany reinvents himself as a German orphan and joins the Hitler Youth. Based on a true story.

1992 Winner of the Golden Globe for Best Foreign Film

Sisters in Resistance [2000]

d. Maia Wechsler

This story about four French women who showed amazing resilience and courage during the Nazi occupation by participating in the French resistance. They were arrested by the Gestapo and imprisoned at Ravensbruck concentration camp. They survived to tell their stories in this documentary.

Unlikely Heroes [2003]

d. Richard Trank

This documentary narrated by Sir Ben Kingsley tells the stories of seven previously unknown Jewish heroes whose courageous acts saved thousands of lives from the Nazis.

[COMICS]

The Great Dictator [1940]

d. Charlie Chaplin

Charlie Chaplin plays two roles—that of the dictator of Tomania, named Adenoid Hynkel, and a Jewish barber—in his satire on Nazi Germany.

To Be Or Not To Be [1942]

d. Ernst Lubitsch

In Poland during the occupation, two actors (Carole Lombard and Jack Benny) engage in their form of resistance.

The Shop on Main Street (Obchod Na Korze) [1965]

d. Jan Kadar, Elmar Klos

Set in Slovakia during World War II, a small notions shop run by a Jewish woman, Mrs. Lautman, is given to a good-for-nothing young man named Tono. Mrs. Lautman (Ida Kaminska) is old, deaf, and oblivious to her situation and thinks the young man is looking for a job and hires him. As Tono becomes aware of the fate of Jews, he drunkenly makes an effort to save Mrs. Lautman.

1965 Academy Award for Best Foreign Language Film

To Be Or Not To Be [REMAKE (1983)]

d. Alan Johnson

This time it is Mel Brooks and Anne Bancroft as the actors fighting the Nazis in occupied Poland.

[DEATH CAMPS]

Camps of Death [1983]

This film is a collection of actual footage shot by the Allied forces of the death camps of World War II.

[DEATH MARCH]

Colors of Courage: Sons of New Mexico, Prisoners of Japan [2002]

Produced by Tony Martinez and Scott Henry

This film tells the story of the veterans of the New Mexico's 200th and 515 Coast Artilleries who endured the infamous Death March. A Japanese guard, Yukio Yamabe, who took part in the march is interviewed.

Available through Albuquerque's PBS affiliate, KNME-TV Channel 5

A New Mexico Story: From the Bataan Death March to the Atomic Bomb [2003]

d. Aaron Wilson

This documentary gives the oral histories of the men of the New Mexico National Guard who withstood starvation and brutal treatment by their Japanese captors.

McGaffey Films

[DENIAL]

The Man in the Glass Booth [1975]

d. Arthur Hiller

Arthur Goldman (Maximilian Schell) lives a good life in Manhattan, but all changes when Israeli agents hurry him out of the country to stand trial a Nazi war criminal.

The Music Box [1990]

d. Constantin Costas-Gravras

Jessica Lange portrays a Chicago lawyer who defends her father against charges that he was a SS officer for the Nazis. As witnesses come forward she faces a personal crisis as her certainty in his innocence begins to wane.

Death and the Maiden [1994]

d. Roman Polanski

A woman (Sigourney Weaver) is convinced that the man (Sir Ben Kingsley) her husband has brought home is responsible for the rape and kidnapping she endured by the government.

[DEMJANJUK TRIAL]

The State of Israel v. John Ivan Demjanjuk [1988]

This documentary is about the Cleveland auto mechanic, who was accused of being Ivan the Terrible and supervised the gas chambers of Treblinka.

Ergo Media

[DIARIES]

The Diary of Anne Frank [1959]

d. George Stevens

A young Jewish girl (Millie Perkins) hides in an attic with her family and their friend's from the Nazis in occupied Amsterdam.

1959 Academy Award Winner: Best Supporting Actor (Shelley Winters) and Best Set Design

[DISAPPEARANCES]

Fire in the Andes [1985]

d. Ilan Ziv

This documentary investigates the disappearance of thousands of Peruvians targeted as members of the Shining Path by the Peruvian Armed Forces.

First Run/Icarus Films

[HOLOCAUST DRAMAS]

This Land is Mine [1943]

d. Jean Renoir

A schoolteacher (Charles Laughton) in German occupied France is drawn into the resistance.

The Pawnbroker [1964]

d. Sidney Lumet

Rod Steiger plays a holocaust survivor who is shut down emotionally in a self-made prison (he is literally behind bars) in his New York pawnshop.

Ship of Fools [1965]

d. Stanley Kramer

A ship traveling to Europe from Mexico in the 1930s provides an opportunity to look at a cross section of society. Starring Vivian Leigh and Oskar Werner.

1965 Academy Award Winner: Best Art Direction and Best Cinematography

The Damned [1969]
d. Luchino Visconti
This film tells the story of a wealthy Junker family and their demise under the Third Reich.

The Night Porter [1974]
d. Liliana Cavani
A concentration camp survivor (Charlotte Rampling) and her tormentor, now the night porter in a hotel in Vienna, engage in a twisted relationship. This was a controversial film for its time.

Jakob, der Lugner (Jacob the Liar) [1975]
d. Frank Beyer
This East German film is the original about a Jewish man who invents stories heard on his secret radio to bring hope to the Ghetto.

Voyage of the Damned [1976]
d. Stuart Rosenberg
A ship leaves Hamburg, Germany, with 937 German Jews (Faye Dunaway, Oskar Werner) on board seeking refuge in 1939 Havana, Cuba.

The Boys From Brazil [1978]
d. Franklin J. Schaffner
Gregory Peck plays Josef Mengele in this tale of a Nazi hunter in South America who uncovers a plot to restore the Third Reich.

Holocaust [1978]
d. Marvin J. Chomsky
A miniseries detailing the plight of a Jewish family in Nazi Germany contrasted with the rise of a German soldier. Stars Michael Moriarty, Meryl Streep, and Ian Holm.

The Tin Drum [1979]
d. Volker Schlonodorff
Young Oskar Matzerath (David Bennet) in 1930 Danzig cannot abide the society he is in and so at age three decides not to grow up.

1979 Academy Award: Best Foreign Language Film

Das Boot est Voll (The Boat Is Full) [1981]
d. Markus Imhoof
German and Austrian refuges arrive in Switzerland and discover even though the Swiss are not involved in the war they do not want any refuges.

Escape from Sobibor [1987]
d. Jack Gold
This miniseries recreates the escape of Jewish inmates from the Sobibor death camp in Eastern Poland. Stars Rutger Hauer and Alan Arkin.

1988 Golden Globe: Best Mini-series

War and Rememberance [1988]
d. Dan Curtis
This 12-part miniseries is based on the Herman Waulk novel. This series covers the events during World War II and the toll it takes on the Henry family. Robert Mitchum stars.

The Nasty Girl [1990]
d. Michael Verhoeven
A young girl begins to question her town's Nazi past and finds herself shunned by her community.

1992 BAFTA: Best Foreign Language Film

Alfa's Wonder [1993]
d. Luke Matin
This story of a French family's struggles during the Holocaust focuses on the youngest daughter's (Natalie Portman) curiosity about the events occurring around her.

1993 Winner of Grand Jury Prize at Cannes

Schindler's List [1993]
d. Steven Spielberg
Oskar Schindler (Liam Neeson) uses Jews from the concentration camps to run his factory in Poland. He becomes increasingly aware of the horrors inflicted upon them by the Nazi commandant Amon Goeth, (Ralph Fiennes) and with the help of his Jewish bookkeeper (Ben Kingsley) devises a plan to save as many Jews as he can.

1993 Academy Awards: Best Picture, Best Director, Best Editing, Best Art Direction, Best Cinematography, Best Music Score, Best Screenplay Based on Other Material

Shine [1996]
d. Scott Hicks
The life of Australian pianist David Helfgott (Geoffrey Rush), a child prodigy who is driven to the edge by his father, a survivor of the Holocaust.

1996 Academy Award: Best Actor (Geoffrey Rush)

Bent [1997]
d. Sean Mathias
Max (Clive Owen) is gay and sent to Dachau where he denies his homosexuality and is given a yellow star for Jews. His friend Horst wears the pink star (for gay) and this story tells of their struggle for survival. Based on the stage play of the same name. Mick Jagger and Sir Ian McKellen co-star.

Life Is Beautiful [1997]
d. Roberto Benigni
A Jewish man brings his love for life and his sense of humor to a Nazi death camp in order to help his young son survive.

1999 Academy Awards: Best Foreign Language Film, Best Actor, (Roberto Benigni), Best Music Score

Left Luggage [1998]
d. Jeroen Krabbe
A Jewish girl becomes the nanny of a young mentally disabled Jewish boy and becomes very close to him. Stars Isabella Rossellini, Maximilian Schell, and Topol.

Aimee and Jaguar [1999]
d. Max Farberbock
A Jewish woman (Jaguar) using a false identity falls in love with the wife of a German soldier (Aimee).

Sunshine [1999]
d. Istvan Szabo
This film follows a Jewish family in Hungary through three generations from humble beginnings to wealth and prosperity and loss again. Stars Ralph Fiennes.

Conspiracy [2001]
d. Frank Pierson
The Wannsee Conference where the Final Solution of the Nazi's Holocaust plan is discussed is told through this film starring Stanley Tucci, Kenneth Branagh, and Colin Firth.

Nowhere in Africa [2001]
d. Caroline Link
A German Jewish family moves to Kenya just before the start of World War II to run a farm. The change is difficult to adjust to but events in Germany make it impossible to return.

2002 Academy Award for Best Foreign Language Film

The Pianist [2002]
d. Roman Polanski
The true story of Polish Jewish pianist, Wladyslaw Szpilman (Adrien Brody), and his struggle to survive after escaping from the Warsaw ghetto during World War II.

2003 Academy Awards: Best Director (Roman Polanski), Best Screenplay Based on Other Material, Best Actor (Adrien Brody)

[EAST TIMOR]

Death of a Nation: The Timor Conspiracy [1994]
d. John Pilger
This documentary film covers the genocide in East Timor by the Indonesian army using Western arms.

[EICHMANN TRIAL]

The Trial of Adolf Eichmann [1997]
This documentary uses actual trial footage as well as the recollections of key witnesses.

[EL SALVADOR]

El Salvador: Another Vietnam [1981]
d. Glen Siber and Tete Vasconcellos
A documentary that focuses on the civil war in El Salvador.

El Salvador: The Seeds of Liberty [1981]
d. Glen Siber and Tete Vasconcellos
This film focuses on the four U.S. churchwomen who were raped and murdered by the Slavadoran National Guard in 1980.

First Run/Icarus Films

[ERITEA]

The Forbidden Land [1990]
d. Daniele Lacourse and Yvan Patry
The human cost of the war for independence is the focus of this film.

Eritea: Hope in the Horn of Africa [1993]
By Grassroots International
The dawn of a new nation after a long fought war for independence.

First Run/Icarus Films

[ETHNIC CLEANSING]

Genocide [1981]
d. Arnold Schwartzman
Film documentary about the Holocaust. Narrated by Elizabeth Taylor and Orson Welles.

1982 Academy Award: Best Documentary

The Genocide Factor [2000]
d. Robert J. Emery
This documentary covers four periods from the Biblical to the Holocaust through the more recent twentieth century killing fields of Cambodia and East Timor.

[ETHNOCIDE/ CULTURAL GENOCIDE]

The Searchers [1956]
d. John Ford
John Wayne searches for five years for his niece (Natalie Wood), who kidnapped and raised by Comanche Indians.

Five Centuries Later [1992]
d. German Gutierrez
This documentary features Rigoberta Menchu, the 1992 Nobel Peace Prize winner, and focuses on the status of Central American aboriginal cultures five hundred years after the arrival of Europeans.

First Run/Icarus Films

[FEMALE INFANTICIDE]

Gift of a Girl: Female Infanticide [1997]
d. Jo Smith and Mayyassa Al-Malazi
This film examines the practice of female infanticide in southern India.

Matrubhoomi [2003]
d. Manish Jha
First time writer-director Manish Jha presents a story of an India without enough women due to female infanticide. The result is a rich landlord is forced to buy a young woman from her father for his five sons with tragic consequences.

[FILM AS PROPAGANDA]

Triumph of the Will [1934]
d. Leni Riefenstahl
This Nazi propaganda film focuses on the 1934 Nazi Party
Congress in Nuremberg for which a well rehearsed,
perfectly executed rally and parade was staged. This is
considered to be one of the most accomplished
propaganda films ever made.

The Eternal Jew [1940]
d. Fritz Hippler
Another of the Third Reich's propaganda films, this one is
done in documentary style, giving it a look of
authenticity that describes Jews worldwide in terms of
an infestation of rats.

The Ducktators [1942]
d. Norm McCabe
Mel Blanc provides the voices of Hitler Duck, Hirohito
Duck, and Mussolini Duck all trying to take over the
barnyard. The Allies are portrayed as the Dove of Peace.

[EUGENICS]

Ninteen Eighty-Four [1984]
d. Michael Radford
George Orwell's classic story of a totalitarian society where
a man (John Hurt) rewrites history for a living then
does the unthinkable and falls in love.

[GUATEMALA]

Under the Gun: Democracy in Guatemala [1987]
d. Pat Goudvis and Robert Richter
A inside look at life in Guatemala where military and
civilians fight for control and human rights issues
remain.

First Run/Icarus films

The Man We Called Juan Carlos [2001]
d. Heather MacAndrew and David Springbett
This film tells the story of Wenceslao Armira, a man called
Juan Carlos, whose two children were murdered by
death squads.

Bullfrog Films

[HIROSHIMA]

No More Hiroshima [1984]
d. Martin Duckworth
A documentary of the hibakusha's (survivors) of
Hiroshima.

[IRAQ]

Paying the Price: Killing the Children of Iraq [2000]
d. John Pilger
This film reveals the devastation that the sanctions on Iraq
have had on its children.

[IRAN]

The Tree That Remembers [2002]
d. Masoud Raouf
A young Iranian student hangs himself from a tree outside
a town in Ontario, Canada. This film investigates what
his life and those who feel betrayed by the 1979 Iranian
revolution.

Bullfrog Films

[KOSOVO]

Kosovo: Rebuilding the Dream [2003]
This documentary looks at efforts to rebuild Kosovo under
the protection of the UN Interim Administration
Mission.

First Run/Icarus Films

[KURDS]

In the Name of Honour [2000]
d. Alex Gabbay
This documentary looks at the oppression of the minority
Kurds in northern Iraq and how violence is being
directed more at women.

Bullfrog Films

[NUREMBERG TRIALS]

Judgment at Nuremberg [1961]
d. Stanley Kramer
The trial of the Nazi war criminals by a U.S. court in 1948
Germany.

1961 Academy Awards: Best Screenplay and Best
Supporting Actor (Maximilian Schell)

[P.O.W. CAMPS]

Stalag 17 [1953]
d. Billy Wilder
A film about Allied prisoners in a German POW camp,
starring William Holden as the cocky American
outwitting the Germans.

The Bridge on the River Kwai [1957]
d. David Lean
British soldiers are forced into labor to build a bridge for
their Japanese captors that the Allied forces plan to
blow up.

1957 Academy Awards: Best Picture, Best Director, Best
Screenplay Based on other Material, Best Editing and
Cinematography, Best Music Score and Best Actor, (Alec
Guinness)

The Great Escape [1963]
d. John Sturges
The Allied soldiers in a German POW camp make a daring
escape. An all-star cast lead by Steve McQueen.

[ROMANIA]

Diamonds in the Dark [1999]
d. Olivia Carrescia

Life before and after the Ceausescus regime as told by ten Romanian women.

[ROMANIS]

A Cry for Roma [2003]
d. Gillian Darling Kovanic

A stark look at the continued persecution of Europe's most reviled minority, the Romani's.

[RWANDA]

Rwandan Nightmare [1994]
d. Simon Gallimore

A documentary that probes the slaughter of over a million Rwandans.

Chronicle of a Genocide Foretold [1996]
d. Daniele Lacourse and Yvan Patry

The massacre of 800,000 Tutsi men, women, and children are the focus of this film.

[STALIN]

The War Symphonies [1997]
d. Larry Weinstein

This film focuses on Stalin's bloody purges and Shostakovich's musical response.

[WAR CRIMES]

The Deer Hunter [1978]
d. Michael Cimino

Harrowing film of the horrors of war during the Vietnam era. This story follows three friends from a small mining town in Pennsylvania and the impact their tour of duty has on them. Robert de Niro and Christopher Walken star.

1978 Academy Award Winner: Best Picture, Best Sound, Best Director, Best Editing and Best Supporting Actor (Christopher Walken).

Apocalypse Now [1979]
d. Francis Ford Coppola

This film based on Joseph Conrad's Heart of Darkness, focuses on a mission assigned to Captain Willard (Martin Sheen) to kill a renegade Green Beret (Marlon Brando).

1997 Academy Award winner: Best Sound, Best Cinematography

Platoon [1986]
d. Oliver Stone

The story of a young recruit (Charlie Sheen) in Vietnam and the horrors of war he experiences.

1986 Academy Award winner: Best Picture, Best Director, Best Editing, Best Sound

Full Metal Jacket [1987]
d. Stanley Kubrick

A group of soldiers in Vietnam become dehumanized by their experiences of war.

Kim's Story: The Road From Vietnam [1996]
d. Shelley Saywell

This film is the story of the little girl, Kim Phuc, whose photo of her running naked down the street burned from napalm fueled the antiwar movement and what became of her.

The Quiet American [2002]
d. Phillip Noyce

This film takes place in Vietnam before the war when U.S. interests and a British reporter collide over the love of a woman.

primary sources

Table of Contents

historical texts

Charter of the International Military Tribunal

SOURCE The Avalon Project at Yale Law School website. Available from http://www.yale.edu/lawweb/avalon/avalon.htm.

INTRODUCTION The Charter of the International Military Tribunal was adopted by the London Conference, held from June until early August 1945. Only four countries, the United States, the United Kingdom, France, and the Soviet Union, participated in the conference, although the Charter was subsequently ratified by several other countries. It was the first international criminal tribunal, and the Charter itself included many innovations, including controversial new definitions of war crimes, crimes against peace and crimes against humanity. The concept of crimes against humanity, first elaborated in the Nuremberg Charter, was meant to address atrocities committed by the Nazis against their own civilian populations, and more specifically the attempt to exterminate the Jews. The participants at the London Conference were nervous about establishing a precedent by which gross violations of human rights could be prosecuted under international law, and they consequently limited the concept of crimes against humanity to acts committed in the context of an illegal international war. It was largely in reaction to this that other states, in 1946, proposed a definition of genocide that recognized it could be committed in peacetime as well as during armed conflict.

I. Constitution of the International Military Tribunal

Article 1

In pursuance of the Agreement signed on the 8th day of August 1945 by the Government of the United States of America, the Provisional Government of the French Republic, the Government of the United Kingdom of Great Britain and Northern Ireland and the Government of the Union of Soviet Socialist Republics, there shall be established an International Military Tribunal (hereinafter called "the Tribunal") for the just and prompt trial and punishment of the major war criminals of the European Axis.

Article 2

The Tribunal shall consist of four members, each with an alternate. One member and one alternate shall be appointed by each of the Signatories. The alternates shall, so far as they are able, be present at all sessions of the Tribunal. In case of illness of any member of the Tribunal or his incapacity for some other reason to fulfill his functions, his alternate shall take his place.

Article 3

Neither the Tribunal, its members nor their alternates can be challenged by the prosecution, or by the Defendants or their Counsel. Each Signatory may replace its members of the Tribunal or his alternate for reasons of health or for other good reasons, except that no replacement may take place during a Trial, other than by an alternate.

Article 4

(a) The presence of all four members of the Tribunal or the alternate for any absent member shall be necessary to constitute the quorum.

(b) The members of the Tribunal shall, before any trial begins, agree among themselves upon the selection from their number of a President, and the President shall hold office during the trial, or as may otherwise be agreed by a vote of not less than three members. The principle of rotation of presidency for successive trials is agreed. If, however, a session of the Tribunal takes place on the territory of one of the four Signatories, the representative of that Signatory on the Tribunal shall preside.

(c) Save as aforesaid the Tribunal shall take decisions by a majority vote and in case the votes are evenly divided, the vote of the President shall be decisive: provided always that convictions and sentences shall only be imposed by affirmative votes of at least three members of the Tribunal.

Article 5

In case of need and depending on the number of the matters to be tried, other Tribunals may be set up; and the establishment, functions, and procedure of each Tribunal shall be identical, and shall be governed by this Charter.

II. Jurisdiction and General Principles

Article 6

The Tribunal established by the Agreement referred to m Article 1 hereof for the trial and punishment of the major war criminals of the European Axis countries shall have the power to try and punish persons who, acting in the interests of the European Axis countries, whether as individuals or as members of organizations, committed any of the following crimes.

The following acts, or any of them, are crimes coming within the jurisdiction of the Tribunal for which there shall be individual responsibility:

(a) Crimes Against Peace: namely, planning, preparation, initiation or waging of a war of aggression, or a war in violation of international treaties, agreements or assurances, or participation in a common plan or conspiracy for the accomplishment of any of the foregoing;

(b) War Crimes: namely, violations of the laws or customs of war. Such violations shall include, but not be limited to, murder, ill treatment or deportation to slave labor or for any other purpose of civilian population of or in occupied territory, murder or ill treatment of prisoners of war or persons on the seas, killing of hostages, plunder of public or private property, wanton destruction of cities, towns or villages, or devastation not justified by military necessity;

(c) Crimes Against Humanity: namely, murder, extermination, enslavement, deportation, and other inhumane acts committed against any civilian population, before or during the war; or persecutions on political, racial or religious grounds in execution of or in connection with any crime within the jurisdiction of the Tribunal, whether or not in violation of the domestic law of the country where perpetrated.

Leaders, organizers, instigators and accomplices participating in the formulation or execution of a common plan or conspiracy to commit any of the foregoing crimes are responsible for all acts performed by any persons in execution of such plan.

Article 7

The official position of defendants, whether as Heads of State or responsible officials in Government Departments, shall not be considered as freeing them from responsibility or mitigating punishment.

Article 8

The fact that the Defendant acted pursuant to order of his Government or of a superior shall not free him from responsibility, but may be considered in mitigation of punishment if the Tribunal determines that justice so requires.

Article 9

At the trial of any individual member of any group or organization the Tribunal may declare (in connection with any act of which the individual may be convicted) that the group or organization of which the individual was a member was a criminal organization.

After the receipt of the Indictment the Tribunal shall give such notice as it thinks fit that the prosecution intends to ask the Tribunal to make such declaration and any member of the organization will be entitled to apply to the Tribunal for leave to be heard by the Tribunal upon the question of the criminal character of the organization. The Tribunal shall have power to allow or reject the application. If the application is allowed, the Tribunal may direct in what manner the applicants shall be represented and heard.

Article 10

In cases where a group or organization is declared criminal by the Tribunal, the competent national authority of any Signatory shall have the right to bring individual to trial for membership therein before national, military or occupation courts. In any such case the criminal nature of the group or organization is considered proved and shall not be questioned.

Article 11

Any person convicted by the Tribunal may be charged before a national, military or occupation court, referred to in Article 10 of this Charter, with a crime other than of membership in a criminal group or organization and such court may, after convicting him, impose upon him punishment independent of and additional to the punishment imposed by the Tribunal for participation in the criminal activities of such group or organization.

Article 12

The Tribunal shall have the right to take proceedings against a person charged with crimes set out in Article 6 of this Charter in his absence, if he has not been found or if the Tribunal, for any reason, finds it necessary, in the interests of justice, to conduct the hearing in his absence.

Article 13

The Tribunal shall draw up rules for its procedure. These rules shall not be inconsistent with the provisions of this Charter.

III. Committee for the Investigation and Prosecution of Major War Criminals.

Article 14

Each Signatory shall appoint a Chief Prosecutor for the investigation of the charges against and the prosecution of major war criminals.

The Chief Prosecutors shall act as a committee for the following purposes:

(a) to agree upon a plan of the individual work of each of the Chief Prosecutors and his staff,

(b) to settle the final designation of major war criminals to be tried by the Tribunal,

(c) to approve the Indictment and the documents to be submitted therewith,

(d) to lodge the Indictment and the accompany documents with the Tribunal,

(e) to draw up and recommend to the Tribunal for its approval draft rules of procedure, contemplated by Article 13 of this Charter. The Tribunal shall have the power to accept, with or without amendments, or to reject, the rules so recommended.

The Committee shall act in all the above matters by a majority vote and shall appoint a Chairman as may be convenient and in accordance with the principle of rotation: provided that if there is an equal division of vote concerning the designation of a Defendant to be tried by the Tribunal, or the crimes with which he shall be charged, that proposal will be adopted which was made by the party which proposed that the particular Defendant be tried, or the particular charges be preferred against him.

Article 15

The Chief Prosecutors shall individually, and acting in collaboration with one another, also undertake the following duties:

(a) investigation, collection and production before or at the Trial of all necessary evidence,

(b) the preparation of the Indictment for approval by the Committee in accordance with paragraph (c) of Article 14 hereof,

(c) the preliminary examination of all necessary witnesses and of all Defendants,

(d) to act as prosecutor at the Trial,

(e) to appoint representatives to carry out such duties as may be assigned them,

(f) to undertake such other matters as may appear necessary to them for the purposes of the preparation for and conduct of the Trial.

It is understood that no witness or Defendant detained by the Signatory shall be taken out of the possession of that Signatory without its assent.

IV. FAIR TRIAL FOR DEFENDANTS

Article 16

In order to ensure fair trial for the Defendants, the following procedure shall be followed:

(a) The Indictment shall include full particulars specifying in detail the charges against the Defendants. A copy of the Indictment and of all the documents lodged with the Indictment, translated into a language which he understands, shall be furnished to the Defendant at reasonable time before the Trial.

(b) During any preliminary examination or trial of a Defendant he will have the right to give any explanation relevant to the charges made against him.

(c) A preliminary examination of a Defendant and his Trial shall be conducted in, or translated into, a language which the Defendant understands.

(d) A Defendant shall have the right to conduct his own defense before the Tribunal or to have the assistance of Counsel.

(e) A Defendant shall have the right through himself or through his Counsel to present evidence at the Trial in support of his defense, and to cross-examine any witness called by the Prosecution.

V. POWERS OF THE TRIBUNAL AND CONDUCT OF THE TRIAL

Article 17

The Tribunal shall have the power

(a) to summon witnesses to the Trial and to require their attendance and testimony and to put questions to them

(b) to interrogate any Defendant,

(c) to require the production of documents and other evidentiary material,

(d) to administer oaths to witnesses,

(e) to appoint officers for the carrying out of any task designated by the Tribunal including the power to have evidence taken on commission.

Article 18

The Tribunal shall

(a) confine the Trial strictly to an expeditious hearing of the cases raised by the charges,

(b) take strict measures to prevent any action which will cause reasonable delay, and rule out irrelevant issues and statements of any kind whatsoever,

(c) deal summarily with any contumacy, imposing appropriate punishment, including exclusion of any Defendant or his Counsel from some or all further proceedings, but without prejudice to the determination of the charges.

Article 19

The Tribunal shall not be bound by technical rules of evidence. It shall adopt and apply to the greatest possible extent expeditious and nontechnical procedure, and shall admit any evidence which it deems to be of probative value.

Article 20

The Tribunal may require to be informed of the nature of any evidence before it is entered so that it may rule upon the relevance thereof.

Article 21

The Tribunal shall not require proof of facts of common knowledge but shall take judicial notice thereof. It shall also take judicial notice of official governmental documents and reports of the United Nations, including the acts and documents of the committees set up in the various allied countries for the investigation of war crimes, and of records and findings of military or other Tribunals of any of the United Nations.

Article 22

The permanent seat of the Tribunal shall be in Berlin. The first meetings of the members of the Tribunal and of the Chief Prosecutors shall be held at Berlin in a place to be designated by the Control Council for Germany. The first trial shall be held at Nuremberg, and any subsequent trials shall be held at such places as the Tribunal may decide.

Article 23

One or more of the Chief Prosecutors may take part in the prosecution at each Trial. The function of any Chief Prosecutor may be discharged by him personally, or by any person or persons authorized by him. The function of Counsel for a Defendant may be discharged at the Defendant's request by any Counsel professionally qualified to conduct cases before the Courts of his own country, or by any other person who may be specially authorized thereto by the Tribunal.

Article 24

The proceedings at the Trial shall take the following course:

(a) The Indictment shall be read in court.

(b) The Tribunal shall ask each Defendant whether he pleads "guilty" or "not guilty."

(c) The prosecution shall make an opening statement.

(d) The Tribunal shall ask the prosecution and the defense what evidence (if any) they wish to submit to the Tribunal, and the Tribunal shall rule upon the admissibility of any such evidence.

(e) The witnesses for the Prosecution shall be examined and after that the witnesses for the Defense. Thereafter such rebutting evidence as may be held by the Tribunal to be admissible shall be called by either the Prosecution or the Defense.

(f) The Tribunal may put any question to any witness and to any defendant, at any time.

(g) The Prosecution and the Defense shall interrogate and may crossexamine any witnesses and any Defendant who gives testimony.

(h) The Defense shall address the court.

(i) The Prosecution shall address the court.

(j) Each Defendant may make a statement to the Tribunal.

(k) The Tribunal shall deliver judgment and pronounce sentence.

Article 25

All official documents shall be produced, and all court proceedings conducted, in English, French and Russian, and in the language of the Defendant. So much of the record and of the proceedings may also be translated into the language of any country in which the Tribunal is sitting, as the Tribunal is sitting, as the Tribunal considers desirable in the interests of the justice and public opinion.

VI. JUDGMENT AND SENTENCE

Article 26

The judgment of the Tribunal as to the guilt or the innocence of any Defendant shall give the reasons on which it is based, and shall be final and not subject to review.

Article 27

The Tribunal shall have the right to impose upon a Defendant, on conviction, death or such other punishment as shall be determined by it to be just.

Article 28

In addition to any punishment imposed by it, the Tribunal shall have the right to deprive the convicted person of any stolen property and order its delivery to the Control Council for Germany.

Article 29

In case of guilt, sentences shall be carried out in accordance with the orders of the Control Council for Germany, which may at any time reduce or otherwise alter the sentences, but may not increase the severity thereof. If the Control Council for Germany, after any Defendant has been convicted and sentenced, discovers fresh evidence which, in its opinion, would found a fresh charge against him, the Council shall report accordingly to the Committee established under Article 14 hereof, for such action as they may consider proper, having regard to the interests of justice.

VII. EXPENSES

Article 30

The expenses of the Tribunal and of the Trials, shall be charged by the Signatories against the funds allotted for maintenance of the Control Council of Germany.

Circular Letter from the Orgburo TsK RK(b) Concerning Relations with the Cossacks

INTRODUCTION During World War II Stalin ordered the deportation of a large part of this population which was incorporated in Russia since 1654, accusing the Cossacks to sympathize with Germany.

24 January 1919
Circular. Secret.

The latest events on different fronts in the Cossack regions — our advance into the interior of the Cossack settlements and the disintegration among the Cossack hosts — compels us to give instructions to party workers about the character of their work during the reestablishment and strengthening of Soviet power in the said regions. It is necessary to recognize, based on the experience of the civil war with the Cossacks, that the most merciless struggle with all the upper layers of the Cossacks through their extermination to a man is the only correct policy. No compromises or half-heartedness whatsoever are acceptable.

Therefore it is necessary:

1. To carry out mass terror against wealthy Cossacks, exterminating them to a man; to carry out merciless mass terror in relations to all Cossacks have taken part in any way directly or indirectly in the struggle with the Soviet power. Against the middle Cossacks it is necessary to take all those measures which give a guarantee against any attempt on their part [to join] a new attack on Soviet power.

2. To confiscate grain and force [them] to gather all surpluses in designated points; this applies both to grain and all other agricultural products.

3. To take all measures assisting the resettlement of newly arrived poor, organizing this settlement where possible.

4. To equalize newly arrive Inogorodnie with the Cossacks in land and in all other relations.

5. To carry out complete disarmament, shooting those who after the time of handing over are found to have arms.

6. To give arms only to reliable elements from the Inogorodnie.

7. Armed detachments are to be stationed in Cossack stanitsas henceforward until the establishment of complete order.

8. To order all commissars appointed to this or that Cossack settlement to show maximum firmness and to carry out the present orders unswervingly.

TsK imposes the obligation on Narkomzem to work out quickly practical measures concerning the mass resettlement of poor on Cossack land to be carried out through the corresponding soviet institutions.

Central Committee RKP RGASPI f.17, op.4. d. 7, l.5.

Control Council Law No. 10

SOURCE The Avalon Project at Yale Law School. Available from http://www.yale.edu/lawweb/avalon/avalon.htm

INTRODUCTION After the victory over the Nazis, a government of occupation was established under what was known as the Control Council. Although the International Military Tribunal at Nuremberg was responsible for prosecuting the major Nazi war criminals, the Control Council issued Law No. 10 to provide a legal framework for the trials of 'lesser' Nazis. Many prosecutions were subsequently carried out, the most well-known being a series of specialized trials organized by the United States. These were held in the same courthouse at Nuremberg where the trial of the major criminals had taken place. Collective trials were held of Nazi judges and prosecutors, businessmen, military commanders, civilian administrators, and leaders of the SS. Control Council Law No. 10 is broadly similar to the Charter of the Nuremberg Tribunal.

PUNISHMENT OF PERSONS GUILTY OF WAR CRIMES, CRIMES AGAINST PEACE AND AGAINST HUMANITY

In order to give effect to the terms of the Moscow Declaration of 30 October 1943 and the London Agreement of 8 August 1945, and the Charter issued pursuant thereto and in order to establish a uniform legal basis in Germany for the prosecution of war criminals and other similar offenders, other than those dealt with by the International Military Tribunal, the Control Council enacts as follows:

Article I

The Moscow Declaration of 30 October 1943 "Concerning Responsibility of Hitlerites for Committed Atrocities" and the London Agreement of 8 August 1945 "Concerning Prosecution and Punishment of Major War Criminals of European Axis" are made integral parts of this Law. Adherence to the provisions of the London Agreement by any of the United Nations, as provided for in Article V of that Agreement, shall not entitle such Nation to participate or interfere in the operation of this Law within the Control Council area of authority in Germany.

Article II

1. Each of the following acts is recognized as a crime:

(a) Crimes against Peace. Initiation of invasions of other countries and wars of aggression in violation of international laws and treaties, including but not limited to planning, preparation, initiation or waging a war of aggression, or a war of violation of international treaties, agreements or assurances, or participation in a common plan or conspiracy for the accomplishment of any of the foregoing.

(b) War Crimes. Atrocities or offenses against persons or property constituting violations of the laws or customs of war, including but not limited to, murder, ill treatment or deportation to slave labour or for any other purpose, of civilian population from occupied territory, murder or ill treatment of prisoners of war or persons on the seas, killing of hostages, plunder of public or private property, wanton destruction of cities, towns or villages, or devastation not justified by military necessity.

(c) Crimes against Humanity. Atrocities and offenses, including but not limited to murder, extermination, enslavement, deportation, imprisonment, torture, rape, or other inhumane acts committed against any civilian population, or persecutions on political, racial or religious grounds whether or not in violation of the domestic laws of the country where perpetrated.

(d) Membership in categories of a criminal group or organization declared criminal by the International Military Tribunal.

2. Any person without regard to nationality or the capacity in which he acted, is deemed to have committed a crime as defined in paragraph 1 of this Article, if he was (a) a principal or (b) was an accessory to the commission of any such crime or ordered or abetted the same or (c) took a consenting part therein or (d) was connected with plans or enterprises involving its commission or (e) was a member of any organization or group connected with the commission of any such crime or (f) with reference to paragraph 1 (a) if he held a high political, civil or military (including General Staff) position in Germany or in one of its Allies, co-belligerents or satellites or held high position in the financial, industrial or economic life of any such country.

3. Any persons found guilty of any of the crimes above mentioned may upon conviction be punished as shall be determined by the tribunal to be just. Such punishment may consist of one or more of the following:

(a) Death.

(b) Imprisonment for life or a term of years, with or without hard labor.

(c) Fine, and imprisonment with or without hard labour, in lieu thereof.

(d) Forfeiture of property.

(e) Restitution of property wrongfully acquired.

(f) Deprivation of some or all civil rights.

Any property declared to be forfeited or the restitution of which is ordered by the Tribunal shall be delivered to the Control Council for Germany, which shall decide on its disposal.

4. (a) The official position of any person, whether as Head of State or as a responsible official in a Government Department, does not free him from responsibility for a crime or entitle him to mitigation of punishment. (b) The fact that any person acted pursuant to the order of his Government or of a superior does not free him from responsibility for a crime, but may be considered in mitigation.

5. In any trial or prosecution for a crime herein referred to, the accused shall not be entitled to the benefits of any statute of limitation in respect to the period from 30 January 1933 to 1 July 1945, nor shall any immunity, pardon or amnesty granted under the Nazi regime be admitted as a bar to trial or punishment.

Article III

1. Each occupying authority, within its Zone of Occupation,

(a) shall have the right to cause persons within such Zone suspected of having committed a crime, including those charged with crime by one of the United Nations, to be arrested and shall take under control the property, real and personal, owned or controlled by the said persons, pending decisions as to its eventual disposition.

(b) shall report to the Legal Directorate the name of all suspected criminals, the reasons for and the places of their detention, if they are detained, and the names and location of witnesses.

(c) shall take appropriate measures to see that witnesses and evidence will be available when required.

(d) shall have the right to cause all persons so arrested and charged, and not delivered to another authority as herein provided, or released, to be brought to trial before an appropriate tribunal. Such tribunal may, in the case of crimes committed by persons of German citizenship or nationality against other persons of German citizenship or nationality, or stateless persons, be a German Court, if authorized by the occupying authorities.

2. The tribunal by which persons charged with offenses hereunder shall be tried and the rules and procedure thereof shall be determined or designated by each Zone Commander for his respective Zone. Nothing herein is intended to, or shall impair or limit the Jurisdiction or power of any court or tribunal now or hereafter established in any Zone by the Commander thereof, or of the International Military Tribunal established by the London Agreement of 8 August 1945.

3. Persons wanted for trial by an International Military Tribunal will not be tried without the consent of the Committee of Chief Prosecutors. Each Zone Commander will deliver such persons who are within his Zone to that committee upon request and will make witnesses and evidence available to it.

4. Persons known to be wanted for trial in another Zone or outside Germany will not be tried prior to decision under Article IV unless the fact of their apprehension has been reported in accordance with Section 1 (b) of this Article, three months have elapsed thereafter, and no request for delivery of the type contemplated by Article IV has been received by the Zone Commander concerned.

5. The execution of death sentences may be deferred by not to exceed one month after the sentence has become final when the Zone Commander concerned has reason to believe that the testimony of those under sentence would be of value in the investigation and trial of crimes within or without his zone.

6. Each Zone Commander will cause such effect to be given to the judgments Of courts of competent jurisdiction, with respect to the property taken under his control pursuant thereto, as he may deem proper in the interest of Justice.

Article IV

1. When any person in a Zone in Germany is alleged to have committed a crime, as defined in Article II, in a country other than Germany or in another Zone, the government of that nation or the Commander of the latter Zone, as the case may be, may request the Commander of the Zone which the person is located for his arrest and delivery for trial to the country or Zone in which the crime was committed. Such request for delivery shall be granted by the Commander receiving it unless he believes such person is wanted for trial or as a witness by an International Military Tribunal, or in Germany, or in a nation other than the one making the request, or the Commander is not satisfied that delivery should be made, in any of which cases he shall have the right to forward the said request to the Legal Directorate of the Allied Control Authority. A similar procedure shall apply to witnesses, material exhibits and other forms of evidence.

2. The Legal Directorate shall consider all requests referred to it, and shall determine the same in accordance with the following principles, its determination to be communicated to the Zone Commander.

(a) A person wanted for trial or as a witness by an International Military Tribunal shall not be delivered for trial or required to give evidence outside Germany, as the case may be, except upon approval by the Committee of Chief Prosecutors acting under the London Agreement of 8 August 1945.

(b) A person wanted for trial by several authorities (other than an International Military Tribunal) shall be disposed of in accordance with the following priorities:

(1) If wanted for trial in the Zone in which he is, he should not be delivered unless arrangements are made for his return after trial elsewhere;

(2) If wanted for trial in a Zone other than that in which he is, he should be delivered to that Zone in preference to delivery outside Germany unless arrangements are made for his return to that Zone after trial elsewhere;

(3) If wanted for trial outside Germany by two or more of the United Nations, of one of which he is a citizen, that one should have priority;

(4) If wanted for trial outside Germany by several countries, not all of which are United Nations, United Nations should have priority;

(5) If wanted for trial outside Germany by two or more of the United Nations, then, subject to Article IV 2 (b) (3) above, that which has the most serious charges against him, which are moreover supported by evidence, should have priority.

Article V

The delivery, under Article IV of this law, of persons for trial shall be mades on demands of the Governments or Zone Commanders in such a manner that the delivery of criminals to one jurisdiction will not become the means of defeating or unnecessarily delaying the carrying out of justice in another place. If within six months the delivered person has not been convicted by the Court of the Zone or country to which he has been delivered, then such person shall be returned upon demand of the Commander of the Zone where the person was located prior to delivery.

Done at Berlin, 20 December 1945.
(Signed) Joseph T. McNarney
JOSEPH T. MCNARNEY
General, U. S. Armyt

(Signed) Bernard B. Montgomery
BERNARD B. MONTGOMERY Field Marshall

(Signed) Louis Koeltz, General d'Corps de Armee for PIEIRR KOENIG
General d'Armee

(Signed) Georgi Zhukov GEORGI ZHUKOV
Marshall of the Soviet Union

General Lothar Von Trotha Extermination Order against the Herero

SOURCE Gewalt, Jan-Bart, trans. (1999). *Herero Heroes.* Oxford, U.K.: James Currey. See pages 172–173. Also available from Namibian National Archives Windhoek, ZBU (Zentralbureau) D.1.a Band 3–4, leaf 165.

INTRODUCTION The order given by General Lothar von Trotha is one of the first documented instances of a policy of genocide. The order was ruthlessly carried out and resulted in the extermination of nearly 90 percent of the Herero. The descendants of the the survivors are seeking reparations for the genocide.

October 2, 1904

I the great General of the German troops send this letter to the Herero people.

The Herero are no longer German subjects. They have murdered and stolen, they have cut off the ears, noses and other body parts of wounded soldiers, now out of captain will receive 1000 Mark, whoever delivers Samuel will receive 5000 Mark. The Herero people must however leave the land. If the populace does not do this I will force them with the *Groot Rohr* [cannon]. Within the German borders every Herero, with or without a gun, with or without cattle, will be shot. I will no longer accept women and children, I will drive them back to their people or I will let them be shot at.

These are my words to the Herero people.

The great General of the mighty German Kaiser.

January 11, 1994, Cable of General Dallaire to UN Headquarters

SOURCE Available from http://www.gwu.edu/~nsarchiv/ NSAEBB/NSAEBB53/rw011194.pdf.

INTRODUCTION On January 10, 1994, General Romeo Dallaire, the Force Commander for UNAMIR in Rwanda, received the most important information from the Chief Trainer of the Interahamwe, the militia of the MRND party, indicating a plot to subvert the peace agreement, slaughter Tutsis at the rate of 1,000 Tutsis every 20 minutes, and kill ten Belgian soldiers to induce the Belgian government to withdraw its peacekeeping contingent. He also informed UNAMIR of four large stocks weapons. In addition, he said that there was a spy on the UN Secretary-General's Special Representative's (Jacques Roger Booh-Booh) staff. In return for revealing the locations of the arms caches, the informer requested that he and his family be provided with asylum in the West. When General Dallaire informed New York headquarters (see the cable below) of his plans to go after the arms caches, the plan was immediately vetoed. Further, Dallaire was instructed to inform President Habyarimana immediately about the information. In investigations afterwards, and in spite of plenty of information that the cable was seen as a crucial item, Riza and Annan first claimed not to have any recollection of the cable, and later said that they received so much information that they did not realize its significance. However, they never ordered any further investigation. The suppression of the cable and follow-up action was the most blatant example of a missed early warning opportunity so necessary to the prevention and mitigation of genocide.

Date: 11 January 1994

To: Baril/DPKO/UNATIONS NEW YORK

From: Dallaire/UNAMIR/KIGALI

Subject: Request for protection for informant

Attn: MGen Baril Room No.2052

Force commander put in contact with informant by very very important government politician. Informant is a top level trainer in the cadre of Interhamwe-armed militia of MRND.

He informed us he was in charge of last Saturday's demonstrations which aims were to target deputies of opposition parties coming to ceremonies and Belgian soldiers. They hoped to provoke the RPF BN to engage (being fired upon) the demonstrators and provoke a civil war. Deputies were to be assassinated upon entry or exit from Parliament. Belgian troops were to be provoked and if Belgians soldiers resorted to force a number of them were to be killed and thus guarantee Belgian withdrawal from Rwanda.

Informant confirmed 48 RGF CDO and a few members of the Gendarmerie participated in demonstrations in plain clothes. Also at least one minister of the MRND and the Sous-Prefect of Kigali were in the demonstration. RGF and Interhamwe provided radio communications.

Informant is a former security member of the president. He also stated he is paid RF150,000 per month by the MRND party to train Interhamwe. Direct link is to Chief of Staff RGF and president of the MRND for financial and material support.

Interhamwe has trained 1700 men in RGF military camps outside the capital. The 1700 are scattered in groups of 40 throughout Kigali. Since UNAMIR deployed he has trained 300 personnel in three week training sessions at RGF camps. Training focus was discipline, weapons, explosives, close combat and tactics.

Principal aim of Interhamwe in the past was to protect Kigali from RPF. Since unamir mandate he has been ordered to register all Tutsi in Kigali. He suspects it is for their extermination. Example he gave was that in 20 minutes his personnel could kill up to 1000 Tutsis.

Informant states he disagrees with anti-Tutsi extermination. He supports opposition to RPF, but cannot support killing of innocent persons. He also stated that he believes the president does not have full control over all elements of his old party/faction.

Informant is prepared to provide location of major weapons cache with at least 135 weapons. He already has distributed 110 weapons including 35 with ammunition and can give us details of their location. Type of weapons are G3 and AK47 provided by RGF. He was ready to go to the arms cache tonight—if we gave him the following guarantee. He requests that he and his family (his wife and four children) be placed under our protection.

It is our intention to take action within the next 36 hours with a possible H-Hr of Wednesday at dawn (local). Informant states that hostilities may commence again if political deadlock ends. Violence could take place day of the ceremonies or the day after. Therefore, Wednesday will give greatest chance of success and also be most timely to provide significant input to ongoing political negotiations.

It is recommended the informant be granted protection and evacuated out of Rwanda. This HQ does not have previous UN experience in such matters and urgently requests guidance. No contact has as yet been made to any embassy in order to inquire if they are prepared to protect him for a period of time by granting diplomatic immunity in their embassy in Kigali before moving him and his family out of the country.

Force Commander will be meeting with the very very important political person tomorrow morning in order to ensure that this individual is conscious of all parameters of his involvement. Force Commander does have certain reservations on the suddenness of the change of heart of the informant to come clean with this information. Recce of armed cache and detailed planning of raid to go on late tomorrow. Possibility of a trap not fully excluded, as this may be a set-up against the very very important political person. Force Commander to inform SRSG first thing in morning to ensure his support.

Nazi-Era Identity Cards

INTRODUCTION The Nazi regime introduced laws and regulations designed to classify all persons by race, making it easier to target Jews and other disfavored minorities. The ultimate result was genocide. The identity documents here distinguish between "Aryan" and "Jew."

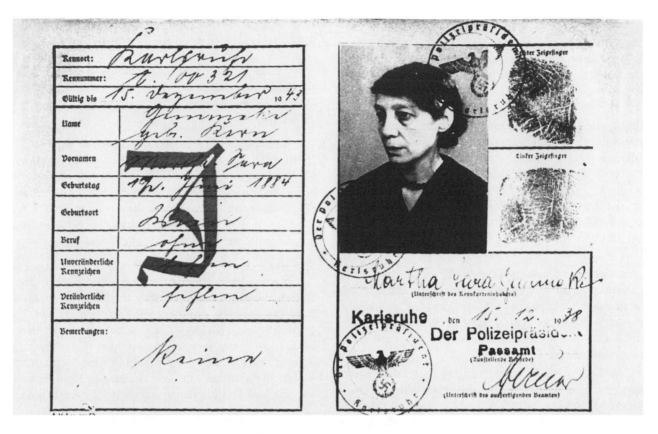

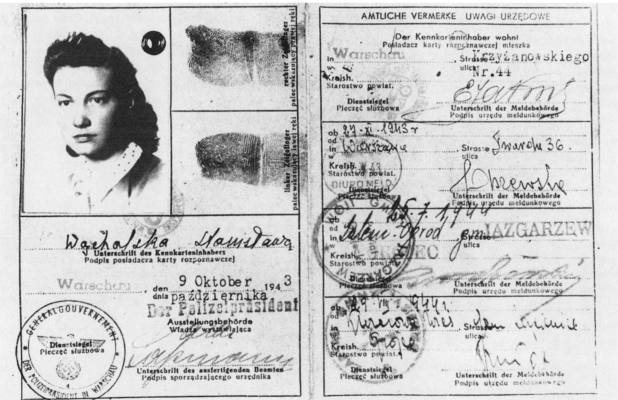

The identity card required by the Nazis soon singled out all Jews living in Germany and other countries invaded by the Third Reich. (top). False identification card issued in name of Stanislawa Wachalska, that was used by Feigele Peltel (now Vladka Meed) while serving as a courier for the Jewish underground in Warsaw (bottom). [USHMM]

Order by the Commander of the Military Division of the Mississippi, January 15, 1865

INTRODUCTION General Sherman issued the following order to General Rufus Saxton to divide land confiscated from rebellious landowners in Southern States into forty-acre tracts and distribute them to slaves freed under President Abraham Lincoln's Emancipation Proclamation. The government was to loan out mules to help work the land. The order and land titles were rescinded by President Andrew Johnson after the assassination of President Lincoln, despite the fact that some 40,000 free men had been provided with homes under the Order's provisions. Many of those who had received land were later forcibly removed. General Sherman's Order and its implementation remain in discussion as one basis of claims for slave reparations.

THE FIELD, SAVANNAH, GA., January 16th, 1865.

SPECIAL FIELD ORDERS, No. 15.

I. The islands from Charleston, south, the abandoned rice fields along the rivers for thirty miles back from the sea, and the country bordering the St. Johns river, Florida, are reserved and set apart for the settlement of the negroes now made free by the acts of war and the proclamation of the President of the United States.

II. At Beaufort, Hilton Head, Savannah, Fernandina, St. Augustine and Jacksonville, the blacks may remain in their chosen or accustomed vocations—but on the islands, and in the settlements hereafter to be established, no white person whatever, unless military officers and soldiers detailed for duty, will be permitted to reside; and the sole and exclusive management of affairs will be left to the freed people themselves, subject only to the United States military authority and the acts of Congress. By the laws of war, and orders of the President of the United States, the negro is free and must be dealt with as such. He cannot be subjected to conscription or forced military service, save by the written orders of the highest military authority of the Department, under such regulations as the President or Congress may prescribe. Domestic servants, blacksmiths, carpenters and other mechanics, will be free to select their own work and residence, but the young and able-bodied negroes must be encouraged to enlist as soldiers in the service of the United States, to contribute their share towards maintaining their own freedom, and securing their rights as citizens of the United States.

Negroes so enlisted will be organized into companies, battalions and regiments, under the orders of the United States military authorities, and will be paid, fed and clothed according to law. The bounties paid on enlistment may, with the consent of the recruit, go to assist his family and settlement in procuring agricultural implements, seed, tools, boots, clothing, and other articles necessary for their livelihood.

III. Whenever three respectable negroes, heads of families, shall desire to settle on land, and shall have selected for that purpose an island or a locality clearly defined, within the limits above designated, the Inspector of Settlements and Plantations will himself, or by such subordinate officer as he may appoint, give them a license to settle such island or district, and afford them such assistance as he can to enable them to establish a peaceable agricultural settlement. The three parties named will subdivide the land, under the supervision of the Inspector, among themselves and such others as may choose to settle near them, so that each family shall have a plot of not more than (40) forty acres of tillable ground, and when it borders on some water channel, with not more than 800 feet water front, in the possession of which land the military authorities will afford them protection, until such time as they can protect themselves, or until Congress shall regulate their title. The Quartermaster may, on the requisition of the Inspector of Settlements and Plantations, place at the disposal of the Inspector, one or more of the captured steamers, to ply between the settlements and one or more of the commercial points heretofore named in orders, to afford the settlers the opportunity to supply their necessary wants, and to sell the products of their land and labor.

IV. Whenever a negro has enlisted in the military service of the United States, he may locate his family in any one of the settlements at pleasure, and acquire a homestead, and all other rights and privileges of a settler, as though present in person. In like manner, negroes may settle their families and engage on board the gunboats, or in fishing, or in the navigation of the inland waters, without losing any claim to land or other advantages derived from this system. But no one, unless an actual settler as above defined, or unless absent on Government service, will be entitled to claim any right to land or property in any settlement by virtue of these orders.

V. In order to carry out this system of settlement, a general officer will be detailed as Inspector of Settlements and Plantations, whose duty it shall be to visit the settlements, to regulate their police and general management, and who will furnish personally to each head of a family, subject to the approval of the President of the United States, a possessory title in writing, giving as near as possible the description of boundaries;

and who shall adjust all claims or conflicts that may arise under the same, subject to the like approval, treating such titles altogether as possessory. The same general officer will also be charged with the enlistment and organization of the negro recruits, and protecting their interests while absent from their settlements; and will be governed by the rules and regulations prescribed by the War Department for such purposes.

VI. Brigadier General R. SAXTON is hereby appointed Inspector of Settlements and Plantations, and will at once enter on the performance of his duties. No change is intended or desired in the settlement now on Beaufort [Port Royal] Island, nor will any rights to property heretofore acquired be affected thereby.

BY ORDER OF MAJOR GENERAL W. T. SHERMAN:

Special Field Orders, No. 15, Headquarters Military Division of the Mississippi, 16 Jan. 1865, Orders & Circulars, ser. 44, Adjutant General's Office, Record Group 94, National Archives.

Principles of International Law Recognized in the Charter of the Nuremberg Tribunal

INTRODUCTION The Nuremberg Principles were adopted by the International Law Commission, acting under instructions from the United Nations General Assembly. They confirm a number of important principles, including the prohibition of the defense of superior orders, the denial of immunity for heads of state, and the liability of accomplices. In the *Eichmann* trial, the Israeli Supreme Court said that the Nuremberg Principles have become part of the law of nations and must be regarded as having been rooted in it also in the past.

Principles of International Law Recognized in the Charter of the Nuremberg Tribunal and in the Judgment of the Tribunal

Principle I

Any person who commits an act which constitutes a crime under international law is responsible therefore and liable to punishment.

Principle II

The fact that internal law does not impose a penalty for an act which constitutes a crime under international law does not relieve the person who committed the act from responsibility under international law.

Principle III

The fact that a person who committed an act which constitutes a crime under international law acted as Head of State or responsible Government official does not relieve him from responsibility under international law.

Principle IV

The fact that a person acted pursuant to order of his Government or of a superior does not relieve him from responsibility under international law, provided a moral choice was in fact possible to him.

Principle V

Any person charged with a crime under international law has the right to a fair trial on the facts and law.

Principle VI

The crimes hereinafter set out are punishable as crimes under international law:

(a) Crimes against peace:

(i) Planning, preparation, initiation or waging of a war of aggression or a war in violation of international treaties, agreements or assurances;

(ii) Participation in a common plan or conspiracy for the accomplishment of any of the acts mentioned under (i).

(b) War crimes:

Violations of the laws or customs of war which include, but are not limited to, murder, ill treatment or deportation to slave-labour or for any other purpose of civilian population of or in occupied territory; murder or ill treatment of prisoners of war, of persons on the Seas, killing of hostages, plunder of public or private property, wanton destruction of cities, towns, or villages, or devastation not justified by military necessity.

(c) Crimes against humanity:

Murder, extermination, enslavement, deportation and other inhuman acts done against any civilian population, or persecutions on political, racial or religious grounds, when such acts are done or such persecutions are carried on in execution of or in connection with any crime against peace or any war crime.

Principle VII

Complicity in the commission of a crime against peace, a war crime, or a crime against humanity as set forth in Principle VI is a crime under international law.

* Text adopted by the Commission at its second session, in 1950, and submitted to the General Assembly as a part of the Commission's report covering the work of that session. The report, which also contains commentaries on the principles, appears in Yearbook of the International Law Commission, 1950, vol. II.

Resolution of the Council of People's Commissars of the Ukrainaian Soviet Socialist Republic and the Central Committee of the Communist Party (Bolshevik) of Ukraine on Blacklisting Villages That Mailiciously Sabotage the Collection of Grain

Addendum to the minutes of Politburo [meeting] No. 93.

In view of the shameful collapse of grain collection in the more remote regions of Ukraine, the Council of People's Commissars and the Central Committee call upon the oblast executive committees and the oblast [party] committees as well as the raion executive committees and the raion [party] committees: to break up the sabotage of grain collection, which has been organized by kulak and counterrevolutionary elements; to liquidate the resistance of some of the rural communists, who in fact have become the leaders of the sabotage; to eliminate the passivity and complacency toward the saboteurs, incompatible with being a party member; and to ensure, with maximum speed, full and absolute compliance with the plan for grain collection.

The Council of People's Commissars and the Central Committee resolve:

To place the following villages on the black list for overt disruption of the grain collection plan and for malicious sabotage, organized by kulak and counter-revolutionary elements:

1. village of Verbka in Pavlograd raion, Dnepropetrovsk oblast.

5. village of Sviatotroitskoe in Troitsk raion, Odessa oblast.

6. village of Peski in Bashtan raion, Odessa oblast.

The following measures should be undertaken with respect to these villages:

1. Immediate cessation of delivery of goods, complete suspension of cooperative and state trade in the villages, and removal of all available goods from cooperative and state stores.

2. Full prohibition of collective farm trade for both collective farms and collective farmers, and for private farmers.

3. Cessation of any sort of credit and demand for early repayment of credit and other financial obligations.

4. Investigation and purge of all sorts of foreign and hostile elements from cooperative and state institutions, to be carried out by organs of the Workers and Peasants Inspectorate.

5. Investigation and purge of collective farms in these villages, with removal of counterrevolutionary elements and organizers of grain collection disruption.

The Council of People's Commissars and the Central Committee call upon all collective and private farmers who are honest and dedicated to Soviet rule to organize all their efforts for a merciless struggle against kulaks and their accomplices in order to: defeat in their villages the kulak sabotage of grain collection; fulfill honestly and conscientiously their grain collection obligations to the Soviet authorities; and strengthen collective farms.

CHAIRMAN OF THE COUNCIL OF PEOPLE'S COMMISSARS OF THE UKRAINIAN SOVIET SOCIALIST REPUBLIC – V. CHUBAR'. SECRETARY OF THE CENTRAL COMMITTEE OF THE COMMUNIST PARTY (BOLSHEVIK) OF UKRAINE – S. KOSIOR.

6 December 1932.

UN General Assembly Resolution on Genocide

SOURCE Available from http://www.un.org/documents/ga/res/1/ares1.htm.

INTRODUCTION General Assembly Resolution 96(I) elevated the term *genocide*, first proposed by Raphael Lemkin in a scholarly work published two years earlier, to an internationally recognized crime. Resolution 96(I) mandated the United Nations to prepare a convention on the subject, and this process was completed two years later, in December 1948. The Resolution was initially proposed by Cuba, India, and Panama, who expressed their frustration with the definition of crimes against humanity used at Nuremberg. They argued that such serious atrocities should be punishable in peacetime as well as during war. Moreover, they urged the principle of universal jurisdiction over genocide, allowing its prosecution even by states with no direct link to the crime through either territory or nationality. The Resolution eliminated the troubling limitation to armed conflict that had been applied at Nuremberg, but failed to endorse the principle of universal jurisdiction. For reasons that remain obscure, the definition of genocide included political groups, but this was subsequently removed in the 1948 Convention.

Genocide is a denial of the right of existence of entire human groups, as homicide is the denial of the right to live of individual human beings; such denial of the right of existence shocks the conscience of mankind, results in great losses to humanity in the form of cultural and other contributions represented by these human groups, and is contrary to moral law and to the spirit and aims of the United nations.

Many instances of such crimes of genocide have occurred when racial, religious, political and other groups have been destroyed, entirely or in part.

The punishment of the crime of genocide is a matter of international concern.

The General Assembly, therefore,

Affirms that genocide is a crime under international law which the civilized world condemns, and for the commission of which principals and accomplices — whether private individuals, public officials or statesmen, and whether the crime is committed on religious, racial, political or any other grounds — are punishable;

Invites the Member States to enact the necessary legislation for the prevention and punishment of this crime;

Recommends that international co-operation be organized between States with a view to facilitating the speedy prevention and punishment of the crime of genocide, and, to this end,

Requests the Economic and Social Council to undertake the necessary studies, with a view to drawing up a draft convention on the crime of genocide to be submitted to the next regular session of the General Assembly.

Fifty-fifth plenary meeting,

11 December 1946.

Whitaker Report on Genocide, 1985

SOURCE Prevent Genocide International. Available from http://www.preventgenocide.org/prevent/UNdocs/whitaker/.

INTRODUCTION There have been two major United Nation documents on genocide, the Ruhashyankiko report of 1978 and the Whitaker report of 1985. Both are major studies of genocide from the standpoint of the Sub-Commission on Prevention of Discrimination and Protection of Minorities (presently the Sub-Commission on Promotion and Protection of Human Rights), with the second report intended as a corrective to the former. Due to political pressure, the Ruhashyankiko report had been forced to delete any mention of the Armenian genocide. The Whitaker report, in contrast, concluded that the Armenian massacres had constituted genocide. The official cites for the reports are: Nicodeme Ruhashyankiko, "Report to the UN Sub-Commission on Prevention of Discrimination and Protection of National Minorities: Study of the Question of the Prevention and Punishment of the Crime of Genocide" (E/CN.4/Sub. 2/416, 4 July 1978), 186 pages; Ben Whitaker, "Re-

vised and Updated Report on the Question of the Prevention and Punishment of the Crime of Genocide" (E/CN.4/Sub. 2/416/1985/6, 2 July 1985), 62 pages.

The Report on genocide prepared by Ben Whitaker in 1985, for what is now called the United Nations Sub-Commission on the Promotion and Protection of Human Rights is one of the major contributions to the evolving law in this area. The Sub-Commission is an expert body which operates very much as a 'think tank' for the Commission on Human Rights. In the early 1970s, it mandated Nicodeme Ruhashyankiko to prepare a study on genocide that was to focus on the application and interpretation of the 1948 Convention. Ruhashyankiko's final report, presented in 1979, was very controversial because he had buckled to Turkish pressure and removed all references to the genocide of the Armenians. Subsequently, the Sub-Commission appointed Whitaker to prepare a revised and updated version, that rectified the omission of the Armenian genocide and also made many other innovative proposals. Whitaker's suggestion that the reference in the definition of genocide to destruction of a group 'in whole or in part' might refer not only to a numerically substantial proportion of the group, but also to a 'significant' part of the group, such as its intellectual, political or religious and cultural leadership, has been endorsed in subsequent judicial decisions.

PART I: HISTORICAL SURVEY

A. The crime of genocide and the purpose of this study

14. Genocide is the ultimate crime and the gravest violation of human rights it is possible to commit. Consequently, it is difficult to conceive of a heavier responsibility for the international community and the Human Rights bodies of the United Nations than to undertake any effective steps possible to prevent and punish genocide in order to deter its recurrence.

15. It has rightly been said that those people who do not learn from history, are condemned to repeat it. This belief underpins much of the Human Rights work of the United Nations. In order to prescribe the optimal remedies to prevent future genocide, it can be of positive assistance to diagnose past cases in order to analyse their causation together with such lessons as the international community may learn from the history of these events.

16. Genocide is a constant threat to peace, and it is essential to exercise the greatest responsibility when discussing a subject so emotive. It is certainly not the intention of this Study in anyway to comment on poli-

tics or to awaken bitterness or feelings of revenge. The purpose and hope of this Study is exactly the opposite: to deter future violence by strengthening collective international responsibility and remedies. It would undermine this purpose, besides violating historical truth as well as the integrity of United Nations Studies, were anybody guilty of genocide to believe that international concern might be averted or historical records changed because of political or other pressure. If such an attempt were to succeed, that would serve to encourage those in the future who may be contemplating similar crimes. Equally, it is necessary to warn that nothing in these historical events should be used to provide an excuse for further violence or vendettas: this Study is a warning directed against violence. Its object is to deter terrorism or killing of whatever scale, and to encourage understanding and reconciliation. The scrutiny of world opinion and an honest recognition of the truth about painful past events have been the starting point for a foundation of reconciliation, with, for example, post-war Germany, which will help to make the future more secure for humanity.

B. The concept of genocide

17. Amongst all human rights, the primacy of the right to life is unanimously agreed to be pre-eminent and essential: it is the sine qua non, for all other human rights (apart from that to one's posthumous reputation) depend for their potential existence on the preservation of human life. Every right can also only survive as a consequence of the exercise of responsibilities. The right of a person or people not to be killed or avoidably left to die depends upon the reciprocal duty of other people to render protection and help to avert this. The concept of this moral responsibility and interdependence in human society has in recent times received increasing international recognition and affirmation. In cases of famine in other countries, for example, the States parties to the International Covenant on Economic, Social and Cultural Rights in "recognizing the fundamental right of everyone to be free from hunger" have assumed responsibility to take "individually and through international co-operation" the measures required "to ensure an equitable distribution of world food supplies in relation to need".(1) The core of the right not to [Page 6] starve to death is a corollary of the right not to be killed, concerning which the duty of safeguarding life is recognized to extend not just to the individual's or group's own Government but to the international community as well.

18. More serious problems arise when the body responsible for threatening and causing death is — or is in complicity with — a State itself.(2) The potential victims in such cases need to turn individually and col-

lectively for protection not to, but from, their own Government. Groups subject to extermination have a right to receive something more helpful than tears and condolences from the rest of the world. Action under the Charter of the United Nations is indeed specifically authorized by the Convention on the Prevention and Protection of the Crime of Genocide, and might as appropriate be directed for example to the introduction of United Nations trusteeship. States have an obligation, besides not to commit genocide, in addition to prevent and punish violations of the crime by others; and in cases of failure in this respect too, the 1948 Convention recognizes that intervention may be justified to prevent or suppress such acts and to punish those responsible "whether they are constitutionally responsible rulers, public officials or private individuals".

19. The Convention on Genocide was unanimously adopted by the United Nations General Assembly on 9 December 1948, and therefore preceded albeit by one day the Universal Declaration of Human Rights itself. While the word "genocide" is a comparatively recent neologism for an old crime,(3) the Convention's preamble notes that "at all periods of history genocide has inflicted great losses on humanity, and being convinced that, in order to liberate mankind from such an odious scourge, international co-operation is required".

20. Throughout recorded human history, war has been the predominant cause or pretext for massacres of national, ethnic, racial or religious groups. War in ancient and classical eras frequently aimed to exterminate if not enslave other peoples. Religious intolerance could also be a predisposing factor: in [Page 7] religious wars of the Middle Ages as well as in places in the Old Testament, some genocide was sanctioned by Holy Writ. The twentieth century equally has seen examples of "total wars" involving the destruction of civilian populations and which the development of nuclear weapons makes an almost inevitable matrix for future major conflicts. In the nuclear era, indeed the logical conclusion of this may be "omnicide".

21. Genocide, particularly of indigenous peoples, has also often occurred as a consequence of colonialism, with racism and ethnic prejudice commonly being predisposing factors. In some cases occupying forces maintained their authority by the terror of a perpetual threat of massacre.(5) Examples could occur either at home or overseas: the English for example massacred native populations in Ireland, Scotland and Wales in order to deter resistance and to "clear" land for seizure, and the British also almost wholly exterminated the indigenous people when colonizing Tasmania as late as the start of the nineteenth century. Africa, Australasia and the Americas witnessed numerous other examples.

The effect of genocide can be achieved in different ways: today, insensitive economic exploitation can threaten the extinction of some surviving indigenous peoples.

22. But genocide, far from being only a matter of historical study, is an aberration which also is a modern danger to civilization. No stronger evidence that the problem of genocide has — far from receding — grown in contemporary relevance is required than the fact that the gravest documented example of this crime is among the most recent, and furthermore occurred in the so-called developed world. Successive advances in killing-power underline that the need for international action against genocide is now more urgent than ever. It has been estimated that the Nazi holocaust in Europe slaughtered some 6 million Jews, 5 million Protestants, 3 million Catholics and half a million Gypsies. This was the product not of international warfare, but a calculated State political policy of mass murder that has been termed "a structural and systematic destruction of innocent people by a State bureaucratic apparatus".(6) The Nazi intention to destroy particular human nations, races, religions, sexual groups, classes and political opponents as a premeditated plan was manifested before the Second World War. The war later offered the Nazi German leaders an opportunity to extend this policy from their own country to the peoples of occupied Poland, parts of the Soviet Union and elsewhere, with an intention of Germanizing their territories. The "final solution" included (as evidenced at the Nuremberg trial), "delayed-action genocide" aimed at destroying groups' biological future through sterilization, castration, abortion, and the forcible transfer of their [Page 8] children.(7) The term genocide, with also its concept as an international crime, was first used officially at the subsequent International Tribunal at Nuremberg. The indictment of 8 October 1945 of the major German war criminals charged that the defendant had: "conducted deliberate" (8)

The concluding speech by the British Prosecutor stated that: "Genocide was not restricted to extermination of the" (9)

23. The present two German Governments have been unflinching in their acknowledgment and condemnation of these guilty events, in their efforts to guard against any repetition of them or of Nazism. The Government of the Federal Republic of Germany had stated that official action will be taken, without the need for complaint from any member of the public, to prosecute people who seek to deny the truth about the Nazi crimes. President von Weizsacker in a forthright recent speech to the Bundestag made clear his belief that his countrymen must have known during the war

of the fate of the Jews: "The genocide of the Jews is without example in history . . . at the end of the war, the whole unspeakable truth of the holocaust emerged. Too many said they knew nothing, or had only an inkling of it. There is no guilt or innocence of a whole people because guilt, like innocence, is not collective but individual. All those who lived through that time with full awareness should ask themselves today, quietly, about their involvement."(10)

24. Toynbee stated that the distinguishing characteristics of the twentieth century in evolving the development of genocide "are that it is committed in cold blood by the deliberate fiat of holders of despotic political power, and that the perpetrators of genocide employ all the resources of present-day technology and organization to make their planned massacres systematic and complete". (11) The Nazi aberration has unfortunately not been the only case of genocide in the twentieth century. Among other examples which can be cited as qualifying are the German massacre of Hereros in 1904, (12) the Ottoman massacre of Armenians in 1915–1916, (13) the Ukrainian pogrom of Jews in 1919, (14) the Tutsi massacre of Hutu in Burundi in 1965 and 1972, (15) the Paraguayan massacre of Ache Indians prior to 1974, (16) the Khmer Rouge massacre in Kampuchea between 1975 and 1978, (17) and the contemporary Iranian killings of Baha'is. (18) Apartheid is considered separately in paragraphs 43–46 below. A number of other cases may be suggested. It could seem pedantic to argue that some terrible mass-killings are legalistically not genocide, but on the other hand it could be counter-productive to devalue genocide through over-diluting its definition.

PART III: FUTURE PROGRESS: POSSIBLE WAYS FORWARD

D. Conclusions

91. The reforms recommended will, like most things worthwhile in human progress, not be easy. They would however be the best living memorial to all the past victims of genocide. To do nothing, by contrast, would be to invite responsibility for helping cause future victims.

PART IV: LIST OF RECOMMENDATIONS

92. The principal recommendations of the present Special Rapporteur are contained in paragraphs 50, 55, 57, 41, 55, 54, 64, 70, 79, 80, 81, 82, 83–84, 85, 86–8), 90 and 91 supra.

international texts

Convention Against Torture and Other Cruel, Inhuman or Degrading Treatment or Punishment

SOURCE The Avalon Project at Yale Law School. Available from http://www.yale.edu/lawweb/avalon/avalon.htm

INTRODUCTION This treaty was adopted by the UN General Assembly on December 10, 1974 and is designed to prevent and punish torture when committed with the involvement of public officials, whether directly acting or acquiescing or condoning the acts when committed by private parties. The Convention adds to international law by defining precisely the act of torture and setting forth the obligations of states parties to combat it. The Convention declares expressly that there are "no exceptional circumstances whatsoever" that would justify torture and that no orders from superior officers may provide a justification. The Convention also sets forth a set of measures and institutions at the international level to supervise compliance by states with the legal obligations contained in the agreement.

The States Parties to this Convention,

Considering that, in accordance with the principles proclaimed in the Charter of the United Nations, recognition of the equal and inalienable rights of all members of the human family is the foundation of freedom, justice and peace in the world,

Recognizing that those rights derive from the inherent dignity of the human person,

Considering the obligation of States under the Charter, in particular Article 55, to promote universal respect for, and observance of, human rights and fundamental freedoms,

Having regard to article 5 of the Universal Declaration of Human Rights and article 7 of the International Covenant on Civil and Political Rights, both of which provide that no one may be subjected to torture or to cruel, inhuman or degrading treatment or punishment,

Having regard also to the Declaration on the Protection of All Persons from Being Subjected to Torture and Other Cruel, Inhuman or Degrading Treatment or Punishment, adopted by the General Assembly on 9 December 1975 (resolution 3452 (XXX)),

Desiring to make more effective the struggle against torture and other cruel, inhuman or degrading treatment or punishment throughout the world,

Have agreed as follows:

Part I

Article 1

1. For the purposes of this Convention, torture means any act by which severe pain or suffering, whether physical or mental, is intentionally inflicted on a person for such purposes as obtaining from him or a third person information or a confession, punishing him for an act he or a third person has committed or is suspected of having committed, or intimidating or coercing him or a third person, or for any reason based on discrimination of any kind, when such pain or suffering is inflicted by or at the instigation of or with the consent or acquiescence of a public official or other person acting in an official capacity. It does not include pain or suffering arising only from, inherent in or incidental to lawful sanctions.

2. This article is without prejudice to any international instrument or national legislation which does or may contain provisions of wider application.

Article 2

1. Each State Party shall take effective legislative, administrative, judicial or other measures to prevent acts of torture in any territory under its jurisdiction.

2. No exceptional circumstances whatsoever, whether a state of war or a threat or war, internal political instability or any other public emergency, may be invoked as a justification of torture.

3. An order from a superior officer or a public authority may not be invoked as a justification of torture.

Article 3

1. No State Party shall expel, return ("refouler") or extradite a person to another State where there are substantial grounds for believing that he would be in danger of being subjected to torture.

2. For the purpose of determining whether there are such grounds, the competent authorities shall take into account all relevant considerations including, where applicable, the existence in the State concerned of a consistent pattern of gross, flagrant or mass violations of human rights.

Article 4

1. Each State Party shall ensure that all acts of torture are offences under its criminal law. The same shall apply to an attempt to commit torture and to an act by any person which constitutes complicity or participation in torture.

2. Each State Party shall make these offences punishable by appropriate penalties which take into account their grave nature.

Article 5

1. Each State Party shall take such measures as may be necessary to establish its jurisdiction over the offences referred to in article 4 in the following cases:

(a) When the offences are committed in any territory under its jurisdiction or on board a ship or aircraft registered in that State;

(b) When the alleged offender is a national of that State;

(c) When the victim os a national of that State if that State considers it appropriate.

2. Each State Party shall likewise take such measures aa may be necessary to establish its jurisdiction over such offences in cases where the alleged offender is present in any territory under its jurisdiction and it does not extradite him pursuant to article 8 to any of the States mentioned in Paragraph 1 of this article.

3. This Convention does not exclude any criminal jurisdiction exercised in accordance with internal law.

Article 6

1. Upon being satisfied, after an examination of information available to it, that the circumstances so warrant, any State Party in whose territory a person alleged to have committed any offence referred to in article 4 is present, shall take him into custody or take other legal measures to ensure his presence. The custody and other legal measures shall be as provided in the law of that State but may be continued only for such time as is necessary to enable any criminal or extradition proceedings to be instituted.

2. Such State shall immediately make a preliminary inquiry into the facts.

3. Any person in custody pursuant to paragraph 1 of this article shall be assisted in communicating immediately with the nearest appropriate representative of the State of which he is a national, or, if he is a stateless person, to the representative of the State where he usually resides.

4. When a State, pursuant to this article, has taken a person into custody, it shall immediately notify the States referred to in article 5, paragraph 1, of the fact that such person is in custody and of the circumstances which warrant his detention. The State which makes the preliminary inquiry contemplated in paragraph 2 of this article shall promptly report its findings to the said State and shall indicate whether it intends to exercise jurisdiction.

Article 7

1. The State Party in territory under whose jurisdiction a person alleged to have committed any offence referred to in article 4 is found, shall in the cases contemplated in article 5, if it does not extradite him, submit the case to its competent authorities for the purpose of prosecution.

2. These authorities shall take their decision in the same manner as in the case of any ordinary offence of a serious nature under the law of that State. In the cases referred to in article 5, paragraph 2, the standards of evidence required for prosecution and conviction shall in no way be less stringent than those which apply in the cases referred to in article 5, paragraph 1.

3. Any person regarding whom proceedings are brought in connection with any of the offences referred to in article 4 shall be guaranteed fair treatment at all stages of the proceedings.

Article 8

1. The offences referred to in article 4 shall be deemed to be included as extraditable offences in any extradition treaty existing between States Parties. States Parties undertake to include such offences as extraditable offences in every extradition treaty to be concluded between them.

2. If a State Party which makes extradition conditional on the existence of a treaty receives a request for extradition from another State Party with which it has no extradition treaty, it may consider this Convention as the legal basis for extradition in respect of such offenses. Extradition shall be subject to the other conditions provided by the law of the requested State.

3. States Parties which do not make extradition conditional on the existence of a treaty shall recognize such offences as extraditable offences between themselves subject to the conditions provided by the law of the requested state.

4. Such offences shall be treated, for the purpose of extradition between States Parties, as if they had been committed not only in the place in which they occurred but also in the territories of the States required to establish their jurisdiction in accordance with article 5, paragraph 1.

Article 9

1. States Parties shall afford one another the greatest measure of assistance in connection with civil proceedings brought in respect of any of the offences referred to in article 4, including the supply of all evidence at their disposal necessary for the proceedings.

2. States Parties shall carry out their obligations under paragraph 1 of this article in conformity with any treaties on mutual judicial assistance that may exist between them.

Article 10

1. Each State Party shall ensure that education and information regarding the prohibition against torture are fully included in the training of law enforcement personnel, civil or military, medical personnel, public officials and other persons who may be involved in the custody, interrogation or treatment of any individual subjected to any form of arrest, detention or imprisonment.

2. Each State Party shall include this prohibition in the rules or instructions issued in regard to the duties and functions of any such persons.

Article 11

Each State Party shall keep under systematic review interrogation rules, instructions, methods and practices as well as arrangements for the custody and treatment of persons subjected to any form of arrest, detention or imprisonment in any territory under its jurisdiction, with a view to preventing any cases of torture.

Article 12

Each State Party shall ensure that its competent authorities proceed to a prompt and impartial investigation, wherever there is reasonable ground to believe that an act of torture has been committee in any territory under its jurisdiction.

Article 13

Each State Party shall ensure that any individual who alleges he has been subjected to torture in any territory under its jurisdiction has the right to complain to and to have his case promptly and impartially examined its competent authorities. Steps shall be taken to ensure that the complainant and witnesses are protected against all ill-treatment or intimidation as a consequence of his complaint or any evidence given.

Article 14

1. Each State Party shall ensure in its legal system that the victim of an act of torture obtains redress and has an enforceable right to fair and adequate compensation including the means for as full rehabilitation as possible. In the event of the death of the victim as a result of an act of torture, his dependents shall be entitled to compensation.

2. Nothing in this article shall affect any right of the victim or other person to compensation which may exist under national law.

Article 15

Each State Party shall ensure that any statement which is established to have been made as a result of torture shall not be invoked as evidence in any proceedings, except against a person accused of torture as evidence that the statement was made.

Article 16

1. Each State Party shall undertake to prevent in any territory under its jurisdiction other acts of cruel, inhuman or degrading treatment or punishment which do not amount to torture as defined in article 1, when such acts are committed by or at the instigation of or with the consent or acquiescence of a public official or other person acting in an official capacity. In particular, the obligations contained in articles 10, 11, 12 and 13 shall apply with the substitution for references to torture or references to other forms of cruel, inhuman or degrading treatment or punishment.

2. The provisions of this Convention are without prejudice to the provisions of any other international instrument or national law which prohibit cruel, inhuman or degrading treatment or punishment or which relate to extradition or expulsion.

Part II

Article 17

1. There shall be established a Committee against Torture (hereinafter referred to as the Committee) which shall carry out the functions hereinafter provided. The Committee shall consist of 10 experts of high moral standing and recognized competence in the field of human rights, who shall serve in their personal capacity. The experts shall be elected by the States Parties, consideration being given to equitable geographical distribution and to the usefulness of the participation of some persons having legal experience.

2. The members of the Committee shall be elected by secret ballot from a list of persons nominated by States Parties. Each State Party may nominate one person from among its own nationals. States Parties shall bear in mind the usefulness of nominating persons who are also members of the Human Rights Committee established under the International Covenant on Civil and Political Rights and are willing to serve on the Committee against Torture.

3. Elections of the members of the Committee shall be held at biennial meetings of States Parties convened by the Secretary-General of the United Nations. At those meetings, for which two thirds of the States Parties shall constitute a quorum, the persons elected to the Committee shall be those who obtain the largest number of votes and an absolute majority of the votes of the representatives of States Parties present and voting.

4. The initial election shall be held no later than six months after the date of the entry into force of this

Convention. At least four months before the date of each election, the Secretary-General of the United Nations shall address a letter to the States Parties inviting them to submit their nominations within three months. The Secretary-General shall prepare a list in alphabetical order of all persons thus nominated, indicating the States Parties which have nominated them, and shall submit it to the States Parties.

5. The members of the Committee shall be elected for a term of four years. They shall be eligible for re-election if renominated. However, the term of five of the members elected at the first election shall expire at the end of two years; immediately after the first election the names of these five members shall be chosen by lot by the chairman of the meeting referred to in paragraph 3.

6. If a member of the Committee dies or resigns or for any other cause can no longer perform his Committee duties, the State Party which nominated him shall appoint another expert from among its nationals to serve for the remainder of his term, subject to the approval of the majority of the States Parties. The approval shall be considered given unless half or more of the States Parties respond negatively within six weeks after having been informed by the Secretary-General of the United Nations of the proposed appointment.

7. States Parties shall be responsible for the expenses of the members of the Committee while they are in performance of Committee duties.

Article 18

1. The Committee shall elect its officers for a term of two years. They may be re-elected.

2. The Committee shall establish its own rules of procedure, but these rules shall provide, inter alia, that

(a) Six members shall constitute a quorum; (b) Decisions of the Committee shall be made by a majority vote of the members present.

3. The Secretary-General of the United Nations shall provide the necessary staff and facilities for the effective performance of the functions of the Committee under this Convention.

4. The Secretary-General of the United Nations shall convene the initial meeting of the Committee. After its initial meeting, the Committee shall meet at such times as shall be provided in its rules of procedure.

5. The State Parties shall be responsible for expenses incurred in connection with the holding of meetings of the States Parties and of the Committee, including reimbursement of the United Nations for any expenses, such as the cost of staff and facilities, incurred by the United Nations pursuant to paragraph 3 above.

Article 19

1. The States Parties shall submit to the Committee, through the Secretary-General of the United Nations, reports on the measures they have taken to give effect to their undertakings under this Convention, within one year after the entry into force of this Convention for the State Party concerned. Thereafter the States Parties shall submit supplementary reports every four years on any new measures taken, and such other reports as the Committee may request.

2. The Secretary-General shall transmit the reports to all States Parties.

[3. Each report shall be considered by the Committee which may make such comments or suggestions on the report as it considers appropriate, and shall forward these to the State Party concerned. That State Party may respond with any observations it chooses to the Committee.

4. The Committee may, at its discretion, decide to include any comments or suggestions made by it in accordance with paragraph 3, together with the observations thereon received from the State Party concerned, in its annual report made in accordance with article 24. If so requested by the State Party concerned, the Committee may also include a copy of the report submitted under paragraph 1.]

Article 20

1. If the Committee receives reliable information which appears to it to contain well-founded indications that torture is being systematically practised in the territory of a State Party, the Committee shall invite that State Party to co-operate in the examination of the information and to this end to submit observations with regard to the information concerned.

2. Taking into account any observations which may have been submitted by the State Party concerned as well as any other relevant information available to it, the Committee may, if it decides that this is warranted, designate one or more of its members to make a confidential inquiry and to report to the Committee urgently.

3. If an inquiry is made in accordance with paragraph 2, the Committee shall seek the co-operation of the State Party concerned. In agreement with that State Party, such an inquiry may include a visit to its territory.

4. After examining the findings of its member or members submitted in accordance with paragraph 2,

the Committee shall transmit these findings to the State Party concerned together with any comments or suggestions which seem appropriate in view of the situation.

5. All the proceedings of the Committee referred to in paragraphs 1 to 4 of this article shall be confidential, and at all stages of the proceedings the cooperation of the State Party shall be sought. After such proceedings have been completed with regard to an inquiry made in accordance with paragraph 2, the Committee may, after consultations with the State Party concerned, decide to include a summary account of the results of the proceedings in its annual report made in accordance with article 24.

Article 21

1. A State Party to this Convention may at any time declare under this article 3 that it recognizes the competence of the Committee to receive and consider communications to the effect that a State Party claims that another State Party is not fulfilling its obligations under this Convention. Such communications may be received and considered according to the procedures laid down in this article only if submitted by a State Party which has made a declaration recognizing in regard to itself the competence of the Committee. No communication shall be dealt with by the Committee under this article if it concerns a State Party which has not made such a declaration. Communications received under this article shall be dealt with in accordance with the following procedure:

(a) If a State Party considers that another State Party is not giving effect to the provisions of this Convention, it may, by written communication, bring the matter to the attention of that State Party. Within three months after the receipt of the communication the receiving State shall afford the State which sent the communication an explanation or any other statement in writing clarifying the matter which should include, to the extent possible and pertinent, references to domestic procedures and remedies taken, pending, or available in the matter.

(b) If the matter is not adjusted to the satisfaction of both States Parties concerned within six months after the receipt by the receiving State of the initial communication, either State shall have the right to refer the matter to the Committee by notice given to the Committee and to the other State.

(c) The Committee shall deal with a matter referred to it under this article only after it has ascertained that all domestic remedies have been invoked and exhausted in the matter, in conformity with the generally recognized principles of international law. This shall not be the rule where the application of the remedies is unreasonably prolonged or is unlikely to bring effective relief to the person who is the victim of the violation of this Convention.

(d) The Committee shall hold closed meetings when examining communications under this article.

(e) Subject to the provisions of subparagraph (c), the Committee shall make available its good offices to the States Parties concerned with a view to a friendly solution of the matter on the basis of respect for the obligations provided for in the present Convention. For this purpose, the Committee may, when appropriate, set up an ad hoc conciliation commission.

(f) In any matter referred to it under this article, the Committee may call upon the States Parties concerned, referred to in subparagraph (b), to supply any relevant information.

(g) The States Parties concerned, referred to in subparagraph (b), shall have the right to be represented when the matter is being considered by the Committee and to make submissions orally and/or in writing.

(h) The Committee shall, within 12 months after the date of receipt of notice under subparagraph (b), submit a report.

(i) If a solution within the terms of subparagraph (e) is reached, the Committee shall confine its report to a brief statement of the facts and of the solution reached.

(ii) If a solution within the terms of subparagraph (e) is not reached, the Committee shall confine its report to a brief statement of the facts; the written submissions and record of the oral submissions made by the States Parties concerned shall be attached to the report. In every matter, the report shall be communicated to the States Parties concerned.

2. The provisions of this article shall come into force when five States Parties to this Convention have made declarations under paragraph 1 of this article. Such declarations shall be deposited by the States Parties with the Secretary-General of the United Nations, who shall transmit copies thereof to the other States Parties. A declaration may be withdrawn at any time by notification to the Secretary-General. Such a withdrawal shall not prejudice the consideration of any matter which is the subject of a communication already trans-

mitted under this article; no further communication by any State Party shall be received under this article after the notification of withdrawal of the declaration has been received by the Secretary-General, unless the State Party concerned has made a new declaration.

Article 22

1. A State Party to this Convention may at any time declare under this article that it recognizes the competence of the Committee to receive and consider communications from or on behalf of individuals subject to its jurisdiction who claim to be victims of a violation by a State Party of the provisions of the Convention. No communication shall be received by the Committee if it concerns a State Party to the Convention which has not made such a declaration.

2. The Committee shall consider inadmissible any communication under this article which is anonymous, or which it considers to be an abuse of the right of submission of such communications or to be incompatible with the provisions of this Convention.

3. Subject to the provisions of paragraph 2, the Committee shall bring any communication submitted to it under this article to the attention of the State Party to this Convention which has made a declaration under paragraph 1 and is alleged to be violating any provisions of the Convention. Within six months, the receiving State shall submit to the Committee written explanations or statements clarifying the matter and the remedy, if any, that may have been taken by that State.

4. The Committee shall consider communications received under this article in the light of all information made available to it by or on behalf of the individual and by the State Party concerned.

5. The Committee shall not consider any communication from an individual under this article unless it has ascertained that:

(a) The same matter has not been, and is not being examined under another procedure of international investigation or settlement;

(b) The individual has exhausted all available domestic remedies; this shall not be the rule where the application of the remedies is unreasonably prolonged or is unlikely to bring effective relief to the person who is the victim of the violation of this Convention.

6. The Committee shall hold closed meetings when examining communications under this article.

7. The Committee shall forward its views to the State Party concerned and to the individual.

8. The provisions of this article shall come into force when five States Parties to this Convention have made declarations under paragraph 1 of this article. Such declarations shall be deposited by the States Parties with the Secretary-General of the United Nations, who shall transmit parties thereof to the other States Parties. A declaration may be withdrawn at any time by notification to the Secretary-General. Such a withdrawal shall not prejudice the consideration of any matter which is the subject of a communication already transmitted under this article; no further communication by or on behalf of an individual shall be received under this article after the notification of withdrawal of the declaration has been received by the Secretary-General, unless the State Party concerned has made a new declaration.

Article 23

The members of the Committee, and of the ad hoc conciliation commissions which may be appointed under article 21, paragraph 1 (e), shall be entitled to the facilities, privileges and immunities of experts on missions for the United Nations as laid down in the relevant sections of the Convention on the Privileges and Immunities of the United Nations.

Article 24

The Committee shall submit an annual report on its activities under this Convention to the States Parties and to the General Assembly of the United Nations.

Part III

Article 25

1. This Convention is open for signature by all States.

2. This Convention is subject to ratification. Instruments of ratification shall be deposited with the Secretary-General of the United Nations.

Article 26

This Convention is open to accession by all States. Accession shall be effected by the deposit of an instrument of accession with the Secretary-General of the United Nations.

Article 27

1. This Convention shall enter into force on the thirtieth day after the date of the deposit with the Secretary-General of the United Nations of the twentieth instrument of ratification or accession.

2. For each State ratifying this Convention or acceding to it after the deposit of the twentieth instrument of ratification or accession, the Convention shall enter into force on the thirtieth day after the date of the deposit of its own instrument of ratification or accession.

Article 28

1. Each State may, at the time of signature or ratification of this Convention or accession thereto, declare that it does not recognize the competence of the Committee provided for in article 20.

2. Any State Party having made a reservation in accordance with paragraph 1 of this article may, at any time, withdraw this reservation by notification to the Secretary-General of the United Nations.

Article 29

1. Any State Party to this Convention may propose an amendment and file it with the Secretary-General of the United Nations. The Secretary-General shall thereupon communicate the proposed amendment to the States Parties to this Convention with a request that they notify him whether they favour a conference of States Parties for the purpose of considering and voting upon the proposal. In the event that within four months from the date of such communication at least one third of the State Parties favours such a conference, the Secretary-General shall convene the conference under the auspices of the United Nations. Any amendment adopted by a majority of the States Parties present and voting at the conference shall be submitted by the Secretary-General to all the States Parties for acceptance.

2. An amendment adopted in accordance with paragraph 1 shall enter into force when two thirds of the States Parties to this Convention have notified the Secretary-General of the United Nations that they have accepted it in accordance with their respective constitutional processes.

3. When amendments enter into force, they shall be binding on those States Parties which have accepted them, other States Parties still being bound by the provisions of this Convention and any earlier amendments which they have accepted.

Article 30

1. Any dispute between two or more States Parties concerning the interpretation or application of this Convention which cannot be settled through negotiation, shall, at the request of one of them, be submitted to arbitration. If within six months from the date of the request for arbitration the Parties are unable to agree on the organization of the arbitration, any one of those Parties may refer the dispute to the International Court of Justice by request in conformity with the Statute of the Court.

2. Each State may at the time of signature or ratification of this Convention or accession thereto, declare that it does not consider itself bound by the preceding paragraph. The other States Parties shall not be bound by the preceding paragraph with respect to any State Party having made such a reservation.

3. Any State Party having made a reservation in accordance with the preceding paragraph may at any time withdraw this reservation by notification to the Secretary-General of the United Nations.

Article 31

1. A State Party may denounce this Convention by written notification to the Secretary-General of the United Nations. Denunciation becomes effective one year after the date of receipt of the notification by the Secretary-General.

2. Such a denunciation shall not have the effect of releasing the State Party from its obligations under this Convention in regard to any act or omission which occurs prior to the date at which the denunciation becomes effective. Nor shall denunciation prejudice in any way the continued consideration of any matter which is already under consideration by the Committee prior to the date at which the denunciation becomes effective.

3. Following the date at which the denunciation of a State Party becomes effective, the Committee shall not commence consideration of any new matter regarding that State.

Article 32

The Secretary-General of the United Nations shall inform all members of the United Nations and all States which have signed this Convention or acceded to it, or the following particulars:

(a) Signatures, ratifications and accessions under articles 25 and 26;

(b) The date of entry into force of this Convention under article 27, and the date of the entry into force of any amendments under article 29;

(c) Denunciations under article 31.

Article 33

1. This Convention, of which the Arabic, Chinese, English, French, Russian and Spanish texts are equally authentic, shall be deposited in the archives of the United Nations.

2. The Secretary-General of the United Nations shall transmit certified copies of this Convention to all States.

On February 4, 1985, the Convention was opened for signature at United Nations Headquarters in New York. At that time, representatives of the following countries signed it: Afghanistan, Argentina, Belgium,

Bolivia, Costa Rica, Denmark, Dominican Republic, Finland, France, Greece, Iceland, Italy, Netherlands, Norway, Portugal, Senegal, Spain, Sweden, Switzerland and Uruguay. Subsequently, signatures were received from Venezuela on February 15, from Luxembourg and Panama on February 22, from Austria on March 14, and from the United Kingdom on March 15, 1985.

Convention on the Prevention and Punishment of the Crime of Genocide; December 9, 1948

SOURCE The Avalon Project at Yale Law School. Available from http://www.yale.edu/lawweb/avalon/avalon.htm

INTRODUCTION The Genocide Convention was adopted by the General Assembly of the United Nations on 9 December 1948, only hours before it passed the Universal Declaration of Human Rights. Its preparation had been mandated by the General Assembly in Resolution 96(I), which was adopted two years earlier. Although there were several stages in its preparation, most of the detailed work, and the final decisions, was carried out by the Sixth Committee of the General Assembly in late 1948. After its adoption, the Convention soon obtained the requisite twenty ratifications for its entry into force, which occurred in early 1951. The definition of genocide in article II is a narrow one, and for this reason it has frequently been criticized. Nevertheless, both international bodies and national lawmakers have been loathe to tamper with it. Article II is repeated verbatim in many treaties, as well as in the criminal codes of many countries.

Adopted by Resolution 260 (III) A of the United Nations General Assembly on 9 December 1948.

The Contracting Parties,

Having considered the declaration made by the General Assembly of the United Nations in its resolution 96 (I) dated 11 December 1946 that genocide is a crime under international law, contrary to the spirit and aims of the United Nations and condemned by the civilized world;

Recognizing that at all periods of history genocide has inflicted great losses on humanity; and

Being convinced that, in order to liberate mankind from such an odious scourge, international co-operation is required;

Hereby agree as hereinafter provided.

Art. 1.

The Contracting Parties confirm that genocide, whether committed in time of peace or in time of war, is a crime under international law which they undertake to prevent and to punish.

Art. 2.

In the present Convention, genocide means any of the following acts committed with intent to destroy, in whole or in part, a national, ethnical, racial or religious group, as such:

(a) Killing members of the group; (b) Causing serious bodily or mental harm to members of the group; (c) Deliberately inflicting on the group conditions of life calculated to bring about its physical destruction in whole or in part; (d) Imposing measures intended to prevent births within the group; (e) Forcibly transferring children of the group to another group.

Art. 3.

The following acts shall be punishable:

(a) Genocide; (b) Conspiracy to commit genocide; (c) Direct and public incitement to commit genocide; (d) Attempt to commit genocide; (e) Complicity in genocide.

Art. 4.

Persons committing genocide or any of the other acts enumerated in Article 3 shall be punished, whether they are constitutionally responsible rulers, public officials or private individuals.

Art. 5.

The Contracting Parties undertake to enact, in accordance with their respective Constitutions, the necessary legislation to give effect to the provisions of the present Convention and, in particular, to provide effective penalties for persons guilty of genocide or any of the other acts enumerated in Article 3.

Art. 6.

Persons charged with genocide or any of the other acts enumerated in Article 3 shall be tried by a competent tribunal of the State in the territory of which the act was committed, or by such international penal tribunal as may have jurisdiction with respect to those Contracting Parties which shall have accepted its jurisdiction.

Art. 7.

Genocide and the other acts enumerated in Article 3 shall not be considered as political crimes for the purpose of extradition.

The Contracting Parties pledge themselves in such cases to grant extradition in accordance with their laws and treaties in force.

Art. 8.

Any Contracting Party may call upon the competent organs of the United Nations to take such action under the Charter of the United Nations as they consider appropriate for the prevention and suppression of acts of genocide or any of the other acts enumerated in Article 3.

Art. 9.

Disputes between the Contracting Parties relating to the interpretation, application or fulfillment of the present Convention, including those relating to the responsibility of a State for genocide or any of the other acts enumerated in Article 3, shall be submitted to the International Court of Justice at the request of any of the parties to the dispute.

Art. 10.

The present Convention, of which the Chinese, English, French, Russian and Spanish texts are equally authentic, shall bear the date of 9 December 1948. Art. 11.

The present Convention shall be open until 31 December 1949 for signature on behalf of any Member of the United Nations and of any non-member State to which an invitation to sign has been addressed by the General Assembly.

The present Convention shall be ratified, and the instruments of ratification shall be deposited with the Secretary-General of the United Nations.

After 1 January 1950, the present Convention may be acceded to on behalf of any Member of the United Nations and of any non-member State which has received an invitation as aforesaid.

Instruments of accession shall be deposited with the Secretary-General of the United Nations.

Art. 12.

Any Contracting Party may at any time, by notification addressed to the Secretary-General of the United Nations, extend the application of the present Convention to all or any of the territories for the conduct of whose foreign relations that Contracting Party is responsible.

Art. 13.

On the day when the first twenty instruments of ratification or accession have been deposited, the Secretary-General shall draw up a process-verbal and transmit a copy of it to each Member of the United Nations and to each of the non-member States contemplated in Article 11.

The present Convention shall come into force on the ninetieth day following the date of deposit of the twentieth instrument of ratification or accession.

Any ratification or accession effected subsequent to the latter date shall become effective on the ninetieth day following the deposit of the instrument of ratification or accession.

Art. 14.

The present Convention shall remain in effect for a period of ten years as from the date of its coming into force.

It shall thereafter remain in force for successive periods of five years for such Contracting Parties as have not denounced it at least six months before the expiration of the current period.

Denunciation shall be effected by a written notification addressed to the Secretary-General of the United Nations.

Art. 15.

If, as a result of denunciations, the number of Parties to the present Convention should become less than sixteen, the Convention shall cease to be in force as from the date on which the last of these denunciations shall become effective.

Art. 16.

A request for the revision of the present Convention may be made at any time by any Contracting Party by means of a notification in writing addressed to the Secretary-General.

The General Assembly shall decide upon the steps, if any, to be taken in respect of such request.

Art. 17.

The Secretary-General of the United Nations shall notify all Members of the United Nations and the non-member States contemplated in Article 11 of the following:

(a) Signatures, ratifications and accessions received in accordance with Article 11; (b) Notifications received in accordance with Article 12; (c) The date upon which the present Convention comes into force in accordance with Article 13; (d) Denunciations received in accordance with Article 14; (e) The abrogation of the Convention in accordance with Article 15; (f) Notifications received in accordance with Article 16.

Art. 18.

The original of the present Convention shall be deposited in the archives of the United Nations.

A certified copy of the Convention shall be transmitted to all Members of the United Nations and to the non-member States contemplated in Article 11.

Art. 19.

The present Convention shall be registered by the Secretary-General of the United Nations on the date of its coming into force.

Geneva Convention IV: Civilian Persons in Time of War (August 12, 1949)

SOURCE The Avalon Project at Yale Law School. Available from http://www.yale.edu/lawweb/avalon/avalon.htm

INTRODUCTION The four Geneva Conventions were adopted on August 12, 1949. For many years, they have enjoyed near-universal ratification, and they are often spoken of as a codification of customary international law. The other three conventions deal with different categories of war victims, namely the wounded on land (I), the wounded at sea (II) and prisoners of war (III). The first Convention was inspired by a Swiss businessman, Henry Dunant, in the mid-nineteenth century. The fundamental principle underlying Convention IV is that when a territory is occupied during an international armed conflict, civilians are to be protected from abuse and persecution. The Convention provides only limited coverage to noninternational armed conflicts, or civil wars, although this shortcoming was partially rectified in a protocol to the Convention adopted in 1977.

CONVENTION (IV) RELATIVE TO THE PROTECTION OF CIVILIAN PERSONS IN TIME OF WAR

Signed at Geneva, 12 August 1949

Table of Contents

Part I. General Provisions

Part II. General Protection of Populations against certain consequences of war

Part III. Status and Treatment of Protected Persons

Part IV. Execution of the Convention

Annex I: Draft Agreement relating to Hospital and Safety Zones and Localities

Annex II: Draft Regulations concerning Collective Relief

Annex III: Cards Correspondence [not included]

The undersigned Plenipotentiaries of the Governments represented at the Diplomatic Conference held at Geneva from 21 April to 12 August 1949, for the purpose of establishing a Convention for the Protection of Civilians in Time of War, have agreed as follows:

PART I

GENERAL PROVISIONS

Article 1. The High Contracting Parties undertake to respect and to ensure respect for the present Convention in all circumstances.

Art. 2. In addition to the provisions which shall be implemented in peace-time, the present Convention shall apply to all cases of declared war or of any other armed conflict which may arise between two or more of the High Contracting Parties, even if the state of war is not recognized by one of them.

The Convention shall also apply to all cases of partial or total occupation of the territory of a High Contracting Party, even if the said occupation meets with no armed resistance.

Although one of the Powers in conflict may not be a party to the present Convention, the Powers who are parties thereto shall remain bound by it in their mutual relations. They shall furthermore be bound by the Convention in relation to the said Power, if the latter accepts and applies the provisions thereof.

Art. 3. In the case of armed conflict not of an international character occurring in the territory of one of the High Contracting Parties, each Party to the conflict shall be bound to apply, as a minimum, the following provisions:

(1) Persons taking no active part in the hostilities, including members of armed forces who have laid down their arms and those placed hors de combat by sickness, wounds, detention, or any other cause, shall in all circumstances be treated humanely, without any adverse distinction founded on race, colour, religion or faith, sex, birth or wealth, or any other similar criteria. To this end the following acts are and shall remain prohibited at any time and in any place whatsoever with respect to the above-mentioned persons: (a) violence to life and person, in particular murder of all kinds, mutilation, cruel treatment and torture; (b) taking of hostages; (c) outrages upon personal dignity, in particular humiliating and degrading treatment; (d) the passing of sentences and the carrying out of executions without previous judgment pronounced by a regularly constituted court, affording all the judicial guarantees which are recognized as indispensable by civilized peoples.

(2) The wounded and sick shall be collected and cared for.

An impartial humanitarian body, such as the International Committee of the Red Cross, may offer its services to the Parties to the conflict.

The Parties to the conflict should further endeavour to bring into force, by means of special agreements, all or part of the other provisions of the present Convention.

The application of the preceding provisions shall not affect the legal status of the Parties to the conflict.

Art. 4. Persons protected by the Convention are those who, at a given moment and in any manner whatsoever, find themselves, in case of a conflict or occupation, in the hands of a Party to the conflict or Occupying Power of which they are not nationals.

Nationals of a State which is not bound by the Convention are not protected by it. Nationals of a neutral State who find themselves in the territory of a belligerent State, and nationals of a co-belligerent State, shall not be regarded as protected persons while the State of which they are nationals has normal diplomatic representation in the State in whose hands they are.

The provisions of Part II are, however, wider in application, as defined in Article 13.

Persons protected by the Geneva Convention for the Amelioration of the Condition of the Wounded and Sick in Armed Forces in the Field of 12 August 1949, or by the Geneva Convention for the Amelioration of the Condition of Wounded, Sick and Shipwrecked Members of Armed Forces at Sea of 12 August 1949, or by the Geneva Convention relative to the Treatment of Prisoners of War of 12 August 1949, shall not be considered as protected persons within the meaning of the present Convention.

Art. 5 Where in the territory of a Party to the conflict, the latter is satisfied that an individual protected person is definitely suspected of or engaged in activities hostile to the security of the State, such individual person shall not be entitled to claim such rights and privileges under the present Convention as would, if exercised in the favour of such individual person, be prejudicial to the security of such State.

Where in occupied territory an individual protected person is detained as a spy or saboteur, or as a person under definite suspicion of activity hostile to the security of the Occupying Power, such person shall, in those cases where absolute military security so requires, be regarded as having forfeited rights of communication under the present Convention.

In each case, such persons shall nevertheless be treated with humanity and, in case of trial, shall not be deprived of the rights of fair and regular trial prescribed by the present Convention. They shall also be granted the full rights and privileges of a protected person under the present Convention at the earliest date consistent with the security of the State or Occupying Power, as the case may be.

Art. 6. The present Convention shall apply from the outset of any conflict or occupation mentioned in Article 2.

In the territory of Parties to the conflict, the application of the present Convention shall cease on the general close of military operations.

In the case of occupied territory, the application of the present Convention shall cease one year after the general close of military operations; however, the Occupying Power shall be bound, for the duration of the occupation, to the extent that such Power exercises the functions of government in such territory, by the provisions of the following Articles of the present Convention: 1 to 12, 27, 29 to 34, 47, 49, 51, 52, 53, 59, 61 to 77, 143.

Protected persons whose release, repatriation or re-establishment may take place after such dates shall meanwhile continue to benefit by the present Convention. Art. 7. In addition to the agreements expressly provided for in Articles 11, 14, 15, 17, 36, 108, 109, 132, 133 and 149, the High Contracting Parties may conclude other special agreements for all matters concerning which they may deem it suitable to make separate provision. No special agreement shall adversely affect the situation of protected persons, as defined by the present Convention, not restrict the rights which it confers upon them.

Protected persons shall continue to have the benefit of such agreements as long as the Convention is applicable to them, except where express provisions to the contrary are contained in the aforesaid or in subsequent agreements, or where more favourable measures have been taken with regard to them by one or other of the Parties to the conflict.

Art. 8. Protected persons may in no circumstances renounce in part or in entirety the rights secured to them by the present Convention, and by the special agreements referred to in the foregoing Article, if such there be.

Art. 9. The present Convention shall be applied with the cooperation and under the scrutiny of the Protecting Powers whose duty it is to safeguard the interests of the Parties to the conflict. For this purpose, the Protecting Powers may appoint, apart from their diplomatic or consular staff, delegates from amongst their own nationals or the nationals of other neutral Powers. The said delegates shall be subject to the approval of the Power with which they are to carry out their duties.

The Parties to the conflict shall facilitate to the greatest extent possible the task of the representatives or delegates of the Protecting Powers. The representatives or delegates of the Protecting Powers shall not in any case exceed their mission under the present Convention.

They shall, in particular, take account of the imperative necessities of security of the State wherein they carry out their duties.

Art. 10. The provisions of the present Convention constitute no obstacle to the humanitarian activities which the International Committee of the Red Cross or any other impartial humanitarian organization may, subject to the consent of the Parties to the conflict concerned, undertake for the protection of civilian persons and for their relief.

Art. 11. The High Contracting Parties may at any time agree to entrust to an international organization which offers all guarantees of impartiality and efficacy the duties incumbent on the Protecting Powers by virtue of the present Convention.

When persons protected by the present Convention do not benefit or cease to benefit, no matter for what reason, by the activities of a Protecting Power or of an organization provided for in the first paragraph above, the Detaining Power shall request a neutral State, or such an organization, to undertake the functions performed under the present Convention by a Protecting Power designated by the Parties to a conflict.

If protection cannot be arranged accordingly, the Detaining Power shall request or shall accept, subject to the provisions of this Article, the offer of the services of a humanitarian organization, such as the International Committee of the Red Cross, to assume the humanitarian functions performed by Protecting Powers under the present Convention.

Any neutral Power or any organization invited by the Power concerned or offering itself for these purposes, shall be required to act with a sense of responsibility towards the Party to the conflict on which persons protected by the present Convention depend, and shall be required to furnish sufficient assurances that it is in a position to undertake the appropriate functions and to discharge them impartially.

No derogation from the preceding provisions shall be made by special agreements between Powers one of which is restricted, even temporarily, in its freedom to negotiate with the other Power or its allies by reason of military events, more particularly where the whole, or a substantial part, of the territory of the said Power is occupied.

Whenever in the present Convention mention is made of a Protecting Power, such mention applies to substitute organizations in the sense of the present Article.

The provisions of this Article shall extend and be adapted to cases of nationals of a neutral State who are in occupied territory or who find themselves in the territory of a belligerent State in which the State of which they are nationals has not normal diplomatic representation.

Art. 12. In cases where they deem it advisable in the interest of protected persons, particularly in cases

of disagreement between the Parties to the conflict as to the application or interpretation of the provisions of the present Convention, the Protecting Powers shall lend their good offices with a view to settling the disagreement.

For this purpose, each of the Protecting Powers may, either at the invitation of one Party or on its own initiative, propose to the Parties to the conflict a meeting of their representatives, and in particular of the authorities responsible for protected persons, possibly on neutral territory suitably chosen. The Parties to the conflict shall be bound to give effect to the proposals made to them for this purpose. The Protecting Powers may, if necessary, propose for approval by the Parties to the conflict a person belonging to a neutral Power, or delegated by the International Committee of the Red Cross, who shall be invited to take part in such a meeting.

PART II

GENERAL PROTECTION OF POPULATIONS AGAINST CERTAIN CONSEQUENCES OF WAR

Art. 13. The provisions of Part II cover the whole of the populations of the countries in conflict, without any adverse distinction based, in particular, on race, nationality, religion or political opinion, and are intended to alleviate the sufferings caused by war.

Art. 14. In time of peace, the High Contracting Parties and, after the outbreak of hostilities, the Parties thereto, may establish in their own territory and, if the need arises, in occupied areas, hospital and safety zones and localities so organized as to protect from the effects of war, wounded, sick and aged persons, children under fifteen, expectant mothers and mothers of children under seven.

Upon the outbreak and during the course of hostilities, the Parties concerned may conclude agreements on mutual recognition of the zones and localities they have created. They may for this purpose implement the provisions of the Draft Agreement annexed to the present Convention, with such amendments as they may consider necessary.

The Protecting Powers and the International Committee of the Red Cross are invited to lend their good offices in order to facilitate the institution and recognition of these hospital and safety zones and localities.

Art. 15. Any Party to the conflict may, either direct or through a neutral State or some humanitarian organization, propose to the adverse Party to establish, in the regions where fighting is taking place, neutralized zones intended to shelter from the effects of war the following persons, without distinction: (a) wounded and sick combatants or non-combatants; (b) civilian persons who take no part in hostilities, and who, while they reside in the zones, perform no work of a military character.

When the Parties concerned have agreed upon the geographical position, administration, food supply and supervision of the proposed neutralized zone, a written agreement shall be concluded and signed by the representatives of the Parties to the conflict. The agreement shall fix the beginning and the duration of the neutralization of the zone.

Art. 16. The wounded and sick, as well as the infirm, and expectant mothers, shall be the object of particular protection and respect.

As far as military considerations allow, each Party to the conflict shall facilitate the steps taken to search for the killed and wounded, to assist the shipwrecked and other persons exposed to grave danger, and to protect them against pillage and ill-treatment.

Art. 17. The Parties to the conflict shall endeavour to conclude local agreements for the removal from besieged or encircled areas, of wounded, sick, infirm, and aged persons, children and maternity cases, and for the passage of ministers of all religions, medical personnel and medical equipment on their way to such areas.

Art. 18. Civilian hospitals organized to give care to the wounded and sick, the infirm and maternity cases, may in no circumstances be the object of attack but shall at all times be respected and protected by the Parties to the conflict. States which are Parties to a conflict shall provide all civilian hospitals with certificates showing that they are civilian hospitals and that the buildings which they occupy are not used for any purpose which would deprive these hospitals of protection in accordance with Article 19.

Civilian hospitals shall be marked by means of the emblem provided for in Article 38 of the Geneva Convention for the Amelioration of the Condition of the Wounded and Sick in Armed Forces in the Field of 12 August 1949, but only if so authorized by the State.

The Parties to the conflict shall, in so far as military considerations permit, take the necessary steps to make the distinctive emblems indicating civilian hospitals clearly visible to the enemy land, air and naval forces in order to obviate the possibility of any hostile action.

In view of the dangers to which hospitals may be exposed by being close to military objectives, it is recommended that such hospitals be situated as far as possible from such objectives.

Art. 19. The protection to which civilian hospitals are entitled shall not cease unless they are used to commit, outside their humanitarian duties, acts harmful to the enemy. Protection may, however, cease only after due warning has been given, naming, in all appropriate cases, a reasonable time limit and after such warning has remained unheeded. The fact that sick or wounded members of the armed forces are nursed in these hospitals, or the presence of small arms and ammunition taken from such combatants which have not yet been handed to the proper service, shall not be considered to be acts harmful to the enemy.

Art. 20. Persons regularly and solely engaged in the operation and administration of civilian hospitals, including the personnel engaged in the search for, removal and transporting of and caring for wounded and sick civilians, the infirm and maternity cases shall be respected and protected. In occupied territory and in zones of military operations, the above personnel shall be recognizable by means of an identity card certifying their status, bearing the photograph of the holder and embossed with the stamp of the responsible authority, and also by means of a stamped, water-resistant armlet which they shall wear on the left arm while carrying out their duties. This armlet shall be issued by the State and shall bear the emblem provided for in Article 38 of the Geneva Convention for the Amelioration of the Condition of the Wounded and Sick in Armed Forces in the Field of 12 August 1949.

Other personnel who are engaged in the operation and administration of civilian hospitals shall be entitled to respect and protection and to wear the armlet, as provided in and under the conditions prescribed in this Article, while they are employed on such duties. The identity card shall state the duties on which they are employed.

The management of each hospital shall at all times hold at the disposal of the competent national or occupying authorities an up-to-date list of such personnel.

Art. 21. Convoys of vehicles or hospital trains on land or specially provided vessels on sea, conveying wounded and sick civilians, the infirm and maternity cases, shall be respected and protected in the same manner as the hospitals provided for in Article 18, and shall be marked, with the consent of the State, by the display of the distinctive emblem provided for in Article 38 of the Geneva Convention for the Amelioration of the Condition of the Wounded and Sick in Armed Forces in the Field of 12 August 1949.

Art. 22. Aircraft exclusively employed for the removal of wounded and sick civilians, the infirm and maternity cases or for the transport of medical personnel and equipment, shall not be attacked, but shall be respected while flying at heights, times and on routes specifically agreed upon between all the Parties to the conflict concerned.

They may be marked with the distinctive emblem provided for in Article 38 of the Geneva Convention for the Amelioration of the Condition of the Wounded and Sick in Armed Forces in the Field of 12 August 1949.

Unless agreed otherwise, flights over enemy or enemy occupied territory are prohibited.

Such aircraft shall obey every summons to land. In the event of a landing thus imposed, the aircraft with its occupants may continue its flight after examination, if any.

Art. 23. Each High Contracting Party shall allow the free passage of all consignments of medical and hospital stores and objects necessary for religious worship intended only for civilians of another High Contracting Party, even if the latter is its adversary. It shall likewise permit the free passage of all consignments of essential foodstuffs, clothing and tonics intended for children under fifteen, expectant mothers and maternity cases.

The obligation of a High Contracting Party to allow the free passage of the consignments indicated in the preceding paragraph is subject to the condition that this Party is satisfied that there are no serious reasons for fearing: (a) that the consignments may be diverted from their destination, (b) that the control may not be effective, or (c) that a definite advantage may accrue to the military efforts or economy of the enemy through the substitution of the above-mentioned consignments for goods which would otherwise be provided or produced by the enemy or through the release of such material, services or facilities as would otherwise be required for the production of such goods. The Power which allows the passage of the consignments indicated in the first paragraph of this Article may make such permission conditional on the distribution to the persons benefited thereby being made under the local supervision of the Protecting Powers.

Such consignments shall be forwarded as rapidly as possible, and the Power which permits their free passage shall have the right to prescribe the technical arrangements under which such passage is allowed.

Art. 24. The Parties to the conflict shall take the necessary measures to ensure that children under fifteen, who are orphaned or are separated from their families as a result of the war, are not left to their own resources, and that their maintenance, the exercise of their religion and their education are facilitated in all circumstances. Their education shall, as far as possible, be entrusted to persons of a similar cultural tradition.

The Parties to the conflict shall facilitate the reception of such children in a neutral country for the duration of the conflict with the consent of the Protecting Power, if any, and under due safeguards for the observance of the principles stated in the first paragraph.

They shall, furthermore, endeavour to arrange for all children under twelve to be identified by the wearing of identity discs, or by some other means.

Art. 25. All persons in the territory of a Party to the conflict, or in a territory occupied by it, shall be enabled to give news of a strictly personal nature to members of their families, wherever they may be, and to receive news from them. This correspondence shall be forwarded speedily and without undue delay.

If, as a result of circumstances, it becomes difficult or impossible to exchange family correspondence by the ordinary post, the Parties to the conflict concerned shall apply to a neutral intermediary, such as the Central Agency provided for in Article 140, and shall decide in consultation with it how to ensure the fulfilment of their obligations under the best possible conditions, in particular with the cooperation of the National Red Cross (Red Crescent, Red Lion and Sun) Societies.

If the Parties to the conflict deem it necessary to restrict family correspondence, such restrictions shall be confined to the compulsory use of standard forms containing twenty-five freely chosen words, and to the limitation of the number of these forms dispatched to one each month.

Art. 26. Each Party to the conflict shall facilitate enquiries made by members of families dispersed owing to the war, with the object of renewing contact with one another and of meeting, if possible. It shall encourage, in particular, the work of organizations engaged on this task provided they are acceptable to it and conform to its security regulations.

PART III

STATUS AND TREATMENT OF PROTECTED PERSONS

SECTION I

Provisions Common to the Territories of the Parties to the Conflict and to Occupied Territories Art. 27. Protected persons are entitled, in all circumstances, to respect for their persons, their honour, their family rights, their religious convictions and practices, and their manners and customs. They shall at all times be humanely treated, and shall be protected especially against all acts of violence or threats thereof and against insults and public curiosity.

Women shall be especially protected against any attack on their honour, in particular against rape, enforced prostitution, or any form of indecent assault.

Without prejudice to the provisions relating to their state of health, age and sex, all protected persons shall be treated with the same consideration by the Party to the conflict in whose power they are, without any adverse distinction based, in particular, on race, religion or political opinion.

However, the Parties to the conflict may take such measures of control and security in regard to protected persons as may be necessary as a result of the war.

Art. 28. The presence of a protected person may not be used to render certain points or areas immune from military operations.

Art. 29. The Party to the conflict in whose hands protected persons may be, is responsible for the treatment accorded to them by its agents, irrespective of any individual responsibility which may be incurred.

Art. 30. Protected persons shall have every facility for making application to the Protecting Powers, the International Committee of the Red Cross, the National Red Cross (Red Crescent, Red Lion and Sun) Society of the country where they may be, as well as to any organization that might assist them.

These several organizations shall be granted all facilities for that purpose by the authorities, within the bounds set by military or security considerations. Apart from the visits of the delegates of the Protecting Powers and of the International Committee of the Red Cross, provided for by Article 143, the Detaining or Occupying Powers shall facilitate, as much as possible, visits to protected persons by the representatives of other organizations whose object is to give spiritual aid or material relief to such persons.

Art. 31. No physical or moral coercion shall be exercised against protected persons, in particular to obtain information from them or from third parties.

Art. 32. The High Contracting Parties specifically agree that each of them is prohibited from taking any measure of such a character as to cause the physical suffering or extermination of protected persons in their hands. This prohibition applies not only to murder, torture, corporal punishments, mutilation and medical or scientific experiments not necessitated by the medical treatment of a protected person, but also to any other measures of brutality whether applied by civilian or military agents.

Art. 33. No protected person may be punished for an offence he or she has not personally committed. Collective penalties and likewise all measures of intimidation or of terrorism are prohibited.

Pillage is prohibited.

Reprisals against protected persons and their property are prohibited.

Art. 34. The taking of hostages is prohibited.

SECTION II

Aliens in the Territory of a Party to the Conflict Art. 35. All protected persons who may desire to leave the territory at the outset of, or during a conflict, shall be entitled to do so, unless their departure is contrary to the national interests of the State. The applications of such persons to leave shall be decided in accordance with regularly established procedures and the decision shall be taken as rapidly as possible. Those persons permitted to leave may provide themselves with the necessary funds for their journey and take with them a reasonable amount of their effects and articles of personal use.

If any such person is refused permission to leave the territory, he shall be entitled to have refusal reconsidered, as soon as possible by an appropriate court or administrative board designated by the Detaining Power for that purpose.

Upon request, representatives of the Protecting Power shall, unless reasons of security prevent it, or the persons concerned object, be furnished with the reasons for refusal of any request for permission to leave the territory and be given, as expeditiously as possible, the names of all persons who have been denied permission to leave.

Art. 36. Departures permitted under the foregoing Article shall be carried out in satisfactory conditions as regards safety, hygiene, sanitation and food. All costs in connection therewith, from the point of exit in the territory of the Detaining Power, shall be borne by the country of destination, or, in the case of accommodation in a neutral country, by the Power whose nationals are benefited. The practical details of such movements may, if necessary, be settled by special agreements between the Powers concerned.

The foregoing shall not prejudice such special agreements as may be concluded between Parties to the conflict concerning the exchange and repatriation of their nationals in enemy hands.

Art. 37. Protected persons who are confined pending proceedings or subject to a sentence involving loss of liberty, shall during their confinement be humanely treated.

As soon as they are released, they may ask to leave the territory in conformity with the foregoing Articles.

Art. 38. With the exception of special measures authorized by the present Convention, in particularly by Article 27 and 41 thereof, the situation of protected persons shall continue to be regulated, in principle, by the provisions concerning aliens in time of peace. In any case, the following rights shall be granted to them: (1) they shall be enabled to receive the individual or collective relief that may be sent to them. (2) they shall, if their state of health so requires, receive medical attention and hospital treatment to the same extent as the nationals of the State concerned. (3) they shall be allowed to practise their religion and to receive spiritual assistance from ministers of their faith. (4) if they reside in an area particularly exposed to the dangers of war, they shall be authorized to move from that area to the same extent as the nationals of the State concerned. (5) children under fifteen years, pregnant women and mothers of children under seven years shall benefit by any preferential treatment to the same extent as the nationals of the State concerned.

Art. 39. Protected persons who, as a result of the war, have lost their gainful employment, shall be granted the opportunity to find paid employment. That opportunity shall, subject to security considerations and to the provisions of Article 40, be equal to that enjoyed by the nationals of the Power in whose territory they are.

Where a Party to the conflict applies to a protected person methods of control which result in his being unable to support himself, and especially if such a person is prevented for reasons of security from finding paid employment on reasonable conditions, the said Party shall ensure his support and that of his dependents.

Protected persons may in any case receive allowances from their home country, the Protecting Power, or the relief societies referred to in Article 30. Art. 40. Protected persons may be compelled to work only to the same extent as nationals of the Party to the conflict in whose territory they are.

If protected persons are of enemy nationality, they may only be compelled to do work which is normally necessary to ensure the feeding, sheltering, clothing, transport and health of human beings and which is not directly related to the conduct of military operations.

In the cases mentioned in the two preceding paragraphs, protected persons compelled to work shall have the benefit of the same working conditions and of the same safeguards as national workers in particular as regards wages, hours of labour, clothing and equipment, previous training and compensation for occupational accidents and diseases.

If the above provisions are infringed, protected persons shall be allowed to exercise their right of complaint in accordance with Article 30.

Art. 41. Should the Power, in whose hands protected persons may be, consider the measures of control mentioned in the present Convention to be inadequate, it may not have recourse to any other measure of control more severe than that of assigned residence or internment, in accordance with the provisions of Articles 42 and 43.

In applying the provisions of Article 39, second paragraph, to the cases of persons required to leave their usual places of residence by virtue of a decision placing them in assigned residence, by virtue of a decision placing them in assigned residence, elsewhere, the Detaining Power shall be guided as closely as possible by the standards of welfare set forth in Part III, Section IV of this Convention.

Art. 42. The internment or placing in assigned residence of protected persons may be ordered only if the security of the Detaining Power makes it absolutely necessary.

If any person, acting through the representatives of the Protecting Power, voluntarily demands internment, and if his situation renders this step necessary, he shall be interned by the Power in whose hands he may be.

Art. 43. Any protected person who has been interned or placed in assigned residence shall be entitled to have such action reconsidered as soon as possible by an appropriate court or administrative board designated by the Detaining Power for that purpose. If the internment or placing in assigned residence is maintained, the court or administrative board shall periodically, and at least twice yearly, give consideration to his or her case, with a view to the favourable amendment of the initial decision, if circumstances permit.

Unless the protected persons concerned object, the Detaining Power shall, as rapidly as possible, give the Protecting Power the names of any protected persons who have been interned or subjected to assigned residence, or who have been released from internment or assigned residence. The decisions of the courts or boards mentioned in the first paragraph of the present Article shall also, subject to the same conditions, be notified as rapidly as possible to the Protecting Power.

Art. 44. In applying the measures of control mentioned in the present Convention, the Detaining Power shall not treat as enemy aliens exclusively on the basis of their nationality de jure of an enemy State, refugees who do not, in fact, enjoy the protection of any government.

Art. 45. Protected persons shall not be transferred to a Power which is not a party to the Convention.

This provision shall in no way constitute an obstacle to the repatriation of protected persons, or to their return to their country of residence after the cessation of hostilities.

Protected persons may be transferred by the Detaining Power only to a Power which is a party to the present Convention and after the Detaining Power has satisfied itself of the willingness and ability of such transferee Power to apply the present Convention. If protected persons are transferred under such circumstances, responsibility for the application of the present Convention rests on the Power accepting them, while they are in its custody. Nevertheless, if that Power fails to carry out the provisions of the present Convention in any important respect, the Power by which the protected persons were transferred shall, upon being so notified by the Protecting Power, take effective measures to correct the situation or shall request the return of the protected persons. Such request must be complied with.

In no circumstances shall a protected person be transferred to a country where he or she may have reason to fear persecution for his or her political opinions or religious beliefs.

The provisions of this Article do not constitute an obstacle to the extradition, in pursuance of extradition treaties concluded before the outbreak of hostilities, of protected persons accused of offences against ordinary criminal law.

Art. 46. In so far as they have not been previously withdrawn, restrictive measures taken regarding protected persons shall be cancelled as soon as possible after the close of hostilities.

Restrictive measures affecting their property shall be cancelled, in accordance with the law of the Detaining Power, as soon as possible after the close of hostilities.

SECTION III

Occupied Territories Art. 47. Protected persons who are in occupied territory shall not be deprived, in any case or in any manner whatsoever, of the benefits of the present Convention by any change introduced, as the result of the occupation of a territory, into the institutions or government of the said territory, nor by any agreement concluded between the authorities of the occupied territories and the Occupying Power, nor by any annexation by the latter of the whole or part of the occupied territory.

Art. 48. Protected persons who are not nationals of the Power whose territory is occupied, may avail themselves of the right to leave the territory subject to the provisions of Article 35, and decisions thereon shall be taken in accordance with the procedure which the Occupying Power shall establish in accordance with the said Article.

Art. 49. Individual or mass forcible transfers, as well as deportations of protected persons from occupied territory to the territory of the Occupying Power or to that of any other country, occupied or not, are prohibited, regardless of their motive.

Nevertheless, the Occupying Power may undertake total or partial evacuation of a given area if the security of the population or imperative military reasons so demand. Such evacuations may not involve the displacement of protected persons outside the bounds of the occupied territory except when for material reasons it is impossible to avoid such displacement. Persons thus evacuated shall be transferred back to their homes as soon as hostilities in the area in question have ceased.

The Occupying Power undertaking such transfers or evacuations shall ensure, to the greatest practicable extent, that proper accommodation is provided to receive the protected persons, that the removals are effected in satisfactory conditions of hygiene, health, safety and nutrition, and that members of the same family are not separated.

The Protecting Power shall be informed of any transfers and evacuations as soon as they have taken place.

The Occupying Power shall not detain protected persons in an area particularly exposed to the dangers of war unless the security of the population or imperative military reasons so demand.

The Occupying Power shall not deport or transfer parts of its own civilian population into the territory it occupies.

Art. 50. The Occupying Power shall, with the co-operation of the national and local authorities, facilitate the proper working of all institutions devoted to the care and education of children.

The Occupying Power shall take all necessary steps to facilitate the identification of children and the registration of their parentage. It may not, in any case, change their personal status, nor enlist them in formations or organizations subordinate to it.

Should the local institutions be inadequate for the purpose, the Occupying Power shall make arrangements for the maintenance and education, if possible by persons of their own nationality, language and religion, of children who are orphaned or separated from their parents as a result of the war and who cannot be adequately cared for by a near relative or friend.

A special section of the Bureau set up in accordance with Article 136 shall be responsible for taking all necessary steps to identify children whose identity is in doubt. Particulars of their parents or other near relatives should always be recorded if available.

The Occupying Power shall not hinder the application of any preferential measures in regard to food, medical care and protection against the effects of war which may have been adopted prior to the occupation in favour of children under fifteen years, expectant mothers, and mothers of children under seven years.

Art. 51. The Occupying Power may not compel protected persons to serve in its armed or auxiliary forces. No pressure or propaganda which aims at securing voluntary enlistment is permitted.

The Occupying Power may not compel protected persons to work unless they are over eighteen years of age, and then only on work which is necessary either for the needs of the army of occupation, or for the public utility services, or for the feeding, sheltering, clothing, transportation or health of the population of the occupied country. Protected persons may not be compelled to undertake any work which would involve them in the obligation of taking part in military operations. The Occupying Power may not compel protected persons to employ forcible means to ensure the security of the installations where they are performing compulsory labour.

The work shall be carried out only in the occupied territory where the persons whose services have been requisitioned are. Every such person shall, so far as possible, be kept in his usual place of employment. Workers shall be paid a fair wage and the work shall be proportionate to their physical and intellectual capacities. The legislation in force in the occupied country concerning working conditions, and safeguards as regards, in particular, such matters as wages, hours of work, equipment, preliminary training and compensation for occupational accidents and diseases, shall be applicable to the protected persons assigned to the work referred to in this Article.

In no case shall requisition of labour lead to a mobilization of workers in an organization of a military or semi-military character.

Art. 52. No contract, agreement or regulation shall impair the right of any worker, whether voluntary or not and wherever he may be, to apply to the representatives of the Protecting Power in order to request the said Power's intervention.

All measures aiming at creating unemployment or at restricting the opportunities offered to workers in an occupied territory, in order to induce them to work for the Occupying Power, are prohibited.

Art. 53. Any destruction by the Occupying Power of real or personal property belonging individually or collectively to private persons, or to the State, or to other public authorities, or to social or cooperative organizations, is prohibited, except where such destruction is rendered absolutely necessary by military operations.

Art. 54. The Occupying Power may not alter the status of public officials or judges in the occupied territories, or in any way apply sanctions to or take any measures of coercion or discrimination against them, should they abstain from fulfilling their functions for reasons of conscience.

This prohibition does not prejudice the application of the second paragraph of Article 51. It does not affect the right of the Occupying Power to remove public officials from their posts.

Art. 55. To the fullest extent of the means available to it, the Occupying Power has the duty of ensuring the food and medical supplies of the population; it should, in particular, bring in the necessary foodstuffs, medical stores and other articles if the resources of the occupied territory are inadequate.

The Occupying Power may not requisition foodstuffs, articles or medical supplies available in the occupied territory, except for use by the occupation forces and administration personnel, and then only if the requirements of the civilian population have been taken into account. Subject to the provisions of other international Conventions, the Occupying Power shall make arrangements to ensure that fair value is paid for any requisitioned goods.

The Protecting Power shall, at any time, be at liberty to verify the state of the food and medical supplies in occupied territories, except where temporary restrictions are made necessary by imperative military requirements.

Art. 56. To the fullest extent of the means available to it, the public Occupying Power has the duty of ensuring and maintaining, with the cooperation of national and local authorities, the medical and hospital establishments and services, public health and hygiene in the occupied territory, with particular reference to the adoption and application of the prophylactic and preventive measures necessary to combat the spread of contagious diseases and epidemics. Medical personnel of all categories shall be allowed to carry out their duties. If new hospitals are set up in occupied territory and if the competent organs of the occupied State are not operating there, the occupying authorities shall, if necessary, grant them the recognition provided for in Article 18. In similar circumstances, the occupying authorities shall also grant recognition to hospital personnel and transport vehicles under the provisions of Articles 20 and 21.

In adopting measures of health and hygiene and in their implementation, the Occupying Power shall take into consideration the moral and ethical susceptibilities of the population of the occupied territory.

Art. 57. The Occupying Power may requisition civilian hospitals of hospitals only temporarily and only in cases of urgent necessity for the care of military wounded and sick, and then on condition that suitable arrangements are made in due time for the care and treatment of the patients and for the needs of the civilian population for hospital accommodation.

The material and stores of civilian hospitals cannot be requisitioned so long as they are necessary for the needs of the civilian population.

Art. 58. The Occupying Power shall permit ministers of religion to give spiritual assistance to the members of their religious communities.

The Occupying Power shall also accept consignments of books and articles required for religious needs and shall facilitate their distribution in occupied territory.

Art. 59. If the whole or part of the population of an occupied territory is inadequately supplied, the Occupying Power shall agree to relief schemes on behalf of the said population, and shall facilitate them by all the means at its disposal.

Such schemes, which may be undertaken either by States or by impartial humanitarian organizations such as the International Committee of the Red Cross, shall consist, in particular, of the provision of consignments of foodstuffs, medical supplies and clothing.

All Contracting Parties shall permit the free passage of these consignments and shall guarantee their protection.

A Power granting free passage to consignments on their way to territory occupied by an adverse Party to the conflict shall, however, have the right to search the consignments, to regulate their passage according to prescribed times and routes, and to be reasonably satisfied through the Protecting Power that these consignments are to be used for the relief of the needy population and are not to be used for the benefit of the Occupying Power.

Art. 60. Relief consignments shall in no way relieve the Occupying Power of any of its responsibilities under Articles 55, 56 and 59. The Occupying Power shall in no way whatsoever divert relief consignments from the purpose for which they are intended, except in cases of urgent necessity, in the interests of the population of the occupied territory and with the consent of the Protecting Power.

Art. 61. The distribution of the relief consignments referred to in the foregoing Articles shall be carried out with the cooperation and under the supervision of the Protecting Power. This duty may also be delegated, by agreement between the Occupying Power and the Protecting Power, to a neutral Power, to the International Committee of the Red Cross or to any other impartial humanitarian body.

Such consignments shall be exempt in occupied territory from all charges, taxes or customs duties unless these are necessary in the interests of the economy of the territory. The Occupying Power shall facilitate the rapid distribution of these consignments.

All Contracting Parties shall endeavour to permit the transit and transport, free of charge, of such relief consignments on their way to occupied territories.

Art. 62. Subject to imperative reasons of security, protected persons in occupied territories shall be permitted to receive the individual relief consignments sent to them.

Art. 63. Subject to temporary and exceptional measures imposed for urgent reasons of security by the Occupying Power:

(a) recognized National Red Cross (Red Crescent, Red Lion and Sun) Societies shall be able to pursue their activities in accordance with Red Cross principles, as defined by the International Red Cross Conferences. Other relief societies shall be permitted to continue their humanitarian activities under similar conditions; (b) the Occupying Power may not require any changes in the personnel or structure of these societies, which would prejudice the aforesaid activities.

The same principles shall apply to the activities and personnel of special organizations of a non-military character, which already exist or which may be established, for the purpose of ensuring the living conditions of the civilian population by the maintenance of the essential public utility services, by the distribution of relief and by the organization of rescues.

Art. 64. The penal laws of the occupied territory shall remain in force, with the exception that they may be repealed or suspended by the Occupying Power in cases where they constitute a threat to its security or an obstacle to the application of the present Convention.

Subject to the latter consideration and to the necessity for ensuring the effective administration of justice, the tribunals of the occupied territory shall continue to function in respect of all offences covered by the said laws. The Occupying Power may, however, subject the population of the occupied territory to provisions which are essential to enable the Occupying Power to fulfil its obligations under the present Convention, to maintain the orderly government of the territory, and to ensure the security of the Occupying Power, of the members and property of the occupying forces or administration, and likewise of the establishments and lines of communication used by them. Art. 65. The penal provisions enacted by the Occupying Power shall not come into force before they have been published and brought to the knowledge of the inhabitants in their own language. The effect of these penal provisions shall not be retroactive.

Art. 66. In case of a breach of the penal provisions promulgated by it by virtue of the second paragraph of Article 64 the Occupying Power may hand over the accused to its properly constituted, non-political military courts, on condition that the said courts sit in the occupied country. Courts of appeal shall preferably sit in the occupied country.

Art. 67. The courts shall apply only those provisions of law which were applicable prior to the offence, and which are in accordance with general principles of law, in particular the principle that the penalty shall be proportionate to the offence. They shall take into consideration the fact the accused is not a national of the Occupying Power.

Art. 68. Protected persons who commit an offence which is solely intended to harm the Occupying Power, but which does not constitute an attempt on the life or limb of members of the occupying forces or administration, nor a grave collective danger, nor seriously damage the property of the occupying forces or administration or the installations used by them, shall be liable to internment or simple imprisonment, provided the duration of such internment or imprisonment is proportionate to the offence committed. Furthermore, internment or imprisonment shall, for such offences, be the only measure adopted for depriving protected persons of liberty. The courts provided for under Article 66 of the present Convention may at their discretion convert a sentence of imprisonment to one of internment for the same period.

The penal provisions promulgated by the Occupying Power in accordance with Articles 64 and 65 may impose the death penalty on a protected person only in cases where the person is guilty of espionage, of serious acts of sabotage against the military installations of the Occupying Power or of intentional offences which have caused the death of one or more persons, provided that such offences were punishable by death under the law of the occupied territory in force before the occupation began.

The death penalty may not be pronounced on a protected person unless the attention of the court has been particularly called to the fact that since the accused is not a national of the Occupying Power, he is not bound to it by any duty of allegiance.

In any case, the death penalty may not be pronounced on a protected person who was under eighteen years of age at the time of the offence.

Art. 69. In all cases the duration of the period during which a protected person accused of an offence is under arrest awaiting trial or punishment shall be deducted from any period of imprisonment of awarded.

Art. 70. Protected persons shall not be arrested, prosecuted or convicted by the Occupying Power for acts committed or for opinions expressed before the occupation, or during a temporary interruption thereof, with the exception of breaches of the laws and customs of war.

Nationals of the occupying Power who, before the outbreak of hostilities, have sought refuge in the territory of the occupied State, shall not be arrested, prosecuted, convicted or deported from the occupied territory, except for offences committed after the outbreak of hostilities, or for offences under common law committed before the outbreak of hostilities which, according to the law of the occupied State, would have justified extradition in time of peace.

Art. 71. No sentence shall be pronounced by the competent courts of the Occupying Power except after a regular trial.

Accused persons who are prosecuted by the Occupying Power shall be promptly informed, in writing, in a language which they understand, of the particulars of the charges preferred against them, and shall be brought to trial as rapidly as possible. The Protecting Power shall be informed of all proceedings instituted by the Occupying Power against protected persons in respect of charges involving the death penalty or imprisonment for two years or more; it shall be enabled, at any time, to obtain information regarding the state of such proceedings. Furthermore, the Protecting Power shall be entitled, on request, to be furnished with all particulars of these and of any other proceedings instituted by the Occupying Power against protected persons.

The notification to the Protecting Power, as provided for in the second paragraph above, shall be sent immediately, and shall in any case reach the Protecting Power three weeks before the date of the first hearing. Unless, at the opening of the trial, evidence is submitted that the provisions of this Article are fully complied with, the trial shall not proceed. The notification shall include the following particulars: (a) description of the accused; (b) place of residence or detention; (c) specification of the charge or charges (with mention of the penal provisions under which it is brought); (d) designation of the court which will hear the case; (e) place and date of the first hearing.

Art. 72. Accused persons shall have the right to present evidence necessary to their defence and may, in particular, call witnesses. They shall have the right to be assisted by a qualified advocate or counsel of their own choice, who shall be able to visit them freely and shall enjoy the necessary facilities for preparing the defence.

Failing a choice by the accused, the Protecting Power may provide him with an advocate or counsel. When an accused person has to meet a serious charge and the Protecting Power is not functioning, the Occupying Power, subject to the consent of the accused, shall provide an advocate or counsel.

Accused persons shall, unless they freely waive such assistance, be aided by an interpreter, both during preliminary investigation and during the hearing in court. They shall have at any time the right to object to the interpreter and to ask for his replacement.

Art. 73. A convicted person shall have the right of appeal provided for by the laws applied by the court. He shall be fully informed of his right to appeal or petition and of the time limit within which he may do so.

The penal procedure provided in the present Section shall apply, as far as it is applicable, to appeals. Where the laws applied by the Court make no provision for appeals, the convicted person shall have the right to petition against the finding and sentence to the competent authority of the Occupying Power.

Art. 74. Representatives of the Protecting Power shall have the right to attend the trial of any protected person, unless the hearing has, as an exceptional measure, to be held in camera in the interests of the security of the Occupying Power, which shall then notify the Protecting Power. A notification in respect of the date and place of trial shall be sent to the Protecting Power.

Any judgement involving a sentence of death, or imprisonment for two years or more, shall be communicated, with the relevant grounds, as rapidly as possible to the Protecting Power. The notification shall contain a reference to the notification made under Article 71 and, in the case of sentences of imprisonment, the name of the place where the sentence is to be served. A record of judgements other than those referred to above shall be kept by the court and shall be open to inspection by representatives of the Protecting Power. Any period allowed for appeal in the case of sentences involving the death penalty, or imprisonment of two years or more, shall not run until notification of judgement has been received by the Protecting Power.

Art. 75. In no case shall persons condemned to death be deprived of the right of petition for pardon or reprieve.

No death sentence shall be carried out before the expiration of a period of a least six months from the date of receipt by the Protecting Power of the notification of the final judgment confirming such death sentence, or of an order denying pardon or reprieve.

The six months period of suspension of the death sentence herein prescribed may be reduced in individual cases in circumstances of grave emergency involving an organized threat to the security of the Occupying Power or its forces, provided always that the Protecting Power is notified of such reduction and is given reasonable time and opportunity to make representations to the competent occupying authorities in respect of such death sentences.

Art. 76. Protected persons accused of offences shall be detained in the occupied country, and if convicted they shall serve their sentences therein. They shall, if possible, be separated from other detainees and shall enjoy conditions of food and hygiene which will be sufficient to keep them in good health, and which will be at least equal to those obtaining in prisons in the occupied country. They shall receive the medical attention required by their state of health. They shall also have the right to receive any spiritual assistance which they may require.

Women shall be confined in separate quarters and shall be under the direct supervision of women.

Proper regard shall be paid to the special treatment due to minors. Protected persons who are detained shall have the right to be visited by delegates of the Protecting Power and of the International Committee of the Red Cross, in accordance with the provisions of Article 143.

Such persons shall have the right to receive at least one relief parcel monthly.

Art. 77. Protected persons who have been accused of offences or convicted by the courts in occupied territory, shall be handed over at the close of occupation, with the relevant records, to the authorities of the liberated territory.

Art. 78. If the Occupying Power considers it necessary, for imperative reasons of security, to take safety measures concerning protected persons, it may, at the most, subject them to assigned residence or to internment.

Decisions regarding such assigned residence or internment shall be made according to a regular procedure to be prescribed by the Occupying Power in accordance with the provisions of the present Convention. This procedure shall include the right of appeal for the parties concerned. Appeals shall be decided with the least possible delay. In the event of the decision being upheld, it shall be subject to periodical review, if possible every six months, by a competent body set up by the said Power.

Protected persons made subject to assigned residence and thus required to leave their homes shall enjoy the full benefit of Article 39 of the present Convention.

SECTION IV
Regulations for the Treatment of Internees

CHAPTER I

General Provisions Art. 79. The Parties to the conflict shall not intern protected persons, except in accordance with the provisions of Articles 41, 42, 43, 68 and 78.

Art. 80. Internees shall retain their full civil capacity and shall exercise such attendant rights as may be compatible with their status.

Art. 81. Parties to the conflict who intern protected persons shall be bound to provide free of charge for their maintenance, and to grant them also the medical attention required by their state of health.

No deduction from the allowances, salaries or credits due to the internees shall be made for the repayment of these costs.

The Detaining Power shall provide for the support of those dependent on the internees, if such dependents are without adequate means of support or are unable to earn a living.

Art. 82. The Detaining Power shall, as far as possible, accommodate the internees according to their nationality, language and customs. Internees who are nationals of the same country shall not be separated merely because they have different languages.

Throughout the duration of their internment, members of the same family, and in particular parents and children, shall be lodged together in the same place of internment, except when separation of a temporary nature is necessitated for reasons of employment or health or for the purposes of enforcement of the provisions of Chapter IX of the present Section. Internees may request that their children who are left at liberty without parental care shall be interned with them.

Wherever possible, interned members of the same family shall be housed in the same premises and given separate accommodation from other internees, together with facilities for leading a proper family life.

CHAPTER II

Places of Internment Art. 83. The Detaining Power shall not set up places of internment in areas particularly exposed to the dangers of war.

The Detaining Power shall give the enemy Powers, through the intermediary of the Protecting Powers, all useful information regarding the geographical location of places of internment.

Whenever military considerations permit, internment camps shall be indicated by the letters IC, placed so as to be clearly visible in the daytime from the air. The Powers concerned may, however, agree upon any other system of marking. No place other than an internment camp shall be marked as such.

Art. 84. Internees shall be accommodated and administered separately from prisoners of war and from persons deprived of liberty for any other reason.

Art. 85. The Detaining Power is bound to take all necessary and possible measures to ensure that protected persons shall, from the outset of their internment, be accommodated in buildings or quarters which afford every possible safeguard as regards hygiene and health, and provide efficient protection against the rigours of the climate and the effects of the war. In no case shall permanent places of internment be situated in unhealthy areas or in districts, the climate of which is injurious to the internees. In all cases where the district, in which a protected person is temporarily interned, is an unhealthy area or has a climate which is harmful to his health, he shall be removed to a more suitable place of internment as rapidly as circumstances permit.

The premises shall be fully protected from dampness, adequately heated and lighted, in particular between dusk and lights out. The sleeping quarters shall be sufficiently spacious and well ventilated, and the internees shall have suitable bedding and sufficient blankets, account being taken of the climate, and the age, sex, and state of health of the internees.

Internees shall have for their use, day and night, sanitary conveniences which conform to the rules of hygiene, and are constantly maintained in a state of cleanliness. They shall be provided with sufficient water and soap for their daily personal toilet and for washing their personal laundry; installations and facilities necessary for this purpose shall be granted to them. Showers or baths shall also be available. The necessary time shall be set aside for washing and for cleaning.

Whenever it is necessary, as an exceptional and temporary measure, to accommodate women internees who are not members of a family unit in the same place of internment as men, the provision of separate sleeping quarters and sanitary conveniences for the use of such women internees shall be obligatory. Art. 86. The Detaining Power shall place at the disposal of interned persons, of whatever denomination, premises suitable for the holding of their religious services.

Art. 87. Canteens shall be installed in every place of internment, except where other suitable facilities are available. Their purpose shall be to enable internees to make purchases, at prices not higher than local market prices, of foodstuffs and articles of everyday use, including soap and tobacco, such as would increase their personal well-being and comfort.

Profits made by canteens shall be credited to a welfare fund to be set up for each place of internment, and administered for the benefit of the internees attached to such place of internment. The Internee Committee provided for in Article 102 shall have the right to check the management of the canteen and of the said fund.

When a place of internment is closed down, the balance of the welfare fund shall be transferred to the welfare fund of a place of internment for internees of the same nationality, or, if such a place does not exist, to a central welfare fund which shall be administered for the benefit of all internees remaining in the custody of the Detaining Power. In case of a general release, the said profits shall be kept by the Detaining Power, subject to any agreement to the contrary between the Powers concerned.

Art. 88. In all places of internment exposed to air raids and other hazards of war, shelters adequate in number and structure to ensure the necessary protection shall be installed. In case of alarms, the measures internees shall be free to enter such shelters as quickly as possible, excepting those who remain for the protection of their quarters against the aforesaid hazards. Any protective measures taken in favour of the population shall also apply to them. All due precautions must be taken in places of internment against the danger of fire.

CHAPTER III

Food and Clothing Art. 89. Daily food rations for internees shall be sufficient in quantity, quality and variety to keep internees in a good state of health and prevent the development of nutritional deficiencies. Account shall also be taken of the customary diet of the internees.

Internees shall also be given the means by which they can prepare for themselves any additional food in their possession.

Sufficient drinking water shall be supplied to internees. The use of tobacco shall be permitted.

Internees who work shall receive additional rations in proportion to the kind of labour which they perform.

Expectant and nursing mothers and children under fifteen years of age, shall be given additional food, in proportion to their physiological needs.

Art. 90. When taken into custody, internees shall be given all facilities to provide themselves with the necessary clothing, footwear and change of underwear, and later on, to procure further supplies if required. Should any internees not have sufficient clothing, account being taken of the climate, and be unable to procure any, it shall be provided free of charge to them by the Detaining Power.

The clothing supplied by the Detaining Power to internees and the outward markings placed on their own clothes shall not be ignominious nor expose them to ridicule.

Workers shall receive suitable working outfits, including protective clothing, whenever the nature of their work so requires.

CHAPTER IV

Hygiene and Medical Attention Art. 91. Every place of internment shall have an adequate infirmary, under the direction of a qualified doctor, where internees may have the attention they require, as well as appropriate diet. Isolation wards shall be set aside for cases of contagious or mental diseases.

Maternity cases and internees suffering from serious diseases, or whose condition requires special treatment, a surgical operation or hospital care, must be admitted to any institution where adequate treatment can be given and shall receive care not inferior to that provided for the general population. Internees shall, for preference, have the attention of medical personnel of their own nationality.

Internees may not be prevented from presenting themselves to the medical authorities for examination. The medical authorities of the Detaining Power shall, upon request, issue to every internee who has undergone treatment an official certificate showing the nature of his illness or injury, and the duration and nature of the treatment given. A duplicate of this certificate shall be forwarded to the Central Agency provided for in Article 140.

Treatment, including the provision of any apparatus necessary for the maintenance of internees in good health, particularly dentures and other artificial appliances and spectacles, shall be free of charge to the internee.

Art. 92. Medical inspections of internees shall be made at least once a month. Their purpose shall be, in particular, to supervise the general state of health, nutrition and cleanliness of internees, and to detect contagious diseases, especially tuberculosis, malaria, and venereal diseases. Such inspections shall include, in particular, the checking of weight of each internee and, at least once a year, radioscopic examination.

CHAPTER V

Religious, Intellectual and Physical Activities Art. 93. Internees shall enjoy complete latitude in the exercise of their religious duties, including attendance at the services of their faith, on condition that they comply with the disciplinary routine prescribed by the detaining authorities.

Ministers of religion who are interned shall be allowed to minister freely to the members of their community. For this purpose the Detaining Power shall ensure their equitable allocation amongst the various places of internment in which there are internees speaking the same language and belonging to the same religion. Should such ministers be too few in number, the Detaining Power shall provide them with the necessary facilities, including means of transport, for moving from one place to another, and they shall be authorized to visit any internees who are in hospital. Ministers of religion shall be at liberty to correspond on matters concerning their ministry with the religious authorities in the country of detention and, as far as possible, with the international religious organizations of their faith. Such correspondence shall not be considered as forming a part of the quota mentioned in Article 107. It shall, however, be subject to the provisions of Article 112.

When internees do not have at their disposal the assistance of ministers of their faith, or should these latter be too few in number, the local religious authorities of the same faith may appoint, in agreement with the Detaining Power, a minister of the internees' faith or, if such a course is feasible from a denominational point of view, a minister of similar religion or a qualified layman. The latter shall enjoy the facilities granted to the ministry he has assumed. Persons so appointed shall comply with all regulations laid down by the Detaining Power in the interests of discipline and security.

Art. 94. The Detaining Power shall encourage intellectual, educational and recreational pursuits, sports and games amongst internees, whilst leaving them free to take part in them or not. It shall take all practicable measures to ensure the exercise thereof, in particular by providing suitable premises. All possible facilities shall be granted to internees to continue their studies or to take up new subjects. The education of children and young people shall be ensured; they shall be allowed to attend schools either within the place of internment or outside.

Internees shall be given opportunities for physical exercise, sports and outdoor games. For this purpose, sufficient open spaces shall be set aside in all places of internment. Special playgrounds shall be reserved for children and young people.

Art. 95. The Detaining Power shall not employ internees as workers, unless they so desire. Employment which, if undertaken under compulsion by a protected person not in internment, would involve a breach of Articles 40 or 51 of the present Convention, and employment on work which is of a degrading or humiliating character are in any case prohibited.

After a working period of six weeks, internees shall be free to give up work at any moment, subject to eight days' notice.

These provisions constitute no obstacle to the right of the Detaining Power to employ interned doctors, dentists and other medical personnel in their professional capacity on behalf of their fellow internees, or to employ internees for administrative and maintenance work in places of internment and to detail such persons for work in the kitchens or for other domestic tasks, or to require such persons to undertake duties connected with the protection of internees against aerial bombardment or other war risks. No internee may, however, be required to perform tasks for which he is, in the opinion of a medical officer, physically unsuited.

The Detaining Power shall take entire responsibility for all working conditions, for medical attention, for the payment of wages, and for ensuring that all employed internees receive compensation for occupational accidents and diseases. The standards prescribed for the said working conditions and for compensation shall be in accordance with the national laws and regulations, and with the existing practice; they shall in no case be inferior to those obtaining for work of the same nature in the same district. Wages for work done shall be determined on an equitable basis by special agreements between the internees, the Detaining Power, and, if the case arises, employers other than the Detaining Power to provide for free maintenance of internees and for the medical attention which their state of health may require. Internees permanently detailed for categories of work mentioned in the third paragraph of this Article, shall be paid fair wages by the Detaining Power. The working conditions and the scale of compensation for occupational accidents and diseases to internees, thus detailed, shall not be inferior to those applicable to work of the same nature in the same district.

Art. 96. All labour detachments shall remain part of and dependent upon a place of internment. The competent authorities of the Detaining Power and the commandant of a place of internment shall be responsible for the observance in a labour detachment of the provisions of the present Convention. The commandant shall keep an up-to-date list of the labour detachments subordinate to him and shall communicate it to the delegates of the Protecting Power, of the International Committee of the Red Cross and of other humanitarian organizations who may visit the places of internment.

CHAPTER VI

Personal Property and Financial Resources Art. 97. Internees shall be permitted to retain articles of personal use. Monies, cheques, bonds, etc., and valuables in their possession may not be taken from them except in accordance with established procedure. Detailed receipts shall be given therefore.

The amounts shall be paid into the account of every internee as provided for in Article 98. Such amounts may not be converted into any other currency unless legislation in force in the territory in which the owner is interned so requires or the internee gives his consent.

Articles which have above all a personal or sentimental value may not be taken away.

A woman internee shall not be searched except by a woman.

On release or repatriation, internees shall be given all articles, monies or other valuables taken from them during internment and shall receive in currency the balance of any credit to their accounts kept in accordance with Article 98, with the exception of any articles or amounts withheld by the Detaining Power by virtue of its legislation in force. If the property of an internee is so withheld, the owner shall receive a detailed receipt.

Family or identity documents in the possession of internees may not be taken away without a receipt being given. At no time shall internees be left without identity documents. If they have none, they shall be issued with special documents drawn up by the detaining authorities, which will serve as their identity papers until the end of their internment.

Internees may keep on their persons a certain amount of money, in cash or in the shape of purchase coupons, to enable them to make purchases.

Art. 98. All internees shall receive regular allowances, sufficient to enable them to purchase goods and articles, such as tobacco, toilet requisites, etc. Such allowances may take the form of credits or purchase coupons.

Furthermore, internees may receive allowances from the Power to which they owe allegiance, the Protecting Powers, the organizations which may assist them, or their families, as well as the income on their property in accordance with the law of the Detaining Power. The amount of allowances granted by the Power to which they owe allegiance shall be the same for each category of internees (infirm, sick, pregnant women, etc.) but may not be allocated by that Power or distributed by the Detaining Power on the basis of discriminations between internees which are prohibited by Article 27 of the present Convention.

The Detaining Power shall open a regular account for every internee, to which shall be credited the allowances named in the present Article, the wages earned and the remittances received, together with such sums taken from him as may be available under the legislation in force in the territory in which he is interned. Internees shall be granted all facilities consistent with the legislation in force in such territory to make remittances to their families and to other dependants. They may draw from their accounts the amounts necessary for their personal expenses, within the limits fixed by the Detaining Power. They shall at all times be afforded reasonable facilities for consulting and obtaining copies of their accounts. A statement of accounts shall be furnished to the Protecting Power, on request, and shall accompany the internee in case of transfer.

CHAPTER VII

Administration and Discipline Art. 99. Every place of internment shall be put under the authority of a responsible officer, chosen from the regular military forces or the regular civil administration of the Detaining Power. The officer in charge of the place of internment must have in his possession a copy of the present Convention in the official language, or one of the official languages, of his country and shall be responsible for its application. The staff in control of internees shall be instructed in the provisions of the present Convention and of the administrative measures adopted to ensure its application.

The text of the present Convention and the texts of special agreements concluded under the said Convention shall be posted inside the place of internment, in a language which the internees understand, or shall be in the possession of the Internee Committee.

Regulations, orders, notices and publications of every kind shall be communicated to the internees and posted inside the places of internment, in a language which they understand.

Every order and command addressed to internees individually must, likewise, be given in a language which they understand.

Art. 100. The disciplinary regime in places of internment shall be consistent with humanitarian principles, and shall in no circumstances include regulations imposing on internees any physical exertion dangerous to their health or involving physical or moral victimization. Identification by tattooing or imprinting signs or markings on the body, is prohibited.

In particular, prolonged standing and roll-calls, punishment drill, military drill and manoeuvres, or the reduction of food rations, are prohibited. Art. 101. Internees shall have the right to present to the authorities in whose power they are, any petition with regard to the conditions of internment to which they are subjected.

They shall also have the right to apply without restriction through the Internee Committee or, if they consider it necessary, direct to the representatives of the Protecting Power, in order to indicate to them any points on which they may have complaints to make with regard to the conditions of internment.

Such petitions and complaints shall be transmitted forthwith and without alteration, and even if the latter are recognized to be unfounded, they may not occasion any punishment.

Periodic reports on the situation in places of internment and as to the needs of the internees may be sent by the Internee Committees to the representatives of the Protecting Powers.

Art. 102. In every place of internment, the internees shall freely elect by secret ballot every six months, the members of a Committee empowered to represent them before the Detaining and the Protecting Powers, the International Committee of the Red Cross and any other organization which may assist them. The members of the Committee shall be eligible for re-election.

Internees so elected shall enter upon their duties after their election has been approved by the detaining authorities. The reasons for any refusals or dismissals shall be communicated to the Protecting Powers concerned.

Art. 103. The Internee Committees shall further the physical, spiritual and intellectual well-being of the internees.

In case the internees decide, in particular, to organize a system of mutual assistance amongst themselves, this organization would be within the competence of the Committees in addition to the special duties entrusted to them under other provisions of the present Convention.

Art. 104. Members of Internee Committees shall not be required to perform any other work, if the ac-complishment of their duties is rendered more difficult thereby.

Members of Internee Committees may appoint from amongst the internees such assistants as they may require. All material facilities shall be granted to them, particularly a certain freedom of movement necessary for the accomplishment of their duties (visits to labour detachments, receipt of supplies, etc.).

All facilities shall likewise be accorded to members of Internee Committees for communication by post and telegraph with the detaining authorities, the Protecting Powers, the International Committee of the Red Cross and their delegates, and with the organizations which give assistance to internees. Committee members in labour detachments shall enjoy similar facilities for communication with their Internee Committee in the principal place of internment. Such communications shall not be limited, nor considered as forming a part of the quota mentioned in Article 107.

Members of Internee Committees who are transferred shall be allowed a reasonable time to acquaint their successors with current affairs.

CHAPTER VIII

Relations with the Exterior Art. 105. Immediately upon interning protected persons, the Detaining Powers shall inform them, the Power to which they owe allegiance and their Protecting Power of the measures taken for executing the provisions of the present Chapter. The Detaining Powers shall likewise inform the Parties concerned of any subsequent modifications of such measures.

Art. 106. As soon as he is interned, or at the latest not more than one week after his arrival in a place of internment, and likewise in cases of sickness or transfer to another place of internment or to a hospital, every internee shall be enabled to send direct to his family, on the one hand, and to the Central Agency provided for by Article 140, on the other, an internment card similar, if possible, to the model annexed to the present Convention, informing his relatives of his detention, address and state of health. The said cards shall be forwarded as rapidly as possible and may not be delayed in any way.

Art. 107. Internees shall be allowed to send and receive letters and cards. If the Detaining Power deems it necessary to limit the number of letters and cards sent by each internee, the said number shall not be less than two letters and four cards monthly; these shall be drawn up so as to conform as closely as possible to the models annexed to the present Convention. If limitations must be placed on the correspondence addressed to internees, they may be ordered only by the Power to which such internees owe allegiance, possibly at the request of the Detaining Power. Such letters and cards must be conveyed with reasonable dispatch; they may not be delayed or retained for disciplinary reasons.

Internees who have been a long time without news, or who find it impossible to receive news from their relatives, or to give them news by the ordinary postal route, as well as those who are at a considerable distance from their homes, shall be allowed to send telegrams, the charges being paid by them in the currency at their disposal. They shall likewise benefit by this provision in cases which are recognized to be urgent.

As a rule, internees' mail shall be written in their own language. The Parties to the conflict may authorize correspondence in other languages.

Art. 108. Internees shall be allowed to receive, by post or by any other means, individual parcels or collective shipments containing in particular foodstuffs, clothing, medical supplies, as well as books and objects of a devotional, educational or recreational character which may meet their needs. Such shipments shall in no way free the Detaining Power from the obligations imposed upon it by virtue of the present Convention.

Should military necessity require the quantity of such shipments to be limited, due notice thereof shall be given to the Protecting Power and to the International Committee of the Red Cross, or to any other organization giving assistance to the internees and responsible for the forwarding of such shipments.

The conditions for the sending of individual parcels and collective shipments shall, if necessary, be the subject of special agreements between the Powers concerned, which may in no case delay the receipt by the internees of relief supplies. Parcels of clothing and foodstuffs may not include books. Medical relief supplies shall, as a rule, be sent in collective parcels.

Art. 109. In the absence of special agreements between Parties to the conflict regarding the conditions for the receipt and distribution of collective relief shipments, the regulations concerning collective relief which are annexed to the present Convention shall be applied.

The special agreements provided for above shall in no case restrict the right of Internee Committees to take possession of collective relief shipments intended for internees, to undertake their distribution and to dispose of them in the interests of the recipients. Nor shall such agreements restrict the right of representatives of the Protecting Powers, the International Committee of the Red Cross, or any other organization giving assistance to internees and responsible for the forwarding

of collective shipments, to supervise their distribution to the recipients.

Art. 110. An relief shipments for internees shall be exempt from import, customs and other dues.

All matter sent by mail, including relief parcels sent by parcel post and remittances of money, addressed from other countries to internees or dispatched by them through the post office, either direct or through the Information Bureaux provided for in Article 136 and the Central Information Agency provided for in Article 140, shall be exempt from all postal dues both in the countries of origin and destination and in intermediate countries. To this effect, in particular, the exemption provided by the Universal Postal Convention of 1947 and by the agreements of the Universal Postal Union in favour of civilians of enemy nationality detained in camps or civilian prisons, shall be extended to the other interned persons protected by the present Convention. The countries not signatory to the abovementioned agreements shall be bound to grant freedom from charges in the same circumstances.

The cost of transporting relief shipments which are intended for internees and which, by reason of their weight or any other cause, cannot be sent through the post office, shall be borne by the Detaining Power in all the territories under its control. Other Powers which are Parties to the present Convention shall bear the cost of transport in their respective territories.

Costs connected with the transport of such shipments, which are not covered by the above paragraphs, shall be charged to the senders.

The High Contracting Parties shall endeavour to reduce, so far as possible, the charges for telegrams sent by internees, or addressed to them.

Art. 111. Should military operations prevent the Powers concerned from fulfilling their obligation to ensure the conveyance of the mail and relief shipments provided for in Articles 106, 107, 108 and 113, the Protecting Powers concerned, the International Committee of the Red Cross or any other organization duly approved by the Parties to the conflict may undertake to ensure the conveyance of such shipments by suitable means (rail, motor vehicles, vessels or aircraft, etc.). For this purpose, the High Contracting Parties shall endeavour to supply them with such transport, and to allow its circulation, especially by granting the necessary safe-conducts.

Such transport may also be used to convey: (a) correspondence, lists and reports exchanged between the Central Information Agency referred to in Article 140 and the National Bureaux referred to in Article 136; (b) correspondence and reports relating to internees which the Protecting Powers, the International Committee of the Red Cross or any other organization assisting the internees exchange either with their own delegates or with the Parties to the conflict.

These provisions in no way detract from the right of any Party to the conflict to arrange other means of transport if it should so prefer, nor preclude the granting of safe-conducts, under mutually agreed conditions, to such means of transport.

The costs occasioned by the use of such means of transport shall be borne, in proportion to the importance of the shipments, by the Parties to the conflict whose nationals are benefited thereby.

Art. 112. The censoring of correspondence addressed to internees or dispatched by them shall be done as quickly as possible.

The examination of consignments intended for internees shall not be carried out under conditions that will expose the goods contained in them to deterioration. It shall be done in the presence of the addressee, or of a fellow-internee duly delegated by him. The delivery to internees of individual or collective consignments shall not be delayed under the pretext of difficulties of censorship.

Any prohibition of correspondence ordered by the Parties to the conflict either for military or political reasons, shall be only temporary and its duration shall be as short as possible.

Art. 113. The Detaining Powers shall provide all reasonable execution facilities for the transmission, through the Protecting Power or the Central Agency provided for in Article 140, or as otherwise required, of wills, powers of attorney, letters of authority, or any other documents intended for internees or dispatched by them.

In all cases the Detaining Powers shall facilitate the execution and authentication in due legal form of such documents on behalf of internees, in particular by allowing them to consult a lawyer.

Art. 114. The Detaining Power shall afford internees all facilities to enable them to manage their property, provided this is not incompatible with the conditions of internment and the law which is applicable. For this purpose, the said Power may give them permission to leave the place of internment in urgent cases and if circumstances allow.

Art. 115. In all cases where an internee is a party to proceedings in any court, the Detaining Power shall, if he so requests, cause the court to be informed of his detention and shall, within legal limits, ensure that all necessary steps are taken to prevent him from being in any way prejudiced, by reason of his internment, as regards the preparation and conduct of his case or as regards the execution of any judgment of the court.

Art. 116. Every internee shall be allowed to receive visitors, especially near relatives, at regular intervals and as frequently as possible.

As far as is possible, internees shall be permitted to visit their homes in urgent cases, particularly in cases of death or serious illness of relatives.

CHAPTER IX

Penal and Disciplinary Sanctions Art. 117. Subject to the provisions of the present Chapter, the laws in force in the territory in which they are detained will continue to apply to internees who commit offences during internment.

If general laws, regulations or orders declare acts committed by internees to be punishable, whereas the same acts are not punishable when committed by persons who are not internees, such acts shall entail disciplinary punishments only. No internee may be punished more than once for the same act, or on the same count.

Art. 118. The courts or authorities shall in passing sentence take as far as possible into account the fact that the defendant is not a national of the Detaining Power. They shall be free to reduce the penalty prescribed for the offence with which the internee is charged and shall not be obliged, to this end, to apply the minimum sentence prescribed.

Imprisonment in premises without daylight, and, in general, all forms of cruelty without exception are forbidden.

Internees who have served disciplinary or judicial sentences shall not be treated differently from other internees.

The duration of preventive detention undergone by an internee shall be deducted from any disciplinary or judicial penalty involving confinement to which he may be sentenced.

Internee Committees shall be informed of all judicial proceedings instituted against internees whom they represent, and of their result.

Art. 119. The disciplinary punishments applicable to internees shall be the following: (1) a fine which shall not exceed 50 per cent of the wages which the internee would otherwise receive under the provisions of Article 95 during a period of not more than thirty days. (2) discontinuance of privileges granted over and above the treatment provided for by the present Convention (3) fatigue duties, not exceeding two hours daily, in connection with the maintenance of the place of internment. (4) confinement.

In no case shall disciplinary penalties be inhuman, brutal or dangerous for the health of internees. Account shall be taken of the internee's age, sex and state of health.

The duration of any single punishment shall in no case exceed a maximum of thirty consecutive days, even if the internee is answerable for several breaches of discipline when his case is dealt with, whether such breaches are connected or not.

Art. 120. Internees who are recaptured after having escaped or when attempting to escape, shall be liable only to disciplinary punishment in respect of this act, even if it is a repeated offence.

Article 118, paragraph 3, notwithstanding, internees punished as a result of escape or attempt to escape, may be subjected to special surveillance, on condition that such surveillance does not affect the state of their health, that it is exercised in a place of internment and that it does not entail the abolition of any of the safeguards granted by the present Convention.

Internees who aid and abet an escape or attempt to escape, shall be liable on this count to disciplinary punishment only.

Art. 121. Escape, or attempt to escape, even if it is a repeated offence, shall not be deemed an aggravating circumstance in cases where an internee is prosecuted for offences committed during his escape.

The Parties to the conflict shall ensure that the competent authorities exercise leniency in deciding whether punishment inflicted for an offence shall be of a disciplinary or judicial nature, especially in respect of acts committed in connection with an escape, whether successful or not.

Art. 122. Acts which constitute offences against discipline shall be investigated immediately. This rule shall be applied, in particular, in cases of escape or attempt to escape. Recaptured internees shall be handed over to the competent authorities as soon as possible.

In cases of offences against discipline, confinement awaiting trial shall be reduced to an absolute minimum for all internees, and shall not exceed fourteen days. Its duration shall in any case be deducted from any sentence of confinement.

The provisions of Articles 124 and 125 shall apply to internees who are in confinement awaiting trial for offences against discipline.

Art. 123. Without prejudice to the competence of courts and higher authorities, disciplinary punishment may be ordered only by the commandant of the place of internment, or by a responsible officer or official who replaces him, or to whom he has delegated his disciplinary powers.

Before any disciplinary punishment is awarded, the accused internee shall be given precise information regarding the offences of which he is accused, and given an opportunity of explaining his conduct and of defending himself. He shall be permitted, in particular, to call witnesses and to have recourse, if necessary, to the services of a qualified interpreter. The decision shall be announced in the presence of the accused and of a member of the Internee Committee.

The period elapsing between the time of award of a disciplinary punishment and its execution shall not exceed one month.

When an internee is awarded a further disciplinary punishment, a period of at least three days shall elapse between the execution of any two of the punishments, if the duration of one of these is ten days or more.

A record of disciplinary punishments shall be maintained by the commandant of the place of internment and shall be open to inspection by representatives of the Protecting Power.

Art. 124. Internees shall not in any case be transferred to penitentiary establishments (prisons, penitentiaries, convict prisons, etc.) to undergo disciplinary punishment therein.

The premises in which disciplinary punishments are undergone shall conform to sanitary requirements: they shall in particular be provided with adequate bedding. Internees undergoing punishment shall be enabled to keep themselves in a state of cleanliness.

Women internees undergoing disciplinary punishment shall be confined in separate quarters from male internees and shall be under the immediate supervision of women.

Art. 125. Internees awarded disciplinary punishment shall be allowed to exercise and to stay in the open air at least two hours daily.

They shall be allowed, if they so request, to be present at the daily medical inspections. They shall receive the attention which their state of health requires and, if necessary, shall be removed to the infirmary of the place of internment or to a hospital.

They shall have permission to read and write, likewise to send and receive letters. Parcels and remittances of money, however, may be withheld from them until the completion of their punishment; such consignments shall meanwhile be entrusted to the Internee Committee, who will hand over to the infirmary the perishable goods contained in the parcels.

No internee given a disciplinary punishment may be deprived of the benefit of the provisions of Articles 107 and 143 of the present Convention.

Art. 126. The provisions of Articles 71 to 76 inclusive shall apply, by analogy, to proceedings against internees who are in the national territory of the Detaining Power.

CHAPTER X

Transfers of Internees Art. 127. The transfer of internees shall always be effected humanely. As a general rule, it shall be carried out by rail or other means of transport, and under conditions at least equal to those obtaining for the forces of the Detaining Power in their changes of station. If, as an exceptional measure, such removals have to be effected on foot, they may not take place unless the internees are in a fit state of health, and may not in any case expose them to excessive fatigue.

The Detaining Power shall supply internees during transfer with drinking water and food sufficient in quantity, quality and variety to maintain them in good health, and also with the necessary clothing, adequate shelter and the necessary medical attention. The Detaining Power shall take all suitable precautions to ensure their safety during transfer, and shall establish before their departure a complete list of all internees transferred.

Sick, wounded or infirm internees and maternity cases shall not be transferred if the journey would be seriously detrimental to them, unless their safety imperatively so demands.

If the combat zone draws close to a place of internment, the internees in the said place shall not be transferred unless their removal can be carried out in adequate conditions of safety, or unless they are exposed to greater risks by remaining on the spot than by being transferred.

When making decisions regarding the transfer of internees, the Detaining Power shall take their interests into account and, in particular, shall not do anything to increase the difficulties of repatriating them or returning them to their own homes.

Art. 128. In the event of transfer, internees shall be officially advised of their departure and of their new postal address. Such notification shall be given in time for them to pack their luggage and inform their next of kin. They shall be allowed to take with them their personal effects, and the correspondence and parcels which have arrived for them. The weight of such baggage may be limited if the conditions of transfer so require, but in no case to less than twenty-five kilograms per internee.

Mail and parcels addressed to their former place of internment shall be forwarded to them without delay.

The commandant of the place of internment shall take, in agreement with the Internee Committee, any measures needed to ensure the transport of the internees' community property and of the luggage the internees are unable to take with them in consequence of restrictions imposed by virtue of the second paragraph.

CHAPTER XI

Deaths Art. 129. The wills of internees shall be received for safe-keeping by the responsible authorities; and if the event of the death of an internee his will shall be transmitted without delay to a person whom he has previously designated.

Deaths of internees shall be certified in every case by a doctor, and a death certificate shall be made out, showing the causes of death and the conditions under which it occurred.

An official record of the death, duly registered, shall be drawn up in accordance with the procedure relating thereto in force in the territory where the place of internment is situated, and a duly certified copy of such record shall be transmitted without delay to the Protecting Power as well as to the Central Agency referred to in Article 140.

Art. 130. The detaining authorities shall ensure that internees who die while interned are honourably buried, if possible according to the rites of the religion to which they belonged and that their graves are respected, properly maintained, and marked in such a way that they can always be recognized. Deceased internees shall be buried in individual graves unless unavoidable circumstances require the use of collective graves. Bodies may be cremated only for imperative reasons of hygiene, on account of the religion of the deceased or in accordance with his expressed wish to this effect. In case of cremation, the fact shall be stated and the reasons given in the death certificate of the deceased. The ashes shall be retained for safe-keeping by the detaining authorities and shall be transferred as soon as possible to the next of kin on their request.

As soon as circumstances permit, and not later than the close of hostilities, the Detaining Power shall forward lists of graves of deceased internees to the Powers on whom deceased internees depended, through the Information Bureaux provided for in Article 136. Such lists shall include all particulars necessary for the identification of the deceased internees, as well as the exact location of their graves.

Art. 131. Every death or serious injury of an internee, caused or suspected to have been caused by a sentry, another internee or any other person, as well as any death the cause of which is unknown, shall be immediately followed by an official enquiry by the Detaining Power.

A communication on this subject shall be sent immediately to the Protecting Power. The evidence of any witnesses shall be taken, and a report including such evidence shall be prepared and forwarded to the said Protecting Power. If the enquiry indicates the guilt of one or more persons, the Detaining Power shall take all necessary steps to ensure the prosecution of the person or persons responsible.

CHAPTER XII

Release, Repatriation and Accommodation in Neutral Countries Art. 132. Each interned person shall be released by the Detaining Power as soon as the reasons which necessitated his internment no longer exist.

The Parties to the conflict shall, moreover, endeavour during the course of hostilities, to conclude agreements for the release, the repatriation, the return to places of residence or the accommodation in a neutral country of certain classes of internees, in particular children, pregnant women and mothers with infants and young children, wounded and sick, and internees who have been detained for a long time.

Art. 133. Internment shall cease as soon as possible after the close of hostilities.

Internees in the territory of a Party to the conflict against whom penal proceedings are pending for offences not exclusively subject to disciplinary penalties, may be detained until the close of such proceedings and, if circumstances require, until the completion of the penalty. The same shall apply to internees who have been previously sentenced to a punishment depriving them of liberty.

By agreement between the Detaining Power and the Powers concerned, committees may be set up after the close of hostilities, or of the occupation of territories, to search for dispersed internees.

Art. 134. The High Contracting Parties shall endeavour, upon the Repatriation close of hostilities or occupation, to ensure the return of all internees to their last place of residence, or to facilitate their residence repatriation.

Art. 135. The Detaining Power shall bear the expense of returning released internees to the places where they were residing when interned, or, if it took them into custody while they were in transit or on the high seas, the cost of completing their journey or of their return to their point of departure.

Where a Detaining Power refuses permission to reside in its territory to a released internee who previously had his permanent domicile therein, such Detaining Power shall pay the cost of the said internee's repatria-

tion. If, however, the internee elects to return to his country on his own responsibility or in obedience to the Government of the Power to which he owes allegiance, the Detaining Power need not pay the expenses of his journey beyond the point of his departure from its territory. The Detaining Power need not pay the cost of repatriation of an internee who was interned at his own request.

If internees are transferred in accordance with Article 45, the transferring and receiving Powers shall agree on the portion of the above costs to be borne by each.

The foregoing shall not prejudice such special agreements as may be concluded between Parties to the conflict concerning the exchange and repatriation of their nationals in enemy hands.

SECTION V

Information Bureaux and Central Agency Art. 136. Upon the outbreak of a conflict and in all cases of occupation, each of the Parties to the conflict shall establish an official Information Bureau responsible for receiving and transmitting information in respect of the protected persons who are in its power.

Each of the Parties to the conflict shall, within the shortest possible period, give its Bureau information of any measure taken by it concerning any protected persons who are kept in custody for more than two weeks, who are subjected to assigned residence or who are interned. It shall, furthermore, require its various departments concerned with such matters to provide the aforesaid Bureau promptly with information concerning all changes pertaining to these protected persons, as, for example, transfers, releases, repatriations, escapes, admittances to hospitals, births and deaths.

Art. 137. Each national Bureau shall immediately forward information concerning protected persons by the most rapid means to the Powers in whose territory they resided, through the intermediary of the Protecting Powers and likewise through the Central Agency provided for in Article 140. The Bureaux shall also reply to all enquiries which may be received regarding protected persons.

Information Bureaux shall transmit information concerning a protected person unless its transmission might be detrimental to the person concerned or to his or her relatives. Even in such a case, the information may not be withheld from the Central Agency which, upon being notified of the circumstances, will take the necessary precautions indicated in Article 140.

All communications in writing made by any Bureau shall be authenticated by a signature or a seal.

Art. 138. The information received by the national Bureau and transmitted by it shall be of such a character as to make it possible to identify the protected person exactly and to advise his next of kin quickly. The information in respect of each person shall include at least his surname, first names, place and date of birth, nationality last residence and distinguishing characteristics, the first name of the father and the maiden name of the mother, the date, place and nature of the action taken with regard to the individual, the address at which correspondence may be sent to him and the name and address of the person to be informed.

Likewise, information regarding the state of health of internees who are seriously ill or seriously wounded shall be supplied regularly and if possible every week.

Art. 139. Each national Information Bureau shall, furthermore, be responsible for collecting all personal valuables left by protected persons mentioned in Article 136, in particular those who have been repatriated or released, or who have escaped or died; it shall forward the said valuables to those concerned, either direct, or, if necessary, through the Central Agency. Such articles shall be sent by the Bureau in sealed packets which shall be accompanied by statements giving clear and full identity particulars of the person to whom the articles belonged, and by a complete list of the contents of the parcel. Detailed records shall be maintained of the receipt and dispatch of all such valuables.

Art. 140. A Central Information Agency for protected persons, in particular for internees, shall be created in a neutral country. The International Committee of the Red Cross shall, if it deems necessary, propose to the Powers concerned the organization of such an Agency, which may be the same as that provided for in Article 123 of the Geneva Convention relative to the Treatment of Prisoners of War of 12 August 1949.

The function of the Agency shall be to collect all information of the type set forth in Article 136 which it may obtain through official or private channels and to transmit it as rapidly as possible to the countries of origin or of residence of the persons concerned, except in cases where such transmissions might be detrimental to the persons whom the said information concerns, or to their relatives. It shall receive from the Parties to the conflict all reasonable facilities for effecting such transmissions.

The High Contracting Parties, and in particular those whose nationals benefit by the services of the Central Agency, are requested to give the said Agency the financial aid it may require.

The foregoing provisions shall in no way be interpreted as restricting the humanitarian activities of the International Committee of the Red Cross and of the relief Societies described in Article 142.

Art. 141. The national Information Bureaux and the Central Information Agency shall enjoy free postage for all mail, likewise the exemptions provided for in Article 110, and further, so far as possible, exemption from telegraphic charges or, at least, greatly reduced rates.

PART IV

EXECUTION OF THE CONVENTION

SECTION I

General Provisions Art. 142. Subject to the measures which the Detaining Powers may consider essential to ensure their security or to meet any other reasonable need, the representatives of religious organizations, relief societies, or any other organizations assisting the protected persons, shall receive from these Powers, for themselves or their duly accredited agents, all facilities for visiting the protected persons, for distributing relief supplies and material from any source, intended for educational, recreational or religious purposes, or for assisting them in organizing their leisure time within the places of internment. Such societies or organizations may be constituted in the territory of the Detaining Power, or in any other country, or they may have an international character.

The Detaining Power may limit the number of societies and organizations whose delegates are allowed to carry out their activities in its territory and under its supervision, on condition, however, that such limitation shall not hinder the supply of effective and adequate relief to all protected persons. The special position of the International Committee of the Red Cross in this field shall be recognized and respected at all times.

Art. 143. Representatives or delegates of the Protecting Powers shall have permission to go to all places where protected persons are, particularly to places of internment, detention and work.

They shall have access to all premises occupied by protected persons and shall be able to interview the latter without witnesses, personally or through an interpreter.

Such visits may not be prohibited except for reasons of imperative military necessity, and then only as an exceptional and temporary measure. Their duration and frequency shall not be restricted.

Such representatives and delegates shall have full liberty to select the places they wish to visit. The Detaining or Occupying Power, the Protecting Power and when occasion arises the Power of origin of the persons to be visited, may agree that compatriots of the internees shall be permitted to participate in the visits.

The delegates of the International Committee of the Red Cross shall also enjoy the above prerogatives. The appointment of such delegates shall be submitted to the approval of the Power governing the territories where they will carry out their duties.

Art. 144. The High Contracting Parties undertake, in time of peace as in time of war, to disseminate the text of the present Convention as widely as possible in their respective countries, and, in particular, to include the study thereof in their programmes of military and, if possible, civil instruction, so that the principles thereof may become known to the entire population.

Any civilian, military, police or other authorities, who in time of war assume responsibilities in respect of protected persons, must possess the text of the Convention and be specially instructed as to its provisions.

Art. 145. The High Contracting Parties shall communicate to one another through the Swiss Federal Council and, during hostilities, through the Protecting Powers, the official translations of the present Convention, as well as the laws and regulations which they may adopt to ensure the application thereof.

Art. 146. The High Contracting Parties undertake to enact any legislation necessary to provide effective penal sanctions for persons committing, or ordering to be committed, any of the grave breaches of the present Convention defined in the following Article.

Each High Contracting Party shall be under the obligation to search for persons alleged to have committed, or to have ordered to be committed, such grave breaches, and shall bring such persons, regardless of their nationality, before its own courts. It may also, if it prefers, and in accordance with the provisions of its own legislation, hand such persons over for trial to another High Contracting Party concerned, provided such High Contracting Party has made out a prima facie case.

Each High Contracting Party shall take measures necessary for the suppression of all acts contrary to the provisions of the present Convention other than the grave breaches defined in the following Article.

In all circumstances, the accused persons shall benefit by safeguards of proper trial and defence, which shall not be less favourable than those provided by Article 105 and those following of the Geneva Convention relative to the Treatment of Prisoners of War of 12 August 1949. Art. 147. Grave breaches to which the preceding Article relates shall be those involving any of the following acts, if committed against persons or property protected by the present Convention: wilful killing, torture or inhuman treatment, including biological experiments, wilfully causing great suffering or serious injury to body or health, unlawful deportation or transfer or unlawful confinement of a protected person, compelling a protected person to serve in the forces of a hostile Power, or wilfully depriving a protected person of the rights of fair and regular trial prescribed in the present Convention, taking of hostages and extensive destruction and appropriation of property, not justified by military necessity and carried out unlawfully and wantonly.

Art. 148. No High Contracting Party shall be allowed to absolve itself or any other High Contracting Party of any liability incurred by itself or by another High Contracting Party in respect of breaches referred to in the preceding Article.

Art. 149. At the request of a Party to the conflict, an enquiry shall be instituted, in a manner to be decided between the interested Parties, concerning any alleged violation of the Convention.

If agreement has not been reached concerning the procedure for the enquiry, the Parties should agree on the choice of an umpire who will decide upon the procedure to be followed.

Once the violation has been established, the Parties to the conflict shall put an end to it and shall repress it with the least possible delay.

SECTION II

Final Provisions

Art. 150. The present Convention is established in English and in French. Both texts are equally authentic.

The Swiss Federal Council shall arrange for official translations of the Convention to be made in the Russian and Spanish languages.

Art. 151. The present Convention, which bears the date of this day, is open to signature until 12 February 1950, in the name of the Powers represented at the Conference which opened at Geneva on 21 April 1949.

Art. 152. The present Convention shall be ratified as soon as possible and the ratifications shall be deposited at Berne.

A record shall be drawn up of the deposit of each instrument of ratification and certified copies of this record shall be transmitted by the Swiss Federal Council to all the Powers in whose name the Convention has been signed, or whose accession has been notified.

Art. 153. The present Convention shall come into force six months after not less than two instruments of ratification have been deposited.

Thereafter, it shall come into force for each High Contracting Party six months after the deposit of the instrument of ratification.

Art. 154. In the relations between the Powers who are bound by the Hague Conventions respecting the Laws and Customs of War on Land, whether that of 29 July 1899, or that of 18 October 1907, and who are parties to the present Convention, this last Convention shall be supplementary to Sections II and III of the Regulations annexed to the above-mentioned Conventions of The Hague.

Art. 155. From the date of its coming into force, it shall be open to any Power in whose name the present Convention has not been signed, to accede to this Convention.

Art. 156. Accessions shall be notified in writing to the Swiss Federal Council, and shall take effect six months after the date on which they are received. The Swiss Federal Council shall communicate the accessions to all the Powers in whose name the Convention has been signed, or whose accession has been notified.

Art. 157. The situations provided for in Articles 2 and 3 shall effective immediate effect to ratifications deposited and accessions notified by the Parties to the conflict before or after the beginning of hostilities or occupation. The Swiss Federal Council shall communicate by the quickest method any ratifications or accessions received from Parties to the conflict.

Art. 158. Each of the High Contracting Parties shall be at liberty to denounce the present Convention.

The denunciation shall be notified in writing to the Swiss Federal Council, which shall transmit it to the Governments of all the High Contracting Parties. The denunciation shall take effect one year after the notification thereof has been made to the Swiss Federal Council. However, a denunciation of which notification has been made at a time when the denouncing Power is involved in a conflict shall not take effect until peace has been concluded, and until after operations connected with release, repatriation and re-establishment of the persons protected by the present Convention have been terminated.

The denunciation shall have effect only in respect of the denouncing Power. It shall in no way impair the obligations which the Parties to the conflict shall remain bound to fulfil by virtue of the principles of the law of nations, as they result from the usages established among civilized peoples, from the laws of humanity and the dictates of the public conscience.

Art. 159. The Swiss Federal Council shall register the present Convention with the Secretariat of the United Nations. The Swiss Federal Council shall also inform the Secretariat of the United Nations of all ratifications, accessions and denunciations received by it with respect to the present Convention. In witness whereof the undersigned, having deposited their respective full powers, have signed the present Convention.

Done at Geneva this twelfth day of August 1949, in the English and French languages. The original shall be deposited in the Archives of the Swiss Confederation. The Swiss Federal Council shall transmit certified copies thereof to each of the signatory and acceding States.

ANNEX I

Draft Agreement Relating to Hospital and Safety Zones and Localities

Art. 1. Hospital and safety zones shall be strictly reserved for the persons mentioned in Article 23 of the Geneva Convention for the Amelioration of the Condition of the Wounded and Sick in Armed Forces in the Field of 12 August 1949, and in Article 14 of the Geneva Convention relative to the Protection of Civilian Persons in Time of War of 12 August 1949, and for the personnel entrusted with the organization and administration of these zones and localities, and with the care of the persons therein assembled.

Nevertheless, persons whose permanent residence is within such zones shall have the right to stay there.

Art. 2. No persons residing, in whatever capacity, in a hospital and safety zone shall perform any work, either within or without the zone, directly connected with military operations or the production of war material.

Art. 3. The Power establishing a hospital and safety zone shall take all necessary measures to prohibit access to all persons who have no right of residence or entry therein.

Art. 4. Hospital and safety zones shall fulfil the following conditions: (a) they shall comprise only a small part of the territory governed by the Power which has established them (b) they shall be thinly populated in relation to the possibilities of accommodation (c) they shall be far removed and free from all military objectives, or large industrial or administrative establishments (d) they shall not be situated in areas which, according to every probability, may become important for the conduct of the war.

Art. 5. Hospital and safety zones shall be subject to the following obligations:

(a) the lines of communication and means of transport which they possess shall not be used for the transport of military personnel or material, even in transit

(b) they shall in no case be defended by military means.

encyclopedia of GENOCIDE *and* CRIMES AGAINST HUMANITY

Art. 6. Hospital and safety zones shall be marked by means of oblique red bands on a white ground, placed on the buildings and outer precincts.

Zones reserved exclusively for the wounded and sick may be marked by means of the Red Cross (Red Crescent, Red Lion and Sun) emblem on a white ground.

They may be similarly marked at night by means of appropriate illumination.

Art. 7. The Powers shall communicate to all the High Contracting Parties in peacetime or on the outbreak of hostilities, a list of the hospital and safety zones in the territories governed by them. They shall also give notice of any new zones set up during hostilities.

As soon as the adverse party has received the above-mentioned notification, the zone shall be regularly established.

If, however, the adverse party considers that the conditions of the present agreement have not been fulfilled, it may refuse to recognize the zone by giving immediate notice thereof to the Party responsible for the said zone, or may make its recognition of such zone dependent upon the institution of the control provided for in Article 8.

Art. 8. Any Power having recognized one or several hospital and safety zones instituted by the adverse Party shall be entitled to demand control by one or more Special Commissions, for the purpose of ascertaining if the zones fulfil the conditions and obligations stipulated in the present agreement.

For this purpose, members of the Special Commissions shall at all times have free access to the various zones and may even reside there permanently. They shall be given all facilities for their duties of inspection.

Art. 9. Should the Special Commissions note any facts which they consider contrary to the stipulations of the present agreement, they shall at once draw the attention of the Power governing the said zone to these facts, and shall fix a time limit of five days within which the matter should be rectified. They shall duly notify the Power which has recognized the zone.

If, when the time limit has expired, the Power governing the zone has not complied with the warning, the adverse Party may declare that it is no longer bound by the present agreement in respect of the said zone.

Art. 10. Any Power setting up one or more hospital and safety zones, and the adverse Parties to whom their existence has been notified, shall nominate or have nominated by the Protecting Powers or by other neutral Powers, persons eligible to be members of the Special Commissions mentioned in Articles 8 and 9.

Art. 11. In no circumstances may hospital and safety zones be the object of attack. They shall be protected and respected at all times by the Parties to the conflict.

Art. 12. In the case of occupation of a territory, the hospital and safety zones therein shall continue to be respected and utilized as such.

Their purpose may, however, be modified by the Occupying Power, on condition that all measures are taken to ensure the safety of the persons accommodated.

Art. 13. The present agreement shall also apply to localities which the Powers may utilize for the same purposes as hospital and safety zones.

ANNEX II
Draft Regulations concerning Collective Relief

Article 1. The Internee Committees shall be allowed to distribute collective relief shipments for which they are responsible to all internees who are dependent for administration on the said Committee's place of internment, including those internees who are in hospitals, or in prison or other penitentiary establishments.

Art. 2. The distribution of collective relief shipments shall be effected in accordance with the instructions of the donors and with a plan drawn up by the Internee Committees. The issue of medical stores shall, however, be made for preference in agreement with the senior medical officers, and the latter may, in hospitals and infirmaries, waive the said instructions, if the needs of their patients so demand. Within the limits thus defined, the distribution shall always be carried out equitably.

Art. 3. Members of Internee Committees shall be allowed to go to the railway stations or other points of arrival of relief supplies near their places of internment so as to enable them to verify the quantity as well as the quality of the goods received and to make out detailed reports thereon for the donors.

Art. 4. Internee Committees shall be given the facilities necessary for verifying whether the distribution of collective relief in all subdivisions and annexes of their places of internment has been carried out in accordance with their instructions.

Art. 5. Internee Committees shall be allowed to complete, and to cause to be completed by members of the Internee Committees in labour detachments or by the senior medical officers of infirmaries and hospitals, forms or questionnaires intended for the donors, relating to collective relief supplies (distribution, requirements, quantities, etc.). Such forms and questionnaires, duly completed, shall be forwarded to the donors without delay.

Art. 6. In order to secure the regular distribution of collective relief supplies to the internees in their place of internment, and to meet any needs that may arise through the arrival of fresh parties of internees, the Internee Committees shall be allowed to create and maintain sufficient reserve stocks of collective relief. For this purpose, they shall have suitable warehouses at their disposal; each warehouse shall be provided with two locks, the Internee Committee holding the keys of one lock, and the commandant of the place of internment the keys of the other.

Art. 7. The High Contracting Parties, and the Detaining Powers in particular, shall, so far as is in any way possible and subject to the regulations governing the food supply of the population, authorize purchases of goods to be made in their territories for the distribution of collective relief to the internees. They shall likewise facilitate the transfer of funds and other financial measures of a technical or administrative nature taken for the purpose of making such purchases.

Art. 8. The foregoing provisions shall not constitute an obstacle to the right of internees to receive collective relief before their arrival in a place of internment or in the course of their transfer, nor to the possibility of representatives of the Protecting Power, or of the International Committee of the Red Cross or any other humanitarian organization giving assistance to internees and responsible for forwarding such supplies, ensuring the distribution thereof to the recipients by any other means they may deem suitable.

Genocide Convention Implementation Act of 1987

INTRODUCTION Although the United States participated very actively in the preparation of the 1948 Genocide Convention, and signed the Convention at the time of its adoption, ratification by Congress would take four decades. The indefatigable proponent of ratification was Senator William Proxmire, who took the floor virtually every day for many years in his call for ratification. When the enabling legislation was finally adopted, in 1987, it was called the Proxmire Act in his honor. The legislation provides for the prosecution of genocide within United States law, and sets out the applicable penalties. It also provides detailed definitions of many of the terms that are used in the Convention.

United States Code

TITLE 18 — CRIMES AND CRIMINAL PROCEDURE

PART I — CRIMES

CHAPTER 50A — GENOCIDE

U.S. Code as of: 01/22/02
Section 1091. Genocide

(a) Basic Offense. Whoever, whether in time of peace or in time of war, in a circumstance described in subsection (d) and with the specific intent to destroy, in whole or in substantial part, a national, ethnic, racial, or religious group as such

(1) kills members of that group;

(2) causes serious bodily injury to members of that group;

(3) causes the permanent impairment of the mental faculties of members of the group through drugs, torture, or similar techniques;

(4) subjects the group to conditions of life that are intended to cause the physical destruction of the group in whole or in part;

(5) imposes measures intended to prevent births within the group; or

(6) transfers by force children of the group to another group;

or attempts to do so, shall be punished as provided in subsection

(b) Punishment for Basic Offense. The punishment for an offense under subsection (a) is

(1) in the case of an offense under subsection

(2) a fine of not more than $1,000,000 or imprisonment for not more than twenty years, or both, in any other case.

(c) Incitement Offense. Whoever in a circumstance described in subsection (d) directly and publicly incites another to violate subsection (a) shall be fined not more than $500,000 or imprisoned not more than five years, or both.

(d) Required Circumstance for Offenses. The circumstance referred to in subsections (a) and (c) is that

(1) the offense is committed within the United States; or

(2) the alleged offender is a national of the United States (as defined in section 101 of the Immigration and Nationality Act (8 U.S.C. 1101)).

(e) Nonapplicability of Certain Limitations. Notwithstanding section 3282 of this title, in the case of an offense under subsection (a)(1), an indictment may be found, or information instituted, at any time without limitation.

International Convention on the Suppression and Punishment of the Crime of Apartheid (July 18, 1976)

SOURCE The Avalon Project at Yale Law School. Available from http://www.yale.edu/lawweb/avalon/avalon.htm

INTRODUCTION The Apartheid Convention was adopted by the United Nations General Assembly in 1973, but with a large number of abstentions by Western countries and negative votes from Portugal, South Africa, the United Kingdom, and the United States. Apartheid is described, in article I, as a crime against humanity, a determination later confirmed in the 1998 Rome Statute of the International Criminal Court.

The States Parties to the present Convention, Recalling the provisions of the Charter of the United Nations, in which all Members pledged themselves to take joint and separate action in co-operation with the Organization for the achievement of universal respect for, and observance of, human rights and fundamental freedoms for all without distinction as to race, sex, language or religion,

Considering the Universal Declaration of Human Rights, which states that all human beings are born free and equal in dignity and rights and that everyone is entitled to all the rights and freedoms set forth in the Declaration, without distinction of any kind, such as race, colour or national origin,

Considering the Declaration on the Granting of Independence to Colonial Countries and Peoples, in which the General Assembly stated that the process of liberation is irresistible and irreversible and that, in the interests of human dignity, progress and justice, an end must be put to colonialism and all practices of segregation and discrimination associated therewith,

Observing that, in accordance with the International Convention on the Elimination of All Forms of Racial Discrimination, States particularly condemn racial segregation and apartheid and undertake to prevent, prohibit and eradicate all practices of this nature in territories under their jurisdiction, Observing that, in the Convention on the Prevention and Punishment of the Crime of Genocide, certain acts which may also be qualified as acts of apartheid constitute a crime under international law,

Observing that, in the Convention on the Non-Applicability of Statutory Limitations to War Crimes and Crimes against Humanity, "inhuman acts resulting from the policy of apartheid" are qualified as crimes against humanity, Observing that the General Assembly of the United Nations has adopted a number of resolutions in which the policies and practices of apartheid are condemned as a crime against humanity,

Observing that the Security Council has emphasized that apartheid and its continued intensification and expansion seriously disturb and threaten international peace and security, Convinced that an International Convention on the Suppression and Punishment of the Crime of Apartheid would make it possible to take more effective measures at the international and national levels with a view to the suppression and punishment of the crime of apartheid,

Have agreed as follows:

Article I

1. The States Parties to the present Convention declare that apartheid is a crime against humanity and that inhuman acts resulting from the policies and practices of apartheid and similar policies and practices of racial segregation and discrimination, as defined in article II of the Convention, are crimes violating the principles of international law, in particular the purposes and principles of the Charter of the United Nations, and constituting a serious threat to international peace and security.

2. The States Parties to the present Convention declare criminal those organizations, institutions and individuals committing the crime of apartheid.

Article II

For the purpose of the present Convention, the term "the crime of apartheid", which shall include similar policies and practices of racial segregation and discrimination as practised in southern Africa, shall apply to the following inhuman acts committed for the purpose of establishing and maintaining domination by one racial group of persons over any other racial group of persons and systematically oppressing them:

(a) Denial to a member or members of a racial group or groups of the right to life and liberty of person:

(i) By murder of members of a racial group or groups;

(ii) By the infliction upon the members of a racial group or groups of serious bodily or mental harm, by the infringement of their freedom or dignity, or by subjecting them to torture or to cruel, inhuman or degrading treatment or punishment;

(iii) By arbitrary arrest and illegal imprisonment of the members of a racial group or groups;

(b) Deliberate imposition on a racial group or groups of living conditions calculated to cause its or their physical destruction in whole or in part;

(c) Any legislative measures and other measures calculated to prevent a racial group or groups from participation in the political, social, economic and cultural life of the country and the deliberate creation of conditions preventing the full development of such a group or groups, in particular by denying to members of a racial group or groups basic human rights and freedoms, including the right to work, the right to form recognized trade unions, the right to education, the right to leave and to return to their country, the right to a nationality, the right to freedom of movement and residence, the right to freedom of opinion and expression, and the right to freedom of peaceful assembly and association;

(d) Any measures, including legislative measures, designed to divide the population along racial lines by the creation of separate reserves and ghettos for the members of a racial group or groups, the prohibition of mixed marriages among members of various racial groups, the expropriation of landed property belonging to a racial group or groups or to members thereof;

(e) Exploitation of the labour of the members of a racial group or groups, in particular by submitting them to forced labour;

(f) Persecution of organizations and persons, by depriving them of fundamental rights and freedoms, because they oppose apartheid.

Article III

International criminal responsibility shall apply, irrespective of the motive involved, to individuals, members of organizations and institutions and representatives of the State, whether residing in the territory of the State in which the acts are perpetrated or in some other State, whenever they:

(a) Commit, participate in, directly incite or conspire in the commission of the acts mentioned in article II of the present Convention;

(b) Directly abet, encourage or co-operate in the commission of the crime of apartheid.

Article IV

The States Parties to the present Convention undertake:

(a) To adopt any legislative or other measures necessary to suppress as well as to prevent any encouragement of the crime of apartheid and similar segregationist policies or their manifestations and to punish persons guilty of that crime;

(b) To adopt legislative, judicial and administrative measures to prosecute, bring to trial and punish in accordance with their jurisdiction persons responsible for, or accused of, the acts defined in article II of the present Convention, whether or not such persons reside in the territory of the State in which the acts are committed or are nationals of that State or of some other State or are stateless persons.

Article V

Persons charged with the acts enumerated in article II of the present Convention may be tried by a competent tribunal of any State Party to the Convention which may acquire jurisdiction over the person of the accused or by an international penal tribunal having jurisdiction with respect to those States Parties which shall have accepted its jurisdiction.

Article VI

The States Parties to the present Convention undertake to accept and carry out in accordance with the Charter of the United Nations the decisions taken by the Security Council aimed at the prevention, suppression and punishment of the crime of apartheid, and to co-operate in the implementation of decisions adopted by other competent organs of the United Nations with a view to achieving the purposes of the Convention.

Article VII

1. The States Parties to the present Convention undertake to submit periodic reports to the group established under article IX on the legislative, judicial, administrative or other measures that they have adopted and that give effect to the provisions of the Convention.

2. Copies of the reports shall be transmitted through the Secretary-General of the United Nations to the Special Committee on Apartheid.

Article VIII

Any State Party to the present Convention may call upon any competent organ of the United Nations to take such action under the Charter of the United Nations as it considers appropriate for the prevention and suppression of the crime of apartheid.

Article IX

1. The Chairman of the Commission on Human Rights shall appoint a group consisting of three members of the Commission on Human Rights, who are also representatives of States Parties to the present Convention, to consider reports submitted by States Parties in accordance with article VII.

2. If, among the members of the Commission on Human Rights, there are no representatives of States Parties to the present Convention or if there are fewer than three such representatives, the Secretary-General

of the United Nations shall, after consulting all States Parties to the Convention, designate a representative of the State Party or representatives of the States Parties which are not members of the Commission on Human Rights to take part in the work of the group established in accordance with paragraph 1 of this article, until such time as representatives of the States Parties to the Convention are elected to the Commission on Human Rights.

3. The group may meet for a period of not more than five days, either before the opening or after the closing of the session of the Commission on Human Rights, to consider the reports submitted in accordance with article VII.

Article X

1. The States Parties to the present Convention empower the Commission on Human Rights:

(a) To request United Nations organs, when transmitting copies of petitions under article 15 of the International Convention on the Elimination of All Forms of Racial Discrimination, to draw its attention to complaints concerning acts which are enumerated in article II of the present Convention;

(b) To prepare, on the basis of reports from competent organs of the United Nations and periodic reports from States Parties to the present Convention, a list of individuals, organizations, institutions and representatives of States which are alleged to be responsible for the crimes enumerated in article II of the Convention, as well as those against whom legal proceedings have been undertaken by States Parties to the Convention;

(c) To request information from the competent United Nations organs concerning measures taken by the authorities responsible for the administration of Trust and Non-Self-Governing Territories, and all other Territories to which General Assembly resolution 1514 (XV) of 14 December 1960 applies, with regard to such individuals alleged to be responsible for crimes under article II of the Convention who are believed to be under their territorial and administrative jurisdiction.

2. Pending the achievement of the objectives of the Declaration on the Granting of Independence to Colonial Countries and Peoples, contained in General Assembly resolution 1514 (XV), the provisions of the present Convention shall in no way limit the right of petition granted to those peoples by other international instruments or by the United Nations and its specialized agencies.

Article XI

1. Acts enumerated in article II of the present Convention shall not be considered political crimes for the purpose of extradition.

2. The States Parties to the present Convention undertake in such cases to grant extradition in accordance with their legislation and with the treaties in force.

Article XII

Disputes between States Parties arising out of the interpretation, application or implementation of the present Convention which have not been settled by negotiation shall, at the request of the States parties to the dispute, be brought before the International Court of Justice, save where the parties to the dispute have agreed on some other form of settlement.

Article XIII

The present Convention is open for signature by all States. Any State which does not sign the Convention before its entry into force may accede to it.

Article XIV

1. The present Convention is subject to ratification. Instruments of ratification shall be deposited with the Secretary-General of the United Nations.

2. Accession shall be effected by the deposit of an instrument of accession with the Secretary-General of the United Nations.

Article XV

1. The present Convention shall enter into force on the thirtieth day after the date of the deposit with the Secretary-General of the United Nations of the twentieth instrument of ratification or accession.

2. For each State ratifying the present Convention or acceding to it after the deposit of the twentieth instrument of ratification or instrument of accession, the Convention shall enter into force on the thirtieth day after the date of the deposit of its own instrument of ratification or instrument of accession.

Article XVI

A State Party may denounce the present Convention by written notification to the Secretary-General of the United Nations. Denunciation shall take effect one year after the date of receipt of the notification by the Secretary-General.

Article XVII

1. A request for the revision of the present Convention may be made at any time by any State Party by means of a notification in writing addressed to the Secretary-General of the United Nations.

2. The General Assembly of the United Nations shall decide upon the steps, if any, to be taken in respect of such request.

Article XVIII

The Secretary-General of the United Nations shall inform all States of the following particulars:

(a) Signatures, ratifications and accessions under articles XIII and XIV;

(b) The date of entry into force of the present Convention under article XV;

(c) Denunciations under article XVI;

(d) Notifications under article XVII.

Article XIX

1. The present Convention, of which the Chinese, English, French, Russian and Spanish texts are equally authentic, shall be deposited in the archives of the United Nations.

2. The Secretary-General of the United Nations shall transmit certified copies of the present Convention to all States.

Rome Statute of the International Criminal Court

SOURCE Available from http://www.un.org/law.

INTRODUCTION The Rome Statute of the International Criminal Court was adopted on July 17, 1998, and entered into force on July 1, 2002, following the sixtieth ratification. The Statute creates the first permanent international criminal tribunal with jurisdiction over genocide and crimes against humanity. There had been proposals for an international court since the mid-nineteenth century, and some successful efforts to establish such a body, but on an *ad hoc* basis. The Nuremberg court, used to judge the Nazi leaders, is the first such example. Parties to the Rome Statute agree to subject their territory, and their citizens, to the jurisdiction of the International Court. If the courts of these countries fail to render justice themselves, the International Court is entitled to intervene and prosecute the crimes itself. The Rome Statute also imposes various obligations upon States in terms of the apprehension of suspects and the gathering of evidence.

PART 1. ESTABLISHMENT OF THE COURT

Article 1

The Court An International Criminal Court ("the Court") is hereby established. It shall be a permanent institution and shall have the power to exercise its jurisdiction over persons for the most serious crimes of international concern, as referred to in this Statute, and shall be complementary to national criminal jurisdictions. The jurisdiction and functioning of the Court shall be governed by the provisions of this Statute.

Article 2

Relationship of the Court with the United Nations The Court shall be brought into relationship with the United Nations through an agreement to be approved by the Assembly of States Parties to this Statute and thereafter concluded by the President of the Court on its behalf.

Article 3

Seat of the Court 1. The seat of the Court shall be established at The Hague in the Netherlands ("the host State").

2. The Court shall enter into a headquarters agreement with the host State, to be approved by the Assembly of States Parties and thereafter concluded by the President of the Court on its behalf.

3. The Court may sit elsewhere, whenever it considers it desirable, as provided in this Statute.

Article 4

Legal status and powers of the Court 1. The Court shall have international legal personality. It shall also have such legal capacity as may be necessary for the exercise of its functions and the fulfillment of its purposes.

2. The Court may exercise its functions and powers, as provided in this Statute, on the territory of any State Party and, by special agreement, on the territory of any other State.

PART 2. JURISDICTION, ADMISSIBILITY AND APPLICABLE LAW

Article 5

Crimes within the jurisdiction of the Court 1. The jurisdiction of the Court shall be limited to the most serious crimes of concern to the international community as a whole. The Court has jurisdiction in accordance with this Statute with respect to the following crimes:

(a) The crime of genocide;

(b) Crimes against humanity;

(c) War crimes;

(d) The crime of aggression.

2. The Court shall exercise jurisdiction over the crime of aggression once a provision is adopted in accordance with articles 121 and 123 defining the crime

and setting out the conditions under which the Court shall exercise jurisdiction with respect to this crime. Such a provision shall be consistent with the relevant provisions of the Charter of the United Nations.

Article 6

Genocide For the purpose of this Statute, "genocide" means any of the following acts committed with intent to destroy, in whole or in part, a national, ethnical, racial or religious group, as such:

(a) Killing members of the group;

(b) Causing serious bodily or mental harm to members of the group;

(c) Deliberately inflicting on the group conditions of life calculated to bring about its physical destruction in whole or in part;

(d) Imposing measures intended to prevent births within the group;

(e) Forcibly transferring children of the group to another group.

Article 7

Crimes against humanity 1. For the purpose of this Statute, "crime against humanity" means any of the following acts when committed as part of a widespread or systematic attack directed against any civilian population, with knowledge of the attack:

(a) Murder;

(b) Extermination;

(c) Enslavement;

(d) Deportation or forcible transfer of population;

(e) Imprisonment or other severe deprivation of physical liberty in violation of fundamental rules of international law;

(f) Torture;

(g) Rape, sexual slavery, enforced prostitution, forced pregnancy, enforced sterilization, or any other form of sexual violence of comparable gravity;

(h) Persecution against any identifiable group or collectivity on political, racial, national, ethnic, cultural, religious, gender as defined in paragraph 3, or other grounds that are universally recognized as impermissible under international law, in connection with any act referred to in this paragraph or any crime within the jurisdiction of the Court;

(i) Enforced disappearance of persons;

(j) The crime of apartheid;

(k) Other inhumane acts of a similar character intentionally causing great suffering, or serious injury to body or to mental or physical health.

2. For the purpose of paragraph 1:

(a) "Attack directed against any civilian population" means a course of conduct involving the multiple commission of acts referred to in paragraph 1 against any civilian population, pursuant to or in furtherance of a State or organizational policy to commit such attack;

(b) "Extermination" includes the intentional infliction of conditions of life, inter alia the deprivation of access to food and medicine, calculated to bring about the destruction of part of a population;

(c) "Enslavement" means the exercise of any or all of the powers attaching to the right of ownership over a person and includes the exercise of such power in the course of trafficking in persons, in particular women and children;

(d) "Deportation or forcible transfer of population" means forced displacement of the persons concerned by expulsion or other coercive acts from the area in which they are lawfully present, without grounds permitted under international law;

(e) "Torture" means the intentional infliction of severe pain or suffering, whether physical or mental, upon a person in the custody or under the control of the accused; except that torture shall not include pain or suffering arising only from, inherent in or incidental to, lawful sanctions;

(f) "Forced pregnancy" means the unlawful confinement of a woman forcibly made pregnant, with the intent of affecting the ethnic composition of any population or carrying out other grave violations of international law. This definition shall not in any way be interpreted as affecting national laws relating to pregnancy;

(g) "Persecution" means the intentional and severe deprivation of fundamental rights contrary to international law by reason of the identity of the group or collectivity;

(h) "The crime of apartheid" means inhumane acts of a character similar to those referred to in paragraph 1, committed in the context of an institutionalized regime of systematic oppression and domination by one racial group over any other racial group or groups and committed with the intention of maintaining that regime;

(i) "Enforced disappearance of persons" means the arrest, detention or abduction of persons by, or with the authorization, support or acquiescence of, a State or a political organization, followed by a refusal to acknowledge that deprivation of freedom or to give information on the fate or whereabouts of those persons, with the intention of removing them from the protection of the law for a prolonged period of time.

3. For the purpose of this Statute, it is understood that the term "gender" refers to the two sexes, male and female, within the context of society. The term "gender" does not indicate any meaning different from the above.

Article 8

War crimes 1. The Court shall have jurisdiction in respect of war crimes in particular when committed as part of a plan or policy or as part of a large-scale commission of such crimes.

2. For the purpose of this Statute, "war crimes" means:

(a) Grave breaches of the Geneva Conventions of 12 August 1949, namely, any of the following acts against persons or property protected under the provisions of the relevant Geneva Convention:

(i) Willful killing;

(ii) Torture or inhuman treatment, including biological experiments;

(iii) Willfully causing great suffering, or serious injury to body or health;

(iv) Extensive destruction and appropriation of property, not justified by military necessity and carried out unlawfully and wantonly;

(v) Compelling a prisoner of war or other protected person to serve in the forces of a hostile Power;

(vi) Willfully depriving a prisoner of war or other protected person of the rights of fair and regular trial;

(vii) Unlawful deportation or transfer or unlawful confinement;

(viii) Taking of hostages.

(b) Other serious violations of the laws and customs applicable in international armed conflict, within the established framework of international law, namely, any of the following acts:

(i) Intentionally directing attacks against the civilian population as such or against individual civilians not taking direct part in hostilities;

(ii) Intentionally directing attacks against civilian objects, that is, objects which are not military objectives;

(iii) Intentionally directing attacks against personnel, installations, material, units or vehicles involved in a humanitarian assistance or peacekeeping mission in accordance with the Charter of the United Nations, as long as they are entitled to the protection given to civilians or civilian objects under the international law of armed conflict;

(iv) Intentionally launching an attack in the knowledge that such attack will cause incidental loss of life or injury to civilians or damage to civilian objects or widespread, long-term and severe damage to the natural environment which would be clearly excessive in relation to the concrete and direct overall military advantage anticipated;

(v) Attacking or bombarding, by whatever means, towns, villages, dwellings or buildings which are undefended and which are not military objectives;

(vi) Killing or wounding a combatant who, having laid down his arms or having no longer means of defence, has surrendered at discretion;

(vii) Making improper use of a flag of truce, of the flag or of the military insignia and uniform of the enemy or of the United Nations, as well as of the distinctive emblems of the Geneva Conventions, resulting in death or serious personal injury;

(viii) The transfer, directly or indirectly, by the Occupying Power of parts of its own civilian population into the territory it occupies, or the deportation or transfer of all or parts of the population of the occupied territory within or outside this territory;

(ix) Intentionally directing attacks against buildings dedicated to religion, education, art, science or charitable purposes, historic monuments, hospitals and places where the sick and wounded are collected, provided they are not military objectives;

(x) Subjecting persons who are in the power of an adverse party to physical mutilation or to medical or scientific experiments of any kind which are neither justified by the medical, dental or hospital treatment of the person concerned nor carried out in his or her interest, and which cause death to or seriously endanger the health of such person or persons;

(xi) Killing or wounding treacherously individuals belonging to the hostile nation or army;

(xii) Declaring that no quarter will be given;

(xiii) Destroying or seizing the enemy's property unless such destruction or seizure be imperatively demanded by the necessities of war;

(xiv) Declaring abolished, suspended or inadmissible in a court of law the rights and actions of the nationals of the hostile party;

(xv) Compelling the nationals of the hostile party to take part in the operations of war directed against their own country, even if they were in the belligerent's service before the commencement of the war;

(xvi) Pillaging a town or place, even when taken by assault;

(xvii) Employing poison or poisoned weapons;

(xviii) Employing asphyxiating, poisonous or other gases, and all analogous liquids, materials or devices;

(xix) Employing bullets which expand or flatten easily in the human body, such as bullets with a hard envelope which does not entirely cover the core or is pierced with incisions;

(xx) Employing weapons, projectiles and material and methods of warfare which are of a nature to cause superfluous injury or unnecessary suffering or which are inherently indiscriminate in violation of the international law of armed conflict, provided that such weapons, projectiles and material and methods of warfare are the subject of a comprehensive prohibition and are included in an annex to this Statute, by an amendment in accordance with the relevant provisions set forth in articles 121 and 123;

(xxi) Committing outrages upon personal dignity, in particular humiliating and degrading treatment;

(xxii) Committing rape, sexual slavery, enforced prostitution, forced pregnancy, as defined in article 7, paragraph 2 (f), enforced sterilization, or any other form of sexual violence also constituting a grave breach of the Geneva Conventions;

(xxiii) Utilizing the presence of a civilian or other protected person to render certain points, areas or military forces immune from military operations;

(xxiv) Intentionally directing attacks against buildings, material, medical units and transport, and personnel using the distinctive emblems of the Geneva Conventions in conformity with international law;

(xxv) Intentionally using starvation of civilians as a method of warfare by depriving them of objects indispensable to their survival, including willfully impeding relief supplies as provided for under the Geneva Conventions;

(xxvi) Conscripting or enlisting children under the age of fifteen years into the national armed forces or using them to participate actively in hostilities.

(c) In the case of an armed conflict not of an international character, serious violations of article 3 common to the four Geneva Conventions of 12 August 1949, namely, any of the following acts committed against persons taking no active part in the hostilities, including members of armed forces who have laid down their arms and those placed hors de combat by sickness, wounds, detention or any other cause:

(i) Violence to life and person, in particular murder of all kinds, mutilation, cruel treatment and torture;

(ii) Committing outrages upon personal dignity, in particular humiliating and degrading treatment;

(iii) Taking of hostages;

(iv) The passing of sentences and the carrying out of executions without previous judgment pronounced by a regularly constituted court, affording all judicial guarantees which are generally recognized as indispensable.

(d) Paragraph 2 (c) applies to armed conflicts not of an international character and thus does not apply to situations of internal disturbances and tensions, such as riots, isolated and sporadic acts of violence or other acts of a similar nature.

(e) Other serious violations of the laws and customs applicable in armed conflicts not of an international character, within the established framework of international law, namely, any of the following acts:

(i) Intentionally directing attacks against the civilian population as such or against individual civilians not taking direct part in hostilities;

(ii) Intentionally directing attacks against buildings, material, medical units and transport, and personnel using the distinctive emblems of the Geneva Conventions in conformity with international law;

(iii) Intentionally directing attacks against personnel, installations, material, units or vehicles involved in a humanitarian assistance or peacekeeping mission in accordance with the Charter of the United Nations, as long as they are entitled to the protection given to civilians or civilian objects under the international law of armed conflict;

(iv) Intentionally directing attacks against buildings dedicated to religion, education, art, science or charitable purposes, historic monuments, hospitals and places where the sick and wounded are collected, provided they are not military objectives;

(v) Pillaging a town or place, even when taken by assault;

(vi) Committing rape, sexual slavery, enforced prostitution, forced pregnancy, as defined in article

7, paragraph 2 (f), enforced sterilization, and any other form of sexual violence also constituting a serious violation of article 3 common to the four Geneva Conventions;

(vii) Conscripting or enlisting children under the age of fifteen years into armed forces or groups or using them to participate actively in hostilities;

(viii) Ordering the displacement of the civilian population for reasons related to the conflict, unless the security of the civilians involved or imperative military reasons so demand;

(ix) Killing or wounding treacherously a combatant adversary;

(x) Declaring that no quarter will be given;

(xi) Subjecting persons who are in the power of another party to the conflict to physical mutilation or to medical or scientific experiments of any kind which are neither justified by the medical, dental or hospital treatment of the person concerned nor carried out in his or her interest, and which cause death to or seriously endanger the health of such person or persons;

(xii) Destroying or seizing the property of an adversary unless such destruction or seizure be imperatively demanded by the necessities of the conflict;

(f) Paragraph 2 (e) applies to armed conflicts not of an international character and thus does not apply to situations of internal disturbances and tensions, such as riots, isolated and sporadic acts of violence or other acts of a similar nature. It applies to armed conflicts that take place in the territory of a State when there is protracted armed conflict between governmental authorities and organized armed groups or between such groups.

3. Nothing in paragraph 2 (c) and (e) shall affect the responsibility of a Government to maintain or reestablish law and order in the State or to defend the unity and territorial integrity of the State, by all legitimate means.

Article 9

Elements of Crimes 1. Elements of Crimes shall assist the Court in the interpretation and application of articles 6, 7 and 8. They shall be adopted by a two-thirds majority of the members of the Assembly of States Parties.

2. Amendments to the Elements of Crimes may be proposed by:

(a) Any State Party;

(b) The judges acting by an absolute majority;

(c) The Prosecutor.

Such amendments shall be adopted by a two-thirds majority of the members of the Assembly of States Parties.

3. The Elements of Crimes and amendments thereto shall be consistent with this Statute.

Article 10

Nothing in this Part shall be interpreted as limiting or prejudicing in any way existing or developing rules of international law for purposes other than this Statute.

Article 11

Jurisdiction ratione temporis 1. The Court has jurisdiction only with respect to crimes committed after the entry into force of this Statute.

2. If a State becomes a Party to this Statute after its entry into force, the Court may exercise its jurisdiction only with respect to crimes committed after the entry into force of this Statute for that State, unless that State has made a declaration under article 12, paragraph 3.

Article 12

Preconditions to the exercise of jurisdiction 1. A State which becomes a Party to this Statute thereby accepts the jurisdiction of the Court with respect to the crimes referred to in article 5.

2. In the case of article 13, paragraph (a) or (c), the Court may exercise its jurisdiction if one or more of the following States are Parties to this Statute or have accepted the jurisdiction of the Court in accordance with paragraph 3:

(a) The State on the territory of which the conduct in question occurred or, if the crime was committed on board a vessel or aircraft, the State of registration of that vessel or aircraft;

(b) The State of which the person accused of the crime is a national.

3. If the acceptance of a State which is not a Party to this Statute is required under paragraph 2, that State may, by declaration lodged with the Registrar, accept the exercise of jurisdiction by the Court with respect to the crime in question. The accepting State shall cooperate with the Court without any delay or exception in accordance with Part 9.

Article 13

Exercise of jurisdiction The Court may exercise its jurisdiction with respect to a crime referred to in article 5 in accordance with the provisions of this Statute if:

(a) A situation in which one or more of such crimes appears to have been committed is referred to the Prosecutor by a State Party in accordance with article 14;

(b) A situation in which one or more of such crimes appears to have been committed is referred to the Prosecutor by the Security Council acting under Chapter VII of the Charter of the United Nations; or

(c) The Prosecutor has initiated an investigation in respect of such a crime in accordance with article 15.

Article 14

Referral of a situation by a State Party 1. A State Party may refer to the Prosecutor a situation in which one or more crimes within the jurisdiction of the Court appear to have been committed requesting the Prosecutor to investigate the situation for the purpose of determining whether one or more specific persons should be charged with the commission of such crimes.

2. As far as possible, a referral shall specify the relevant circumstances and be accompanied by such supporting documentation as is available to the State referring the situation.

Article 15

Prosecutor 1. The Prosecutor may initiate investigations proprio motu on the basis of information on crimes within the jurisdiction of the Court.

2. The Prosecutor shall analyse the seriousness of the information received. For this purpose, he or she may seek additional information from States, organs of the United Nations, intergovernmental or non-governmental organizations, or other reliable sources that he or she deems appropriate, and may receive written or oral testimony at the seat of the Court.

3. If the Prosecutor concludes that there is a reasonable basis to proceed with an investigation, he or she shall submit to the Pre-Trial Chamber a request for authorization of an investigation, together with any supporting material collected. Victims may make representations to the Pre-Trial Chamber, in accordance with the Rules of Procedure and Evidence.

4. If the Pre-Trial Chamber, upon examination of the request and the supporting material, considers that there is a reasonable basis to proceed with an investigation, and that the case appears to fall within the jurisdiction of the Court, it shall authorize the commencement of the investigation, without prejudice to subsequent determinations by the Court with regard to the jurisdiction and admissibility of a case.

5. The refusal of the Pre-Trial Chamber to authorize the investigation shall not preclude the presenta-

tion of a subsequent request by the Prosecutor based on new facts or evidence regarding the same situation.

6. If, after the preliminary examination referred to in paragraphs 1 and 2, the Prosecutor concludes that the information provided does not constitute a reasonable basis for an investigation, he or she shall inform those who provided the information. This shall not preclude the Prosecutor from considering further information submitted to him or her regarding the same situation in the light of new facts or evidence.

Article 16

Deferral of investigation or prosecution No investigation or prosecution may be commenced or proceeded with under this Statute for a period of 12 months after the Security Council, in a resolution adopted under Chapter VII of the Charter of the United Nations, has requested the Court to that effect; that request may be renewed by the Council under the same conditions.

Article 17

Issues of admissibility 1. Having regard to paragraph 10 of the Preamble and article 1, the Court shall determine that a case is inadmissible where:

(a) The case is being investigated or prosecuted by a State which has jurisdiction over it, unless the State is unwilling or unable genuinely to carry out the investigation or prosecution;

(b) The case has been investigated by a State which has jurisdiction over it and the State has decided not to prosecute the person concerned, unless the decision resulted from the unwillingness or inability of the State genuinely to prosecute;

(c) The person concerned has already been tried for conduct which is the subject of the complaint, and a trial by the Court is not permitted under article 20, paragraph 3;

(d) The case is not of sufficient gravity to justify further action by the Court.

2. In order to determine unwillingness in a particular case, the Court shall consider, having regard to the principles of due process recognized by international law, whether one or more of the following exist, as applicable:

(a) The proceedings were or are being undertaken or the national decision was made for the purpose of shielding the person concerned from criminal responsibility for crimes within the jurisdiction of the Court referred to in article 5;

(b) There has been an unjustified delay in the proceedings which in the circumstances is inconsistent with an intent to bring the person concerned to justice;

(c) The proceedings were not or are not being conducted independently or impartially, and they were or are being conducted in a manner which, in the circumstances, is inconsistent with an intent to bring the person concerned to justice.

3. In order to determine inability in a particular case, the Court shall consider whether, due to a total or substantial collapse or unavailability of its national judicial system, the State is unable to obtain the accused or the necessary evidence and testimony or otherwise unable to carry out its proceedings.

Article 18

Preliminary rulings regarding admissibility 1. When a situation has been referred to the Court pursuant to article 13 (a) and the Prosecutor has determined that there would be a reasonable basis to commence an investigation, or the Prosecutor initiates an investigation pursuant to articles 13 (c) and 15, the Prosecutor shall notify all States Parties and those States which, taking into account the information available, would normally exercise jurisdiction over the crimes concerned. The Prosecutor may notify such States on a confidential basis and, where the Prosecutor believes it necessary to protect persons, prevent destruction of evidence or prevent the absconding of persons, may limit the scope of the information provided to States.

2. Within one month of receipt of that notification, a State may inform the Court that it is investigating or has investigated its nationals or others within its jurisdiction with respect to criminal acts which may constitute crimes referred to in article 5 and which relate to the information provided in the notification to States. At the request of that State, the Prosecutor shall defer to the State's investigation of those persons unless the Pre-Trial Chamber, on the application of the Prosecutor, decides to authorize the investigation.

3. The Prosecutor's deferral to a State's investigation shall be open to review by the Prosecutor six months after the date of deferral or at any time when there has been a significant change of circumstances based on the State's unwillingness or inability genuinely to carry out the investigation.

4. The State concerned or the Prosecutor may appeal to the Appeals Chamber against a ruling of the Pre-Trial Chamber, in accordance with article 82. The appeal may be heard on an expedited basis.

5. When the Prosecutor has deferred an investigation in accordance with paragraph 2, the Prosecutor may request that the State concerned periodically inform the Prosecutor of the progress of its investigations and any subsequent prosecutions. States Parties shall respond to such requests without undue delay.

6. Pending a ruling by the Pre-Trial Chamber, or at any time when the Prosecutor has deferred an investigation under this article, the Prosecutor may, on an exceptional basis, seek authority from the Pre-Trial Chamber to pursue necessary investigative steps for the purpose of preserving evidence where there is a unique opportunity to obtain important evidence or there is a significant risk that such evidence may not be subsequently available.

7. A State which has challenged a ruling of the Pre-Trial Chamber under this article may challenge the admissibility of a case under article 19 on the grounds of additional significant facts or significant change of circumstances.

Article 19

Challenges to the jurisdiction of the Court or the admissibility of a case 1. The Court shall satisfy itself that it has jurisdiction in any case brought before it. The Court may, on its own motion, determine the admissibility of a case in accordance with article 17.

2. Challenges to the admissibility of a case on the grounds referred to in article 17 or challenges to the jurisdiction of the Court may be made by:

(a) An accused or a person for whom a warrant of arrest or a summons to appear has been issued under article 58;

(b) A State which has jurisdiction over a case, on the ground that it is investigating or prosecuting the case or has investigated or prosecuted; or

(c) A State from which acceptance of jurisdiction is required under article 12.

3. The Prosecutor may seek a ruling from the Court regarding a question of jurisdiction or admissibility. In proceedings with respect to jurisdiction or admissibility, those who have referred the situation under article 13, as well as victims, may also submit observations to the Court.

4. The admissibility of a case or the jurisdiction of the Court may be challenged only once by any person or State referred to in paragraph 2. The challenge shall take place prior to or at the commencement of the trial. In exceptional circumstances, the Court may grant leave for a challenge to be brought more than once or at a time later than the commencement of the trial. Challenges to the admissibility of a case, at the commencement of a trial, or subsequently with the leave of the Court, may be based only on article 17, paragraph 1 (c).

5. A State referred to in paragraph 2 (b) and (c) shall make a challenge at the earliest opportunity.

6. Prior to the confirmation of the charges, challenges to the admissibility of a case or challenges to the

jurisdiction of the Court shall be referred to the Pre-Trial Chamber. After confirmation of the charges, they shall be referred to the Trial Chamber. Decisions with respect to jurisdiction or admissibility may be appealed to the Appeals Chamber in accordance with article 82.

7. If a challenge is made by a State referred to in paragraph 2 (b) or (c), the Prosecutor shall suspend the investigation until such time as the Court makes a determination in accordance with article 17.

8. Pending a ruling by the Court, the Prosecutor may seek authority from the Court:

(a) To pursue necessary investigative steps of the kind referred to in article 18, paragraph 6;

(b) To take a statement or testimony from a witness or complete the collection and examination of evidence which had begun prior to the making of the challenge; and

(c) In cooperation with the relevant States, to prevent the absconding of persons in respect of whom the Prosecutor has already requested a warrant of arrest under article 58.

9. The making of a challenge shall not affect the validity of any act performed by the Prosecutor or any order or warrant issued by the Court prior to the making of the challenge.

10. If the Court has decided that a case is inadmissible under article 17, the Prosecutor may submit a request for a review of the decision when he or she is fully satisfied that new facts have arisen which negate the basis on which the case had previously been found inadmissible under article 17.

11. If the Prosecutor, having regard to the matters referred to in article 17, defers an investigation, the Prosecutor may request that the relevant State make available to the Prosecutor information on the proceedings. That information shall, at the request of the State concerned, be confidential. If the Prosecutor thereafter decides to proceed with an investigation, he or she shall notify the State to which deferral of the proceedings has taken place.

Article 20

Ne bis in idem 1. Except as provided in this Statute, no person shall be tried before the Court with respect to conduct which formed the basis of crimes for which the person has been convicted or acquitted by the Court.

2. No person shall be tried by another court for a crime referred to in article 5 for which that person has already been convicted or acquitted by the Court.

3. No person who has been tried by another court for conduct also proscribed under article 6, 7 or 8 shall be tried by the Court with respect to the same conduct unless the proceedings in the other court:

(a) Were for the purpose of shielding the person concerned from criminal responsibility for crimes within the jurisdiction of the Court; or

(b) Otherwise were not conducted independently or impartially in accordance with the norms of due process recognized by international law and were conducted in a manner which, in the circumstances, was inconsistent with an intent to bring the person concerned to justice.

Article 21

Applicable law 1. The Court shall apply:

(a) In the first place, this Statute, Elements of Crimes and its Rules of Procedure and Evidence;

(b) In the second place, where appropriate, applicable treaties and the principles and rules of international law, including the established principles of the international law of armed conflict;

(c) Failing that, general principles of law derived by the Court from national laws of legal systems of the world including, as appropriate, the national laws of States that would normally exercise jurisdiction over the crime, provided that those principles are not inconsistent with this Statute and with international law and internationally recognized norms and standards.

2. The Court may apply principles and rules of law as interpreted in its previous decisions.

3. The application and interpretation of law pursuant to this article must be consistent with internationally recognized human rights, and be without any adverse distinction founded on grounds such as gender as defined in article 7, paragraph 3, age, race, colour, language, religion or belief, political or other opinion, national, ethnic or social origin, wealth, birth or other status.

PART 3. GENERAL PRINCIPLES OF CRIMINAL LAW

Article 22

Nullum crimen sine lege 1. A person shall not be criminally responsible under this Statute unless the conduct in question constitutes, at the time it takes place, a crime within the jurisdiction of the Court.

2. The definition of a crime shall be strictly construed and shall not be extended by analogy. In case of ambiguity, the definition shall be interpreted in favour of the person being investigated, prosecuted or convicted.

3. This article shall not affect the characterization of any conduct as criminal under international law independently of this Statute.

Article 23

Nulla poena sine lege A person convicted by the Court may be punished only in accordance with this Statute.

Article 24

Non-retroactivity ratione personae 1. No person shall be criminally responsible under this Statute for conduct prior to the entry into force of the Statute.

2. In the event of a change in the law applicable to a given case prior to a final judgement, the law more favourable to the person being investigated, prosecuted or convicted shall apply.

Article 25

Individual criminal responsibility 1. The Court shall have jurisdiction over natural persons pursuant to this Statute.

2. A person who commits a crime within the jurisdiction of the Court shall be individually responsible and liable for punishment in accordance with this Statute.

3. In accordance with this Statute, a person shall be criminally responsible and liable for punishment for a crime within the jurisdiction of the Court if that person:

(a) Commits such a crime, whether as an individual, jointly with another or through another person, regardless of whether that other person is criminally responsible;

(b) Orders, solicits or induces the commission of such a crime which in fact occurs or is attempted;

(c) For the purpose of facilitating the commission of such a crime, aids, abets or otherwise assists in its commission or its attempted commission, including providing the means for its commission;

(d) In any other way contributes to the commission or attempted commission of such a crime by a group of persons acting with a common purpose. Such contribution shall be intentional and shall either:

(i) Be made with the aim of furthering the criminal activity or criminal purpose of the group, where such activity or purpose involves the commission of a crime within the jurisdiction of the Court; or

(ii) Be made in the knowledge of the intention of the group to commit the crime;

(e) In respect of the crime of genocide, directly and publicly incites others to commit genocide;

(f) Attempts to commit such a crime by taking action that commences its execution by means of a substantial step, but the crime does not occur because of circumstances independent of the person's intentions. However, a person who abandons the effort to commit the crime or otherwise prevents the completion of the crime shall not be liable for punishment under this Statute for the attempt to commit that crime if that person completely and voluntarily gave up the criminal purpose.

4. No provision in this Statute relating to individual criminal responsibility shall affect the responsibility of States under international law.

Article 26

Exclusion of jurisdiction over persons under eighteen The Court shall have no jurisdiction over any person who was under the age of 18 at the time of the alleged commission of a crime.

Article 27

Irrelevance of official capacity 1. This Statute shall apply equally to all persons without any distinction based on official capacity. In particular, official capacity as a Head of State or Government, a member of a Government or parliament, an elected representative or a government official shall in no case exempt a person from criminal responsibility under this Statute, nor shall it, in and of itself, constitute a ground for reduction of sentence.

2. Immunities or special procedural rules which may attach to the official capacity of a person, whether under national or international law, shall not bar the Court from exercising its jurisdiction over such a person.

Article 28

Responsibility of commanders and other superiors In addition to other grounds of criminal responsibility under this Statute for crimes within the jurisdiction of the Court:

(a) A military commander or person effectively acting as a military commander shall be criminally responsible for crimes within the jurisdiction of the Court committed by forces under his or her effective command and control, or effective authority and control as the case may be, as a result of his or her failure to exercise control properly over such forces, where:

(i) That military commander or person either knew or, owing to the circumstances at the time, should have known that the forces were committing or about to commit such crimes; and

(ii) That military commander or person failed to take all necessary and reasonable measures within his or her power to prevent or repress their commission or to submit the matter to the competent authorities for investigation and prosecution.

(b) With respect to superior and subordinate relationships not described in paragraph (a), a superior shall be criminally responsible for crimes within the jurisdiction of the Court committed by subordinates under his or her effective authority and control, as a result of his or her failure to exercise control properly over such subordinates, where:

(i) The superior either knew, or consciously disregarded information which clearly indicated, that the subordinates were committing or about to commit such crimes;

(ii) The crimes concerned activities that were within the effective responsibility and control of the superior; and

(iii) The superior failed to take all necessary and reasonable measures within his or her power to prevent or repress their commission or to submit the matter to the competent authorities for investigation and prosecution.

Article 29

Non-applicability of statute of limitations The crimes within the jurisdiction of the Court shall not be subject to any statute of limitations.

Article 30

Mental element 1. Unless otherwise provided, a person shall be criminally responsible and liable for punishment for a crime within the jurisdiction of the Court only if the material elements are committed with intent and knowledge.

2. For the purposes of this article, a person has intent where:

(a) In relation to conduct, that person means to engage in the conduct;

(b) In relation to a consequence, that person means to cause that consequence or is aware that it will occur in the ordinary course of events.

3. For the purposes of this article, "knowledge" means awareness that a circumstance exists or a consequence will occur in the ordinary course of events. "Know" and "knowingly" shall be construed accordingly.

Article 31

Grounds for excluding criminal responsibility 1. In addition to other grounds for excluding criminal re-

sponsibility provided for in this Statute, a person shall not be criminally responsible if, at the time of that person's conduct:

(a) The person suffers from a mental disease or defect that destroys that person's capacity to appreciate the unlawfulness or nature of his or her conduct, or capacity to control his or her conduct to conform to the requirements of law;

(b) The person is in a state of intoxication that destroys that person's capacity to appreciate the unlawfulness or nature of his or her conduct, or capacity to control his or her conduct to conform to the requirements of law, unless the person has become voluntarily intoxicated under such circumstances that the person knew, or disregarded the risk, that, as a result of the intoxication, he or she was likely to engage in conduct constituting a crime within the jurisdiction of the Court;

(c) The person acts reasonably to defend himself or herself or another person or, in the case of war crimes, property which is essential for the survival of the person or another person or property which is essential for accomplishing a military mission, against an imminent and unlawful use of force in a manner proportionate to the degree of danger to the person or the other person or property protected. The fact that the person was involved in a defensive operation conducted by forces shall not in itself constitute a ground for excluding criminal responsibility under this subparagraph;

(d) The conduct which is alleged to constitute a crime within the jurisdiction of the Court has been caused by duress resulting from a threat of imminent death or of continuing or imminent serious bodily harm against that person or another person, and the person acts necessarily and reasonably to avoid this threat, provided that the person does not intend to cause a greater harm than the one sought to be avoided. Such a threat may either be:

(i) Made by other persons; or

(ii) Constituted by other circumstances beyond that person's control.

2. The Court shall determine the applicability of the grounds for excluding criminal responsibility provided for in this Statute to the case before it.

3. At trial, the Court may consider a ground for excluding criminal responsibility other than those referred to in paragraph 1 where such a ground is derived from applicable law as set forth in article 21. The procedures relating to the consideration of such a ground shall be provided for in the Rules of Procedure and Evidence.

Article 32

Mistake of fact or mistake of law 1. A mistake of fact shall be a ground for excluding criminal responsibility only if it negates the mental element required by the crime.

2. A mistake of law as to whether a particular type of conduct is a crime within the jurisdiction of the Court shall not be a ground for excluding criminal responsibility. A mistake of law may, however, be a ground for excluding criminal responsibility if it negates the mental element required by such a crime, or as provided for in article 33.

Article 33

Superior orders and prescription of law 1. The fact that a crime within the jurisdiction of the Court has been committed by a person pursuant to an order of a Government or of a superior, whether military or civilian, shall not relieve that person of criminal responsibility unless:

(a) The person was under a legal obligation to obey orders of the Government or the superior in question;

(b) The person did not know that the order was unlawful; and

(c) The order was not manifestly unlawful.

2. For the purposes of this article, orders to commit genocide or crimes against humanity are manifestly unlawful.

Security Council Resolution 808

SOURCE UN Documentation Center. Available from http://www.un.org/documents.

INTRODUCTION Unlike most international courts, the ICTY and ICTR were not established by treaty. Instead, they exist as a consequence of decisions taken by the UN Security Council under the authority granted it by the UN Charter to maintain or restore international peace and security. The resolutions thus fall under UN Charter Chapter VII which makes them legally binding on UN member states; the statutes were similarly approved by the UN Security Council under its Chapter VII authority.

Adopted by the Security Council at its 3175th meeting, on 22 February 1993

The Security Council,

Reaffirming its resolution 713 (1991) of 25 September 1991 and all subsequent relevant resolutions,

Recalling paragraph 10 of its resolution 764 (1992) of 13 July 1992, in which it reaffirmed that all parties are bound to comply with the obligations under international humanitarian law and in particular the Geneva Conventions of 12 August 1949, and that persons who commit or order the commission of grave breaches of the Conventions are individually responsible in respect of such breaches,

Recalling also its resolution 771 (1992) of 13 August 1992, in which, *inter alia,* it demanded that all parties and others concerned in the former Yugoslavia, and all military forces in Bosnia and Herzegovina, immediately cease and desist from all breaches of international humanitarian law,

Recalling further its resolution 780 (1992) of 6 October 1992, in which it requested the Secretary-General to establish, as a matter of urgency, an impartial Commission of Experts to examine and analyse the information submitted pursuant to resolutions 771 (1992) and 780 (1992), together with such further information as the Commission of Experts may obtain, with a view to providing the Secretary-General with its conclusions on the evidence of grave breaches of the Geneva Conventions and other violations of international humanitarian law committed in the territory of the former Yugoslavia,

Having considered the interim report of the Commission of Experts established by resolution 780 (1992) (S/25274), in which the Commission observed that a decision to establish an ad hoc international tribunal in relation to events in the territory of the former Yugoslavia would be consistent with the direction of its work,

Expressing once again its grave alarm at continuing reports of widespread violations of international humanitarian law occurring within the territory of the former Yugoslavia, including reports of mass killings and the continuance of the practice of "ethnic cleansing",

Determining that this situation constitutes a threat to international peace and security,

Determined to put an end to such crimes and to take effective measures to bring to justice the persons who are responsible for them,

Convinced that in the particular circumstances of the former Yugoslavia the establishment of an international tribunal would enable this aim to be achieved and would contribute to the restoration and maintenance of peace,

Noting in this regard the recommendation by the Co-Chairmen of the Steering Committee of the International Conference on the Former Yugoslavia for the establishment of such a tribunal (S/25221),

Noting also with grave concern the "report of the European Community investigative mission into the

treatment of Muslim women in the former Yugoslavia"
(S/25240, annex I),

Noting further the report of the committee of jurists
submitted by France (S/25266), the report of the commission of jurists submitted by Italy (S/25300), and the
report transmitted by the Permanent Representative of
Sweden on behalf of the Chairman-in-Office of the
Conference on Security and Cooperation in Europe
(CSCE) (S/25307),

1.*Decides* that an international tribunal shall be established for the prosecution of persons responsible for
serious violations of international humanitarian law
committed in the territory of the former Yugoslavia
since 1991;

2. *Requests* the Secretary-General to submit for
consideration by the Council at the earliest possible
date, and if possible no later than 60 days after the
adoption of the present resolution, a report on all aspects of this matter, including specific proposals and
where appropriate options for the effective and expeditious implementation of the decision contained in paragraph 1 above, taking into account suggestions put forward in this regard by Member States;

3. *Decides* to remain actively seized of the matter.

Security Council Resolution 827

SOURCE UN Documentation Center. Available from http://
www.un.org/documents.

*Adopted by the Security Council at its 3217th meet-
ing, on 25 May 1993*

The Security Council,

Reaffirming its resolution 713 (1991) of 25 September 1991 and all subsequent relevant resolutions,

Having considered the report of the Secretary-
General (S/25704 and Add..1) pursuant to paragraph 2
of resolution 808 (1993),

Expressing once again its grave alarm at continuing
reports of widespread and flagrant violations of international humanitarian law occurring within the territory
of the former Yugoslavia, and especially in the Republic
of Bosnia and Herzegovina, including reports of mass
killings, massive, organized and systematic detention
and rape of women, and the continuance of the practice
of "ethnic cleansing", including for the acquisition and
the holding of territory,

Determining that this situation continues to constitute a threat to international peace and security,

Determined to put an end to such crimes and to
take effective measures to bring to justice the persons
who are responsible for them,

Convinced that in the particular circumstances of
the former Yugoslavia the establishment as an ad hoc
measure by the Council of an international tribunal and
the prosecution of persons responsible for serious violations of international humanitarian law would enable
this aim to be achieved and would contribute to the restoration and maintenance of peace,

Believing that the establishment of an international
tribunal and the prosecution of persons responsible for
the above-mentioned violations of international humanitarian law will contribute to ensuring that such violations are halted and effectively redressed,

Noting in this regard the recommendation by the
Co-Chairmen of the Steering Committee of the International Conference on the Former Yugoslavia for the establishment of such a tribunal (S/25221),

Reaffirming in this regard its decision in resolution
808 (1993) that an international tribunal shall be established for the prosecution of persons responsible for serious violations of international humanitarian law committed in the territory of the former Yugoslavia since
1991,

Considering that, pending the appointment of the
Prosecutor of the International Tribunal, the-
Commission of Experts established pursuant to resolution 780 (1992) should continue on an urgent basis the
collection of information relating to evidence of grave
breaches of the Geneva Conventions and other violations of international humanitarian law as proposed in
its interim report (S/25274),

Acting under Chapter VII of the Charter of the
United Nations,

1. *Approves,* the report of the Secretary-General;

2. *Decides* hereby to establish an international tribunal for the sole purpose of prosecuting persons responsible for serious violations of international humanitarian law committed in the territory of the former
Yugoslavia between 1 January 1991 and a date to be determined by the Security Council upon the restoration
of peace and to this end to adopt the Statute of the International Tribunal annexed to the above-mentioned
report;

3. *Requests* the Secretary-General to submit to the
judges of the International Tribunal, upon their election, any suggestions received from States for the rules
of procedure and evidence called for in Article 15 of the
Statute of the International Tribunal;

4. *Decides* that all States shall cooperate fully with
the International Tribunal and its organs in accordance
with the present resolution and the Statute of the International Tribunal and that consequently all States shall

take any measures necessary under their domestic law to implement the provisions of the present resolution and the Statute, including the obligation of States to comply with requests for assistance or orders issued by a Trial Chamber under Article 29 of the Statute;

5. *Urges* States and intergovernmental and non-governmental organizations to contribute funds, equipment and services to the International Tribunal, including the offer of expert personnel;

6. *Decides* that the determination of the seat of the International Tribunal is subject to the conclusion of appropriate arrangements between the United Nations and the Netherlands acceptable to the Council, and that the International Tribunal may sit elsewhere when it considers it necessary for the efficient exercise of its functions;

7. *Decides* also that the work of the International Tribunal shall be carried out without prejudice to the right of the victims to seek, through appropriate means, compensation for damages incurred as a result of violations of international humanitarian law;

8. *Requests* the Secretary-General to implement urgently the present resolution and in particular to make practical arrangements for the effective functioning of the International Tribunal at the earliest time and to report periodically to the Council;

9. *Decides* to remain actively seized of the matter.

Security Council Resolution 955

SOURCE UN Documentation Center. Available from http://www.un.org/documents.

Adopted by the Security Council at its 3453rd meeting, on 8 November 1994

The Security Council,

Reaffirming all its previous resolutions on the situation in Rwanda,

Having considered the reports of the Secretary-General pursuant to paragraph 3 of resolution 935 (1994) of 1 July 1994 (S/1994/879 and S/1994/906), and having taken note of the reports of the Special Rapporteur for Rwanda of the United Nations Commission on Human Rights (S/1994/1157, annex I and annex II),

Expressing appreciation for the work of the Commission of Experts established pursuant to resolution 935 (1994), in particular its preliminary report on violations of international humanitarian law in Rwanda transmitted by the Secretary-General's letter of 1 October 1994 (S/1994/1125),

Expressing once again its grave concern at the reports indicating that genocide and other systematic, widespread and flagrant violations of international humanitarian law have been committed in Rwanda,

Determining that this situation continues to constitute a threat to international peace and security,

Determined to put an end to such crimes and to take effective measures to bring to justice the persons who are responsible for them,

Convinced that in the particular circumstances of Rwanda, the prosecution of persons responsible for serious violations of international humanitarian law would enable this aim to be achieved and would contribute to the process of national reconciliation and to the restoration and maintenance of peace,

Believing that the establishment of an international tribunal for the prosecution of persons responsible for genocide and the other above-mentioned violations of international humanitarian law will contribute to ensuring that such violations are halted and effectively redressed,

Stressing also the need for international cooperation to strengthen the courts and judicial system of Rwanda, having regard in particular to the necessity for those courts to deal with large numbers of suspects,

Considering that the Commission of Experts established pursuant to resolution 935 (1994) should continue on an urgent basis the collection of information relating to evidence of grave violations of international humanitarian law committed in the territory of Rwanda and should submit its final report to the Secretary-General by 30 November 1994,

Acting under Chapter VII of the Charter of the United Nations,

1. *Decides* hereby, having received the request of the Government of Rwanda (S/1994/1115), to establish an international tribunal for the sole purpose of prosecuting persons responsible for genocide and other serious violations of international humanitarian law committed in the territory of Rwanda and Rwandan citizens responsible for genocide and other such violations committed in the territory of neighbouring States, between 1 January 1994 and 31 December 1994 and to this end to adopt the Statute of the International Criminal Tribunal for Rwanda annexed hereto;

2. *Decides* that all States shall cooperate fully with the International Tribunal and its organs in accordance with the present resolution and the Statute of the International Tribunal and that consequently all States shall take any measures necessary under their domestic law to implement the provisions of the present resolution and the Statute, including the obligation of States to comply with requests for assistance or orders issued by

a Trial Chamber under Article 28 of the Statute, and requests States to keep the Secretary-General informed of such measures;

3. *Considers* that the Government of Rwanda should be notified prior to the taking of decisions under articles 26 and 27 of the Statute;

4. *Urges* States and intergovernmental and non-governmental organizations to contribute funds, equipment and services to the International Tribunal, including the offer of expert personnel;

5. *Requests* the Secretary-General to implement this resolution urgently and in particular to make practical arrangements for the effective functioning of the International Tribunal, including recommendations to the Council as to possible locations for the seat of the International Tribunal at the earliest time and to report periodically to the Council;

6. *Decides* that the seat of the International Tribunal shall be determined by the Council having regard to considerations of justice and fairness as well as administrative efficiency, including access to witnesses, and economy, and subject to the conclusion of appropriate arrangements between the United Nations and the State of the seat, acceptable to the Council, having regard to the fact that the International Tribunal may meet away from its seat when it considers it necessary for the efficient exercise of its functions; and decides that an office will be established and proceedings will be conducted in Rwanda, where feasible and appropriate, subject to the conclusion of similar appropriate arrangements;

7. *Decides* to consider increasing the number of judges and Trial Chambers of the International Tribunal if it becomes necessary;

8. *Decides* to remain actively seized of the matter.

Annex
Statute of the International Tribunal for Rwanda

Having been established by the Security Council acting under Chapter VII of the Charter of the United Nations, the International Criminal Tribunal for the Prosecution of Persons Responsible for Genocide and Other Serious Violations of International Humanitarian Law Committed in the Territory of Rwanda and Rwandan citizens responsible for genocide and other such violations committed in the territory of neighbouring States, between 1 January 1994 and 31 December 1994 (hereinafter referred to as "the International Tribunal for Rwanda") shall function in accordance with the provisions of the present Statute.

Article 1
Competence of the International Tribunal for Rwanda

The International Tribunal for Rwanda shall have the power to prosecute persons responsible for serious violations of international humanitarian law committed in the territory of Rwanda and Rwandan citizens responsible for such violations committed in the territory of neighbouring States, between 1 January 1994 and 31 December 1994, in accordance with the provisions of the present Statute.

Article 2
Genocide

1. The International Tribunal for Rwanda shall have the power to prosecute persons committing genocide as defined in paragraph 2 of this article or of committing any of the other acts enumerated in paragraph 3 of this article.

2. Genocide means any of the following acts committed with intent to destroy, in whole or in part, a national, ethnical, racial or religious group, as such:

(a) Killing members of the group;

(b) Causing serious bodily or mental harm to members of the group;

(c) Deliberately inflicting on the group conditions of life calculated to bring about its physical destruction in whole or in part;

(d) Imposing measures intended to prevent births within the group;

(e) Forcibly transferring children of the group to another group.

3. The following acts shall be punishable:

(a) Genocide;

(b) Conspiracy to commit genocide;

(c) Direct and public incitement to commit genocide;

(d) Attempt to commit genocide;

(e) Complicity in genocide.

Article 3
Crimes against humanity

The International Tribunal for Rwanda shall have the power to prosecute persons responsible for the following crimes when committed as part of a widespread or systematic attack against any civilian population on national, political, ethnic, racial or religious grounds:

(a) Murder;

(b) Extermination;

(c) Enslavement;

(d) Deportation;

(e) Imprisonment;

(f) Torture;

(g) Rape;

(h) Persecutions on political, racial and religious grounds;

(i) Other inhumane acts.

Article 4
Violations of Article 3 common to the Geneva Conventions and of Additional Protocol II

The International Tribunal for Rwanda shall have the power to prosecute persons committing or ordering to be committed serious violations of Article 3 common to the Geneva Conventions of 12 August 1949 for the Protection of War Victims, and of Additional Protocol II thereto of 8 June 1977. These violations shall include, but shall not be limited to:

(a) Violence to life, health and physical or mental well-being of persons, in particular murder as well as cruel treatment such as torture, mutilation or any form of corporal punishment;

(b) Collective punishments;

(c) Taking of hostages;

(d) Acts of terrorism;

(e) Outrages upon personal dignity, in particular humiliating and degrading treatment, rape, enforced prostitution and any form of indecent assault;

(f) Pillage;

(g) The passing of sentences and the carrying out of executions without previous judgement pronounced by a regularly constituted court, affording all the judicial guarantees which are recognized as indispensable by civilized peoples;

(h) Threats to commit any of the foregoing acts.

Article 5
Personal jurisdiction

The International Tribunal for Rwanda shall have jurisdiction over natural persons pursuant to the provisions of the present Statute.

Article 6

Individual criminal responsibility

1. A person who planned, instigated, ordered, committed or otherwise aided and abetted in the planning, preparation or execution of a crime referred to in articles 2 to 4 of the present Statute, shall be individually responsible for the crime.

2. The official position of any accused person, whether as Head of State or Government or as a responsible Government official, shall not relieve such person of criminal responsibility nor mitigate punishment.

3. The fact that any of the acts referred to in articles 2 to 4 of the present Statute was committed by a subordinate does not relieve his or her superior of criminal responsibility if he or she knew or had reason to know that the subordinate was about to commit such acts or had done so and the superior failed to take the necessary and reasonable measures to prevent such acts or to punish the perpetrators thereof.

4. The fact that an accused person acted pursuant to an order of a Government or of a superior shall not relieve him or her of criminal responsibility, but may be considered in mitigation of punishment if the International Tribunal for Rwanda determines that justice so requires.

Article 7
Territorial and temporal jurisdiction

The territorial jurisdiction of the International Tribunal for Rwanda shall extend to the territory of Rwanda including its land surface and airspace as well as to the territory of neighbouring States in respect of serious violations of international humanitarian law committed by Rwandan citizens. The temporal jurisdiction of the International Tribunal for Rwanda shall extend to a period beginning on 1 January 1994 and ending on 31 December 1994.

Article 8
Concurrent jurisdiction

1. The International Tribunal for Rwanda and national courts shall have concurrent jurisdiction to prosecute persons for serious violations of international humanitarian law committed in the territory of Rwanda and Rwandan citizens for such violations committed in the territory of neighbouring States, between 1 January 1994 and 31 December 1994.

2. The International Tribunal for Rwanda shall have primacy over the national courts of all States. At any stage of the procedure, the International Tribunal for Rwanda may formally request national courts to defer to its competence in accordance with the present Statute and the Rules of Procedure and Evidence of the International Tribunal for Rwanda.

Article 9
Non bis in idem

1. No person shall be tried before a national court for acts constituting serious violations of international humanitarian law under the present Statute, for which he or she has already been tried by the International Tribunal for Rwanda.

2. A person who has been tried by a national court for acts constituting serious violations of international

humanitarian law may be subsequently tried by the International Tribunal for Rwanda only if:

(a) The act for which he or she was tried was characterized as an ordinary crime; or

(b) The national court proceedings were not impartial or independent, were designed to shield the accused from international criminal responsibility, or the case was not diligently prosecuted

3. In considering the penalty to be imposed on a person convicted of a crime under the present Statute, the International Tribunal for Rwanda shall take into account the extent to which any penalty imposed by a national court on the same person for the same act has already been served.

Article 10
Organization of the International Tribunal for Rwanda

The International Tribunal for Rwanda shall consist of the following organs:

(a) The Chambers, comprising two Trial Chambers and an Appeals Chamber;

(b) The Prosecutor; and

(c) A Registry.

Article 11
Composition of the Chambers

The Chambers shall be composed of eleven independent judges, no two of whom may be nationals of the same State, who shall serve as follows:

(a) Three judges shall serve in each of the Trial Chambers;

(b) Five judges shall serve in the Appeals Chamber.

Article 12
Qualification and election of judges

1. The judges shall be persons of high moral character, impartiality and integrity who possess the qualifications required in their respective countries for appointment to the highest judicial offices. In the overall composition of the Chambers due account shall be taken of the experience of the judges in criminal law, international law, including international humanitarian law and human rights law.

2. The members of the Appeals Chamber of the International Tribunal for the Prosecution of Persons Responsible for Serious Violations of International Humanitarian Law Committed in the Territory of the Former Yugoslavia since 1991 (hereinafter referred to as "the International Tribunal for the Former Yugoslavia") shall also serve as the members of the Appeals Chamber of the International Tribunal for Rwanda.

3. The judges of the Trial Chambers of the International Tribunal for Rwanda shall be elected by the General Assembly from a list submitted by the Security Council, in the following manner:

(a) The Secretary-General shall invite nominations for judges of the Trial Chambers from States Members of the United Nations and non-member States maintaining permanent observer missions at United Nations Headquarters;

(b) Within thirty days of the date of the invitation of the Secretary-General, each State may nominate up to two candidates meeting the qualifications set out in paragraph 1 above, no two of whom shall be of the same nationality and neither of whom shall be of the same nationality as any judge on the Appeals Chamber;

(c) The Secretary-General shall forward the nominations received to the Security Council. From the nominations received the Security Council shall establish a list of not less than twelve and not more than eighteen candidates, taking due account of adequate representation on the International Tribunal for Rwanda of the principal legal systems of the world;

(d) The President of the Security Council shall transmit the list of candidates to the President of the General Assembly. From that list the General Assembly shall elect the six judges of the Trial Chambers. The candidates who receive an absolute majority of the votes of the States Members of the United Nations and of the non-Member States maintaining permanent observer missions at United Nations Headquarters, shall be declared elected. Should two candidates of the same nationality obtain the required majority vote, the one who received the higher number of votes shall be considered elected.

4. In the event of a vacancy in the Trial Chambers, after consultation with the Presidents of the Security Council and of the General Assembly, the Secretary-General shall appoint a person meeting the qualifications of paragraph 1 above, for the remainder of the term of office concerned.

5. The judges of the Trial Chambers shall be elected for a term of four years. The terms and conditions of service shall be those of the judges of the International Tribunal for the Former Yugoslavia. They shall be eligible for re-election.

Article 13
Officers and members of the Chambers

1. The judges of the International Tribunal for Rwanda shall elect a President.

2. After consultation with the judges of the International Tribunal for Rwanda, the President shall assign the judges to the Trial Chambers. A judge shall serve only in the Chamber to which he or she was assigned.

3. The judges of each Trial Chamber shall elect a Presiding Judge, who shall conduct all of the proceedings of that Trial Chamber as a whole.

Article 14
Rules of procedure and evidence

The judges of the International Tribunal for Rwanda shall adopt, for the purpose of proceedings before the International Tribunal for Rwanda, the rules of procedure and evidence for the conduct of the pre-trial phase of the proceedings, trials and appeals, the admission of evidence, the protection of victims and witnesses and other appropriate matters of the International Tribunal for the Former Yugoslavia with such changes as they deem necessary.

Article 15
The Prosecutor

1. The Prosecutor shall be responsible for the investigation and prosecution of persons responsible for serious violations of international humanitarian law committed in the territory of Rwanda and Rwandan citizens responsible for such violations committed in the territory of neighbouring States, between 1 January 1994 and 31 December 1994.

2. The Prosecutor shall act independently as a separate organ of the International Tribunal for Rwanda. He or she shall not seek or receive instructions from any Government or from any other source.

3. The Prosecutor of the International Tribunal for the Former Yugoslavia shall also serve as the Prosecutor of the International Tribunal for Rwanda. He or she shall have additional staff, including an additional Deputy Prosecutor, to assist with prosecutions before the International Tribunal for Rwanda. Such

staff shall be appointed by the Secretary-General on the recommendation of the Prosecutor.

Article 16
The Registry

1. The Registry shall be responsible for the administration and servicing of the International Tribunal for Rwanda.

2. The Registry shall consist of a Registrar and such other staff as may be required.

3. The Registrar shall be appointed by the Secretary-General after consultation with the President of the International Tribunal for Rwanda. He or she shall

serve for a four-year term and be eligible for reappointment. The terms and conditions of service of the Registrar shall be those of an Assistant Secretary-General of the United Nations.

4. The staff of the Registry shall be appointed by the Secretary-General on the recommendation of the Registrar.

Article 17
Investigation and preparation of indictment

1. The Prosecutor shall initiate investigations ex-officio or on the basis of information obtained from any source, particularly from Governments, United Nations organs, intergovernmental and non-governmental organizations. The Prosecutor shall assess the information received or obtained and decide whether there is sufficient basis to proceed.

2. The Prosecutor shall have the power to question suspects, victims and witnesses, to collect evidence and to conduct on-site investigations. In carrying out these tasks, the Prosecutor may, as appropriate, seek the assistance of the State authorities concerned.

3. If questioned, the suspect shall be entitled to be assisted by counsel of his or her own choice, including the right to have legal assistance assigned to the suspect without payment by him or her in any such case if he or she does not have sufficient means to pay for it, as well as to necessary translation into and from a language he or she speaks and understands.

4. Upon a determination that a prima facie case exists, the Prosecutor shall prepare an indictment containing a concise statement of the facts and the crime or crimes with which the accused is charged under the Statute. The indictment shall be transmitted to a judge of the Trial Chamber.

Article 18
Review of the indictment

1. The judge of the Trial Chamber to whom the indictment has been transmitted shall review it. If satisfied that a prima facie case has been established by the Prosecutor, he or she shall confirm the indictment. If not so satisfied, the indictment shall be dismissed.

2. Upon confirmation of an indictment, the judge may, at the request of the Prosecutor, issue such orders and warrants for the arrest, detention, surrender or transfer of persons, and any other orders as may be required for the conduct of the trial.

Article 19
Commencement and conduct of trial proceedings

1. The Trial Chambers shall ensure that a trial is fair and expeditious and that proceedings are conduct-

ed in accordance with the rules of procedure and evidence, with full respect for the rights of the accused and due regard for the protection of victims and witnesses.

2. A person against whom an indictment has been confirmed shall, pursuant to an order or an arrest warrant of the International Tribunal for Rwanda, be taken into custody, immediately informed of the charges against him or her and transferred to the International Tribunal for Rwanda.

3. The Trial Chamber shall read the indictment, satisfy itself that the rights of the accused are respected, confirm that the accused understands the indictment, and instruct the accused to enter a plea. The Trial Chamber shall then set the date for trial.

4. The hearings shall be public unless the Trial Chamber decides to close the proceedings in accordance with its rules of procedure and evidence.

Article 20
Rights of the accused

1. All persons shall be equal before the International Tribunal for Rwanda.

2. In the determination of charges against him or her, the accused shall be entitled to a fair and public hearing, subject to article 21 of the Statute.

3. The accused shall be presumed innocent until proved guilty according to the provisions of the present Statute.

4. In the determination of any charge against the accused pursuant to the present Statute, the accused shall be entitled to the following minimum guarantees, in full equality:

(a) To be informed promptly and in detail in a language which he or she understands of the nature and cause of the charge against him or her;

(b) To have adequate time and facilities for the preparation of his or her defence and to communicate with counsel of his or her own choosing;

(c) To be tried without undue delay;

(d) To be tried in his or her presence, and to defend himself or herself in person or through legal assistance of his or her own choosing; to be informed, if he or she does not have legal assistance, of this right; and to have legal assistance assigned to him or her, in any case where the interests of justice so require, and without payment by him or her in any such case if he or she does not have sufficient means to pay for it;

(e) To examine, or have examined, the witnesses against him or her and to obtain the attendance and examination of witnesses on his or her behalf under the same conditions as witnesses against him or her;

(f) To have the free assistance of an interpreter if he or she cannot understand or speak the language used in the International Tribunal for Rwanda;

(g) Not to be compelled to testify against himself or herself or to confess guilt.

Article 21
Protection of victims and witnesses

The International Tribunal for Rwanda shall provide in its rules of procedure and evidence for the protection of victims and witnesses. Such protection measures shall include, but shall not be limited to, the conduct of in camera proceedings and the protection of the victim's identity.

Article 22
Judgement

1. The Trial Chambers shall pronounce judgements and impose sentences and penalties on persons convicted of serious violations of international humanitarian law.

2. The judgement shall be rendered by a majority of the judges of the Trial Chamber, and shall be delivered by the Trial Chamber in public. It shall be accompanied by a reasoned opinion in writing, to which separate or dissenting opinions may be appended.

Article 23
Penalties

1. The penalty imposed by the Trial Chamber shall be limited to imprisonment. In determining the terms of imprisonment, the Trial Chambers shall have recourse to the general practice regarding prison sentences in the courts of Rwanda.

2. In imposing the sentences, the Trial Chambers should take into account such factors as the gravity of the offence and the individual circumstances of the convicted person.

3. In addition to imprisonment, the Trial Chambers may order the return of any property and proceeds acquired by criminal conduct, including by means of duress, to their rightful owners.

Article 24
Appellate proceedings

1. The Appeals Chamber shall hear appeals from persons convicted by the Trial Chambers or from the Prosecutor on the following grounds:

(a) An error on a question of law invalidating the decision; or

(b) An error of fact which has occasioned a miscarriage of justice.

2. The Appeals Chamber may affirm, reverse or revise the decisions taken by the Trial Chambers.

Article 25
Review proceedings

Where a new fact has been discovered which was not known at the time of the proceedings before the Trial Chambers or the Appeals Chamber and which could have been a decisive factor in reaching the decision, the convicted person or the Prosecutor may submit to the International Tribunal for Rwanda an application for review of the judgement.

Article 26
Enforcement of sentences

Imprisonment shall be served in Rwanda or any of the States on a list of States which have indicated to the Security Council their willingness to accept convicted persons, as designated by the International Tribunal for Rwanda. Such imprisonment shall be in accordance with the applicable law of the State concerned, subject to the supervision of the International Tribunal for Rwanda.

Article 27
Pardon or commutation of sentences

If, pursuant to the applicable law of the State in which the convicted person is imprisoned, he or she is eligible for pardon or commutation of sentence, the State concerned shall notify the International Tribunal for Rwanda accordingly. There shall only be pardon or commutation of sentence if the President of the International Tribunal for Rwanda, in consultation with the judges, so decides on the basis of the interests of justice and the general principles of law.

Article 28
Cooperation and judicial assistance

1. States shall cooperate with the International Tribunal for Rwanda in the investigation and prosecution of persons accused of committing serious violations of international humanitarian law.

2. States shall comply without undue delay with any request for assistance or an order issued by a Trial Chamber, including, but not limited to:

(a) The identification and location of persons;

(b) The taking of testimony and the production of evidence;

(c) The service of documents;

(d) The arrest or detention of persons;

(e) The surrender or the transfer of the accused to the International Tribunal for Rwanda.

Article 29
The status, privileges and immunities of the International Tribunal for Rwanda

1. The Convention on the Privileges and Immunities of the United Nations of 13 February 1946 shall apply to the International Tribunal for Rwanda, the judges, the Prosecutor and his or her staff, and the Registrar and his or her staff.

2. The judges, the Prosecutor and the Registrar shall enjoy the privileges and immunities, exemptions and facilities accorded to diplomatic envoys, in accordance with international law.

3. The staff of the Prosecutor and of the Registrar shall enjoy the privileges and immunities accorded to officials of the United Nations under articles V and VII of the Convention referred to in paragraph 1 of this article.

4. Other persons, including the accused, required at the seat or meeting place of the International Tribunal for Rwanda shall be accorded such treatment as is necessary for the proper functioning of the International Tribunal for Rwanda.

Article 30
Expenses of the International Tribunal for Rwanda

The expenses of the International Tribunal for Rwanda shall be expenses of the Organization in accordance with Article 17 of the Charter of the United Nations.

Article 31
Working languages

The working languages of the International Tribunal shall be English and French.

Article 32
Annual report

The President of the International Tribunal for Rwanda shall submit an annual report of the International Tribunal for Rwanda to the Security Council and to the General Assembly.

Supplementary Convention on the Abolition of Slavery, the Slave Trade, and Institutions and Practices Similar to Slavery; September 7, 1956

SOURCE The Avalon Project at Yale Law School. Available from http://www.yale.edu/lawweb/avalon/avalon.htm

INTRODUCTION The Supplementary Convention on the Abolition of Slavery was adopted in 1956 and entered into force the next year. It defines "institutions and practices similar to slavery," requiring State to take steps towards their progressive abolition of abandonment. States are also required to create criminal offenses for transporting slaves, marking or mutilating persons with a view to their subjugation, and enslavement itself.

PREAMBLE

The States Parties to the present Convention

Considering that freedom is the birthright of every human being; Mindful that the peoples of the United Nations reaffirmed in the Charter their faith in the dignity and worth of the human person;

Considering that the Universal Declaration of Human Rights, proclaimed by the General Assembly of the United Nations as a common standard of achievement for all peoples and all nations, states that no one shall be held in slavery or servitude and that slavery and the slave trade shall be prohibited in all their forms;

Recognizing that, since the conclusion of the Slavery Convention signed at Geneva on 25 September 1926, which was designed to secure the abolition of slavery and of the slave trade, further progress has been made towards this end;

Having regard to the Forced Labour Convention of 1930 and to subsequent action by the International Labour Organisation in regard to forced or compulsory labour;

Being aware, however, that slavery, the slave trade and institutions and practices similar to slavery have not yet been eliminated in all parts of the world;

Having decided, therefore, that the Convention of 1926, which remains operative, should now be augmented by the conclusion of a supplementary convention designed to intensify national as well as international efforts towards the abolition of slavery, the slave trade and institutions and practices similar to slavery;

Have agreed as follows:

SECTION I — INSTITUTIONS AND PRACTICES SIMILAR TO SLAVERY

Article 1

Each of the States Parties to this Convention shall take all practicable and necessary legislative and other measures to bring about progressively and as soon as possible the complete abolition or abandonment of the following institutions and practices, where they still exist and whether or not they are covered by the definition of slavery contained in article 1 of the Slavery Convention signed at Geneva on 25 September 1926:

(a) Debt bondage, that is to say, the status or condition arising from a pledge by a debtor of his personal services or of those of a person under his control as security for a debt, if the value of those services as reasonably assessed is not applied towards the liquidation of the debt or the length and nature of those services are not respectively limited and defined;

(b) Serfdom, that is to say, the condition or status of a tenant who is by law, custom or agreement bound to live and labour on land belonging to another person and to render some determinate service to such other person, whether for reward or not, and is not free to change his status;

(c) Any institution or practice whereby:

(i) A woman, without the right to refuse, is promised or given in marriage on payment of a consideration in money or in kind to her parents, guardian, family or any other person or group; or

(ii) The husband of a woman, his family, or his clan, has the right to transfer her to another person for value received or otherwise; or

(iii) A woman on the death of her husband is liable to be inherited by another person;

(d) Any institution or practice whereby a child or young person under the age of 18 years is delivered by either or both of his natural parents or by his guardian to another person, whether for reward or not, with a view to the exploitation of the child or young person or of his labour.

Article 2

With a view to bringing to an end the institutions and practices mentioned in article 1 (c) of this Convention, the States Parties undertake to prescribe, where appropriate, suitable minimum ages of marriage, to encourage the use of facilities whereby the consent of both parties to a marriage may be freely expressed in the presence of a competent civil or religious authority, and to encourage the registration of marriages.

SECTION II — THE SLAVE TRADE

Article 3

1. The act of conveying or attempting to convey slaves from one country to another by whatever means of transport, or of being accessory thereto, shall be a criminal offence under the laws of the States Parties to this Convention and persons convicted thereof shall be liable to very severe penalties.

2. (a) The States Parties shall take all effective measures to prevent ships and aircraft authorized to fly their flags from conveying slaves and to punish persons guilty of such acts or of using national flags for that purpose.

(b) The States Parties shall take all effective measures to ensure that their ports, airfields and coasts are not used for the conveyance of slaves.

3. The States Parties to this Convention shall exchange information in order to ensure the practical coordination of the measures taken by them in combating the slave trade and shall inform each other of every case of the slave trade, and of every attempt to commit this criminal offence, which comes to their notice.

Article 4

Any slave who takes refuge on board any vessel of a State Party to this Convention shall ipso facto be free.

SECTION III — SLAVERY AND INSTITUTIONS AND PRACTICES SIMILAR TO SLAVERY

Article 5

In a country where the abolition or abandonment of slavery, or of the institutions or practices mentioned in article I of this Convention, is not yet complete, the act of mutilating, branding or otherwise marking a slave or a person of servile status in order to indicate his status, or as a punishment, or for any other reason, or of being accessory thereto, shall be a criminal offence under the laws of the States Parties to this Convention and persons convicted thereof shall be liable to punishment.

Article 6

1. The act of enslaving another person or of inducing another person to give himself or a person dependent upon him into slavery, or of attempting these acts, or being accessory thereto, or being a party to a conspiracy to accomplish any such acts, shall be a criminal offence under the laws of the States Parties to this Convention and persons convicted thereof shall be liable to punishment.

2. Subject to the provisions of the introductory paragraph of article 1 of this Convention, the provisions of paragraph 1 of the present article shall also apply to the act of inducing another person to place himself or a person dependent upon him into the servile status resulting from any of the institutions or practices mentioned in article 1, to any attempt to perform such acts, to bring accessory thereto, and to being a party to a conspiracy to accomplish any such acts.

SECTION IV — DEFINITIONS

Article 7

For the purposes of the present Convention:

(a) "Slavery" means, as defined in the Slavery Convention of 1926, the status or condition of a person over whom any or all of the powers attaching to the right of ownership are exercised, and "slave" means a person in such condition or status;

(b) "A person of servile status" means a person in the condition or status resulting from any of the institutions or practices mentioned in article 1 of this Convention;

(c) "Slave trade" means and includes all acts involved in the capture, acquisition or disposal of a person with intent to reduce him to slavery; all acts involved in the acquisition of a slave with a view to selling or exchanging him; all acts of disposal by sale of exchange of a person acquired with a view to being sold or exchanged; and, in general, every act of trade or transport in slaves by whatever means of conveyance.

SECTION V — CO-OPERATION BETWEEN STATES PARTIES AND COMMUNICATION OF INFORMATION

Article 8

1. The States Parties to this Convention undertake to co-operate with each other and with the United Nations to give effect to the foregoing provisions.

2. The Parties undertake to communicate to the Secretary-General of the United Nations copies of any laws, regulations and administrative measures enacted or put into effect to implement the provisions of this Convention.

3. The Secretary-General shall communicate the information received under paragraph 2 of this article to the other Parties and to the Economic and Social Council as part of the documentation for any discussion which the Council might undertake with a view to making further recommendations for the abolition of slavery, the slave trade or the institutions and practices which are the subject of this Convention.

SECTION VI — FINAL CLAUSES

Article 9

No reservations may be made to this Convention.

Article 10

Any dispute between States Parties to this Convention relating to its interpretation or application, which is not settled by negotiation, shall be referred to the International Court of Justice at the request of any one of the parties to the dispute, unless the parties concerned agree on another mode of settlement.

Article 11

1. This Convention shall be open until 1 July 1957 for signature by any State Member of the United Nations or of a specialized agency. It shall be subject to ratification by the signatory States, and the instruments of ratification shall be deposited with the Secretary-General of the United Nations, who shall inform each signatory and acceding State.

2. After 1 July 1957 this Convention shall be open for accession by any State Member of the United Nations or of a specialized agency, or by any other State to which an invitation to accede has been addressed by the General Assembly of the United Nations. Accession shall be effected by the deposit of a formal instrument with the Secretary-General of the United Nations, who shall inform each signatory and acceding State.

Article 12

1. This Convention shall apply to all non-self-governing, trust, colonial and other non-metropolitan territories for the international relations of which any State Party is responsible; the Party concerned shall, subject to the provisions of paragraph 2 of this article, at the time of signature, ratification or accession declare the non-metropolitan territory or territories to which the Convention shall apply ipso facto as a result of such signature, ratification or accession.

2. In any case in which the previous consent of a non-metropolitan territory is required by the constitutional laws or practices of the Party or of the non-metropolitan territory, the Party concerned shall endeavour to secure the needed consent of the non-metropolitan territory within the period of twelve months from the date of signature of the Convention by the metropolitan State, and when such consent has been obtained the Party shall notify the Secretary-General. This Convention shall apply to the territory or territories named in such notification from the date of its receipt by the Secretary-General.

3. After the expiry of the twelve month period mentioned in the preceding paragraph, the States Parties concerned shall inform the Secretary-General of the results of the consultations with those non-metropolitan territories for whose international relations they are responsible and whose consent to the application of this Convention may have been withheld.

Article 13

1. This Convention shall enter into force on the date on which two States have become Parties thereto.

2. It shall thereafter enter into force with respect to each State and territory on the date of deposit of the instrument of ratification or accession of that State or notification of application to that territory.

Article 14

1. The application of this Convention shall be divided into successive periods of three years, of which the first shall begin on the date of entry into force of the Convention in accordance with paragraph I of article 13.

2. Any State Party may denounce this Convention by a notice addressed by that State to the Secretary-General not less than six months before the expiration of the current three-year period. The Secretary-General shall notify all other Parties of each such notice and the date of the receipt thereof.

3. Denunciations shall take effect at the expiration of the current three-year period.

4. In cases where, in accordance with the provisions of article 12, this Convention has become applicable to a non-metropolitan territory of a Party, that Party may at any time thereafter, with the consent of the territory concerned, give notice to the Secretary-General of the United Nations denouncing this Convention separately in respect of that territory. The denunciation shall take effect one year after the date of the receipt of such notice by the Secretary-General, who shall notify all other Parties of such notice and the date of the receipt thereof.

Article 15

This Convention, of which the Chinese, English, French, Russian and Spanish texts are equally authentic, shall be deposited in the archives of the United Nations Secretariat. The Secretary-General shall prepare a certified copy thereof for communication to States Parties to this Convention, as well as to all other States Members of the United Nations and of the specialized agencies. IN WITNESS WHEREOF the undersigned, being duly authorized thereto by their respective Governments, have signed this Convention on the date appearing opposite their respective signatures.

DONE at the European Office of the United Nations at Geneva, this seventh day of September one thousand nine hundred and fifty-six.

Universal Declaration of Human Rights

SOURCE The Avalon Project at Yale Law School. Available from http://www.yale.edu/lawweb/avalon/avalon.htm

INTRODUCTION Adopted by the General Assembly of the United Nations on December 10, 1948, the Universal Declaration of Human Rights his described in its preamble as constituting a "common standard of achievement," Those who prepared it relied upon a study of national constitutions in an attempt to distill a common denominator of human rights that would be of universal application. The U.S. representative to the UN Commission on Human Rights, Eleanor Roosevelt, presided over the process, but she was assisted by personalities from Europe, Africa, Asia, Latin America, and the Arab world. The Declaration's significance has been reaffirmed subsequently in various treaties and declarations, and it retains its universal significance. Some experts describe the Declaration as a codification of customary international law, while others have argued that it is an authoritative interpretation of the more laconic human rights clauses found in the Charter of the United Nations.

Preamble

WHEREAS recognition of the inherent dignity and of the equal and inalienable rights of all members of the human family is the foundation of freedom, justice and peace in the world,

WHEREAS disregard and contempt for human rights have resulted in barbarous acts which have outraged the conscience of mankind, and the advent of a world in which human beings shall enjoy freedom of speech and belief and freedom from fear and want has been proclaimed as the highest aspiration of the common people,

WHEREAS it is essential, if man is not to be compelled to have recourse, as a last resort, to rebellion against tyranny and oppression, that human rights should be protected by the rule of law,

WHEREAS it is essential to promote the development of friendly relations between nations,

WHEREAS the peoples of the United Nations have in the Charter reaffirmed their faith in fundamental human rights, in the dignity and worth of the human person and in the equal rights of men and women and have determined to promote social progress and better standards of life in larger freedom,

WHEREAS Member States have pledged themselves to achieve, in co-operation with the United Nations, the promotion of universal respect for and observance of human rights and fundamental freedoms,

WHEREAS a common understanding of these rights and freedoms is of the greatest importance for the full realization of this pledge,

Now, Therefore,

The General Assembly

proclaims

This Universal Declaration of Human Rights as a common standard of achievement for all peoples and all nations, to the end that every individual and every organ of society, keeping this Declaration constantly in mind, shall strive by teaching and education to promote respect for these rights and freedoms and by progressive measures, national and international, to secure their universal and effective recognition and observance, both among the peoples of Member States themselves and among the peoples of territories under their jurisdiction.

Article 1

All human beings are born free and equal in dignity and rights. They are endowed with reason and conscience and should act towards one another in a spirit of brotherhood.

Article 2

Everyone is entitled to all the rights and freedoms set forth in this Declaration, without distinction of any kind, such as race, colour, sex, language, religion, political or other opinion, national or social origin, property, birth or other status.

Furthermore, no distinction shall be made on the basis of the political, jurisdictional or international status of the country or territory to which a person belongs, whether it be independent, trust, non-self-governing or under any other limitation of sovereignty.

Article 3

Everyone has the right to life, liberty and security of person.

Article 4

No one shall be held in slavery or servitude; slavery and the slave trade shall be prohibited in all their forms.

Article 5

No one shall be subjected to torture or to cruel, inhuman or degrading treatment or punishment.

Article 6

Everyone has the right to recognition everywhere as a person before the law.

Article 7

All are equal before the law and are entitled without any discrimination to equal protection of the law. All are entitled to equal protection against any discrimination in violation of this Declaration and against any incitement to such discrimination.

Article 8

Everyone has the right to an effective remedy by the competent national tribunals for acts violating the fundamental rights granted him by the constitution or by law.

Article 9

No one shall be subjected to arbitrary arrest, detention or exile.

Article 10

Everyone is entitled in full equality to a fair and public hearing by an independent and impartial tribunal, in the determination of his rights and obligations and of any criminal charge against him.

Article 11

(1) Everyone charged with a penal offence has the right to be presumed innocent until proved guilty according to law in a public trial at which he has had all the guarantees necessary for his defence.

(2) No one shall be held guilty of any penal offence on account of any act or omission which did not constitute a penal offence, under national or international law, at the time when it was committed. Nor shall a heavier penalty be imposed than the one that was applicable at the time the penal offence was committed.

Article 12

No one shall be subjected to arbitrary interference with his privacy, family, home or correspondence, nor to attacks upon his honour and reputation. Everyone has the right to the protection of the law against such interference or attacks.

Article 13

(1) Everyone has the right to freedom of movement and residence within the borders of each State.

(2) Everyone has the right to leave any country, including his own, and to return to his country.

Article 14

(1) Everyone has the right to seek and to enjoy in other countries asylum from persecution.

(2) This right may not be invoked in the case of prosecutions genuinely arising from non-political crimes or from acts contrary to the purposes and principles of the United Nations.

Article 15

(1) Everyone has the right to a nationality.

(2) No one shall be arbitrarily deprived of his nationality nor denied the right to change his nationality.

Article 16

(1) Men and women of full age, without any limitation due to race, nationality or religion, have the right to marry and to found a family. They are entitled to equal rights as a marriage, during marriage and at its dissolution.

(2) Marriage shall be entered into only with the free and full consent of the intending spouses.

(3) The family is the natural and fundamental group unit of society and is entitled to protection by society and the State.

Article 17

(1) Everyone has the right to own property alone as well as in association with others.

(2) No one shall be arbitrarily deprived of his property.

Article 18

Everyone has the right to freedom of thought, conscience and religion; this right includes freedom to change his religion or belief, and freedom, either alone or in community with others and in public or private, to manifest his religion or belief in teaching, practice, worship and observance.

Article 19

Everyone has the right to freedom of opinion and expression; this right includes freedom to hold opinions without interference and to seek, receive and impart information and ideas through any media and regardless of frontiers.

Article 20

(1) Everyone has the right to freedom of peaceful assembly and association.

(2) No one may be compelled to belong to an association.

Article 21

(1) Everyone has the right to take part in the government of his country, directly or through freely chosen representatives.

(2) Everyone has the right of equal access to public service in his country.

(3) The will of the people shall be the basis of the authority of the government; this will shall be expressed in periodic and genuine elections which shall be by universal and equal suffrage and shall be held by secret vote or by equivalent free voting procedures.

Article 22

Everyone, as a member of society, has the right to social security and is entitled to realization, through national effort and international co-operation and in accordance with the organization and resources of each State, of the economic, social and cultural rights indispensable for his dignity and the free development of his personality.

Article 23

(1) Everyone has the right to work, to free choice of employment, to just and favourable conditions of work and to protection against unemployment.

(2) Everyone, without any discrimination, has the right to equal pay for equal work.

(3) Everyone who works has the right to just and favourable remuneration ensuring for himself and his family an existence worthy of human dignity, and supplemented, if necessary, by other means of social protection.

(4) Everyone has the right to form and to join trade unions for the protection of his interests.

Article 24

Everyone has the right to rest and leisure, including reasonable limitation of working hours and periodic holidays with pay.

Article 25

(1) Everyone has the right to a standard of living adequate for the health and well-being of himself and of his family, including food, clothing, housing, and medical care and necessary social services, and the right to security in the event of unemployment, sickness, disability, widowhood, old age, or other lack of livelihood in circumstances beyond his control.

(2) Motherhood and childhood are entitled to special care and assistance. All children, whether born in or out of wedlock, shall enjoy the same social protection.

Article 26

(1) Everyone has the right to education. Education shall be free, at least in the elementary and fundamental stages. Elementary education shall be compulsory. Technical and professional education shall be made generally available and higher education shall be equally accessible to all on the basis of merit.

(2) Education shall be directed to the full development of the human personality and to the strengthening of respect for human rights and fundamental freedoms. It shall promote understanding, tolerance and friendship among all nations, racial or religious groups, and shall further the activities of the United Nations for the maintenance of peace.

(3) Parents have a prior right to choose the kind of education that shall be given to their children.

Article 27

(1) Everyone has the right freely to participate in the cultural life of the community, to enjoy the arts and to share in scientific advancement and its benefits.

(2) Everyone has the right to the protection of the moral and material interests resulting from any scientific, literary or artistic production of which he is the author.

Article 28

Everyone is entitled to a social and international order in which the rights and freedoms set forth in this Declaration can be fully realized.

Article 29

(1) Everyone has duties to the community in which alone the free and full development of his personality is possible.

(2) In the exercise of his rights and freedoms, everyone shall be subject only to such limitations as are determined by law solely for the purpose of securing due recognition and respect for the rights and freedoms and others and of meeting the just requirements of morality, public order and the general welfare in a democratic society.

(3) These rights and freedoms may in no case be exercised contrary to the purposes and principles of the United Nations.

Article 30

Nothing in this Declaration may be interpreted as implying for any State, group or person any right to engage in any activity or to perform any act aimed at the destruction of any of the rights and freedoms set forth herein.

judicial decisions

Amistad

SOURCE The Avalon Project at Yale Law School. Available from http://www.yale.edu/lawweb/avalon/avalon.htm

INTRODUCTION In 1839 Africans from Sierra Leone were abducted by Portuguese slave traders and taken to Havana, where they were put on a Cuban ship, the *Amistad*. The Africans seized the ship, and attempted to return to Africa, when they were seized by a U.S. naval vessel. Litigation relating to the ship and ownership of the Africans proceeded in a Federal District Court in Connecticut, and subsequently before the Supreme Court. The Africans were defended by President John Quincy Adams, who successfully argued they should be freed. The Court said they had been kidnapped illegally, and had never been slaves. Justice Story had written earlier that ". . . it was the ultimate right of all human beings in extreme cases to resist oppression, and to apply force against ruinous injustice," although the somewhat narrower reasoning of the judgment recognized the Africans right to resist unlawful slavery.

U.S. Supreme Court
THE AMISTAD, 40 U.S. 518 (1841)
40 U.S. 518 (Pet.)
The AMISTAD.
UNITED STATES, Appellants,
v.
The LIBELLANTS AND CLAIMANTS of the
SCHOONER AMISTAD, her tackle, apparel and
furniture, together with her cargo, and the
AFRICANS mentioned and described in the
several libels and claims, Appellees.
January Term, 1841

In 1839, Africans from Sierra Leone were abducted by Portuguese slave traders and taken to Havana, where they were put on a Cuban ship, the *Amistad*. The Africans seized the ship, and attempted to return to Africa, when they were seized by a United States naval vessel. Litigation relating to the ship and ownership of the Africans proceeded in a Federal District Court in Connecticut, and subsequently before the Supreme Court. The Africans were defended by former President John Quincy Adams, who successfully argued they should be freed. The Court said they had been kidnapped illegally, and had never been slaves. Justice Story had written earlier that '...it was the ultimate right of all human beings in extreme cases to resist oppression, and to apply force against ruinous injustice', although the somewhat narrower reasoning of the judgment recognized the Africans right to resist "unlawful" slavery.

[40 U.S. 518, 521] APPEAL from the Circuit Court of Connecticut. On the 23d day of January 1840, Thomas R. Gedney and Richard W. Meade, officers of the United States surveying brig Washington, on behalf of themselves and the officers and crew of the brig Washington, and of others interested and entitled, filed a libel in the district court of the United States for the district of Connecticut, stating, that off Culloden Point, near Montauk Point, they took possession of a vessel which proved to be a Spanish schooner, called the Amistad, of Havana, in the Island of Cuba, of about 120 tons burden; and the said libellants found said schooner was manned by forty-five negroes, some of whom had landed near the said point for water, [40 U.S. 518, 522] and there were also on board, two Spanish gentlemen, who represented themselves to be, and as the libellants verily believed, were, part owners of the cargo, and of the negroes on board, who were slaves belonging to said Spanish gentlemen; that the schooner Amistad sailed, on the 28th day of June, A. D. 1839, from the port of Havana, bound to a port in the province of Principe, both in the island of Cuba, under the command of Raymon Ferrer, as master thereof; that the schooner had on board and was laden with a large and valuable cargo, and provisions, to the amount, in all, of $40,000, and also money to the sum and amount of about $250; and also fifty-four slaves, to wit, fifty-one male slaves, and three young female slaves, who were worth $25,000; and while on the voyage from Havana to Principe, the slaves rose upon the master and crew of the schooner, and killed and murdered the master and one of the crew, and two more of the crew escaped and got away from the schooner; that the two Spaniards on board, to wit, Pedro Montez and Jose Ruiz, remained alive on board the schooner, after the murder of the master, and after the negroes had taken possession of the vessel and cargo; that their lives were spared, to as-

sist in the sailing of the vessel; and it was directed by the negroes, that the schooner should be navigated for the coast of Africa; and Pedro Montez and Jose Ruiz did, accordingly, steer as thus directed and compelled by the negroes, at the peril of their lives, in the day-time, and in the night, altered their course and steered for the American shore; but after two months on the ocean, they succeeded in coming round Montauk Point, when they were discovered and boarded by the libellants, and the two Spanish gentlemen begged for and claimed the aid and protection of the libellants. That the schooner was accordingly taken possession of, and re-captured from the hands and possession of the negroes who had taken the same: that the schooner was brought into the port of New London, where she now was; and the schooner would, with great difficulty, exposure and danger, have been taken by the libellants, but for the surprise upon the blacks who had possession thereof, a part of whom were on shore; and but for the aid and assistance and services of the libellants, the vessel and cargo would have been wholly lost to the respective owners thereof. That the cargo [40 U.S. 518, 523] belonged to divers Spanish merchants and others, resident in the island of Cuba, and to Pedro Montez and Jose Ruiz, the latter owning most of the slaves. The libellants stated, that having saved the schooner Amistad and cargo, and the slaves, with considerable danger, they prayed that process should be issued against the same, and that the usual proceedings might be had by the court, by which a reasonable salvage should be decreed out of the property so saved.

Afterwards, Henry Green and Pelatiah Fordham and others, filed a petition and answer to the libel, claiming salvage out of the property proceeded against by Thomas R. Gedney and others, and stating, that before the Amistad was seen or boarded by the officers and crew of the Washington, they had secured a portion of the negroes who had come on shore, and had thus aided in saving the vessel and cargo.

On the 29th of August 1839, Jose Ruiz and Pedro Montez, of Cuba, filed claims to all the negroes on board of the Amistad, except Antonio, as their slaves. A part of the merchandize on board the vessel was also claimed by them. They alleged, that the negroes had risen on the master of the schooner, and had murdered him; and that afterwards, they, Ruiz and Montez, had brought her into the United States. They claimed, that the negroes and merchandize ought to be restored to them, under the treaty with Spain; and denied salvage to Lieutenant Gedney, and to all other persons claiming salvage. Afterwards, Ruiz and Montez each filed in the district court, a separate libel, stating more at large the circumstances of the voyage of the Amistad, the murder of the master by the negroes, and that the negroes afterwards compelled them to steer the vessel towards Africa, but that they contrived to bring her to the coast of the United States, where she was captured by the United States brig Washington: Ruiz, in his libel, stated the negroes belonging to him to have been forty-nine in number, 'named and known at Havana, as follows: Antonio, Simon, Jose, Pedro, Martin, Manuel, Andreo, Edwards, Celedonia, Burtolono, Ramia, Augustin, Evaristo, Casamero, Merchoi, Gabriel, Santorin, Escolastico, Rascual, Estanislao, Desidero, Nicholas, Estevan, Thomas, Cosme, Luis, Bartolo, Julian, Federico, Salustiano, [40 U.S. 518, 524] Ladislao, Celestino, Epifanio, Eduardo, Benancico, Felepe, Francisco, Hipoleto, Berreto, Isidoro, Vecente, Deconisco, Apolonio, Esequies, Leon, Julio, Hipoleto and Zenon; of whom several have died.' Their present names, Ruiz stated, he had been informed, were, 'Cinque, Burnah 1st, Carpree, Dammah, Fourrie 1st, Shumah, Conomah, Choolay, Burnah 2d, Baah, Cabbah, Poomah, Kimbo, Peea, Bang-ye-ah, Saah, Carlee, Parale, Morrah, Yahome, Narquor, Quarto, Sesse, Con, Fourrie 2d, Kennah, Lammane, Fajanah, Faah, Yahboy, Faquannah, Berrie, Fawnu, Chockammaw and Gabbow.' The libel of Pedro Montez stated, that the names of three negroes on board the Amistad, belonging to him, were Francisco, Juan and Josepha; the Spanish name of the fourth was not mentioned; and the four were now called Teme, Mahgra, Kene and Carria. All these were stated to be slaves, and the property of the claimants, purchased by them at Havana, where slavery was tolerated and allowed by law; and they and the merchandize on board the vessel, the claimants alleged, by the laws and usages of nations, and of the United States of America, and according to the treaties between Spain and the United States, ought to be restored to the claimants, without diminution, and entire.

The vessel, negroes and merchandize were taken into his possession, by the marshal of the district of Connecticut, under process issued by order of the court. 1

On the 19th of September 1837, William S. Holabird, Esq., attorney of the United States for the district, filed a suggestion in the district court, stating, that since the libel aforesaid of Thomas R. Gedney, Esq., was filed in this court, viz: within the present month of September, in the year of our Lord 1839, the duly accredited minister to the United States of her Catholic Majesty, the Queen of Spain, had officially presented to the proper department of the United States government, a claim, which was then pending, upon the United States, setting forth, that 'the vessel aforesaid, called the Amistad, and her cargo aforesaid, together with cer-

tain slaves on board the said vessel, all being the same as described in the libel aforesaid, are the property of Spanish subjects, and that the said vessel, cargo and slaves, while so being the property of the said Spanish subjects, arrived [40 U.S. 518, 525] within the jurisdictional limits of the United States, and were taken possession of by the said public armed brig of the United States, under such circumstances as make it the duty of the United States to cause the same vessel, cargo and slaves, being the property of said Spanish subjects, to be restored to the true proprietors and owners of the same, without further hindrance or detention, as required by the treaty now subsisting between the United States and Spain.' The attorney of the United States, in behalf of the United States, prayed the court, on its being made legally to appear that the claim of the Spanish minister was well founded, and was conformable to the treaty, that the court make such order for the disposal of the said vessel, cargo and slaves as might best enable the United States in all respect to comply with their treaty stipulations, and preserve the public faith inviolate. But if it should be made to appear, that the persons described as slaves, were negroes and persons of color, who had been transported from Africa, in violation of the laws of the United States, and brought within the United States, contrary to the same laws, the attorney, in behalf of the United States, claimed, that in such case, the court would make such further order in the premises, as would enable the United States, if deemed expedient, to remove such persons to the coast of Africa, to be delivered there to such agent or agents as might be authorized to receive and provide for them, pursuant to the laws of the United States, in such case provided, or to make such other order as to the court might seem fit, right and proper in the premises.

On the same day, September 19th, 1839, the negroes, by their counsel, filed an answer to the libel of Lieutenant Gedney and others, claiming salvage, and to the claim of Ruiz and Montez, claiming them as slaves, as also to the intervention of the United States, on the application of the minister of Spain; in which they said, that they were natives of Africa, and were born free, and ever since had been, and still of right were and ought to be, free and not slaves; that they were never domiciled in the island of Cuba, or in the dominions of the Queen of Spain, nor subject to the laws thereof. That on or about the 15th day of April 1839, they were, in the land of their nativeity, unlawfully kidnapped, and forcibly and wrongfully, by certain persons to them unknown, [40 U.S. 518, 526] who were there unlawfully and piratically engaged in the slave-trade between the coast of Africa and the island of Cuba, contrary to the will of these respondents, unlawfully, and under circumstances of great cruelty, transported to the island of Cuba, for the unlawful purpose of being sold as slaves, and were there illegally landed for that purpose. That Jose Ruiz, one of the libellants, well knowing all the premises, and confederating with the persons by whom the respondents were unlawfully taken and holden as slaves, and intending to deprive the respondents severally of their liberty, made a pretended purchase of the respondents, except the said Carria, Teme, Kene and Mahgra; and that Pedro Montez, also well knowing all the premises, and confederating with the said persons, for the purpose aforesaid, made a pretended purchase of the said Carria, Teme, Kene and Mahgra; that the pretended purchases were made from persons who had no right whatever to the respondents, or any of them, and that the same were null and void, and conferred no right or title on Ruiz or Montez, or right of control over the respondents, or either of them. That on or about the 28th day of June 1839, Ruiz and Montez, confederating with each other, and with and Ramon Ferrer, now deceased, master of the schooner Amistad, and others of the crew thereof, caused respondents, severally, without law or right, under color of certain false and fraudulent papers by them procured and fraudulently used for that purpose, to be placed by force on board the schooner, to be transported, with said Ruiz and Montez, to some place unknown to the respondents, and there enslaved for life. That the respondents, being treated on board said vessel, by said Ruiz and Montez and their confederates, with great cruelty and oppression, and being of right free, as aforesaid, were incited by the love of liberty natural to all men, and by the desire of returning to their families and kindred, to take possession of said vessel, while navigating the high seas, as they had a right to do, with the intent to return therein to their native country, or to seek an asylum in some free state, where slavery did not exist, in order that they might enjoy their liberty under the protection of its government; that the schooner, about the 26th of August 1839, arrived, in the possession of the respondents, at Culloden Point, near Montauk, and was there anchored near the shore of Long Island, within [40 U.S. 518, 527] hailing distance thereof, and within the waters and territory of the state of New York; that the respondents, Cinque, Carlee, Dammah, Baah, Monat, Nahguis, Quato, Con, Fajanah, Berrie, Gabbo, Fouleaa, Kimbo, Faquannah, Cononia, otherwise called Ndzarbla, Yaboi, Burnah 1st, Shuma, Fawne, Peale, Ba and Sheele, while said schooner lay at anchor as aforesaid, went on shore, within the state of New York to procure provisions and other necessaries, and while there, in a state where slavery is unlawful and does not exist, under the protection of the government and laws of said state, by which they were all free, whether on board of said schooner or no shore,

the respondents were severally seized, as well those who were on shore as aforesaid, as those who were on board of and in possession of said schooner, by Lieutenant Gedney, his officers and crew, of the United States brig Washington, without any lawful warrant or authority whatever, at the instance of Ruiz and Montez, with the intent to keep and secure them as slaves to Ruiz and Montez, respectively, and to obtain an award of salvage therefore from this honorable court, as for a meritorious act. That for that purpose, the respondents were, by Lieutenant Gedney, his officers and crew, brought to the port of New London; and while there, and afterwards, under the subsequent proceedings in this honorable court, taken into the custody of the marshal of said district of Connecticut, and confined and held in the jails in the cities of New Haven and Hartford, respectively, as aforesaid. Wherefore, the respondents prayed, that they might be set free, as they or right were and ought to be, and that they be released from the custody of the marshal, under the process of this honorable court, under which, or under color of which, they were holden as aforesaid.

Jose Antonio Tellincas, and Aspe and Laca, subjects of Spain, and merchants of Cuba, presented claims for certain merchandize which was on board the Amistad, when taken possession of by Lieutenant Gedney; denying all claims to salvage, and asking that the property should be restored to them.

On the 23d day of January, the district judge made a decree, having taken into his consideration all the libels, claims and the suggestion of the district-attorney of the United States, and the claim preferred by him that the negroes should be delivered to [40 U.S. 518, 528] the Spanish authorities, the negroes to be sent by them to Cuba, or that the negroes should be placed under the authority of the President of the United States, to be transported to Africa. The decree rejected the claim of Green and others to salvage, with costs. The claim of Lieutenant Gedney and others to salvage on the alleged slaves, was dismissed. The libels and claims of Ruiz and Montez, being included under the claim of the minister of Spain, were ordered to be dismissed, with costs taxed against Ruiz and Montez respectively. 'That that part of the claim of the minister of Spain which demands the surrender of Cinques and others, who are specifically named in the answer filed as aforesaid, be dismissed, without cost.' That the claim of the vice-consul of Spain, demanding the surrender to the Spanish government of Antonio, a slave owned by the heirs of Captain Ferrer, should be sustained; and ordered that Antonio should be delivered to the government of Spain, or its agent, without costs. The claims of Tellincas, and Aspe and Laca, for the restoration of the goods specified by them, being part of the cargo of the Amistad, was sustained, and that the same goods be restored to them, deducting one-third of the gross appraised value of them, which was allowed as salvage to the officers and crew of the Washington. A like salvage of one-third of the gross value of the Amistad, and the other merchandize on board of her, was also adjudged to the salvors. The costs were to be deducted from the other two-thirds.

'And whereas, the duly-accredited minister of Spain, resident in the United States, hath, in behalf of the government of Spain, for the owners of said schooner, and the residue of said goods, claimed that the same be restored to that government, for the said owners, they being Spanish subjects, under the provisions of the treaty subsisting between the United States and Spain: And whereas, it hath been made to appear to this court, that the said schooner is lawfully owned by the subjects of Spain, as also the residue of said goods, not specifically claimed: And whereas, the aforesaid Don Pedro Montez and Jose Ruiz have in person ceased to prosecute their claim as specified in their respective libels, and their said claims fall within the demand [40 U.S. 518, 529] and claim of the Spanish minister, made as aforesaid, And whereas, the seizure of the said schooner and goods by the said Thomas R. Gedney and others, was made on the high seas, in a perilous condition, and they were first brought into the port of New London, within the district of Connecticut, and libeled for salvage.' The decree then proceeded to adjudge to Lieutenant Gedney and others, as salvage, one-third of the gross proceeds of the vessel and cargo, according to an appraisement which had been made thereof; and, if not paid, directed the property to be sold, and that proportion of the gross proceeds of the sale to be paid over to the captors, the residue, after payment of all costs, to be paid to the respective owners of the same.

Upon the answers of the negroes, and the representations of the district-attorney of the United States, and of Montez and Ruiz, the decree proceeded: 'This court having fully heard the parties appearing, with their proofs, do find, that the respondents, severally answering as aforesaid, are each of them natives of Africa, and were born free, and ever since have been, and still of right are free, and not slaves, as is in said several libels claims or representations alleged or surmised; that they were never domiciled in the Island of Cuba, or the dominions of the Queen of Spain, or subject to the laws thereof; that they were severally kidnapped in their native country, and were, in violation of their own rights, and of the laws of Spain, prohibiting the African slave-trade, imported into the island of Cuba, about the 12th June 1839, and were there unlawfully held and trans-

ferred to the said Ruiz and Montez, respectively; that said respondents were, within fifteen days after their arrival at Havana, aforesaid, by said Ruiz and Montez, put on board said schooner Amistad, to be transported to some port in said island of Cuba, and there unlawfully held as slaves; that the respondents, or some of them, influenced by the desire of recovering their liberty, and of returning to their families and kindred in their native country, took possession of said schooner Amistad, killed the captain and cook, and severely wounded said Montez, while on her voyage from Havana, as aforesaid, and that the respondents arrived, in possession of said schooner, at Culloden Point, near Montauk, and there anchored [40 U.S. 518, 530] said schooner on the high seas, at the distance of half a mile from the shore of Long Island, and were there, while a part of the respondents were, as is alleged in their said answer, on shore, in quest of water and other necessaries, and about to sail in said schooner for the coast of Africa, seized by said Lieutenant Gedney, and his officers and crew, and brought into the port of New London, in this district. And this court both further find, that it hath ever been the intention of the said Montez and Ruiz, since the said Africans were put on board the said schooner, to hold the said Africans as slaves; that at the time when the said Cinque and others, here making answer, were imported from Africa, into the dominions of Spain, there was a law of Spain prohibiting such importations, declaring the persons so imported to be free; that said law was in force when the claimants took the possession of the said Africans and put them on board said schooner, and the same has ever since been in force.' The decree of the district court recited the decree of the government of Spain, of December 1817, prohibiting the slave-trade, and declaring all negroes brought into the dominions of Spain by slave-traders to be free; and enjoining the execution of the decree on all the officers of Spain in the dominions of Spain. The decree of the district court proceeded: 'And this court doth further find, that when the said Africans were shipped on board the said schooner, by the said Montez and Ruiz, the same were shipped under the passports signed by the governor-general of the Island of Cuba, in the following words, viz: Description. Size. Age. Color. Hair. Forehead. Eyebrows. Eyes. Nose. Mouth. Beard. Peculiar signs. Havana, June 22d, 1839.

I grant permission to carry three black ladinos, named Juana, Francisco, and Josefa, property of Dr. Pedro Montez, to Puerto Principe, by sea. They must present themselves to the respective territorial judge with this permit.

Duty, 2 reals. ESPLETA. (Indorsed)-Commander of Matria.

Let pass, in the schooner Amistad, to Guanaja, Ferrer, master. Havana, June 27th, 1839. MART. & CO. [40 U.S. 518, 531] Description. Size. Age. Color. Hair. Forehead. Eyebrows. Eyes. Nose. Mouth. Beard. Peculiar signs. Havana, June 26th, 1839.

I grant permission to carry forty-nine black ladinos, named Antonio, Simon, Lucas, Jose, Pedro, Martin, Manuel, Andrios, Edwardo, Celedernnio, Bartolo, Raman, Augustin, Evaristo, Casimero, Meratio, Gabriel, Santome, Ecclesiastico, Pasenal, Stanislao, Desiderio, Nicolas, Estevan, Tomas, Cosme, Luis, Bartolo, Julian, Federico, Saturdino, Ladislas, Celestino, Epifano, Froneric, Venaniro, Feligre, Francisco, Hypolito, Benito, Isdoro, Vicente, Dioniceo, Apolino, Eseuie l, Leon, Julio, Hipolito y Raman, property of Dr. Jose Ruiz, to Puerto Principe; by sea. They must present themselves with this permit to the respective territorial judge.'

ESPLETA. Duty, 2 reals.

(Indorsed) Commander of Matria.

Let pass, in the schooner Amistad, to Guanaja, Ferrer, master. Havana, June 27th, 1839. MART. & CO.

Which said passports do not truly describe the said persons shipped under the same. Whereupon, the said claim of the minister of Spain, as set forth in the two libels filed in the name of the United States, by the said district-attorney, for and in behalf of the government of Spain and her subjects, so far as the same relate to the said Africans named in said claim, be dismissed. And upon the libel filed by said district-attorney, in behalf of the United States, claiming the said Africans libeled as aforesaid, and now in the custody of the marshal of the district of Connecticut, under and by virtue of process issued from this court, that they may be delivered to the president of the United States to be transported to Africa: It is decreed, that the said Africans now in the custody of said marshal, and libeled and claimed as aforesaid (excepting Antonio Ferrer), be delivered to the president of the United States, by the marshal of the district of Connecticut, to be by him transported to Africa, in pursuance of [40 U.S. 518, 532] the law of congress, passed March 3d, 1819, entitled "an act in addition to the acts prohibiting the slave-trade."

After the decree was pronounced, the United States, 'claiming in pursuance of a demand made upon them by the duly-accredited minister of her Catholic Majesty, the Queen of Spain, to the United States, moved an appeal from the whole and every part of the said decree, except the part of the same in relation to the slave Antonio, to the circuit court' of Connecticut. Antonio Tellincas, and Aspe and Laca, claimants, &c.,

also appealed from the decree to the circuit court, except for so much of the decree as sustained their claims to the goods, &c. The Africans, by their African names, moved in the circuit court, in April 1840, that so much of the appeal of the district-attorney of the United States, from so much of the decree of the district court as related to them severally, might be dismissed; 'because they say, that the United States do not claim, nor have they ever claimed, any interest in the appellees, respectively, or either of them, and have no right, either by the law of nations, or by the constitution or laws of the United States, to appear in the courts of the United States, to institute or prosecute claims to property, in behalf of the subjects of the Queen of Spain, under the circumstances appearing on the record in this case; much less to enforce the claims of the subject of a foreign government, to the persons of the said appellees, respectively, as the slaves of the said foreign subjects, under the circumstances aforesaid.' The circuit court refused the motion.

The circuit court affirmed the decree of the district court, pro forma, except so far as respected the claims of Tellincas, and Aspe and Laca.

After this decree of the circuit court, the United States, claiming in pursuance of a demand made upon them by the duly-accredited minister of her Catholic Majesty, the Queen of Spain, to the United States, moved an appeal from the whole and every part of the decree of the court, affirming the decree of the district court, to the supreme court of the United States, to be holden at the city of Washington, on the second Monday of January, A. D. 1841; and it was allowed. [40 U.S. 518, 533] The court, as far as respected the decree of the district court allowing salvage on the goods on board the Amistad, continued the case, to await the decision of the supreme court, on that part of the decree appealed from.

The circuit court, in the decree, proceeded to say, that 'they had inspected certain depositions and papers remaining as of record in said circuit court, and to be used as evidence, before the supreme court of the United States, on the trial of said appeal.' Among the depositions, were the following: 'I, Richard Robert Madden, a British subject, having resided for the last three years and upwards, at Havana, where I have held official situations under the British government, depose and say, that I have held the office of superintendent of liberated Africans, during that term, and still hold it; and have held for the term of one year, the office there, of British commissioner, in the mixed court of justice. The duties of my office and of my avocation, have led me to become well acquainted with Africans recently imported from Africa. I have seen and had in my charge many hundreds of them. I have also seen the Africans in the custody of the marshal of the district of Connecticut, except the small children. I have examined them and observed their language, appearance and manners; and I have no doubt of their having been, very recently, brought from Africa. To one of them, I spoke, and repeated a Mohammedan form of prayer, in the Arabic language; the man immediately recognised the language, and repeated a few words of it, after me, and appeared to understand it, particularly the words 'Allah akbar,' or God is great. The man who was beside this negro, I also addressed in Arabic, saying, 'salaam alikoem,' or peace be to you; he immediately, in the customary oriental salutations, replied, 'alikoem salaam,' or peace be on you. From my knowledge of oriental habits, and of the appearance of the newly-imported slaves in Cuba, I have no doubt of those negroes of the Amistad being bon a fide Bozal negroes, quite newly imported from Africa. I have a full knowledge of the subject of slavery-slave-trade in Cuba; and I know that no law exists, or has existed, since the year 1820, that sanctions the introduction of negroes into the island of Cuba, from Africa, for the purpose of making slaves, or being held in slavery; and that [40 U.S. 518, 534] all such Bozal negroes, as those recently imported are called, are legally free; and no law, common or statute, exists there, by which they can be held in slavery. Such Africans, long settled in Cuba, and acclimated, are called ladinos, and must have been introduced before 1820, and are so called, in contradistinction to the term creole, which is applied to the negroes born in the island. I have seen, and now have before me, a document, dated 26th June 1839, purporting to be signed by Ezpeleta, who is captain-general of the island, to identify which, I have put my name to the left-hand corner of the document, in presence of the counsel of the Africans; this document, or 'traspasso,' purporting to be a permit granted to Don I. Ruiz, to export from Havana to Puerto Principe, forty-nine negroes, designated by Spanish names, and called therein ladinos, a term totally inapplicable to newly-imported Africans. I have seen, and now have before me, another document, dated 22d June 1839, and signed in the same manner, granted to Don Pedro Montez, for the removal of three negro children from Havana to Puerto Principe, also designated by Spanish names, and likewise called 'ladinos,' and wholly inapplicable to young African children, who could not have been acclimated, and long settled in the island; which document, I have identified in the same manner as the former. To have obtained these documents from the governor, for bon a fide Bozal negroes, and have described them in the application for it, as ladinos, was evidently a fraud; but nothing more than such an application and the payment of the necessary

fees would be required to procure it, as there is never any inquiry or inspection of the negroes, on the part of the governor, or his officer, nor is there any oath required from the applicant. I further state that the above documents are manifestly inapplicable to the Africans of the Amistad I have seen here and in New Haven; but such documents are commonly obtained by similar applications at the Havana, and by these means, the negroes recently and illegally introduced, are thus removed to the different ports of the island, and the danger obviated of their falling in with English cruisers, and then they are illegally carried into slavery. One of the largest dealers and importers of the island of Cuba, in African slaves, is the notorious house of Martines & Co., of Havana; and for years past, as at present, they have [40 U.S. 518, 535] been deeply engaged in this traffic; and the Bozal Africans, imported by these and all other slave-traders, when brought to the Havana, are immediately taken to the barracoons, or slave-marts; five of which are situated in the immediate vicinity of the governor's county house, about one mile and a half from the walls of Havana; and from these barracoons, they are taken and removed to the different parts of the island, when sold; and having examined the endorsements on the back of the traspasso, or permits for the removal of the said negroes of the Amistad, the signature to that endorsement appears to be that of Martines & Co.; and the document purports to be a permit or pass for the removal of the said negroes. The handwriting of Martines & Co., I am not acquainted with. These barracoons, outside the city walls, are fitted up exclusively for the reception and sale of Bozal negroes; one of these barracoons or slave-marts, called la miserecordia, or 'mercy,' kept by a man, named Riera, I visited the 24th September last, in company with a person well acquainted with this establishment; and the factor or major domo of the master, in the absence of the latter, said to me, that the negroes of the Amistad had been purchased there; that he knew them well; that they had been bought by a man from Puerto Principe, and had been embarked for that place; and speaking of the said negroes, he said, 'che lastima,' or what pity it is, which rather surprised me; the man further explained himself, and said, his regret was for the loss of so many valuable Bozals, in the event of their being emancipated in the United States. One of the houses most openly engaged, and notoriously implicated in the slave-trade transactions, is that of Martines & Co.; and their practice is, to remove their newly-arrived negroes from the slave ships to these barracoons, where they commonly remain two or three weeks, before sold, as these negroes of the Amistad, illegally introduced by Martines & Co., were, in the present instance, as is generally reported and believed in the Havana. Of the Africans which I have seen and examined, from the necessity which my office imposes on me at the Havana, of assisting at the registry of the newly-imported Bozals, emancipated by the mixed court, I can speak with tolerable certainty of the ages of these people, with the exception of the children, whom [40 U.S. 518, 536] have not seen. Sa, about 17; Ba, 21; Luckawa, 19; Tussi, 30; Beli, 18; Shuma, 26; Nama, 20; Tenquis, 21; the others, I had not time to take a note of their ages. With respect to the mixed commission, its jurisdiction extends only to cases of captured negroes brought in by British or Spanish cruisers; and notwithstanding the illegalities of the traffic in slaves, from twenty to twenty-five thousand slaves have been introduced into the island, during the last three years; and such is the state of society, and of the administration of the laws there, that hopeless slavery is the inevitable result of their removal into the interior.'

On his cross-examination, the witness stated, that he was not acquainted with the dialects of the African tribes, but was slightly acquainted with the Arabic language. Lawful slaves of the island are not offered for sale generally, nor often placed in the barracoons, or man-marts. The practice in Havana is to use the barracoons 'for Bozal negroes only.' Barracoons are used for negroes recently imported, and for their reception and sale. The native language of the Africans is not often continued for a long time, on certain plantations. 'It has been to me a matter of astonishment, at the shortness of time in which the language of the negroes is disused, and the Spanish language adopted and acquired. I speak this, from a very intimate knowledge of the condition of the negroes in Cuba, from frequent visits to plantations, and journeys in the interior; and on this subject, I think I can say, my knowledge is as full as any person's can be.' 'There are five or six barracoons within pistol-shot of the country residence of the captain-general of Cuba. On every other part of the coast where the slave-trade is carried on, a barracoon or barracoons must likewise exist. They are a part of the things necessary to the slave-trade, and are for its use only, for instance, near Matanzas, there is a building or shed of this kind and used for this purpose. Any negroes landed in the island since 1820, and carried into slavery, have been illegally introduced; and the transfer of them under false names, such as calling Bozal, ladinos, is, necessarily, a fraud. Unfortunately, there is no interference on the part of the local authorities; they connive at it, and collude with the slave-traders; the governor alone, at the Havana, receiving a [40 U.S. 518, 537] bounty or impost on each negro thus illegally introduced, of $10 a head. As to the mixed commission, once the negroes clandestinely introduced are landed, they no longer have cognisance of the violation of the treaty; the governor has cognisance of this and every other bearing of the Spanish law, on Spanish soil. This head-money has not the sanction of any Spanish law for its imposition; and the proof of this is, it is called a voluntary contribution.'

Also, a statement, given by the district-attorney, W. S. Holabird, Esq., of what was made to him by A. G. Vega, Esq., Spanish consul, January 10th, 1840: 'That he is a Spanish subject; that he resided in the island of Cuba several years; that he knows the laws of that island on the subject of slavery; that there was no law that was considered in force in the island of Cuba, that prohibited the bringing in African slaves; that the court of mixed commissioners had no jurisdiction, except in cases of capture on the sea; that newly-imported African negroes were constantly brought to the island, and after landing, were bon a, fide transferred from one owner to another, without any interference by the local authorities or the mixed commission, and were held by the owners, and recognised as lawful property; that slavery was recognised in Cuba, by all the laws that were considered in force there; that the native language of the slaves was kept up on some plantations, for years. That the barracoons are public markets, where all descriptions of slaves are sold and bought; that the papers of the Amistad are genuine, and are in the usual form; that it was not necessary to practise any fraud, to obtain such papers from the proper officers of the government; that none of the papers of the Amistad are signed by Martines, spoken of by R. R. Madden in his deposition; that he (Martines) did not hold the office from whence that paper issued.'

Also, a deposition of James Ray, a mariner on board of the Washington, stating the circumstances of the taking possession of the Amistad, and the Africans, which supported the allegations in the several libels, in all essential circumstances. The documents exhibited as the passports of the Spanish authorities at Havana, and other papers relating to the Amistad, and her clearance from Havana, were also annexed to the decree of the circuit court, in the original Spanish.

Translations of all [40 U.S. 518, 538] of these which were deemed of importance in the cause, are given in the decree of the district court.

Sullivan Haley stated in his deposition, that he heard Ruiz say, that 'none of the negroes could speak Spanish; they are just from Africa.'

James Covey, a colored man, deposed, that 'he was born at Berong-Mendi country; left there seven and a half years ago; was a slave, and carried to Lumboko. All these Africans were from Africa. Never saw them until now. I could talk with them. They appeared glad, because they could speak the same language. I could understand all but two or three. They say, they from Lumboko; three moons. They all have Mendi names, and their names all mean something; Carle, means bone; Kimbo, means cricket. They speak of rivers which I know; said they sailed from Lumboko; two or three speak different language from the others; the Timone language. Say-ang-wa rivers spoken of; these run through the Vi country. I learned to speak English, at Sierre Leone. Was put on board a man-of-war, one year and a half. They all agree as to where they sailed form. I have no doubt they are Africans. I have been in this country six months; came in a British man-of-war; have been in this town (New Haven) four months, with Mr. Bishop; he calls on me for no money, and do not know who pays my board. I was stolen by a black man, who stole ten of us. One man carried us two months' walk. Have conversed with Sinqua; Barton has been in my town, Gorang. I was sailing for Havana, when the British man-of-war captured us.' The testimony of Cinque and the negroes of the Amistad, supported the statements in their answers.

The respondents also gave in evidence the 'treaty between Great Britain and Spain, for the abolition of the slave-trade, signed at Madrid, 23d September 1817.'

The case was argued, for the United States, by Gilpin, Attorney-General; and by Baldwin and Adams, for the appellees; Jones, on the part of Lieutenant Gedney and others, of the United States brig Washington, was not required by the court to argue the claims to salvage. [40 U.S. 518, 539] Gilpin, Attorney-General, for the United States, reviewed the evidence, as set out in the record, of all the facts connected with the case, from the first clearance of the schooner Amistad, at Havana, on the 18th May 1838, down to the 23d January 1840, when the final decree of the district court of the United States for the district of Connecticut, was rendered.

The attorney-general proceeded to remark, that on the 23d January 1840, the case stood thus: The vessel, cargo and negroes were in possession of the marshal, under process from the district court, to answer to five separate claims; those of Lieutenant Gedney, and Messrs. Green & Fordham for salvage; that of the United States, at the instance of the Spanish minister, for the vessel, cargo and negroes, to be restored to the Spanish owners, in which claim those of Messrs. Ruiz and Montez were merged; that of the Spanish vice-consul, for the slave Antonio, to be restored to the Spanish owner; and that of Messrs. Tellincas, and Aspe and Laca, for the restoration of a part of the cargo belonging to them. The decree of the district court found, that the vessel and the goods on board, were the property of the Spanish subjects, and that the passports under which the ne-

groes were shipped at Havana, were signed by the governor-general of Cuba. It denied the claims of Lieutenant Gedney, and Messrs. Green and Fordham, to salvage on the slaves, but allowed the claims of the officers and crew of the Washington to salvage on the Amistad, and on the merchandize on board of that vessel. It also decreed, that the residue of the goods, and the vessel, should be delivered to the Spanish minister, to be restored to the Spanish owners; and that the slave Antonio should be delivered to the Spanish vice-consul, for the same purpose. As to the negroes, claimed by Ruiz and Montes, it dismissed the claims of those persons, on the ground, that they were included under that of the minister of Spain. The libel of the United States, claiming the delivery of the negroes to the Spanish minister, was dismissed, on the ground, that they were not slaves, but were kidnapped and imported into Cuba; and that at the time they were so imported, there was a law of Spain declaring persons so imported to be free. The alternative prayer of the United States, claiming the delivery of the negroes, to be transported to Africa, was granted.

As soon as this decree was made, an appeal was taken by the [40 U.S. 518, 540] United States to the circuit court, from the whole of it, except so far as it related to Antonio. At the succeeding term of the circuit court, the negroes moved that the appeal of the United States might be dismissed, on the ground, that they had no interest in the negroes; and also, on the ground, that they had no right to prosecute claims to property in behalf of subjects of the Queen of Spain. That motion, however, was refused by the circuit court, which proceeded to affirm the decree of the district court, on the libel of the United States.

It is from this decree of the circuit court, that the present appeal to the supreme court is prosecuted.

Was the decree of the circuit court correct? The state of the facts, as found by the decree, and not denied, was this: The vessel and the goods on board, were the property of Spanish subjects, in Havana, on the 27th June 1839. At that time, slavery was recognised and in existence in the Spanish dominions. The negroes in question are certified, at that time, in a document signed by the governor-general of Cuba, to be ladinos negroes — that is, slaves — the property of Spanish subjects. As such, permission is given by the governor-general, to their owners, to take them by sea, to Puerto Principe, in the same island. The vessel, with these slaves, thus certified, on board, in charge of their alleged owners, regularly cleared and sailed from Havana, the documentary evidence aforesaid, and the papers of the vessel being also on board. During this voyage, the negroes rose, killed the master, and took possession of the vessel. On the 26th August, the vessel, cargo and negroes were rescued and taken on the high seas, by a public officer of the United States, and brought into a port of the United States, where they await the decision of the judicial tribunals.

In this position of things, the minister of Spain demands that the vessel, cargo and negroes be restored, pursuant to the 9th article of the treaty of 27th October 1795, which provides (1 Laws U. S. 268), that 'all ships and merchandize of what nature soever, which shall be rescued out of the hands of any pirates or robbers, on the high seas, shall be brought into some port of either state, and shall be delivered into the custody of the officers of that port, in order to be taken care of and restored entire to the true proprietor, as soon as due [40 U.S. 518, 541] and sufficient proof shall be made concerning the property thereof.' The only inquiries, then, that present themselves, are: 1. Has 'due and sufficient proof concerning the property thereof' been made? 2. If so, have the United States a right to interpose in the manner they have done, to obtain its restoration to the Spanish owners? If these inquiries result in the affirmative, then the decree of the circuit court was erroneous, and ought to be reversed.

I. It is submitted, that there has been due and sufficient proof concerning the property, to authorize its restoration. It is not denied, that, under the laws of Spain, negroes may be held as slaves, as completely as they are in any of the states of this Union; nor will it be denied, if duly proved to be such, they are subject to restoration, as much as other property, when coming under the provisions of this treaty. Now, these negroes are declared, by the certificates of the governor-general, to be slaves, and the property of the Spanish subjects therein named. That officer (1 White's New Rec. 369, 371; 8 Pet. 310) is the highest functionary of the government in Cuba; his public acts are the highest evidence of any facts stated by him, within the scope of his authority. It is within the scope of his authority, to declare what is property, and what are the rights of the subjects of Spain, within his jurisdiction, in regard to property.

Now, in the intercourse of nations, there is no rule better established than this, that full faith is to be given to such acts — to the authentic evidence of such acts. The question is not, whether the act is right or wrong; it is, whether the act has been done, and whether it is an act within the scope of the authority. We are to inquire only whether the power existed, and whether it was exercised, and how it was exercised; not whether it was rightly or wrongly exercised. The principle is universally admitted, that, wherever an authority is delegated to any public officer, to be exercised at his discretion, under his own judgment, and upon his own responsibility, the acts done in the appropriate exercise of that authority, are binding as to the subject-matter. Without such a rule, there could be no peace or comity among nations; all harmony, all mutual [40 U.S. 518, 542] respect, would be destroyed; the courts and tribunals of one country would become the judges of the local laws and property of others. Nor is it to be supposed, that so important a principle would not be recognised by courts of justice. They have held, that, whether the act of the foreign functionary be executive, legislative or judicial, it is, if exercised within its appropriate sphere, binding as to the subject-matter; and the authentic record of such act is full and complete evidence thereof. In the case of Marbury v. Madison, 1 Cranch 170, this court held, that a commission was conclusive evidence of an executive appointment; and that a party from whom it was withheld might obtain it through the process of a court, as being such evidence of his rights. In the case of Thompson v. Tolmie, 2 Pet. 167, this court sustained the binding and sufficient character of a decision, made by a competent tribunal, and not reversed, whether that decision was in itself right or wrong. In the case of the United States v. Arredondo, 6 Ibid. 719, the whole doctrine on this subject is most forcibly stated. Indeed, nothing can be clearer than the principles thus laid down; nor can they apply more directly to any case than the present. Here is the authentic certificate or record of the highest officer known to the Spanish law, declaring, in terms, that these negroes are the property of the several Spanish subjects. We have it countersigned by another of the principal officers. We have it executed and delivered, as the express evidence of property, to these persons. It is exactly the same as that deemed sufficient for the vessel and for the cargo. Would it not have been complete and positive evidence in the island of Cuba? If so, the principle laid down by this court makes it such here.

But this general principle is strengthened by the particular circumstances of the case. Where property on board of a vessel is brought into a foreign port, the documentary evidence, whether it be a judicial decree, or the ship's papers, accompanied by possession, is the best evidence of ownership, and that to which courts of justice invariably look. In the case of Bernadi v. Motteux, Doug. 575, Lord MANSFIELD laid down the rule, that a decree of a foreign court was conclusive as to the right of property under it. In that of The Virgilantia, 1 Rob. 3, 11, the necessity or propriety of producing the ship's papers, as the first [40 U.S. 518, 543] evidence of her character and property, and of ascertaining her national character from her passport, is expressly recognised. In that of The Cosmopolite, 3 Rob. 269, the title of the claimant, who was a Dane, to the vessel, was a decree of a French court against an American vessel; the court refused to inquire into the circumstances of the condemnation, but held the decree sufficient evidence for them. In that of The Sarah, 3 Rob. 266, the captors of a prize applied to be allowed to give proof of the property being owned by persons other than those stated in the ship's documents, but it was refused. In that of The Henrick and Maria, 4 Rob. 43, the very question was made, whether the court would not look into the validity of a title, derived under a foreign court of admiralty, and it was refused.

These principles are fully sustained by our own courts. In the case of The Resolution, 2 Dall. 22-3, possession of property on board of a vessel is held to be presumptive evidence of ownership; and the ship's papers, bills of lading, and other documents, are pri a facie evidence of the facts they speak. It is in this evidence that vessels are generally acquitted or condemned. In that of The Ann Green, 1 Gallis. 281-84, it is laid down as the rule, that the first and proper evidence in prize cases is the ship's papers; and that only in cases of doubt, is further testimony to be received. The court there say, that as a general rule, they would pronounce for the inadmissibility of such further evidence. So, in that of The Diana, 2 Gallis. 97, the general rule laid down is, that no claim is to be admitted in opposition to the ship's papers; the exceptions stand upon very particular grounds. In that of Ohl v. Eagle Insurance Company, 4 Mason 172, parol evidence was held not to be admissible to contradict a ship's papers. In that of McGrath v. The Candelero, Bee 60, a decree of restitution in a foreign court of admiralty was held to be full evidence of the ownership, and such as was to be respected in all other countries. In that of Catlett v. Pacific Insurance Company, 1 Paine 612, the register was held to be conclusive evidence of the national character of the vessel; and a similar rule was held to exist in regard to a pass, in the case of Barker v. Phoenix Insurance Company, 8 Johns. 307.

Similar principles have been adopted in this court. [40 U.S. 518, 544] The decree of a foreign court of admiralty, on a question of blockade, was allowed in the case of Croudson v. Leonard, 4 Cranch 434, to be contradicted in the court below; but this court reversed that decision, and held it to be conclusive. In that of The Mary, 9 Cranch 142, this court sustained the proof of property founded on the register, against a decree of a foreign court of admiralty. In that of The Pizarro, 2 Wheat. 227, the court look to the documentary evidence, as that to be relied on to prove ownership; and although the papers were not strictly correct, they still relied on them, in preference to further extraneous proof. Add to all this, the 12th article of the treaty which Spain (1 Laws U. S. 270) which makes passports and certificates evidence of property; and the principle may be regarded as established beyond a question, that the regular documents are the best and primary evidence in regard to all property on board of vessels. This is, indeed, especially the case, when they are merely coasting vessels, or such as are brought in on account of distress, shipwreck or other accident. The injustice of requiring further evidence in such cases, is too apparent, to need any argument on the subject. Nor is it a less settled rule of international law, that when a vessel puts in by reason of distress or any similar cause, she is not to be judged by the municipal law. The unjust results to which a different rule would lead are most apparent. Could we tolerate it, that if one of our own coasters was obliged to put into Cuba, and had regular coasting papers, the courts of that country should look beyond them, as to proof of property?

If this point be established, is there any difference between property in slaves and other property? They existed as property, at the time of the treaty, in, perhaps, every nation of the globe; they still exist as property in Spain and the United States; they can be demanded as property, in the states of this Union to which they fly, and where by the laws they would not, if domiciliated, be property. If, then, they are property, the rules laid down in regard to property extend to them. If they are found on board of a vessel, the evidence of property should be that which is recognised as the best in other cases of property — the vessel's papers, accompanied by possession. In the cases of The Louis, [40 U.S. 518, 545] 2 Dods. 238, slaves are treated of, by Sir WILLIAM SCOTT, in express terms, as property, and he directed that those taken unlawfully from a foreigner should be restored. In the case of The Antelope, 10 Wheat. 119, the decision in the case of The Louis is recognised, and the same principle was fully and completely aced upon. It was there conceded (10 Wheat. 124), that possession on board of a vessel was evidence of property. In the case of Johnson v. Tompkins, 1 Bald. 577, it was held, that, even where it was a question of freedom or slavery, the same rules of evidence prevailed as in other cases relative to the right of property. In the case of Choat v. Wright, 2 Dev. 289, a sale of a slave, accompanied by delivery, is valid, though there be no bill of sale. And it is well settled, that a title to them is vested by the statute of limitations, as in other cases of property. 5 Cranch 358, 361; 11 Wheat. 361.

If, then, the same law exists in regard to property in slaves as in other things; and if documentary evidence, from the highest authority of the country where the property belonged, accompanied with possession, is produced; it follows, that the title to the ownership of this property is as complete as is required by law.

But it is said, that this evidence is insufficient, because it is, in point of fact, fraudulent and untrue. The ground of this assertion is, that the slaves were not property in Cuba, at the date of the document signed by the governor-general; because they had been lately introduced into that island from Africa, and persons so introduced were free. To this it is answered, that if it were so, this court will not look beyond the authentic evidence under the official certificate of the governor-general; that, if it would, there is not such evidence as this court can regard to be sufficient to overthrow the positive statement of that document; and that, if the evidence were even deemed sufficient to show the recent introduction of the negroes, it does not establish that they were free at the date of the certificate.

1. This court will not look behind the certificate of the governor-general. It does not appear to be alleged, that it is fraudulent in itself. It is found by the district court to have been signed by him, and countersigned by the officer of the customs. [40 U.S. 518, 546] It was issued by them, in the appropriate exercise of their functions. It resembles an American register or coasting license. Now, all the authorities that have been cited show, that these documents are received as the highest species of evidence, and that, even if there is error in the proceedings on which they are founded. The correction must be made from the tribunal from which it emanates. Where should we stop, if we were to refuse to give faith to the documents of public officers? All national intercourse, all commerce, must be at an end. If there is error in issuing these papers, the matter must be sent to the tribunals of Spain for correction.

2. But if this court will look behind this paper, is the evidence sufficient to contradict it? The official declaration to be contradicted is certainly of a character not to be lightly set aside in the courts of a foreign country. The question is not, as to the impression we may derive from the evidence; but how far is it sufficient to justify us in declaring a fact, in direct contradiction to such an official declaration. It is not evidence that could be received, according to the established admiralty practice. Seamen (1 Pet. Adm. 211) on board of a vessel cannot be witnesses for one another, in matters where they have a common interest. Again, the principal part of this evidence is not taken under oath. That of Dr. Madden, which is mainly relied upon, is chiefly hearsay; and is contradicted, in some its most essential particulars, by that of other witnesses. Would this court be justified, on evidence such as this, in setting aside the admitted certificate of the governor-

general? Would such evidence, on one of our own courts, be deemed adequate to set aside a judicial proceeding, or an act of a public functionary, done in the due exercise of his office? How, then, can it be adequate to such an end, before the tribunals of a foreign country, when they pass upon the internal municipal acts of another government; and when the endeavor is made to set them aside, in a mater relating to their own property and people?

3. But admit this evidence to be competent and sufficient; admit these negroes were brought into Cuba, a few weeks before the certificate was given; still, were they not slaves, under the Spanish laws? It is not denied, that negroes imported from [40 U.S. 518, 547] Africa into Cuba, might be slaves. If they are not, it is on account of some special law or decree. Has such a law been produced in the present case? The first document produced is the treaty with England, of 23d September 1817. But that has no such effect. It promises, indeed, that Spain will take into consideration the means of preventing the slave-trade, and it points out those means, so far as the trade on the coast of Africa is concerned. But it carefully limits the ascertainment of any infringement to two special tribunals, one at Sierra Leone, and the other at Havana. The next is the decree of December 1817, which authorizes negroes, brought in against the treaty, to 'be declared free.' The treaty of 28th June 1835, which is next adduced, is confined entirely to the slave-trade on the coast of Africa, or the voyage from there. Now, it is evident, that none of these documents show that these negroes were free in Cuba. They had not been 'declared free,' by any competent tribunal. Even had they been taken actually on board of a vessel engaged in the slave-trade, they must have been adjudicated upon at one of the two special courts, and nowhere else. Can this court, then, undertake to decide this question of property, when it has not even been decided by the Spanish courts; and make such decision, in the face of the certificate of the highest functionary of the island?

It is submitted, then, that if is this court does go behind the certificate of the governor-general, and look into the fact, whether or not these persons were slaves on the 18th June 1839, yet there is no sufficient evidence on which they could adjudge it to untrue. If this be so, the proof concerning the property is sufficient to bring the case within the intention and provisions of the treaty.

The next question is, did the United States legally intervene to obtain the decree of the court for the restoration of the property, in order that it might be delivered to the Spanish owners, according to the stipulations of the treaty?

They did! because the property of foreigners, thus brought under the cognisance of the courts, is, of right, deliverable to the public functionaries of the government to which such foreigners belong; because those functionaries have required the interposition of the United States on their behalf; and because the United States were authorized, [40 U.S. 518, 548] on that request, to interpose, pursuant to their treaty obligations. That the property of foreigners, under such circumstances, may be delivered to the public functionaries, is so clearly established, by the decisions of this court, that it is unnecessary to discuss the point. In the case (2 Mason 411-12, 463) of La Jeune Eugenie, there was a libel of the vessel, as in this case, and a claim interposed be the French consul, and also by the owners themselves. The court there directed the delivery of the property to the public functionary. In that of The Divina Pastora, 4 Wheat. 52, the Spanish consul interposed. In that of The Antelope, 10 Ibid. 68, there were claims interposed, very much as in this case, by the captain as captor, and by the vice-consuls of Spain and Portugal, for citizens of their respective countries; and by the United States. The court directed their delivery, partly to the consul of Spain, and partly to the United States. It is thus settled, that the public functionaries are entitled to intervene in such cases, on behalf of the citizens of their countries. In the present one, the Spanish minister did so intervene by applying to the United States to adopt, on his behalf, the necessary proceedings; and, upon his doing so, Ruiz and Montez withdrew their separate claims. The United States, on their part, acted as the treaty required. The executive is their agent, in all such transactions, and on him devolved the obligation to see this property restored entire, if due proof concerning it was made. The form of proceeding was already established by precedent and by law. The course adopted was exactly that pursued in the case of McFadden v. The Exchange, 7 Cranch 116, where a vessel was libeled in a port of the United States. Being a public vessel of a foreign sovereign, which the government was bound to protect, they intervened exactly in the same way. The libel was dismissed, and the vessel restored to the custody of the public officers of France.

It is, therefore, equally clear, that the United States, in this instance, has pursued the course required by the laws of nations; and if the court are satisfied, on the first point, that there is due proof concerning the property, then it ought to be delivered entire, so that it may be restored to the Spanish owners. If this be so, the court below has erred, because it has not decreed any part of [40 U.S. 518, 549] the property to be delivered entire, except the boy Antonio. From the vessel and cargo, it has deducted the salvage, diminishing them by that amount; and the negroes it has entirely refused to direct to be delivered.

Baldwin, for the defendants in error. — In preparing to address this honorable court, on the questions arising upon this record, in behalf of the humble Africans whom I represent — contending, as they are, for freedom and for life, with two powerful governments arrayed against them — it has been to me a source of high gratification, in this unequal contest, that those questions will be heard and decided by a tribunal, not only elevated far above the influence of executive power and popular prejudice, but, from its very constitution, exempt from liability to those imputations to which a court, less happily constituted, or composed only of members from one section of the Union, might, however unjustly, be exposed.

This case is not only one of deep interest in itself, as affecting the destiny of the unfortunate Africans whom I represent, but it involves considerations deeply affecting our national character in the eyes of the whole civilized world, as well as questions of power on the part of the government of the United States, which are regarded with anxiety and alarm by a large portion of our citizens. It presents, for the first time, the question, whether that government, which was established for the promotion of justice, which was founded on the great principles of the revolution, as proclaimed in the Declaration of Independence, can, consistently with the genius of our institutions, become a party to proceedings for the enslavement of human beings cast upon our shores, and found, in the condition of freemen, within the territorial limits of a free and sovereign state?

In the remarks I shall have occasion to make, it will be my design to appeal to no sectional prejudices, and to assume no positions in which I shall not hope to be sustained by intelligent minds from the south as well as from the north.

Although I am in favor of the broadest liberty of inquiry and discussion — happily secured by our constitution to every citizen, subject only to his individual responsibility to the laws for its abuse; I have ever been of the opinion, that the exercise of that liberty, by [40 U.S. 518, 550] citizens of one state, in regard to the institutions of another, should always be guided by discretion, and tempered with kindness. Mr. Baldwin here proceeded to state all the facts of the case, and the proceedings in the district and circuit courts, in support of the motion to dismiss the appeal. As no decision was given by the court on the motion, this part of the argument is, necessarily, omitted.

Mr. Baldwin continued, if the government of the United States could appear in any case as the representative of foreigners claiming property in the court of admiralty, it has no right to appear in their behalf, to aid them in the recovery of fugitive slaves, even when domiciled in the country from which they escaped; much less the recent victims of the African slave-trade, who have sought an asylum in one of the free states of the Union, without any wrongful act on our part, or for which, as in the case of the Antelope, we are in any way responsible. The recently-imported Africans of the Amistad, if they were ever slaves, which is denied, were in the actual condition of freedom, when they came within the jurisdictional limits of the state of New York. They came there, without any wrongful act on the part of any officer or citizen of the United States. They were in a state where, not only no law existed to make them slaves, but where, by an express statute, all persons, except fugitives, & c., from a sister state, are declared to be free. They were under the protection of the laws of a state, which, in the language of the supreme court, in the case of City of New York v. Miln, 11 Pet. 139, 'has the same undeniable and unlimited jurisdiction over all persons and things within its territorial limits, as any foreign nation, when that jurisdiction is not surrendered or restrained by the constitution of the United States.'

The American people have never imposed it as a duty on the government of the United States, to become actors in an attempt to reduce to slavery, men found in a state of freedom, by giving extra-territorial force to a foreign slave law.

Such a duty would not only be repugnant to the feelings of a large portion of the citizens of the United States, but it would be wholly inconsistent with the fundamental principles of our government, and the purposes [40 U.S. 518, 551] for which it was established, as well as with its policy in prohibiting the slave-trade and giving freedom to its victims. The recovery of slaves for their owners, whether foreign or domestic, is a matter with which the executive of the United States has no concern. The constitution confers upon the government no power to establish or legalize the institution of slavery. It recognises it as existing, in regard to persons held to service by the laws of the states which tolerate it; and contains a compact between the states, obliging them to respect the rights acquired under the slave laws of other states, in the cases specified in the constitution. But it imposes no duty, and confers no power, on the government of the United States, to act in regard to it. So far as the compact extends, the courts of the United States, whether sitting in a free state or a slave state, will give effect to it. Beyond that, all persons within the limits of a state are entitled to the protection of its laws.

If these Africans have been taken from the possession of their Spanish claimants, and wrongfully brought into the United States by our citizens, a question would have been presented similar to that which existed in the case of The Antelope. But when men have come here voluntarily, without any wrong on the part of the government or citizens of the United States, in withdrawing them from the jurisdiction of the Spanish laws, why should this government be required to become active in their restoration? They appear here as freemen. They are in a state where they are presumed to be free. They stand before our courts on equal ground with their claimants; and when the courts, after an impartial hearing, with all parties in interest before them, have pronounced them free, it is neither the duty nor the right of the executive of the United States, to interfere with the decision.

The question of the surrender of fugitive slaves to a foreign claimant, if the right exists at all, is left to the comity of the states which tolerate slavery. The government of the United States has nothing to do with it. In the letter of instructions addressed by Mr. Adams, when secretary of state, to Messrs. Gallatin and Rush, dated November 2d, 1818, in relation to a proposed arrangement with Great Britain, for a more active co-operation in the suppression of the slave-trade, he assigns as a [40 U.S. 518, 552] reason for rejecting the proposition for a mixed commission, 'that the disposal of the negroes found on board the slave-trading vessels, which might be condemned by the sentence of the mixed courts, cannot be carried into effect by the United States.' 'The condition of the blacks being, in this Union, regulated by the municipal laws of the separate states, the government of the United States can neither guaranty their liberty in the states where they could only be received as slaves, nor control them in the states where they would be recognised as free.' Doc. 48, H. Rep. 2 sess. 16th Cong. p. 15.

It may comport with the interest or feelings of a slave state, to surrender a fugitive slave to a foreigner, or, at least, to expel him from their borders. But the people of New England, except so far as they are bound by the compact, would cherish and protect him. To the extent of the compact, we acknowledge our obligation, and have passed laws for its fulfillment. Beyond that, our citizens would be unwilling to go. A state has no power to surrender a fugitive criminal to a foreign government for punishment; because that is necessarily a matter of national concern. The fugitive is demanded for a national purpose. But the question of the surrender of fugitive slaves concerns individuals merely. They are demanded as property only, and for private purposes. It is therefore, a proper subject for the action of the state, and not of the national authorities. The surrender of neither is demandable of right, unless stipulated by treaty. See, as to the surrender of fugitive criminals, 2 Brock. 493; 2 Summ. 482; 14 Pet. 540; Doc. 199, H. R. 26 Cong. p. 53-70; 10 Am. State Pap. 151-153, 433; 3 Hall's Law Jour. 135. An overture was once made by the government of the United States to negotiate a treaty with Great Britain, for the mutual surrender of fugitive slaves. But it was instantly repelled by the British government. It may well be doubted, whether such a stipulation is within the treaty making power under the constitution of the United States. 'The power to make treaties,' says Chief Justice TANEY, 14 Pet. 569, 'is given in general terms,' 'and consequently, it was designed to include all those subjects which, in the ordinary intercourse of nations, had usually been made subjects [40 U.S. 518, 553] of negotiation and treaty; and which are consistent with the nature of our institutions, and the distribution of powers between the general and state government.' See Holmes v. Jennison, 14 Pet. 569. But however this may be, the attempt to introduce it is evidence that, unless provided for by treaty, the obligation to surrender was not deemed to exist.

We deny that Ruiz and Montez, Spanish subjects, had a right to call on any officer or court of the United States to use the force of the government, or the process of the law, for the purpose of again enslaving those who have thus escaped from foreign slavery, and sought an asylum here. We deny that the seizure of these persons by Lieutenant Gedney for such a purpose was a legal or justifiable act. How would it be — independently of the treaty between the United States and Spain — upon the principles of our government, of the common law, or of the law of nations? If a foreign slave vessel, engaged in a traffic which by our laws is denounced as inhuman and piratical, should be captured by the slaves, while on her voyage from Africa to Cuba, and they should succeed in reaching our shores, have the constitution or laws of the United States imposed upon our judges, our naval officers, or our executive, the duty of seizing the unhappy fugitives and delivering them up to their oppressors? Did the people of the United States, whose government is based on the great principles of the revolution, proclaimed in the Declaration of Independence, confer upon the federal, executive or judicial tribunals, the power of making our nation accessories to such atrocious violations of human rights? Is there any principle of international law, or law of comity, which requires it? Are our courts bound, and if not, are they at liberty, to give effect here to the slave-trade laws of a foreign nation; to laws affecting strangers, never domiciled there, when, to give them such effect, would be to violate the natural rights of men?

These questions are answered in the negative by all the most approved writers on the laws of nations. 1 Burg. Confl. 741; Story, Confl. 92. By the law of France, the slaves of their colonies, immediately on their arrival in France, become free. In the case of [40 U.S. 518, 554] Forbes v. Cochrane, 2 Barn. & Cres. 463, this question is elaborately discussed and settled by the English court of king's bench. By the law of the state of New York, a foreign slave escaping into that state becomes free. And the courts of the United States, in acting upon the personal rights of men found within the jurisdiction of a free state, are bound to administer the laws as they would be administered by the state courts, in all cases in which the laws of the state do not conflict with the laws or obligations of the United States. The United States, as a nation, have prohibited the slave-trade, as inhuman and piratical, and they have no law authorizing the enslaving of its victims. It is a maxim, to use the words of an eminent English judge, in the case of Forbes v. Cochrane, 2 Barn. & Cres. 448, 'that which is called comitas inter communitates, cannot prevail in any case, where it violates the law of our own country, the law of nature, or the law of God.' 9 Eng. C. L. 149. And that the laws of a nation, proprio vigore, have no force beyond its own territories, except so far as respects its own citizens, who owe it allegiance, is too familiarly settled, to need the citation of authorities. See The Apollon, 9 Wheat. 366; 2 Mason 151-8. The rules on this subject adopted in the English court of admiralty are the same which prevail in their courts of common law, though they have decided in the case of The Louis, 2 Dods. 238, as the supreme court did in the case of The Antelope, 10 Wheat. 66, that as the slave-trade was not, at that time, prohibited by the law of nations, if a foreign slaver was captured by an English ship, it was a wrongful act, which it would be the duty of the court of admiralty to repair, by restoring the possession. The principle of amoveas manus, adopted in these cases, has no application to the case of fugitives from slavery.

But it is claimed, that if these Africans, though 'recently imported into Cuba,' were, by the laws of Spain, the property of Ruiz and Montez, the government of the United States is bound by the treaty to restore them; and that, therefore, the intervention of the executive in these proceedings is proper for that purpose. It has already, it is believed, been shown, that even if the case were within the treaty, the intervention of the executive, as a party before the judicial tribunals, was unnecessary and improper, [40 U.S. 518, 555] since the treaty provides for its own execution by the courts, on the application of the parties in interest. And such a resort is expressly provided in the 20th article of the treaty of 1794 with Great Britain, and in the 26th article of the treaty of 1801, with the French republic, both of which are in other respects similar to the 9th article of the Spanish treaty, on which the attorney-general has principally relied.

The 6th article of the Spanish treaty has received a judicial construction in the case of The Santissima Trinidad, 7 Wheat. 284, where it was decided, that the obligation assumed is simply that of protecting belligerent vessels from capture, within our jurisdiction. It can have no application, therefore, to a case like the present. The 9th article of that treaty provides, 'that all ships and merchandize, of what nature soever, which shall be rescued out of the hands of pirates or robbers, on the high seas, shall be brought into some port of either state, and shall be delivered to the custody of the officers of that port, in order to be taken care of, and restored entire to the true proprietors, as soon as due and sufficient proof shall be made concerning the property thereof.' To render this clause of the treaty applicable to the case under consideration, it must be assumed, that under the term 'merchandize' the contracting parties intended to include slaves; and that slaves, themselves the recent victims of piracy, who by a successful revolt, have achieved their deliverance from slavery, on the high seas, and have availed themselves of the means of escape of which they have thus acquired the possession, are to be deemed 'pirates and robbers,' 'from whose hands' such 'merchandize has been rescued.' It is believed, that such a construction of the words of the treaty is not in accordance with the rules of interpretation which ought to govern our courts; and that when there is no special reference to human beings, as property, who are not acknowledged as such by the law or comity of nations, generally, but only by the municipal laws of the particular nations which tolerate slavery, it cannot be presumed, that the contracting parties intended to include them under the general term 'merchandize.' As has already been remarked, it may well be doubted, [40 U.S. 518, 556] whether such a stipulation would be within the treaty-making power of the United States. It is to be remembered, that the government of the United States is based on the principles promulgated in the Declaration of Independence, by the congress of 1776; 'that all men are created equal; that they are endowed by their Creator with certain inalienable rights; that among these are life, liberty and the pursuit of happiness; and that to secure these rights, governments are instituted.'

The convention which formed the federal constitution, though they recognised slavery as existing in regard to persons held to labor by the laws of the states which tolerated it, were careful to exclude from that instrument every expression that might be construed into an admission that there could be property in men. It appears by the report of the proceedings of the convention (3 Madison Papers 1428), that the first clause of 9, art. 1, which provides for the imposition of a tax or duty on the importation of such persons as any of the states, then existing, might think proper to admit, &c., 'not exceeding ten dollars for each person,' was adopted in its present form, in consequence of the opposition by Roger Sherman and James Madison to the clause as it was originally reported, on the ground, 'that it admitted, that there could be property in men;' an idea which Mr. Madison said, 'he thought it wrong to admit in the constitution.' The words reported by the committee, and striken out on this objection, were: 'a tax or duty may be imposed on such migration or importation, at a rate not exceeding the average of the duties laid upon imports.' The constitution as it now stands will be searched in vain for an expression recognising human beings as merchandize, or legitimate subjects of commerce. In the case of New York v. Miln, 11 Pet. 104, 136, Judge BARBOUR, in giving the opinion of the court, expressly declares, in reference to the power 'to regulate commerce' conferred on congress by the constitution, that 'persons are not the subjects of commerce.' Judging from the public sentiment which prevailed at the time of the adoption of the constitution, it is probable, that the first act of the government, in the exercise of its power to regulate commerce, would have been to prohibit the slave-trade, if the had not been restrained, until 1808, from prohibiting the importation of such persons as any of the states, [40 U.S. 518, 557] then existing, should think proper to admit. But could congress have passed an act authorizing the importation of slaves as articles of commerce, into any state, in opposition to a law of the state, prohibiting their introduction? If they could, they may now force slavery into every state. For no state can prohibit the introduction of legitimate objects of foreign commerce, when authorized by congress. The United States must be regarded as comprehending free states as well as slave states; states which do not recognise slaves as property, as well as states which do so regard them. When all speak as a nation, general expressions ought to be construed to mean what all understand to be included in them; at all events, what may be included consistently with the law of nations.

The ninth article of the Spanish treaty was copied from the 16th article of the treaty with France, concluded in 1778, in the midst of the war of the revolution, in which the great principles of liberty proclaimed in the Declaration of Independence were vindicated by our fathers. By 'merchandize rescued from pirates,' the contracting parties must have had in view property, which it would be the duty of the public ships of the

United States to rescue from its unlawful possessors. Because, if it is taken from those who are rightfully in possession, the capture would be wrongful, and it would be our duty to restore it. But is it a duty which our naval officers owe to a nation tolerating the slave-trade, to subdue for their kidnappers the revolted victims of their cruelty? Could the people of the United States, consistently with their principles as a nation, have ever consented to a treaty stipulation which would impose such a duty on our naval officers? a duty which would drive every citizen of a free state from the service of his country? Has our government, which has been so cautious as not to oblige itself to surrender the most atrocious criminals, who have sought an asylum in the United States, bound itself, under the term 'merchandize,' to seize and surrender fugitive slaves? The subject of the delivery of fugitives was under consideration before and during the negotiation of the treaty of San Lorenzo; and was purposely omitted in the treaty: 10, Waite's State Papers, 151, 433. Our treaties with Tunis and Algiers contain similar expressions, in which both parties stipulate [40 U.S. 518, 558] for the protection of the property of the subjects of each, within the jurisdiction of the other. The Algerine regarded his Spanish captive as property; but was it ever supposed, that if an Algerine corsair should be seized by the captive slaves on board of her, it would be the duty of our naval officers, or our courts of admiralty, to re-capture and restore them? The phraseology of the entire article in the treaty, clearly shows that it was intended to apply only to inanimate things, or irrational animals; such as are universally regarded as property. It is 'merchandize rescued from the hands of pirates and robbers on the high seas' that is to be restored. There is no provision for the surrender of the pirates themselves. And the reason is, because the article has reference only to those who are 'hostes humani generis,' whom it is lawful for, and the duty of, all nations to capture and to punish. If these Africans were 'pirates' or sea robbers, whom our naval officers might lawfully seize, it would be our duty to detain them for punishment; and then what would become of the 'merchandize?'

But they were not pirates, nor in any sense hostes humani generis. Cinque, the master-spirit who guided them, had a single object in view. That object was — not piracy or robbery — but the deliverance of himself and his companions in suffering, from unlawful bondage. They owed no allegiance to Spain. They were on board of the Amistad, by constraint. Their object was to free themselves from the fetters that bound them, in order that they might return to their kindred and their home. In so doing, they were guilty of no crime, for which they could be held responsible as pirates. See Bee 273. Suppose, they had been impressed American sea-

men, who had regained their liberty in a similar manner, would they in that case have been deemed guilty of piracy and murder? Not! in the opinion of Chief Justice MARSHALL. In his celebrated speech in justification of the surrender by President Adams of Nash, under the British treaty, he says: 'Had Thomas Nash been an impressed American, the homicide on board the Hermione would most certainly not have been murder. The act of impressing a American is an act of lawless violence. The confinement on board a vessel is a continuation of that violence, and an additional outrage. Death [40 U.S. 518, 559] committed within the United States, in resisting such violence, would not have been murder.' Bee 290.

The United States, as a nation, is to be regarded as a free state. And all men being presumptively free, when 'merchandize' is spoken of in the treaty of a free state, it cannot be presumed, that human beings are intended to be included as such. Hence, whenever our government have intended to speak of negroes as property, in their treaties, they have been specifically mentioned, as in the treaties with Great Britain of 1783 and 1814. It was on the same principle, that Judge DRAYTON, of South Carolina, decided, in the case of Almeida, who had captured, during the last war, an English vessel with slaves, that the word 'property' in the prize act, did not include negroes, and that they must be regarded as prisoners of war, and not sold or distributed as merchandize. 5 Hall's Law Jour. 459. And it was for the same reason, that it was deemed necessary, in the constitution, to insert an express stipulation in regard to fugitives from service. The law of comity would have obliged each state to protect and restore property belonging to a citizen of another, without such stipulation; but it would not have required the restoration of fugitive slaves from a sister state, unless they had been expressly mentioned.

In the interpretation of treaties, we ought always to give such a construction to the words as is most consistent with the customary use of language; most suitable to the subject, and to the legitimate powers of the contracting parties; most conformable to the declared principles of the government; such a construction as will not lead to injustice to others, or in any way violate the laws of nature. These are, in substance, the rules of interpretation as given by Vattel, lib. 2, ch. 17. The construction claimed in behalf of the Spanish libellants, in the present case, is at war with them all.

It would be singular, indeed, if the tribunals of a government which has declared the slave-trade piracy, and has bound itself by a solemn treaty with Great Britain, in 1814, to make continued efforts 'to promote its entire abolition, as a traffic irreconcilable with the principles of humanity and justice,' should construe the general expressions of a treaty which, since that period, [40 U.S. 518, 560] has been revised by the contracting parties, as obliging this nation to commit the injustice of treating as property, the recent victims of this horrid traffic; more especially, when it is borne in mind, that the government of Spain, anterior to the revision of the treaty in 1819, had formally notified our government, that Africans were no longer the legitimate objects of trade; with a declaration that 'His Majesty felt confident that a measure so completely in harmony with the sentiments of this government, and of all the inhabitants of this republic, could not fail to be equally agreeable to the president.' Doc. 48, 2 sess. 16 Cong. p. 8. Would the people of the United States, in 1819, have assented to such a treaty? Would it not have furnished just ground of complaint by Great Britain, as a violation of the 10th article of the treaty of Ghent?

But even if the treaty, in its terms, were such as to oblige us to violate towards strangers the immutable laws of justice, it would, according to Vattel, impose no obligation. Vattel, c. 1, 9; lib. 2, c. 12, 161; c. 17, 311. The law of nature and the law of nations bind us as effectually to render justice to the African, as the treaty can to the Spaniard. Before a foreign tribunal, the parties litigating the question of freedom or slavery, stand on equal ground. And in a case like this, where it is admitted, that the Africans were recently imported, and consequently, never domiciled in Cuba, and owe no allegiance to its laws, their rights are to be determined by that law which is of universal obligation — the law of nature. If, indeed, the vessel in which they sailed had been driven upon our coast by stress of weather, or other unavoidable cause, and they had arrived here, in the actual possession of their alleged owners, and had been slaves by the law of the country from which they sailed, and where they were domiciled, it would have been a very different question, whether the courts of the United States could interfere to liberate them, as was done at Bermuda by the colonial tribunal, in the case of The Enterprise. But in this case, there has been no possession of these Africans by their claimants, within our jurisdiction, of which they have been deprived, by the act of our government or its officers; and neither by the law of comity, nor by force of the treaty, are the [40 U.S. 518, 561] officers or courts of the United States required, or by the principles of our government permitted, to become actors in reducing them to slavery.

These preliminary questions have been made on account of the important principles involved in them, and not from any unwillingness to meet the question between the Africans and their claimants, upon the facts in evidence, and on those alone, to vindicate their claims to freedom. Suppose, then, the case to be properly here; and that Ruiz and Montez, unprejudiced by the decree of the court below, were at liberty to take issue with the Africans upon their answer, and to call upon this court to determine the question of liberty or property, how stands the case on the evidence before the court?

The Africans, when found by Lieutenant Gedney, were in a free state, where all men are presumed to be free, and were in the actual condition of freemen. The burden of proof, therefore, rests on those who assert them to be slaves. 10 Wheat. 66; 2 Mason 459. When they call on the courts of the United States to reduce to slavery men who are apparently free, they must show some law, having force in the place where they were taken, which makes them slaves, or that the claimants are entitled in our courts to have some foreign law, obligatory on the Africans as well as on the claimants, enforced in respect to them, and that by such foreign law they are slaves. It is not pretended, that there was any law existing in the place where they were found, which made them slaves, but it is claimed, that by the laws of Cuba, they were slaves to Ruiz and Montez; and that those laws are to be here enforced. But before the laws of Cuba, if any such there be, can be applied, to affect the personal status of individuals within a foreign jurisdiction, it is very clear, that it must be shown that they were domiciled in Cuba.

It is admitted and proved, in this case, that these negroes are natives of Africa, and recently imported into Cuba. Their domicile of origin is, consequently, the place of their birth, in Africa. And the presumption of law is, always, that the domicile of origin is retained, until the change is proved. 1 Burge's Conflict 34. [40 U.S. 518, 562] The burden of proving the change is cast on him who alleges it. 5 Ves. 787. The domicile of origin prevails, until the party has not only acquired another, but has manifested and carried into execution an intention of abandoning his former domicile, and acquiring another, as his sole domicile. As it is the will or intention of the party which alone determines what is the real place of domicile which he has chosen, it follows, that a former domicile is not abandoned, by residence in another, if that residence be not voluntarily chosen. Those who are in exile, or in prison, as they are never presumed to have abandoned all hope of return, retain their former domicile. 1 Burge 46. That these victims of fraud and piracy — husbands torn from their wives and families — children from their parents and kindred — neither intended to abandon the land of their nativity, nor had lost all hope of recovering it, sufficiently appears from the facts on this record. It cannot, surely, be claimed, that a residence, under such circumstances, of these helpless beings, for ten days, in a slave barracoon, before hey were transferred to the Amistad, changed their native domicile for that of Cuba.

It is not only incumbent on the claimants to prove that the Africans are domiciled in Cuba, and subject to its laws, but they must show that some law existed there, by which 'recently imported Africans' can be lawfully held in slavery. Such a law is not to be presumed, but the contrary. Comity would seem to require of us to presume, that a traffic so abhorrent to the feelings of the whole civilized world, is not lawful in Cuba. These respondents having been born free, and having been recently imported into Cuba, have a right to be everywhere regarded as free, until some law obligatory on them is produced, authorizing their enslavement. Neither the law of nature, nor the law of nations, authorizes the slave-trade; although it was holden in the case of The Antelope, that the law of nations did not at that time actually prohibit it. If they are slaves, then, it must be by some positive law of Spain, existing at the time of their recent importation. No such law is exhibited. On the contrary, it is proved by the deposition of Dr. Madden, one of the British commissioners resident at Havana, that since the year 1820, there has been no such law in force there, either statute or common law. [40 U.S. 518, 563] But we do not rest the case here. We are willing to assume the burden of proof. On the 14th of May 1818, the Spanish government, by their minister, announced to the government of the United States, that the slave-trade was prohibited by Spain; and by express command of the king of Spain, Don Onis communicated to the president of the United States, the treaty with Great Britain of September 23d, 1817, by which the king of Spain, moved partly by motives of humanity, and partly in consideration of 400, 000l. sterling, paid to him by the British government, for the accomplishment of so desirable an object, engaged that the slave-trade should be abolished throughout the dominions of Spain, on the 30th May 1820. By the ordinance of the king of Spain, of December 1817, it is directed, that every African imported into any of the colonies of Spain, in violation of the treaty, shall be declared free in the first port at which he shall arrive. By the treaty between Great Britain and Spain, of the 28th of June 1835, which is declared to be made for the purpose of 'rendering the means taken for abolishing the inhuman traffic is slaves more effective,' and to be in the spirit of the treaty contracted between both powers on the 23d of September 1817, 'the slave-trade is again declared, on the part of Spain, to be henceforward totally and finally abolished, in all parts of the world.' And by the royal ordinance of November 2d, 1838, the gover-

nor and the naval officers having command on the coast of Cuba, are stimulated to greater vigilance to suppress it.

Such, then, being the laws in force in all the dominions of Spain, and such the conceded facts in regard to the nativity and recent importation of these Africans, upon what plausible ground can it be claimed by the government of the United States, that they were slaves in the island of Cuba, and are here to be treated as property, and not as human beings? The only evidence exhibited to prove them slaves, are the papers of the Amistad, giving to Jose Ruiz permission to transport forty-nine ladinos belonging to him, from Havana to Puerto Principe; and a like permit to Pedro Montez, to transport three ladinos. For one of the four Africans, claimed by Montez (the boy Ka-le), there is no permit at all.

It has been said in an official opinion by the late attorney-general [40 U.S. 518, 564] (Mr. Grundy), that 'as this vessel cleared out from one Spanish port to another Spanish port, with papers regularly authenticated by the proper officers at Havana, evidencing that these negroes were slaves, and that the destination of the vessel was to another Spanish port, the government of the United States would not be authorized to go into an investigation for the purpose of ascertaining whether the facts stated in those papers by the Spanish officers are true or not'—'that if it were to permit itself to go behind the papers of the schooner Amistad, it would place itself in the embarrassing condition of judging upon Spanish laws, their force, effect and application to the case under consideration.' In support of this opinion, a reference is made to the opinion of this court, in the case of Arredondo, 6 Pet. 729, where it is stated to be 'a universal principle, that where power or jurisdiction is delegated to any public officer or tribunal over a subject-matter, and its exercise is confided to his or their discretion, the acts so done are binding and valid as to the subject-matter; and individual rights will not be disturbed collaterally, for anything done in the exercise of that discretion within the authority conferred. The only questions which can arise between an individual claiming a right under the acts done, and the public, or any person denying its validity, are power in the officer, and fraud in the party.' The principle thus stated, was applicable to the case then before the court, which related to the validity of a grant made by a public officer; but it does not tend to support the position for which it is cited in the present case. For, in the first place, there was no jurisdiction over these newly-imported Africans, by the laws of Spain, to make them slaves, any more than if they had been white men. The ordinance of the king declared them free. Secondly, there was no intentional exercise of jurisdiction over them for such a purpose, by the officer who granted the permits. And thirdly, the permits were fraudulently obtained, and fraudulently used, by the parties claiming to take benefit of them. For the purposes for which they are attempted to be applied, the permits are as inoperative as would be a grant from a public officer, fraudulently obtained, where the state had no title to the thing granted, and the officer no authority to issue the grant. See 6 Pet. 730; 5 Wheat. 303. [40 U.S. 518, 565] But it is said, we have no right to place ourselves in the position of judging upon the Spanish laws. How can our courts do otherwise, when Spanish subjects call upon them to enforce rights which, if they exist at all, must exist by force of Spanish laws? For what purpose did the government of Spain communicate to the government of the United States, the fact of the prohibition of the slave-trade, unless it was, that it might be known and acted upon by our courts? Suppose, the permits to Ruiz and Montez had been granted for the express purpose of consigning to perpetual slavery, these recent victims of this prohibited trade, could the government of Spain now ask the government or the courts of the United States, to give validity to the acts of a colonial officer, in direct violation of that prohibition; and thus make us aiders and abettors in what we know to be an atrocious wrong? It may be admitted, that even after such an annunciation, our cruisers could not lawfully seize a Spanish slaver, cleared out as such by the governor of Cuba; but if the Africans on board of her could effect their own deliverance, and reach our shores, has not the government of Spain authorized us to treat them with hospitality, as freemen? Could the Spanish minister, without offence, ask the government of the United States to seize these victims of fraud and felony, and treat them as property, because a colonial governor had thought proper to violate the ordinance of his king, in granting a permit to a slaver?

But in this case, we make no charge upon the governor of Cuba. A fraud upon him is proved to have been practised by Ruiz and Montez. He never undertook to assume jurisdiction over these Africans as slaves, or to decide any question in regard to them. He simply issued, on the application of Ruiz and Montez, passports for ladino slaves from Havana to Puerto Principe. When, under color of those passports, they fraudulently put on board the Amistad, Bozals, who by the laws of Spain could not be slaves, we surely manifest no disrespect to the acts of the governor, by giving efficacy to the laws of Spain, and denying to Ruiz and Montez the benefit of their fraud. The custom-house license, to which the name of Espeleta in print was appended, was not a document given or intended to be used as evidence of property between Ruiz and Montez, and the

[40 U.S. 518, 566] Africans; any more than a permit from our custom-house would be to settle conflicting claims of ownership to the articles contained in the manifest. As between the government and the shippers, it would be evidence, if the negroes described in the passport were actually put on board, and were, in truth, the property of Ruiz and Montez, that they were legally shipped; that the custom-house forms had been complied with; and nothing more. But in view of facts as they appear, and are admitted in the present case, the passports seem to have been obtained by Ruiz and Montez, only as a part of the necessary machinery for the completion of a slave-voyage. The evidence tends strongly to prove, that Ruiz, at least, was concerned in the importation of these Africans, and that the re-shipment of them, under color of passports obtained for ladinos, as the property of Ruiz and Montez, in connection with the false representation on the papers of the schooner, that they were 'passengers for the government,' was an artifice resorted to by these slave-traders, for the double purpose of evading the scrutiny of British cruisers, and legalizing the transfer of their victims to the place of their ultimate destination. It is a remarkable circumstance, that though more than a year has elapsed, since the decree of the district court denying the title of Ruis and Montez, and pronouncing the Africans free, not a particle of evidence has since been produced in support of their claims. And yet, strange as it may seem, during all this time, not only the sympathies of the Spanish minister, but the powerful aid of our own government have been enlisted in their behalf!

It was the purpose of the reporter to insert the able and interesting argument of Mr. Adams, for the African appellees; and the publication of the 'reports' has been postponed in the hope of obtaining it, prepared by himself. It has not been received. As many of the points presented by Mr. Adams, in the discussion of the cause, were not considered by the court essential to its decision: and were not taken notice of in the opinion of the court, delivered by Mr. Justice STORY, the necessary omission of the argument is submitted to with less regret. [40 U.S. 518, 567] Gilpin, Attorney-General in reply. — The judiciary act, which gives to this court its powers, so far as they depend on the legislature, directs that, on an appeal from the decree of an inferior court, this court shall render such judgment as the court below did, or should have rendered. It is to obtain from it such a decree in this case, that the United States present themselves here as appellants.

At the threshold of their application, the right so to present themselves is denied. They are to be turned away, as suitors having no claim to such interposition. The argument has gone a step farther; it seems now to be contended, that their appearance in the court below, which was not then objected to, is to be regarded as destitute of right, equally with their present appearance here. They are not even mere interlopers, seeking justice without warrant; they are dictators, in the form of supplicants, and their suggestions to the court, and their application for its judgment, upon solemn and important questions of fact, are distorted by an ingenious logic, which it is difficult to follow. Applications, made without the slightest expression of a wish, except to obtain that judgment, and in a form which, it might be supposed, would secure admission into any court, are repudiated, under the harsh name of 'executive interference.' Yet in what single respect do the facts of this case sustain such allegations? How can it be justly said, that there has been any 'executive interference,' not resulting from the adoption of that course which public duty made incumbent; and conducted in the manner, and in that manner only, which was required by that sense of public duty, from which, no officer, possessing a due regard for the obligations of his trust, will ever shrink?

In what situation is the case, when it is first presented to the notice of the government of the United States? On nearly, if not exactly, the same day, that the secretary of state receives from the minister of Spain an official communication, dated at New York, and stating the facts connected with the schooner L'Amistad, then just brought within the territory of the United States; stating also, that the vessel is a Spanish vessel, laden with merchandize, and with sundry negro slaves on board, accompanied with all the documents required by the laws of Spain, for navigating a vessel, and for proving ownership of [40 U.S. 518, 568] property; and then making an application to the government of the United States to interpose, so that the property thus within our territory, might be restored to its owners pursuant to the treaty; and asserting also, that the negroes, who were guilty, as he contended, of a crime for which they ought to be punished, ought to be delivered up on that account, too, pursuant to the law of nations — on or about the same day, the letter of the district — attorney, which, though dated a day earlier, is written in Connecticut, also reaches the department of state, conveying the information that this same property and these same negroes are already within the custody and authority of the judicial tribunals of the United States, by virtue of process, civil and criminal, issued by a judge of the United States, after solemn and deliberate inquiry. The vessel, the cargo and the negroes, had been all taken possession of, by a warrant issued by the court, 'as property;' they were then, at that very time, in the custody, keeping and possession of the court, as property, without the slightest suggestion

having been made by the executive branch of the government, or even a knowledge of the fact on its part; and when its interposition is formally solicited, its first information relative to the case received, it finds the subject of the demand already under the control of the judicial branch.

In this situation, the executive government, thus appealed to, and thus informed, looks to its treaty stipulations, the most solemn and binding compacts that nations know among each other, and the obligations of which can never be treated lightly, so long as good faith forms the first duty of every community. Those stipulations, entered into in 1795 (1 Laws U. S. 266), provide, in the first place (article 6), that each party to the treaty, the United States and Spain, shall 'endeavor, by all means in their power, to protect and defend and vessels and other effects belonging to the citizens or subjects of the other, which shall be within the extent of the jurisdiction.' Again, in the eighth article, it is declared, that 'in case the subjects or inhabitants of either country shall, with their shipping, he forced, through stress of weather, or any other urgent necessity for seeking shelter, to enter any port of the other, they shall enjoy all favor, protection and help.' Again, in the ninth article, it is provided, that 'all ships and merchandize, of what nature soever, [40 U.S. 518, 569] which shall be rescued out of the hands of any pirates or robbers, on the high seas, shall be brought into some port of either state, and shall be delivered into the custody of the officers of that port, in order to be taken care of, and restored entire to the true proprietor, as soon as due and sufficient proof shall be made concerning the property thereof.' In the 16th article, it is further declared, that the liberty of navigation and commerce meant by the treaty, shall extend to all kinds of merchandize, excepting those only which are contraband, and they are expressly enumerated; and it the 22d article, the object of the treaty is declared to be 'the extension of mutual commerce.' When these stipulations were thus made, slaves were a notorious article of merchandize and traffic in each country; not only were they so in the United States, but there was a constitutional provision, prohibiting congress from interfering to prevent their importation, as such, from abroad. This treaty, with these provisions thus solemnly and carefully framed, was renewed in 1819; was declared to be still in existence and force. It is declared (7 Laws U. S. 624), that every one of the articles above quoted 'remains confirmed.' It stands exactly as it stood in 1795; and, in the year 1821, after both governments had abolished the slave-trade, the provisions adopted in 1795 are thus, as to 'every clause and article thereof,' so renewed, solemnly ratified and confirmed by the president and senate of the United States. No clause is introduced to vary the nature or character of the merchandize; none to lessen or change the obligations, as would have been the case, had any such change been contemplated; but the two treaties, having the final date of 1821, bear the character of a single instrument.

Now, these are stipulations too clear to be misunderstood; too imperative to be wantonly neglected. Could we not ask of Spain the fulfillment of every one of them towards our own citizens? If so, were we not bound, at least, to see that, through some public functionary, or by some means in which nations fulfill mutual obligations, they were performed by us to the subjects of Spain, whenever the casus foederis should arise? Did it arise in this case? Here were, unquestionably, as the representative of Spain believed and stated, a vessel and effects [40 U.S. 518, 570] of subjects of that country, within our jurisdiction; here was a vessel and merchandize, rescued, as he alleged, from the hands of robbers, brought into one of our ports, and already in the custody of public officers. Did not a treaty stipulation require the United States to 'endeavor by all means in their power to protect and defend this property?' Did not a treaty stipulation require us to 'extend to them all favor, protection and help?' Did not a treaty stipulation bind us to 'restore, entire, the property, to the true proprietors, as soon as due and sufficient proof should be made concerning the same?' If not, then is there no force and meaning in language; and the words of solemn treaties are an idle breath, of which nations may be as regardless as of the passing wind.

The case then had arisen, where it was the duty of the United States, as parties to this treaty, to interfere and see that its stipulations were performed. How were they to interfere? Certainly, at the instance of the executive, through the medium of the judiciary, in whose custody and under whose control the property claimed already was. The questions incident to due and sufficient proof of property are clearly judicial questions; but when that property is already in the custody and under the jurisdiction of a court, they are so, from necessity, as it is desirable they always should be, from choice. This position, never denied, was eloquently urged by the counsel of these negroes, when they first addressed the executive on the subject (Cong. Doc. No. 185, p. 64), and to that view they added the request that he 'would submit the question for adjudication to the tribunals of the land.' He did so! He interposed, at the instance of the Spanish minister, to fulfill a treaty stipulation, by causing a suggestion to be filed in the court which had already taken cognisance of the subject-matter, and which had the property in its custody. That suggestion stated the allegation of the Spanish minister, that this was property which ought to be restored

under the treaty; prayed in effect an inquiry of the court into that fact; and requested such a decree, after such inquiry, as might enable the United States, as a nation, to fulfill their treaty obligations to the Spanish nation. This has been called 'executive interference' and 'executive dictation.' To answer such a charge in [40 U.S. 518, 571] any other way than by appealing to the facts, would be to trespass on the patience of the court.

As if such charges were felt to be insufficient, an attempt is made, by argument, to prove that the government of the United States had no right thus to interpose — no right to make this suggestion to the district court. And why not?

It is said, because there is no law giving this power, and it cannot be implied; because in a question of private property, it must be left to the parties alone to prosecute their rights, and the parties in this case were already doing so for themselves; and because it was an interference and encroachment of the executive on the province of the court, not sanctioned by any precedent. These are the grounds that have been taken, and it might be sufficient to say, that although every one of them existed in as full force, when the case was tried in the district court, none of them were there taken; although every one of them was known, before the plea and answer of the respondents, they started none of these objections. After the decree and judgment of the court below, it is too late to start them. But there is nothing in them, whenever made.

I. The executive government was bound to take the proper steps for having the treaty executed, and these were the proper steps. A treaty is the supreme law; the executive duty is especially to take care that the laws be faithfully executed; no branch of this duty is more usual or apparent, than that which is executed in connection with the proceedings and decrees of courts. What special assignment, by act of congress, has been made of the executive duties, in the fulfillment of laws, through the decrees and judgments of the judiciary? Yet it is matter of daily occurrence. What gives the district-attorney a right to file his libel against a package of goods, which the law says shall be forfeited, on proof being made that they are falsely invoiced, any more than to file his libel against a vessel and her cargo, which a treaty (a still higher law) declares shall be restored, on proof concerning the property thereof? In the one case, it is the execution of a law, by an executive officer, through the medium or in connection with the courts; in the other case, it is the execution of a treaty in a similar manner. But in the latter, the duty is, if possible, more imperative, since the execution of treaties, [40 U.S. 518, 572] being connected with public and foreign relations, is devolved upon the executive branch. These principles are clearly stated by this court in the case of The Peggy, 1 Cranch 103; and more fully in that of Williams v. Suffolk Insurance Company, 13 Pet. 420.

As to its being a question of private property, which the parties might themselves prosecute, it is not perceived how this impairs the right, or even lessens the obligation, of the United States to interfere, to the extent and in the manner they did, especially, when solicited by the minister representing these parties; they appear on behalf, or at the instance, of a foreign sovereignty in alliance with them, which assumes itself the rights and interests of the parties; those parties withdraw, as this record expressly shows, when they so appear; no act of theirs occurs, after the interposition of the United States, at the instance of the Spanish minister, and it is expressly stated, that they so withdrew, because their claims were merged in that which was thus presented. This appearance of the United States is not, as has been argued, a substitution of themselves as parties in interest; it is a substitution, under a treaty obligation; a substitution assumed in their public character to perform a public duty, by means of which the further prosecution of the individuals is (as the treaty intended it should be) rendered unnecessary. Besides, what is there to show that all the parties having an interest in this property were before the court? It is nowhere so stated; and if they were not, the objections totally fail.

How this proceeding is an interference by the executive with the court; how it a n encroachment on the judicial department; how it is a dicatation to the court, or advice to it to do its duty, it is difficult to conceive; and therefore, difficult to reply to such constructions of an act, analogous to the conduct of every proceeding in a court, rendered necessary to, or imperative upon, the executive, in the execution of the laws. If this libel, so definite in what it alleges and what it asks, founded on the official request of a public functionary, and intended to obtain the execution of a definite treaty obligation, be an infringement of judicial authority, it will be scarcely possible for a district-attorney, hereafter, to file an information, or present an indictment. [40 U.S. 518, 573] Nor is it, as is alleged, without precedent.

In fact, every case of a libel filed by the United States, soliciting the examination and decree of a court in rem, is a precedent, so far as any principle is concerned. But the cases of The Exchange, The Cassius, and The Eugenia, are not to be distinguished on any ground. They were cases of property in court, under libels of private suitors; the United States interposed, under their obligations to foreign powers. That those obligations were general, not arising by special treaty provisions, makes the cases less strong. It is said, that

the property in litigation in those cases, was to be delivered to the sovereign; is this property less in that position, when it is asked for by the representative of the sovereign? It is said, they were not delivered up as property; the Exchange and Cassius were so delivered, as public property of 'the Emperor Napoleon,' so stated in terms, and of the French republic. The Eugenia was delivered to the consul of France, that it might be proceeded against in rem, if desired. In the forms of proceeding by the United States, and in the decrees, everything resembles what has been done or sought for in this case.

But, in fact, every instance of interposition of foreign functionaries, consuls and others, affords a precedent. They have no right of property. They are no parties in interest. They interpose in behalf of the citizen. Did not this court, in the case of The Bello Corrunes, 6 Wheat. 152, where the express point was made, and the interposition of the Spanish consul, on behalf of his fellow-citizens, was resisted, sustain his right, as a public functionary, although it was admitted, he could show no special authority in the particular proceeding? So, in the case of The Antelope, 10 Wheat. 66, the consul was allowed to interpose for Spanish subjects, who were actually unknown. It will hardly be denied, that where the foreign functionary may thus come into our courts, to prosecute for the party in interest, our own functionaries may do the same. As to the case of Nash, Bee 266, it clearly sustains, so far as the course of proceeding, by means of the judiciary, is concerned, the right and duty of the executive thus to interpose. This was an application for the restoration of a criminal under treaty stipulations. The main question was, whether this surrender belonged exclusively to the executive, or was to be effected through the medium of the judiciary, [40 U.S. 518, 574] and while Chief Justice MARSHALL sustained the authority of the executive, as founded on the casus foederis, he admitted, that the aid of the judiciary might, in some cases, be called in. If this were so, as to persons, it is at least equally so, in regard to property. In respect to both, proof is to be made; without proof, neither the restoration of the one nor the other can be effected; that proof is appropriately made to, and passed upon by, the judicial tribunals; but as the execution of the treaty stipulation is vested in the executive, if the case is proved to the satisfaction of the judiciary, its interposition, so far as is necessary to that end, forms a proper part of the judicial proceedings.

It seems clear, then, that these objections to the duty of the executive to interpose, where the property to be restored is in the custody of the court, cannot be sustained, either by principle or authority. And such appears to be the sentiment of the counsel for the appellees, from the zeal with which they have pressed another argument, to reach the same end. That argument is, that the United States could not interpose, because the Spanish minister never had asked for the restoration of the slaves as property; and because, if he had, he had sought it solely from the executive department, and denied the jurisdiction of the court. Now, suppose this were so, it would be a sufficient answer to say, that, independent of the request of the foreign functionary, the United States had a treaty obligation to perform, which they were bound to perform; and that, if a request in regard to its performance was made, upon grounds not tenable, this did not release the United States from their obligation, on grounds which, as they knew, did properly exist. But, in point of fact, the Spanish minister did, from the first, demand these negroes, as property belonging to Spanish subjects, which ought to be restored as property, under the treaty of 1795.

Passages have been culled from the letters of Mr. Calderon, and Mr. Argaiz, to show that their surrender, as criminals, was only sought for; but the correspondence, taken together, bears no such construction. It is true, they were demanded as criminals; the alleged crime had been committed on Spanish subjects, and on board of a Spanish ship; by the law of nations and by the judgment of this court, such a case was within Spanish jurisdiction. Whether a nation has a right, by the public law, [40 U.S. 518, 575] under such circumstances, to require the extradition of the criminal, is a point on which jurists have differed; but most independent nations, if not all, have properly assumed and maintained the right to determine the question for themselves; denying the existence of any such obligation. To make the request, however, is a matter of constant occurrence; to sustain it by appeals to the law of nations, as conferring a right, is usual; we have, in our own government, asked for such extradition, at the very time we have denied the existence of the obligation. That the Spanish minister should, therefore, request the delivery of these persons as criminals; that he should sustain his request as one consonant to the law of nations, is not in the least a matter of surprise But did that interfere with his demand for them also, as property? There is no reason why it should do so, and the correspondence shows that it did not, in point of fact.

The very first letter of Mr. Calderon, that of 6th September 1839, quoted and commented upon by the counsel for the appellees, commences with a reference to the treaty stipulation, as one of the foundations and causes of his application. It is his imperious duty, he says, to claim an observance of the law of nations, and

of the treaties existing between the United States and Spain. Then follow, throughout the letter, repeated references to the double character of the demand for the slaves; references which it seems scarcely possible to misconceive. He declares, officially declares, that the vessel, 'previous to her departure, obtained her clearance from the customhouse, the necessary permit from the authorities for the transportation of the negroes, a passport, and all the other documents required by the law of Spain for navigating a vessel, and for proving ownership of property; a circumstance particularly important,' in his opinion.

So Mr. Argaiz, in his letter of the 26th November 1839, evidently pursues the same double demand; that they should be surrendered under the treaty, as property, and that they are also subject to delivery, as criminals. If there were a doubt as to his meaning, it must be removed, by observing his course on the passage of the resolutions adopted unanimously by the American senate, on the 15th of April last. Those resolutions declared:

1. That a ship or vessel on the high seas, in time of peace, engaged in a lawful voyage, is, according to the law of nations, [40 U.S. 518, 576] under the exclusive jurisdiction of the state to which the flag belongs; as much so, as if constituting a part of its own domain.

2. That if such ship or vessel should be forced, by stress of weather, or other unavoidable cause, into the port and under the jurisdiction of a friendly power, she and her cargo, and persons on board, with their property, and all the rights belonging to their personal relations, as established by the laws of the state to which they belong, would be placed under the protection which the laws of nations extend to the unfortunate under such circumstances.

On the passage of these resolutions, so evidently referring to the slaves as property, adopted in relation to the slaves carried into Bermuda and there set free, Mr. Argaiz claimed, for the owners of the slaves on board the Amistad, the application of the same rules. To complete the chain of evidence derived from the correspondence, we have a letter addressed by him to the secretary of state, on the first moment that the allegation of the request being for their delivery as criminals, was made official, by the motion of the appellees lately filed in this court — we have a note to the secretary of state, explicitly renewing his demand in the double relation.

It is evident, then, that there was a clear, distinct and formal request, on the part of the Spanish minister, for the delivery of these negroes, by virtue of the treaty, as the property of Spanish subjects. This fact, it has

Amistad

been endeavored to establish from the correspondence, because it has been alleged, that the executive of the United States has given a construction to the request of the Spanish minister, at variance with that stated in the libel of the district-attorney. As to any legal bearing on the case, it does not appear to be material. So far as the courts of justice are concerned, no principle is better settled, than that, in relation to the political operations of the government, the judiciary adopts the construction given to their own acts and those of foreign representatives, by the proper executive departments. The opinion of this court to that effect, is apparent in the decisions, already cited, in the cases of The Peggy and the Suffolk Insurance Co.; and when, in the case of Garcia v. Lee, the whole matter was received, with special reference to the construction of treaties, it was solemnly and deliberately affirmed. That the department [40 U.S. 518, 577] of state regarded this request as one for the delivery of property, is evident, not merely from the libel of the district-attorney, but from the whole correspondence. To obtain a different view, we must, indeed, pick out sentences separate from their context, and give to particular phrases a meaning not consistent with the whole scope of the documents in which they are found.

But as if the allegation, that the Spanish minister never required the restoration of these slaves as property, under the treaty, was not to be clearly established by the correspondence, it is endeavored to be sustained by the fact, that he refused to submit to the judgment of the court, as definitive of the rights of Spain and her subjects, under the treaty. How this refusal changes the character of his demand, on the one hand, or the proper mode of proceeding by the executive, on the other, it is not easy to perceive. No nation looks, in its intercourse, under a treaty, with another to any but the executive government. Every nation has a right to say with what act she will be satisfied as fulfilling a treaty stipulation, the other party to the treaty reserving the same right. Has not our executive, over and over again, demanded redress for acts sanctioned by decrees of foreign tribunals? Have we not sought that redress, by applications made directly to their executives? Has it ever been heard, that the claims of American citizens for redress from foreign governments, are precluded, because foreign courts have decided upon them? Such has not been the case, in point of fact, and such is not the course authorized by the aw, and adopted in the intercourse, of nations. To say, therefore, that Spain would not recognise a decree of a court, which should award her less than the treaty, in her opinion, stipulated she should receive, does not, as it must appear, affect, in any manner whatever, the rights under it, or the mode of proceeding to be adopted by our own executive.

With the latter, the course was plain. The matter was already before the judiciary, a component and independent branch of the government to which it appropriately belonged. Its action is calmly waited for, as affording the just and only basis of ultimate decision by the executive.

Viewed, then, on every ground of treaty obligation, of constitutional duty, of precedent, or of international intercourse, the [40 U.S. 518, 578] interposition of the executive in the mode adopted, so far from being 'unnecessary and improper,' was one of duty and propriety, on receiving from the Spanish minister his official representation, and from the district-attorney the information that the matter was already in charge of the court.

And now it may be asked, whether there is anything in these facts to justify the censure so largely cast upon the executive for the course which it was deemed a duty to pursue; anything that authorizes 'its arraignment,' to use the language of the counsel for the appellees, before the judicial tribunals, 'for their judgment and censure?' Performing cautiously an international obligation; passing upon no rights, private or public; submitting to the courts of justice the facts made known officially to it; seeking the decrees of the legitimate tribunals; communicating to foreign functionaries, that by these decrees its course would be governed — it is these acts which are argued upon, as ground for censure and denunciation. With what justice, may be well tested, by placing another government in the position of our own. Let us recollect, that there is among nations, as among men, a golden rule; let us do to them, as we wish them to do to us; let us ask how we would have our own minister and representative in a foreign land to act by us, if we were thrown in like manner on a foreign shore — if a citizen of South Carolina, sailing to New Orleans with his slaves, were thus attacked, his associates killed, himself threatened with death, and carried for months in a vessel scarcely seaworthy, beneath a tropical sun.

Should we blame the American minister who had asked the interposition of the courts? Should we blame the foreign government that facilitated that interposition? Look at the case of the negroes carried to Bermuda; have we there — as we are now denounced for not doing — have we there gone as private suitors into the courts, or have we sought redress, as nations seek it for their citizens? The question of freedom or slavery was there brought, exactly as it was here, before the judicial tribunals, at the instance of persons who took up the cause of the slaves; the owners did not pursue their claims as a mere matter of private right; the government of the United States, through its minister, appealed to the executive government of Great Britain; sought redress from [40 U.S. 518, 579] that quarter; and received it. The value of the slaves was paid, not to the individuals, but to our own government, who took their business upon themselves, exactly as the Spanish minister has assumed that of Ruiz and Montez. Let us then be just; let us not demand one mode of proceeding for ourselves, and practise another towards those who have an equal right to claim similar conduct at our hands.

II. The attorney-general then proceeded to reply to the position of the counsel for the appellees, that whatever might be the right of the United States as parties to the proceedings in the district and circuit courts, they had yet no authority to appeal, in such a case, from the decrees of those courts, to this tribunal, and that, therefore, the present appeal should be dismissed. As no decision was given by the court on this point, and the argument in support of the motion, and on behalf of the apellees, has not been reported, that in reply, and in behalf of the United States, as appellants, is also necessarily omitted. The position contended for by the attorney-general was, that the case was before this court — coram judice; and that the case itself, the parties to it, and the mode of bringing it up, were all in accordance with the law authorizing appeals. If so, he submitted, that this court had jurisdiction of it, and would revise the decree that had been pronounced by the circuit court, which was all that was solicited. That the highest judicial tribunal should pronounce upon the facts set out in this record, was all that the executive could desire; they presented questions that appropriately belonged to the judiciary, as the basis of executive action; they related to the rights of property, and the proofs concerning it; and when the decision of that co-ordinate branch of the government, to which the examination of such questions appropriately belonged, should be made, the course of executive action would be plain.

III. The only question, then, that remains to be considered, is, was the decree erroneous? The decree, as it stands, and as it now comes up for examination, is, that this vessel and her cargo shall be delivered up to the Spanish minister, for the Spanish owners, not entire, but after deducting one-third for salvage, to be given to Lieutenant Gedney and his associates; and that the negroes, except Antonio, shall be delivered to the president of the United States, to be [40 U.S. 518, 580] sent to Africa, pursuant to the provisions of the act of 3d March 1819, 2. (2 Story's Laws 1752.) Now, it is submitted, that this decree is erroneous, because the vessel, cargo and negroes were all the property of Spanish subjects, rescued from robbers, and brought into a port of the United States, and due proof concerning the property in them was made; that, therefore, the decree should have been, that they be delivered to the Spanish owners, or to the Spanish minister, for the owners, according to the stipulations of the ninth article of the treaty of 1795.

The vessel and cargo are admitted to be merchandize or property, within the meaning of the treaty. Are slaves also property or merchandize, within its meaning? That they are not, has been very elaborately argued by the counsel for the appellees; yet, it is confidently submitted, that both by the laws of Spain and of the United States, slaves are property; and a fair construction of the treaty shows, that it was intended to embrace every species of property recognised by the laws of the two contracting nations. We are asked for a law to this effect; a law establishing the existence of slavery in the Spanish dominions. It might be sufficient to say, that what is matter of notorious history will be recognised by this court, without producing a statutory regulation; but the royal decree of 1817, which promulgates the abolition of the foreign slave-trade, refers throughout to the existence of slavery in the Spanish Indies, and this court, in many of its adjudications, has recognised its existence.

If slaves, then, were property by the laws of Spain, it might be justly concluded, that even if they were not so recognized by the United States, still they are property, within the meaning of the treaty, because the intention of the treaty was to protect the property of each nation. But, in fact, slaves were, and are, as clearly recognised by them to be property, as they ever were by Spain. Our citizens hold them as property; buy and sell them as property; legislate upon them as property. State after state has been received into this Union, with the solemn and deliberate assent of the national legislature, whose constitutions, previously submitted to and sanctioned by that legislature, recognise slaves as merchandize; to be held as such, carried as such from place to place, and bought and sold as such. It has been argued, that this government, as a government, never has [40 U.S. 518, 581] recognised property in slaves.

To this it is answered, that if no other proof could be adduced, these acts of the national government are evidence that it has done so. The constitution of the United States leaves to the states the regulation of their internal property, of which slaves were, at the time it was formed, a well-known portion.

It also guarantied and protected the rights of the states to increase this property, up to the year 1808, by importation from abroad. How, then, can it be said, that this government, as a government, never has recognised this property? But if slaves be not so regarded, by what authority did the general government demand indemnity for slaves set free in Bermuda, by the British government? Is not this an act, recent in date, and deliberate in conduct, showing the settled construction put upon slaves as property. Is not the resolution of the senate (the unanimous resolution) a declaration, that slaves, though liberated as persons, and so adjudged by a foreign court, are, in fact, by the law of nations, property, if so allowed to be held in the country to which the owner belongs?

But it is contended, that although they may have been recognised as property by the two nations, they were not such property as was subject to restoration by the treaty. Now, to this it may be answered, in the first place, that every reason which can be suggested for the introduction of the treaty stipulations to protect and restore property, applies as fully to slaves as to any other. It is, in states where slavery exists, a valuable species of property; it is an object of traffic; it is transported from place to place. Can it be supposed, that the citizen of Virginia, sailing to New Orleans with his slaves, less needs the benefit of these treaty stipulations for them, than for any other property he may have on board, if he is carried into a port of Cuba, under any of the adverse circumstances for which the treaty was intended to provide? But again, is not the treaty so broad and general in its terms, that one of the contracting parties has no right to make an exclusion of this property, without the assent of the other? The 16th article of the treaty says, it is to extend to 'all kinds' of merchandize, except that which is contraband. Was not a slave a kind of merchandize, then recognized as such by each nation, and allowed to be imported into each nation, by their respective laws?

The treaty of 1819, which was ratified in 1821, after the slave-trade [40 U.S. 518, 582] was abolished, but while slave property was held in both countries' renews this article as it stood in 1795. Is it possible to imagine, that if a new policy was to be adopted, there would not have been an express stipulation or change in regard to this, as there was in regard to other articles of the old treaty? If further proof were wanting, it would be found in the fact, that the executive authorities of both nations, at once and unequivocally, considered the terms of the treaty as extending to slave property. Independently of the authority which this decision on the political construction of a treaty will have with this court, upon the principles it has laid down, it may be regarded as strong evidence of the intentions of the contracting parties; and when we see our own government and the senate of the United States, seriously examining how far a similar case is one that falls within the class of international obligations independent of treaty, we may give to its deliberate judgment, in the proper construction of this treaty, the highest weight.

The next inquiry is, whether the property in question was 'rescued out of the hands of any pirates or robbers, on the high seas, and brought into any port of the United States?' That the vessel was at anchor, below low-water mark, when taken possession of, and consequently, upon the high seas, as defined by the law of nations, is a fact not controverted; but it is objected, that the negroes by whom she was held were not pirates or robbers, in the sense of the treaty, and that if they were, its provisions could not apply to them, because they were themselves the persons who were rescued. That the acts committed by the negroes amount to piracy and robbery, seems too clear to be questioned. Piracy is an offence defined and ascertained by the law of nations; it is 'forcible depredation on the sea, animo furandi.' United States v. Smith, 5 Wheat. 153.

Every ingredient necessary to constitute a crime, thus defined, is proved in the present case. It was the intention of the treaty, that whenever, by an act of piracy, a vessel and property were run away with — taken from the owners, who are citizens of the United States or Spain — it should, if it came into the possession of the other party, be kept by that party and restored entire. Slaves differ from other property, in the fact, that they are persons as well as property; that they may be actors in the piracy; but it is not perceived, how [40 U.S. 518, 583] this act, of itself, changes the rights of the owners, where they exist and are recognised by law. If they are property, they are property rescued from pirates, and are to be restored, if brought by the necessary proof within the provisions of the treaty.

What are those provisions? That 'due and sufficient proof must be made concerning the property thereof.' The first inquiry 'concerning property,' is its identity. Is there any doubt as to the identity of these slaves? There is clearly none. Are they proved to have been slaves, owned by Spanish subjects? They are negroes, in a country where slavery exists, passing from one port of the Spanish dominions to another, in a regularly documented coasting vessel; and they are proved to be, at the time they leave Havana, in the actual possession of the persons claiming to be their owners. So far as all the prima facie evidence extends, derived from the circumstances of the case at that time, they may be regarded as slaves, as much as the negroes who accompany a planter between any two ports of the United States. This, then, is the first evidence of property — their actual existence in a state of slavery, and in the possession of their alleged owners, in a place where slavery is recognised, and exists by law.

In addition to this evidence derived from possession, Ruiz and Montez had, according to the statement of the Spanish minister, which was read by the counsel for the appellees, 'all the documents required by the laws of Spain for proving ownership of property.' They have a certificate, under the signature of the governor-general, countersigned or attested by the captain of the port, declaring that these negroes are the property of the Spanish citizens who are in possession of them. It has already been shown, by reference to the laws of Spain, that the powers of a governor-general in a Spanish colony are of a most plenary character. That his powers are judicial, was expressly recognised by this court, in the case of Keene v. McDonough, 8 Pet. 310. If such are the powers of this officer, and if this be a document established as emanating from him, it must be regarded as conclusive, in a foreign country. The cases already cited, establish the two positions, that, as regards property on board of a vessel, the accompanying documents are the first and best evidence, especially, when attended with possession; and that a [40 U.S. 518, 584] decree or judgment, or declaration of a foreign tribunal, made within the scope of its authority, is evidence, beyond which the courts of another country will not look. These rules are essential to international intercourse. Could it be tolerated, that where vessels, on a coasting voyage, from one port of a country to another, are driven, without fault of their own, to take refuge in the harbor of another country, the authentic evidences of property in their own country are to be disregarded? That foreign courts are to execute the municipal laws of another country, according to their construction of them? Can it be, that the courts of this country will refuse to recognise the evidence of property, which is recognised and deemed sufficient in the country to which that property belongs? We have unquestionable evidence, that such documents as these are regarded as adequate proofs of property in Cuba. But it is said, this certificate is a mere passport, and no proof of property. To this it is replied, that it is recognised as the necessary and usual evidence of property, as appears by the testimony referred to. It is true, it is a passport for Ruiz, but it is not a mere personal passport; it is one to take property with him, and it ascertains and describes that property.

But we are told, it must be regarded as fraudulent by this court; and the grounds on which this assertion is made, are the evidence adduced to show that these negroes have been imported into Cuba from Africa, since the treaty between Great Britain and Spain. Is this evidence legal and sufficient to authorize this court to declare the particular fact for which it is vouched — that the negroes were imported into Cuba contrary to law? If it be sufficient for this, does such illegal importation make the negroes free men in the island of Cuba? If it does, will this court declare the certificate to be null and void, or leave that act to the decision of the appropriate Spanish tribunals?

In the argument submitted on the part of the United States, in opening the case, the nature of this evidence has been commented upon. It is such chiefly as is not legal evidence in the courts of the United States. Now the question is not as to the impression derived from such evidence, but it is whether, on testimony not legally sufficient, the declaration of a competent foreign functionary will be set aside? As if there were doubt, whether a court of the United States would so do, the admissions of Ruiz, and [40 U.S. 518, 585] of the attorney of the United States are vouched. Yet it is apparent, that these were admissions, not of facts known to themselves, but of impressions derived from evidence which is as much before this court as it was before them. To neither one nor the other was the fact in question personally known. It was inferred by them, from evidence now for the most part before this court.

But, admitting the fact of the recent importation from Africa, still, nothing has been adduced to controvert the position, taken in opening, that the laws of Spain required, in such a case, and even in the case of negroes actually seized on board of a Spanish vessel, on her voyage from Africa, a declaration by a court expressly recognised by Spain, to establish their freedom. However much we may abhor the African slave-trade, all nations have left to those in whose vessels it is carried on, the regulation and punishment of it. The extent to which Spain was willing to permit any other nation to interpose, where her vessels or her subjects were concerned, is carefully determined in this very treaty. The principal witness of the appellees expressly admits, that when negroes are landed, though in known violation of the treaty, it is a subject to be disposed of by the municipal law. Now, it is not pretended here, that, even if these negroes were unlawfully introduced, they have been declared free. Can, then, this court adjudge that these negroes were free in the island of Cuba, even if the fact of their recent importation be proved? Much more, can they assume to do it, by putting their construction on a treaty, not of the United States, but between two foreign nations; a treaty which those nations have the sole right to construe and act upon for themselves?

But, if satisfied that the governor-general has been imposed upon, and the documents fraudulently obtained, still, is the fraud to be punished and the error to be rectified in our courts, or in those of Spain? What says Sir WILLIAM SCOTT, in the case of The Louis, when asked what is to be done, if a French ship, laden with slaves, in violation of the laws of that country, is brought into an English port: 'I answer,' says he, 'without hesitation, restore the possession which has been unlawfully divested; rescind the illegal act done by your own subject, and leave the foreigner to the justice of his own country.'

Can a rule more directly applicable to the present case be found? 'The courts of no [40 U.S. 518, 586] country,' says Chief Justice MARSHALL, in the case of The Antelope, 'execute the penal laws of another.' In the case of The Eugenia, where a French vessel was liable to forfeiture, under the laws of France, for violating the laws prohibiting the slave-trade, Judge STORY directed, not that she should be condemned in our own courts, but that she should be sent to France. 'This,' says he, 'enables the foreign sovereign to exercise complete jurisdiction, if he shall prefer to have it remitted to his own courts for adjudication.' 'This,' he afterwards adds, 'makes our own country, not a principal, but an auxiliary, in enforcing the interdict of France, and subserves the great interests of universal justice.'

Are not these the true principles which should govern nations in their intercourse with each other; principles sanctioned by great and venerated names? Are not these the principles by which we would require other nations to be governed, when our citizens are charged, in a foreign country, with a breach of our own municipal laws? And is it not productive of the same result? Do we doubt, that the courts and officers of Spain will justly administer her own laws? Will this court act on the presumption, that the tribunals of a foreign and friendly nation will fail to pursue that course which humanity, justice and the sacred obligations of their own laws demand? No nation has a right so to presume, in regard to another; and notwithstanding the distrust that has been repeatedly expressed in the progress of this cause, in regard to the Spanish tribunals and the Spanish functionaries; yet a just respect towards another and a friendly nation; the common courtesy which will not suppose in advance, that it will intentionally do wrong; oblige us to believe, and warrant us in so doing, that if the laws of Spain have been violated; if its officers have been deceived; and if these negroes are really free; these facts will be there ascertained and acted upon, and we shall as 'auxiliaries,' not principals, best 'subserve the cause of universal justice.'

If this view be correct, and if the evidence is sufficient to prove the property of the Spanish subjects in the island of Cuba, the only question that remains to be considered is, whether the acts of the slaves during the voyage changed their condition. It has been argued strongly, that they were free; that they were 'in the actual condition of freedom;' but how can [40 U.S. 518, 587] that be maintained? If slaves by the laws of Spain, they were so on board of a Spanish vessel, as much as on her soil; and will it be asserted, that the same acts in the island of Cuba would have made them free? This will hardly be contended. No nation, recognising slavery, admits the sufficiency of forcible emancipation. In what respect, were these slaves, if such by the laws of Spain, released from slavery by their own acts of aggression upon their masters, any more than a slave becomes free in Pennsylvania, who forcibly escapes from his owner in Virginia? For this court to say, that these acts constituted a release from slavery, would be to establish for another country municipal regulations in regard to her property; and not that only, but to establish them directly in variance with our own laws, in analogous cases. If the negroes in this case were free, it was because they were not slaves, when placed on board the Amistad, not because of the acts there committed by them.

It is submitted, then, that so far as this court is concerned, there is sufficient evidence concerning this property, to warrant its restoration pursuant to the provisions of the treaty with Spain; and that, therefore, the judgment of the court below should be reversed, and a decree made by this court for the entire restoration of the property.

STORY, Justice, delivered the opinion of the court.

This is the case of an appeal from the decree of the circuit court of the district of Connecticut, sitting in admiralty. The leading facts, as he appear upon the transcript of the proceedings, are as follows: On the 27th of June 1839, the schooner L'Amistad, being the property of Spanish subjects, cleared out from the port of Havana, in the island of Cuba, for Puerto Principe, in the same island. On board of the schooner were the master, Ramon Ferrer, and Jose Ruiz and Pedro Montez, all Spanish subjects. The former had with him a negro boy, named Antonio, claimed to be his slave. Jose Ruiz had with him forty-nine negroes, claimed by him as his slaves, and stated to be his property, in a certain pass or document, signed by the governor-general of Cuba. Pedro Montez had with him four other negroes, also claimed by him as his slaves, and stated to be his property, in a similar pass or document, also signed by the governor- general [40 U.S. 518, 588] of Cuba. On the voyage, and before the arrival of the vessel at her port of destination, the negroes rose, killed the master, and took possession of her. On the 26th of August, the vessel was discovered by Lieutenant Gedney, of the United States brig Washington, at anchor on the high seas, at the distance of half a mile from the shore of Long Island. A part of the negroes were then on shore, at Culloden Point, Long Island; who were seized by

Lieutenant Gedney, and brought on board. The vessel, with the negroes and other persons on board, was brought by Lieutenant Gedney into the district of Connecticut, and there libeled for salvage in the district court of the United States. A libel for salvage was also filed by Henry Green and Pelatiah Fordham, of Sag Harbor, Long Island. On the 18th of September, Ruiz and Montez filed claims and libels, in which they asserted their ownership of the negroes as their slaves, and of certain parts of the cargo, and prayed that the same might be 'delivered to them, or to the representatives of her Catholic Majesty, as might be most proper.' On the 19th of September, the attorney of the United States for the district of Connecticut, filed an information or libel, setting forth, that the Spanish minister had officially presented to the proper department of the government of the United States, a claim for the restoration of the vessel, cargo and slaves, as the property of Spanish subjects, which had arrived within the jurisdictional limits of the United States, and were taken possession of by the said public armed brig of the United States, under such circumstances as made it the duty of the United States to cause the same to be restored to the true proprietors, pursuant to the treaty between the United States and Spain; and praying the court, on its being made legally to appear that the claim of the Spanish minister was well founded, to make such order for the disposal of the vessel, cargo and slaves, as would best enable the United States to comply with their treaty stipulations. But if it should appear, that the negroes were persons transported from Africa, in violation of the laws of the United States, and brought within the United States, contrary to the same laws; he then prayed the court to make such order for their removal to the cost of Africa, pursuant to the laws of the United States, as it should deem fit.

On the 19th of November, the attorney of the United States [40 U.S. 518, 589] filed a second information or libel, similar to the first, with the exception of the second prayer above set forth in his former one. On the same day, Antonio G. Vega, the vice-consul of Spain for the state of Connecticut, filed his libel, alleging that Antonio was a slave, the property of the representatives of Ramon Ferrer, and praying the court to cause him to be delivered to the said vice-consul, that he might be returned by him to his lawful owner in the island of Cuba.

On the 7th of January 1840, the negroes, Cinque and others, with the exception of Antonio, by their counsel, filed an answer, denying that they were slaves, or the property of Ruiz and Montez, or that the court could, under the constitution or laws of the United States, or under any treaty, exercise any jurisdiction

over their persons, by reason of the premises; and praying that they might be dismissed. They specially set forth and insisted in this answer, that they were native-born Africans; born free, and still, of right, ought to be free and not slaves; that they were, on or about the 15th of April 1839, unlawfully kidnapped, and forcibly and wrongfully carried on board a certain vessel, on the coast of Africa, which was unlawfully engaged in the slave-trade, and were unlawfully transported in the same vessel to the island of Cuba, for the purpose of being there unlawfully sold as slaves; that Ruiz and Montez, well knowing the premises, made a pretended purchase of them; that afterwards, on or about the 28th of June 1839, Ruiz and Montez, confederating with Ferrer (master of the Amistad), caused them, without law or right, to be placed on board of the Amistad, to be transported to some place unknown to them, and there to be enslaved for life; that, on the voyage, they rose on the master, and took possession of the vessel, intending to return therewith to their native country, or to seek an asylum in some free state; and the vessel arrived, about the 26th of August 1839, off Montauk Point, near Long Island; a part of them were sent on shore, and were seized by Lieutenant Gedney, and carried on board; and all of them were afterwards brought by him into the district of Connecticut.

On the 7th of January 1840, Jose Antonio Tellincas, and Messrs. Aspe and Laca, all Spanish subjects, residing in Cuba, filed their [40 U.S. 518, 590] claims, as owners to certain portions of the goods found on board of the schooner L'Amistad. On the same day, all the libellants and claimants, by their counsel, except Jose Ruiz and Pedro Montez (whose libels and claims, as stated of record, respectively, were pursued by the Spanish minister, the same being merged in his claims), appeared, and the negroes also appeared by their counsel; and the case was heard on the libels, claims, answers and testimony of witnesses.

On the 23d day of January 1840, the district court made a decree. By that decree, the court rejected the claim of Green and Fordham for salvage, but allowed salvage to Lieutenant Gedney and others, on the vessel and cargo, of one-third of the value thereof, but not on the negroes, Cinque and others; it allowed the claim of Tellincas, and Aspe and Laca, with the exception of the above-mentioned salvage; it dismissed the libels and claims of Ruiz and Montez, with costs, as being included under the claim of the Spanish minister; it allowed the claim of the Spanish vice-consul, for Antonio, on behalf of Ferrer's representatives; it rejected the claims of Ruiz and Montez for the delivery of the negroes, but admitted them for the cargo, with the exception of the above-mentioned salvage; it rejected the claim made by the attorney of the United States on behalf of the Spanish minister, for the restoration of the negroes, under the treaty; but it decreed, that they should be delivered to the president of the United States, to be transported to Africa, pursuant to the act of 3d March 1819.

From this decree, the district-attorney, on behalf of the United States, appealed to the circuit court, except so far as related to the restoration of the slave Antonio. The claimants, Tellincas, and Aspe and Laca, also appealed from that part of the decree which awarded salvage on the property respectively claimed by them. No appeal was interposed by Ruiz or Montez, nor on behalf of the representatives of the owners of the Amistad. The circuit court by a mere pro forma decree, affirmed the decree of the district court, reserving the question of salvage upon the claims of Tellincas, and Aspe and Laca. And from that decree, the present appeal has been brought to this court.

The cause has been very elaborately argued, as well upon the [40 U.S. 518, 591] merits, as upon a motion of behalf of the appellees to dismiss the appeal. On the part of the United States, it has been contended: 1. That due and sufficient proof concerning the property has been made, to authorize the restitution of the vessel, cargo and negroes to the Spanish subjects on whose behalf they are claimed, pursuant to the treaty with Spain, of the 27th of October 1795. 2. That the United States had a right to intervene in the manner in which they have done, to obtain a decree for the restitution of the property, upon the application of the Spanish minister. These propositions have been strenuously denied on the other side. Other collateral and incidental points have been stated, upon which it is not necessary at this moment to dwell.

Before entering upon the discussion of the main points involved in this interesting and important controversy, it may be necessary to say a few words as to the actual posture of the case as it now stands before us. In the first place, then, the only parties now before the court on one side, are the United States, intervening for the sole purpose of procuring restitution of the property, as Spanish property, pursuant to the treaty, upon the grounds stated by the other parties claiming the property in their respective libels. The United States do not assert any property in themselves, nor any violation of their own rights, or sovereignty or laws, by the acts complained of. They do not insist that these negroes have been imported into the United States, in contravention of our own slave-trade acts. They do not seek to have these negroes delivered up, for the purpose of being transferred to Cuba, as pirates or robbers, or as fugitive criminals found within our territories, who have been guilty of offences against the laws of

Spain. They do not assert that the seizure and bringing the vessel, and cargo and negroes, into port, by Lieutenant Gedney, for the purpose of adjudication, is a tortuous act. They simply confine themselves to the right of the Spanish claimants to the restitution of their property, upon the facts asserted in their respective allegations.

In the next place, the parties before the court, on the other side, as appellees, are Lieutenant Gedney, on his libel for salvage, and the negroes (Cinque and others), asserting themselves, in their answer, not to be slaves, but free native Africans, kidnapped [40 U.S. 518, 592] in their own country, and illegally transported by force from that country; and now entitled to maintain their freedom.

No question has been here made, as to the proprietary interests in the vessel and cargo. It is admitted, that they belong to Spanish subjects, and that they ought to be restored. The only point on this head is, whether the restitution ought to be upon the payment of salvage, or not? The main controversy is, whether these negroes are the property of Ruiz and Montez, and ought to be delivered up; and to this, accordingly, we shall first direct our attention. It has been argued on behalf of the United States, that the court are bound to deliver them up, according to the treaty of 1795, with Spain, which has in this particular been continued in full force, by the treaty of 1819, ratified in 1821. The sixth article of that treaty seems to have had, principally in view, cases where the property of the subjects of either state had been taken possession of within the territorial jurisdiction of the other, during war. The eighth article provides for cases where the shipping of the inhabitants of either state are forced, through stress of weather, pursuit of pirates or enemies, or any other urgent necessity, to seek shelter in the ports of the other. There may well be some doubt entertained, whether the present case, in its actual circumstances, falls within the purview of this article. But it does not seem necessary, for reasons hereafter stated, absolutely to decide it. The ninth article provides, 'that all ships and merchandize, of what nature soever, which shall be rescued out of the hands of any pirates or robbers, on the high seas, shall be brought into some port of either state, and shall be delivered to the custody of the officers of that port, in order to be taken care of and restored, entire, to the true proprietor, as soon as due and sufficient proof shall be made concerning the property thereof.' This is the article on which the main reliance is placed on behalf of the United States, for the restitution of these negroes. To bring the case within the article, it is essential to establish: 1st, That these negroes, under all the circumstances, fall within the description of merchandize, in the sense of the treaty. 2d, That there has been a rescue of them on the high seas, out of the hands of the pirates and robbers; which, in the present case, can only be, by showing that they [40 U.S. 518, 593] themselves are pirates and robbers: and 3d, That Ruiz and Montez, the asserted proprietors, are the true proprietors, and have established their title by competent proof.

If these negroes were, at the time, lawfully held as slaves, under the laws of Spain, and recognised by those laws as property, capable of being lawfully bought and sold; we see no reason why they may not justly be deemed, within the intent of the treaty, to be included under the denomination of merchandize, and as such ought to be restored to the claimants; for upon that point the laws of Spain would seem to furnish the proper rule of interpretation. But admitting this, it is clear, in our opinion, that neither of the other essential facts and requisites has been established in proof; and the onus probandi of both lies upon the claimants to give rise to the casus foederis. It is plain, beyond controversy, if we examine the evidence, that these negroes never were the lawful slaves of Ruiz or Montez, or of any other Spanish subjects. They are natives of Africa, and were kidnapped there, and were unlawfully transported to Cuba, in violation of the laws and treaties of Spain, and the most solemn edicts and declarations of that government. By those laws and treaties, and edicts, the African slave trade is utterly abolished; the dealing in that trade is deemed a heinous crime; and the negroes thereby introduced into the dominions of Spain, are declared to be free. Ruiz and Montez are proved to have made the pretended purchase of these negroes, with a full knowledge of all the circumstances. And so cogent and irresistible is the evidence in this respect, that the district-attorney has admitted in open court, upon the record, that these negroes were native Africans, and recently imported into Cuba, as alleged in their answers to the libels in the case. The supposed proprietary interest of Ruiz and Montez is completely displaced, if we are at liberty to look at the evidence, or the admissions of the district-attorney.

If then, these negroes are not slaves, but are kidnapped Africans, who, by the laws of Spain itself, are entitled to their freedom, and were kidnapped and illegally carried to Cuba, and illegally detained and restrained on board the Amistad; there is no pretence to say, that they are pirates or robbers. We may lament the dreadful acts by which they asserted their liberty, and took possession of the Amistad, and endeavored to regain their native [40 U.S. 518, 594] country; but they cannot be deemed pirates or robbers, in the sense of the law of nations, or the treaty with Spain, or the laws of Spain itself; at least, so far as those laws have been brought to our knowledge. Nor do the libels of Ruiz or Montez assert them to be such.

This posture of the facts would seem, of itself, to put an end to the whole inquiry upon the merits. But it is argued, on behalf of the United States, that the ship and cargo, and negroes, were duly documented as belonging to Spanish subjects, and this court have no right to look behind these documents; that full faith and credit is to be given to them; and that they are to be held conclusive evidence in this cause, even although it should be established by the most satisfactory proofs, that they have been obtained by the grossest frauds and impositions upon the constituted authorities of Spain. To this argument, we can, in no wise, assent. There is nothing in the treaty which justifies or sustains the argument. We do not here meddle with the point, whether thee h as been any connivance in this illegal traffic, on the part of any of the colonial authorities or subordinate officers of Cuba; because, in our view, such an examination is unnecessary, and ought not to be pursued, unless it were indispensable to public justice, although it has been strongly pressed at the bar. What we proceed upon is this, that although public documents of the government, accompanying property found on board of the private ships of a foreign nation, certainly are to be deemed prim a facie evidence of the facts which they purport to state, yet they are always open to be impugned for fraud; and whether that fraud be in the original obtaining of these documents, or in the subsequent fraudulent and illegal use of them, when once it is satisfactorily established, it overthrows all their sanctity, and destroys them as proof. Fraud will vitiate any, even the most solemn, transactions; and an asserted title to property, founded upon it, is utterly void. The very language of the ninth article of the treaty of 1795, requires the proprietor to make due and sufficient proof of his property. And how can that proof be deemed either due or sufficient, which is but a connected and stained tissue of fraud? This is not a mere rule of municipal jurisprudence. Nothing is more clear in the law of nations, as an established rule to regulate their rights and duties, [40 U.S. 518, 595] and intercourse, than the doctrine, that the ship's papers are but prim a facie evidence, and that, if they are shown to be fraudulent, they are not to be held proof of any valid title. This rule is familiarly applied, and, indeed, is of every-day's occurrence in cases of prize, in the contests between belligerents and neutrals, as is apparent from numerous cases to be found in the reports of this court; and it is just as applicable to the transactions of civil intercourse between nations, in times of peace. If a private ship, clothed with Spanish papers, should enter the ports of the United States, claiming the privileges and immunities, and rights, belonging the bona fide subjects of Spain, under our treaties or laws, and she should, in reality, belong to the subjects of another nation, which was not entitled to any such privileges, immunities or rights, and the proprietors were seeking, by fraud, to cover their own illegal acts, under the flag of Spain; there can be no doubt, that it would be the duty of our courts to strip off the disguise, and to look at the case, according to its naked realities. In the solemn treaties between nations, it can never be presumed, that either state intends to provide the means of perpetrating or protecting frauds; but all the provisions are to be construed intended to be applied to bon a fide transactions. The 17th article of the treaty with Spain, which provides for certain passports and certificates, as evidence of property on board of the ships of both states, is, in its terms, applicable only to cases where either of the parties is engaged in a war. This article required a certain form of passport to be agreed upon by the parties, and annexed to the treaty; it never was annexed; and therefore, in the case of The Amiable Isabella, 6 Wheat. 1, it was held inoperative.

It is also a most important consideration, in the present case, which ought not to be lost sight of, that, supposing these African negroes not to be slaves, but kidnapped, and free negroes, the treaty with Spain cannot be obligatory upon them; and the United States are bound to respect their rights as much as those of Spanish subjects. The conflict of rights between the parties, under such circumstances, becomes positive and inevitable, and must be decided upon the eternal principles of justice and international law. If the contest were about any goods on board of this ship, to which American citizens asserted a title, which was [40 U.S. 518, 596] denied by the Spanish claimants, there could be no doubt of the right to such American citizens to litigate their claims before any competent American tribunal, notwithstanding the treaty with Spain. A fortiori, the doctrine must apply, where human life and human liberty are in issue, and constitute the very essence of the controversy. The treaty with Spain never could have intended to take away the equal rights of all foreigners, who should contest their claims before any of our courts, to equal justice; or to deprive such foreigners of the protection given them by other treaties, or by the general law of nations. Upon the merits of the case, then, there does not seem to us to be any ground for doubt, that these negroes ought to be deemed free; and that the Spanish treaty interposes no obstacle to the just assertion of their rights.

There is another consideration, growing out of this part of the case, which necessarily rises in judgment. It is observable, that the United States, in their original claim, filed it in the alternative, to have the negroes, if slaves and Spanish property, restored to the proprietors; or, if not slaves, but negroes who had been transported from Africa, in violation of the laws of the United States, and brought into the United States, contrary to the same laws, then the court to pass an order to enable the United States to remove such persons to the coast of Africa, to be delivered there to such agent as may be authorized to receive and provide for them. At a subsequent period, this last alternative claim was not insisted on, and another claim was interposed, omitting it; from which the conclusion naturally arises, that it was abandoned.

The decree of the district court, however, contained an order for the delivery of the negroes to the United States, to be transported to the coast of Africa, under the act of the 3d of March 1819, ch. 224. The United States do not now insist upon any affirmance of this part of the decree; and in our judgment, upon the admitted facts, there is no ground to assert, that the case comes within the purview of the act of 1819, or of any other of our prohibitory slave-trade acts.

These negroes were never taken from Africa, or brought to the United States, in contravention of those acts. When the Amistad arrived, she was in possession of the negroes, asserting their freedom; and in no sense could they possibly intend to import themselves here, as [40 U.S. 518, 597] slaves, or for sale as slaves. In this view of the matter, that part of the decree of the district court is unmaintainable, and must be reversed.

The view which has been thus taken of this case, upon the merits, under the first point, renders it wholly unnecessary for us to give any opinion upon the other point, as to the right of the United States to intervene in this case in the manner already stated. We dismiss this, therefore, as well as several minor points made at the argument.

As to the claim of Lieutenant Gedney for the salvage service, it is understood, that the United States do not now desire to interpose any obstacle to the allowance of it, if it is deemed reasonable by the court. It was a highly meritorious and useful service to the proprietors of the ship and cargo; and such as, by the general principles of maritime law, is always deemed a just foundation for salvage. The rate allowed by the court, does not seem to us to have been beyond the exercise of a sound discretion, under the very particular and embarrassing circumstances of the case.

Upon the whole, our opinion is, that the decree of the circuit court, affirming that of the district court, ought to be affirmed, except so far as it directs the negroes to be delivered to the president, to be transported to Africa, in pursuance of the act of the 3d of March 1819; and as to this, it ought to be reversed: and that the said negroes be declared to be free, and be dismissed from the custody of the court, and go without day.

BALDWIN, Justice, dissented.

THIS cause came on to be heard, on the transcript of the record from the circuit court of the United States for the district of Connecticut, and was argued by counsel: On consideration whereof, it is the opinion of this court, that there is error in that art of the decree of the circuit court, affirming the decree of the district court, which ordered the said negroes to be delivered to the president of the United States, to be transported to Africa, in pursuance of the act of congress of the 3d of March 1819; and that, as to that part, it ought to be reversed: and in all other respects, that the said decree of the [40 U.S. 518, 598] circuit court ought to be affirmed. It is, therefore, ordered, adjudged and decreed by this court, that the decree of the said circuit court be and the same is hereby affirmed, except as to the part aforesaid, and as to that part, that it be reversed; and that the cause be remanded to the circuit court, with directions to enter, in lieu of that part, a decree, that the said negroes be and are hereby declared to be free, and that they be dismissed from the custody of the court, and be discharged from the suit, and go thereof quit, without day.

Celebici

INTRODUCTION Celebici is a town in Central Bosnia, strategically located roughly halfway from Sarajevo to Mostar. In 1993, during the war in Bosnia and Herzegovina Serb elements lost military control to the combined forces of Muslims and Croats. A concentration camp was established in a factory complex where Serb prisoners were subjected to a range of abuses and atrocities. Several of those involved in the administration and supervision of the camp were tried in one of the first prosecutions before the International Criminal Tribunal for the former Yugoslavia. The November 1998 convictions of several of the accused were upheld by the Appeals Chamber in 2001.

International Tribunal for the Prosecution of Persons Responsible for Serious Violations of International Humanitarian Law Committed in the Territory of the Former Yugoslavia since 1991

Case No.: IT-96-21-A

Date: 20 February 2001

IN THE APPEALS CHAMBER

Before: Judge David Hunt, Presiding ; Judge Fouad Riad; Judge Rafael Nieto-Navia; Judge Mohamed Bennouna; Judge Fausto Pocar

Registrar: Mr. Hans Holthuis

Judgement of: 20 February 2001

PROSECUTOR V Zejnil DELALIC, Zdravko MUCIC (aka 'PAVO'), Hazim DELIC and Esad LANDZO (aka 'ZENGA') ('CELEBICI Case')

JUDGEMENT

Counsel for the Accused:

Mr. John Ackerman and Ms Edina Residovic for Zejnil Delalic Mr. Tomislav Kuzmanovic and Mr. Howard Morrison for Zdravko Mucic Mr. Salih Karabdic and Mr. Tom Moran for Hazim Delic Ms Cynthia Sinatra and Mr. Peter Murphy for Esad Landzo

The Office of the Prosecutor:

Mr. Upawansa Yapa Mr. William Fenrick Mr. Christopher Staker Mr. Norman Farrell Ms Sonja Boelaert-Suominen Mr Roeland Bos

Case No.: IT-96-21-A 20 February 2001

The Appeals Chamber of the International Tribunal for the Prosecution of Persons Responsible for Serious Violations of International Humanitarian Law Committed in the Territory of the Former Yugoslavia since 1991 ('International Tribunal") is seized of appeals against the Judgement rendered by Trial Chamber II on 16 November 1998 in the case of *Prosecutor v Zejnil Delalic, Zdravko Mucic also known as 'Pavo", Hazim Delic, Esad Land'o also known as 'Zenga"* ('Trial Judgement").

Having considered the written and oral submissions of the Parties, the Appeals Chamber

HEREBY RENDERS ITS JUDGEMENT.

I. INTRODUCTION

1. The Indictment against *Zejnil Delalic, Zdravko Mucic, Hazim Delic* and *Esad Land'o*, confirmed on 21 March 1996, alleged serious violations of humanitarian law that occurred in 1992 when Bosnian Muslim and Bosnian Croat forces took control of villages within the Konjic municipality in central Bosnia and Herzegovina. The present appeal concerns events within the Konjic municipality, where persons were detained in a former Yugoslav People's Army ('JNA") facility: the Celebici camp. The Trial Chamber found that detainees were killed, tortured, sexually assaulted, beaten and otherwise subjected to cruel and inhumane treatment by Mucic, Delic and Land'o. Mucic was found to have been the commander of the Celebici camp, Delic the deputy commander and Land'o a prison guard.

2. In various forms, Delalic was co-ordinator of Bosnian Muslim and Bosnian Croat forces in the Konjic area between approximately April and September 1992. He was found not guilty of twelve counts of grave breaches of the Geneva Conventions of 1949 and violations of the laws or customs of war. The Trial Chamber concluded that Delalic did not have sufficient command and control over the Celebici camp or the guards that worked there to entail his criminal responsibility for their actions.

3. Mucic was found guilty of grave breaches of the Geneva Conventions and of violations of the laws or customs of war for crimes including murder, torture, inhuman treatment and unlawful confinement, principally on the basis of his superior responsibility as commander of the Celebici camp, but also, in respect of certain counts, for his direct participation in the crimes. Mucic was sentenced to seven years imprisonment. Delic was found guilty of grave breaches of the Geneva Conventions and violations of the laws or customs of war for his direct participation in crimes including murder, torture, and inhuman treatment. Delic was sentenced to twenty years imprisonment. Landzo was found guilty of grave breaches of the Geneva Conventions and violations of the laws or customs of war, for crimes including murder, torture, and cruel treatment, and sentenced to fifteen years imprisonment.

4. The procedural background of the appeal proceedings is found in Annex A, which also contains a complete list of the grounds of appeal. Certain of the grounds of appeal of the individual parties dealt with substantially the same subject matter, and certain grounds of appeal of Land'o were joined by Mucic and Delic. For that reason, this judgement considers the various grounds of appeal grouped by subject matter, which was also the way the different grounds of appeal were dealt with during oral argument.

Trial Judgement, pp 447-449.

II. GROUNDS OF APPEAL RELATING TO ARTICLE 2 OF THE STATUTE

5. Delic, Mucic and Landzo have raised two closely related issues in relation to the findings of the Trial Chamber based on Article 2 of the Statute. The first is the question of the legal test for determining the nature of the conflict, and the second, that of the criteria for establishing whether a person is 'protected" under Geneva Convention IV. Delic has raised a third issue as to whether Bosnia and Herzegovina was a party to the Geneva Conventions at the time of the events alleged in the Indictment.

A. Whether the Trial Chamber Erred in Holding that the Armed Conflict in Bosnia and Herzegovina at the Time Relevant to the Indictment was of an International Character

6. Delic, Mucic, and Land'o challenge the Trial Chamber's finding that the armed conflict in Bosnia and Herzegovina was international at all times relevant to the Indictment. Relying upon the reasoning of the majority in the *Tadic* and *Aleksovski* first instance Judgements, the appellants argue that the armed conflict was internal at all times. It is submitted that the Trial Chamber used an incorrect legal test to determine the nature of the conflict and that the test set out by the majority of the *Tadic* Trial Chamber, the 'effective control" test, based on *Nicaragua*, is the appropriate test. In the appellants' opinion, applying this correct test, the facts as found by the Trial Chamber do not support a finding that the armed conflict was international. Consequently, the appellants seek a reversal of the verdict of guilty on the counts of the Indictment based upon Article 2 of the Statute.

7. The Prosecution submits that these grounds of appeal should be dismissed. It submits that the correct legal test for determining whether an armed conflict is international was set forth by the Appeals Chamber in the *Tadic* Appeal Judgement, which rejected the 'effective control" test in relation to acts of armed forces or paramilitary units. Relying upon the *Aleksovski* Appeal Judgement, the Prosecution contends that the Appeals Chamber should follow its previous decision.

8. As noted by the Prosecution, the issue of the correct legal test for determining whether an armed conflict is international was addressed by the Appeals Chamber in the *Tadic* Appeal Judgement. In the *Aleksovski* Appeal Judgement, the Appeals Chamber found that 'in the interests of certainty and predictability, the Appeals Chamber should follow its previous decisions, but should be free to depart from them for cogent reasons in the interests of justice". Elaborating on this principle, the Chamber held:

> Instances of situations where cogent reasons in the interests of justice require a departure from a previous decision include cases where the previous decision has been decided on the basis of a wrong legal principle or cases where a previous decision has been given *per incuriam*, that is a judicial decision that has been 'wrongly decided, usually because the judge or judges were ill-informed about the applicable law."

> It is necessary to stress that the normal rule is that previous decisions are to be followed, and departure from them is the exception. The Appeals Chamber will only depart from a previous decision

after the most careful consideration has been given to it, both as to the law, including the authorities cited, and the facts.

What is followed in previous decisions is the legal principle (*ratio decidendi*), and the obligation to follow that principle only applies in similar cases, or substantially similar cases. This means less that the facts are similar or substantially similar, than that the question raised by the facts in the subsequent case is the same as the question decided by the legal principle in the previous decision. There is no obligation to follow previous decisions which may be distinguished for one reason or another from the case before the court.

In light of this finding, the *Aleksovski* Appeals Chamber followed the legal test set out in the *Tadic* Appeal Judgement in relation to internationality.

9. Against this background, the Appeals Chamber will turn to the question of the applicable law for determining whether an armed conflict is international.

1. What is the Applicable Law? 10. The Appeals Chamber now turns to a consideration of the *Tadic* Appeal Judgement, and to the relevant submissions of the parties in this regard, in order to determine whether, applying the principle set forth in the *Aleksovski* Appeal Judgement, there are any cogent reasons in the interests of justice for departing from it.

11. From the outset, the Appeals Chamber notes that the findings of the Trial Chamber majorities in the *Tadic* and *Aleksovski* Judgements, upon which the appellants rely, were overturned on appeal.

12. In the *Tadic* case, the Appeals Chamber was concerned with, inter *alia*, the legal criteria for establishing when, in an armed conflict which is *prima facie* internal, armed forces may be regarded as acting on behalf of a foreign power, thereby rendering the conflict international.

13. The Appeals Chamber saw the question of internationality as turning on the issue of whether the Bosnian Serb forces 'could be considered as de iure or *de facto* organs of a foreign power, namely the FRY". The important question was 'what degree of authority or control must be wielded by a foreign State over armed forces fighting on its behalf in order to render international an armed conflict which is prima facie internal". The Chamber considered, after a review of various cases including *Nicaragua*, that international law does not always require the same degree of control over armed groups or private individuals for the purpose of determining whether they can be regarded as a *de facto* organ of the State. The Appeals Chamber found that there were three different standards of control under

which an entity could be considered *de facto* organ of the State, each differing according to the nature of the entity. Using this framework, the Appeals Chamber determined that the situation with which it was concerned fell into the second category it identified, which was that of the acts of armed forces or militias or paramilitary units.

14. The Appeals Chamber determined that the legal test which applies to this category was the 'overall control" test:

In order to attribute the acts of a military or paramilitary group to a State, it must be proved that the State wields *overall control* over the group, not only by equipping and financing the group, but also by co-ordinating or helping in the general planning of its military activity. [...] However, it is not necessary that, in addition, the State should also issue, either to the head or to members of the group, instructions for the commission of specific acts contrary to international law.

15. Overall control was defined as consisting of more than 'the mere provision of financial assistance or military equipment or training". Further, the Appeals Chamber adopted a flexible definition of this test, which allows it to take into consideration the diversity of situations on the field in present-day conflicts:

This requirement, however, does not go so far as to include the issuing of specific orders by the State, or its direction of each individual operation. Under international law it is by no means necessary that the controlling authorities should plan all the operations of the units dependent on them, choose their targets, or give specific instructions concerning the conduct of military operations and any alleged violations of international humanitarian law. The control required by international law may be deemed to exist when a State (or in the context of an armed conflict, the Party to the conflict) *has a role in organising, coordinating or planning the military actions* of the military group, in addition to financing, training and equipping or providing operational support to that group. Acts performed by the group or members thereof may be regarded as acts of *de facto* State organs regardless of any specific instruction by the controlling State concerning the commission of each of those acts.

16. The Appeals Chamber in *Tadic* considered *Nicaragua* in depth, and based on two grounds, held that the 'effective control" test enunciated by the ICJ was not persuasive.

17. Firstly, the Appeals Chamber found that the *Nicaragua* 'effective control" test did not seem to be

consonant with the 'very logic of the entire system of international law on State responsibility", which is 'not based on rigid and uniform criteria". In the Appeals Chamber's view, 'the whole body of international law on State responsibility is based on a realistic concept of accountability, which disregards legal formalities". Thus, regardless of whether or not specific instructions were issued, the international responsibility of the State may be engaged.

18. Secondly, the Appeals Chamber considered that the *Nicaragua* test is at variance with judicial and State practice. Relying on a number of cases from claims tribunals, national and international courts, and State practice, the Chamber found that, although the 'effective control" test was upheld by the practice in relation to individuals or unorganised groups of individuals acting on behalf of States, it was not the case in respect of military or paramilitary groups.

19. The Appeals Chamber found that the armed forces of the Republika Srpska were to be regarded as acting under the overall control of, and on behalf of, the FRY, sharing the same objectives and strategy, thereby rendering the armed conflict international.

20. The Appeals Chamber, after considering in depth the merits of the *Nicaragua* test, thus rejected the 'effective control" test, in favour of the less strict 'overall control" test. This may be indicative of a trend simply to rely on the international law on the use of force, jus ad bellum, when characterising the conflict. The situation in which a State, the FRY, resorted to the indirect use of force against another State, Bosnia and Herzegovina, by supporting one of the parties involved in the conflict, the Bosnian Serb forces, may indeed be also characterised as a proxy war of an international character. In this context, the 'overall control" test is utilised to ascertain the foreign intervention, and consequently, to conclude that a conflict which was prima facie internal is internationalised.

21. The appellants argue that the findings of the *Tadic* Appeal Judgement which rejected the 'correct legal test" set out in *Nicaragua* are erroneous as the Tribunal is bound by the ICJ's precedent. It is submitted that when the ICJ has determined an issue, the Tribunal should follow it, (1) because of the ICJ's position within the United Nations Charter, and (2) because of the value of precedent. Further, even if the ICJ's decisions are not binding on the Tribunal, the appellants submits that it is 'undesirable to have two courts (...) having conflicting decisions on the same issue".

22. The Prosecution rebuts this argument with the following submissions: (1) The two courts have different jurisdictions, and in addition, the ICJ Statute does not provide for precedent. It would thus be odd that the decisions of the ICJ which are not strictly binding on itself would be binding on the Tribunal which has a different jurisdiction.31 (2) The Appeals Chamber in the *Tadic* appeal made specific reference to *Nicaragua* and held it not to be persuasive. (3) Judge Shahabuddeen in a dissenting opinion in an ICTR decision found that the differences between the Tribunal and the ICJ do not prohibit recourse to the relevant jurisprudence on relevant matters, and that the Tribunal can draw some persuasive value from the ICJ's decisions, without being bound by them.

23. The Appeals Chamber is not persuaded by the appellants' argument. The Appeals Chamber in *Tadic*, addressing the argument that it should not follow the *Nicaragua* test in relation to the issue at hand as the two courts have different jurisdiction, held:

> What is at issue is not the distinction between two classes of responsibility. What is at issue is a preliminary question: that of the conditions on which under international law an individual may be held to act as a *de facto* organ of a State.

24. The Appeals Chamber agrees that 'so far as international law is concerned, the operation of the desiderata of consistency, stability, and predictability does not stop at the frontiers of the Tribunal. [...] The Appeals Chamber cannot behave as if the general state of the law in the international community whose interests it serves is none of its concern". However, this Tribunal is an autonomous international judicial body, and although the ICJ is the 'principal judicial organ" within the United Nations system to which the Tribunal belongs, there is no hierarchical relationship between the two courts. Although the Appeals Chamber will necessarily take into consideration other decisions of international courts, it may, after careful consideration, come to a different conclusion.

25. An additional argument submitted by Land'o is that the Appeals Chamber in the *Tadic* Jurisdiction Decision accurately decided that the conflict was internal. The Appeals Chamber notes that this argument was previously raised by the appellants at trial. The Trial Chamber then concluded that it is 'incorrect to contend that the Appeals Chamber has already settled the matter of the nature of the conflict in Bosnia and Herzegovina. In the *Tadic* Jurisdiction Decision the Chamber found that 'the conflicts in the former Yugoslavia have both internal and international aspects' and deliberately left the question of the nature of particular conflicts open for the Trial Chamber to determine". The Appeals Chamber fully agrees with this conclusion.

26. Applying the principle enunciated in the *Aleksovski* Appeal Judgement, this Appeals Chamber is unable to conclude that the decision in the *Tadic* was arrived at on the basis of the application of a wrong legal principle, or arrived at *per incuriam*. After careful consideration of the arguments put forward by the appellants, this Appeals Chamber is unable to find cogent reasons in the interests of justice to depart from the law as identified in the *Tadic* Appeal Judgement. The 'overall control" test set forth in the *Tadic* Appeal Judgement is thus the applicable criteria for determining the existence of an international armed conflict.

27. The Appeals Chamber will now examine the Trial Judgement in order to ascertain what test was applied.

2. Has the Trial Chamber Applied the 'Overall Control' Test? 28. The Appeals Chamber first notes that the *Tadic* Appeal Judgement which set forth the 'overall control" test had not been issued at the time of the delivery of the Trial Judgement. The Appeals Chamber will thus consider whether the Trial Chamber, although not, from a formal viewpoint, having applied the 'overall control" test as enunciated by the Appeals Chamber in *Tadic*, based its conclusions on a legal reasoning consistent with it.

29. The issue before the Trial Chamber was whether the armed forces of the Bosnian Serbs could be regarded as acting on behalf of the FRY, in order to determine whether after its withdrawal in May 1992 the conflict continued to be international or instead became internal. More specifically, along the lines of *Tadic*, the relevant issue is whether the Trial Chamber came to the conclusion that the Bosnian Serb armed forces could be regarded as having been under the overall control of the FRY, going beyond the mere financing and equipping of such forces, and involving also participation in the planning and supervision of military operations after 19 May 1992.

30. The Prosecution submits that the test applied by the Trial Chamber is consistent with the 'overall control" test. In the Prosecution's submission, the Trial Chamber adopted the "same approach" as subsequently articulated by the Appeals Chamber in *Tadic* and *Aleksovski*. Further, the Trial Judgement goes through the "exact same facts, almost as we found in the *Tadic* decision". The Prosecution contends that the Appeals Chamber has already considered the same issues and facts in the *Tadic* appeal, and found that the same conflict was international after May 1992. In the Prosecution's opinion, the Trial Chamber's conclusion that "the government of the FRY was the [...] controlling force behind the VRS" is consistent with *Tadic*.

3. The Nature of the Conflict Prior to 19 May 1992 31. The Trial Chamber first addressed the question of whether there was an international armed conflict in Bosnia and Herzegovina in May 1992 and whether it continued throughout the rest of that year, *i.e.*, at the time relevant to the charges alleged in the Indictment.

32. The Trial Chamber found that a "significant numbers of [JNA] troops were on the ground when the [BH] government declared the State's independence on 6 March 1992". Further, "there is substantial evidence that the JNA was openly involved in combat activities in Bosnia and Herzegovina from the beginning of March and into April and May of 1992." The Trial Chamber therefore concluded that:

> [...] an international armed conflict existed in Bosnia and Herzegovina at the date of its recognition as an independent State on 6 April 1992. There is no evidence to indicate that the hostilities which occurred in the Konjic municipality at that time were part of a separate armed conflict and, indeed, there is some evidence of the involvement of the JNA in the fighting there.

33. The Trial Chamber's finding as to the nature of the conflict prior to 19 May 1992 is based on a finding of a direct participation of one State on the territory of another State. This constitutes a plain application of the holding of the Appeals Chamber in *Tadic* that it "is indisputable that an armed conflict is international if it takes place between two or more States", which reflects the traditional position of international law. The Appeals Chamber is in no doubt that there is sufficient evidence to justify the Trial Chamber's finding of fact that the conflict was international prior to 19 May 1992.

4. The Nature of the Conflict After 19 May 1992 34. The Trial Chamber then turned to the issue of the character of the conflict after the alleged withdrawal of the external forces it found to be involved prior to 19 May 1992. Based upon, amongst other matters, an analysis of expert testimony and of Security Council resolutions, it found that after 19 May 1992, the aims and objectives of the conflict remained the same as during the conflict involving the FRY and the JNA prior to that date, *i.e.*, to expand the territory which would form part of the Republic. The Trial Chamber found that "[t]he FRY, at the very least, despite the purported withdrawal of its forces, maintained its support of the Bosnian Serbs and their army and exerted substantial influence over their operations".

35. The Trial Chamber concluded that "[d]espite the formal change in status, the command structure of the new Bosnian Serb army was left largely unaltered from that of the JNA, from which the Bosnian Serbs re-

ceived their arms and equipment as well as through local SDS organisations".

36. In discussing the nature of the conflict, the Trial Chamber did not rely on *Nicaragua*, noting that, although "this decision of the ICJ constitutes an important source of jurisprudence on various issues of international law", the ICJ is "a very different judicial body concerned with rather different circumstances from the case in hand".

37. The Trial Chamber described its understanding of the factual situation upon which it was required to make a determination as being

> [...] characterised by the breakdown of previous State boundaries and the creation of new ones. Consequently, the question which arises is one of *continuity of control of particular forces*. The date which is consistently raised as the turning point in this matter is that of 19 May 1992, when the JNA apparently withdrew from Bosnia and Herzegovina.

38. It continued:

The Trial Chamber must keep in mind that the forces constituting the VRS had a prior identity as an actual organ of the SFRY, as the JNA. When the FRY took control of this organ and subsequently severed the formal link between them, by creating the VJ and VRS, the *presumption* remains that these forces retained their link with it, unless otherwise demonstrated.

39. Along the lines of Judge McDonald's Dissenting Opinion in the *Tadic* case (which it cited), the Trial Chamber found that:

> [...] the withdrawal of JNA troops who were not of Bosnian citizenship, and the creation of the VRS and VJ, constituted a deliberate attempt to mask the continued involvement of the FRY in the conflict while its Government remained in fact the controlling force behind the Bosnian Serbs. From the level of strategy to that of personnel and logistics the operations of the JNA persisted in all but name. It would be wholly artificial to sever the period before 19 May 1992 from the period thereafter in considering the nature of the conflict and applying international humanitarian law.

40. The appellants submit that the Trial Chamber did not rely on any legal test to classify the conflict, *i.e.*, it failed to pronounce its own test to determine whether an intervening State has sufficient control over insurgents to render an internal conflict international. On the other hand, the Prosecution submits that the Trial Chamber classified the conflict on the basis of whether the Prosecution had proved that the FRY/VJ was the "controlling force behind the Bosnian Serbs".

41. The Appeals Chamber disagrees with the appellants' submission that the Trial Chamber did not rely on any legal test to determine the issue. The Trial Chamber appears to have relied on a "continuity of control" test in considering the evidence before it, in order to determine whether the nature of the conflict in Bosnia and Herzegovina, which was international until a point in May 1992, had subsequently changed. The Trial Chamber thus relied on a "control" test, evidently less strict than the "effective control" test. The Trial Chamber did not focus on the issuance of specific instructions, which underlies the "effective control" test. In assessing the evidence, however, the Trial Chamber clearly had regard to all the elements pointing to the influence and control retained over the VRS by the VJ, as required by the "overall control" test.

42. The method employed by the Trial Chamber was later considered as the correct approach in *Aleksovski*. The *Aleksovski* Appeals Chamber indeed interpreted the "overall control" test as follows:

> The "overall control" test calls for an assessment of all the elements of control taken as a whole, and a determination to be made on that basis as to whether there was the required degree of control. Bearing in mind that the Appeals Chamber in the *Tadic* Judgement arrived at this test against the background of the "effective control" test set out by the decision of the ICJ in *Nicaragua*, and the "specific instructions" test used by the Trial Chamber in *Tadic*, the Appeals Chamber considers it appropriate to say that the standard established by the "overall control" test is not as rigorous as those tests.

43. The Appeals Chamber finds that the Trial Chamber's assessment of the effect in reality of the formal withdrawal of the FRY army after 19 May 1992 was based on a careful examination of the evidence before it. That the Trial Chamber indeed relied on this approach is evidenced by the use of phrases such as "despite the attempt at camouflage by the authorities of the FRY", or "despite the formal change in status" in the discussion of the evidence before it.

44. An additional argument submitted by Land'o in support of his contention that the Trial Chamber decided the issue wrongly is based on the agreement concluded under the auspices of the ICRC on 22 May 1992. In Land'o's opinion, this agreement, which was based on common Article 3 of the Geneva Conventions, shows that the conflict was considered by the parties to it to be internal. The Appeals Chamber fully concurs with the Trial Chamber's finding that the *Tadic* Jurisdiction Decision's reference to the agreement "merely demonstrates that some of the norms applica-

ble to international armed conflicts were specifically brought into force by the parties to the conflict in Bosnia and Herzegovina, some of whom may have wished it to be considered internal, and does not show that the conflict must therefore have been internal in nature".

45. The appellants further argue that the Trial Chamber relied on a "presumption" that the FRY/VJ still exerted control over the VRS after 19 May 1992 to determine the nature of the conflict. The Trial Chamber thus used an "incorrect legal test" when it concluded that because of the former existing links between the FRY and the VRS, the FRY/VJ retained control over the VRS. The Prosecution responds that it is unfounded to suggest that the Trial Chamber shifted to the Defence the burden of proving that the conflict did not remain international after the withdrawal of the JNA.

46. The Appeals Chamber is of the view that although the use of the term "presumption" by the Trial Chamber may not be appropriate, the approach it followed, i.e., assessing all of the relevant evidence before it, including that of the previous circumstances, is correct. This approach is clearly in keeping with the Appeals Chamber's holding in Tadic that in determining the issue of the nature of the conflict, structures put in place by the parties should not be taken at face value. There it held:

> Undue emphasis upon the ostensible structures and overt declarations of the belligerents, as opposed to a nuanced analysis of the reality of their relationship, may tacitly suggest to groups who are in de facto control of military forces that responsibility for the acts of such forces can be evaded merely by resort to a superficial restructuring of such forces or by a facile declaration that the reconstituted forces are henceforth independent of their erstwhile sponsors.

47. The Trial Chamber's finding is also consistent with the holding of the Appeals Chamber in Tadic that "[w]here the controlling State in question is an adjacent State with territorial ambitions on the State where the conflict is taking place, and the controlling State is attempting to achieve its territorial enlargement through the armed forces which it controls, it may be easier to establish the threshold". The "overall control" test could thus be fulfilled even if the armed forces acting on behalf of the "controlling State" had autonomous choices of means and tactics although participating in a common strategy along with the "controlling State".

48. Although the Trial Chamber did not formally apply the "overall control" test set forth by the Tadic Appeal Judgement, the Appeals Chamber is of the view

that the Trial Chamber's legal reasoning is entirely consistent with the previous jurisprudence of the Tribunal. The Appeals Chamber will now turn to an additional argument of the parties concerning the Trial Chamber's factual findings.

49. Despite submissions in their briefs that suggested that the appellants wished the Appeals Chamber to review the factual findings of the Trial Chamber in addition to reviewing its legal conclusion, the appellants submitted at the hearing that they "just ask the Court to apply the proper legal test to the facts that were found by the Trial Chamber". The Appeals Chamber will thus not embark on a general assessment of the Trial Chamber's factual findings.

50. The Trial Chamber came to the conclusion, as in the Tadic case, that the armed conflict taking place in Bosnia and Herzegovina after 19 May 1992 could be regarded as international because the FRY remained the controlling force behind the Bosnian Serbs armed forces after 19 May 1992. It is argued by the parties that the facts relied upon in the present case are very similar to those found in the Tadic case. As observed previously, however, a general review of the evidence before the Trial Chamber does not fall within the scope of this appeal. It suffices to say that this Appeals Chamber is satisfied that the facts as found by the Trial Chamber fulfil the legal conditions as set forth in the Tadic case.

51. The Appeals Chamber therefore finds that Delic's Ground 8, Mucic's Ground 5, and Land'o's Ground 5 must fail.

B. Whether the Bosnian Serbs Detained in the Celebici Camp were Protected Persons Under Geneva Convention IV

52. Delalic, Mucic, Delic and Land'o submit that the Trial Chamber erred in law in finding that the Bosnian Serbs detainees at the Celebici camp could be considered not to be nationals of Bosnia and Herzegovina for the purposes of the category of persons protected under Geneva Convention IV. They contend that the Trial Chamber's conclusions are inconsistent with international law and Bosnian law. The appellants request that the Appeals Chamber enter judgements of acquittal on all counts based on Article 2 of the Statute.

53. The Prosecution submits that the appellants' grounds of appeal have no merit and that the Appeals Chamber should follow its previous jurisprudence on the issue, as set out in the Tadic Appeal Judgement, and confirmed by the Aleksovski Appeal Judgement. It submits that it is now settled in that jurisprudence that in an international conflict victims may be considered as not being nationals of the party in whose hands they find themselves, even if, as a matter of national law,

they were nationals of the same State as the persons by whom they are detained. Further, the Prosecution submits that the test applied by the Trial Chamber is consistent with the *Tadic* Appeal Judgement.

54. As noted by the Prosecution, the Appeals Chamber in *Tadic* has previously addressed the issue of the criteria for establishing whether a person is "protected" under Geneva Convention IV. In accordance with the principle set out in the *Aleksovski* Appeal Judgement, as enunciated in paragraph 8 of this Judgement, the Appeals Chamber will follow the law in relation to protected persons as identified in the *Tadic* Appeal Judgement, unless cogent reasons in the interests of justice exist to depart from it.

55. After considering whether cogent reasons exist to depart from the *Tadic* Appeal Judgement, the Appeals Chamber will turn to an analysis of the Trial Chamber's findings so as to determine whether it applied the correct legal principles to determine the nationality of the victims for the purpose of the application of the grave breaches provisions.

1. What is the Applicable Law?

56. Article 2 of the Statute of the Tribunal provides that it has the power to prosecute persons who committed grave breaches of the Geneva Conventions "against persons or property *protected under the provisions of the relevant Geneva Conventions*". The applicable provision to ascertain whether Bosnian Serbs detained in the Celebici camp can be regarded as victims of grave breaches is Article 4(1) of Geneva Convention IV on the protection of civilians, which defines "protected persons" as "those in the hands of a Party to the conflict or Occupying Power of which they are not nationals." The Appeals Chamber in *Tadic* found that:

> [...] the Convention intends to protect civilians (in enemy territory, occupied territory or the combat zone) who do not have the nationality of the belligerent in whose hands they find themselves, or who are stateless persons. In addition, as is apparent from the preparatory work, the Convention also intends to protect those civilians in occupied territory who, while having the nationality of the Party to the conflict in whose hands they find themselves, are refugees and thus no longer owe allegiance to this Party and no longer enjoy its diplomatic protection....

57. The Appeals Chamber held that "already in 1949 *the legal bond of nationality was not regarded as crucial* and allowance was made for special cases". Further, relying on a teleological approach, it continued:

58. The Appeals Chamber in *Aleksovski* endorsed the *Tadic* reasoning holding that "Article 4 may be

given a wider construction so that a person may be accorded protected status, notwithstanding the fact that he is of the same nationality as his captors."

59. The appellants submit that the Appeals Chamber decisions in *Tadic* and *Aleksovski* wrongly interpreted Article 4 of Geneva Convention IV, and that the *Tadic* and *Aleksovski* Trial Chamber Judgements are correct. It is essentially submitted that in order for victims to gain "protected persons" status, Geneva Convention IV requires that the person in question be of a different nationality than the perpetrators of the alleged offence, based on the national law on citizenship of Bosnia and Herzegovina. This interpretation is based on a "strict" interpretation of the Convention which is, in the appellants' view, mandated by the "traditional rules of treaty interpretation".

60. The Prosecution contends that the Appeals Chamber in *Aleksovski* already adopted the approach used in the *Tadic* Appeal Judgement, and that the appellants in this case have not demonstrated any "cogent reasons in the interests of justice" that could justify a departure by the Appeals Chamber from its previous decisions on the issue.

61. Before turning to these arguments, the Appeals Chamber will consider an additional argument submitted by the appellants which goes to the status of the *Tadic* Appeal Judgement statement of the law and may be conveniently addressed as a preliminary matter.

62. The appellants submit that the *Tadic* statements on the meaning of protected persons are dicta, as in their view the Appeals Chamber in *Tadic* and *Aleksovski* cases derived the protected persons status of the victims from the finding that the perpetrators were acting on behalf of the FRY or Croatia. The Prosecution on the other hand submits that the Appeals Chamber's statement in *Tadic* was part of the ratio *decidendi*.

63. While the Appeals Chamber in *Tadic* appears to have reached a conclusion as to the status of the victims as protected persons based on the previous finding that the Bosnian Serbs acted as *de facto* organs of another State, the FRY, it set forth a clear statement of the law as to the applicable criteria to determine the nationality of the victims for the purposes of the Geneva Conventions. The Appeals Chamber is satisfied that this statement of the applicable law, which was endorsed by the Appeals Chamber in *Aleksovski*, falls within the scope of the *Aleksovski* statement in relation to the practice of following previous decisions of the Appeals Chamber.

64. The Appeals Chamber now turns to the main arguments relied upon by the appellants, namely that the Appeals Chamber's interpretation of the nationality

requirement is wrong as it is (1) contrary to the "traditional rules of treaty interpretation"; and (2) inconsistent with the national laws of Bosnia and Herzegovina on citizenship.

65. The appellants submit that "the traditional rules of treaty interpretation" should be applied to interpret strictly the nationality requirement set out in Article 4 of Geneva Convention IV. The word "national" should therefore be interpreted according to its natural and ordinary meaning. The appellants submit in addition that if the Geneva Conventions are now obsolete and need to be updated to take into consideration a "new reality", a diplomatic conference should be convened to revise them.

66. The Prosecution on the other hand contends that the Vienna Convention on the Law of Treaties of 1969 provides that the ordinary meaning is the meaning to be given to the terms of the treaty in their context and in the light of their object and purpose. It is submitted that the Appeals Chamber in *Tadic* found that the legal bond of nationality was not regarded as crucial in 1949, *i.e.*, that there was no intention at the time to determine that nationality was the sole criteria. In addition, adopting the appellants' position would result in the removal of protections from the Geneva Conventions contrary to their very object and purpose.

67. The argument of the appellants relates to the interpretative approach to be applied to the concept of nationality in Geneva Convention IV. The appellants and the Prosecution both rely on the Vienna Convention in support of their contentions. The Appeals Chamber agrees with the parties that it is appropriate to refer to the Vienna Convention as the applicable rules of interpretation, and to Article 31 in particular, which sets forth the general rule for the interpretation of treaties. The Appeals Chamber notes that it is generally accepted that these provisions reflect customary rules. The relevant part of Article 31 reads as follows:

A treaty shall be interpreted in good faith in accordance with the ordinary meaning to be given to the terms of the treaty in their context and in the light of its object and purpose.

68. The Vienna Convention in effect adopted a textual, contextual *and* a teleological approach of interpretation, allowing for an interpretation of the natural and ordinary meaning of the terms of a treaty in their context, while having regard to the object and purpose of the treaty.

69. In addition, Article 32 of the Vienna Convention, entitled "Supplementary means of interpretation", provides that:

Recourse may be had to supplementary means of interpretation, including the preparatory work of

the treaty and the circumstances of its conclusion, in order to confirm the meaning resulting from the application of article 31, or to determine the meaning when the interpretation according to article 31:

(a) leaves the meaning ambiguous and obscure; or

(b) leads to a result which is manifestly absurd or unreasonable.

70. Where the interpretative rule set out in Article 31 does not provide a satisfactory conclusion recourse may be had to the *travaux preparatoires* as a subsidiary means of interpretation.

71. In finding that ethnicity may be taken into consideration when determining the nationality of the victims for the purposes of the application of Geneva Convention IV, the Appeals Chamber in *Tadic* concluded:

Under these conditions, the requirement of nationality is even less adequate to define protected persons. In such conflicts, *not only the text and the drafting history of the Convention but also, and more importantly, the Convention's object and purpose* suggest that allegiance to a Party to the conflict and, correspondingly, control by this Party over persons in a given territory, may be regarded as the crucial test.

72. This reasoning was endorsed by the Appeals Chamber in *Aleksovski*:

73. The Appeals Chamber finds that this interpretative approach is consistent with the rules of treaty interpretation set out in the Vienna Convention. Further, the Appeals Chamber in *Tadic* only relied on the *travaux preparatoires* to reinforce its conclusion reached upon an examination of the overall context of the Geneva Conventions. The Appeals Chamber is thus unconvinced by the appellants' argument and finds that the interpretation of the nationality requirement of Article 4 in the *Tadic* Appeals Judgement does not constitute a rewriting of Geneva Convention IV or a "recreation" of the law. The nationality requirement in Article 4 of Geneva Convention IV should therefore be ascertained within the context of the object and purpose of humanitarian law, which "is directed to the protection of civilians to the maximum extent possible". This in turn must be done within the context of the changing nature of the armed conflicts since 1945, and in particular of the development of conflicts based on ethnic or religious grounds.

74. The other set of arguments submitted by the appellants relates to the national laws of Bosnia and Herzegovina on citizenship, and the applicable criteria to ascertain nationality. The appellants contend that the term "national" in Geneva Convention IV refers to

nationality as defined by domestic law. It is argued that according to the applicable law of Bosnia and Herzegovina on citizenship at the time relevant to the Indictment, the Bosnian Serbs were of Bosnian nationality. In the appellants' submission, all former citizens of the former Socialist Republic of Bosnia and Herzegovina (including those of Serbian ethnic origin), one of the constituent republics of the SFRY, became Bosnian nationals when the SFRY was dissolved and Bosnia and Herzegovina was recognised as an independent State in April 1992. Further, FRY citizenship was limited to residents in its constituent parts, and the law of Bosnia and Herzegovina did not provide a possibility for its citizens of Serb ethnic background to opt for FRY citizenship. Delalic submits that in addition, the Bosnian Serbs subsequently agreed to the Dayton Agreement, which provides that they are nationals of Bosnia and Herzegovina.

75. The appellants' arguments go to the issue of whether domestic laws are relevant to determining the nationality of the victims for the purpose of applying the Geneva Conventions. As observed above, however, the nationality requirement of Article 4 of Geneva Convention IV is to be interpreted within the framework of humanitarian law.

76. It is a settled principle of international law that the effect of domestic laws on the international plane is determined by international law. As noted by the Permanent Court of International Justice in the *Case of Certain German Interests in Polish Upper Silesia*, "[f]rom the standpoint of International Law and of the Court which is its organ, municipal laws are merely facts which express the will and constitute the activities of States, in the same manner as do legal decisions or administrative measures". In relation to the admissibility of a claim within the context of the exercise of diplomatic protection based on the nationality granted by a State, the ICJ held in *Nottebohm*:

> But the issue which the Court must decide is not one which pertains to the legal system of Liechtenstein. It does not depend on the law or on the decision of Liechtenstein whether that State is entitled to exercise its protection, in the case under consideration. To exercise protection, to apply to the Court, is to place oneself on the plane of international law. It is international law which determines whether a State is entitled to exercise protection and to seize the Court.

77. The ICJ went on to state that "[i]nternational practice provides many examples of acts performed by States in the exercise of their domestic jurisdiction which do not necessarily or automatically have international effect". To paraphrase the ICJ in *Nottebohm*, the

question at issue must thus be decided on the basis of international law; to do so is consistent with the nature of the question and with the nature of the Tribunal's own functions. Consequently, the nationality granted by a State on the basis of its domestic laws is not automatically binding on an international tribunal which is itself entrusted with the task of ascertaining the nationality of the victims for the purposes of the application of international humanitarian law. Article 4 of Geneva Convention IV, when referring to the absence of national link between the victims and the persons in whose hands they find themselves, may therefore be considered as referring to a nationality link defined for the purposes of international humanitarian law, and not as referring to the domestic legislation as such. It thus falls squarely within the competence of this Appeals Chamber to ascertain the effect of the domestic laws of the former Yugoslavia within the international context in which this Tribunal operates.

78. Relying on the ICRC Commentary to Article 4 of Geneva Convention IV, the appellants further argue that international law cannot interfere in a State's relations with its own nationals, except in cases of genocide and crimes against humanity. In the appellants' view, in the situation of an internationalised armed conflict where the victims and the perpetrators are of the same nationality, the victims are only protected by their national laws.

79. The purpose of Geneva Convention IV in providing for universal jurisdiction only in relation to the grave breaches provisions was to avoid interference by domestic courts of other States in situations which concern only the relationship between a State and its own nationals. The ICRC Commentary (GC IV), referred to by the appellants, thus stated that Geneva Convention IV is "faithful to a recognised principle of international law: it does not interfere in a State's relations with its own nationals". The Commentary did not envisage the situation of an internationalised conflict where a foreign State supports one of the parties to the conflict, and where the victims are detained because of their ethnicity, and because they are regarded by their captors as operating on behalf of the enemy. In these circumstances, the formal national link with Bosnia and Herzegovina cannot be raised before an international tribunal to deny the victims the protection of humanitarian law. It may be added that the government of Bosnia and Herzegovina itself did not oppose the prosecution of Bosnian nationals for acts of violence against other Bosnians based upon the grave breaches regime.

80. It is noteworthy that, although the appellants emphasised that the "nationality" referred to in Geneva Convention IV is to be understood as referring to the

legal citizenship under domestic law, they accepted at the hearing that in the former Yugoslavia "nationality", in everyday conversation, refers to ethnicity.

81. The Appeals Chamber agrees with the Prosecution that depriving victims, who arguably are of the same nationality under domestic law as their captors, of the protection of the Geneva Conventions solely based on that national law would not be consistent with the object and purpose of the Conventions. Their very object could indeed be defeated if undue emphasis were placed on formal legal bonds, which could also be altered by governments to shield their nationals from prosecution based on the grave breaches provisions of the Geneva Conventions. A more purposive and realistic approach is particularly apposite in circumstances of the dissolution of Yugoslavia, and in the emerging State of Bosnia and Herzegovina where various parties were engaged in fighting, and the government was opposed to a partition based on ethnicity, which would have resulted in movements of population, and where, ultimately, the issue at stake was the final shape of the State and of the new emerging entities.

82. In *Tadic*, the Appeals Chamber, relying on a teleological approach, concluded that formal nationality may not be regarded as determinative in this context, whereas ethnicity may reflect more appropriately the reality of the bonds:

> This legal approach, hinging on substantial relations more than on formal bonds, becomes all the more important in present-day international armed conflicts. While previously wars were primarily between well-established States, in modern inter-ethnic armed conflicts such as that in the former Yugoslavia, new States are often created during the conflict and ethnicity rather than nationality may become the grounds for allegiance. Or, put another way, ethnicity may become determinative of national allegiance.

83. As found in previous Appeals Chamber jurisprudence, Article 4 of Geneva Convention IV is to be interpreted as intending to protect civilians who find themselves in the midst of an international, or internationalised, conflict to the maximum extent possible. The nationality requirement of Article 4 should therefore be ascertained upon a review of "the substance of relations" and not based on the legal characterisation under domestic legislation. In today's ethnic conflicts, the victims may be "assimilated" to the external State involved in the conflict, even if they formally have the same nationality as their captors, for the purposes of the application of humanitarian law, and of Article 4 of Geneva Convention IV specifically. The Appeals Chamber thus agrees with the *Tadic* Appeal Judgement that

"even if in the circumstances of the case the perpetrators and the victims were to be regarded as possessing the same nationality, Article 4 would still be applicable".

84. Applying the principle enunciated in *Aleksovski*, the Appeals Chamber sees no cogent reasons in the interests of justice to depart from the *Tadic* Appeal Judgement. The nationality of the victims for the purpose of the application of Geneva Convention IV should not be determined on the basis of formal national characterisations, but rather upon an analysis of the substantial relations, taking into consideration the different ethnicity of the victims and the perpetrators, and their bonds with the foreign intervening State.

85. It is therefore necessary to consider the findings of the Trial Chamber to ascertain whether it applied these principles correctly.

2. Did the Trial Chamber Apply the Correct Legal Principles? 86. As in the section relating to the nature of the conflict, the Appeals Chamber first notes that the *Tadic* Appeal Judgement, which set forth the law applicable to the determination of protected person status, had not been issued at the time of the issue of the Trial Judgement. The Appeals Chamber will thus consider whether the Trial Chamber, although having not, from a formal viewpoint, applied the reasoning of the Appeals Chamber in the *Tadic* Appeal Judgement, based its conclusions on legal reasoning consistent with it.

87. The issue before the Trial Chamber was whether the Bosnian Serb victims in the hands of Bosnian Muslims and Bosnian Croats could be regarded as protected persons, *i.e.*, as having a different nationality from that of their captors.

88. The appellants argue that the Bosnian Serb victims detained in the Celebici camp were clearly nationals of Bosnia and Herzegovina, and cannot be considered as FRY nationals. Thus, the victims could not be considered as "protected persons". The Prosecution on the other hand contends that the test applied by the Trial Chamber was consistent with the *Tadic* Appeal Judgement.

89. It is first necessary to address a particular argument before turning to an examination of the Trial Chamber's findings. Delalic submits, contrary to the Prosecution's assertions, the *Tadic* Appeal Judgement does not govern the protected persons issue in this case, because the facts of the two cases are dramatically different. The Appeals Chamber in *Aleksovski* observed that the principle that the Appeals Chamber will follow its previous decisions "only applies in similar cases, or substantially similar cases. This means less that the facts are similar or substantially similar, than that the

question raised by the facts in the subsequent case is the same as the question decided by the legal principle in the previous decision".

90. In *Tadic* and *Aleksovski* the perpetrators were regarded as acting on behalf of an external party, the FRY and Croatia respectively, and the Bosnian Muslim victims were considered as protected persons by virtue of the fact that they did not have the nationality of the party in whose hands they found themselves. By contrast, in this case, where the accused are Bosnian Muslim or Bosnian Croat, no finding was made that they were acting on behalf of a foreign State, whereas the Bosnian Serb victims could be regarded as having links with the party (the Bosnian Serb armed forces) acting on behalf of a foreign State (the FRY). However, although the factual circumstances of these cases are different, the legal principle which is applicable to the facts is identical. The Appeals Chamber therefore finds the appellant's argument unconvincing.

91. The Trial Chamber found that the Bosnian Serb victims could be regarded "as having been in the hands of a party to the conflict of which they were not nationals, being Bosnian Serbs detained during an international armed conflict by a party to that conflict, the State of Bosnia and Herzegovina". The Trial Chamber essentially relied on a broad and purposive approach to reach its conclusion, rejecting the proposition that a determination of the nationality of the victims should be based on the domestic laws on citizenship.

92. The Trial Chamber first emphasised the role played by international law in relation to nationality, holding that "the International Tribunal may choose to refuse to recognise (or give effect to) a State's grant of its nationality to individuals for the purposes of applying international law". It then nevertheless found that "[a]n analysis of the relevant laws on nationality in Bosnia and Herzegovina in 1992 does not, however, reveal a clear picture. At that time, as we have discussed, the State was struggling to achieve its independence and all the previous structures of the SFRY were dissolving. In addition, an international armed conflict was tearing Bosnia and Herzegovina apart and the very issue which was being fought over concerned the desire of certain groups within its population to separate themselves from that State and join with another". The Trial Chamber also noted that "the Bosnian Serbs, in their purported constitution of the SRBH, proclaimed that citizens of the Serb Republic were citizens of Yugoslavia".

93. The Trial Chamber also declined to rely upon the argument presented by the Prosecution's expert Professor Economides that there is an emerging doctrine in international law of the right to the nationality of one's own choosing. Finding that the principle of a right of option was not a settled rule of international law, the Trial Chamber held that this principle could not be, of itself, determinative in viewing the Bosnian Serbs to be non-nationals of Bosnia and Herzegovina.

94. The Trial Chamber discussed the nationality link in the light of the *Nottebohm* case and concluded:

> Assuming that Bosnia and Herzegovina had granted its nationality to the Bosnian Serbs, Croats and Muslims in 1992, there may be an insufficient link between the Bosnian Serbs and that State for them to be considered Bosnian nationals by this Trial Chamber in the adjudication of the present case. The granting of nationality occurred within the context of the dissolution of a State and a consequent armed conflict. Furthermore, the Bosnian Serbs had clearly expressed their wish not to be nationals of Bosnia and Herzegovina by proclaiming a constitution rendering them part of Yugoslavia and engaging in this armed conflict in order to achieve that aim. Such finding would naturally be limited to the issue of the application of international humanitarian law and would be for no wider purpose. It would also be in the spirit of that law by rendering it as widely applicable as possible.

95. In the light of its finding on the international character of the conflict, the Trial Chamber held that it is "possible to regard the Bosnian Serbs as acting on behalf of the FRY in its continuing armed conflict against the authorities of Bosnia and Herzegovina". The Bosnian Serb victims could thus be considered as having a different nationality from that of their captors.

96. That the Trial Chamber relied upon a broad and purposive, and ultimately realistic, approach is indicated by the following references which concluded its reasoning:

> [T]his Trial Chamber wishes to emphasise the necessity of considering the requirements of article 4 of the Fourth Geneva Convention in a more flexible manner. The provisions of domestic legislation on citizenship in a situation of violent State succession cannot be determinative of the protected status of persons caught up in conflicts which ensue from such events. The Commentary to the Fourth Geneva Convention charges us not to forget that "the Conventions have been drawn up first and foremost to protect individuals, and not to serve State interests" and thus it is the view of this Trial Chamber that their protections should be applied to as broad a category of persons as possible. It would indeed be contrary to the intention of the Security Council, which was concerned with effec-

tively addressing a situation that it had determined to be a threat to international peace and security, and with ending the suffering of all those caught up in the conflict, for the International Tribunal to deny the application of the Fourth Geneva Convention to any particular group of persons solely on the basis of their citizenship status under domestic law.

97. The Appeals Chamber finds that the legal reasoning adopted by the Trial Chamber is consistent with the *Tadic* reasoning. The Trial Chamber rejected an approach based upon formal national bonds in favour of an approach which accords due emphasis to the object and purpose of the Geneva Conventions. At the same time, the Trial Chamber took into consideration the realities of the circumstances of the conflict in Bosnia and Herzegovina, holding that "(t)he law must be applied to the reality of the situation". Although in some respects the legal reasoning of the Trial Chamber may appear to be broader than the reasoning adopted by the Appeals Chamber, this Appeals Chamber is satisfied that the conclusions reached fall within the scope of the *Tadic* reasoning. As submitted by the Prosecution, the Trial Chamber correctly sought to establish whether the victims could be regarded as belonging to the opposing side of the conflict.

98. The Appeals Chamber particularly agrees with the Trial Chamber's finding that the Bosnian Serb victims should be regarded as protected persons for the purposes of Geneva Convention IV because they "were arrested and detained mainly on the basis of their Serb identity" and "they were clearly regarded by the Bosnian authorities as belonging to the opposing party in an armed conflict and as posing a threat to the Bosnian State".

99. The Trial Chamber's holding that its finding "would naturally be limited to the issue of the application of international humanitarian law and would be for no wider purpose"123 also follows closely the Appeals Chamber's position that the legal test to ascertain the nationality of the victims is applicable within the limited context of humanitarian law, and for the specific purposes of the application of Geneva Convention IV in cases before the Tribunal. Land'o submitted in his brief that the Trial Chamber's finding suggests that a person can have one nationality for the purposes of national law, and another for purposes of international law, which, in his opinion, is contrary to international law. He also contended that the Trial Chamber's holding involuntarily deprives all Bosnian Serbs of their nationality. The argument that the Trial Chamber's findings have the consequence of regulating the nationality of the victims in the national sphere is unmeritorious.

It should be made clear that the conclusions reached by international judges in the performance of their duties do not have the effect of regulating the nationality of these persons *vis a vis* the State within the national sphere. Nor do they purport to pronounce on the internal validity of the laws of Bosnia and Herzegovina. The Appeals Chamber agrees with the Prosecution that the Trial Chamber did not act unreasonably in not giving weight to the evidence led by the Defence concerning the nationality of the particular victims under domestic law.

100. The appellants submit arguments based upon the "effective link" test derived from the ICJ case *Nottebohm*. In their view, the following indicia should be taken into consideration when assessing the nationality link of the victims with the FRY: place of birth, of education, of marriage, of vote, and habitual residence; the latter being, they submit, the most important criterion.

101. The *Nottebohm* case was concerned with ascertaining the effects of the national link for the purposes of the exercise of diplomatic protection, whereas in the instant case, the Appeals Chamber is faced with the task of determining whether the victims could be considered as having the nationality of a foreign State involved in the conflict, for the purposes of their protection under humanitarian law. It is thus irrelevant to demonstrate, as argued by the appellants, that the victims and their families had their habitual residence in Bosnia and Herzegovina, or that they exercised their activities there. Rather, the issue at hand, in a situation of internationalised armed conflict, is whether the victims can be regarded as not sharing the same nationality as their captors, for the purposes of the Geneva Conventions, even if arguably they were of the same nationality from a domestic legal point of view.

102. Although the Trial Chamber referred to the *Nottebohm* "effective link" test in the course of its legal reasoning, its conclusion as to the nationality of the victims for the purposes of the Geneva Conventions did not depend on that test. The Trial Chamber emphasised that "operating on the international plane, the International Tribunal may choose to refuse to recognise (or give effect to) a State's grant of its nationality to individuals for the purposes of applying international law". Further, the Trial Chamber when assessing the nationality requirement clearly referred to the specific circumstances of the case and to the specific purposes of the application of humanitarian law.

103. Delalic further submitted that the Trial Chamber altered international law in relying upon the "secessionist activities" of the Bosnian Serbs to reach its conclusion, as the right to self-determination is not recognised in international law.

104. It is irrelevant to determine whether the activities with which the Bosnian Serbs were associated were in conformity with the right to self-determination or not. As previously stated, the question at issue is not whether this activity was lawful or whether it is in compliance with the right to self-determination. Rather, the issue relevant to humanitarian law is whether the civilians detained in the Celebici camp were protected persons in accordance with Geneva Convention IV.

105. Delic also submits that the Trial Chamber's finding that the Bosnian Serb victims were not Bosnian nationals is at odds with its factual conclusions that Bosnian Serbs were Bosnian citizens for the purpose of determining the existence of an international armed conflict.127 This argument has no merit. Contrary to the Appellant's contention, the findings of the Trial Chamber are not contradictory. In finding that the conflict which took place in Bosnia and Herzegovina was of an international character, the Trial Chamber merely concluded that a foreign State was involved and was supporting one of the parties in a conflict that was *prima facie* internal. This finding did not purport to make a determination as to the nationality of the party engaged in fighting with the support of the foreign State.

3. **Conclusion** 106. The Appeals Chamber finds that the legal reasoning applied by the Trial Chamber is consistent with the applicable legal principles identified in the *Tadic* Appeal Judgement. For the purposes of the application of Article 2 of the Statute to the present case, the Bosnian Serb victims detained in the Celebici camp must be regarded as having been in the hands of a party to the conflict, Bosnia and Herzegovina, of which they were not nationals. The appellants' grounds of appeal therefore fail.

C. Whether Bosnia and Herzegovina was a Party to the Geneva Conventions at the Time of the Events Alleged in the Indictment

107. Delic challenges the Trial Chamber's findings of guilt based on Article 2 of the Statute, which vests the Tribunal with the jurisdiction to prosecute grave breaches of the 1949 Geneva Conventions. Delic contends that because Bosnia and Herzegovina did not "accede" to the Geneva Conventions until 31 December 1992, *i.e.*, after the events alleged in the Indictment, his acts committed before that date cannot be prosecuted under the treaty regime of grave breaches. Delic also argues that the Geneva Conventions do not constitute customary law. Therefore, in his opinion, the application of the Geneva Conventions to acts which occurred before the date of Bosnia and Herzegovina's "accession" to them would violate the principle of legality or *nullem crimen sine lege*. All counts based on Article 2 of the

Statute in the Indictment should, he argues, thus be dismissed.

108. The Prosecution contends that regardless of whether or not Bosnia and Herzegovina was bound by the Geneva Conventions *qua* treaty obligations at the relevant time, the grave breaches provisions of the Geneva Conventions reflected customary international law at all material times. Further, Bosnia and Herzegovina was bound by the Geneva Conventions as a result of their instrument of succession deposited on 31 December 1992, which took effect on the date on which Bosnia and Herzegovina became independent, 6 March 1992.

109. The Appeals Chamber first takes note of the "declaration of succession" deposited by Bosnia and Herzegovina on 31 December 1992 with the Swiss Federal Council in its capacity as depositary of the 1949 Geneva Conventions.

110. Bosnia and Herzegovina's declaration of succession may be regarded as a "notification of succession" which is now defined by the 1978 Vienna Convention on Succession of States in Respect of Treaties as "any notification, however phrased or named, made by a successor State expressing its consent to be considered as bound by the treaty".132 Thus, in the case of the replacement of a State by several others, "a newly independent State which makes a notification of succession [...] shall be considered a party to the treaty from the date of the succession of States or from the date of entry into force of the treaty, whichever is the later date.133 The date of 6 March 1992 is generally accepted as the official date of Bosnia and Herzegovina's independence (when it became a sovereign State) and it may be considered that it became an official party to the Geneva Conventions from this date". Indeed, the Swiss Federal Council subsequently notified the State parties to the Geneva Conventions that Bosnia and Herzegovina "became a party to the Conventions [...] at the date of its independence, *i.e.* on 6 March 1992".135 In this regard, the argument put forward by the appellants appears to confuse the concepts of "accession" and "succession".

111. Although Article 23(2) of the Convention also provides that pending notification of succession, the operation of the treaty in question shall be considered "suspended" between the new State and other parties to the treaty, the Appeals Chamber finds that in the case of this type of treaty, this provision is not applicable. This is because, for the following reasons, the Appeals Chamber confirms that the provisions applicable are binding on a State from creation. The Appeals Chamber is of the view that irrespective of any findings as to formal succession, Bosnia and Herzegovina would

in any event have succeeded to the Geneva Conventions under customary law, as this type of convention entails automatic succession, *i.e.*, without the need for any formal confirmation of adherence by the successor State. It may be now considered in international law that there is automatic State succession to multilateral humanitarian treaties in the broad sense, *i.e.*, treaties of universal character which express fundamental human rights. It is noteworthy that Bosnia and Herzegovina itself recognised this principle before the ICJ.

Convention on 23 July 1993. Although the Convention was not in force at the time relevant to the issue at hand, the provisions of relevance to the issue before the Appeals Chamber codify rules of customary international law, as has been recognised by State. *See, e.g.*, Declaration of Tanganyika, 1961, and the subsequent declarations made by new States since then (United Nations Legislative Series, ST/LEG/SER.B/14 p 177). The Appeals Chamber notes that the practice of international organisations (UN, ILO, ICRC) and States shows that there was a customary norm on succession *de jure* of States to general treaties, which applies automatically to human rights treaties.

112. It is indisputable that the Geneva Conventions fall within this category of universal multilateral treaties which reflect rules accepted and recognised by the international community as a whole. The Geneva Conventions enjoy nearly universal participation.

113. In light of the object and purpose of the Geneva Conventions, which is to guarantee the protection of certain fundamental values common to mankind in times of armed conflict, and of the customary nature of their provisions, the Appeals Chamber is in no doubt that State succession has no impact on obligations arising out from these fundamental humanitarian conventions. In this regard, reference should be made to the Secretary-General's Report submitted at the time of the establishment of the Tribunal, which specifically lists the Geneva Conventions among the international humanitarian instruments which are "beyond any doubt part of customary law so that the problem of adherence of some but not all States to specific conventions does not arise". The Appeals Chamber finds further support for this position in the *Tadic* Jurisdiction Decision.

114. For these reasons the Appeals Chamber finds that there was no gap in the protection afforded by the Geneva Conventions, as they, and the obligations arising therefrom, were in force for Bosnia and Herzegovina at the time of the acts alleged in the Indictment.

115. The Appeals Chamber dismisses this ground of appeal.

III. GROUNDS OF APPEAL RELATING TO ARTICLE 3 OF THE STATUTE

116. Delalic, Mucic and Delic challenge the Trial Chamber's findings that (1) offences within common Article 3 of the Geneva Conventions of 1949 are encompassed within Article 3 of the Statute; (2) common Article 3 imposes individual criminal responsibility; and (3) that common Article 3 is applicable to international armed conflicts. The appellants argue that the Appeals Chamber should not follow its previous conclusions in the *Tadic* Jurisdiction Decision, which, it is submitted, was wrongly decided. That Decision determined that violations of common Article 3 were subjected to the Tribunal's jurisdiction under Article 3 of its Statute, and that, as a matter of customary law, common Article 3 was applicable to both internal and international conflicts and entailed individual criminal responsibility. The Prosecution submits that the appellants' grounds should be rejected because they are not consistent with the *Tadic* Jurisdiction Decision, which the Appeals Chamber should follow. The Prosecution contends that the grounds raised by the appellants for reopening the Appeals Chamber's previous reasoning are neither founded nor sufficient.

117. As noted by the parties, the issues raised in this appeal were previously addressed by the Appeals Chamber in the *Tadic* Jurisdiction Decision. In accordance with the principle set out in the *Aleksovski* Appeal Judgement, as enunciated in paragraph 8 of this Judgement, the Appeals Chamber will follow its *Tadic* jurisprudence on the issues, unless there exist cogent reasons in the interests of justice to depart from it.

118. The grounds presented by the appellants raise three different issues in relation to common Article 3 of the Geneva Conventions: (1) whether common Article 3 falls within the scope of Article 3 of the Tribunal's Statute; (2) whether common Article 3 is applicable to international armed conflicts; (3) whether common Article 3 imposes individual criminal responsibility. After reviewing the *Tadic* Jurisdiction Decision in respect of each of these issues to determine whether there exist cogent reasons to depart from it, the Appeals Chamber will turn to an analysis of the Trial Judgement to ascertain whether it applied the correct legal principles in disposing of the issues before it.

119. As a preliminary issue, the Appeals Chamber will consider one of the appellants' submissions concerning the status of the *Tadic* Jurisdiction Decision, which is relevant to the discussion of all three issues.

120. In their grounds of appeal, the appellants invite the Appeals Chamber to reverse the position it took in the *Tadic* Jurisdiction Decision concerning the applicability of common Article 3 of the Geneva Conven-

tions under Article 3 of the Statute, and thus to revisit the issues raised. Delalic inter alia submits that the Appeals Chamber did not conduct a rigorous analysis at the time (suggesting also that there is a difference in nature between interlocutory appeals and post-judgement appeals) and that many of the issues raised now were not briefed or considered in the *Tadic* Jurisdiction Decision. In the appellants' view, the Decision was rendered *per incuriam*. Such a reason affecting a judgement was envisaged in the *Aleksovski* Appeal Judgement as providing a basis for departing from an earlier decision.

121. As to the contention that the arguments which the appellants make now were not before the Appeals Chamber in *Tadic*, the Prosecution submits that it is not the case that they were not considered in the *Tadic* Jurisdiction Decision: the essence of most of the arguments now submitted by the appellants was addressed and decided by the Appeals Chamber in that Decision. In relation to the argument that the *Tadic* Jurisdiction Decision was not based on a rigorous analysis, the Prosecution submits that that Decision contains detailed reasoning and that issues decided in an interlocutory appeal should not be regarded as having any lesser status than a decision of the Appeals Chamber given after the Trial Chamber's judgement. Further, the Decision was not given *per incuriam*, as the Appeals Chamber focused specifically on this issue, the arguments were extensive and many authorities were referred to. In the Prosecution's submission, there are therefore no reasons to depart from it.

122. This Appeals Chamber is of the view that there is no reason why interlocutory decisions of the Appeals Chamber should be considered, as a matter of principle, as having any lesser status than a final decision on appeal. The purpose of an appeal, whether on an interlocutory or on a final basis, is to determine the issues raised with finality. There is therefore no basis in the interlocutory status of the *Tadic* Jurisdiction Decision to consider it as having been made *per incuriam*.

A. Whether Common Article 3 of the Geneva Conventions Falls Within the Scope of Article 3 of the Statute

1. What is the Applicable Law? 123. Article 3 of the Statute entitled "Violations of the Laws or Customs of War" reads:

> The International Tribunal shall have the power to prosecute persons violating the laws or customs of war. Such violations shall include, but not be limited to:
>
> (a) employment of poisonous weapons or other weapons calculated to cause unnecessary suffering;

> (b) wanton destruction of cities, towns or villages, or devastation not justified by military necessity;
>
> (c) attack, or bombardment, by whatever means, of undefended towns, villages, dwellings, or buildings;
>
> (d) seizure of, destruction or willful damage done to institutions dedicated to religion, charity and education, the arts and science, historic monuments and works of art and science;
>
> (e) plunder of public or private property.

124. Common Article 3 of the Geneva Conventions provides in relevant parts that:

> In the case of armed conflict not of an international character occurring in the territory of one of the High Contracting Parties, each Party to the conflict shall be bound to apply, as a minimum, the following provisions:
>
> (1) Persons taking no active part in the hostilities, including members of armed forces who have laid down their arms and those placed hors de combat by sickness, wounds, detention, or any other cause, shall in all circumstances be treated humanely, without any adverse distinction founded on race, colour, religion or faith, sex, birth or wealth, or any other similar criteria.
>
> To this end, the following acts are and shall remain prohibited at any time and in anyplace whatsoever with respect to the above-mentioned persons:
>
> (a) Violence to life and person, in particular murder of all kinds, mutilation, cruel treatment and torture;
>
> (b) Taking of hostages;
>
> (c) Outrages upon personal dignity, in particular humiliating and degrading treatment;
>
> (d) The passing of sentences and the carrying out of executions without previous judgement pronounced by a regularly constituted court, affording all the judicial guarantees which are recognised as indispensable by civilised peoples.
>
> (2) The wounded and the sick shall be collected and cared for.

125. In relation to the scope of Article 3 of the Statute, the Appeals Chamber in the *Tadic* Jurisdiction Decision held that Article 3 "is a general clause covering all violations of humanitarian law not falling under Article 2 or covered by Articles 4 and 5". It went on:

> Article 3 thus confers on the International Tribunal jurisdiction over any serious offence against international humanitarian law not covered by Arti-

cles 2, 4 or 5. Article 3 is a fundamental provision laying down that any "serious violation of international humanitarian law" must be prosecuted by the International Tribunal. In other words, Article 3 functions as a residual clause designed to ensure that no serious violation of international humanitarian law is taken away from the jurisdiction of the International Tribunal. Article 3 aims to make such jurisdiction watertight and inescapable.

126. The conclusion of the Appeals Chamber was based on a careful analysis of the Secretary-General's Report. The Appeals Chamber *inter alia* emphasised that the Secretary-General acknowledged that the Hague Regulations, annexed to the 1907 Hague Convention (IV) Respecting the Laws and Customs of War on Land, which served as a basis for Article 3 of the Statute, "have a broader scope than the Geneva Conventions, in that they cover not only the protection of victims of armed violence (civilians) or of those who no longer take part in the hostilities (prisoners of war), but also the conduct of hostilities". The Appeals Chamber noted that, although the Secretary-General's Report subsequently indicated "that the violations explicitly listed in Article 3 relate to Hague law not contained in the Geneva Conventions", Article 3 contains the phrase "shall include but not be limited to". The Appeals Chamber concluded: "Considering this list in the general context of the Secretary-General's discussion of the Hague Regulations and international humanitarian law, we conclude that this list may be construed to include other infringements of international humanitarian law."

127. In support of its conclusion, the Appeals Chamber also relied on statements made by States in the Security Council at the time of the adoption of the Statute of the Tribunal, which "can be regarded as providing an authoritative interpretation of Article 3 to the effect that its scope is much broader than the enumerated violations of Hague law". The Appeals Chamber also relied on a teleological approach in its analysis of the provisions of the Statute. Reference was also made to the context and purpose of the Statute as a whole, and in particular to the fact that the Tribunal was established to prosecute "serious violations of international humanitarian law". It continued: "Thus, if correctly interpreted, Article 3 fully realises the primary purpose of the establishment of the International Tribunal, that is, not to leave unpunished any person guilty of any such serious violation, whatever the context within which it may have been committed". The Appeals Chamber concluded that Article 3 is intended to incorporate violations of both Hague (conduct of war) and Geneva (protection of victims) law provided that cer-

tain conditions, *inter alia* relating to the customary status of the rule, are met.

128. The Appeals Chamber then went on to specify four requirements that must be met in order for a violation of international humanitarian law to be subject to Article 3 of the Statute. The Appeals Chamber then considered the question of which such violations, when committed in internal conflicts, met these requirements. It discussed in depth the existence of customary international humanitarian rules applicable to internal conflicts, and found that State practice had developed since the 1930s, to the effect that customary rules exist applicable to non-international conflicts. These rules include common Article 3 but also go beyond it to include rules relating to the methods of warfare.

129. The Appeals Chamber will now turn to the arguments of the appellants which discuss the *Tadic* Jurisdiction Decision conclusions in order to determine whether there exist cogent reasons in the interests of justice to depart from them.

130. In support of their submission that violations of common Article 3 are not within the jurisdiction of the Tribunal, the appellants argue that in adopting Article 3 of the Statute, the Security Council never intended to permit prosecutions under this Article for violations of common Article 3, and, had the Security Council intended to include common Article 3 within the ambit of Article 3, it would have expressly included it in Article 2 of the Statute, which deals with the law related to the protection of victims. In their opinion, an analysis of Article 3 of the Statute shows that it is limited to Hague law. A related argument presented by the appellants is that Article 3 can only be expanded to include offences which are comparable and lesser offences than those already listed, and not to include offences of much greater magnitude and of a completely different character. In support of their argument, the appellants also rely on a comparison of the ICTY and ICTR Statutes, as Article 4 of the ICTR Statute *explicitly* includes common Article 3. The appellants further argue that the Security Council viewed the conflict taking place in the former Yugoslavia as international, and accordingly provided for the prosecution of serious violations of humanitarian law in the context of an international conflict only. The Prosecution submits that the Appeals Chamber should follow its previous conclusion in the *Tadic* Jurisdiction Decision.

131. As to the appellants' argument based on the intention of the Security Council, the Appeals Chamber is of the view that the Secretary-General's Report and the statements made by State representatives in the Security Council at the time of the adoption of the Statute, as analysed in *Tadic*, clearly support a conclusion

that the list of offences listed in Article 3 was meant to cover violations of *all* of the laws or customs of war, understood broadly, in addition to those mentioned in the Article by way of example. Recourse to interpretative statements made by States at the time of the adoption of a resolution may be appropriately made by an international court when ascertaining the meaning of the text adopted, as they constitute an important part of the legislative history of the Statute. These statements may shed light on some aspects of the drafting and adoption of the Statute as well as on its object and purpose, when no State contradicts that interpretation, as noted in *Tadic*.166 This is consistent with the accepted rules of treaty interpretation.

132. The Appeals Chamber is similarly unconvinced by the appellants' submission that it is illogical to incorporate violations of common Article 3 which are "Geneva law" rules, within Article 3 which covers "Hague law" rules. The Appeals Chamber in *Tadic* discussed the evolution of the meaning of the expression "war crimes". It found that war crimes have come to be understood as covering both Geneva and Hague law, and that violations of the laws or customs of war cover both types of rules. The traditional law of warfare concerning the protection of persons (both taking part and not taking part in hostilities) and property is now more correctly termed "international humanitarian law" and has a broader scope, including, for example, the Geneva Conventions. The ICRC Commentary (GC IV) indeed stated that "the Geneva Conventions form part of what are generally called the laws and customs of war, violations of which are commonly called war crimes". Further, Additional Protocol I contains rules of both Geneva and Hague origin.

133. Recent confirmation that a strict separation between Hague and Geneva law in contemporary international humanitarian law based on the "type" of rules is no longer warranted may be found in Article 8 of the ICC Statute. This Article covers "War crimes" generally, namely grave breaches and "other serious violations of the laws and customs of war applicable in international armed conflict"; violations of common Article 3 in non-international armed conflicts; and "other serious violations of the laws and customs of war applicable in non-international armed conflict". The Appeals Chamber thus confirms the view expressed in the *Tadic* Appeal Judgement that the expression "laws and customs of war" has evolved to encompass violations of Geneva law at the time the alleged offences were committed, and that consequently, Article 3 of the Statute may be interpreted as intending the incorporation of Geneva law rules. It follows that the appellants' argument that violations of common Article 3 cannot be included in Article 3 as they are of a different fails.

134. Turning next to the appellants' argument that common Article 3 would more logically be incorporated in Article 2 of the Statute, the Appeals Chamber observes that the Geneva Conventions themselves make a distinction between the grave breaches and other violations of their provisions. The offences enumerated in common Article 3 may be considered as falling into the category of other serious violations of the Geneva Conventions, and are thus included within the general clause of Article 3. There is thus no apparent inconsistency in not including them in the scope of Article 2 of the Statute. This approach based on a distinction between the grave breaches of the Geneva Conventions and other serious violations of the Conventions, has also later been followed in the ICC Statute.

135. As will be discussed below, the appellants' argument that the Security Council viewed the conflict as international, even if correct, would not be determinative of the issue, as the prohibitions listed under common Article 3 are also applicable to international conflicts. It is, however, appropriate to note here that the Appeals Chamber does not share the view of the appellants that the Security Council and the Secretary-General determined that the conflict in the former Yugoslavia at the time of the creation of the Tribunal was international. In the Appeals Chamber's view, the Secretary-General's Report does not take a position as to whether the various conflicts within the former Yugoslavia were international in character for purposes of the applicable law as of a particular date. The Statute was worded neutrally. Article 1 of the Statute entitled "Competence of the International Tribunal" vests the Tribunal with the power to prosecute "serious violations of international humanitarian law committed in the territory of the former Yugoslavia since 1991", making no reference to the nature of the conflict. This supports the interpretation that the Security Council in adopting the Statute was of the view that the question of the nature of the conflict should be judicially determined by the Tribunal itself, the issue involving factual and legal questions.

136. The Appeals Chamber thus finds no cogent reasons in the interests of justice to depart from its previous jurisprudence concerning the question of whether common Article 3 of the Geneva Conventions is included in the scope of Article 3 of the Statute.

2. Did the Trial Chamber Follow the *Tadic* Jurisdiction Decision? 137. The Trial Chamber generally relied on the *Tadic* Jurisdiction Decision as it found "no reason to depart" from it. That the Trial Chamber accepted that common Article 3 is incorporated in Article 3 of the Statute appears clearly from the following findings. The Trial Chamber referred to paragraphs 87 and 91 of the *Tadic* Jurisdiction Decision to describe the "division of labour between Articles 2 and 3 of the Statute". The Trial Chamber went on to hold that "this Trial Chamber is in no doubt that the intention of the Security Council was to ensure that all serious violations of international humanitarian law, committed within the relevant geographical and temporal limits, were brought within the jurisdiction of the International Tribunal."

138. In respect of the customary status of common Article 3, the Trial Chamber found:

> While in 1949 the insertion of a provision concerning internal armed conflicts into the Geneva Conventions may have been innovative, there can be no question that the protections and prohibitions enunciated in that provision have come to form part of customary international law. As discussed at length by the Appeals Chamber, a corpus of law concerning the regulation of hostilities and protection of victims in internal armed conflicts is now widely recognised.

139. The Appeals Chamber therefore finds that the Trial Chamber correctly adopted the Appeals Chamber's statement of the law in disposing of this issue.

B. Whether Common Article 3 is Applicable to International Armed Conflicts

1. What is the Applicable Law? 140. In the course of its discussion of the existence of customary rules of international humanitarian law governing internal armed conflicts, the Appeals Chamber in the *Tadic* Jurisdiction Decision observed a tendency towards the blurring of the distinction between interstate and civil wars as far as human beings are concerned. It then found that some treaty rules, and common Article 3 in particular, which constitutes a mandatory minimum code applicable to internal conflicts, had gradually become part of customary law. In support of its position that violations of common Article 3 are applicable regardless of the nature of the conflict, the Appeals Chamber referred to the ICJ holding in *Nicaragua* that the rules set out in common Article 3 reflect "elementary considerations of humanity" applicable under customary international law to any conflict. The ICJ in *Nicaragua* discussed the customary status of common Article 3 to the Geneva Conventions and held:

> Article 3 which is common to all four Geneva Conventions of 12 August 1949 defines certain rules to be applied in the armed conflicts of a non-international character. There is no doubt that, in the event of international armed conflicts, these rules also constitute a minimum yardstick, in addi-

tion to the more elaborate rules which are also to apply to international conflicts; and they are rules which, in the Court's opinion, reflect what the Court in 1949 called "elementary considerations of humanity" (Corfu Channel, Merits, I.C.J. Reports 1949, p. 22; paragraph 215).

Thus, relying on *Nicaragua*, the Appeals Chamber concluded:

> Therefore at least with respect to the minimum rules in common Article 3, the character of the conflict is irrelevant.

141. The Appeals Chamber also considered that the procedural mechanism, provided for in common Article 3, inviting parties to internal conflicts to agree to abide by the rest of the Conventions, "reflect an understanding that certain fundamental rules should apply regardless of the nature of the conflict." The Appeals Chamber also found that General Assembly resolutions corroborated the existence of certain rules of war concerning the protection of civilians and property applicable in both internal and international armed conflicts.

142. Referring to the *Tadic* Jurisdiction Decision, which the Trial Chamber followed, Delalic argues that the Appeals Chamber failed to properly consider the status of common Article 3, and in particular failed to analyse state practice and *opinio juris*, in support of its conclusion that it was, as a matter of customary international law, applicable to international armed conflicts. Further, in his opinion, the findings of the ICJ on the customary status of common Article 3 and its applicability to both internal and international conflicts are *dicta*. The Prosecution is of the view that, as stated by the ICJ in *Nicaragua*, it is because common Article 3 gives expression to elementary considerations of humanity, which are applicable irrespective of the nature of the conflict, that common Article 3 is applicable to international conflicts.

143. It is indisputable that common Article 3, which sets forth a minimum core of mandatory rules, reflects the fundamental humanitarian principles which underlie international humanitarian law as a whole, and upon which the Geneva Conventions in their entirety are based. These principles, the object of which is the respect for the dignity of the human person, developed as a result of centuries of warfare and had already become customary law at the time of the adoption of the Geneva Conventions because they reflect the most universally recognised humanitarian principles. These principles were codified in common Article 3 to constitute the minimum core applicable to internal conflicts, but are so fundamental that they are

regarded as governing both internal and international conflicts. In the words of the ICRC, the purpose of common Article 3 was to "ensur(e) respect for the few essential rules of humanity which all civilised nations consider as valid everywhere and under all circumstances and as being above and outside war itself". These rules may thus be considered as the "quintessence" of the humanitarian rules found in the Geneva Conventions as a whole.

144. It is these very principles that the ICJ considered as giving expression to fundamental standards of humanity applicable in *all* circumstances.

145. That these standards were considered as reflecting the principles applicable to the Conventions in their entirety and as constituting substantially similar core norms applicable to both types of conflict is clearly supported by the ICRC Commentary (GC IV):

> This minimum requirement in the case of non-international conflict, is *a fortiori* applicable in international armed conflicts. It proclaims the guiding principle common to all four Geneva Conventions, and from it each of them derives the essential provision around which it is built.

146. This is entirely consistent with the logic and spirit of the Geneva Conventions; it is a "logical application of its fundamental principle". Specifically, in relation to the substantive rules set out in subparagraphs (1) (a)-(d) of common Article 3, the ICRC Commentary continues:

> The value of the provision is not limited to the field dealt with in Article 3. Representing, as it does, the minimum which must be applied in the least determinate of conflicts, its terms must *a fortiori* be respected in the case of international conflicts proper, when all the provisions of the Convention are applicable. For "the greater obligation includes the lesser", as one might say.

147. Common Article 3 may thus be considered as the "minimum yardstick" of rules of international humanitarian law of similar substance applicable to both internal and international conflicts. It should be noted that the rules applicable to international conflicts are not limited to the minimum rules set out in common Article 3, as international conflicts are governed by more detailed rules. The rules contained in common Article 3 are considered as applicable to international conflicts because they constitute the core of the rules applicable to such conflicts. There can be no doubt that the acts enumerated in *inter alia* subparagraphs (a), violence to life, and (c), outrages upon personal dignity, are heinous acts "which the world public opinion finds particularly revolting". These acts are also prohibited

in the grave breaches provisions of Geneva Convention IV, such as Article 147. Article 75 of Additional Protocol I, applicable to international conflicts, also provides a minimum of protection to any person unable to claim a particular status. Its paragraph 75(2) is directly inspired by the text of common Article 3.

148. This interpretation is further confirmed by a consideration of other branches of international law, and more particularly of human rights law.

149. Both human rights and humanitarian law focus on respect for human values and the dignity of the human person. Both bodies of law take as their starting point the concern for human dignity, which forms the basis of a list of fundamental minimum standards of humanity. The ICRC Commentary on the Additional Protocols refers to their common ground in the following terms: "This irreducible core of human rights, also known as 'non-derogable rights' corresponds to the lowest level of protection which can be claimed by anyone at anytime [...]".

The universal and regional human rights instruments and the Geneva Conventions share a common "core" of fundamental standards which are applicable at all times, in all circumstances and to all parties, and from which no derogation is permitted. The object of the fundamental standards appearing in both bodies of law is the protection of the human person from certain heinous acts considered as unacceptable by all civilised nations in all circumstances.

150. It is both legally and morally untenable that the rules contained in common Article 3, which constitute mandatory minimum rules applicable to internal conflicts, in which rules are less developed than in respect of international conflicts, would not be applicable to conflicts of an international character. The rules of common Article 3 are encompassed and further developed in the body of rules applicable to international conflicts. It is logical that this minimum be applicable to international conflicts as the substance of these core rules is identical. In the Appeals Chamber's view, something which is prohibited in internal conflicts is necessarily outlawed in an international conflict where the scope of the rules is broader. The Appeals Chamber is thus not convinced by the arguments raised by the appellants and finds no cogent reasons to depart from its previous conclusions.

2. Did the Trial Chamber Follow the *Tadic* Jurisdiction Decision? 151. The Trial Chamber found:

> While common Article 3 of the Geneva Conventions was formulated to apply to internal armed conflicts, it is also clear from the above discussion that its substantive prohibitions apply equally in

situations of international armed conflicts. Similarly, and as stated by the Appeals Chamber, the crimes falling under Article 3 of the Statute of the International Tribunal may be committed in either kind of conflicts. The Trial Chamber's finding that the conflict in Bosnia and Herzegovina in 1992 was of an international nature does not, therefore, impact upon the application of Article 3.

152. The Trial Chamber therefore clearly followed the Appeals Chamber jurisprudence.

C. Whether Common Article 3 Imposes Individual Criminal Responsibility

1. What is the Applicable Law? 153. The Appeals Chamber in the *Tadic* Jurisdiction Decision, in analysing whether common Article 3 attracts individual criminal responsibility first noted that "common Article 3 of the Geneva Conventions contains no explicit reference to criminal liability for violation of its provisions". Referring however to the findings of the International Military Tribunal at Nuremberg that a finding of individual criminal responsibility is not barred by the absence of treaty provisions on punishment of breaches, provided certain conditions are fulfilled, it found:

> Applying the foregoing criteria to the violations at issue here, we have no doubt that they entail individual criminal responsibility, regardless of whether they are committed in internal or international conflicts. Principles and rules of humanitarian law reflect "elementary considerations of humanity" widely recognised as the mandatory minimum for conduct in armed conflict of any kind. No one can doubt the gravity of the acts at issue, nor the interest of the international community in their prohibition.

154. In the Appeals Chamber's opinion, this conclusion was also supported by "many elements of international practice (which) show that States intend to criminalise serious breaches of customary rules and principles on internal conflicts". Specific reference was made to prosecutions before Nigerian courts, national military manuals, national legislation (including the law of the former Yugoslavia adopted by Bosnia and Herzegovina after its independence),204 and resolutions adopted unanimously by the Security Council.

155. The Appeals Chamber found further support for its conclusion in the law of the former Yugoslavia as it stood at the time of the offences alleged in the Indictment:

> Nationals of the former Yugoslavia as well as, at present, those of Bosnia-Herzegovina were therefore aware, or should have been aware, that they were amenable to the jurisdiction of their national criminal courts in cases of violation of international humanitarian law.

156. Reliance was also placed by the Appeals Chamber on the agreement reached under the auspices of the ICRC on 22 May 1992, in order to conclude that the breaches of international law occurring within the context of the conflict, regarded as internal by the agreement, could be criminally sanctioned.

157. The appellants contend that the evidence presented in the *Tadic* Jurisdiction Decision does not establish that common Article 3 is customary international law that creates individual criminal responsibility because there is no showing of State practice and *opinio juris*. Additionally, the appellants submit that at the time of the adoption of the Geneva Conventions in 1949, common Article 3 was excluded from the grave breaches system and thus did not fall within the scheme providing for individual criminal responsibility. In their view, the position had not changed at the time of the adoption of Additional Protocol II in 1977. It is further argued that common Article 3 imposes duties on States only and is meant to be enforced by domestic legal systems.

158. In addition, the appellants argue that solid evidence exists which demonstrates that common Article 3 is *not* a rule of customary law which imposes liability on natural persons. Particular emphasis is placed on the ICTR Statute and the Secretary-General's Report which states that common Article 3 was criminalised for the first time in the ICTR Statute.

159. The Prosecution argues that the *Tadic* Jurisdiction Decision previously disposed of the issue and should be followed. The Prosecution submits that, if violations of the international laws of war have traditionally been regarded as criminal under international law, there is no reason of principle why once those laws came to be extended to the context of internal armed conflicts, their violation in that context should not have been criminal, at least in the absence of clear indications to the contrary. It is further submitted that since 1949, customary law and international humanitarian law have developed to such an extent that today universal jurisdiction does not only exist in relation to the grave breaches of the Geneva Conventions but also in relation to other types of serious violations of international humanitarian law. The Prosecution contends that this conclusion is not contrary to the principle of legality, which does not preclude development of criminal law, so long as those developments do not criminalise conduct which at the time it was committed could reasonably have been regarded as legitimate.

160. Whereas, as a matter of strict treaty law, provision is made only for the prosecution of grave breaches committed within the context of an international conflict, the Appeals Chamber in *Tadic* found that as a matter of customary law, breaches of international humanitarian law committed in internal conflicts, including violations of common Article 3, could also attract individual criminal responsibility.

161. Following the appellants' argument, two different regimes of criminal responsibility would exist based on the different legal characterisation of an armed conflict. As a consequence, the same horrendous conduct committed in an internal conflict could not be punished. The Appeals Chamber finds that the arguments put forward by the appellants do not withstand scrutiny.

162. As concluded by the Appeals Chamber in *Tadic*, the fact that common Article 3 does not contain an explicit reference to individual criminal liability does not necessarily bear the consequence that there is no possibility to sanction criminally a violation of this rule. The IMT indeed followed a similar approach, as recalled in the *Tadic* Jurisdiction Decision when the Appeals Chamber found that a finding of individual criminal responsibility is not barred by the absence of treaty provisions on punishment of breaches. The Nuremberg Tribunal clearly established that individual acts prohibited by international law constitute criminal offences even though there was no provision regarding the jurisdiction to try violations: "Crimes against international law are committed by men, not by abstract entities, and only by punishing individuals who commit such crimes can the provisions of international law be enforced".

163. The appellants argue that the exclusion of common Article 3 from the Geneva Conventions grave breaches system, which provides for universal jurisdiction, has the necessary consequence that common Article 3 attracts no individual criminal responsibility. This is misconceived. In the Appeals Chamber's view, the appellants' argument fails to make a distinction between two separate issues, the issue of criminalisation on the one hand, and the issue of jurisdiction on the other. Criminalisation may be defined as the act of outlawing or making illegal certain behaviour. Jurisdiction relates more to the judicial authority to prosecute those criminal acts. These two concepts do not necessarily always correspond. The Appeals Chamber is in no doubt that the acts enumerated in common Article 3 were intended to be criminalised in 1949, as they were clearly intended to be illegal within the international legal order. The language of common Article 3 clearly prohibits fundamental offences such as murder and tor-

ture. However, no jurisdictional or enforcement mechanism was provided for in the Geneva Conventions at the time.

164. This interpretation is supported by the provisions of the Geneva Conventions themselves, which impose on State parties the duty "to respect and ensure respect for the present Conventions in all circumstances". Common Article 1 thus imposes upon State parties, upon ratification, an obligation to implement the provisions of the Geneva Conventions in their domestic legislation. This obligation clearly covers the Conventions in their entirety and this obligation thus includes common Article 3. The ICJ in the *Nicaragua* case found that common Article 1 also applies to internal conflicts.

165. In addition, the third paragraph of Article 146 of Geneva Convention IV, after setting out the universal jurisdiction mechanism applicable to grave breaches, provides:

> Each High Contracting Party shall take measures necessary for the suppression of all acts contrary to the provisions of the present Convention other than the grave breaches defined in the following Article.

166. The ICRC Commentary (GC IV) stated in relation to this provision that "there is no doubt that what is primarily meant is the repression of breaches other than the grave breaches listed and only in the second place administrative measures to ensure respect for the provisions of the Convention". It then concluded:

> This shows that all breaches of the Convention should be repressed by national legislation. The Contracting Parties who have taken measures to repress the various grave breaches of the Convention and have fixed an appropriate penalty in each case should at least insert in their legislation a general clause providing for the punishment of other breaches. Furthermore, under the terms of this paragraph, the authorities of the Contracting Parties should give all those subordinate to them instructions in conformity with the Convention and should institute judicial or disciplinary punishment for breaches of the Convention.

167. This, in the Appeals Chamber's view, clearly demonstrates that, as these provisions do not provide for exceptions, the Geneva Conventions envisaged that violations of common Article 3 could entail individual criminal responsibility under domestic law, which is accepted by the appellants. The absence of such legislation providing for the repression of such violations would, arguably, be inconsistent with the general obligation contained in common Article 1 of the Conventions.

168. As referred to by the Appeals Chamber in the *Tadic* Jurisdiction Decision, States have adopted domestic legislation providing for the prosecution of violations of common Article 3. Since 1995, several more States have adopted legislation criminalising violations of common Article 3, thus further confirming the conclusion that States regard violations of common Article 3 as constituting crimes. Prosecutions based on common Article 3 under domestic legislation have also taken place.

169. The Appeals Chamber is also not convinced by the appellants' submission that sanctions for violations of common Article 3 are intended to be enforced at the national level only. In this regard, the Appeals Chambers refers to its previous conclusion on the customary nature of common Article 3 and its incorporation in Article 3 of the Statute.

170. The argument that the ICTR Statute, which is concerned with an internal conflict, made violations of common Article 3 subject to prosecution at the international level, in the Appeals Chamber's opinion, reinforces this interpretation. The Secretary-General's statement that violations of common Article 3 of the Geneva Conventions were criminalised for the first time, meant that provisions for international jurisdiction over such violations were *expressly* made for the first time. This is so because the Security Council when it established the ICTR was not creating new law but was *inter alia* codifying existing customary rules for the purposes of the jurisdiction of the ICTR. In the Appeals Chamber's view, in establishing this Tribunal, the Security Council simply created an international mechanism for the prosecution of crimes which were already the subject of individual criminal responsibility.

171. The Appeals Chamber is unable to find any reason of principle why, once the application of rules of international humanitarian law came to be extended (albeit in an attenuated form) to the context of internal armed conflicts, their violation in that context could not be criminally enforced at the international level. This is especially true in relation to prosecution conducted by an international tribunal created by the UN Security Council, in a situation where it specifically called for the prosecution of persons responsible for violations of humanitarian law in an armed conflict regarded as constituting a threat to international peace and security pursuant to Chapter VII of the UN Charter.

172. In light of the fact that the majority of the conflicts in the contemporary world are internal, to maintain a distinction between the two legal regimes and their criminal consequences in respect of similarly egregious acts because of the difference in nature of the conflicts would ignore the very purpose of the Geneva Conventions, which is to protect the dignity of the human person.

173. The Appeals Chamber is similarly unconvinced by the appellants' argument that such an interpretation of common Article 3 violates the principle of legality. The scope of this principle was discussed in the *Aleksovski* Appeal Judgement, which held that the principle of *nullem crimen sine lege* does not prevent a court from interpreting and clarifying the elements of a particular crime. It is universally acknowledged that the acts enumerated in common Article 3 are wrongful and shock the conscience of civilised people, and thus are, in the language of Article 15(2) of the ICCPR, "criminal according to the general principles of law recognised by civilised nations."

174. The Appeals Chamber is unable to find any cogent reasons in the interests of justice to depart from the conclusions on this issue in the *Tadic* Jurisdiction Decision.

2. Did the Trial Chamber Apply the Correct Legal Principles? 175. The Appeals Chamber notes that the appellants raised before the Trial Chamber the same arguments now raised in this appeal. The Trial Chamber held:

Once again, this is a matter which has been addressed by the Appeals Chamber in the *Tadic* Jurisdiction Decision and the Trial Chamber sees no reason to depart from its findings. In its Decision, the Appeals Chamber examines various national laws as well as practice, to illustrate that there are many instances of penal provisions for violations of the laws applicable in internal armed conflicts. From these sources, the Appeals Chamber extrapolates that there is nothing inherently contrary to the concept of individual criminal responsibility for violations of common Article 3 of the Geneva Conventions and that, indeed, such responsibility does ensue.

176. It then concluded:

The fact that the Geneva Conventions themselves do not expressly mention that there shall be criminal liability for violations of common Article 3 clearly does not in itself preclude such liability. Furthermore, identification of the violation of certain provisions of the Conventions as constituting "grave breaches" and thus subject to mandatory universal jurisdiction, certainly cannot be interpreted as rendering all of the remaining provisions of the Conventions as without criminal sanction. While "grave breaches" *must* be prosecuted and punished by all States, "other" breaches of the Geneva Conventions *may* be so. Consequently, an international tribunal such as this must also be permitted to prosecute and punish such violations of the Conventions.

177. In support of this conclusion, which fully accords with the position taken by the Appeals Chamber, the Trial Chamber went on to refer to the ILC Draft Code of Crimes against the Peace and Security of Mankind and the ICC Statute. The Trial Chamber was careful to emphasise that although "these instruments were all drawn up after the acts alleged in the Indictment, they serve to illustrate the widespread conviction that the provisions of common Article 3 are not incompatible with the attribution of individual criminal responsibility".

178. In relation to the ICTR Statute and the Secretary-General's statement in his ICTR report that common Article 3 was criminalised for the first time, the Trial Chamber held: "the United Nations cannot 'criminalise' any of the provisions of international humanitarian law by the simple act of granting subject-matter jurisdiction to an international tribunal. The International Tribunal merely identifies and applies existing customary international law and, as stated above, this is not dependent upon an express recognition in the Statute of the content of that custom, although express reference may be made, as in the Statute of the ICTR". This statement is fully consistent with the Appeals Chamber's finding that the lack of explicit reference to common Article 3 in the Tribunal's Statute does not warrant a conclusion that violations of common Article 3 may not attract individual criminal responsibility.

179. The Trial Chamber's holding in respect of the principle of legality is also consonant with the Appeals Chamber's position. The Trial Chamber made reference to Article 15 of the ICCPR, and to the Criminal Code of the SFRY, adopted by Bosnia and Herzegovina, before concluding:

It is undeniable that acts such as murder, torture, rape and inhuman treatment are criminal according to "general principles of law" recognised by all legal systems. Hence the caveat contained in Article 15, paragraph 2, of the ICCPR should be taken into account when considering the application of the principle of *nullum crimen sine lege* in the present case. The purpose of this principle is to prevent the prosecution and punishment of an individual for acts which he reasonably believed to be lawful at the time of their commission. It strains credibility to contend that the accused would not recognise the criminal nature of the acts alleged in the Indictment. The fact that they could not foresee the cre-

ation of an International Tribunal which would be the forum for prosecution is of no consequence.

180. The Appeals Chamber fully agrees with this statement and finds that the Trial Chamber applied the correct legal principles in disposing of the issues before it.

181. It follows that the appellants' grounds of appeal fail.

IV. GROUNDS OF APPEAL CONCERNING COMMAND RESPONSIBILITY

182. In the present appeal, Mucic and the Prosecution have filed grounds of appeal which relate to the principles of command responsibility. Article 7(3) of the Statute, "Individual criminal responsibility", provides that:

The fact that any of the acts referred to in articles 2 to 5 of the present Statute was committed by a subordinate does not relieve his superior of criminal responsibility if he knew or had reason to know that the subordinate was about to commit such acts or had done so and the superior failed to take the necessary and reasonable measures to prevent such acts or to punish the perpetrators thereof.

A. The Ninth Ground of Appeal of Mucic

183. The ninth ground of Mucic's appeal alleges both a legal and factual error on the part of the Trial Chamber in finding that Mucic had, at the time when the crimes concerned in this case were being committed, the *de facto* authority of a commander in the Celebici camp. Most of the arguments presented by Mucic are concerned with the Trial Chamber's factual findings. The Prosecution argues that Mucic's ground be denied.

184. The Appeals Chamber understands that the remedy desired by the appellant in this ground of appeal is an acquittal of those convictions based on his command responsibility.

185. The Appeals Chamber will first consider the issue of whether a superior may be held liable for the acts of subordinates on the basis of *de facto* authority, before turning to the arguments relating to alleged errors of fact.

1. *de facto* Authority as a Basis for a Finding of Superior Responsibility in International Law 186. In his brief, Mucic appeared to contest the issue of whether a *de facto* status is sufficient for the purpose of ascribing criminal responsibility under Article 7(3) of the Statute. It is submitted that *de facto* status must be equivalent to *de jure* status in order for a superior to be held responsible for the acts of subordinates. He submits that a person in a position of *de facto* authority must be shown to wield the same kind of control over subordinates as *de jure* superiors. In the appellant's view, the approach taken by the Trial Chamber that the absence of formal legal authority, in relation to civilian and military structures, does not preclude a finding of superior responsibility, "comes too close to the concept of strict responsibility". Further, Mucic interprets Article 28 of the ICC Statute as limiting the application of the doctrine of command responsibility to "commanders or those effectively acting as commanders". He submits that "the law relating to *de jure/de facto* command responsibility is far from certain" and that the Appeals Chamber should address the issue.

187. The Prosecution argues that Mucic has failed to adduce authorities to support his argument that the Trial Chamber erred in finding Mucic to be a *de facto* superior. In its view, the finding of the *de facto* responsibility does not amount to a form of strict liability, and *de facto* authority does not have to possess certain features of *de jure* authority. It is submitted that Mucic has not identified any legal basis for alleging that the Trial Chamber has erred in holding that the doctrine of command responsibility applies to civilian superiors.

188. The Trial Chamber found:

[...] a *position of command is indeed a necessary precondition* for the imposition of command responsibility. However, this statement must be qualified by the recognition that the existence of such a position *cannot be determined by reference to formal status alone*. Instead, the factor that determines liability for this type of criminal responsibility is the *actual possession, or non-possession, of powers of control over the actions of subordinates*. Accordingly, formal designation as a commander should not be considered to be a necessary prerequisite for command responsibility to attach, as such responsibility may be imposed by virtue of a person's *de facto*, as well as *de jure*, position as a commander.

189. It is necessary to consider first the notion of command or superior authority within the meaning of Article 7(3) of the Statute before examining the specific issue of *de facto* authority. Article 87(3) of Additional Protocol I to the 1949 Geneva Conventions provides:

The High Contracting Parties and Parties to the conflict shall require any commander who is aware that subordinates or other persons *under his control* are going to commit or have committed a breach of the Conventions or of his Protocol, to initiate such steps as are necessary to prevent such violations of the Conventions or this Protocol, and, where appropriate, to initiate disciplinary or penal action against violators thereof.

190. The *Blaskic* Judgement, referring to the Trial Judgement and to Additional Protocol I, construed control in terms of the material ability of a commander to punish:

What counts is his material ability, which instead of issuing orders or taking disciplinary action may entail, for instance, submitting reports to the competent authorities in order for proper measures to be taken.

191. In respect of the meaning of a commander or superior as laid down in Article 7(3) of the Statute, the Appeals Chamber held in *Aleksovski*:

Article 7(3) provides the legal criteria for command responsibility, thus giving the word "commander" a juridical meaning, in that the provision becomes applicable only where a superior with the required mental element failed to exercise his powers to prevent subordinates from committing offences or to punish them afterwards. This necessarily implies that a superior must have such powers prior to his failure to exercise them. If the facts of a case meet the criteria for the authority of a superior as laid down in Article 7(3), the legal finding would be that an accused is a superior within the meaning of that provision.

192. Under Article 7(3), a commander or superior is thus the one who possesses the power or authority in either a *de jure* or a *de facto* form to prevent a subordinate's crime or to punish the perpetrators of the crime after the crime is committed.

193. The power or authority to prevent or to punish does not solely arise from *de jure* authority conferred through official appointment. In many contemporary conflicts, there may be only *de facto*, self-proclaimed governments and therefore *de facto* armies and paramilitary groups subordinate thereto. Command structure, organised hastily, may well be in disorder and primitive. To enforce the law in these circumstances requires a determination of accountability not only of individual offenders but of their commanders or other superiors who were, based on evidence, in control of them without, however, a formal commission or appointment. A tribunal could find itself powerless to enforce humanitarian law against *de facto* superiors if it only accepted as proof of command authority a formal letter of authority, despite the fact that the superiors acted at the relevant time with all the powers that would attach to an officially appointed superior or commander.

194. In relation to Mucic's responsibility, the Trial Chamber held:

[...] whereas formal appointment is an important aspect of the exercise of command authority or superior authority, the actual exercise of authority in the absence of a formal appointment is sufficient for the purpose of incurring criminal responsibility. Accordingly, the factor critical to the exercise of command responsibility is the actual possession, or non-possession, of powers of control over the actions of the subordinates.

195. The Trial Chamber, prior to making this statement in relation to the case of Mucic, had already considered the origin and meaning of *de facto* authority with reference to existing practice. Based on an analysis of World War II jurisprudence, the Trial Chamber also concluded that the principle of superior responsibility reflected in Article 7(3) of the Statute encompasses political leaders and other civilian superiors in positions of authority. The Appeals Chamber finds no reason to disagree with the Trial Chamber's analysis of this jurisprudence. The principle that military and other superiors may be held criminally responsible for the acts of their subordinates is well-established in conventional and customary law. The standard of control reflected in Article 87(3) of Additional Protocol I may be considered as customary in nature. In relying upon the wording of Articles 86 and 87 of Additional Protocol I to conclude that "it is clear that the term 'superior' is sufficiently broad to encompass a position of authority based on the existence of *de facto* powers of control", the Trial Chamber properly considered the issue in finding the applicable law.

196. "Command", a term which does not seem to present particular controversy in interpretation, normally means powers that attach to a military superior, whilst the term "control", which has a wider meaning, may encompass powers wielded by civilian leaders. In this respect, the Appeals Chamber does not consider that the rule is controversial that civilian leaders may incur responsibility in relation to acts committed by their subordinates or other persons under their effective control. Effective control has been accepted, including in the jurisprudence of the Tribunal, as a standard for the purposes of determining superior responsibility. The *Blaškic* Trial Chamber for instance endorsed the finding of the Trial Judgement to this effect. The showing of effective control is required in cases involving both *de jure* and *de facto* superiors. This standard has more recently been reaffirmed in the ICC Statute, Article 28 of which reads in relevant parts:

> In addition to other grounds of criminal responsibility under this Statute for crimes within the jurisdiction of the Court;
>
> (a) A military commander or person effectively acting as a military commander shall be criminally responsible for crimes within the jurisdiction of the

Court committed by forces under his or her effective command and control, or effective authority and control as the case may be, as a result of his or her failure to exercise control properly over such forces, [...]

> (b) With respect to superior and subordinate relationships not described in paragraph (a), a superior shall be criminally responsible for crimes within the jurisdiction of the Court committed by subordinates under his or her effective authority and control, as a result of his or her failure to exercise control properly over such subordinates [...]

197. In determining questions of responsibility it is necessary to look to effective exercise of power or control and not to formal titles. This would equally apply in the context of criminal responsibility. In general, the possession of *de jure* power in itself may not suffice for the finding of command responsibility if it does not manifest in effective control, although a court may presume that possession of such power *prima facie* results in effective control unless proof to the contrary is produced. The Appeals Chamber considers that the ability to exercise effective control is necessary for the establishment of *de facto* command or superior responsibility and thus agrees with the Trial Chamber that the absence of formal appointment is not fatal to a finding of criminal responsibility, provided certain conditions are met. Mucic's argument that *de facto* status must be equivalent to *de jure* status for the purposes of superior responsibility is misplaced. Although the degree of control wielded by a *de jure* or *de facto* superior may take different forms, a *de facto* superior must be found to wield substantially similar powers of control over subordinates to be held criminally responsible for their acts. The Appeals Chamber therefore agrees with the Trial Chamber's conclusion:

> While it is, therefore, the Trial Chamber's conclusion that a superior, whether military or civilian, may be held liable under the principle of superior responsibility on the basis of his *de facto* position of authority, the fundamental considerations underlying the imposition of such responsibility must be borne in mind. *The doctrine of command responsibility is ultimately predicated upon the power of the superior to control the acts of his subordinates. A duty is placed upon the superior to exercise this power so as to prevent and repress the crimes committed by his subordinates, and a failure by him to do so in a diligent manner is sanctioned by the imposition of individual criminal responsibility in accordance with the doctrine. It follows that there is a threshold at which persons cease to possess the necessary powers of control over the actual perpetrators*

of offences and, accordingly, cannot properly be considered their "superiors" within the meaning of Article 7(3) of the Statute. While the Trial Chamber must at all times be alive to the realities of any given situation and be prepared to pierce such veils of formalism that may shield those individuals carrying the greatest responsibility for heinous acts, *great care must be taken lest an injustice be committed in holding individuals responsible for the acts of others in situations where the link of control is absent or too remote.*

Accordingly, it is the Trial Chamber's view that, in order for the principle of superior responsibility to be applicable, *it is necessary that the superior have effective control over the persons committing the underlying violations of international humanitarian law, in the sense of having the material ability to prevent and punish the commission of these offences.* With the caveat that such authority can have a *de facto* as well as a *de jure* character, the Trial Chamber accordingly shares the view expressed by the International Law Commission that the doctrine of superior responsibility extends to civilian superiors only to the extent that they exercise a degree of control over their subordinates which is similar to that of military commanders.

198. As long as a superior has effective control over subordinates, to the extent that he can prevent them from committing crimes or punish them after they committed the crimes, he would be held responsible for the commission of the crimes if he failed to exercise such abilities of control.

199. The remainder of Mucic's ground of appeal concerns the sufficiency of the evidence regarding the existence of his *de facto* authority. This poses a question of fact, which the Appeals Chamber will now consider.

2. The Trial Chamber's Factual Findings 200. At the appeal hearing, Mucic argued that the Trial Chamber's reliance on the evidence cited in the Trial Judgement in support of the finding that he exercised superior authority was unreasonable. He made a number of arguments which were ultimately directed to his central contention that the evidence was insufficient to support a conclusion that he was a *de facto* commander for the entire period of time set forth in the Indictment. His submissions particularly emphasised that he had no authority in the camp during the months of May, June, or July of 1992.

201. At the hearing, the Prosecution submitted that it was open to a reasonable Trial Chamber to conclude from the evidence as a whole that Mucic was commander of the Celebici camp throughout the period referred to in the Indictment. It was argued that Mucic has not shown that the Trial Chamber has been unreasonable in its evaluation of evidence, and that it is a reasonable inference of the Trial Chamber that Mucic wielded a degree of control and authority in the Celebici camp, drawn from the fact that he had the ability to assist detainees.

3. Discussion 202. In respect of a factual error alleged on appeal, the *Tadic* Appeal Judgement provides the test that:

It is only where the evidence relied on by the Trial Chamber could not reasonably have been accepted by any reasonable person that the Appeals Chamber can substitute its own finding for that of the Trial Chamber.

203. In the appeal of *Furund'ija*, the Appeals Chamber declined to conduct an independent assessment of the evidence admitted at trial, as requested by the appellants, understood as a request for *de novo* review, and took the view that "[t]his Chamber does not operate as a second Trial Chamber."

204. In paragraphs 737-767 of the Trial Judgement, a thorough analysis of evidence led the Trial Chamber to conclude that Mucic "had all the powers of a commander" in the camp. The conclusion was also based on Mucic's own admission that he had "necessary disciplinary powers". Mucic, who disputes this conclusion on appeal, must persuade the Appeals Chamber that the conclusion is one which could not have reasonably been made by a reasonable tribunal of fact, so that a miscarriage of justice has occurred.

205. The Appeals Chamber notes that Mucic argued at trial to the effect that, in the absence of any document formally appointing him to the position of commander or warden of the camp, it was not shown what authority he had over the camp personnel. On appeal, he repeats this argument, and reiterates some of his objections made at trial in respect of the Prosecution evidence which was accepted by the Trial Chamber as showing that he had *de facto* authority in the camp in the period alleged in the Indictment.

206. Having concluded that "the actual exercise of authority in the absence of a formal appointment is sufficient for the purpose of incurring criminal responsibility" provided that the *de facto* superior exercises actual powers of control, the Trial Chamber considered the argument of Mucic that he had no "formal authority". It looked at the following factors to establish that Mucic had *de facto* authority: Mucic's acknowledgement of his having authority over the Celebici camp since 27 July 1992, the submission in the defence closing brief that Mucic used his "limited" authority to pre-

vent crimes and to order that the detainees not be mistreated and that the offenders tried to conceal offences from him, the defence statement that when Mucic was at the camp, there was "far greater" discipline than when he was absent, the evidence that co-defendant Delic told the detainees that Mucic was commander, the evidence that he arranged for the transfer of detainees, his classifying of detainees for the purpose of continued detention or release, his control of guards, and the evidence that he had the authority to release prisoners. At trial, the Trial Chamber accepted this body of evidence. The Appeals Chamber considers that it has not been shown that the Trial Chamber erred in accepting the evidence which led to the finding that Mucic was commander of the camp and as such exercised command responsibility.

207. Mucic argues that the Trial Chamber failed to explain on what date he became commander of the camp. The Trial Chamber found:

208. The Appeals Chamber can see no reason why the Trial Chamber's conclusion that it was unnecessary to make a finding as to the exact date of his appointment — as opposed to his status during the relevant period — was unreasonable.

209. Mucic claims that he had no authority of whatever nature during the months of May, June and July of 1992. The Indictment defined the relevant period in which Mucic was commander of the camp to be "from approximately May 1992 to November 1992". The offences of subordinates upon which the relevant charges against Mucic were based took place during that period. The Appeals Chamber notes that the Trial Judgement considered the objection of Mucic to the evidence which was adduced to show that he was present in the camp in May 1992. The objection was made through the presentation of defence evidence, which was rejected by the Trial Chamber as being inconclusive. On this point, the Appeals Chamber observes that Mucic did not challenge the testimony of certain witnesses which was adduced to show that Mucic was not only present in the camp but in a position of authority in the months of May, June and July of 1992. Reference is made to the evidence given by Witness D, who was a member of the Military Investigative Commission in the camp and worked closely with Mucic in the classification of the detainees. The Trial Chamber was "completely satisfied" with this evidence. The witness testified that Mucic was present at the meeting of the Military Investigative Commission held in early June 1992 to discuss the classification and continued detention or release of the detainees. It is also noteworthy that, in relation to a finding in the case of Delic, it was found that the Military Investigative Commission only

conducted interviews with detainees after informing Mucic, or Delic when the former was absent, and that only Mucic and Delic had access to the files of the Commission. Further, Mucic conceded in his interview with the Prosecution that he went to the camp as early as 20 May 1992. Moreover, Grozdana Jecez, a former detainee at the camp, was interrogated by Mucic in late May or early June 1992. The Appeals Chamber is satisfied that the evidence relied upon by the Trial Chamber constitutes adequate support for its findings.

210. The Appeals Chamber is satisfied that it was open to the Trial Chamber to find that from "before the end of May 1992" Mucic was exercising *de facto* authority over the camp and its personnel.

211. In addition, Mucic submitted:

(i) The Trial Chamber failed to consider the causal implications of the acquittal of the co-defendant Delalic from whom the Prosecution alleged Mucic obtained his necessary authority; and (ii) The Trial Chamber gave wrongful and/or undue weight to the acts of benefice [sic] attributed to Mucic at, *inter alia*, paragraph 1247 of the Trial Judgement, to found command responsibility, instead of treating them as acts of compassion coupled with the strength of personal character which constitute some other species of authority.

212. The first argument appears to be based on an assumption that Mucic's authority rested in some formal way on that of Delalic. This argument has no merit. It is clear that the Trial Chamber found that, regardless of the way Mucic was appointed, he in fact exercised *de facto* authority, irrespective of Delalic's role in relation to the camp.

213. The second point lacks merit in that the acts related to in paragraph 1247 of the Trial Judgement were considered by the Trial Chamber for the purpose of sentencing, rather than conviction; and that acts beneficial to detainees done by Mucic referred to by the Trial Chamber may reasonably be regarded as strengthening its view that Mucic was in a position of authority to effect "greater discipline" in the camp than when he was absent. Although potentially compassionate in nature, these acts are nevertheless evidence of the powers which Mucic exercised and thus of his authority.

4. **Conclusion** 214. For the foregoing reasons, the Appeals Chamber dismisses this ground of appeal and upholds the finding of the Trial Chamber that Mucic was the *de facto* commander of the Celebici camp during the relevant period indicated in the Indictment.

B. The Prosecution Grounds of Appeal

215. The Prosecution has filed three grounds of appeal relating to command responsibility.

1. Mental Element — "Knew or had Reason to Know"

216. The Prosecution's first ground of appeal is that the Trial Chamber has erred in law by its interpretation of the standard of "knew or had reason to know" as laid down in Article 7(3) of the Statute.

217. Delalic argues that the Trial Chamber's interpretation of "had reason to know" is *obiter dicta* and does not affect the finding concerning Delalic that he never had a superior-subordinate relationship with Delic, Mucic, and Land'o. He submits that the Trial Chamber did not determine the matter of the mental element of command responsibility in terms of customary law. The ground should therefore not be considered. He argues that if the Appeals Chamber proceeds to deal with this ground, Delalic will agree with the interpretation given by the Trial Chamber in this regard.

218. Acknowledging Delalic's submission, the Prosecution asks the Appeals Chamber to deal with the mental element as a matter of general significance to the Tribunal's jurisprudence. The Trial Chamber, it contends, determined the matter in terms of the customary law applicable at the time of the offences. The Prosecution does not argue for a mental standard based on strict liability.

219. Delic agrees with the Prosecution's position that Articles 86 and 87 of Additional Protocol I reflect customary law as established through the post Second World War cases. A commander has a duty to be informed, but not every failure in this duty gives rise to command responsibility.

220. The issues raised by this ground of appeal of the Prosecution include:

(i) whether in international law, the duty of a superior to control his subordinates includes a duty to be apprised of their action, *i.e.* a duty to know of their action and whether neglect of such duty will always result in criminal liability;

(ii) whether the standard of "had reason to know" means either the commander had information indicating that subordinates were about to commit or had committed offences or he did not have this information due to dereliction of his duty; and

(iii) whether international law acknowledges any distinction between military and civil leaders in relation to the duty to be informed.

221. The Appeals Chamber takes note of the fact that this ground of appeal is raised by the Prosecution for its general importance to the "jurisprudence of the Tribunal". Considering that this ground concerns an important element of command responsibility, that the Prosecution alleges an error on the part of the Trial Chamber in respect of a finding as to the applicable law, that the parties have made extensive submissions on it, and that it is indeed an issue of general importance to the proceedings before the Tribunal, the Appeals Chamber will consider it by reference to Article 7(3) of the Statute and customary law at the time of the offences alleged in the Indictment.

(i) The Mental Element Articulated by the Statute

222. Article 7(3) of the Statute provides that a superior may incur criminal responsibility for criminal acts of subordinates "if he knew or had reason to know that the subordinate was about to commit such acts or had done so" but fails to prevent such acts or punish those subordinates.

223. The Trial Chamber held that a superior:

[...] may possess the *mens rea* for command responsibility where: (1) he had actual knowledge, established through direct or circumstantial evidence, that his subordinates were committing or about to commit crimes referred to under Articles 2 through 5 of the Statute, or (2) where he had in his possession information of a nature, which at the least, would put him on notice of the risk of such offences by indicating the need for additional investigation in order to ascertain whether such crimes were committed or were about to be committed by his subordinates.

224. The Prosecution position is essentially that the reference to "had reason to know" in Article 7(3) of the Statute, refers to two possible situations. First, a superior had information which put him on notice or which suggested to him that subordinates were about to commit or had committed crimes. Secondly, a superior lacked such information as a result of a serious dereliction of his duty to obtain the information within his reasonable access. As acknowledged by the Prosecution, only the second situation is not encompassed by the Trial Chamber's findings. Delalic argues to the effect that the Trial Chamber was correct in its statement of the law in this regard, and that the second situation envisaged by the Prosecution was in effect an argument based on strict liability. Delic agrees with the Prosecution's assessment of customary law that "the commander has an international duty to be informed", but argues that the Statute was designed by the UN Security Council in such a way that the jurisdiction of the Tribunal was limited to cases where the commander had actual knowledge or such knowledge that it gave him reason to know of subordinate offences, which was a rule inconsistent with customary law laid down in the military trials conducted after the Second World War.

225. The literal meaning of Article 7(3) is not difficult to ascertain. A commander may be held criminally

liable in respect of the acts of his subordinates in violation of Articles 2 to 5 of the Statute. Both the subordinates and the commander are individually responsible in relation to the impugned acts. The commander would be tried for failure to act in respect of the offences of his subordinates in the perpetration of which he did not directly participate.

226. Article 7(3) of the Statute is concerned with superior liability arising from failure to act in spite of knowledge. Neglect of a duty to acquire such knowledge, however, does not feature in the provision as a separate offence, and a superior is not therefore liable under the provision for such failures but only for failing to take necessary and reasonable measures to prevent or to punish. The Appeals Chamber takes it that the Prosecution seeks a finding that "reason to know" exists on the part of a commander if the latter is seriously negligent in his duty to obtain the relevant information. The point here should not be that knowledge may be presumed if a person fails in his *duty* to obtain the relevant information of a crime, but that it may be presumed if he had the *means* to obtain the knowledge but deliberately refrained from doing so. The Prosecution's argument that a breach of the duty of a superior to remain constantly informed of his subordinates actions will necessarily result in *criminal* liability comes close to the imposition of criminal liability on a strict or negligence basis. It is however noted that although a commander's failure to remain apprised of his subordinates' action, or to set up a monitoring system may constitute a neglect of duty which results in liability within the military disciplinary framework, it will not necessarily result in criminal liability.

227. As the Tribunal is charged with the application of customary law, the Appeals Chamber will briefly consider the case-law in relation to whether there is a duty in customary law to know of all subordinate activity, breach of which will give rise to criminal responsibility in the context of command or superior responsibility.

(ii) Duty to Know In Customary Law 228. In the *Yamashita* case, the United States Military Commission found that:

> Clearly, assignment to command military troops is accompanied by broad authority and heavy responsibility [...]. It is absurd, however, to consider a commander a murderer or rapist because one of his soldiers commits a murder or a rape. Nevertheless, where murder and rape and vicious, revengeful actions are widespread offences, and there is no effective attempt by a commander to discover and control the criminal acts, such a commander may be held responsible, even criminally liable, for the lawless acts of his troops, depending upon their nature and the circumstances surrounding them.

The Military Commission concluded that proof of widespread offences, and secondly of the failure of the commander to act in spite of the offences, may give rise to liability. The second factor suggests that the commander needs to discover and control. But it is the first factor that is of primary importance, in that it gives the commander a reason or a basis to discover the scope of the offences. In the *Yamashita* case, the fact stood out that the atrocities took place between 9 October 1944 to 3 September 1945, during which General Yamashita was the commander-in-chief of the 14th Army Group including the Military Police. This length of time begs the question as to how the commander and his staff could be ignorant of large-scale atrocities spreading over this long period. The statement of the commission implied that it had found that the circumstances demonstrated that he had enough notice of the atrocities to require him to proceed to investigate further and control the offences. The fact that widespread offences were committed over a long period of time should have put him on notice that crimes were being or had been committed by his subordinates.

229. On the same case, the United Nations War Crimes Commission commented:

> [...] the crimes which were shown to have been committed by Yamashita's troops were so widespread, both in space and in time, that they could be regarded as providing either prima facie evidence that the accused *knew* of their perpetration, or evidence that he must have failed to fulfill a duty to *discover* the standard of conduct of his troops.

This last sentence deserves attention. However, having considered several cases decided by other military tribunals, it went on to qualify the above statement:

> Short of maintaining that a Commander has a duty to *discover* the state of discipline prevailing among his troops, Courts dealing with cases such as those at present under discussion may in suitable instances have regarded *means of knowledge* as being the same as knowledge itself.

In summary, it pointedly stated that "the law on this point awaits further elucidation and consolidation". Contrary to the Trial Chamber's conclusion, other cases discussed in the Judgement do not show a consistent trend in the decisions that emerged out of the military trials conducted after the Second World War. The citation from the Judgement in the case of *United States v Wilhelm List* ("*Hostage case*") indicates that List failed to acquire "supplementary reports to apprise him of all the pertinent facts". The tribunal in the case found that if a commander of occupied territory "fails to require and obtain *complete* information" he is guilty of a dereliction of his duty. List was found to be charged with notice of the relevant crimes because of reports which had been made to him. Therefore, List had in his possession information that should have prompted him to investigate further the situation under his command. The Trial Chamber also quoted from the *Pohl* case. The phrase quoted is also meant to state a different point than that suggested by the Trial Chamber. In that case, the accused Mummenthey pleaded ignorance of fact in respect of certain aspects of the running of his business which employed concentration camp prisoners. Having refuted this plea by invoking evidence showing that the accused knew fully of those aspects, the tribunal stated:

> Mummenthey's assertions that he did not know what was happening in the labor camps and enterprises under his jurisdiction does not exonerate him. It was his duty to know.

That statement, when read in the context of that part of the judgement, means that the accused was under a duty arising from his position as an SS officer and business manager in charge of a war-time enterprise to know what was happening in his business, including the conditions of the labour force who worked in that business. Any suggestion that the tribunal used that statement to express that the accused had a duty under international law to know would be *obiter* in light of the finding that he had knowledge. In the *Roechling* case, which was also referred to by the Trial Chamber, the court concluded that Roechling had a "duty to keep himself informed about the treatment of the deportees." However, it also noted that "Roechling [...] had repeated opportunities during the inspection of his concerns to ascertain the fate meted out to his personnel, since he could not fail to notice the prisoner's uniform on those occasions". This was information which would put him on notice. It is to be noted that the courts which referred to the existence of a "duty to know" at the same time found that the accused were put on notice of subordinates' acts.

230. Further, the Field Manual of the US Department of Army 1956 (No. 27-10, Law of Land Warfare) provides:

> The commander is...responsible, if he had actual knowledge, or *should have had knowledge, through reports received by him or through other means,* that troops or other persons subject to his control are about to commit or have committed a war crime and he fails to use the means at his disposal to insure compliance with the law of war.

The italicised clause is clear that the commander should be presumed to have had knowledge if he had reports or other means of communication; in other words, he *had already information* as contained in reports or through other means, which put him on notice. On the basis of this analysis, the Appeals Chamber must conclude, in the same way as did the United Nations War Crimes Commission, that the then customary law did not impose in the criminal context a general duty to know upon commanders or superiors, breach of which would be sufficient to render him responsible for subordinates' crimes.

231. The anticipated elucidation and consolidation of the law on the question as to whether there was a duty under customary law for the commander to obtain the necessary information came with Additional Protocol I. Article 86(2) of the protocol provides:

> The fact that a breach of the Conventions or of this Protocol was committed by a subordinate does not absolve his superiors from penal or disciplinary responsibility, as the case may be, if they knew, or *had information which should have enabled them to conclude in the circumstances at the time,* that he was committing or was going to commit such a breach and if they did not take all feasible measures within their power to prevent or repress the breach.

232. The phrase, "had reason to know", is not as clear in meaning as that of "had information enabling them to conclude", although it may be taken as effectively having a similar meaning. The latter standard is more explicit, and its rationale is plain: failure to conclude, or conduct additional inquiry, in spite of alarming information constitutes knowledge of subordinate offences. Failure to act when required to act with such knowledge is the basis for attributing liability in this category of case.

233. The phrase "had information", as used in Article 86(2) of Additional Protocol I, presents little difficulty for interpretation. It means that, at the critical time, the commander had in his possession such information that should have put him on notice of the fact that an unlawful act was being, or about to be, committed by a subordinate. As observed by the Trial Chamber, the apparent discrepancy between the French version, which reads *"des informations leur permettant de conclure"* (literally: information enabling them to conclude), and the English version of Article 86(2) does not undermine this interpretation. This is a reference to information, which, if at hand, would oblige the commander to obtain more information (*i.e.* conduct further inquiry), and he therefore "had reason to know".

234. As noted by the Trial Chamber, the formulation of the principle of superior responsibility in the ILC Draft Code is very similar to that in Article 7(3) of the Statute. Further, as the ILC comments on the draft articles drew from existing practice, they deserve close attention. The ILC comments on the *mens rea* for command responsibility run as follows:

Article 6 provides two criteria for determining whether a superior is to be held criminally responsible for the wrongful conduct of a subordinate. First, a superior must have known or had reason to know *in the circumstances at the time* that a subordinate was committing or was going to commit a crime. This criterion indicates that a superior may have the *mens rea* required to incur criminal responsibility in two different situations. In the first situation, a superior has actual knowledge that his subordinate is committing or is about to commit a crime...In the second situation, he has *sufficient relevant information to enable him to conclude under the circumstances at the time* that his subordinates are committing or are about to commit a crime. The ILC further explains that "[t]he phrase 'had reason to know' is taken from the statutes of the ad hoc tribunals and should be understood as having the same meaning as the phrase 'had information enabling them to conclude' which is used in the Additional Protocol I. The Commission decided to use the former phrase to ensure an objective rather than a subjective interpretation of this element of the first criterion."

235. The consistency in the language used by Article 86(2) of Additional Protocol I, and the ILC Report and the attendant commentary, is evidence of a consensus as to the standard of the *mens rea* of command responsibility. If "had reason to know" is interpreted to mean that a commander has a duty to inquire further, on the basis of information of a general nature he has in hand, there is no material difference between the standard of Article 86(2) of Additional Protocol I and the standard of "should have known" as upheld by certain cases decided after the Second World War.

236. After surveying customary law and especially the drafting history of Article 86 of Additional Protocol I, the Trial Chamber concluded that:

An interpretation of the terms of this provision [Article 86 of Additional Protocol I] in accordance with their ordinary meaning thus leads to the conclusion, confirmed by the *travaux preparatoires*, that a superior can be held criminally responsible only if some specific information was in fact available to him which would provide notice of offences committed by his subordinates. This information

need not be such that it by itself was sufficient to compel the conclusion of the existence of such crimes. It is sufficient that the superior was put on further inquiry by the information, or, in other words, that it indicated the need for additional investigation in order to ascertain whether offences were being committed or about to be committed by his subordinates. This standard, which must be considered to reflect the position of customary law at the time of the offences alleged in the Indictment, is accordingly controlling for the construction of the *mens rea* standard established in Article 7(3). The Trial Chamber thus makes no finding as to the present content of customary law on this point.

237. The Prosecution contends that the Trial Chamber relied improperly upon reference to the object and purpose of Additional Protocol I. The ordinary meaning of the language of Article 86(2) regarding the knowledge element of command responsibility is clear. Though adding little to the interpretation of the language of the provision, the context of the provision as provided by Additional Protocol I simply confirms an interpretation based on the natural meaning of its provisions. Article 87 requires parties to a conflict to impose certain duties on commanders, including the duty in Article 87(3) to "initiate disciplinary or penal action" against subordinates or other persons under their control who have committed a breach of the Geneva Conventions or of the Protocol. That duty is limited by the terms of Article 87(3) to circumstances where the commander "is aware" that his subordinates are going to commit or have committed such breaches. Article 87 therefore interprets Article 86(2) as far as the duties of the commander or superior are concerned, but the criminal offence based on command responsibility is defined in Article 86(2) only.

238. Contrary to the Prosecution's submission, the Trial Chamber did not hold that a superior needs to have information on subordinate offences in his actual possession for the purpose of ascribing criminal liability under the principle of command responsibility. A showing that a superior had some general information in his possession, which would put him on notice of possible unlawful acts by his subordinates would be sufficient to prove that he "had reason to know". The ICRC Commentary (Additional Protocol I) refers to "reports addressed to (the superior), [...] the tactical situation, the level of training and instruction of subordinate officers and their troops, and their character traits" as potentially constituting the information referred to in Article 86(2) of Additional Protocol I. As to the form of the information available to him, it may

be written or oral, and does not need to have the form of specific reports submitted pursuant to a monitoring system. This information does not need to provide specific information about unlawful acts committed or about to be committed. For instance, a military commander who has received information that some of the soldiers under his command have a violent or unstable character, or have been drinking prior to being sent on a mission, may be considered as having the required knowledge.

239. Finally, the relevant information only needs to have been provided or available to the superior, or in the Trial Chamber's words, "in the possession of". It is not required that he actually acquainted himself with the information. In the Appeals Chamber's view, an assessment of the mental element required by Article 7(3) of the Statute should be conducted in the specific circumstances of each case, taking into account the specific situation of the superior concerned at the time in question. Thus, as correctly held by the Trial Chamber,341 as the element of knowledge has to be proved in this type of cases, command responsibility is not a form of strict liability. A superior may only be held liable for the acts of his subordinates if it is shown that he "knew or had reason to know" about them. The Appeals Chamber would not describe superior responsibility as a vicarious liability doctrine, insofar as vicarious liability may suggest a form of strict imputed liability.

(iii) **Civilian Superiors** 240. The Prosecution submits that civilian superiors are under the same duty to know as military commanders. If, as found by the Appeals Chamber, there is no such "duty" to know in customary law as far as military commanders are concerned, this submission lacks the necessary premise. Civilian superiors undoubtedly bear responsibility for subordinate offences under certain conditions, but whether their responsibility contains identical elements to that of military commanders is not clear in customary law. As the Trial Chamber made a factual determination that Delalic was not in a position of superior authority over the Celebici camp in any capacity, there is no need for the Appeals Chamber to resolve this question.

(iv) **Conclusion** 241. For the foregoing reasons, this ground of appeal is dismissed. The Appeals Chamber upholds the interpretation given by the Trial Chamber to the standard "had reason to know", that is, a superior will be criminally responsible through the principles of superior responsibility only if information was available to him which would have put him on notice of offences committed by subordinates. This is consistent with the customary law standard of *mens rea* as existing at the time of the offences charged in the Indictment.

2. Whether Delalic Exercised Superior Responsibility

242. The Prosecution's second ground of appeal alleges an error of law in the Trial Chamber's interpretation of the nature of the superior-subordinate relationship which must be established to prove liability under Article 7(3) of the Statute. The Prosecution contends that the Trial Chamber wrongly "held that the doctrine of superior responsibility requires the perpetrator to be part of a subordinate unit in a direct chain of command under the superior." This legal error, it is said, led to the erroneous finding that Delalic did not exercise superior responsibility over the Celebici camp and thus was not responsible for the offences of the camp staff.

243. The Prosecution argues that, contrary to the finding of the Trial Chamber, the doctrine of command responsibility does not require the existence of a direct chain of command under the superior, and that other forms of *de jure* and *de facto* control, including forms of influence, may suffice for ascribing liability under the doctrine. The criterion for superior responsibility is actual control, which entails the ability to prevent violations, rather than direct subordination. Delalic was in a special position in that the facts found by the Trial Chamber established that he "act[ed] on behalf of the War Presidency, he act[ed] on behalf of the supreme command in Sarajevo, he act[ed] on behalf of the investigating commission with respect to prisoners, he issued orders with respect to the functioning of the Celebici prison". It concludes that, as the Trial Chamber found him to have knowledge of the ill-treatment in the camp, and yet failed to prevent or punish the violations, the Appeals Chamber may substitute verdicts of guilty on those counts under which command responsibility was charged.

244. The Prosecution submits that, if the Appeals Chamber applies the correct test to all of the facts found by the Trial Chamber, the *only* conclusion it could reach is that Delalic was a superior and was guilty of the crimes charged, which would permit it to reverse the verdict of acquittal. If the Appeals Chamber finds that the facts found by the Trial Chamber do not permit it to reach that conclusion, it should remit the case to a newly constituted Trial Chamber to determine the relevant counts.

245. In the alternative, the Prosecution requests leave to be granted to present additional evidence which had been "wrongly excluded by the Trial Chamber", being evidence that it sought to call in rebuttal. The documentary evidence which had not been admitted was annexed to the Prosecution Brief. The submission in relation to admission of wrongfully excluded evidence as expressed in the Prosecution Brief initially

suggested that this course was proposed as an alternative *remedy* which would fall for consideration only should the Appeals Chamber accept the argument that the Trial Chamber made an error of law in its statement of the nature of the superior-subordinate relationship. However, it was also stated that the Prosecution alleges that the Trial Chamber's exclusion of the evidence constituted a distinct error of law, and in subsequent written and oral submissions it was made apparent that, although not expressed as a separate ground of appeal, the submissions as to erroneous exclusion of evidence constitute an independent basis for challenging the Trial Chamber's finding that Delalic was not a superior. As Delalic in fact answered this Prosecution argument, no prejudice will result if the Appeals Chamber deals with this alternative submission as an independent allegation of error of law.

246. Delalic contends that in any event the evidence of the position of Delalic in relation to the Celebici camp demonstrates that he had no superior authority there, and that the Prosecution's theory of "influence responsibility" is not supported by customary law. He argues that a revision of the judgement by the Appeals Chamber can only concern errors of law, and that, where there is a mix of factual and legal errors, the appropriate remedy is that a new trial be ordered. Delalic submits that the Trial Chamber was correct in refusing the to allow the proposed Prosecution witnesses to testify as rebuttal witnesses and in rejecting the Prosecution motion to re-open the proceedings.

247. The Prosecution's argument relating to the Trial Chamber's findings as to the nature of the superior-subordinate relationship is considered first before turning to the second argument relating to the exclusion of evidence which was sought to be admitted as rebuttal or fresh evidence.

(i) The Superior-Subordinate Relationship in the Doctrine of Command Responsibility 248. The Prosecution interprets the Trial Chamber to have held that, in cases involving command or superior responsibility, the perpetrator must be "part of a subordinate unit in a direct chain of command under the superior" for the superior to be held responsible. The Prosecution submissions do not refer to any specific express statement of the Trial Chamber to this effect but appear to consider that this was the overall effect of the Trial Chamber's findings. The Prosecution first refers to, and apparently accepts, the finding of the Trial Chamber that:

> [...] in order for the principle of superior responsibility to be applicable, it is necessary that the superior have effective control over the persons committing the underlying violations of international humanitarian law, in the sense of having the mate-

rial ability to prevent and punish the commission of these offences [...] such authority can have a *de facto* or *de jure* character.

249. The Prosecution then refers to certain subsequent conclusions of the Trial Chamber which it apparently regards as supporting its interpretation that the Trial Chamber held that the doctrine of superior responsibility requires the perpetrator to be part of a subordinate unit in a direct chain of command under the superior. First, the Prosecution refers to the Trial Chamber's statement that, in the case of the exercise of *de facto* authority, it must be

> [...] accompanied by the trappings of the exercise of *de jure* authority. By this, the Trial Chamber means that the perpetrator of the underlying offence must be the subordinate of the person of higher rank *and under his direct or indirect control*.

The section of the judgement cited and relied upon in the Prosecution Brief, however, omits the italicised portion of the passage. This qualification expressly conveys the Trial Chamber's view that the relationship of subordination required by the doctrine of command responsibility may be direct *or indirect*.

250. The Trial Chamber also referred to the ICRC Commentary (Additional Protocols), where it is stated that the superior-subordinate relationship should be seen "in terms of a hierarchy encompassing the concept of control". Noting that Article 87 of Additional Protocol I establishes that the duty of a military commander to prevent violations of the Geneva Conventions extends not only to his subordinates but also to "other persons under his control", the Trial Chamber stated that:

> This type of superior-subordinate relationship is described in the Commentary to the Additional Protocols by reference to the concept of "indirect subordination", in contrast to the link of "direct subordination" which is said to relate the tactical commander to his troops.

251. Two points are clear from the Trial Chamber's consideration of the issue. First, the Trial Chamber found that a *de facto* position of authority suffices for the purpose of ascribing command responsibility. Secondly, it found that the superior-subordinate relationship is based on the notion of control within a hierarchy and that this control can be exercised in a direct or indirect manner, with the result that the superior-subordinate relationship itself may be both direct and indirect. Neither these findings, nor anything else expressed within the Trial Judgement, demonstrates that the Trial Chamber considered that, for the necessary superior-subordinate relationship to exist, the perpe-

trator must be in a direct chain of command under the superior.

252. Examining the actual findings of the Trial Chamber on the issue, it is therefore far from apparent that it found that the doctrine of superior responsibility requires the perpetrator to be part of a subordinate unit in a *direct* chain of command under the superior; nor is such a result a necessary implication of its findings. This seems to have been implicitly recognised by the Prosecution in its oral submissions on this ground of appeal at the hearing. The Appeals Chamber regards the Trial Chamber as having recognised the possibility of both indirect as well as direct relationships subordination and agrees that this may be the case, with the proviso that effective control must always be established.

253. However, the argument of the Prosecution goes further than challenging the perceived requirement of *direct* subordination. The key focus of the Prosecution argument appears to be the Trial Chamber's rejection of the Prosecution theory that persons who can exert "substantial influence" over a perpetrator who is not necessarily a subordinate may, by virtue of that influence, be held responsible under the principles of command responsibility. The Prosecution does not argue that *anyone* of influence may be held responsible in the context of superior responsibility, but that a superior encompasses someone who "may exercise a substantial degree of influence over the perpetrator or over the entity to which the perpetrator belongs."

254. The Trial Chamber understood the Prosecution at trial to be seeking "to extend the concept of the exercise of superior authority to persons over whom the accused can exert substantial influence in a given situation, who are clearly not subordinates", which is essentially the approach taken by the Prosecution on appeal. The Trial Chamber also rejected the idea, which it apparently regarded as being implicit in the Prosecution view, that a superior-subordinate relationship could exist in the absence of a subordinate:

> The view of the Prosecution that a person may, in the absence of a subordinate unit through which authority is exercised, incur responsibility for the exercise of a superior authority seems to the Trial Chamber a novel proposition clearly at variance with the principle of command responsibility. The law does not know of a universal superior without a corresponding subordinate. The doctrine of command responsibility is clearly articulated and anchored on the relationship between superior and subordinate, and the responsibility of the commander for actions of members of his troops. It is a species of vicarious responsibility through which

military discipline is regulated and ensured. This is why a subordinate unit of the superior or commander is a sine qua non for superior responsibility.

The Trial Chamber thus unambiguously required that the perpetrator be subordinated to the superior. While it referred to hierarchy and chain of command, it was clear that it took a wide view of these concepts:

> The requirement of the existence of a "superior-subordinate relationship" which, in the words of the Commentary to Additional Protocol I, should be seen "in terms of a hierarchy encompassing the concept of control", is particularly problematic in situations such as that of the former Yugoslavia during the period relevant to the present case — situations where previously existing formal structures have broken down and where, during an interim period, the new, possibly improvised, control and command structures may be ambiguous and ill-defined. It is the Trial Chamber's conclusion... that persons effectively in command of such more informal structures, with power to prevent and punish the crimes of persons who are in fact under their control, may under certain circumstances be held responsible for their failure to do so.

The Trial Chamber's references to concepts of subordination, hierarchy and chains of command must be read in this context, which makes it apparent that they need not be established in the sense of formal organisational structures so long as the fundamental requirement of an effective power to control the subordinate, in the sense of preventing or punishing criminal conduct, is satisfied.

255. It is clear that the Trial Chamber drew a considerable measure of assistance from the ICRC Commentary (Additional Protocols) on Article 86 of Additional Protocol I (which refers to the circumstances in which a superior will be responsible for breaches of the Conventions or the Protocol committed by his subordinate) in finding that actual control of the subordinate is a necessary requirement of the superior-subordinate relationship. he Commentary on Article 86 of Additional Protocol I states that:

> we are concerned only with the superior who has a personal responsibility with regard to the perpetrator of the acts concerned because the latter, *being his subordinate, is under his control.* The direct link which must exist between the superior and the subordinate clearly follows from the duty to act laid down in paragraph 1 [of Article 86]. Furthermore only that superior is normally in the position

of having information enabling him to conclude in the circumstances at the time that the subordinate has committed or is going to commit a breach. However it should not be concluded from this that the provision only concerns the commander under whose direct orders the subordinate is placed. The concept of the superior is broader and should be seen in terms of a hierarchy encompassing the concept of control.

The point which the commentary emphasises is the concept of control, which results in a relationship of superior and subordinate.

256. The Appeals Chamber agrees that this supports the Trial Chamber's interpretation of the law on this point. The concept of effective *control* over a subordinate - in the sense of a material ability to prevent or punish criminal conduct, however that control is exercised - is the threshold to be reached in establishing a superior-subordinate relationship for the purpose of Article 7(3) of the Statute.

257. In considering the Prosecution submissions relating to "substantial influence", it can be noted that they are not easily reconcilable with other Prosecution submissions in relation to command responsibility. The Prosecution expressly endorses the requirement that the superior have effective *control* over the perpetrator, but then espouses, apparently as a matter of general application, a theory that in fact "substantial influence" alone may suffice, in that "where a person's powers of influence amount to a *sufficient* degree of authority or control in the circumstances to put that person in a position to take preventative action, a failure to do so may result in criminal liability." This latter standard appears to envisage a lower threshold of control than an effective control threshold; indeed, it is unclear that in its natural sense the concept of "substantial *influence*" entails any necessary notion of control at all. Indeed, certain of the Prosecution submissions at the appeal hearing suggest that the substantial influence standard it proposes is not intended to pose any different standard than that of control in the sense of the ability to prevent or punish:

But we would submit that if there is the substantial influence, which we concede is something which has got to be determined essentially on a case-by-case basis, if this superior does have *the material ability to prevent or punish*, he or she should be within the confines of this doctrine of command responsibility as set forth in Article 7(3).

The Appeals Chamber will consider whether substantial influence has ever been recognised as a foundation of superior responsibility in customary law.

258. The Prosecution relied at trial and on appeal on the Hostage case in support of its position that the perpetrators of the crimes for which the superior is to be held responsible need not be subordinates, and that substantial influence is a sufficient degree of control. The Appeals Chamber concurs with the view of the Trial Chamber that the *Hostage case* is based on a distinction in international law between the duties of a commander for occupied territory and commanders in general. That case was concerned with a commander in occupied territory. The authority of such a commander is to a large extent territorial, and the duties applying in occupied territory are more onerous and far-reaching than those applying to commanders generally. Article 42 of the Regulations Respecting the Laws and Customs of War on Land, annexed to the Hague Convention (IV) Respecting the Laws and Customs of War on Land 1907, provides:

Territory is considered occupied when it is actually placed under the authority of the hostile army.

The occupation extends only to the territory where such authority has been established and can be exercised.

Article 43 provides:

The authority of the legitimate power having in fact passed into the hands of the occupant, the latter shall take all the measures in his power to restore, and ensure, as far as possible, public order and safety, while respecting, unless absolutely prevented, the laws in force in the country.

This clearly does not apply to commanders in general. It was not then alleged, nor could it now be, that Delalic was a commander in occupied territory, and the Trial Chamber found expressly that he was not.

259. The Prosecution emphasises however that it did not rely on the *Hostage case* alone. At trial, and on appeal, the Prosecution relied on the judgement in the *Muto* case before the International Military Tribunal for the Far East. The Appeals Chamber regards the *Muto* case as providing limited assistance for the present purpose. Considering Muto's liability as Chief-of-Staff to General Yamashita, the Tokyo Tribunal found him to be in a position "to influence policy", and for this reason he was held responsible for atrocities by Japanese troops in the Philippines. It is difficult to ascertain from the judgement in that case whether his conviction on Count 55 for his failure to take adequate steps to ensure the observance of the laws of war reflected his participation in the making of that policy or was linked to his conviction on Count 54 which alleged that he "ordered, authorized and permitted" the commission of conventional war crimes. It is possible that the conviction on Count 54 led to that on Count 55.

260. On the other hand, the Military Tribunal V in *United States v Wilhelm von Leeb et al*, states clearly that:

> In the absence of participation in criminal orders or their execution within a command, a Chief of Staff does not become criminally responsible for criminal acts occurring therein. He has no command authority over subordinate units. All he can do in such cases is call those matters to the attention of his commanding general, Command authority and responsibility for its exercise rest definitively upon his commander.

This suggests that a Chief-of-Staff would be found guilty only if he were involved in the execution of criminal policies by writing them into orders that were subsequently signed and issued by the commanding officer. In that case, he could be *directly* liable for aiding and abetting or another form of participation in the offences that resulted from the orders drafted by him. The Appeals Chamber therefore confines itself to stating that the case-law relied on by the Prosecution was not uniform on this point. No force of precedent can be ascribed to a proposition that is interpreted differently by equally competent courts.

261. The Prosecution also relies on the *Hirota* and *Roechling* cases. In the *Hirota* case, the Tokyo Tribunal found that Hirota, the Japanese Foreign Minister at the time of the atrocities committed by Japanese forces during the Rape of Nanking, "was derelict in his duty in not insisting before the Cabinet that immediate action be taken to put an end to the atrocities, failing any other action open to him to bring about the same result." The Trial Chamber found this to be "language indicating powers of persuasion rather than formal authority to order action to be taken".

262. In the *Roechling* case, a number of civilian industrialists were found guilty in respect of the ill-treatment of deportees employed in forced labour, not on the basis that they ordered the treatment but because they "permitted it; and indeed supported it, and in addition, for not having done their utmost to put an end to the abuses". The Trial Chamber referred specifically to the findings in relation to von Gemmingen-Hornberg, who was the president of the Directorate and works manager of the Roechling steel plants. The tribunal at first instance had found that "the high position which he occupied in the corporation, as well as the fact that he was Herman Roechling's son-in-law, gave him certainly sufficient authority to obtain an alleviation in the treatment of these workers", and that this constituted "cause under the circumstances" to find him guilty of inhuman treatment of the workers. The reference to "sufficient authority" was interpreted by the Trial Chamber as indicating "powers of persuasion rather than formal authority", partly because of the tribunal's reference to the fact that the accused was Roechling's son-in-law, and it is upon this interpretation that the Prosecution appears to rely.

263. The Appeals Chamber does not interpret the reference to "sufficient authority" as entailing an acceptance of powers of persuasion or influence alone as being a sufficient basis on which to found command responsibility. The *Roechling* judgement on appeal does not refer to the fact that the accused was Roechling's son-in-law, but it emphasises his senior position as president of the Directorate and his position as works manager, "that is, as the works representative in negotiations with the authorities specially competent to deal with matters relating to labor. His sphere of competence also included contact with the Gestapo in regard to the works police". The judgements suggest that he was found to have powers of control over the conditions of the workers which, although not involving any formal ability to give orders to the works police, exceeded mere powers of persuasion or influence. Thus the Appeals Chamber considers the Trial Chamber's initial characterisation of the case as being "best construed as an example of the imposition of superior responsibility on the basis of *de facto* powers of control possessed by civilian industrial leaders" as being the more accurate one.

264. The Appeals Chamber also considers that the *Pohl* case does not support the proposition of the Prosecution that the substantial influence alone of a superior may suffice for the purpose of command responsibility. The person in question, Karl Mummenthey, an SS officer and a business manager, not only possessed "military power of command" but, more importantly in this case, "control" over the industries where mistreatment of concentration camp labourers occurred. This is apparent even from the passage of the judgement cited by the Prosecution in its Appeal Brief:

> Mummenthey was a definite integral and important figure in the whole concentration camp setup, and, as an SS officer, *wielded military power of command*. If excesses occurred in the industries *under his control* he was in a position not only to know about them, but to do something.

265. In the context of relevant jurisprudence on the question, it should also be noted that the Prosecution also relies on the fact that a Trial Chamber of the International Criminal Tribunal for Rwanda, in *Prosecutor v Kayishema and Ruzindana*, relied on these World War II authorities, and on the references to them in the judgement of the Trial Chamber in *Celebici*, to find that powers of influence are sufficient to impose superior responsibility. The ICTR Trial Chamber stated:

[...] having examined the *Hostage* and *High Command* cases the Chamber in *Celebici* concluded that they authoritatively asserted the principle that, "powers of influence not amounting to formal powers of command provide a sufficient basis for the imposition of command responsibility." This Trial Chamber concurs.

No weight can be afforded to this statement of the ICTR Trial Chamber, as it is based on a misstatement of what the Trial Chamber in *Celebici* actually held. The quoted statement was not a conclusion of the Trial Chamber, nor its interpretation of the *Hostage* and *High Command* cases, but the ICTR Trial Chamber's interpretation of the decision of the Tokyo Tribunal in the *Muto* case. The Trial Chamber in *Celebici* ultimately regarded any "influence" principle which may have been established by *Muto* case as being outweighed by other authorities which suggested that a position of command in the sense of effective control was necessary.

266. The Appeals Chamber considers, therefore, that customary law has specified a standard of *effective* control, although it does not define precisely the means by which the control must be exercised. It is clear, however, that substantial influence as a means of control in any sense which falls short of the possession of effective control over subordinates, which requires the possession of material abilities to prevent subordinate offences or to punish subordinate offenders, lacks sufficient support in State practice and judicial decisions. Nothing relied on by the Prosecution indicates that there is sufficient evidence of State practice or judicial authority to support a theory that substantial influence as a means of exercising command responsibility has the standing of a rule of customary law, particularly a rule by which criminal liability would be imposed.

267. The Appeals Chamber therefore finds that the Trial Chamber has applied the correct legal test in the case of Delalic. There is, therefore, no basis for any further application of that test to the Trial Chamber's findings, whether by the Appeals Chamber or by a reconstituted Trial Chamber.

268. The Prosecution's argument dealt with here is limited to the submission that it was the Trial Chamber's alleged error of law in the legal test which led it to an erroneous conclusion that Delalic did not exercise superior authority. There was no independent allegation in the Prosecution Brief that the Trial Chamber made errors of fact in its factual findings which should be overturned by the Appeals Chamber, although certain submissions at the hearing of the appeal suggest that the Prosecution submits that, even under the standard of effective control (which was in fact applied by the Trial Chamber), the Trial Chamber should have found Delalic to have exercised superior authority. However, nothing raised by the Prosecution would support a finding by the Appeals Chamber that the Trial Chamber's findings, and its ultimate conclusion from those facts that Delalic did not exercise the requisite degree of control, was so unreasonable that no reasonable tribunal of fact could have reached them.

(ii) Whether the Trial Chamber erred in excluding rebuttal or fresh evidence 269. As discussed above, the Prosecution submitted "in the alternative" that the Appeals Chamber should grant leave to the Prosecution to present "additional" evidence that was wrongly excluded by the Trial Chamber. The nature of the "alternative" was described as follows:

> The issue is an issue of an error of law. The issue is whether or not the Trial Chamber applied the correct test for the admission of rebuttal or fresh evidence. If they applied the incorrect test and it's an error of law, then the Trial Chamber erred.

270. As noted above, the Appeals Chamber deals with this argument as an independent allegation of an error of law on behalf of the Trial Chamber.

271. At the request of the Trial Chamber during the case of the last of the accused to present his defence, the Prosecution filed a notification of witnesses proposed to testify in rebuttal. It proposed to call four witnesses, one relating to the case against Landzo and the others relating to the case against Delalic, one of whom was a Prosecution investigator being called essentially to tender a number of documents "not previously available to the prosecution". Oral submissions on the proposal were heard by the Trial Chamber on 24 July 1998, and the Trial Chamber ruled that, with the exception of the witness relating to the case against Landzo, the proposed evidence was not rebuttal evidence, but fresh evidence, and that the Prosecution had not put forward anything which would support an application to admit fresh evidence. This decision was reflected in a written Order which noted that "rebuttal evidence is limited to matters that arise directly and specifically out of defence evidence".

272. The evidence which was not admitted by the Trial Chamber related to Delic, Mucic and Delalic, but the Prosecution submission that the exclusion constituted an error invalidating the decision is limited in application to the effect of this evidence on its case against Delalic. Its overall purpose was to show that Delalic had the requisite degree of control over the Celebici camp. The three proposed witnesses, and the documents they sought to adduce, were as follows:

(i) Rajko Dordic, Sr, to testify as to his release from the Celebici camp pursuant to a release form signed by Delalic and dated 3 July 1992. It was proposed that the witness produce and authenticate the document. This was intended to rebut the evidence of defence witnesses that Delalic was authorised to sign release documents only in exceptional circumstances when the members of the Investigative Commission were not present in Celebici.

(ii) Stephen Chambers, an investigator of the Office of the Prosecutor, to present "documentary evidence not previously available to the Prosecutor" which had been seized from the State Commission for the Search for the Missing in Sarajevo and from the home and work premises of an official of the State Commission for Gathering Facts on War Crimes in Konjic. This was said to rebut the testimony of witnesses that Delalic, as commander of Tactical Group 1, had no authority over the Celebici camp.

(iii) Professor Andrea Stegnar, a handwriting expert, to give expert testimony in relation to a number of the recently obtained documents alleged to bear the signature of the accused. This was not argued to have any independent rebuttal basis.

273. The Trial Chamber characterised the nature of rebuttal evidence as "evidence to refute a particular piece of evidence which has been adduced by the defence", with the result that it is "limited to matters that arise directly and specifically out of defence evidence." This standard is essentially consistent with that used previously and subsequently by other Trial Chambers. The Appeals Chamber agrees that this standard — that rebuttal evidence must relate to a significant issue arising directly out of defence evidence which could not reasonably have been anticipated — is correct. It is in this context that the Appeals Chamber understands the Trial Chamber's statement, made later in its Decision on Request to Reopen, that "evidence available to the Prosecution *ab initio*, the relevance of which does not arise *ex improviso*, and which remedies a defect in the case of the Prosecution, is generally not admissible." Although the Appeals Chamber would not itself use that particular terminology, it sees, contrary to the Prosecution submission, no error in that statement when read in context.

274. The Trial Chamber's particular reasons for rejecting the evidence as rebuttal evidence, as expressed in the oral hearing on 24 July, were, in relation to category (i), that the other evidence heard by the Trial Chamber was that Delalic had signed such documents only on behalf of the Investigating Commission and not in his own capacity. As the relevant release document also was acknowledged to state that Delalic was signing "for" the Commission, the Trial Chamber queried how

it could be considered to rebut what had already been put in evidence. The Trial Chamber appeared to assess the document as having such low probative value in relation to the fundamental matter that the Prosecution was trying to prove — namely, Delalic's authority to release prisoners in his own capacity — that it could not be considered to rebut the defence evidence identified by the Prosecution. This assessment was reasonably open to the Trial Chamber.

275. In relation to category (ii), the Trial Chamber rejected the characterisation of the evidence as rebuttal evidence on the basis that it was better characterised as fresh evidence. While it may have been desirable for the Trial Chamber to state more specifically its view as to why the evidence did not refute a particular matters arising directly and specifically out of defence evidence, the Appeals Chamber agrees that it was open to regard the evidence as not being evidence in rebuttal. It is first noteworthy that the Prosecution, in applying to adduce the evidence, described it first as "fresh evidence, not previously available to the prosecution" and gave only a fairly cursory description of how in its view the evidence rebutted defence evidence. It said that the evidence would rebut the evidence of witnesses "who all stated that Zejnil Delalic as Commander of Tactical Group 1 had no *de facto* authority, or any other authority whatsoever" over the Celebici camp. Thus the evidence was intended to establish that Delalic did in fact exercise such authority. As such, it went to a matter which was a fundamental part of the case the Prosecution was required to prove in relation to its counts under Article 7(3). Such evidence should be brought as part of the Prosecution case in chief and not in rebuttal. As the Trial Chamber correctly observed, where the evidence which "is itself evidence probative of the guilt of the accused, and where it is reasonably foreseeable by the Prosecution that some gap in the proof of guilt needs to be filled by the evidence called by it", it is inappropriate to admit it in rebuttal, and the Prosecution "cannot call additional evidence merely because its case has been met by certain evidence to contradict it."

276. Where such evidence could not have been brought as part of the Prosecution case in chief because it was not in the hands of the Prosecution at the time, this does not render it admissible as rebuttal evidence. The fact that evidence is newly obtained, if that evidence does not meet the standard for admission of rebuttal evidence, will not render it admissible as rebuttal evidence. It merely puts it into the category of fresh evidence, to which a different basis of admissibility applies. This is essentially what the Trial Chamber found. There is therefore no merit in the Prosecution's submission that the evidence should have been admitted as

"the reason for not adducing it during the Prosecution's case [was] not due to the failure to foresee the issues that may arise during the Defence case." The issue as to whether the evidence should have been admitted as fresh evidence is considered below.

277. The admission of the testimony of the handwriting expert referred to in category (iii) essentially relied on the admission of the category (ii) evidence, so it need not be further considered.

278. Following the Trial Chamber's rejection of the evidence as rebuttal evidence, the Prosecution filed an alternative request to re-open the Prosecution case. The Trial Chamber rejected this alternative orally, issuing its written reasons on 19 August 1998. The Prosecution filed applications under Rule 73 for leave to appeal the Order of 30 July and the Decision of 4 August, on 6 August and 17 August, respectively. A Bench of the Appeals Chamber denied leave to appeal in respect of both applications on the basis that it saw no issue that would cause such prejudice to the case of the Prosecution as could not be cured by the final disposal of the trial including post-judgement appeal, or which assumed general importance to the proceedings of the Tribunal or in international law generally, these being the two tests established by Rule 73(B) regarding the granting or withholding of leave to appeal.

279. In its Decision on Request to Reopen the Trial Chamber, after considering the basis on which evidence could be admitted as rebuttal evidence, acknowledged the possibility that the Prosecution "may further be granted leave to re-open its case in order to present new evidence not previously available to it." It stated:

> Such fresh evidence is properly defined not merely as evidence that was not in fact in the possession of the Prosecution at the time of the conclusion of its case, but as evidence which by the exercise of reasonable diligence could not have been obtained by the Prosecution at that time. The burden of establishing that the evidence sought to be adduced is of this character rests squarely on the Prosecution.

280. The Trial Chamber also identified the factors which it considered relevant to the exercise of its discretion to admit the fresh evidence. These were described as:

> (i) the "advanced stage of the trial"; *i.e.*, the later in the trial that the application is made, the less likely the evidence will be admitted;
>
> (ii) the delay likely to be caused by a re-opening of the Prosecution case, and the suitability of an adjournment in the overall context of the trial; and
>
> (iii) the probative value of the evidence to be presented.

281. Taking these considerations into account the Trial Chamber assessed both the evidence and the Prosecution's explanation for its late application to adduce it and concluded that the Prosecution had not discharged its burden of proving that the evidence could not have been found earlier with the exercise of reasonable diligence. In addition, it found that the admission of the evidence would result in the undue protraction of the trial for up to three months, as the testimony of further witnesses to authenticate the relevant documents could be required as well as the evidence of any witnesses that the defence should be permitted to bring in response. Finally, the Trial Chamber assessed the evidence to be of minimal probative value, consisting of "circumstantial evidence of doubtful validity", with the result that its exclusion would not cause the Prosecution injustice. It concluded generally that "the justice of the case and the fair and expeditious conduct of the proceedings enjoins a rejection of the application."

282. The Prosecution does not challenge the Trial Chamber's definition of fresh evidence as evidence which was not in the possession of the party at the time and which by the exercise of all reasonable diligence could not have been obtained by the relevant party at the conclusion of its case. Nor does it challenge the "general principle of admissibility" used by the Trial Chamber.

283. The Appeals Chamber agrees that the primary consideration in determining an application for re-opening a case to allow for the admission of fresh evidence is the question of whether, with reasonable diligence, the evidence could have been identified and presented in the case in chief of the party making the application. If it is shown that the evidence could *not* have been found with the exercise of reasonable diligence before the close of the case, the Trial Chamber should exercise its discretion as to whether to admit the evidence by reference to the probative value of the evidence and the fairness to the accused of admitting it late in the proceedings. These latter factors can be regarded as falling under the general discretion, reflected in Rule 89 (D) of the Rules, to exclude evidence where its probative value is substantially outweighed by the need to ensure a fair trial. Although this second aspect of the question of admissibility was less clearly stated by the Trial Chamber, the Appeals Chamber, for the reasons discussed below, considers that it applied the correct principles in this respect.

284. The Prosecution contends that although the Trial Chamber was correct in requiring proof of the exercise of reasonable diligence, it should have found that it had exercised such diligence. The Trial Chamber took the view, having considered the reasons put for-

ward by the Prosecution, that the Prosecution had not discharged its burden of demonstrating that even with reasonable diligence the proposed evidence could not have been previously obtained and presented as part of its case in chief. It implicitly expressed its opinion that the Prosecution had not pursued the relevant evidence vigorously until after the close of the Defence case. The Prosecution submits that this finding was "factually incorrect" and represented "a misapprehension of the facts in relation to the efforts of the Prosecution to obtain this evidence", but does not more than reiterate the description of the efforts to obtain the evidence which it had already provided to the Trial Chamber. It does not identify how, in its view, the Trial Chamber's conclusion on the facts were so unreasonable that no reasonable Trial Chamber could have reached it. It is not suggested that the Trial Chamber did not consider the Prosecution's explanation. No such suggestion could be made in light of the obvious demonstrations both in the hearing of the oral submissions on the issue and the Decision on the Request to Reopen that the Trial Chamber did consider the explanations the Prosecution was putting to it. In the Appeals Chamber's view, even making considerable allowances to the Prosecution in relation to the "complexities involved in obtaining the evidence", it is apparent that there were failures to pursue diligently the investigations for which no adequate attempt to provide an explanation was made.

285. Two examples demonstrate this problem. A number of the documents which were sought to be admitted had been seized in June 1998 from the office and home of Jasminka Dzumhur, a former official of the State Commission for Exchange in Konjic and the Army of Bosnia and Herzegovina 4th Corps Military Investigative Commission. The material provided by the Prosecution in its Request to Reopen to explain its prior effort to obtain documents and information from Ms Dzumhur includes the statement that:

> Between late 1996 and early 1997, the Prosecution contacted Jasminka Dzumhur three times. She consistently refused to provide a statement, but on one occasion, *briefly showed an investigator an untranslated document concerning the transfer of duties in Celebici prison in November 1996,* signed by Zdravko Mucic and Zejnil Delalic. *She said she had other documents, but none of the documents were provided to the Prosecution.*

With this knowledge, obtained in November 1996, that Ms Dzumhur held documents which they considered would be relevant to their case, the next step apparently taken by the Prosecution was four to five months later in mid-April 1997, when it made a formal request for assistance to the Government of Bosnia and Herzegovina. The Prosecution received a response on 23 July 1997, following a reminder in June 1997. On the material provided by the Prosecution, it was almost five months later that it took the next step of issuing a second request to the Government of Bosnia and Herzegovina, which received a relatively rapid response in early January, by providing certain documents. Given that the trial had opened in March 1997, it was open to the Trial Chamber to regard the lapse of these periods of time between the taking of active steps to pursue the documents during after the trial had actually commenced as an indication that reasonable diligence was not being exercised.

286. Secondly, in a case such as the present where the evidence is sought to be presented not only after the close of the case of the Prosecution but long after the close of the case of the relevant accused, it was necessary for the Prosecution to establish that the evidence could not have been obtained, even if after the close of its case, at an earlier stage in the trial. The application to have the new evidence admitted was made many months after the Prosecution gained actual knowledge of the location at which the relevant documents were likely to be held. The information provided by the Prosecution, in its "Alternative Request to Reopen the Prosecution's Case", indicated that the Prosecution gained possession of certain documents from the State Commission for the Search for the Missing on 27 March 1998, which indicated that the relevant documents were in the possession of Jasminka Dzumhur. It was not until 5 May 1998 that the Prosecution took any further step in trying to obtain the documents, when it "informed the authorities that various requests concerning the contacting of officials and former officials of Konjic Municipality, including Jasminka Dzumhur remained outstanding". An application for a search warrant was made to a Judge of the Tribunal on 10 June 1998, after Delalic's defence case had closed. Even making allowances for the complexities of such investigations, allowing a period of over five weeks to elapse between becoming aware of the location of the documents and taking any further active step to obtain them, in light of the advanced state of the defence case, cannot be considered to be the exercise of reasonable diligence. If the Prosecution was in fact taking steps to obtain the information at that time, it did not disclose them to the Trial Chamber and cannot now complain at the assessment that it did not exercise "reasonable diligence" in obtaining and presenting the evidence earlier. Given that the burden of proving that reasonable diligence was exercised in obtaining the evidence lies on the Prosecution, it was open to the Trial Chamber to decide on the information provided to it by the Prosecution that it has not discharged that burden.

287. The Prosecution further submits that the Trial Chamber erred in the exercise of its discretion in certain of the matters it took into account. As the Trial Chamber's finding that reasonable diligence had not been exercised was a sufficient basis on which to dispose of the application, it is not strictly necessary to determine this issue, but as the Trial Chamber expressed its views on this aspect of the application, the Appeals Chamber will consider it here. The Prosecution argues that relevant and probative evidence is only excluded when its admission is substantially outweighed by the need to ensure a fair trial, and cites the provisions of certain national systems in support of this. In relation to these provisions which the Prosecution has selectively drawn from only three national jurisdictions, it can be observed that even if they were to be accepted as a guide to the principles applicable to this issue in the Tribunal, two of them simply confer a discretion on the Trial Chamber *exceptionally* to admit new evidence. The provision cited from the Costa Rican Code of Criminal Procedure states that:

> *Exceptionally*, the court *may* order [...] that new evidence be introduced if, during the trial proceedings new facts or circumstances have arisen that *need to be established*.

The provision relied on from the German Code provides for the admission of new evidence "if this is absolutely necessary".

288. The Trial Chamber stated the principle as being that:

> While it is axiomatic that all evidence must fulfill the requirements of admissibility, for the Trial Chamber to grant the Prosecution permission to reopen its case, the probative value of the proposed evidence must be such that it outweighs any prejudice caused to the accused. Great caution must be exercised by the Trial Chamber lest injustice be done to the accused, and it is therefore only in exceptional circumstances where the justice of the case so demands that the Trial Chamber will exercise its discretion to allow the Prosecution to adduce new evidence after the parties to a criminal trial have closed their case.

The Prosecution argues that the statement of the Trial Chamber that "the probative value of the proposed evidence must be such that it outweighs any prejudice caused to the accused" incorrectly states the applicable principle, which is that stated in Rule 89(D), namely that the need to ensure a fair trial substantially outweighs the probative value of the evidence. The reference by the Trial Chamber to the potential "prejudice caused to the accused" was not, in the view of the Appeals Chamber, the appropriate one in the context. However it is apparent from a reading of the rest of the Decision on Request to Reopen that the Trial Chamber, in referring to prejudice to the accused was turning its mind to matters which may affect the fairness of the accused's trial. This is apparent both from the reference, in the passage cited above, to the need to avoid "injustice to the accused" and the concluding statement in the decision:

> In our view, the justice of the case and the fair and expeditious conduct of the proceedings enjoins a rejection of the application.

289. The Prosecution also argues that the Trial Chamber erred in its assessment of the probative value of the evidence. It contends that the Trial Chamber erred in finding that the evidence was inferential and equivocal. The Prosecution relies on a statement by the Trial Chamber that the documents "cannot be probative". Although this was perhaps unfortunate terminology, it is apparent from the Trial Chamber's decision that after considering the evidence it was of the view not that it could not be probative but that the documents "contain circumstantial evidence of doubtful validity". This was an assessment not that the documents were incapable, as a matter of law, of having probative value, but that, having regard to their contents which did not disclose direct evidence of the matters in dispute but, at best, gave rise to "mere inferences", the documents had a low probative value. This assessment, and more specifically the exercise of balancing the particular degree of probative value disclosed by the documents against the unfairness which would result if the evidence were admitted, is a matter for the Trial Chamber which will not be interfered with on appeal in the absence of convincing demonstration of error. No such demonstration has been made. 290. The Prosecution also specifically challenged the Trial Chamber's conclusion that the trial had reached such a stage that the evidence should not be admitted.452 The stage in the trial at which the evidence is sought to be adduced and the potential delay that will be caused to the trial are matters highly relevant to the fairness to the accused of admission of fresh evidence. This consideration extends not only to Delalic as the accused against whom the evidence was sought to be admitted, but also the three co-accused whose trial would be equally delayed for reasons unrelated to themselves. The Appeals Chamber does not understand the Trial Chamber to have taken the stage of the trial into account in any sense other than its impact on the fairness of the trial of the accused, and, in the circumstances, the Appeals Chamber regards the Trial Chamber as having been fully justified in taking the very late stage of the trial into account.

The Prosecution sought to have this evidence admitted not only after the close of its own case, but well after the close of the defence case of Delalic and only very shortly before the close of the case of the last accused. The Prosecution contends that "none of the accused objected to the potential presentation of the evidence of Mr Chambers."453 This assertion is clearly incorrect. At the hearing of oral submissions on whether the evidence could be admitted as rebuttal or fresh evidence, counsel for Delalic stated:

> His Honour Karibi-Whyte has said what I was thinking and that is that we're in the second year of this trial, and, perhaps, the third or fourth year of investigations concerning these matters. And the Prosecution, despite what they say, despite what reasons they may offer, I think is a matter of law. *It's unfair at this point to produce documents in June, 1998.*

The defence for Delalic also expressed its opposition to the presentation of the fresh evidence in its written response to the request to reopen.

291. The Prosecution also argued that the Trial Chamber was wrong in its finding that the admission of the evidence would cause three months' delay:

> The Prosecutor calculated that the three remaining proposed witnesses would take, on direct examination, less than four hours. It is respectfully submitted that the Trial Chamber's estimation that this would likely postpone the trial for three months is not borne out, given that there were only three witnesses and approximately 22 documents, some only supporting documents for the search warrant.

This submission is disingenuous. The time which the Trial Chamber needed to take into account in determining the effect on the accused was not limited to the time which it may take to examine the three witnesses. The Trial Chamber found that, given the nature of the documents, it was likely that the testimony of further witnesses would be required to authenticate the relevant documents. It would also be necessary to allow for the defence to call appropriate witnesses in response. Further, as noted by the Trial Chamber, the Prosecution had stated in its Request to Reopen, after acknowledging that the defence may need to call witnesses:

> In addition, the Prosecution would seek leave to call witnesses to rebut the testimony of those brought by the Defence.

292. In light of these considerations, it was open to the Trial Chamber — which, having presided over the trial which had already taken over eighteen months, was well-placed to assess the time required taking into account practical considerations such as temporary

witness unavailability — to conclude that the likely delay would be up to three months. In light of this finding, it is apparent that the Trial Chamber considered that the admission of the evidence would create a sufficiently adverse effect on the fairness of the trial of all of the accused, that it outweighed the limited probative value of the evidence. As a secondary matter, it is also apparent that the Trial Chamber was concerned to fulfill its obligation under Article 20 of the Statute to ensure the trial was expeditious. In light of these considerations, the decision not to exercise its discretion to grant the application was open to the Trial Chamber.

293. For the above reasons, the Appeals Chamber finds that the Prosecution has not demonstrated that the Trial Chamber committed any error in the exercise of its discretion. This aspect of this ground of appeal relating to the exclusion of evidence by the Trial Chamber is therefore also dismissed, and with it this ground of appeal in its entirety.

. Delic's Acquittal under Article 7(3) 4. The Prosecution's fifth ground of appeal alleges that the Trial Chamber "erred when it decided... that Hazim Delic was not a 'superior' in the Celebici Prison Camp for the purposes of ascribing criminal responsibility to him under Article 7(3) of the Statute." The Prosecution submits that the Trial Chamber applied the wrong legal test when it held that "the perpetrator of the underlying offence must be the *subordinate* of the person of higher rank" and that "a subordinate unit of the superior or commander is a *sine qua non* for superior responsibility." The Prosecution also submits, apparently in the alternative, that, even if the test formulated by the Trial Chamber for determining who is a superior for the purposes of Article 7(3) was correct, it misapplied the test in this case. The Prosecution refers to the Trial Chamber's findings, including its finding that Delic was the "deputy commander" of the camp, to say that he should have been found to be a superior. Because, it is said, the Trial Chamber's findings also establish that he was aware of the offences of subordinates, and that he failed to prevent or punish them, the Appeals Chamber should find Delic guilty under Article 7(3) on counts 13, 14, 33, 34, 38, 39, 44, 45, 46 and 47.

295. In support of this ground, the Prosecution reiterates its theory that command responsibility entails a superior-subordinate relationship in which the superior effectively controls the subordinate, in the sense that the superior possesses the material ability to prevent or punish the offences and that "[s]uch control can be manifest in powers of influence which permit the superior to intervene". It also argues that the Trial Chamber erred in requiring Delic to be part of the chain of command, as the correct test is whether he has suffi-

cient control, influence, or authority to prevent or punish. If, as the Trial Chamber found, *de facto* control is sufficient in this context, it should assess in each case whether an accused has *de facto* powers or control to prevent or punish.

296. Delic responds that among the elements required for finding a person liable under the doctrine of command responsibility are the requirement of "a hierarchy in which superiors are authorized to control their subordinates to a degree that the superior is responsible for the actions of his subordinates" and that the superior must be "vested with authority to control his subordinates." In the military, the chain of command is a hierarchy of commanders, with deputy commanders being outside this chain of command.

297. Turning to the Trial Chamber's findings on the question of Delic's liability under Article 7(3), it clearly found that Delic held the position of "deputy commander" of the Celebici camp. However, it also found that this was "not dispositive of Delic's status" as the real issue before the Trial Chamber was:

[w]hether the accused had the power to issue orders to subordinates and to prevent or punish the criminal acts of his subordinates, thus placing him within the chain of command. In order to do so the Trial Chamber must look to the actual authority of Hazim Delic as evidenced by his acts in the Celebici prison camp.

298. The Chamber proceeded to consider evidence of the degree of actual authority wielded by Delic in the camp, and concluded that:

[...] this evidence is indicative of *a degree of influence* Hazim Delic had in the Celebici prison-camp on some occasions, in the criminal mistreatment of detainees. However, this influence could be attributable to the guards' fear of an intimidating and morally delinquent individual who was the instigator of and a participant in the mistreatment of detainees, and *is not, on the facts before the Trial Chamber, of itself indicative of the superior authority of. Delic sufficient to attribute superior responsibility to him.*

Having examined more evidence, it further found:

This evidence indicates that Hazim Delic was tasked with assisting Zradvko Mucic by organising and arranging for the daily activities in the Celebici prison-camp. However, it cannot be said to indicate that he had actual command authority in the sense that he could issue orders and punish and prevent the criminal acts of subordinates.

299. The Trial Chamber therefore concluded that, despite Delic's position of deputy commander of the camp, he did not exercise actual authority in the sense of having powers to prevent or punish and therefore was not a superior or commander of the perpetrators of the relevant offences in the sense required by Article 7(3).

300. The Appeals Chamber has already rejected, in its discussion of the Prosecution's second ground of appeal, the Prosecution argument that "substantial influence" is a sufficient measure of "control" for the imposition of liability under Article 7(3). It need only therefore confirm that the Trial Chamber's finding that Delic had powers of influence was not of itself a sufficient basis on which to find him a superior if it was not established beyond reasonable doubt by the evidence that he actually had the ability to exercise effective control over the relevant perpetrators.

301. The remaining issue as to the applicable law raised by the Prosecution in relation to this ground which has not previously been considered is its contention that the Trial Chamber erred because it required Delic to be part of the chain of command and, more generally, it required the perpetrators of the underlying offences to be his "subordinates" before liability under Article 7(3) could be imposed.

302. It is beyond question that the Trial Chamber considered Article 7(3) to impose a requirement that there be a superior with a corresponding subordinate. The Prosecution itself submits that one of the three requirements under Article 7(3) is that of a superior-subordinate relationship. There is therefore a certain difficulty in comprehending the Prosecution submission that the Trial Chamber erred in law in requiring the perpetrator of the underlying offence to be a subordinate of the person of higher rank. The Trial Chamber clearly did understand the relationship of subordination to encompass indirect and informal relationships, as is apparent from its acceptance of the concepts of civilian superiors and *de facto* authority, to which the Appeals Chamber has referred in its discussion of the issue in relation to the Prosecution's second ground of appeal.

303. The Appeals Chamber understands the necessity to prove that the perpetrator was the "subordinate" of the accused, not to import a requirement of *direct or formal* subordination but to mean that the relevant accused is, by virtue of his or her position, senior in some sort of formal or informal hierarchy to the perpetrator. The ability to exercise effective control in the sense of a material power to prevent or punish, which the Appeals Chamber considers to be a minimum requirement for the recognition of the superior-subordinate relationship, will almost invariably not be satisfied unless such a relationship of subordination exists. However,

it is possible to imagine scenarios in which one of two persons of equal status or rank — such as two soldiers or two civilian prison guards — could in fact exercise "effective control" over the other at least in the sense of a purely practical ability to prevent the conduct of the other by, for example, force of personality or physical strength. The Appeals Chamber does not consider the doctrine of command responsibility — which developed with an emphasis on persons who, by virtue of the position which they occupy, have authority over others — as having been intended to impose criminal liability on persons for the acts of other persons of completely equal status.

304. The Appeals Chamber acknowledges that the Trial Chamber's references to the absence of evidence that Delic "lay within" or was "part of" the chain of command may, if taken in isolation, be open to the interpretation that the Trial Chamber believed Article 7(3) to require the accused to have a formal position in a formal hierarchy which directly links him to a subordinate who also holds a formal position within that hierarchy. Given that it has been accepted that the law relating to command responsibility recognises not only civilian superiors, who may not be in any such formal chain of command, and de facto authority, for which no formal appointment is required, the law does not allow for such an interpretation. However, when read in the context of the rest of the Trial Chamber's Judgement, the Appeals Chamber is satisfied that the Trial Chamber was not in fact imposing the requirement of such a formalised position in a formal chain of command, as opposed to requiring that there be proof that Delic was a superior in the sense of having the material ability to prevent or punish the acts of persons subordinate to him. This is apparent from, for example, the Trial Chamber's references to the sufficiency of indirect control (where it amounts to effective control) and its acceptance of de facto authority, to which reference has already been made by the Appeals Chamber in the context of the Prosecution's second ground of appeal.

305. However, the Prosecution has also submitted that, "even on the Trial Chamber's test for the superior-subordinate relationship, Delic should have been convicted as the Trial Chamber misapplied this test to its own findings of fact". The Prosecution, based on its understanding that the Trial Chamber required proof that Delic was exercising authority within a formal chain of command, contends that the facts found by the Trial Chamber establish this. As indicated above, the Appeals Chamber considers that the Trial Chamber essentially applied the correct test — whether Delic exercised effective control in having the material ability to prevent or punish crimes committed by subordinates

— and did not require him to have a formalised position in a direct chain of command over the subordinates. However, the Appeals Chamber will consider the Trial Chamber findings which are relied on by the Prosecution to determine whether those findings must have compelled a conclusion that either standard was satisfied. As this aspect of the appeal involves an allegation that the Trial Chamber erred in its findings of fact, the Prosecution must establish that the conclusion reached by the Trial Chamber (that Delic did not exercise superior authority) was one which no reasonable tribunal of fact could have reached. In order to succeed on its submission that the Appeals Chamber should substitute its own finding for that of the Trial Chamber — that is, that Delic did in fact exercise command responsibility and enter convictions accordingly — it is necessary for the Prosecution to establish that this finding is the only reasonable finding available on the evidence. This standard was acknowledged by the Prosecution.

306. The Prosecution first relies on the Trial Chamber's finding that Delic was deputy commander of the camp. The Appeals Chamber accepts the Trial Chamber's view that this title or position is not dispositive of the issue and that it is necessary to look to whether there was evidence of actual authority or control exercised by Delic. For the same reason, the fact that the detainees regarded him as the deputy commander, and as a person with influence over the guards, is not conclusive evidence of his actual authority.

307. The Prosecution identifies four other findings of the Trial Chamber which it says demonstrate such actual control. The Appeals Chamber considers them in turn.

308. The Trial Chamber referred to testimony of four witnesses to the effect that the guards feared Delic and that he occasionally criticised them severely. This evidence appeared to be accepted by the Trial Chamber, but it was interpreted by the Trial Chamber as showing a "degree of influence" which could be "attributable to the guards' fear of an intimidating and morally delinquent individual" rather than as unambiguous evidence of superior authority. The Appeals Chamber considers that this interpretation of this piece of evidence was open to the Trial Chamber, who, it must be remembered, heard the witnesses and the totality of the evidence itself. There was certainly nothing submitted by the Prosecution which would demonstrate that this conclusion was so unreasonable that no reasonable tribunal of fact could have reached it.

309. The Prosecution also referred to evidence that Delic had ordered the beating of detainees on certain occasions. As the Prosecution itself acknowledges, the

Trial Chamber did not find beyond reasonable doubt that Delic did in fact order guards to conduct the series of beatings which was the subject of the evidence referred to in paragraph 804 of the Trial Judgement. The Trial Chamber referred to the evidence of certain witnesses and concluded that the evidence "*suggests* that Mr. Delic conducted a vindictive beating of the people from Bradina on one particular day and then told at least one other guard, Mr. Landzo to continue this beating."

However, it is *not proven* that the beatings that followed from that day or [*sic*] were 'ordered' by Mr. Delic". In relation to the second occasion referred to in paragraph 805 of the Judgement, the Trial Chamber only referred to the Prosecution allegation of Delic ordering a beating and stated:

> Witness F and Mirko Dordic testified to this incident and indicated that Delic "ordered" or was "commanding" the guards in this collective beating.

The Trial Chamber did not state whether it accepted this evidence, and it made no finding as to whether Delic actually ordered the beating or not. Despite the Prosecution's apparent suggestion that it is enough that "the Trial Chamber made no finding that this evidence was unreliable", this is not a sufficient basis for the Appeals Chamber to take it as a finding by the Trial Chamber that the ordering of the beating was proved beyond reasonable doubt. The Appeals Chamber therefore cannot identify from the matters referred to by the Prosecution any unambiguous findings that it was proven beyond reasonable doubt that Delic ordered guards to mistreat detainees.

310. The Prosecution also refers to the finding that Delic "was tasked with assisting Zdravko Mucic by organising and arranging for the daily activities in the camp." A finding as to such a responsibility for organising and arranging activities in the camp, while potentially demonstrating that Delic had some seniority within the camp, actually provides no information at all as to whether he had authority or effective control over the guards within the camp who were the perpetrators of the offences for which it is sought to make Delic responsible. The Appeals Chamber therefore agrees with the Trial Chamber that it was open to regard this evidence as inconclusive.

311. Finally, the Prosecution refers to evidence given by Delic's co-accused Landzo that he "carried out all of [Delic's] orders out of fear and also because I believed I had to carry [*sic*] execute them". While the Trial Chamber certainly considered this evidence, it did not accept it, as it found that Landzo was not a credible witness and that his evidence could not be relied on unless supported by other evidence. It did not identify any other evidence which it regarded as constituting such support.

312. There were therefore a number of problems with the relevance of the findings or the quality of the underlying evidence relied on by the Prosecution. The weakness of such evidence as the foundation of any finding *beyond reasonable doubt* that Delic exercised superior authority was recognised by the Trial Chamber, which concluded that all this evidence was "indicative of a degree of influence Hazim Delic had in the Celebici prison-camp on some occasions, in the criminal mistreatment of detainees", but that it "is not, on the facts before this Trial Chamber, of itself indicative of the superior authority of Delic sufficient to attribute superior responsibility to him". The Appeals Chamber does not see anything in this conclusion which suggests it is unreasonable, and certainly not that it is so unreasonable that no reasonable tribunal of fact could reach it.

313. Although this conclusion effectively disposes of this ground of appeal, it is necessary to make an observation in relation to one final issue. The Prosecution submitted that, should it be accepted that the Trial Chamber should have found that Delic did in fact exercise superior authority over the guards in the camp, it would then be possible to reverse his acquittals on the basis of the findings in the Trial Judgement. In particular, it submits that it is established that Delic knew or had reason to know on the following basis:

> It cannot seriously be disputed that Delic knew of the crimes being committed in the camp generally. The Trial Chamber said that "The crimes committed in the Celebici prison-camp were so frequent and notorious that there is no way that *Mr. Mucic* could not have known or heard about them." There is also no way that Delic could not have known about them, given that he was himself convicted for directly participating in them, and was involved in the operation of the camp on a daily basis.

It must first be observed that, contrary to this submission, there was *no* finding that Delic directly participated in all of the crimes for which he is sought to be made responsible. Secondly, it cannot be accepted that a finding by the Trial Chamber that a co-accused who was commander of the camp must have known of the crimes committed in the camp can be taken, by some kind of imputation, as a finding beyond reasonable doubt that *Delic* knew or had reason to know of the crimes for which the Prosecution seeks to have convictions entered. The Trial Judgement contains no findings as to Delic's state of knowledge in relation to many of the crimes for which the Prosecution seek a reversal of the acquittal. It is undisputed that command responsibility does not impose strict liability on a superior for the offences of subordinates. Thus, had the Appeals Chamber accepted that the only reasonable conclusion on the evidence was that Delic was a superior, the question of whether he knew or had reason to know of the relevant offences would have remained unresolved, and it would in theory have been necessary to remit the matter to a Trial Chamber for consideration.

314. For the foregoing reasons, the Appeals Chamber dismisses this ground of appeal.

V. UNLAWFUL CONFINEMENT OF CIVILIANS

A. Introduction

315. Count 48 of the Indictment charged Mucic, Delic and Delalic with individual participation in, and superior responsibility for, the unlawful confinement of numerous civilians in the Celebici camp. The offence of unlawful confinement of civilians is punishable under Article 2(g) of the Statute as a grave breach of the Geneva Conventions. Count 48 provided:

> Between May and October 1992, Zejnil DELALIC, Zdravko MUCIC, and Hazim DELIC participated in the unlawful confinement of numerous civilians at Celebici camp. Zejnil DELALIC, Zdravko MUCIC, and Hazim DELIC also knew or had reason to know that persons in positions of subordinate authority to them were about to commit those acts resulting in the unlawful confinement of civilians, or had already committed those acts, and failed either to take the necessary and reasonable steps to prevent those acts or to punish the perpetrators after the acts had been committed. By their acts and omissions, Zejnil DELALIC, Zdravko MUCIC, and Hazim DELIC are responsible for:

> Count 48. A Grave Breach punishable under Article 2(g) (unlawful confinement of civilians) of the Statute of the Tribunal.

316. The Trial Chamber found Mucic guilty of unlawful confinement of civilians as charged in count 48 under both Articles 7(1) and 7(3) of the Statute. It found Delalic and Delic not guilty under this count. The Prosecution appeals against these acquittals. The Prosecution contends in its third ground of appeal that:

> The Trial Chamber erred when it decided in paragraphs 1124-1144 that Zejnil Delalic was not guilty of the unlawful confinement of civilians as charged in count 48 of the Indictment.

> The Prosecution's sixth ground of appeal is that:

> The Trial Chamber erred when it decided in paragraphs 1125-1144 that Hazim Delic was not guilty

of the unlawful confinement of civilians as charged in count 48 of the Indictment.

317. The Prosecution contends that the Trial Chamber applied the wrong legal principle to determine the responsibility of Delalic and Delic for the unlawful confinement of the civilians in the Celebici camp. In the case of Delalic, the Prosecution contends that the Trial Chamber also failed to apply correctly the law relating to aiding and abetting.

318. Mucic appeals against his conviction. He contends in his twelfth ground of appeal that:

> The Trial Chamber erred in fact and law in finding that the detainees, or any of them, within the Celebici camp were unlawfully detained [...]

Mucic also challenges the Trial Chamber's findings that he had the requisite *mens rea* for the offence and that any acts or omissions by him were sufficient to constitute the *actus reus* for the offence.

319. These grounds of appeal, although dealing with different matters, touch on a number of issues which are common to each ground. It is convenient to discuss two of these common legal issues before turning to the specific issues raised discretely by each ground of appeal:

> (i) the legal standard for determining what constitutes the unlawful confinement of civilians; and

> (ii) whether the Trial Chamber was correct in its conclusion that some of the civilians in the Celebici camp were unlawfully detained.

(i) **The unlawful confinement of civilians** 320. The offence of unlawful confinement of a civilian, a grave breach of the Geneva Conventions which is recognised under Article 2(g) of the Statute of the Tribunal, is not further defined in the Statute. As found by the Trial Chamber, however, clear guidance can be found in the provisions of Geneva Convention IV. The Trial Chamber found that the confinement of civilians during armed conflict may be permissible in limited cases, but will be unlawful if the detaining party does not comply with the provisions of Article 42 of Geneva Convention IV, which states:

> The internment or placing in assigned residence of protected persons may be ordered only if the security of the Detaining Power makes it absolutely necessary. If any person, acting through the representatives of the Protecting Power, voluntarily demands internment, and if his situation renders this step necessary, he shall be interned by the Power in whose hands he may be.

Thus the involuntary confinement of a civilian where the security of the Detaining Power does not make this absolutely necessary will be unlawful. Further, an initially lawful internment clearly becomes unlawful if the detaining party does not respect the basic procedural rights of the detained persons and does not establish an appropriate court or administrative board as prescribed in Article 43 of Geneva Convention IV. That article provides:

> Any protected person who has been interned or placed in assigned residence shall be entitled to have such action reconsidered as soon as possible by an appropriate court or administrative board designated by the Detaining Power for that purpose. If the internment or placing in assigned residence is maintained, the court or administrative board shall periodically, and at least twice yearly, give consideration to his or her case, with a view to the favourable amendment of the initial decision, if circumstances permit.

> Unless the protected persons concerned object, the Detaining Power shall, as rapidly as possible, give the Protecting Power the names of any protected persons who have been interned or subjected to assigned residence, or have been released from internment or assigned residence. The decisions of the courts or boards mentioned in the first paragraph of the present Article shall also, subject to the same conditions, be notified as rapidly as possible to the Protecting Power.

321. In its consideration of the law relating to the offence of unlawful confinement, the Trial Chamber also referred to Article 5 of Geneva Convention IV, which imposes certain restrictions on the protections which may be enjoyed by certain individuals under the Convention. It provides, in relevant part:

> Where, in the territory of a Party to the conflict, the latter is satisfied that an individual protected person is *definitely suspected of or engaged in activities hostile to the security of the State*, such individual person shall not be entitled to claim such rights and privileges under the present Convention as would, if exercised in the favour of such individual person, be prejudicial to the security of such State.
> [...]

> In each case, such persons shall nevertheless be treated with humanity, and, in case of trial, shall not be deprived of the rights of fair and regular trial prescribed by the present Convention. They shall also be granted the full rights and privileges of a protected person under the present Convention at the earliest date consistent with the security of the State or Occupying Power, as the case may be.

This provision reinforces the principle behind Article 42, that restrictions on the rights of civilian protected persons, such as deprivation of their liberty by confinement, are permissible only where there are reasonable grounds to believe that the security of the State is at risk.

322. The Appeals Chamber agrees with the Trial Chamber that the exceptional measure of confinement of a civilian will be lawful only in the conditions prescribed by Article 42, and where the provisions of Article 43 are complied with. Thus the detention or confinement of civilians will be unlawful in the following two circumstances:

> (i) when a civilian or civilians have been detained in contravention of Article 42 of Geneva Convention IV, *i.e.* they are detained without reasonable grounds to believe that the security of the Detaining Power makes it absolutely necessary; and

> (ii) where the procedural safeguards required by Article 43 of Geneva Convention IV are not complied with in respect of detained civilians, even where their initial detention may have been justified.

(ii) Was the confinement of the Celebici camp detainees unlawful? 323. As stated above, the Trial Chamber found that the persons detained in the Celebici camp were civilian protected persons for the purposes of Article 4 of Geneva Convention IV. The Trial Chamber accepted evidence that indicated that a number of the civilians in the camp were in possession of weapons at the time of their capture, but refrained from making any finding as to whether the detaining power could legitimately have formed the view that the detention of this category of persons was necessary for the security of that power. However, the Trial Chamber also found that the confinement of a significant number of civilians in the camp could not be justified by any means. Even taking into account the measure of discretion which should be afforded to the detaining power in assessing what may be detrimental to its own security, several of the detained civilians could not reasonably have been considered to pose any sufficiently serious danger as to warrant their detention. The Trial Chamber specifically accepted the evidence of a number of witnesses who had testified that they had not participated in any military activity or even been politically active, including a 42-year old mother of two children. It concluded that at least this category of people were detained in the camp although there existed no serious and legitimate reason to conclude that they seriously prejudiced the security of the detaining party, which indicated that the detention was a collective measure aimed at a specific group of persons, based mainly on their ethnic background.

324. Mucic argues in relation to his ground of appeal, and Delic and Delalic argue in response to the Prosecution's ground of appeal, that the Prosecution failed to prove beyond reasonable doubt that the persons confined in the Celebici camp were unlawfully detained. They reiterate their submission that the detainees were not in fact protected persons, a submission which the Appeals Chamber is rejecting in relation to the ground of appeal based on that argument.

325. The Prosecution responds that the findings of the Trial Chamber that the victims were unlawfully detained must stand unless the accused show that those findings were unreasonable in the sense that no reasonable person could have reached them.

326. Delalic contends that since "the Trial Chamber, in determining that they [the civilians] were protected persons, found that they were not loyal to [...] Bosnia and Herzegovina, then they are virtually *ipso facto* security risks to the Government in that they are supporting the rebel forces". He explains the detention of persons who may not have borne arms on the basis that "if not engaged in actual fighting, then they are certainly in a position to provide food, clothing, shelter and information to those who are".

327. In the Appeals Chamber's view, there is no necessary inconsistency between the Trial Chamber's finding that the Bosnian Serbs were regarded by the Bosnian authorities as belonging to the opposing party in an armed conflict and the finding that some of them could not reasonably be regarded as presenting a threat to the detaining power's security. To hold the contrary would suggest that, whenever the armed forces of a State are engaged in armed conflict, the *entire* civilian population of that State is necessarily a threat to security and therefore may be detained. It is perfectly clear from the provisions of Geneva Convention IV referred to above that there is no such blanket power to detain the entire civilian population of a party to the conflict in such circumstances, but that there must be an assessment that each civilian taken into detention poses a *particular risk* to the security of the State. This is reflected in the ICRC Commentary to Article 42 of Geneva Convention IV:

> [...] the mere fact that a person is a subject of an enemy Power cannot be considered as threatening the security of the country where he is living; it is not therefore a valid reason for interning him or placing him in assigned residence.

Thus the Appeals Chamber agrees with the conclusion reached by the Trial Chamber that "the mere fact that a person is a national of, or aligned with, an enemy party cannot be considered as threatening the security

of the opposing party where he is living, and is not, therefore, a valid reason for interning him."

328. It was contended by Delic that detention in the present case was justified under international law because "[t]he government is clearly entitled to some reasonable time to determine which of the detainees is a danger to the State's security". Although the Appeals Chamber accepts this proposition, it does not share the view apparently taken by Delic as to what is a "reasonable time" for this purpose. The reasonableness of this period is *not* a matter solely to be assessed by the detaining power. The Appeals Chamber recalls that Article 43 of Geneva Convention IV provides that the decision to take measures of detention against civilians must be "reconsidered *as soon as possible* by an appropriate court or administrative board."520 Read in this light, the reasonable time which is to be afforded to a detaining power to ascertain whether detained civilians pose a security risk must be the *minimum* time necessary to make enquiries to determine whether a view that they pose a security risk has any objective foundation such that it would found a "definite suspicion" of the nature referred to in Article 5 of Geneva Convention IV. Although the Trial Chamber made no express finding upon this issue, the Appeals Chamber is satisfied that the only reasonable finding upon the evidence is that the civilians detained in the Celebici camp had been detained for longer than such a minimum time.

329. The Trial Chamber found that a Military Investigative Commission for the crimes allegedly committed by the persons confined in the Celebici camp was established, but that this Commission did not meet the requirements of Article 43 of Geneva Convention IV as it did not have the necessary power to decide finally on the release of prisoners whose detention could not be considered as justified for any serious reason. There is therefore nothing in the activities of the Commission which could justify the continued detention of detainees in respect of whom there was no reason to categorise as a security risk. Indeed, it appears to have recommended the release of several of the Celebici camp detainees, albeit without result. Delic submits that "the government had the right to continue the confinement until it determined that the State's security would not be harmed by release of the detainees." This submission, which carries the implication that civilian detainees may be considered a risk to security which makes their detention absolutely necessary until proved otherwise, completely reverses the onus of justifying detention of civilians. It is upon the detaining power to establish that the particular civilian does pose such a risk to its security that he must be detained, and the obligation lies on it to release the civilian if there is inadequate foundation for such a view.

330. The Trial Chamber, as the trier of facts, is in the best position to assess and weigh the evidence before it, and the Appeals Chamber gives a margin of deference to a Trial Chamber's evaluation of the evidence and findings of facts. Nothing put to the Appeals Chamber indicates that there is anything unreasonable in the relevant sense in the Trial Chamber's findings as to the unlawful nature of the confinement of a number of civilians in the Celebici camp. As observed in the ICRC Commentary, the measure of confinement of civilians is an "exceptionally severe" measure, and it is for that reason that the threshold for its imposition is high — it must, on the express terms of Article 42, be "absolutely necessary". It was open to the Trial Chamber to accept the evidence of a number of witnesses that they had not borne arms, nor been active in political or any other activity which would give rise to a legitimate concern that they posed a security risk. The Appeals Chamber is also not satisfied that the Trial Chamber erred in its conclusion that, even if it were to accept that the initial confinement of the individuals detained in the Celebici prison-camp was lawful, the continuing confinement of these civilians was in violation of international humanitarian law, as the detainees were not granted the procedural rights required by article 43 of Geneva Convention IV.

B. The Prosecution appeals

331. As stated above, the Prosecution claims that the Trial Chamber erred in acquitting Delalic of both direct responsibility under Article 7(1) and superior responsibility under Article 7(3) for the offence of unlawful confinement.

332. The Prosecution requests the Appeals Chamber to reverse the Trial Chamber's acquittal of Delalic and Mucic on count 48, and substitute a verdict of guilty for this count. Delalic and Delic respond that their acquittals on this count were correct in law and should not be disturbed.

1. Article 7(3) Liability 333. The Prosecution argues as part of the third ground of appeal that the Trial Chamber erred in finding that it was not proved that Delalic had superior authority in connection with the unlawful confinement of civilians, and relies for support on its arguments submitted in relation to its second ground of appeal, without more. In relation to the sixth ground of appeal, the Prosecution contends that the Trial Chamber erred in finding that Delic did not have superior responsibility for the unlawful confinement of civilians.

334. The Trial Chamber found that:

Zejnil Delalic and Hazim Delic have respectively been found not to have exercised superior authority over the Celebici prison-camp. For this reason, the Trial Chamber finds that these two accused cannot be held criminally liable as superiors, pursuant to Article 7(3) of the Statute, for the unlawful confinement of civilians in the Celebici prison-camp.

The resolution of this aspect of these grounds therefore rests upon the resolution of the Prosecution's second and fifth grounds of appeal, which challenged the Trial Chamber's finding that Delalic and Delic did not exercise superior authority under Article 7(3) of the Statute. The Appeals Chamber has dismissed those grounds of appeal, with the result that the Trial Chamber's determination that Delalic and Delic were not superiors for the purposes of Article 7(3) of the Statute remains. The present grounds of appeal therefore cannot succeed insofar as they relate to Delalic and Delic's liability for the unlawful confinement of civilians pursuant to Article 7(3) of the Statute.

2. Article 7(1) Liability 335. The Prosecution contends that the Trial Chamber erred in law in the principles it applied in considering when an accused can be held responsible under Article 7 (1) for unlawful confinement of civilians. The Prosecution argues that, had the Trial Chamber applied the correct legal principles in regard to Article 7(1) to the facts it had found, Delalic and Delic would have been liable under Article 7(1) for aiding and abetting in the commission of the unlawful confinement of civilians. It is submitted that the Trial Chamber's findings demonstrate that Delalic and Delic knew that civilians were unlawfully confined in the camp and consciously participated in their continued detention, and that this is sufficient to found their personal liability for the offence.

336. As discussed above, the Trial Chamber found that civilians are unlawfully confined where they are detained in contravention of Articles 42 and 43 of Geneva Convention IV. In relation to the nature of the individual participation in the unlawful confinement which will render an individual personally liable for the offence of unlawful confinement of civilians under Article 2(g) of the Statute, the Trial Chamber, having found that Delalic and Delic did not exercise superior responsibility over the camp, held:

Furthermore, on the basis of these findings, the Trial Chamber must conclude that the Prosecution has failed to demonstrate that Zejnil Delalic and Hazim Delic were in a position to affect the continued detention of civilians in the Celebici prison-camp. In these circumstances, Zejnil Delalic and Hazim Delic cannot be deemed to have participated in this offence. Accordingly, the Trial Chamber finds that Zejnil Delalic and Hazim Delic are not guilty of the unlawful confinement of civilians, as charged in count 48 of the Indictment.

337. On the basis of the italicised portion of the above passage, the Prosecution interprets the Trial Chamber as having applied a test which requires proof of the exercise of superior authority under Article 7(3) of the Statute before an individual could be held responsible under Article 7(1) of the Statute for the offence of unlawful confinement. More generally, the Prosecution submits that the Trial Chamber erred in finding that, as a matter of law, an accused cannot be criminally liable under Article 7(1) for the unlawful confinement of civilians unless that person was "in a position to affect the continued detention of civilians". The Prosecution observes that individual criminal liability extends to any person who committed an offence in the terms of Article 7(1).

338. In relation to the contention that the Trial Chamber found that an accused can be liable under Article 7(1) for the offence of unlawful confinement only if it is proved that he exercises superior authority under Article 7(3), there is some question as to whether the Trial Chamber in fact made such a legal finding. The Trial Chamber's statement that, "on the basis of" its findings that Delalic and Delic could not be held criminally liable under Article 7(3) of the Statute, it "must conclude" that there had been a failure to prove that they had been in a position to affect the continued detention of the civilians in the camp could be interpreted as suggesting that the Trial Chamber believed that, as a *legal* matter, there could be no liability for unlawful confinement under Article 7(1) without superior responsibility under Article 7(3) being established. Such a legal interpretation is clearly incorrect, as it entwines two types of liability, liability under Article 7(1) and liability under Article 7(3). As emphasised by the Secretary-General's Report, the two liabilities are different in nature. Liability under Article 7(1) applies to direct perpetrators of crimes and to accomplices. Article 7(3) applies to persons exercising command or superior responsibility. As has already been acknowledged by the Appeals Chamber in another context, these principles are quite separate and neither is dependent in law upon the other. In the *Aleksovski* Appeal Judgement, the Appeals Chamber rejected a Trial Chamber statement, made in relation to the offence of outrages of personal dignity consisting of the use of detainees for forced labour and as human shields, that the accused "cannot be held responsible under Article 7(1) in circumstances where he does not have direct authority over the main perpetrators of the crimes". There is no reason to believe that, in the context of the offence of unlawful confinement, there would be any special requirement that

a position of superior authority be proved before liability under Article 7(1) could be recognised.

339. However, the Appeals Chamber is not satisfied that this is what the Trial Chamber in fact held. The reference to its findings on the issue of superior authority when concluding that, "[i]n these circumstances, Zejnil Delalic and Hazim Delic cannot be deemed to have participated in this offence" suggests that the Trial Chamber was referring not to its *legal* conclusion that the two accused were not superiors for the purposes of Article 7(3), but to the previous *factual findings* that it had made in that context, which were also relevant to the issue of their individual responsibility for the offence of unlawful confinement. Whether the Trial Chamber was unreasonable in relying on those findings to conclude that Delalic and Delic should be acquitted of the offence under Article 7(1) is a separate issue which is discussed below.

340. The Prosecution also challenges the Trial Chamber's apparent conclusion that, to be responsible for this offence under Article 7(1), the perpetrator must be "in a position to affect the continued detention" of the relevant civilians. Responsibility may be attributed if the accused falls within the terms of Article 7(1) of the Statute, which provides that:

> A person who planned, instigated, ordered, committed or otherwise aided and abetted in the planning, preparation or execution of a crime referred to in articles 2 to 5 of the present Statute, shall be individually responsible for the crime.

341. It is submitted that an accused can be liable under Article 7(1) for committing the crime of unlawful confinement of civilians even if the accused was not the person who could determine which victim would be detained, and whether particular victims would be released. The Prosecution proposes that, in order to establish criminal responsibility for *committing* the offence of unlawful confinement of civilians it is sufficient to prove (i) that civilians were unlawfully confined, (ii) knowledge that the civilians were being unlawfully confined and (iii) participation in the confinement of those persons. The Prosecution submits that, in relation to guards in a prison, the third matter "will be satisfied by showing that the duties of the guard were in themselves in execution or administration of the illegal system."

342. The Appeals Chamber is of the view that to establish that an individual has *committed* the offence of unlawful confinement, something more must be proved than mere knowing "participation" in a general system or operation pursuant to which civilians are confined. In the Appeals Chamber's view, the fact alone

of a role in some capacity, however junior, in maintaining a prison in which civilians are unlawfully detained is an inadequate basis on which to find primary criminal responsibility of the nature which is denoted by a finding that someone has *committed* a crime. Such responsibility is more properly allocated to those who are responsible for the detention in a more direct or complete sense, such as those who actually place an accused in detention without reasonable grounds to believe that he constitutes a security risk; or who, having some powers over the place of detention, accepts a civilian into detention without knowing that such grounds exist; or who, having power or authority to release detainees, fails to do so despite knowledge that no reasonable grounds for their detention exist, or that any such reasons have ceased to exist. In the case of prison guards who are employed or conscripted to supervise detainees, and have no role in the determination of who is detained or released, the Prosecution submits that the presence alone of the camp guards was the "most immediate obstacle to each detainee's liberty" and that the guard's presence in the camp in that capacity alone would therefore constitute commission by them of the crime of unlawful confinement. This, however, poses the question of what such a guard is expected to do under such circumstances. The implication from the Prosecution submissions is that such a guard must release the prisoners. The Appeals Chamber, however, does not accept that a guard's omission to take unauthorised steps to release prisoners will suffice to constitute the commission of the crime of unlawful confinement. The Appeals Chamber also finds it difficult to accept that such a guard must cease to supervise those detained in the camp to avoid such liability, particularly in light of the fact that among the detainees there may be persons who are lawfully confined because they genuinely do pose a threat to the security of the State.

343. It is not necessary for present purposes for the Appeals Chamber to attempt an exhaustive definition of the circumstances which will establish that the offence is *committed*, but it suffices to observe that such liability is reserved for persons responsible in a more direct or complete sense for the civilian's unlawful detention. Lesser degrees of directness of participation obviously remain relevant to liability as an accomplice or a participant in a joint criminal enterprise, which concepts are best understood by reference first to what will establish primary liability for an offence.

344. In relation to accomplice liability, the Prosecution contends that, "[i]n the case of the crime of unlawful confinement of civilians under Article 2(g) of the Statute, a person who, for instance, *instigates* or *aids*

and abets may not ever be in a position to affect the continued detention of the civilians concerned." The Prosecution also observes that many of the crimes within the Tribunal's jurisdiction may in practice be committed jointly by a number of persons if they have the requisite *mens rea* and that the crime of unlawful confinement is a clear example of this as "it was the various camp guards and administrators, acting jointly, who collectively ran the camp and kept the victims confined within it."

345. Although it did not explicitly discuss as a discrete legal matter the exact principles by which individuals will be held individually criminally responsible for the unlawful confinement of civilians, the Trial Chamber did, earlier in its Judgement, discuss the general principles relating to criminal responsibility under Article 7(1) of the Statute. It cited the following statement from the Trial Chamber in the *Tadic* Judgement which the *Celebici* Trial Chamber considered to state accurately "the scope of individual criminal responsibility under Article 7(1)":

> [...] the accused will be found criminally culpable for any conduct where it is determined that he knowingly participated in the commission of an offence that violates international humanitarian law and his participation directly and substantially affected the commission of that offence through supporting the actual commission before, during, or after the incident. He will also be responsible for all that naturally results from the commission of the act in question.

This statement, from its context in the *Tadic* Trial Judgement, although broadly expressed, appears to have been intended to refer to liability for aiding and abetting or all forms of accomplice liability rather than all forms of individual criminal responsibility under Article 7(1) including primary or direct responsibility. In the case of primary or direct responsibility, where the accused himself commits the relevant act or omission, the qualification that his participation must "directly and substantially affect the commission of the offence" is an unnecessary one. The Trial Chamber, in referring to the ability to "affect the continued detention" of the civilians, appears to have been providing a criterion to enable the identification of the person who could have a "direct and substantial effect" on the commission of unlawful confinement of civilians in the sense of the *Tadic* statement.

346. It may have been clearer had the Trial Chamber set out expressly its understanding of the relevant principles in relation to the establishment of primary or direct responsibility for the offence of unlawful confinement of civilians, in relation to which the general

principles of accomplice liability set out earlier in its Judgement would also be applied. However, the Appeals Chamber does not consider that these submissions establish that the Trial Chamber erred in stating that an accused must be in a position to affect the continued detention of the civilians if this is understood, as the Appeals Chamber does, to mean that they must have participated in some significant way in the continued detention of the civilians, whether to a degree which would establish primary responsibility, or to a degree necessary to establish liability as an accomplice or pursuant to a common plan. The particular submissions the Prosecution makes in support of its contention that Delalic and Delic should have been convicted under Article 7(1) for the offence are now considered.

(a) Delalic 347. The Prosecution alleges that Delalic should have been found guilty for aiding and abetting the offence of unlawful confinement. Delalic argues that the Indictment did not charge him with aiding and abetting in Count 48 and that, even if it were to be accepted that he was so charged, the evidence did not show beyond a reasonable doubt that he was guilty as an aider and abettor.

348. The Prosecution responds that Delalic was charged with aiding and abetting in Count 48 of the Indictment by the use of the word "participation". Delalic contends however that "when the Prosecutor intends to charge aiding and abetting it is done so specifically", and he advances some examples of other indictments before the Tribunal that charge aiding and abetting for the offence of unlawful confinement. Delalic refers to Articles 18(4) and 21(4)(a) of the Statute which require that the indictment contain "a concise statement of the facts and the crime or crimes with which the accused is charged under the Statute" and that an accused must be informed of the nature and cause of the charge against him.

349. The Appeals Chamber notes that the alleged offence of unlawful confinement is charged in count 48 of the Indictment as follows:

> Between May and October 1992, Zejnil DELALIC, Zdravko MUCIC, and Hazim DELIC *participated in* the unlawful confinement of numerous civilians at Celebici camp. Zejnil DELALIC, Zrdavko MUCIC, and Hazim DELIC also knew or had reason to know that persons in positions of subordinate authority to them were about to commit those acts resulting in the unlawful confinement of civilians, or had already committed those acts, and failed either to take the necessary and reasonable steps to prevent those acts or to punish the perpetrators after the acts had been committed. By their acts

and omissions, Zejnil DELALIC, Zdravko MUCIC, and Hazim DELIC are responsible for:

> Count 48. A Grave Breach punishable under Article 2(g) (unlawful confinement of civilians) of the Statute of the Tribunal.

Article 7 (1) does not contain the wording used in the Indictment of "participating", but the Prosecution contends that it is evident that a person can participate in a crime through any of the types of conduct referred to in that provision.

350. The Appeals Chamber notes that the language used in Count 48 could (and should) have been expressed with greater precision. Although the accused are clearly charged under both Article 7(1) and Article 7(3) of the Statute, no particular head of Article 7(1) is indicated. The Appeals Chamber has already referred to the difficulties which arise from the failure of the Prosecution to identify exactly the type of responsibility alleged against an accused, and has recommended that the Prosecution "indicate in relation to each individual count precisely and expressly the particular nature of the responsibility alleged". However, it was also accepted in that case that the general reference to the terms of Article 7(1) was, in that context, an adequate basis on which to find that the accused had been charged with aiding and abetting.

351. In relation to use of the word "participate" to describe forms of responsibility, the Appeals Chamber notes that the Report of the Secretary-General mentions the word "participate" in the context of individual criminal responsibility:

> The Secretary-General believes that all persons who participate in the planning, preparation or execution of serious violations of international humanitarian law in the former Yugoslavia contribute to the commission of the violation and are, therefore, individually responsible.

It is clear that Article 7 (1) of the Statute encompasses various modes of participation, some more direct than other. The word "participation" here is a broad enough term to encompass all forms of responsibility which are included within Article 7(1) of the Statute. Although greater specificity in drafting indictments is desirable, failure to identify expressly the exact mode of participation is not necessarily fatal to an indictment if it nevertheless makes clear to the accused the "nature and cause of the charge against him". There has been no suggestion that a complaint was made prior to the trial that Delalic did not know the case that he had to meet. It is too late to make the complaint now on appeal that the Indictment was inadequate to advise the accused that all such forms of responsibility were alleged. The use of the word "participate" is poor drafting, but it should have been understood here as including all forms of participation referred to in Article 7(1) given that superior responsibility was expressed to be an additional form of responsibility.

352. The Trial Chamber therefore correctly interpreted Count 48 of the Indictment and the supporting paragraph as charging the three accused generally with participation in the unlawful confinement of civilians pursuant to Article 7(1) of the Statute, as well as with responsibility as superiors pursuant to Article 7(3) of the Statute. The Trial Chamber had earlier defined aiding and abetting as:

> [including] all acts of assistance that lend encouragement or support to the perpetration of an offence and which are accompanied by the requisite *mens rea*. Subject to the caveat that it be found to have contributed to, or have had an effect on, the commission of the crime, the relevant act of assistance may be removed both in time and place from the actual commission of the offence.

The Prosecution does not challenge that definition. Subject to the observation that the acts of assistance, encouragement or support must have a substantial effect on the perpetration of the crime, the Appeals Chamber also accepts the statement as accurate.

353. As noted above, in its conclusions in relation to the liability of Delalic and Delic under Article 7(1) for the offence of unlawful confinement, the Trial Chamber referred to its earlier findings made in the context of its consideration of their liability as superiors pursuant to Article 7(3) of the Statute. Although those findings were being made for the primary purpose of determining whether superior responsibility was being exercised, it is clear that they involved a broad consideration by the Trial Chamber of the nature of the involvement of the two accused in the affairs of the Celebici camp. The Prosecution indeed contends that the findings made by the Trial Chamber provided an adequate basis on which to determine Delalic's liability for aiding and abetting.

354. The Trial Chamber considered the evidence in relation to the placing of civilians in detention at the camp, but it made no finding that Delalic participated in their arrest or in placing them in detention in the camp. The Prosecution advances no argument that the Trial Chamber erred in this respect.

355. However, the Prosecution argues that Delalic participated in the continued detention of civilians as an aider and abettor. The Trial Chamber found that there was "no evidence that the Celebici prison-camp

came under Delalic's authority by virtue of his appointment as co-ordinator". The Trial Chamber found that the primary responsibility of Delalic in his position as co-ordinator was to provide logistical support for the various formations of the armed forces; that these consisted of, inter alia, supplies of material, equipment, food, communications equipment, railroad access, transportation of refugees and the linking up of electricity grids.

These findings as to the scope of Delalic's role obviously supported its later conclusion that he was not in a position to affect the continued detention of the civilians at the Celebici camp.

356. The Prosecution, however, refers to two specific matters which it says constituted aiding and abetting by Delalic: his role in "publicly justifying and defending the purpose and legality of the camp", and his "participation in the classification and releasing of prisoners".

357. The Prosecution contends that the evidence before the Trial Chamber showed that Delalic was involved in the release of Doctor Gruba~ and Witness P in July 1992, and that he signed orders on 24 and 28 August 1992 for the classification of detainees and their release. However, the Trial Chamber explicitly found that:

> As co-ordinator, Zejnil Delalic had no authority to release prisoners.

The Trial Chamber found that the orders referred to by the Prosecution were not signed in Delalic's capacity as "co-ordinator", as all documents were signed "for" the Head of the Investigating Body of the War Presidency. He had no independent authority to do so.

358. The Appeals Chamber considers that this conclusion has not been shown to be so unreasonable that no reasonable trier of fact could have reached it. The Trial Chamber interpreted those orders explicitly as not constituting evidence that he exercised superior responsibility in relation to the camp. The Trial Chamber appears to have interpreted the orders as being, although indicative of some degree of involvement in the continuing detention or release of detainees, inadequate to establish a degree of participation that would be sufficient to constitute a substantial effect on the continuing detention which would be adequate for the purposes of aiding and abetting. The Appeals Chamber considers that this interpretation of the significance of the orders was open to the Trial Chamber.

359. The Prosecution's submission that the Trial Chamber erred in failing to find that Delalic aided and abetted the commission of the offence of unlawful confinement by publicly justifying and defending the pur-

pose of the camp must be rejected for similar reasons. The Trial Chamber referred to the evidence that Delalic had contacts with the ICRC, and that he had been interviewed by journalists in relation to the camp. Even if it could be accepted that this reference alone constituted a finding by the Trial Chamber that these contacts and interviews occurred, it was open to the Trial Chamber to find that any supportive effect that this had in relation to the detention of civilians in the camp was inadequate to be characterised as having a substantial effect on the commission of the crime.

360. The Prosecution has not referred to any other evidence before the Trial Chamber which would indicate that a finding of guilt for Delalic on this count was the *only reasonable* conclusion to be drawn, a matter which must be established before an acquittal would be overturned on appeal. The Prosecution's third ground of appeal must therefore be dismissed in its entirety.

(b) Delic 361. The Prosecution submits that Delic should have been found guilty under Article 7(1), although its written or oral submissions again emphasise the concept of "participation" and do not clearly identify exactly what mode of participation it contends the Trial Chamber should have found had been established.

362. The Trial Chamber found no evidence which demonstrated beyond reasonable doubt that Delic had any role in the creation of the camp, in the arrest and placing in detention of the civilians. Delic argues that it has not been established that he exercised any role in the decision to detain or release prisoners.

363. Although Delic belonged to the military police of the joint command of the TO and HVO, which the Trial Chamber found had been involved in the creation of the camp, there was no finding by the Trial Chamber that Delic in his position had authority to detain or release civilians or even that as a practical matter he could affect who should be detained or released. The Prosecution does not refer to any evidence which would have established such a finding beyond reasonable doubt. The Trial Chamber did find that the evidence established that Delic was "tasked with assisting Zdravko Mucic by organising and arranging for the daily activities in the Celebici prison-camp."

364. Although the Prosecution appears to contend that the evidence established Delic's primary responsibility for commission of the offence of unlawful confinement of civilians, it does not refer to any evidence which establishes more than that he was aware of the unlawfulness of the detention of at least some of the detainees, and that he, as a guard and deputy commander of the camp, thereby participated in the detention of

the civilians held there. The Prosecution makes the general submission that:

Clearly, any detainee who had attempted to leave the Celebici camp would have been physically prevented from so doing, not by the person in command of the camp, but by one of the camp guards. The most immediate cause of each detainee's confinement, and the most immediate obstacle to each detainee's liberty, was thus the camp guards. Provided that he or she had the requisite *mens rea*, each camp guard who participated in the confinement of civilians in the camp, and prevented them from leaving it, will thus be criminally liable on the basis of Article 7(1) for the unlawful confinement of civilians, whether or not the particular guard, under the regime in force in the camp, had any responsibility for determining who would be detained and who would be released.

Insofar as this may suggest that any prison guard who is aware that there are detainees within the camp who were detained without reasonable grounds to suspect that they were a security risk is, without more, responsible for the crime of unlawful confinement, the Appeals Chamber does not accept this submission. As already indicated above, the Appeals Chamber has concluded that a greater degree of involvement in the confinement of an individual is required to establish primary responsibility, and that, even in relation to aiding and abetting, it must be established that the accused's assistance to the principal must have a substantial effect on the commission of the crime. What will satisfy these requirements will depend on the circumstances of the particular case, but the Appeals Chamber would not accept that the circumstance alone of holding a position as a guard somewhere within a camp in which civilians are unlawfully detained suffices to render that guard responsible for the crime of unlawful confinement of civilians. The Prosecution has not referred to particular evidence which would place Delic's involvement in the confinement of the civilians at the Celebici camp at a level higher than the holding of the offices of guard and deputy-commander.

365. It appears from certain other submissions of the Prosecution that, although is does not put its case in this way, it in fact considers that the doctrine of common criminal purpose or joint criminal enterprise is the most apposite form of responsibility to apply to Delic. However it does not identify any findings of the Trial Chamber on the evidence which would establish the necessary elements of criminal liability through participation in a joint criminal enterprise.

366. Although it may be accepted that the only reasonable finding on the evidence, particularly in relation

to the nature of some of the detainees at the camp, including elderly persons, must have been that Delic was aware that, in respect of at least some of the detainees, there existed no reasonable grounds to believe that they constituted a security risk, this is not the only matter which must be established in relation to an allegation of participation in a common criminal design. The existence of a common concerted plan, design or purpose between the various participants in the enterprise (including the accused) must also be proved. It is also necessary to establish a specific *mens rea*, being a shared intent to further the planned crime, an intent to further the common concerted system of ill-treatment, or an intention to participate in and further the joint criminal enterprise, depending on the circumstances of the case. The Prosecution has not pointed to any evidence before the Trial Chamber which would have made the conclusion that these elements had been proved beyond reasonable doubt the *only reasonable* conclusion on the evidence.

367. As to Delic's relationship to the work of the Military Investigative Commission in charge of granting procedural guarantees to detainees, the Trial Chamber concluded that the role of Delic was to assist Mucic by organising and arranging for detainees to be brought to interrogations. The Trial Chamber made no finding that Delic had participated in the work of the Commission. It also made no finding that Delic himself had either responsibility for ensuring that the procedural review was conducted, or authority or power to release detainees, a power which should have been exercised when the appropriate reviews were not conducted.

368. The Appeals Chamber is satisfied that it was open to the Trial Chamber to assess the evidence before it as not proving beyond reasonable doubt that Delic's acts and omissions constituted any adequate form of "participation" in the offence of unlawful confinement for the purpose of ascribing criminal responsibility under Article 7(1).

369. The Appeals Chamber therefore finds that the Prosecution has not established that the Trial Chamber's conclusion that Delic was not guilty under Article 7 (1) for the offence of unlawful confinement was unreasonable.

C. Mucic's Appeal

370. Mucic, in support of this ground of appeal, adopted "as a substantive appeal against conviction on Count 48" the closing submissions made on behalf of Delalic at trial and made only a limited number of his own submissions on this ground. The Prosecution submits that, as these "incorporated" arguments were filed before the Trial Chamber's Judgement was rendered, they should not be considered.

371. The task of the Appeals Chamber, as defined by Article 25 of the Statute, is to hear appeals from the decisions of Trial Chambers on the grounds of an error on a question of law invalidating the decision or of an error of fact which has occasioned a miscarriage of justice. An appellant must show how the Trial Chamber erred in law or in fact, and the Appeals Chamber expects their submissions to be directed to that end. The submissions "incorporated" by Mucic provide no assistance on the aspects of his ground of appeal which allege an error of fact. However, to the extent that the submissions are relevant to the questions of law raised by Mucic's ground of appeal, the Appeals Chamber has considered them in addition to the submissions made by counsel for Mucic at the hearing of the appeal.

372. Mucic challenges his conviction for the offence of illegal detention or unlawful confinement first with the argument that the detainees of the camp were *lawfully* confined because of suspicion of inciting armed rebellion against the State of Bosnia and Herzegovina. The Appeals Chamber has already considered the submission that the Trial Chamber erred in finding that at least some of the detainees were unlawfully confined, and has rejected it.

373. Mucic then submits that it was not proved that he had the requisite *mens rea* because:

> Given that it is not remotely suggested that the Appellant has, or had, any expert or other knowledge of International Law, it would be a counsel of impossible perfection to conclude that in 1992 he could have known, or did know, that there was a possibility that the confinement of persons at Celebici could, or would be, construed as illegal under an interpretation of an admixture of the Geneva Conventions and Article 2(g) of the Statute of the Tribunal, a Statute not then in existence.

374. The Prosecution notes that it is unclear whether Mucic contends that the knowledge of the law is an element of the crime or whether Mucic is raising a defence of error of law. In either of those cases, the Prosecution argues that there is no general principle of criminal law that knowledge of the law is an element of the *mens rea* of a crime and that no defence of mistake of law is available under international humanitarian law. These submissions miss the real issue raised by Mucic's submission — that he could not have been expected to know that the detention of the Celebici detainees would become illegal at some future time. Mucic's submission has no merit because it is clear from the provisions cited above from Geneva Convention IV that the detention of those persons was illegal at the very time of their detention.

375. Mucic also argued that it was not his function as "prison administrator" to know whether the detention of the victims was unlawful. At the hearing of the appeal, counsel for Mucic placed greater emphasis on the argument that Mucic did not in fact have the requisite *mens rea* for a conviction under Article 7(1) of the Statute, and that the Trial Chamber relied upon evidence which established only that he "had reason to know" as a basis for a positive finding that he did in fact have the requisite knowledge that the detainees were unlawfully detained. The Prosecution argues that, because Mucic knew of the types of people detained in the camp and the circumstances of their arrest, he had the *mens rea* for the commission of the offence.

376. The Trial Chamber found that Mucic, by virtue of his position of command, was the individual with primary responsibility for, and had the ability to affect, the continued detention of civilians in the camp. Mucic submits in this regard that the determination of the legality of the detention is not a function or duty of prison administrators but rather of those who authorize arrests and the placing of arrestees into detention. The Appeals Chamber accepts that it is not open simply to conclude that, because of a position of superior authority somewhere in relation to a prison camp, an accused is also *directly* responsible under Article 7(1) for the offence of unlawful confinement committed anywhere in that camp. The particular circumstances entailing liability under Article 7 (1) have to be specifically established before liability could be imposed. This depends on the particular organisation of duties within a camp, and it is a matter to be determined on the evidence.

377. The Trial Chamber found that some detainees were possibly legally detained ab initio but found that some other detainees were not. The Trial Chamber made no finding that Mucic ordered, instigated, planned or otherwise aided and abetted the process of the arrest and placement of civilians in detention in the camp. However, as observed above, there is a second means by which the offence of unlawful confinement can be committed. The detention of detainees without granting the procedural guarantees required by Article 43 of Geneva Convention IV also constitutes the offence of unlawful confinement, whether the civilians were originally lawfully detained or not. It was this aspect of the offence that the Trial Chamber was relying on when it held:

> Specifically, Zdravko Mucic, in this position, [*i.e.* of superior authority over the camp] had the authority to release detainees. By omitting to ensure that a proper enquiry was undertaken into the status of the detainees, and that those civilians who could not lawfully be detained were immediately

released, Zdravko Mucic participated in the unlawful confinement of civilians in the Celebici prison-camp.

Thus the Trial Chamber appears to have found Mucic guilty on the basis of the denial of procedural guarantees under the second "category" of this offence, and the Appeals Chamber's consideration will be limited to his liability in that context. The Appeals Chamber first notes that, although Mucic contests whether it was his responsibility as camp commander to know whether the detainees were lawfully detained or not, he does not contest on appeal the Trial Chamber's finding that he had the authority to release prisoners. In any case, the Appeals Chamber notes that the Trial Chamber made reference to a variety of evidence in support of this finding. The Appeals Chamber therefore proceeds on the basis that this finding was open to the Trial Chamber and that it is the relevant one.

378. As is evident from the earlier discussion of the law relating to unlawful confinement, the Appeals Chamber considers that a person in the position of Mucic commits the offence of unlawful confinement of civilians where he has the authority to release civilian detainees and fails to exercise that power, where

(i) he has no reasonable grounds to believe that the detainees do not pose a real risk to the security of the state; or

(ii) he knows that they have not been afforded the requisite procedural guarantees (or is reckless as to whether those guarantees have been afforded or not).

379. Where a person who has authority to release detainees knows that persons in continued detention have a right to review of their detention and that they have not been afforded that right, he has a duty to release them. Therefore, failure by a person with such authority to exercise the power to release detainees, whom he knows have not been afforded the procedural rights to which they are entitled, commits the offence of unlawful confinement of civilians, even if he is not responsible himself for the failure to have their procedural rights respected.

380. The Trial Chamber expressly found that the detainees were not afforded the necessary procedural guarantees. It also found that Mucic did in fact have the power to release detainees at the camp. The only remaining question raised by Mucic's ground of appeal is therefore whether the Trial Chamber had found (although it did not refer to it explicitly) that Mucic had the relevant *mens rea*, *i.e.*, he knew that the detainees had a right to review of their detention but had not been afforded this review or was reckless as to whether

they had been afforded it or not. It is not strictly necessary, in relation to an allegation that the offence of unlawful confinement has been committed through non-compliance with the obligation to afford procedural guarantees, to establish that there was also knowledge that the initial detention of the relevant detainees had been unlawful. This is because the obligation to afford procedural guarantees applies to all detainees whether initially lawfully detained or not. However, as is apparent from the discussion below, the Trial Chamber's findings also suggest that it had concluded that Mucic was also aware that no reasonable ground existed for the detention of at least some of the detainees.

381. The Trial Chamber concluded in relation to Mucic that "[b]y *omitting to ensure that a proper enquiry was undertaken into the status of the detainees* and that those civilians who could not lawfully be detained were immediately released, Zdravko Mucic participated in the unlawful confinement of civilians in the Celebici prison-camp." It is implicit in this finding that Mucic knew that a review of the detainees' detention was required but had not been conducted. There are a number of findings of the Trial Chamber on the evidence before it which support this conclusion.

382. Relevant to Mucic's knowledge of the unlawful nature of the confinement of certain of the detainees (both because of absence of review of detention and, in some cases, of the absence of grounds for the initial detention) is his knowledge of the work of the Military Investigative Commission. As noted above, the Trial Chamber found that a Military Investigative Commission was established by the Konjic Joint Command following a decision by the War Presidency of Konjic to investigate crimes allegedly committed by the detainees prior to their arrival at the Celebici camp, and that the Commission did not have the power to finally decide on the release of wrongfully detained prisoners.

383. The Trial Chamber found that the Commission consisted of five members, one of which was Witness D. The Trial Chamber referred to Witness D's testimony that he worked closely with Mucic in the classification of the detainees in the Celebici camp, and that Mucic had a complete list of the detainees which he brought out for members of the Commission. It is apparent from the context of the Trial Chamber's reference that it accepted that evidence. Witness D also testified that Mucic was present early in June when members of the Commission met to discuss how they would go about their work of the classification of the detainees and consideration for their continued detention or release. It is implicit in these findings as to Mucic's awareness of the work of the Commission, and even of its existence as an independent body with a review function

over the camp, that Mucic must have known that such a review was legally required.

384. The Trial Chamber also found that the Commission had prepared a report in June 1992 detailing the "conditions in the prison-camp, including the mistreatment of detainees and the continued incarceration of persons who were peaceful civilians", and the fact that they were unable to correct them. The Trial Chamber cited from the report, which stated, *inter alia*:

Detainees were maltreated and physically abused by certain guards from the moment they were brought in until the time their statement was taken *i.e.* until their interview was conducted. Under such circumstances, Commission members were unable to learn from a large number of detainees all the facts relevant for each detainee and the area from which he had been brought in and where he had been captured. [...] Commission members also interviewed persons arrested outside the combat zone; the Commission did not ascertain the reason for these arrests, but these detainees were subjected to the same treatment [...] Persons who had been arrested under such circumstances stayed in detention even after it had been established that they had been detained for no reason and received the same treatment as persons captured in the combat zone [...] Because self-appointed judges have appeared, any further investigation is pointless until these problems are solved.

385. It is obvious from this report, which the Trial Chamber accepted, that there were persons in the camp in respect of whom no reasons existed to justify their detention and that the Commission was not able to perform the necessary review of the detention of the Celebici camp detainees. The Trial Chamber found that, after working for about one month at the prison-camp, the Commission was in fact disbanded at the instigation of its members as early as the end of June 1992. Although the Trial Chamber made no finding that Mucic had read the Commission's report, in view of its findings that Mucic worked closely with the Commission, it is implicit in the findings taken as a whole that Mucic was aware of the matters that the Commission discussed in the report, including the fact that there were civilians there who had been detained without justification, and that the detainees generally had not had their detention properly reviewed. This knowledge can only have been reinforced by the presence in the camp, of which Mucic must have been aware, of detainees of a kind which would have appeared so unlikely to pose a security risk that it must have raised doubts as to whether any reasonable grounds had ever existed for their initial detention. This included elderly persons

and persons such as Grozdana Cecez, a 42 year old mother of two children.

386. The Appeals Chamber finds that it was open to the Trial Chamber, from its primary findings (which have not been shown to be unreasonable), to conclude that Mucic, by not using his authority to release detainees whom he knew had not had their detention reviewed and had therefore not received the necessary procedural guarantees, committed the offence of unlawful confinement of civilians and was therefore guilty of the offence pursuant to Article 7(1) of the Statute.

387. The Appeals Chamber therefore dismisses this ground of appeal.

D. Conclusion

388. For the foregoing reasons, the Appeals Chamber dismisses the twelfth ground of appeal of Mucic, and the third and sixth grounds of appeal of the Prosecution.

X. SELECTIVE PROSECUTION

596. Landzo alleges that he was the subject of a selective prosecution policy conducted by the Prosecution. He defines a selective prosecution as one "in which the criteria for selecting persons for prosecution are based, not on considerations of apparent criminal responsibility alone, but on extraneous policy reasons, such as ethnicity, gender, or administrative convenience." Specifically, he alleges that he, a young Muslim camp guard, was selected for prosecution, while indictments "against all other Defendants without military rank", who were all "non-Muslims of Serbian ethnicity", were withdrawn by the Prosecution on the ground of changed prosecutorial strategies.

597. The factual background to this contention is that the Prosecutor decided in 1998 to seek the withdrawal of the indictments against fourteen accused who at that stage had neither been arrested nor surrendered to the Tribunal. This application was granted by Judges of the Tribunal in early May 1998. At that stage, the trial in the present proceedings had been underway for a period of over twelve months. The Prosecutor's decision and the grant of leave to withdraw the indictment was announced in a Press Release, which explained the motivation for the decision in the following terms:

> Over recent months there has been a steady increase in the number of accused who have either been arrested or who have surrendered voluntarily to the jurisdiction of the Tribunal.
>
> [...].
>
> The arrest and surrender process has been unavoidably piecemeal and sporadic and it appears

that this is likely to continue. One result of this situation is that accused, who have been jointly indicted, must be tried separately, thereby committing the Tribunal to a much larger than anticipated number of trials.

> In light of that situation, I have re-evaluated all outstanding indictments vis-a-vis the overall investigative and prosecutorial strategies of my Office. Consistent with those strategies, which involve maintaining an investigative focus on persons holding higher levels of responsibility, or on those who have been personally responsible for the [sic] exceptionally brutal or otherwise extremely serious offences, I decided that it was appropriate to withdraw the charges against a number of accused in what have become known as the Omarska and Keraterm indictments, which were confirmed in February 1995 and July 1995 respectively.

Although counsel for Landzo submitted that the Prosecution sought and obtained the withdrawal of indictments against sixteen accused, "some of whom were already in custody" of the Tribunal at the relevant time, this was not the case. Although three people were released from the custody of the Tribunal on 19 December 1997 pursuant to a decision granting the Prosecutor's request to withdraw their indictment, the withdrawal of those indictments was based on the quite different consideration of insufficiency of evidence. Landzo does not appear to have intended to refer to the withdrawal of any indictments other than those referred to in the Press Release, and the submissions proceeded upon that basis.

598. Landzo accordingly submitted, first at trial and now on appeal, that, because the indictment against him was not also withdrawn, he was singled out for prosecution for an impermissible motive and that this selective prosecution contravened his right to a fair trial as guaranteed by Article 21 of the Statute. Citing a decision of the United States of America's Supreme Court, *Yick Wo v Hopkins*, and Article 21(3) of the Rome Statute of the International Criminal Court, Landzo submits that the guarantee of a fair trial under Article 21(1) of the Statute incorporates the principle of equality and that prohibition of selective prosecution is a general principle of customary international criminal law.

599. The Trial Chamber, in its sentencing considerations, referred to Landzo's argument that, because he was an ordinary soldier rather than a person of authority, he should not be subject to the Tribunal's jurisdiction, and then stated:

> [The Trial Chamber] does, however, note that the statement issued in May this year (1998) by the

Tribunal Prosecutor concerning the withdrawal of charges against several indicted persons, quoted by the Defence, indicates that an exception to the new policy of maintaining the investigation and indictment only of persons in positions of some military or political authority, is made for those responsible for exceptionally brutal or otherwise extremely serious offences. From the facts established and the findings of guilt made in the present case, the conduct of Esad Landzo would appear to fall within this exception.

600. The Prosecution argues that the Prosecutor has a broad discretion in deciding which cases should be investigated and which persons should be indicted. In exercising this discretion, the Prosecutor may have regard to a wide range of criteria. It is impossible, it is said, to prosecute all persons placed in the same position and, because of this, the jurisdiction of the International Tribunal is made concurrent with the jurisdiction of national courts by Article 9 of the Statute.

601. Article 16 of the Statute entrusts the responsibility for the conduct of investigation and prosecution of persons responsible for serious violations of international humanitarian law committed in the territory of the former Yugoslavia since 1 January 1991 to the Prosecutor. Once a decision has been made to prosecute, subject to the requirement that the Prosecutor be satisfied that a prima facie case exists, Article 18 and 19 of the Statute require that an indictment be prepared and transmitted to a Judge of a Trial Chamber for review and confirmation if satisfied that a prima facie case has been established by the Prosecutor. Once an indictment is confirmed, the Prosecutor can withdraw it prior to the initial appearance of the accused only with the leave of the Judge who confirmed it, and after the initial appearance only with the leave of the Trial Chamber.

602. In the present context, indeed in many criminal justice systems, the entity responsible for prosecutions has finite financial and human resources and cannot realistically be expected to prosecute every offender which may fall within the strict terms of its jurisdiction. It must of necessity make decisions as to the nature of the crimes and the offenders to be prosecuted. It is beyond question that the Prosecutor has a broad discretion in relation to the initiation of investigations and in the preparation of indictments. This is acknowledged in Article 18(1) of the Statute, which provides:

The Prosecutor shall initiate investigations ex-officio or on the basis of information obtained from any source, particularly from Governments, United Nations organs, intergovernmental and non-governmental organizations. The Prosecutor shall

assess the information received or obtained and *decide whether there is sufficient basis to proceed.*

It is also clear that a discretion of this nature is not unlimited. A number of limitations on the discretion entrusted to the Prosecutor are evident in the Tribunal's Statute and Rules of Procedure and Evidence.

603. The Prosecutor is required by Article 16(2) of the Statute to "act independently as a separate organ of the International Tribunal", and is prevented from seeking or receiving instructions from any government or any other source. Prosecutorial discretion must therefore be exercised entirely independently, within the limitations imposed by the Tribunal's Statute and Rules. Rule 37(A) provides that the Prosecutor "shall perform all the functions provided by the Statute in accordance with the Rules and such Regulations, consistent with the Statute and the Rules, as may be framed by the Prosecutor."

604. The discretion of the Prosecutor at all times is circumscribed in a more general way by the nature of her position as an official vested with specific duties imposed by the Statute of the Tribunal. The Prosecutor is committed to discharge those duties with full respect of the law. In this regard, the Secretary-General's Report stressed that the Tribunal, which encompasses all of its organs, including the Office of the Prosecutor, must abide by the recognised principles of human rights.

605. One such principle is explicitly referred to in Article 21(1) of the Statute, which provides:

All persons shall be equal before the International Tribunal.

This provision reflects the corresponding guarantee of equality before the law found in many international instruments, including the 1948 Universal Declaration of Human Rights, the 1966 International Covenant on Civil and Political Rights, the Additional Protocol I to the Geneva Conventions, and the Rome Statute of the International Criminal Court. All these instruments provide for a right to equality before the law, which is central to the principle of the due process of law. The provisions reflect a firmly established principle of international law of equality before the law, which encompasses the requirement that there should be no discrimination in the enforcement or application of the law. Thus Article 21 and the principle it embodies prohibits discrimination in the application of the law based on impermissible motives such as, *inter alia*, race, colour, religion, opinion, national or ethnic origin. The Prosecutor, in exercising her discretion under the Statute in the investigation and indictment of accused before the Tribunal, is subject to the principle of equality before the law and to this requirement of non-discrimination.

606. This reflects principles which apply to prosecutorial discretion in certain national systems. In the United Kingdom, the limits on prosecutorial discretion arise from the more general principle, applying to the exercise of administrative discretion generally, that the discretion is to be exercised in good faith for the purpose for which it was conferred and not for some ulterior, extraneous or improper purpose. In the United States, where the guarantee of equal protection under the law is a constitutional one, the court may intervene where the accused demonstrates that the administration of a criminal law is "directed so exclusively against a particular class of persons [...] with a mind so unequal and oppressive" that the prosecutorial system amounts to "a practical denial" of the equal protection of the law.

607. The burden of the proof rests on Landzo, as an appellant alleging that the Prosecutor has improperly exercised prosecutorial discretion, to demonstrate that the discretion was improperly exercised in relation to him. Landzo must therefore demonstrate that the decision to prosecute him or to continue his prosecution was based on impermissible motives, such as race or religion, and that the Prosecution failed to prosecute similarly situated defendants.

608. The Prosecution submits that, in order to demonstrate a selective prosecution, Landzo must show that he had been singled out for an impermissible motive, so that the mere existence of similar unprosecuted acts is not enough to meet the required threshold.

609. Landzo submits that a test drawn from United States case-law, and in particular the case *United States of America v Armstrong*, provides the required threshold for selective prosecution claims. Pursuant to this test, the complainant must prove first that he was singled out for prosecution for an improper motive, and secondly, that the Prosecutor elected not to prosecute other similarly situated defendants. There is therefore no significant difference between the applicable standards identified by Landzo and by the Prosecution.

610. As observed by the Prosecution, the test relied on by Landzo in *United States of America v Armstrong*, puts a heavy burden on an appellant. To satisfy this test, Landzo must demonstrate clear evidence of the intent of the Prosecutor to discriminate on improper motives, and that other similarly situated persons were not prosecuted. Other jurisdictions which recognise an ability for judicial review of a prosecutorial discretion also indicate that the threshold is a very high one.

611. It is unnecessary to select between such domestic standards, as it is not appropriate for the Appeals Chamber simply to rely on the jurisprudence of any one jurisdiction in determining the applicable legal principles. The provisions of the Statute referred to above and the relevant principles of international law provide adequate guidance in the present case. The breadth of the discretion of the Prosecutor, and the fact of her statutory independence, imply a presumption that the prosecutorial functions under the Statute are exercised regularly. This presumption may be rebutted by an appellant who can bring evidence to establish that the discretion has in fact not been exercised in accordance with the Statute; here, for example, in contravention of the principle of equality before the law in Article 21. This would require evidence from which a clear inference can be drawn that the Prosecutor was motivated in that case by a factor inconsistent with that principle. Because the principle is one of *equality* of persons before the law, it involves a comparison with the legal treatment of other persons who must be similarly situated for such a comparison to be a meaningful one. This essentially reflects the two-pronged test advocated by Landzo and by the Prosecution of (i) establishing an unlawful or improper (including discriminatory) motive for the prosecution and (ii) establishing that other similarly situated persons were not prosecuted.

612. Landzo argues that he was the only Bosnian Muslim accused without military rank or command responsibility held by the Tribunal, and he contends that he was singled out for prosecution "simply because he was the only person the Prosecutor's office could find to 'represent' the Bosnian Muslims". He was, it is said, prosecuted to give an appearance of "evenhandedness" to the Prosecutor's policy. Landzo alleges that the Prosecutor's decision to seek the withdrawal of indictments against the accused identified in the Press Release, without seeking the discontinuation of the proceedings against Landzo, was evidence of a discriminatory purpose. Landzo rejects the justification given by the Prosecutor in the Press Release of a revaluation of indictments according to changed strategies "in light of the decision to except the one Muslim defendant without military rank or command responsibility from the otherwise complete dismissal of charges against Defendants having that status."

613. The Prosecution argues that a change of prosecutorial tactics, in view of the need to reassign available resources of the Prosecution, cannot be considered as being significative of discriminatory intent. Furthermore, the evidence of discriminatory intent must be coupled with the evidence that the Prosecutor's policy had a discriminatory effect, so that other *similarly-*

situated individuals of other ethnic or religious backgrounds were not prosecuted. The Prosecution observes that those against whom charges were withdrawn had not yet been arrested or surrendered to the Tribunal, whereas Land'o was in custody and his case already mid-trial. The Prosecution adds that even if it was to be considered that the continuation of Landzo's trial resulted in him being singled out, it was in any event for the commission of exceptionally brutal or otherwise serious offences.

614. The crimes of which Landzo was convicted are described both in the Trial Judgement and in the present judgement at paragraphs 565-570. The Appeals Chamber considers that, in light of the unquestionably violent and extreme nature of these crimes, it is quite clear that the decision to continue the trial against Landzo was consistent with the stated policy of the Prosecutor to "focus on persons holding higher levels of responsibility, or on those who have been *personally responsible for the exceptionally brutal or otherwise extremely serious offences.*" A decision, made in the context of a need to concentrate prosecutorial resources, to identify a person for prosecution on the basis that they are believed to have committed exceptionally brutal offences can in no way be described as a discriminatory or otherwise impermissible motive.

615. Given the failure of Landzo to adduce any evidence to establish that the Prosecution had a discriminatory or otherwise unlawful or improper motive in indicting or continuing to prosecute him, it is not strictly necessary to have reference to the additional question of whether there were other similarly situated persons who were not prosecuted or against whom prosecutions were discontinued. However, the facts in relation to this question support the conclusion already drawn that Landzo was not the subject of a discriminatory selective prosecution.

616. All of the fourteen accused against whom charges were withdrawn pursuant to the Prosecutor's change of policy, unlike Landzo, had not been arrested and were not in the custody of the Tribunal. None of the fourteen persons identified in the Press Release as the subject of the withdrawn indictments had been arrested or surrendered to the Tribunal so were not in the Tribunal's custody.

617. At the time at which the decision was taken to withdraw the indictments on the basis of changed prosecutorial strategy, the trial of Landzo and his co-accused had been underway for over twelve months. None of the persons in respect of whom the indictments were withdrawn were facing trial at the time. These practical considerations alone, which demonstrate an important difference in the situation of Land-

zo and the persons against whom indictments were withdrawn, also provide the rational justification for the Prosecutor's decisions at the time. The Appeals Chamber notes that the Prosecutor explicitly stated that accused against whom charges were withdrawn could still be tried at a later stage by the Tribunal or by national courts by virtue of the principle of concurrent jurisdiction. Had Landzo been released with the leave of the Trial Chamber, he would have been subject to trial upon the same or similar charges in Bosnia and Herzegovina.

618. Finally, even if in the hypothetical case that those against whom the indictments were withdrawn were identically situated to Landzo, the Appeals Chamber cannot accept that the appropriate remedy would be to reverse the convictions of Landzo for the serious offences with which he had been found guilty. Such a remedy would be an entirely disproportionate response to such a procedural breach. As noted by the Trial Chamber, it cannot be accepted that "unless all potential indictees who are similarly situated are brought to justice, there should be no justice done in relation to a person who has been indicted and brought to trial".

619. This ground of appeal is therefore dismissed.

Eichmann

SOURCE The Online Casebook. "The Eichmann Case." Available from http://www.his.com/~clight/eichmann.htm.

INTRODUCTION Adolf Eichmann was an important Nazi bureaucrat who oversaw much of the Final Solution. He escaped capture as a war criminal, and eventually fled to Argentina where he lived an obscure life under an alias. Eichmann was eventually tracked down by Israeli intelligence agents. Because of doubts that Argentina would cooperate in his extradition, in 1960 Eichmann was kidnapped and taken secretly to Israel for prosecution. The Eichmann trial heard scores of witnesses about the Nazi atrocities, and was a defining moment in Israel's history. Eichmann unsuccessfully argued that the courts of Israel had no jurisdiction, that the judges were biased, and that he was being punished under retroactive criminal law. Eichmann's conviction was upheld on appeal to the Supreme Court. Appeals to Prime Minister Ben Gurion that he not be executed were rejected. Eichmann was cremated and his ashes scattered on the Mediterranean so as not to create a shrine for his perverse admirers.

The Trial Court Decision
The Supreme Court Decision
Background

Adolf Eichmann was a high ranking SS officer who played a central role in the planning and implementation of the persecution of Jews in Germany, Poland, Hungary and several other countries before and during World War II. At the end of the war he escaped to Argentina where he lived and worked under an alias until May, 1960 when he was kidnapped by Israeli agents. Argentina complained to the Security Council about this clear violation of Argentine sovereignty. The Security Council, while making it clear that it did not condone Eichmann's crimes, declared that "acts such as that under consideration [the kidnapping of Eichmann] which affect the sovereignty of a Member State and therefore cause international friction, may, if repeated, endanger international peace and security." The Security Council requested the Government of Israel "to make appropriate reparation in accordance with the Charter of the United Nations and the rules of international law." Argentina did not demand the return of Eichmann, and in August, 1960. the Argentine and Israeli governments resolved in a joint communique "to regard as closed the incident which arose out of the action taken by citizens of Israel, which infringed the fundamental rights of the State of Argentina." Eichmann was then tried in Israel under Israel's Nazi Collaborators Law (a law enacted after Israel became a state in 1948). He was found guilty and the conviction was subsequently upheld by the Supreme Court of Israel. On May 31, 1962 Eichmann went to the gallows, the only person ever formally executed by the State of Israel.

ATTORNEY GENERAL OF ISRAEL v.
EICHMANN:
Trial Court Decision
36 Intl. L. Rep. 5 (Israel, Dist. Ct. Jerusalem
1961)
Learned defence counsel . . . submits:

(a) that the Israel Law, by imposing punishment for acts done outside the boundaries of the State and before its establishment, against persons who were not Israel citizens, and by a person who acted in the course of duty on behalf of a foreign country ("Act of State"), conflicts with international law and exceeds the powers of the Israel Legislature;

(b) that the prosecution of the accused in Israel following his abduction from a foreign country conflicts with international law and exceeds the jurisdiction of the Court. . . . [The Court ruled that national law would prevail over international law in an Israel court. Nonetheless, it offered a lengthy analysis of the international law questions.]

From the point of view of international law, the power of the State of Israel to enact the Law in question or Israel's "right to punish" is based, with respect to the offences in question, on a dual foundation: the universal character of the crimes in question and their specific character as intended to exterminate the Jewish people.

12. The abhorrent crimes defined in this Law are not crimes under Israel law alone. These crimes, which struck at the whole of mankind and shocked the conscience of nations, are grave offenses against the law of nations itself (delicta jurit gentium). Therefore, so far from international law negating or limiting the jurisdiction of countries with respect to such crimes, international law is, in the absence of an International Court, in need of the judicial and legislative organs of every country to give effect to its criminal interdictions and to bring the criminals to trial. The jurisdiction to try crimes under international law is universal.

[Here the Court discussed piracy, and instances of universality jurisdiction over war crimes. It also referred to "genocide" as having become a crime under customary international law prior to the Genocide Convention; but held that the limitation in the Genocide Convention, Article 6, to trial before the court of the territory, was a treaty rule only, applicable only to offences committed after the Genocide Convention entered into force in 1951.]

26. It is superfluous to add that the "crime against the Jewish people", which constitutes the crime of "genocide", is nothing but the gravest type of "crime against humanity" (and all the more so because both under Israel law and under the Convention a special intention is requisite for its commission, an intention that is not required for the commission of a "crime against humanity"). Therefore, all that has been said in the Nuremberg principles about "crimes against humanity" applies a fortiori to "crime against the Jewish people". . .

27. It is indeed difficult to find a more convincing instance of a just retroactive law than the legislation providing for the punishment of war criminals and perpetrators of crimes against humanity and against the Jewish people, and all the reasons justifying the Nuremberg judgments justify eo ipse the retroactive legislation of the Israel legislator. . . . The accused in this case is charged with the implementation of the plan for the "final solution of the problem of the Jews". Can anyone in his right mind doubt the absolute criminality of such acts? . . .

28. The contention of learned counsel for the defence that it is not the accused but the State on whose behalf he had acted, who is responsible for his criminal acts is only true as to its second part. It is true that under international law Germany bears not only moral, but also legal, responsibility for all the crimes that were committed as its own "acts of State," including the

Eichmann

crimes attributed to the accused. But that responsibility does not detract one iota from the personal responsibility of the accused for his acts.

The repudiation of the argument of "act of State" is one of the principles of international law that were acknowledged by the Charter and judgment of the Nuremberg Tribunal and were unanimously affirmed by the United Nations Assembly in its Resolution of December 11, 1946.

30. We have discussed at length the international character of the crimes in question because this offers the broadest possible, though not the only, basis for Israel's jurisdiction according to the law of nations. No less important from the point of view of international law is the special connection which the State of Israel has with such crimes, since the people of Israel (Am Israel), the Jewish people constituted the target and the victim of most of the said crimes. The State of Israel's "right to punish" the accused derives, in our view, from two cumulative sources: a universal source (pertaining to the whole of mankind), which vests the right to prosecute and punish crimes of this order in every State within the family of nations; and a specific or national source, which gives the victim nation the right to try any who assault its existence.

This second foundation of criminal jurisdiction conforms, according to accepted terminology, to the protective principle.

34. The connection between the State of Israel and the Jewish people needs no explanation. The State of Israel was established and recognized as the State of the Jews.

In view of the recognition by the United Nations of the right of the Jewish people to establish their State, and in the light of the recognition of the established Jewish State by the family of nations, the connection between the Jewish people and the State of Israel constitutes an integral part of the law of nations.

The massacre of millions of Jews by the Nazi criminals that very nearly led to the extinction of the Jewish people in Europe was one of the major causes for the establishment of the State of the survivors. The State cannot be cut off from its roots, which lie deep also in the catastrophe which befell European Jewry.

Half the citizens of the State have immigrated from Europe in recent years, some before and some after the Nazi massacre. There is hardly one of them who has not lost parents, brothers and sisters, and many their spouses and their offspring in the Nazi inferno.

In these circumstances, unprecedented in the annals of any other nation, can there be anyone who would contend that there are not sufficient "linking points" between the crime of the extermination of the Jews of Europe and the State of Israel?

35. Indeed, this crime very deeply concerns the "vital interests" of the State of Israel, and under the "protective principle" this State has the right to punish the criminals.

41. It is an established rule of law that a person being tried for an offence against the laws of a State may not oppose his trial by reason of the illegality of his arrest or of the means whereby he was brought within the jurisdiction of that State. The courts in England, the United States and Israel have constantly held that the circumstances of the arrest and the mode of bringing the accused into the territory of the State have no relevance to his trial, and they have consistently refused in all instances to enter upon an examination of these circumstances.

50. Indeed, there is no escaping the conclusion that the question of the violation of international law by the manner in which the accused was brought into the territory of a country arises at the international level, namely, the relations between the two countries concerned alone, and must find its solution at such level.

52. According to the existing rule of law there is no immunity for a fugitive offender save in the one and only case where he has been extradited by the asylum State to the requesting State for a specific offence, which is not the offence for which he was being tried. The accused was not surrendered to Israel by Argentina, and the State of Israel is not bound by any agreement with Argentina to try the accused for any other specific offence, or not to try him for the offences being tried in the present case. The rights of asylum and immunity belong to the country of asylum and not to the offender, and the accused cannot compel a foreign sovereign State to give him protection against its will. The accused was a wanted war criminal when he escaped to Argentina by concealing his true identity. Only after he was kidnapped and brought to Israel was his identity revealed. After negotiations between the two Governments, the Government of Argentina waved its demand for his return and declared that it viewed the incident as closed. The Government of Argentina thereby refused conclusively to grant the accused any sort of protection. The accused has been brought to trial before the Court of a State which charges him with grave offences against its laws. The accused has no immunity against this trial and must stand trial in accordance with the indictment.

EICHMANN V. ATTORNEY-GENERAL OF
ISRAEL:
Supreme Court Decision
Supreme Court of Israel (1962) 136 I.L.R. 277

Judgment Per Curiam:

' [As to the argument for the appellant that. in the event of a conflict between local legislation and intentional law.] it is imperative to give reference to the principles of international law, we do not agree with this view. According to the law of Israel, which is identical on this point with English law, the relationship between municipal and intentional law is governed by the following rules:

(1) The principle in question becomes incorporated into the municipal law and a part of that law only after it has achieved general international recognition . . .

(2) This, however, only applies where there is no conflict between the provisions of municipal law and a rule of international law. But where such a conflict does exist, it is the duty of the Court to give preference to and apply the laws of the local legislature. True. the presumption must be that the legislature strives to adjust the laws to the principles of international law which have received general recognition. But where a contrary intention clearly emerges from the statute itself, that presumption loses its force and the Court is enjoined to disregard it.

(3) On the other hand, a local statutory provision, which is open to equivocal construction and whose content does not demand another construction, must be construed in accordance with the rules of public international law. . . .

. . . [Concerning the retroactivity argument,] the principle nullum crimen sine lege, nulla poena sine lege, in so far as it negates penal legislation with retroactive effect, has not yet become a rule of customary international law.

It is true that in many countries [it] has been embodied in the Constitution of the State or in its criminal code, because of the considerable moral value inherent in it, and in such countries the Court may not depart from it by one iota. . . . But this state of affairs is not universal. Thus, in the United Kingdom . . . there is no constitutional limitation of the power of the legislature to enact its criminal laws with retrospective effect, and should it do so the court will have no power to invalidate them. . . . [I]n those countries . . . the moral value in the principle . . . has become legally effective only to the extent that the maxim constitutes a rule of the interpretation of statutes — where there is doubt as to

the intention of the legislature the court is directed not to construe the criminal statute under its consideration as to include within its purview an act that was committed prior to its enactment. 4

Therefore, if it is [contended] that we must apply intentional law as it is, and not as it ought to be from the moral point of view, then we must reply that precisely from a legal point of view there is no such provision in it; it follows automatically that the principle cannot be deemed to be part of the Israel municipal law by virtue of international law, but that the extent of its application in this country is the same as in England.

. . . [As to the moral significance of the maxim, the Court considered that it would be a greater affront to moral principles if the type of crime of which the appellant bad been found guilty went unpunished.]

. . . The contention . . . that (since] the State of Israel had not existed at the time of the commission of the offences . . . its competence to impose punishment therefore is limited to its own citizens is equally unfounded. . . . This argument too must be rejected on the basis that the lower court had to apply local legislation.]

. . . [As) to the contention [that] the enactment of a criminal law applicable to an act committed in a foreign country by a foreign national conflicts with the principle of territorial sovereignty, here too we must hold that there is no such rule in international customary law. . . . This is established by the Judgment of the [World) Court in the Lotus case. . . . It was held . . . that the principle of territorial sovereignty merely requires that the State exercise its power to punish within its own borders, not outside them —. That subject to this restriction every State may exercise a wide discretion as to the application of its laws and the jurisdiction of its courts in respect of acts committed outside the State; and that only in so far as it is possible to point to a specific rule prohibiting the exercise of this discretion . . . is a State prevented from exercising it.

That view was based on the following two grounds:

(1) It is precisely the conception of State sovereignty which demands the preclusion of any presumption that there is a restriction on its independence;

(2) Even if it is true that the principle of the territorial character of criminal law is firmly established in various States, it is no less true that in almost all of such States criminal jurisdiction has been extended . . . so as to embrace offences committed outside its territory.

. . . [O]n the question of the jurisdiction of a State to punish persons who are not its nationals for acts committed beyond its borders, there is as yet no intentional accord.

It follows that in the absence of general agreement as to the existence of [such a] rule of international law, . . . there is, again, no escape from the conclusion that it cannot be deemed to be embodied in Israel municipal law, and therefore on that ground, too. the contention fails.

[E]ven if Counsel . . . were right in his view that intentional law prohibits a State from trying a foreign national for an act committed outside its borders, even this would not [help]. The reason for this is that according to the theory of international law, in the absence of an international treaty which vests rights in an individual, that law only recognises the rights of a State; in other words, assuming that there is such a prohibition in intentional law, the violation of it is deemed to be a violation of the rights of the State to which the accused belongs, and not a violation of his own rights.

. . . There was no prohibition whatever by international law of the enactment of the Law of 1950, either because it created ex post facto offences or because such offences are of an extraterritorial character. . . . [But] these contentions are unjustifiable even from a positive approach, namely, that when enacting the Law the Knesset [legislature] only sought to apply the principle of international law and to realise its objectives.

The crimes created by the Law and of which the appellant was convicted must be deemed today to have always borne the stamps of intentional crimes, banned by intentional law and entailing individual criminal liability. It is the particular universal character of these crimes that vests in each State the power to try and punish any who assisted in their commission. [Reference the Genocide Convention and the Nuremberg judgement]. . . . As is well known, the rules of the law of nations are not derived solely from intentional treaties and crystallised international usage. In the absence of a supreme legislative authority and international codes the process of its evolution resembles that of the common law;... its rules are established from case to case, by analogy with the rules embodied in treaties and in intentional custom, on the basis of the " 'general' principles of law recognised by civilised nations," and in the light of the vital international needs that impel an immediate solution. A principle which constitutes a common denominator for the judicial systems of numerous countries must clearly be regarded as a "general principle of law recognised by civilised nations." [C]ustomary international law is never stagnant, but is rather in a process of constant growth.

. . . [As to] the features which identify crimes that have long been recognised by customary international law[,]. . . they constitute acts which damage vital international interests... they impair the foundations and security of the international community; they violate universal moral values and humanitarian principles which are at the root of the systems of criminal law adopted by civilised nations. The underlying principle in intentional law that governs such crimes is that the individual who has committed any of them and who, at the time of his act, may be presumed to have had a thorough understanding of its heinous nature must account in law for his behaviour. It is true that intentional law does not establish explicit and graduated criminal sanctions; that there is not as yet in existence either an intentional Criminal Court, or intentional machinery for the imposition of punishment. But, for the time being, intentional law surmounts these difficulties . . . by authorising the countries of the world to mete out punishment for the violation of its provisions. This they do by enforcing these provisions either directly or by virtue of the municipal legislation which has adopted and integrated them.

The classic example of a "customary" international crime . . . is that of piracy jure gentium. [Another] example . . . is that of a "war crime" in the conventional sense . . . the group of acts committed by members of the armed forces of the enemy which are contrary to the "laws and customs of war." individual criminal responsibility because they undermine the foundations of intentional society and are repugnant to the conscience of civilised nations. When the belligerent State punishes for such acts, it does so not only because persons who were its nationals . . . suffered bodily harm or material damage. but also, and principally, because they involve the perpetration of an intentional crime in the avoidance of which all the nations of the world are interested.

In view of the characteristic traits of intentional crimes and the organic development of the law of nations — a development that advances from case to case under the impact of the humane sentiments common to civilised nations, and under the pressure of the needs that are vital for the survival of mankind and for ensuring the stability of the world order it definitely cannot be said that when the Charter of the Nuremburg International Military Tribunal was signed and the categories of "war crimes" and "crimes against humanity" were defined in it, this merely amounted to an act of legislation by the victorious countries.

. . . [The interest in preventing and imposing punishment for acts comprised in the category in question especially when they are perpetrated on a very large scale — must necessarily extend beyond the borders of the State to which the perpetrators belong and which evinced tolerance or encouragement of their outrages; for such acts can undermine the foundations of the international community as a whole and impair its very stability. . . .

If we are to regard customary international law as a developing progressive system, the criticism becomes devoid of value . . . [E]ver since the Nuremberg Tribunal decided this question, that very decision must be seen as a judicial act which establishes a "precedent" defining the rule of international law. In any event, it would be unseemly for any other court to disregard such a rule and not to follow it.

If there was any doubt as to this appraisal of the "Nuremberg Principles" as principles that have formed part of customary international law 64 since time immemorial, "such doubt" has been removed by . . . the United Nations Resolution on the Affirmation of the Principles of International Law Recognised by the Charter and Judgment of the Nuremberg Tribunal and that affirming that Genocide is a crime under intentional law . . . and as [is seen] in the advisory opinion of 1951 . . . the principles inherent in the [Genocide] Convention — as distinct from the contractual obligations embodied therein — had already been part of customary intentional law at the time of the shocking crimes which led to the. Resolution and the Convention.

. . . [T]he crimes established in the Law of 1950 . . . must be seen today as acts that have always been forbidden by customary international law — acts which are of a "universal" criminal character and entail individual criminal responsibility. . . . [T]he enactment of the Law was not, from the point of view of international law, a legislative act that conflicted with the principle nulla poena or the operation of which was retroactive, but rather one by which the Knesset gave effect to intentional law and its objectives.

. . . [I]t is the universal character of the crimes in question which vests in every State the power to try those who participated in the preparation of such crimes, and to punish them therefore. . . .

One of the principles whereby States assume, in one degree or another, the power to try and punish a person for an offence he has committed is the principle of universality. Its meaning is, in essence, that that power is vested in every State regardless of the fact that the offence was committed outside its territory by a person who did not belong to it, provided he is in its custody at the time he is brought to trial. This principle has wide support and is universally acknowledged with respect to the offence of piracy jure gentium. . . . [One view] holds that it cannot be applied to any other offence, lest this entail excessive interference with the competence of the State in which the offence was committed.

A second school . . . agrees . . . to the extension of the principle to all manner of extraterritorial offences committed by foreign nationals. . . . It is not more than an auxiliary principle to be applied in circumstances in which no resort can be had to the principle of territorial sovereignty or to the nationality principle, both of which are universally agreed to. [Holders of this view] impose various restrictions on the applications of the principle of universal jurisdiction, which are designed to obviate opposition by those States that find themselves competent to punish the offender according to either of the other two principles. [One of these reservations is that the extradition of the offender should be offered to the State where his offence was committed.].

A third school. . . . holds that the rule of universal jurisdiction, which is valid in cases of piracy, logically applies also to all such criminal acts or omissions which constitute offences under the law of nations (delicta juris gentium) without any reservation whatever or, at most, subject to a reservation of the kind Oust] mentioned. . . . This view has been opposed in the past because of the difficulty in securing general agreement as to the offences to be included.

. . . Notwithstanding the differences . . . there is full justification for applying here the principle of universal jurisdiction since the intentional character of the "crimes against humanity" (in the wide meaning of the term) is, in this case, not in doubt, and the unprecedented extent of their injurious and murderous effect is not open to dispute at the present day. In other words, the basic reason for which international law recognises the right of each State to exercise such jurisdiction in piracy offences . . . applies with all the greater force.

[I]t was not the recognition of the universal jurisdiction to try and punish the person who committed "piracy" that justified the viewing of such an act as an international crime sui generis, but it was the agreed vital interest of the international community that justified the exercise of the jurisdiction in question. . . .

It follows that the State which prosecutes and punishes a person for that offence acts solely as the organ and agent of the intentional community, and metes out punishment to the offender for his breach of the prohibition imposed by the law of nations.

. . . We have also taken into consideration the possible desire of other countries to try the appellant in so far as the crimes. . . . were committed in those countries or their evil effects were felt there . . . But . . . we have not heard of a single protest by any of these countries against conducting the trial in Israel. . . . What is more, it is precisely the fact that the crimes . . . and their effects have extended to numerous countries that empties the territorial principle of its content in the present case, and justifies Israel in assuming criminal jurisdiction by virtue of the "universal" principle.

[It is argued by counsel that Article 6 of the Genocide Convention provides that] a person accused of this crime shall be tried by a court of competent jurisdiction of the State in which it was committed . . . Article 6 imposes upon the parties contractual obligations with future effect. . . . obligations which bind them to prosecute for crimes of "genocide" which will be committed within their territories in the future. The obligation. however, has nothing to do with the universal power vested in every State to prosecute for crimes of this type committed in the past — a power which is based on customary international law.

. . . The State of Israel was entitled, pursuant to the principle of universal jurisdiction and acting in the capacity of guardian of international law and agent for its enforcement, to try the appellant. This being so, it is immaterial that the State of Israel did not exist at the time the offences were committed. . . .

[The Tribunal drew attention to Israel's connection to the Jewish people and the Jewish National Home in Palestine.] If we . . . have concentrated on the international and universal character of the crimes for which the appellant has been convicted, one of our reasons for doing so was that some of them were directed against non-Jewish groups. . . .

[As to the circumstances of Eichmann's capture, the Court cited a long list of local, British. American and Continental precedents and reached the following conclusions:]

(a) In the absence of an extradition agreement between the State to which a "fugitive offender" has been brought for trial and the country of "asylum" . . . and even if there existed such an agreement . . . ut the offender was not extradited . . . in accordance therewith — the Court will not investigate, the circumstances in which he was detained and brought to the area of jurisdiction.

(b) This also applies if the offender's contention be that the abduction was carried out by the agents of the State prosecuting him, since in such a case the right violated is not that of the offender, but the sovereign right of the State aggrieved. . . . The issue must therefore find its solution on the intentional level, and is not justiciable before the Court into whose area of jurisdiction the offender has been brought.

(c) From the point of view of international law the aggrieved State may condone the violation of its sovereignty and waive its claims, including the claim for the return of the offender to its territory, and such waiver may be explicit or by acquiescence.

(d) Only in one eventuality has a fugitive offender a right of immunity when he has been extradited by the country of asylum to the country requesting his extradition for a specific offence, which is not the offence for which he is tried. . . .

(g) The right of asylum and immunity belong to the country of asylum, not to the offender . . . .

. . . The appellant is a "fugitive from justice" from the point of view of the law of nations, since the crimes that were attributed to him are of an international character and have been condemned publicly by the civilised world . . . ; therefore, by virtue of the principle of universal jurisdiction, every country has the right to try him. This jurisdiction was automatically vested in the State of Israel on its establishment in 1948 as a sovereign State. Therefore, in bringing the appellant to trial, it functioned as an organ of intentional law and acted to enforce the provisions thereof through its own law. Consequently, it is immaterial that the crimes in question were committed . . . when the State of Israel did not exist, and outside its territory. . . . The moment it is admitted that the State of Israel possesses criminal jurisdiction both according to local I an according to the law of nations. it must also be conceded that the Court is not bound to investigate the manner and legality of the . . . detention. . . . [The Court then turned to the issues of Acts of State, and of superior orders]

. . .Appeal dismissed

Filartiga

INTRODUCTION In 1980 a U.S. Appeals Court breathed new life into an ancient statute, the Alien Tort Statute, originally adopted in 1789. According to the Court, the Statute authorized private lawsuits by victims of human rights abuses under customary international law, such as torture, when directed against defendants who were not United States citizens. The Statute had been almost forgotten when it was invoked by the family of a torture victim to sue the torturer in New York. The case opened the court house door to many human rights victims who found the perpetrators of their abuse living in or visiting the United States. It was subsequently followed by other federal courts in cases against those who committed genocide or crimes against humanity in Rwanda, Ethiopia, Argentina, and parts of the former Yugoslavia.

Dolly M. E. FILARTIGA and Joel
Filartiga, Plaintiffs-Appellants,
v.
Americo Norberto PENA-IRALA,
Defendant-Appellee.
No. 191, Docket 79–6090.
United States Court of Appeals,
Second Circuit.
Argued Oct. 16, 1979. Decided June 30, 1980.

Citizens of the Republic of Paraguay, who had applied for permanent political asylum in the United States, brought action against one also a citizen of Paraguay; who was in United States on a visitor's visa, for wrongfully causing the death of their son allegedly by the use of torture. The United States District Court for the Eastern District of New York, Eugene H. Nickerson, J., dismissed the action for want of subject matter jurisdiction and appeal was taken. The Court of Appeals, Irving R. Kaufman, Circuit Judge, held that deliberate torture perpetrated under the color of official authority violates universally accepted norms of international law of human rights regardless of the nationality of the parties, and, thus, whenever an alleged torturer is found and served with process by an alien within the borders of the United States, the Alien Tort Statute provides federal jurisdiction.

Reversed.

Before FEINBERG, Chief Judge, KAUFMAN and KEARSE, Circuit Judges.

IRVING R. KAUFMAN, Circuit Judge:

Upon ratification of the Constitution, the thirteen former colonies were fused into a single nation, one which, in its relations with foreign states, is bound both to ob. serve and construe the accepted norms of international law, formerly known as the law of nations. Under the Articles of Confederation, the several states had interpreted and applied this body of doctrine as part of their common law, but with the founding of the "more perfect Union" of 1789, the law of nations became preeminently a federal concern.

Implementing the constitutional mandate for national control over foreign relations, the First Congress established original district court jurisdiction over "all causes where an alien sues for a tort only [committed] in violation of the *law* of nations." Judiciary Act of 1789, ch. 20, ¤ 9(b), 1 Stat.73, 77 (1789), *codified* at 28 U.S.C. ¤ 1350.

Construing this rarely-invoked provision, we hold that deliberate torture perpetrated under color of official authority violates universally accepted norms of the international law of human rights, regardless of the nationality of the parties. Thus, whenever an alleged torturer is found and served with process by an alien within our borders, ¤ 1350 provides federal jurisdiction. Accordingly, we reverse the judgment of the district court dismissing the complaint for want of federal jurisdiction.

I

The appellants, plaintiffs below, are citizens of the Republic of Paraguay. Dr. Joel Filartiga, a physician, describes himself as a longstanding opponent of the government of President Alfredo Stroessner, which has held power in Paraguay since 1954. His daughter, Dolly Filartiga, arrived in the United States in 1978 under a visitor's visa, and has since applied for permanent political asylum. The Filartigas brought this action in the Eastern District of New York against Americo Norberto Pena-Irala (Pena), also a citizen of Paraguay, for wrongfully causing the death of Dr. Filartiga's seventeen-year old son, Joelito. Because the district court dismissed the action for want of subject matter jurisdiction; we must accept as true the allegations contained in the Filartigas' complaint and affidavits for purposes of this appeal.

The appellants contend that on March 29, 1976, Joelito Filartiga was kidnapped and tortured to death by Pena, who was then Inspector General of Police in Asuncion, Paraguay. Later that day, the police brought Dolly Filartiga to Pena's home where she was confronted with the body of her brother, which evidenced marks of severe torture. As she fled, horrified, from the house, Pena followed after her shouting, "Here you have what you have been looking for for so long and what you deserve. Now shut up." The Filartigas claim that Joelito was tortured and killed in retaliation for his father's political activities and beliefs.

Shortly thereafter, Dr. Filartiga commenced a criminal action in the Paraguayan courts against Pena and the police for the murder of his son. As a result, Dr. Filartiga's attorney was arrested and brought to police headquarters where, shackled to a wall, Pena threatened him with death. This attorney, it is alleged, has since been disbarred without just cause.

During the course of the Paraguayan criminal proceeding, which is apparently still pending after four years, another man, Hugo Duarte, confessed to the murder. Duarte, who was a member of the Pena household, claimed that he had discovered his wife and Joelito in flagrante *delicto,* and that the crime was one of passion. The Filartigas have submitted a photograph of Joelito's corpse showing injuries they believe refute this claim. Dolly Filartiga, moreover, has stated that she will offer evidence of three independent autopsies demonstrating that her brother's death "was the result of professional methods of torture." Despite his confession, Duarte, we are told, has never been convicted or sentenced in connection with the crime.

In July of 1978, Pena sold his house in Paraguay and entered the United States under a visitor's visa. He was accompanied by Juana Bautista Fernandez Villalba, who had lived with him in Paraguay. The couple remained in the United States beyond the term of their visas, and were living in Brooklyn, New York, when Dolly Filartiga, who was then living in Washington, D.C., learned of their presence. Acting on information provided by Dolly the Immigration and Naturalization Service arrested Pena and his companion, both of whom were subsequently ordered deported on April 5, 1979 following a hearing. They had then resided in the United States for more than nine months.

Almost immediately, Dolly caused Pena to be served with. a summons and civil complaint at the Brooklyn Navy Yard, where he was being held pending deportation. The complaint alleged that Pena had wrongfully caused Joelito's death by torture and sought compensatory and punitive damages of $10,000,000. The Filartigas also sought to enjoin Pena's deportation to ensure his availability for testimony at trial. The cause of action is stated as arising under "wrongful death statutes; the U. N. Charter; the Universal Declaration on Human Rights; the U. N. Declaration Against Torture; the American Declaration of the Rights and Duties of Man; and other pertinent declarations, documents and practices constituting the customary international law of human rights and the law of nations," as well as 28 U.S.C. ¤ 1350, Article II, sec. 2 and the Supremacy Clause of the U. S. Constitution. Jurisdiction is claimed under the general federal question provision, 28 U.S.C. ¤ 1331 and, principally on this appeal, under the Alien Tort Statute, 28 U.S.C. ¤ 1350.

II

[1] Appellants rest their principal argument in support of federal jurisdiction upon the Alien Tort Statute, 8 U.S.C. ¤ 1350, which provides: "The district courts shall have original jurisdiction of any civil action by an alien for a tort only, committed in violation of the, law of nations or a treaty of the United States." Since appellants do not contend that their action arises directly under a treaty of the United States, a threshold question on the jurisdictional issue is whether the conduct alleged violates the law of nations. In light of the universal condemnation of torture in numerous international agreements and the renunciation of torture as an instrument of official policy by virtually all of the nations of the world (in principle if not in practice), we find that an act of torture committed by a state official

against one held in detention violates established norms of the international law of human rights, and hence the law of nations.

[2] The Supreme Court has enumerated the appropriate sources of international law. The law of nations "may be ascertained by consulting the works of jurists, writing professedly on, public law; or by the general usage and practice of nations; or by judicial decisions recognizing and enforcing that law." *United States v. Smith,* 18 U.S. (5 Wheat.) 158, 160–61, 5 L.Ed. 57 (1820); *Lopes v. Reederei Richard Schroder,* 225 F.Supp. 292, 295 (E.D.Pa.1963). In *Smith,* a statute proscribing "the crime of piracy [on the high seas] as defined by the law of nations," 3 Stat. 510(a) (1819), was held sufficiently determinate in meaning to afford the basis for a death sentence. The *Smith* Court discovered among the works of Lord Bacon, Grotius, Bochard and other commentators a genuine consensus that rendered the crime "sufficiently and constitutionally defined." *Smith, supra,* 18 U.S. (5 Wheat.) at 162, 5 L.Ed. 57.

The Paquete Habana, 175 U.S. 677, 20 S.Ct. 290, 44 L.Ed. 320 (1900), reaffirmed that

> where there is no treaty, and no controlling executive or legislative act or judicial decision, resort must be had to the customs and usages of civilized nations; and, as evidence of these, to the works of jurists and commentators, who by years of labor, research and experience, have made themselves peculiarly well acquainted with the subjects of which they treat. Such works are resorted to by judicial tribunals, not for the speculations of their authors concerning what the law ought to be, but for trustworthy evidence of what the law really is.

Id. at 700, 20 S.Ct. at 299. Modern international sources confirm the propriety of this approach.

[3] Habana is particularly instructive for present purposes, for it held that the traditional prohibition against seizure of an enemy's coastal fishing vessels during wartime, a standard that began as one of comity only, had ripened over the preceding century into "a settled rule of international law" by "the general assent of civilized nations." *id.* at 694, 20 S.Ct. at 297; *accord, id.* at 686, 20 S.Ct. at 297. Thus it is clear that courts must interpret international law not as it was in 1789, but as it has evolved and exists among the nations of the world today. *See Ware v. Hylton,* 3 U.S. (3 Dall.) 198, 1 L.Ed. 568 (1796) (distinguishing between "ancient" and "modern" law of nations).

The requirement that a rule command the "general assent of civilized nations" to become binding upon them all is a stringent one. Were this riot so, the courts of one nation might feel free to impose idiosyncratic legal rules upon others, in the name of applying international law. Thus, in *Banco National de Cuba v. Sabbatino,* 376 U.S. 398, 84 S.Ct. 923, 11 L.Ed.2d 804 (1964), the Court declined to pass on the validity of the Cuban government's expropriation of a foreign-owned corporation's assets, noting the sharply conflicting views on the issue propounded by the capital-exporting, capital-importing, socialist and capitalist nations. *Id.* at 428–30, 84 S.Ct. at 940–41.

The case at bar presents us with a situation diametrically opposed to the conflicted state of law that confronted the *Sabbatino* Court. Indeed, to paraphrase that Court's statement, *id.* at 428, 84 S.Ct. at 940, there are few, if any, issues in international law today on which opinion seems to be so united as the limitations on. a state's power to torture persons held in its custody.

The United Nations Charter (a treaty of the United States, *see* 59 Stat. 1033 (1945)) makes it clear that in this modern age a state's treatment of its own citizens is a matter of international concern. It provides:

> With a view to the creation of conditions of stability and well-being which are necessary for peaceful and friendly relations among nations . . . the United Nations shall promote . . . universal respect for, and observance of, human rights and fundamental freedoms for all without distinctions as to race, sex, language or religion.

id. Art. 55. And further:

> All members pledge themselves to take joint and separate action in cooperation with the Organization for the achievement of the purposes' set forth in Article 55.

id. Art. 56.

While this broad mandate has been held not to be wholly self-executing, *Hitai v. Immigration and Naturalization* Service, 343 F.2d 466, 468 (2d Cir. 1965), this observation alone does not end our inquiry. For although there is no universal agreement as to the precise extent of the "human rights and fundamental freedoms" guaranteed to all by the Charter, there is at present no dissent from the view that the guaranties include, at a bare minimum, the right to be free from torture. This prohibition has become part of customary international law, as evidenced and defined by the Universal Declaration of Human Rights, General Assembly Resolution 217 (III)(A) (Dec. 10, 1948) which states, in the plainest of terms, "no one shall be subjected to torture." The General Assembly hass declared that the Charter precepts embodied in this Universal Declaration "constitute basic principles of international law." G.A.Res. 2625 (XXV) (Oct. 24, 1970).

Particularly relevant is the Declaration on the Protection of All Persons from Being Subjected to Torture, General Assembly Resolution 3452,30 U.N. GAOR Supp. (No. 34) 91, U.N.Doc. A/1034 (1975). The Declaration expressly prohibits any state from permitting the dastardly and totally inhuman act of torture. Torture, in turn, is defined as any act by which severe pain and suffering, whether physical or mental, is intentionally inflicted by or at the instigation of a public official on a person for such purposes as . . . intimidating him or other persons." The Declaration goes on to provide that "[w]here it is proved that an act of torture or other cruel, inhuman or degrading treatment or punishment has been committed by or at the instigation of a public official, the victim shall be afforded redress and compensation, in accordance with national law." This Declaration, like the Declaration of Human Rights before it, was adopted without dissent by the General Assembly. Nayar, "Human Rights: The United Nations and United States Foreign Policy," 19, *Harv.Int'l L.J.* 813, 816 n.18 (1978).

These U.N. declarations are significant because they specify with great precision the obligations of member nations under the Charter. Since their adoption, "[m]embers can no longer contend that they do not know what human rights they promised in the Charter to promote." Sohn, "A Short History of United Nations Documents on Human Rights," in *The United Nations and Human Rights, 18th Report of the Commission* (Commission to Study the Organization of Peace ed. 1968). Moreover, a U.N. Declaration is, according to one authoritative definition, "a formal and solemn instrument, suitable for rare occasions when principles of great and lasting importance are being enunciated." 34 U.N. ESCOR, Supp. (No. 8) 15, U.N. Doe. E/cn.4/1/610 (1962) (memorandum of Office of Legal Affairs, U.N. Secretariat). Accordingly, it has been observed that the Universal Declaration of Human Rights "no longer fits into the dichotomy of 'binding treaty' against 'nonbinding. pronouncement,' but is rather an authoritative statement of the international E. Schwelb, *Human Rights and the International Community* 70 (1964).

Thus, a Declaration creates an expectation of adherence, and "insofar as the expectation is gradually justified by State practice, a declaration may by custom become recognized as laying down rules binding upon the States." 34 U.N. ESCOR, *supra* Indeed, several commentators have concluded that the Universal Declaration has become, in toto, a part of binding, customary international law. Nayar, *supra,* at 816–17; Waldlock, "Human Rights in Contemporary International Law and the Significance of the European Convention," *Int'l & Comp. L.Q.,* Supp. Publ. No. 11, at 15 (1965).

Turning to the act of torture, we have little difficulty discerning its universal.renunciation in the modern usage and practice of nations. Smith, *supra*, 18 U.S. (5 Wheat.) at 160–61, 5 L.Ed.57. The international consensus surrounding torture has found expression in numerous international treaties and accords. *E. g., American Convention on Human Rights,* Art. 5, OAS Treaty Series No. 36. at 1, OAS Off. Rec. OEA/Ser 4 v/II 23, doc. 21, rev. 2 (English ed., 1975) ("No one shall be subjected to torture or to cruel, inhuman or degrading punishment or treatment"); International Covenant on Civil and Political Rights, U.N. General Assembly Res. 2200 (XXI)A, U.N. Doc. A/6316 (Dec. 16, 1966) (identical language); European Convention for the Protection of Human Rights and Fundamental Freedoms, Art. 3, Council of Europe, European Treaty Series No. 5 (1968), 213 U.N. T.S.211 (*semble*). The substance of these international agreements is reflected in modern municipal—i.e. national–law as well. Although torture was once a routine concomitant of criminal interrogations in many nations, during the modern and hopefully more enlightened era it has been universally renounced. According to one survey, torture is prohibited, expressly or implicitly, by the constitutions of over fiftyfive nations, including both the United States and Paraguay. Our State Department reports a general recognition of this principle:

> There now exists an international consensus that recognizes basic human rights and obligations owed by all governments to their citizens. . . . There is no doubt that these rights are often violated; but virtually all governments acknowledge their validity.

Department of State, *Country Reports on Human Rights for 1979,* published as Joint Comm. Print, House Comm. on Foreign Affairs, and Senate Comm. on Foreign Relations, 96th Cong. 2d Sess. (Feb. 4, 1980), Introduction at 1. We have been directed to no assertion by any contemporary state of a right to torture its own or another nation's citizens. Indeed, United States diplomatic contacts confirm the universal abhorrence with which torture is viewed:

> In exchanges between United States embassies and all foreign states with which the United States maintains relations, it has been the Department of State's general experience that no government has asserted a right to torture its own nationals. Where reports of torture elicit some credence, a state usually responds by denial or, less frequently, by asserting that the conduct was unauthorized or constituted rough treatment short of torture.

Memorandum of the United States as Amicus Curiae at 16 n.34.

[4] Having examined the sources from which customary international law is derived—the usage of nations, judicial opinions and the works of jurists—we conclude that official torture is now prohibited by the law of nations. The prohibition is clear and unambiguous, and admits of no distinction between treatment of aliens and citizens. Accordingly, we must conclude that the dictum in *Dreyfus v. von Finek, supra,* 534 F.2d at 31, to the effect that "violations of international law do not occur when the aggrieved parties are nationals of the acting state," is clearly out of tune with the current usage and practice of international law. The treaties and accords cited above, as well as the express foreign policy of our own government, all make it clear that international law confers fundamental rights upon all people vis-a-vis their own governments. While the ultimate scope of those rights will be a subject for continuing refinement and elaboration, we hold that the right to be free from torture is now among them. We therefore turn to the question whether the other requirements for jurisdiction are met.

III

Appellee submits that even if the tort alleged is a violation of modern international law, federal jurisdiction may not be exercised consistent with the dictates of Article III of the Constitution. The claim is without merit. Common law courts of general jurisdiction regularly adjudicate transitory tort claims between individuals over whom they exercise personal jurisdiction, wherever the tort occurred. Moreover, as part of an articulated scheme of federal control over external affairs, Congress provided, in the first Judiciary Act, ¤ 9(b), 1 Stat. 73, 77 (1789), for federal jurisdiction over suits by aliens where principles of international law tire in issue. The constitutional basis for the Alien Tort Statute is the law of nations, which has always been part of the federal common law.

[5] It is not extraordinary for a court to adjudicate a tort claim arising outside of its territorial jurisdiction. A state or nation has a legitimate interest in the orderly resolution of disputes among those within its borders, and where the *lex loci delicti commissi* is applied, it is an expression of comity to give effect to the laws of the state where the wrong occurred. Thus, Lord Mansfield in *Mostyn v. Fabrigas,* 1 Cowp. 161 (1774), *quoted in McKenna v. Fisk,* 42 U.S. (1 How.) 241, 248, 11 L.Ed. 117 (1843) said:

> [I]f A becomes indebted to B, or commits a tort upon his person or upon his personal property in Paris, an action in either case may be maintained against A in England, if he is there found . . . . [A]s to transitory actions, there is not a colour of doubt but that any action which is transitory may be laid in any county in England, though the matter arises beyond the seas.

Mostyn came into our law as the original basis for state court jurisdiction over out-of-state torts, *McKenna v. Fisk, supra,* 42 U.S. (1 How.) 241, 11 L.Ed. 117 (personal injury suits *held* transitory); *Dennick v. Railroad Co.,* 103 U.S. 11, 26 L.Ed. 439 (1880) (wrongful death action *held* transitory), and it has not lost its force in suits to recover for a wrongful death occurring upon foreign soil, *Slater v. Mexican National Railroad Co.,* 194 U.S. 120, 24 S.Ct. 581, 48 L.Ed. 900 (1904), as long as the conduct complained of was unlawful where performed. *Restatement (Second) of Foreign Relations Law of the United States* ¤ 19

(1965). Here, where in *personam* jurisdiction has been obtained over the defendant, the parties agree that the acts alleged would violate Paraguayan law, and the policies of the forum are consistent with the foreign law, state court jurisdiction would be proper. Indeed, appellees conceded as much at oral argument.

[10] Although the Alien Tort Statute has rarely been the basis for jurisdiction during its long history, in light of the foregoing discussion, there can be little doubt that this action is properly brought in federal court. This is undeniably an action by an alien, for a tort only, committed in violation of the law of nations. The paucity of suits successfully maintained under the section is readily attributable to the statute's requirement of alleging a "*violation* of the law of nations" (emphasis supplied) at the jurisdictional threshold. Courts have, accordingly, engaged in a more searching preliminary review of the merits than is required,' for example, under the more flexible "arising under" formulation. *Compare O'Reilly de Camara v. Brooke,* 209 U.S. 45, 52, 28 S.Ct. 439, 441, 52 L.Ed. 676 (1907) (question of Alien Tort Statute jurisdiction disposed of "on the merits") (Holmes, J.), with *Bell v. Hood,* 327 U.S. 678, 66 S.Ct. 773, 90 L.Ed. 939 (1946) (general federal question jurisdiction not defeated by the possibility that the averments in the complaint may fail to state a cause of action). Thus, the narrowing construction that the Alien Tort Statute has previously received reflects the fact that earlier cases did not involve such well-established, universally recognized norms of international law that are here at issue.

[11] For example, the statute does not confer jurisdiction over an action by a Luxembourgeois international investment trust's suit for fraud, conversion and corporate waste. *IIT v. Vencap,* 519 F.2d 1001, 1015 (1975). In *IIT,* Judge Friendly astutely noted that the mere fact that every nation's municipal law may prohibit theft does not incorporate "the Eighth Commandment, 'Thou Shalt not steal'. . . [into] the law of nations." It is only where the nations of the world have demonstrated that the wrong is of mutual, and not merely several, concern, by means of express international accords, that a wrong generally recognized becomes an international law violation within the meaning of the statute. Other recent ¤ 1350 cases are similarly distinguishable.

In closing, however, we note that the foreign relations implications of this and other issues the district court will be required to adjudicate on remand underscores the wisdom of the First Congress in vesting jurisdiction over such claims in the federal district courts through the Alien Tort Statute. Questions of this nature are fraught with implications for the nation as a whole, and therefore should not be left to the potentially varying adjudications of the courts of the, fifty states.

In the twentieth century the international community has come to recognize the common danger posed by the flagrant disregard of basic human rights and particularly the right to be free of, torture. Spurred first by the Great War, and then the Second, civilized nations have banded together to prescribe acceptable norms of international behavior. From the ashes of the Second World War arose the United Nations Organization, amid hopes that an era of peace and cooperation had at last begun. Though many of these aspirations have remained elusive goals, that circumstance cannot diminish the true progress that has been made. In the modern age, humanitarian and practical considerations have combined to lead the nations of the world to recognize that respect for fundamental human rights is in their individual and collective interest. Among the rights universally proclaimed by all nations, as we have noted, is the right to be free of physical torture. Indeed, for purposes of civil liability, the torturer has become—like the pirate and slave trader before him—*hostis humani generis,* an enemy of all mankind. Our holding today, giving effect to a jurisdictional provision enacted by our First Congress, is a small but important step in the fulfillment of the ageless dream to free all people from brutal violence.

Krstic

INTRODUCTION The greatest mass killing in Europe since the end of World War II occurred at Srebrenica, located in eastern Bosnia close to the border with Serbia. Historically a Muslim enclave, its existence thwarted Serb plans to create a larger Serb entity that would include major parts of Bosnia and Herzegovina. In July 1995 the Bosnian Serb forces, under the command of General Ratko Mladic, ethnically cleansed the women and children from the area, and then proceeded to summarily execute the men. It is believed that 7,000 to 8,000 unarmed prisoners were murdered within the space of a few days. Radislav Krstic was one of the military leaders involved in the Serb actions in and around Srebrenica. In the first conviction for genocide by the International Criminal Tribunal for the Former Yugoslavia, he was found guilty in August 2001. In April 2004 the Appeals Chamber concluded that Krstic did not intend to exterminate the Muslim population of Srebrenica, but because he assisted Mladic with knowledge of the genocidal plans, he was guilty as an accomplice.

PROSECUTOR v. RADISLAV KRSTIC
(Case No: IT-98-33-A)
JUDGEMENT, 19 April 2004

1. The Appeals Chamber of the International Tribunal for the Prosecution of Persons Responsible for Serious Violations of International Humanitarian Law Committed in the Territory of the Former Yugoslavia Since 1991 is seised of two appeals from the written Judgement rendered by the Trial Chamber on 2 August 2001 in the case of *Prosecutor v. Radislav Krstic*, Case No. IT-98-33-T ("Trial Judgement"). Having considered the written and oral submissions of the Prosecution and the Defence, the Appeals Chamber hereby renders its Judgement.

2. Srebrenica is located in eastern Bosnia and Herzegovina. It gave its name to a United Nations so-called safe area, which was intended as an enclave of safety set up to protect its civilian population from the surrounding war. Since July 1995, however, Srebrenica has also lent its name to an event the horrors of which form the background to this case. The depravity, brutality and cruelty with which the Bosnian Serb Army ("VRS") treated the innocent inhabitants of the safe area are now well known and documented. Bosnian women, children and elderly were removed from the enclave, and between 7,000 – 8,000 Bosnian Muslim men were systematically murdered.

3. Srebrenica is located in the area for which the Drina Corps of the VRS was responsible. Radislav Krstic was a General-Major in the VRS and Commander of the Drina Corps at the time the crimes at issue were committed. For his involvement in these events, the Trial Chamber found Radislav Krstic guilty of genocide; persecution through murders, cruel and inhumane treatment, terrorising the civilian population, forcible transfer and destruction of personal property; and murder as a violation of the laws or customs of war. Radislav Krstic was sentenced to forty-six years of imprisonment.

4. For ease of reference, two annexes are appended to this Judgement. Annex A contains a Procedural Background, detailing the progress of this appeal. Annex B contains a Glossary of Terms, which provides references to and definitions of citations and terms used in this Judgement.

II. THE TRIAL CHAMBER'S FINDING THAT GENOCIDE OCCURRED IN SREBRENICA

1. The Defence appeals Radislav Krstic's conviction for genocide committed against Bosnian Muslims in Srebrenica. The Defence argues that the Trial Chamber both misconstrued the legal definition of genocide and erred in applying the definition to the circumstances of this case. With respect to the legal challenge, the Defence's argument is two-fold. First, Krstic contends that the Trial Chamber's definition of the part of the national group he was found to have intended to destroy was unacceptably narrow. Second, the Defence argues that the Trial Chamber erroneously enlarged the term "destroy" in the prohibition of genocide to include the geographical displacement of a community.

A. The Definition of the Part of the Group

2. Article 4 of the Tribunal's Statute, like the Genocide Convention, covers certain acts done with "intent to destroy, in whole or in part, a national, ethnical, racial or religious group, as such." The Indictment in this case alleged, with respect to the count of genocide, that Radislav Krstic "intend[ed] to destroy a part of the Bosnian Muslim people as a national, ethnical, or religious group." The targeted group identified in the Indictment, and accepted by the Trial Chamber, was that of the Bosnian Muslims. The Trial Chamber determined that the Bosnian Muslims were a specific, distinct national group, and therefore covered by Article 4. This conclusion is not challenged in this appeal.

3. As is evident from the Indictment, Krstic was not alleged to have intended to destroy the entire national group of Bosnian Muslims, but only a part of that group. The first question presented in this appeal is whether, in finding that Radislav Krstic had genocidal intent, the Trial Chamber defined the relevant part of the Bosnian Muslim group in a way which comports with the requirements of Article 4 and of the Genocide Convention.

4. It is well established that where a conviction for genocide relies on the intent to destroy a protected group "in part," the part must be a substantial part of that group. The aim of the Genocide Convention is to prevent the intentional destruction of entire human groups, and the part targeted must be significant enough to have an impact on the group as a whole. Although the Appeals Chamber has not yet addressed this issue, two Trial Chambers of this Tribunal have examined it. In *Jelisic*, the first case to confront the question, the Trial Chamber noted that, "[g]iven the goal of the [Genocide] Convention to deal with mass crimes, it is widely acknowledged that the intention to destroy must target at least a *substantial* part of the group." The

same conclusion was reached by the *Sikirica* Trial Chamber: "This part of the definition calls for evidence of an intention to destroy a substantial number relative to the total population of the group." As these Trial Chambers explained, the substantiality requirement both captures genocide's defining character as a crime of massive proportions and reflects the Convention's concern with the impact the destruction of the targeted part will have on the overall survival of the group.

5. The question has also been considered by Trial Chambers of the ICTR, whose Statute contains an identical definition of the crime of genocide. These Chambers arrived at the same conclusion. In Kayishema, the Trial Chamber concluded, after having canvassed the authorities interpreting the Genocide Convention, that the term "'in part' requires the intention to destroy a considerable number of individuals who are part of the group." This definition was accepted and refined by the Trial Chambers in *Bagilishema* and *Semanza*, which stated that the intent to destroy must be, at least, an intent to destroy a substantial part of the group.

6. This interpretation is supported by scholarly opinion. The early commentators on the Genocide Convention emphasized that the term "in part" contains a substantiality requirement. Raphael Lemkin, a prominent international criminal lawyer who coined the term "genocide" and was instrumental in the drafting of the Genocide Convention, addressed the issue during the 1950 debate in the United States Senate on the ratification of the Convention. Lemkin explained that "the destruction in part must be of a substantial nature so as to affect the entirety." He further suggested that the Senate clarify, in a statement of understanding to accompany the ratification, that "the Convention applies only to actions undertaken on a mass scale." Another noted early commentator, Nehemiah Robinson, echoed this view, explaining that a perpetrator of genocide must possess the intent to destroy a substantial number of individuals constituting the targeted group. In discussing this requirement, Robinson stressed, as did Lemkin, that "the act must be directed toward the destruction of a *group*," this formulation being the aim of the Convention.

7. Recent commentators have adhered to this view. The International Law Commission, charged by the UN General Assembly with the drafting of a comprehensive code of crimes prohibited by international law, stated that "the crime of genocide by its very nature requires the intention to destroy at least a substantial part of a particular group." The same interpretation was adopted earlier by the 1985 report of Benjamin Whitaker, the Special Rapporteur to the United Nations Sub-

Commission on Prevention of Discrimination and Protection of Minorities.

8. The intent requirement of genocide under Article 4 of the Statute is therefore satisfied where evidence shows that the alleged perpetrator intended to destroy at least a substantial part of the protected group. The determination of when the targeted part is substantial enough to meet this requirement may involve a number of considerations. The numeric size of the targeted part of the group is the necessary and important starting point, though not in all cases the ending point of the inquiry. The number of individuals targeted should be evaluated not only in absolute terms, but also in relation to the overall size of the entire group. In addition to the numeric size of the targeted portion, its prominence within the group can be a useful consideration. If a specific part of the group is emblematic of the overall group, or is essential to its survival, that may support a finding that the part qualifies as substantial within the meaning of Article 4.

9. The historical examples of genocide also suggest that the area of the perpetrators' activity and control, as well as the possible extent of their reach, should be considered. Nazi Germany may have intended only to eliminate Jews within Europe alone; that ambition probably did not extend, even at the height of its power, to an undertaking of that enterprise on a global scale. Similarly, the perpetrators of genocide in Rwanda did not seriously contemplate the elimination of the Tutsi population beyond the country's borders. The intent to destroy formed by a perpetrator of genocide will always be limited by the opportunity presented to him. While this factor alone will not indicate whether the targeted group is substantial, it can — in combination with other factors — inform the analysis.

10. These considerations, of course, are neither exhaustive nor dispositive. They are only useful guidelines. The applicability of these factors, as well as their relative weight, will vary depending on the circumstances of a particular case.

11. In this case, having identified the protected group as the national group of Bosnian Muslims, the Trial Chamber concluded that the part the VRS Main Staff and Radislav Krstic targeted was the Bosnian Muslims of Srebrenica, or the Bosnian Muslims of Eastern Bosnia. This conclusion comports with the guidelines outlined above. The size of the Bosnian Muslim population in Srebrenica prior to its capture by the VRS forces in 1995 amounted to approximately forty thousand people. This represented not only the Muslim inhabitants of the Srebrenica municipality but also many Muslim refugees from the surrounding region. Although this population constituted only a small per-

centage of the overall Muslim population of Bosnia and Herzegovina at the time, the importance of the Muslim community of Srebrenica is not captured solely by its size. As the Trial Chamber explained, Srebrenica (and the surrounding Central Podrinje region) were of immense strategic importance to the Bosnian Serb leadership. Without Srebrenica, the ethnically Serb state of Republica Srpska they sought to create would remain divided into two disconnected parts, and its access to Serbia proper would be disrupted. The capture and ethnic purification of Srebrenica would therefore severely undermine the military efforts of the Bosnian Muslim state to ensure its viability, a consequence the Muslim leadership fully realized and strove to prevent. Control over the Srebrenica region was consequently essential to the goal of some Bosnian Serb leaders of forming a viable political entity in Bosnia, as well as to the continued survival of the Bosnian Muslim people. Because most of the Muslim inhabitants of the region had, by 1995, sought refuge within the Srebrenica enclave, the elimination of that enclave would have accomplished the goal of purifying the entire region of its Muslim population.

12. In addition, Srebrenica was important due to its prominence in the eyes of both the Bosnian Muslims and the international community. The town of Srebrenica was the most visible of the "safe areas" established by the UN Security Council in Bosnia. By 1995 it had received significant attention in the international media. In its resolution declaring Srebrenica a safe area, the Security Council announced that it "should be free from armed attack or any other hostile act." This guarantee of protection was re-affirmed by the commander of the UN Protection Force in Bosnia (UNPROFOR) and reinforced with the deployment of UN troops. The elimination of the Muslim population of Srebrenica, despite the assurances given by the international community, would serve as a potent example to all Bosnian Muslims of their vulnerability and defenselessness in the face of Serb military forces. The fate of the Bosnian Muslims of Srebrenica would be emblematic of that of all Bosnian Muslims.

13. Finally, the ambit of the genocidal enterprise in this case was limited to the area of Srebrenica. While the authority of the VRS Main Staff extended throughout Bosnia, the authority of the Bosnian Serb forces charged with the take-over of Srebrenica did not extend beyond the Central Podrinje region. From the perspective of the Bosnian Serb forces alleged to have had genocidal intent in this case, the Muslims of Srebrenica were the only part of the Bosnian Muslim group within their area of control.

14. In fact, the Defence does not argue that the Trial Chamber's characterization of the Bosnian Muslims of Srebrenica as a substantial part of the targeted group contravenes Article 4 of the Tribunal's Statute. Rather, the Defence contends that the Trial Chamber made a further finding, concluding that the part Krstic intended to destroy was the Bosnian Muslim men of military age of Srebrenica. In the Defence's view, the Trial Chamber then engaged in an impermissible sequential reasoning, measuring the latter part of the group against the larger part (the Bosnian Muslims of Srebrenica) to find the substantiality requirement satisfied. The Defence submits that if the correct approach is properly applied, and the military age men are measured against the entire group of Bosnian Muslims, the substantiality requirement would not be met.

15. The Defence misunderstands the Trial Chamber's analysis. The Trial Chamber stated that the part of the group Radislav Krstic intended to destroy was the Bosnian Muslim population of Srebrenica. The men of military age, who formed a further part of that group, were not viewed by the Trial Chamber as a separate, smaller part within the meaning of Article 4. Rather, the Trial Chamber treated the killing of the men of military age as evidence from which to infer that Radislav Krstic and some members of the VRS Main Staff had the requisite intent to destroy all the Bosnian Muslims of Srebrenica, the only part of the protected group relevant to the Article 4 analysis.

16. In support of its argument, the Defence identifies the Trial Chamber's determination that, in the context of this case, "the intent to kill the men (of military age) amounted to an intent to destroy a substantial part of the Bosnian Muslim group." The Trial Chamber's observation was proper. As a specific intent offense, the crime of genocide requires proof of intent to commit the underlying act and proof of intent to destroy the targeted group, in whole or in part. The proof of the mental state with respect to the commission of the underlying act can serve as evidence from which the fact-finder may draw the further inference that the accused possessed the specific intent to destroy.

17. The Trial Chamber determined that Radislav Krstic had the intent to kill the Srebrenica Bosnian Muslim men of military age. This finding is one of intent to commit the requisite genocidal act - in this case, the killing of the members of the protected group, prohibited by Article 4(2)(a) of the Statute. From this intent to kill, the Trial Chamber also drew the further inference that Krstic shared the genocidal intent of some members of the VRS Main Staff to destroy a substantial part of the targeted group, the Bosnian Muslims of Srebrenica.

18. It must be acknowledged that in portions of its Judgement, the Trial Chamber used imprecise language which lends support to the Defence's argument. The Trial Chamber should have expressed its reasoning more carefully. As explained above, however, the Trial Chamber's overall discussion makes clear that it identified the Bosnian Muslims of Srebrenica as the substantial part in this case.

19. The Trial Chamber's determination of the substantial part of the protected group was correct. The Defence's appeal on this issue is dismissed.

B. *The Determination of the Intent to Destroy*

20. The Defence also argues that the Trial Chamber erred in describing the conduct with which Radislav Krstic is charged as genocide. The Trial Chamber, the Defence submits, impermissibly broadened the definition of genocide by concluding that an effort to displace a community from its traditional residence is sufficient to show that the alleged perpetrator intended to destroy a protected group. By adopting this approach, the Defence argues, the Trial Chamber departed from the established meaning of the term genocide in the Genocide Convention — as applying only to instances of physical or biological destruction of a group — to include geographic displacement.

21. The Genocide Convention, and customary international law in general, prohibit only the physical or biological destruction of a human group. The Trial Chamber expressly acknowledged this limitation, and eschewed any broader definition. The Chamber stated: "(C(ustomary international law limits the definition of genocide to those acts seeking the physical or biological destruction of all or part of the group. (A(n enterprise attacking only the cultural or sociological characteristics of a human group in order to annihilate these elements which give to that group its own identity distinct from the rest of the community would not fall under the definition of genocide."

22. Given that the Trial Chamber correctly identified the governing legal principle, the Defence must discharge the burden of persuading the Appeals Chamber that, despite having correctly stated the law, the Trial Chamber erred in applying it. The main evidence underlying the Trial Chamber's conclusion that the VRS forces intended to eliminate all the Bosnian Muslims of Srebrenica was the massacre by the VRS of all men of military age from that community. The Trial Chamber rejected the Defence's argument that the killing of these men was motivated solely by the desire to eliminate them as a potential military threat. The Trial Chamber based this conclusion on a number of factual findings, which must be accepted as long as a reason-able Trial Chamber could have arrived at the same conclusions. The Trial Chamber found that, in executing the captured Bosnian Muslim men, the VRS did not differentiate between men of military status and civilians. Though civilians undoubtedly are capable of bearing arms, they do not constitute the same kind of military threat as professional soldiers. The Trial Chamber was therefore justified in drawing the inference that, by killing the civilian prisoners, the VRS did not intend only to eliminate them as a military danger. The Trial Chamber also found that some of the victims were severely handicapped and, for that reason, unlikely to have been combatants. This evidence further supports the Trial Chamber's conclusion that the extermination of these men was not driven solely by a military rationale.

23. Moreover, as the Trial Chamber emphasized, the term "men of military age" was itself a misnomer, for the group killed by the VRS included boys and elderly men normally considered to be outside that range. Although the younger and older men could still be capable of bearing arms, the Trial Chamber was entitled to conclude that they did not present a serious military threat, and to draw a further inference that the VRS decision to kill them did not stem solely from the intent to eliminate them as a threat. The killing of the military aged men was, assuredly, a physical destruction, and given the scope of the killings the Trial Chamber could legitimately draw the inference that their extermination was motivated by a genocidal intent.

24. The Trial Chamber was also entitled to consider the long-term impact that the elimination of seven to eight thousand men from Srebrenica would have on the survival of that community. In examining these consequences, the Trial Chamber properly focused on the likelihood of the community's physical survival. As the Trial Chamber found, the massacred men amounted to about one fifth of the overall Srebrenica community. The Trial Chamber found that, given the patriarchal character of the Bosnian Muslim society in Srebrenica, the destruction of such a sizeable number of men would "inevitably result in the physical disappearance of the Bosnian Muslim population at Srebrenica." Evidence introduced at trial supported this finding, by showing that, with the majority of the men killed officially listed as missing, their spouses are unable to remarry and, consequently, to have new children. The physical destruction of the men therefore had severe procreative implications for the Srebrenica Muslim community, potentially consigning the community to extinction.

25. This is the type of physical destruction the Genocide Convention is designed to prevent. The Trial Chamber found that the Bosnian Serb forces were

aware of these consequences when they decided to systematically eliminate the captured Muslim men. The finding that some members of the VRS Main Staff devised the killing of the male prisoners with full knowledge of the detrimental consequences it would have for the physical survival of the Bosnian Muslim community in Srebrenica further supports the Trial Chamber's conclusion that the instigators of that operation had the requisite genocidal intent.

26. The Defence argues that the VRS decision to transfer, rather than to kill, the women and children of Srebrenica in their custody undermines the finding of genocidal intent. This conduct, the Defence submits, is inconsistent with the indiscriminate approach that has characterized all previously recognized instances of modern genocide.

27. The decision by Bosnian Serb forces to transfer the women, children and elderly within their control to other areas of Muslim-controlled Bosnia could be consistent with the Defence argument. This evidence, however, is also susceptible of an alternative interpretation. As the Trial Chamber explained, forcible transfer could be an additional means by which to ensure the physical destruction of the Bosnian Muslim community in Srebrenica. The transfer completed the removal of all Bosnian Muslims from Srebrenica, thereby eliminating even the residual possibility that the Muslim community in the area could reconstitute itself. The decision not to kill the women or children may be explained by the Bosnian Serbs' sensitivity to public opinion. In contrast to the killing of the captured military men, such an action could not easily be kept secret, or disguised as a military operation, and so carried an increased risk of attracting international censure.

28. In determining that genocide occurred at Srebrenica, the cardinal question is whether the intent to commit genocide existed. While this intent must be supported by the factual matrix, the offence of genocide does not require proof that the perpetrator chose the most efficient method to accomplish his objective of destroying the targeted part. Even where the method selected will not implement the perpetrator's intent to the fullest, leaving that destruction incomplete, this ineffectiveness alone does not preclude a finding of genocidal intent. The international attention focused on Srebrenica, combined with the presence of the UN troops in the area, prevented those members of the VRS Main Staff who devised the genocidal plan from putting it into action in the most direct and efficient way. Constrained by the circumstances, they adopted the method which would allow them to implement the genocidal design while minimizing the risk of retribution.

29. The Trial Chamber — as the best assessor of the evidence presented at trial — was entitled to conclude that the evidence of the transfer supported its finding that some members of the VRS Main Staff intended to destroy the Bosnian Muslims in Srebrenica. The fact that the forcible transfer does not constitute in and of itself a genocidal act does not preclude a Trial Chamber from relying on it as evidence of the intentions of members of the VRS Main Staff. The genocidal intent may be inferred, among other facts, from evidence of "other culpable acts systematically directed against the same group."

30. The Defence also argues that the record contains no statements by members of the VRS Main Staff indicating that the killing of the Bosnian Muslim men was motivated by genocidal intent to destroy the Bosnian Muslims of Srebrenica. The absence of such statements is not determinative. Where direct evidence of genocidal intent is absent, the intent may still be inferred from the factual circumstances of the crime. The inference that a particular atrocity was motivated by genocidal intent may be drawn, moreover, even where the individuals to whom the intent is attributable are not precisely identified. If the crime committed satisfies the other requirements of genocide, and if the evidence supports the inference that the crime was motivated by the intent to destroy, in whole or in part, a protected group, a finding that genocide has occurred may be entered.

31. In this case, the factual circumstances, as found by the Trial Chamber, permit the inference that the killing of the Bosnian Muslim men was done with genocidal intent. As already explained, the scale of the killing, combined with the VRS Main Staff's awareness of the detrimental consequences it would have for the Bosnian Muslim community of Srebrenica and with the other actions the Main Staff took to ensure that community's physical demise, is a sufficient factual basis for the finding of specific intent. The Trial Chamber found, and the Appeals Chamber endorses this finding, that the killing was engineered and supervised by some members of the Main Staff of the VRS. The fact that the Trial Chamber did not attribute genocidal intent to a particular official within the Main Staff may have been motivated by a desire not to assign individual culpability to persons not on trial here. This, however, does not undermine the conclusion that Bosnian Serb forces carried out genocide against the Bosnian Muslims.

32. Among the grievous crimes this Tribunal has the duty to punish, the crime of genocide is singled out for special condemnation and opprobrium. The crime is horrific in its scope; its perpetrators identify entire human groups for extinction. Those who devise and

implement genocide seek to deprive humanity of the manifold richness its nationalities, races, ethnicities and religions provide. This is a crime against all of humankind, its harm being felt not only by the group targeted for destruction, but by all of humanity.

33. The gravity of genocide is reflected in the stringent requirements which must be satisfied before this conviction is imposed. These requirements — the demanding proof of specific intent and the showing that the group was targeted for destruction in its entirety or in substantial part — guard against a danger that convictions for this crime will be imposed lightly. Where these requirements are satisfied, however, the law must not shy away from referring to the crime committed by its proper name. By seeking to eliminate a part of the Bosnian Muslims, the Bosnian Serb forces committed genocide. They targeted for extinction the forty thousand Bosnian Muslims living in Srebrenica, a group which was emblematic of the Bosnian Muslims in general. They stripped all the male Muslim prisoners, military and civilian, elderly and young, of their personal belongings and identification, and deliberately and methodically killed them solely on the basis of their identity. The Bosnian Serb forces were aware, when they embarked on this genocidal venture, that the harm they caused would continue to plague the Bosnian Muslims. The Appeals Chamber states unequivocally that the law condemns, in appropriate terms, the deep and lasting injury inflicted, and calls the massacre at Srebrenica by its proper name: genocide. Those responsible will bear this stigma, and it will serve as a warning to those who may in future contemplate the commission of such a heinous act.

34. In concluding that some members of the VRS Main Staff intended to destroy the Bosnian Muslims of Srebrenica, the Trial Chamber did not depart from the legal requirements for genocide. The Defence appeal on this issue is dismissed.

index

Boldface page numbers refer to the main entry on the subject. Italic page numbers refer to illustrations, maps, and photos.

American Eugenics Society (AES), 255

American Jewish Joint Distribution Commission (JDC), 1056

American Military Commission in the Far East, 599

American Red Cross, 531–533

American Relief Administration (ARA), 1056

American Revolution, *687, 965*

American Service Members' Protection Act, 546

Améry, Jean, 801

Amin, Idi, 1053, 1054

Amistad case, 965

Amnesty, **31–37**
  Algerians, for crimes committed against, 17, 20
  Armenian genocide, 187, 210, 490–491
  Chile, 737
  Christmas amnesty, 777
  El Mozote massacre, 382
  International Criminal Tribunal for the Former Yugoslavia, 417
  Japanese war criminals, 1034
  Latin America, 736–737
  Peruvian human rights violators, 801
  Pinochet regime, 169
  Polish detainees in the Soviet Union, 607
  Sierra Leone, 949, 954
  South Africa, 491
  torture, 1038
  truth commissions, 1049

Amnesty International, *288, 746*
  accountability, 487
  Ennals, Martin, 287–288
  Israel and the Occupied Territories, investigations of, 752–753
  overview, 749

Amputations, *952, 954, 959, 1036, 1133*

Amursana, 1183

Ana Celis Laureano v. Peru, 262

Anabasis (Xenophon), 683–684

Analysis and investigations, 576

ANC. *See* African National Congress (ANC)

Ancerl, Karel, 718

Ancient world, **37–39**
  Carthage, 149–151
  homosexuality, 461
  slavery, 964
  Sparta, 986–988
  See also Greece, ancient; India, ancient and medieval; Rome, ancient

And the Crooked Shall Be Made Straight (Robinson), 281

Andean Program, 514

Anderson, Hu C, 775

Andersonville Prison, 848

Andes region, 799

Anfal campaign, 584–585

Angels in America (Kushner), 450

Angolan civil war, 724

Angoulvant, Gabriel, 385

"Ani Ma'amin" (song), 711

Annan, Kofi, *546, 1114*
  on Bosnian conflict, 1175
  early warnings, 272
  self-defense as justifiable use of force, 14
  on Wallenberg, Raoul, 1139

Antelope case, 965

Antemortem data collection, 379

Anthony, Scott J., 942

Anthropology, **39–40**, 307, 672

Anti-ballistic missile systems, 760

Anti-Communism, 532, 811, 818

Anti-Personnel Mine Convention, 474

"Anti-Rightist Struggle," 172

Anti-Romanis laws, 920

Anti-Semitism, **40–47**, *41*
  art propaganda, 85
  bystanders, 139
  Catholic Church, 155–156
  Christianity, 880, 882
  films, 356
  German escalation of, 403–404
  ghettos, 409, 410–413
  Goebbels, Joseph, 414–415
  hate propaganda, *826,* 826–828
  Heidegger, Martin, 801–802
  Himmler, Heinrich, 439–441
  Hitler, Adolf, 451–453
  Holocaust denial, 244–246
  incitement, 494
  inter-war period, 399–400
  radio, 859
  rescuing, as barrier to, 895
  Sicherheitsdienst (SD), 407
  South Africa, 979
  Stalin, Joseph, 997, 1066
  stolen art, 83–84
  Strauss, Richard, 712
  Streicher, Julius, 1001–1002
  Der Stürmer, 247–249, *248*
  utopian ideology, 1125, 1126
  Wagner, Richard, 717
  See also Ghettos; Holocaust; Nuremberg Laws; Pogroms

Anti-Stalinist resistance, 904

Anti-Tamil riots, 991–992

Anti-Terrorism Act, 23

Antiabortion laws, 917

Anuaks, 299–300

Anya Nya, 1005

Apartheid, **47–55**
  amnesty, 31
  Article 7, Rome Statute, 3
  as crime against humanity, 215
  denationalization, 243
  forms of, 980–981
  Indians in South Africa, 1085
  Mandela, Nelson, 657–659
  racism, 855
  restitution, 912
  South Africa, 979–982
  United States, 7
  See also Convention on the Suppression and Punishment of the Crime of Apartheid

Apartheid Convention. *See* Convention on the Suppression and Punishment of the Crime of Apartheid

APC (All People's Congress), 947

Apologies
  International Committee of the Red Cross, 538
  residential school system, victims of the, 901

Appeals
  evidence, 325
  International Criminal Tribunal for Rwanda, 550–551
  Prosecutor v. Goran Jelisic, 525–526, 529–530

Appian, 150

Applebaum, Anne, 904

Application of the Genocide Convention case, 910

Aquinas, St. Thomas, 42–43, 471

ARA (American Relief Administration), 1056

Arab persecution, 19, 707–709

Arabization
  of Kurds, 636
  Sudan, 1002–1008

Arabs, Marsh, 585

Arana, Julio, 29

Arapaho, 942

Ararat (film), 361

Arawaks. *See* Taino

Arbeit macht frei from Toitland Europa (Maayan and Yaron), 269

Arbenz Guzmán, Jacobo, 419

Arbitrary deprivation of life, 477–478

Arbitrary detention, 1071–1072

V1: [1–482]; V2: [483–1016]; V3: [1017–1458]

Beecher, Henry, 671

Beijing Platform for Action, 1164

Being and Time (Heidegger), 802

Beirut, Lebanon, 736

Belaunde Terry, Fernando, 799

Belgium
    Congo, colonization of, 617–621
    disappearances, prosecutions
      concerning, 261
    national laws, 729
    national prosecutions, 835
    racism, 858–859
    Rwanda, colonialism in, 925–926
    Rwandan peacekeeping mission,
      1092
    state responsibility, 908
    universal jurisdiction cases, 1120,
      1121

Belzec execution center, 332, 456

Ben M'Hidi, Larbi, 20

Benedict XII, Pope, 154

Benenson, Peter, 749

Bengal, 346

Benigni, Roberto, 362–363, 943

Bent (Sherman), 269

Benzoni, Girolamo, 1017

Beothuk, **120–121**

Berber Algerians, 19

Bergen-Belsen, 330, 1159

Berger, Oscar, 422

Berger, Thomas R., 741

Bergholz, Fred, 1184

Beria, Lavrenti, 606–608

Berlin Conference, 509

Berlin Documents Center, 266

Berlin Jewish Museum, 61–62

Berlin Treaty, 70

Berlin Wall, destruction of the, 477

Berman, Karel, 718

Bernadotte, Folke, 1138

Bernard, Claude, 670

Berning, Heinrich, 805

Beschloss, Michael, 538

Bespuca povijesne zbiljnosti
    (Tudjman), 1051

Bettelheim, Bruno, 971

Better Fewer But Better (Lenin), 647

Bey, Ibrahim, 289

Bhartiya Janata Party (BJP), 507–508

Bhivandi-Jalgaon riots, 507

Bhutto, Zulfiqar Ali, 118

Biafra, **121–124**

Bialik, Chaim Nachman, 814

Bialystok, 457

Biamby, Philippe, 31

Bible
    anti-Semitism, 41
    genocide accounts, 39
    rules of war, 471

Biedermann, 680

Bielski otriad camp, 903

Big Foot, 1166–1167, *1167*

"Big Lie Theory," 828

Bigeard, Marcel, 17

Bihumugani, Leopold, 133

Bikindi, Simon, 860

Biko, Steve, 51

Bilateralism, 698–699, 906

Bill of Particulars, Tokyo Trial,
    1031–1032

Bioethics, 673–674

Biographies, **124–125**

Biological altruism. *See* Altruism,
    biological

Biological and chemical weapons
    Ethiopia, 292–295
    Hague Conventions, 430
    humanitarian law, 474
    Iran-Iraq war, 586
    Japan, 598, 599
    Kurdish genocide, 584–585
    Kurds, use against, 636
    medical experimentation, 671
    reproduction, 894
    See also Gas; Weapons of mass
      destruction

Birkenau, 100

Birth, prevention of, 889

Birth control, government sponsored,
    893

BJP (Bhartiya Janata Party), 507–508

Black Book of Communism (Courtois),
    1060

"Black Codes," 7

Black Hundreds, 815

Black Kettle, Chief, 162–163

The Black Man, 385

The Black Stork (film), 366–367

Blacks (Urban Areas) Consolidation
    Act (South Africa), 50

Blackshirts, 294–295

Blair, Tony, 950

"Blaming the victim," 971

Blanchard, Pascal, 17

Blanche of Castille, 153

Blaskic case, 558, 1013

Blobel, Paul, 109–110

Bloch, Eduard, 451–452

Block Islanders, 789

"Blockleiter Braunmüller" (radio
    program), 944

Blood libel, 42

Bloody News from My Friend
    (Siamanto), 811

Blue Book on the Putumayo
    (Casement), 29

Blue Helmets, 949–950

"Blue Series," 266

Blum, Léon, 385

Boarding-school system, 744

Boban, Mate, 127

Bockarie, Samuel, 948, 950

Boer war, 979

Bogomils, 152

In re Bohne, 337

Bolsheviks
    Cossacks, treatment of, 208–209
    Lenin, Vladimir, 645–647
    October Revolution, 1061
    Russian Civil War, 1062–1063
    utopian ideology, 1125–1126

Boltanski, Christian, 88

Bolton, John, 545–546

Bombing
    aerial, 662, 765
    of Cambodia, 610
    Hague Conventions, 430

Bond Head, Frances, 147

Bone fractures and skeletal injuries,
    58–59

Bone transplantation experiments,
    672

Bonhoeffer, Dietrich, 880

Book burning
    Goebbels, Joseph, 414
    memorials, 680

Bor, Josef, 712

Border War of Eritrea, 291–292,
    296–298

Borovcanin, Ljubomir, 989

Borowski, Tadeusz, 812

Bos, Adriaan, 543

Bosnia and Herzegovina, **125–129,**
    701
    Albanian Kosovars, 623
    artistic representation of genocide,
      88
    Commission on Human Rights
      investigation, 1076–1077
    elections, 1173
    ethnic cleansing, 301, 303
    General Assembly resolution,
      1084
    International Committee of the
      Red Cross, 535
    International Court of Justice,
      requested intervention of, 540

Izetbegovic, Alija, 588–589
Karadzic, Radovan, 605–606
mass graves, 667
Milosevic, Slobodan, 691
Mladic, Ratko, 700–701
national laws, 732
national prosecutions, 737–738, 836
Organization for Security and Cooperation in Europe, 781–783
peacekeeping, 786, 787
racism, 859
religion, 882
restitution, 912–913
safe zones, 941
Security Council response, 1090–1091
sovereignty vote, 1173
state responsibility, 908, 910
Tudjman, Franjo, policy of, 1052
United States foreign policy, 1113–1115
violence against women, 1164–1165
See also International Criminal Tribunal for the Former Yugoslavia (ICTY); Serbs; Yugoslavia, former
Bosnia and Herzegovina v. Yugoslavia, 910, 1084
Bosnian Muslims
Mladic, Ratko, ethnic cleansing by, 700
photography of victims, 803
Srebrenica, attack on, 941
Bosnian National Library, 310
Bosnian refugees, 875, 876
Botha, Pierre Willem, 982
Botswana, 725
Bouhler, Philipp, 315, 805
Boundary construction, 40
Bourhis, R. Y., 329
Bow Street Stipendiary Magistrate and others, ex parte Pinochet Ugarte, 234
Boxer Rebellion, 169–170
Boycotts
Jewish businesses, 828
South Africa, 52
Bozano v. France, 339
Brandt, Karl, 315, 319, 774, 805
Braunsteiner-Ryan, Hermine, 735, 1162
Brazil
Indianist movement, 29
indigenous peoples, 512
Brazilian National Indian Foundation (FUNAI), 29

Brazzaville Conference, 385
Bread queue massacre, 589
Brecht, Bertolt, 944
Breitenfeld, Richard, 712
Bresson, Henri-Cartier, 370
Brevissima Relación (Las Casas), 1017
Brewster, Jonathan, 788
Bride service, 952–953
Bricrly, James, 966
British North American Act (Great Britain), 147
British Red Cross Society, 531
Broadcasting. See Media case; Radio; Television
Broederbond, 981
Brooklyn Jewish Chronic Disease Hospital, 671
Brother Eichmann (Eichmann), 269
Brown v. Board of Education (1954), 9–10
Browne, J. Ross, 1178
Browning, Christopher, 328, 587, 1135
Broz, Josip. See Tito
Bruder Eichmann (Eichmann), 269
Brüning, Heinrich, 818
Brussels Act. See General Act for the Repression of the African Slave Trade
Brussels Conference on the Laws and Customs of War, 388, 470, 474
Bryant, A. T., 1182
Bryant, Gyude, 652
Bryce, Viscount, 252
Buchanwald, 672
Buck v. Bell, 255
Bucyana, Martin, 928
Budapest, Great Synagogue in, 679
Buddhism
ethnocide, 312
Kalmyks, 604–605
Khmer Rouge, persecution of monks by, 612
monks, 1027
Sinhala Buddhists, 990–992
Tibet, 1026–1028
Bugeaud, Thomas, 16
Bukharin, Nikolai, 629, 1064
Bulgaria, 458
Bullock, Alan, 328
Burckhardt, Carl J., 537
Burdenko, N. N., 607
Bureaucracy, 791
Burial, 59
Burkhardt, Carl J., 532

Burleigh,Michael, 368
Burma. See Myanmar
Burr, J. Millard, 1007
al-Burujerdi, Murtada, 585
Burundi, 133–137
ethnic massacres, 11
Hutu, 926
Ndadaye, Melchior, assassination of, 928
Tutsi, 926
United Nations Sub-Commission on Human Rights resolution, 1094
Bush, George W.
International Criminal Court, 545–546, 1110
nuclear weapons policy, 759–760
weapons of mass destruction, 1154–1155
Bushness, Prudence, 973
Business organizations, international, 569
"Butare Four," 553, 729
Buthelezi, Mangosutho, 981
Buyoya, Pierre, 136
Bystanders, 137–140
as perpetrators, 790
as victims, 1132
Byzantium, 220–221, 222–223

[C]

C 100 P bombs, 294
Cable News Network (CNN), 1020
Caesarius of Heisterbach, 154
California, Yuki of, 1177–1178
Caligula (Schwartz), 712
Calley, William, 736, 1148
Cambodia, 141–146
artistic representation of genocide, 89
dissidents, 143, 144
documentation, 266–267
early warning of genocide, 272
estimating victim numbers, 615–617
General Assembly representation, 1080, 1112–1113
International Committee of the Red Cross, 535
reconciliation, 869–870
truth commission, lack of a, 1050
Tuol Sleng Prison, 210, 616
United Nations Sub-Commission on Human Rights, 1094
United States policy, 1111–1113
utopian ideology, 1126
women perpetrators, 792–793
See also Khmer Rouge; Pol Pot

Charter of the Nuremberg Tribunal. *See* London Charter
Charter of the United Nations
Commission on Human Rights, 1073–1074
compensation, 191
human rights, 1068
humanitarian intervention, 465–467
indigenous peoples, 510–511
state-sponsored assassination, 90
Chea, Nuon, 609, 611, 613
Chechens, **159–162**, 872–873, 875
Cheka, 646, 1063
Chelmno, 331–332
Chemical weapons. *See* Biological and chemical weapons; Weapons of mass destruction
Chemical Weapons Convention. *See* Convention on the Prohibition of the Development, Production, Stockpiling and Use of Chemical Weapons and on Their Destruction
Chen Kuei Yuan, 1028
Cherokees, 229, 375, 744, 1043–1045
Cheyenne, **162–163**, 942
Chiang Kai-shek, 170–171
Child abuse, 900–901
Child soldiers, 164, 165–166, 957–960
Children, **163–167**, *164, 166*
Aborigines, assimilation policy for, 103, 513, 901–902
amputation, *1036, 1133*
Commission on Human Rights, 1078
definition, 371–372
disabled, 255–256
forcible transfer, 370–376
linguistic genocide, 653
music of reconciliation, 717
Native American assimilation, 744
as perpetrators, 793
psychology of survivors, 843
refugee camps, *871*
refugees, 876
rescue of, 369
rights of the child, 479
Rwanda, *926*
of survivors, 843–844
Children in the Holocaust and World War II: Their Secret Diaries (Holliday, ed.), 253
Children of the Ghetto (Zangwill), 412
Chile, **167–169**, *168*
amnesty law, 737
film dramatizations, 364
International Committee of the Red Cross, 535

national prosecutions, 737
Pinochet, Augusto, 487, 805–809
transitional justice, 1046, 1047
victims, 1129
Chiles, Lawton, 924–925
China, **169–175**
banned art, 82
Burmese independence, 129
Chinese in Cambodia, 144, 612
civil war, 170–171
famine, 346–347
General Assembly representation, 1080, 1112–1113
homosexuality, 461
Mongol conquests, 702
Nanking massacre, *595, 597,* 598, 663–664, 1149
rules of war, 469
San Francisco conference, 1073–1074
Tibet and, 1026–1028
United Nations, establishment of the, 1068
Zunghars, 1182–1184
See also Mao Zedong
Chinese Communist Party (CCP), 170–173, 659–661
Chinese Indonesians, 519
Chirac, Jacques, 432
Chittagong Hill Tract, **175–176**, 249–250
Chivalry, 469, 471–472
Chivington, John, 162–163, 942
Chmielnicki, Bogdan, **176–177**
Choeun, Chhit, 610–611, 613
Chorzow Factory case, 911
Christianity
Albigensian Crusade, 153–154
Almohad policies toward, 25
anti-Romani sentiment, 921
anti-Semitism, 41–43
Armenian Church, 68–69
Armenian genocide, songs of, 715
Cathars, 151–154
Holocaust, 880, 882
Huguenots, 463–465
Inquisitions, 521–524
Moriscos, persecution of, 707–709
rules of war, 471–472
Spanish Conquest, 105–106
Sudan, 1003
witch hunts, 881
Christians, Roman persecution of, **177–179**
Christmas amnesty, 777
Chronicles of a provisional planet (Gatti), 269
Chrysostom, St. John, 41–42
Chubar, Vlas, 1058, 1060

Church Committee, 91–92
Churchill, Winston, 706, 764–765, 1100
CICIACS (Commission to Investigate Illegal and Clandestine Security Forces), 422
CIOMS (Council for International Organizations of Medical Sciences), 673–674
CIS (Community of Independent States), 308
Citizens for Global Solutions, 751
Citizenship, 762
The City of Slaughter (Bialik), 814
Civil defense forces (Sierra Leone), 947, 948
Civil disobedience. *See* Nonviolent resistance
Civil Liberties Act, 191
Civil litigation
Alien Tort Statute (U.S.), 21–23
Chechens, 160–161
compensation, 191–192
ethnic violence, 305
historical injustices, 446
immunity, 488
Japanese companies, 600
against Japanese companies, 600
reparations, 887
residential schools, 901
Civil Rights Acts, 7
Civil Rights Cases, 6–7
Civil Rights Movement, U.S., 10
Civil War, U.S., 6, 196–197, 847, 1144
Civil wars. *See* Internal conflicts
Civilians
aerial bombing, 765
Geneva Conventions on the Protection of Victims of War, 392
Hiroshima and Nagasaki bombings, 754–755
Special Court for Sierra Leone, 959
superior responsibility, 1011–1012, 1014–1015
World War II, targeting of, 442–443
Claims
collective, 1131
Herero reparations, 438
historical injustices, 444–447
reparations, 884–885, 886–888
restitution, 911, 912–913
Rosewood survivors, 924
Claims Resolution Tribunal, 912
Clandestine detention centers (CDCs), 379

Davison, Neil R., 353

Dawes Act, 744

Dawidziuk, Stanislawa, 896

al-Dawla, Adhud, 32

Dawn (Wiesel), 1159–1160

A Day in the Life of Ivan Denisovich (Solzhenitsyn), 427

Day of Hatred, 614

Day of Liberation, 614

Dayaks, 603

Dayton Accords
Bosnia and Herzegovina, 128–129
map, *218*
restitution, 912–913
Srebrenica massacre, impetus of the, 989
weaknesses, 1175–1176

De Baer, Marcel, 1102

De Bry, Theodore, 1017

De Gaulle, Charles, 19, 20, 432

De Grandy, Miguel, 924

De-individuation, 1023

De Klerk, Frederik W., 31, 54, 659, 816, 982

Deadly force, 477

"Death Fugue" (Celan), 812

Death marches, **226–229**
Bataan Death March, 227, *228*, 599
ethnic cleansing, 303
World War II, 457

Death Mills (film), 370

Death penalty. *See* Capital punishment

Death row phenomenon, 227–228

Death squads, **229–230**
Argentina, 379
Chile, 806
Einsatzgruppen, 281–282, *282*
El Salvador, 285
Liberia, 651
Peru, 800, 801
photography of, 803

Deception, perpetrators', **230–232**, 840

Deception, victims', **232–233**

Declaration of Basic Principles of Justice for Victims of Crime and Abuse of Power, 879, 889

Declaration of Principles on Tolerance, 314

Declaration of St. Petersburg, 1152

Declaration of the Congress of Vienna, 965–966

Declaration of the Rights of Man and the Citizen (France), 286

Declaration on Aggressive Nationalism, Racism, Chauvinism, Xenophobia, and Anti-Semitism, 783

Declaration on Fundamental Principles concerning the Contribution of the Mass Media to Strengthening Peace and International Understanding, to the Promotion of Human Rights and to Countering Racialism, Apartheid and Incitement to War, 824

Declaration on Race and Racial Prejudice (UNESCO), 824

Declaration on Territorial Asylum, 35

Declaration on the Prevention of Nuclear Catastrophe, 758

Declaration on the Prohibition of the Use of Nuclear and Thermo-Nuclear Weapons, 758

Declaration on the Protection of All Persons From Enforced Disappearance, 260

Declaration on the Relation of the Church to Non-Christian Religions (Catholic Church), 158

Declaration on the Right of Peoples to Peace, 15

Declaration on the Rights of Indigenous Peoples, 515

Declaration on the Rights of Persons Belonging to National or Ethnic, Religious, and Linguistic Minorities, 305, 695

Decolonization
ethnicity, 308
mercenaries, 684
racism, 856

Defendants
London Charter, 655
Nuremberg Trials, 766–767
Special Court for Sierra Leone, 957–958
Tokyo Trial, 1030–1033, *1032*

Defense lawyers, 766

Defense mechanisms of victims, 845–846

Defense Systems Ltd., 687

Defenses, **233–238**
extradition, 336–338
rape, 867
See also Heads of state, prosecution of; Self defense; Superior orders

Defiance Campaign, 658

Definition setting, 1074–1075

Definitions
aggression, 13–14
altruism, 26

apartheid, 47
children, 371
conspiracy, 200
crimes against humanity, 211, 767
degrading treatment, 1040
deportations, 560
enslavement, 560
ethnicity, 304
ethnocide, 309–310
euthanasia, 317
excuse, 233
extermination, 560
forcible transfer, 372
genocide, 204–205, 395–397, 483, 644
genocide, philosophical aspects of, 802
ghetto, 408–409, 410
grave breaches, 1146–1147
Holocaust, 453
human rights, 476
indigenous peoples, 509, 510–511
inhuman treatment, 1040
international armed conflict, 34
international law, 565
Jews, biological definition of, 762–763
justification, 233
mass graves, 666
massacres, 661, 663
mercenaries, 683, 685, 688–689
minorities, 692
nongovernmental organizations (NGOs), 746–747
perpetrators, 559
persecution, 561, 794–797
rape, 560–561, 867–868
refugees, 874–875
religious groups, 883
resistance, 903
states, 567–568
torture, 560, 1039–1040
transitional justice, 1046
treachery, 90
treaties, 565–566
United Nations responsibility, 1069–1070
universal jurisdiction, 1116
victim groups, 559, 563
victims, 1129–1132
war crimes, 655, 767, 1103–1104
weapons of mass destruction, 1151–1152

Deforestation, 603

Degenerate art, 81–82, 83

Degesch, 389

Degrading treatment, 844–845, 1040

Dehumanization
psychology of perpetrators, 840
terrorism, 1023

Dejaco, Walter, 100

Dekulakization, 629–630, 1057, 1067

Del Ponte, Carla, **238–240**, 549, 551, 553, 557

Delalic et al., 237, 1011

Delbo, Charlotte, 353

Demilitarized zones, 941

Demjanjuk trial, **240–242**, *241*
  acquittal, 216
  investigation, 574–575
  Israeli national laws, 731
  universal jurisdiction, 1119

Democide, 277, 397

Democracies
  genocide, 272, 822
  South Africa, 983

Democratic Kampuchea. *See* Cambodia

Democratic Republic of the Congo. *See* Congo

Demographics, 59, 615

Demonstrations. *See* Marches and demonstrations

Denationalization, **242–243**

Deng Xiaoping, 172, 173, 174, 1028

Denial, **243–247**
  banned art, 82
  European Court of Human Rights, 830
  free speech and, 497
  genocide courses, 277
  impunity, 489–491
  Irving, David, 586–588
  perpetrators, 793–794
  religion, complicity of, 880
  Turkish denial of the Armenian genocide, 681
  Ukraine famine, 1055
  United States policy towards Cambodia, 1112
  victims, 845
  Where Are My People?, Turkey's response to, 358

Denikin, A. I., 815

Denmark
  hate speech, 435
  rescuers, 459

Denying the Holocaust (Lipstadt), 586–587

Department of Peacekeeping Operations, UN, 786

Department of the Repression of the Slave Trade, 1004

Depayin massacre, 132

Deportations
  Armenians, 73–75, 93, 648
  Bosnia, 301
  Chams, 612
  collusive, 338–339
  crimes against humanity, 214

definition, 560
  Eichmann, Adolf, 279
  European Jews, 455–456
  extradition, 334
  Hungarian Jews, 1137–11139
  Jews, 6286
  kulaks, 629–630
  Kurds, 584, 633, 635
  Moriscos, 709
  Polish POWs, 606
  Romanis, 922
  Stalin, Joseph, 997, 1065

The Deputy (Hochhuth), 809

Dergue, 296–299, 730

Derrida, Jacques, 450

Dersim uprising, 634–635

Descriptive statistics, 575

Destruction, 663–665

The Destruction of the European Jews (Hilberg), 449

Detention
  Indonesia, 520
  International Committee of the Red Cross, 535, 536–537
  Working Group on Arbitrary Detention, 1071–1072

Deterrence
  genocide, 822
  punishment, 846, 852
  terrorism, 1024

Deutch, John, 974

Die Deutsche Wochenschau (film), 368

Developing states, 876

Development as Freedom (Sen), 349

Developmental genocide, **249–250**

Devil's Arithmetic (Yolen), 353

Dewdney, Edgar, 148

al-Dhahab, Suwar, 1005–1006

Dhamma, 502

Diamond mining, 947–952, 954

Diaries, **250–253**

Diaries of a Danish Missionary: Harpoot, 1907-1919 (Jacobsen), 251–252

The Diary of Anne Frank (Frank), 252, 269

The Diary of Dawid Sierakowiak: Five Notebooks from the Lódz Ghetto (Adleson, ed.), 252

Difference, 40

Diffusion of responsibility, 139

Dillon, Edward, 1178

Diminished responsibility defense, 236–237

DINA (*Dirección de Inteligencia Nacional*), 167, 806–807

Dinka, 1006, 1007

Diocletian, 177–179, *178*

Diop, Alioune, 385

Diplomatic immunity, 485–488

Diplomatic protection, 569

Dirección de Inteligencia Nacional (DINA), 167, 806–807

Direct aspect of incitement, 496, 499

Directorate of National Intelligence (DINA), 167, 806–807

Dirty warriors, 65, **65–67**, 322

Disabilities, people with, **253–258**
  eugenics films, 367
  killing techniques, 456
  medical experimentation, 673–675
  Nuremberg Laws, 763
  reproduction, 890

Disappearances, **259–264**
  amnesties, 737
  Argentina, 64, 377, 378–380
  as crime against humanity, 215
  family members as victims, 1130
  forensics and Argentine disappearances, 377, 378–380
  General Assembly resolution, 1085
  International Committee of the Red Cross, 536
  jurisdiction, 336
  Missing (film), 364

Disclosure, prior, 323, 1030, 1033

Discrimination
  as factor in crimes against humanity, 213
  female infanticide and feticide, 350–351
  homosexuals, 461–463
  international human rights law, 479
  persecution and, 795
  See also Anti-Semitism; Racism; Religious persecution

Diseases
  Amazon indigenous peoples, 27, 30
  Aztecs, 105
  Canadian indigenous peoples, 146–147
  Central and South America, 512
  Congo, 620
  Incas, 493
  Taino, 1018
  See also Biological and chemical weapons

Disfranchisement
  African Americans, 7–8
  South Africa, 49–50

Disinformation, 840

Disorientation of victims, 844

encyclopedia of GENOCIDE *and* CRIMES AGAINST HUMANITY

Environmental control and terrorism, 1023

Environmental issues
gold mining effects on Venezuelan rain forest, *28*
indigenous peoples' activism, 514
nuclear weapons, 756
"Plan of Action for the Marshes," 585
Russo-Chechen conflict, 161

Epidemic jaundice experiments, 672

EPLF (Eritrean People's Liberation Front), 290, 296–298

EPRDF (Ethiopian Peoples Revolutionary Democratic Front), 298–299

Epstein, Rob, 370

Equality of arms, 323

Equipo Argentino de Antropologia Forense (EAAF), 378–382

Equivalence fallacy in comparative genocide, 188–189

Eradication and destruction, 664–665

Erb Krank (film), 367, 368

Das Erbe (film), 367

Erdemovic case, 235–236, 988

Eritrea, **289–291**, *290*, 299

Eritrean People's Liberation Front (EPLF), 290, 296–298

Die Ermittlung (Weiss), 269

ERO (Eugenics Record Office), 255, 315

ERP (*Ejército Revolucionario del Pueblo*), 64

ERR (Einsatzstab Reichsleiters Rosenberg), 83–84

Erzberg, Matthias, 399

Escape, gulag, 904

Escuela de Mecánica de la Armada (ESMA), 64

Eser, Albin, 529

ESMA (Escuela de Mecánica de la Armada), 64

Espinoza, Pedro, 737

Espionage, 430–431

"Essay on the Inequality of the Human Races" (Gobineau), 857, 890

Esser, Johann, 710

Estimating victim numbers, **615–617**, 620–621, 998–999

Estrella v. Uruguay, 1039

Et toi, comment as-tu fait? (Delbo), 269

Eternal flames, 679

The Eternal Jew (film), 356, 369, 415

Ethical Guidelines for Biomedical Research Involving Human Subjects (CIOMS), 673

Ethics
altruism, 26–27
bystanders, 137–139
Hiroshima bombing, 443–444
medical experimentation, 669–675
physician perpetrators, 804–805

"Ethics and Clinical Research" (Beecher), 671

Ethiopia, **292–301**, *293*
criminal code, 243
Eritrea and, 289–291
famine, *347*
International Committee of the Red Cross, 532
national laws, 730

Ethiopian Peoples Revolutionary Democratic Front (EPRDF), 298–299

Ethnic Albanians. *See* Albanians, ethnic

Ethnic cleansing, **301–304**
Bosnia and Herzegovina, 125–129
codification and punishment of, 694
Commission on Human Rights investigation, 1076–1077
destruction-and-eradication dynamic, 664–665
ethnicity and, 306
General Assembly resolution, 1084
as genocide, 563
German national laws, 730
International Criminal Tribunal for the Former Yugoslavia, 558
Karadzic, Radovan, 605–606
Kosovar Albanians, 1176
Kurds, 636
Mladic, Ratko, 700–701
national prosecutions, 835–836
Organization for Security and Cooperation in Europe, condemnation by, 783
refugees, 662–663
Security Council resolutions, 1090–1091
Sri Lanka, 991
Stalin, Joseph, 997, 1065

Ethnic conflicts, 665

Ethnic groups, **304–306**
international law, 570
Japan, 596–597

Ethnic identity, 925–927

Ethnic markers, 307

Ethnic nationalism, 989–994

Ethnicity, **306–309**
Liberia, 650–651
South Africa, 979–980

Sparta, 986
Sri Lanka, 989–990
Tibet, 1026
Uganda, 1053

Ethnocide, **309–314**
East Timore, 274
ethnicity and, 306
Japan, 596–597
Kalmyks, 605
Kurds, 635
Native Americans, 744–745

Etter, Phillippe, 537

Eugenics, **315–316**
disabilities, people with, 254–255
euthanasia and, 318–319
physician perpetrators, 804, 805
racism, 857
reproduction, 889–890
social Darwinism, 968–969

Eugenics films, **366–368**

Eugenics Record Office (ERO), 255, 315

Eugenius III, Pope, 221

Euphemisms, 231, 499–500, 643

Europe
African slave trade, 961–962
anti-Semitism, 43–45, 156, 453–454
Beothuk relations with Europeans, 120
developmental genocide, 249–250
ghettos, 409–413
hate speech, 435
Holocaust deniers, 245–246
homosexuality, 461–462
Inquisitions, 521–524
minorities, protection of, 696–698, 696–699
Romanis, 919–922
rules of war, 471–472
slave trade, 964–966
witch hunts, 881
Zulus and, 1181–1182
See also Specific countries; Specific regions

European Charter for Regional or Minority Languages, 697–698

European Commission for Democracy through Law, 698

European Commission of Human Rights
hate speech and freedom of expression, 830
Holocaust deniers, 245–246
torture, 1039

European Committee on Crime Problems (ECCP), 316–317

European Community (EC)
Bosnia and Herzegovina, 128, 1173
Conference on Yugoslavia, 127

European Community (EC)
continued
  international law, 568
European Convention for the
  Prevention of Torture and
  Inhuman or Degrading Treatment
  or Punishment, 207, 1037, 1042
European Convention on Human
  Rights
  death penalty and extradition, 338
  direct victim representation, 1133
  execution, 477
  hate speech, 435, 824
  minorities, protection of, 697
  reparations, 888
  self-defense, 235
  torture, 1037
  victims' rights, 1132
European Convention on the Non-
  Application of Statutory
  Limitations, **316–317**, 1000, 1146
European Court of Human Rights
  Chechens, 160–161
  corporal punishment, 1040
  death penalty, 1041
  extradition, 339
  hate speech, 435, 824, 829, 830
  homosexuality, 463
  inhumane treatment, 1040
  minorities, protection of, 696–698
  permanence, 480
  reparations, 888
  restitution, 912
  torture, 1039, 1042
  victim claims, 1130
European Court of Justice of the
  European Union, 888
European Free Trade Association,
  568
European Union, 817
Euthanasia, **317–320**
  Nazi eugenics films, 367
  Nazi policies, 890
  Nuremberg Laws, 763
  physician perpetrators, 804, 805
  T-4 program, *254*, 315, 331, 456
Evans, John, 942
Evans, Richard, 587
Evian Accords, 19, 626
Evidence, **320–325**
  Armenian genocide, 648
  conspiracy, 201
  Einsatzgruppen trial, 775
  forensics, 376–381
  historiography sources, 447–448
  International Criminal Court,
    544–545
  International Criminal Tribunal
    for the Former Yugoslavia, 562–
    563
  Kosovo conflict, *561*

  mass graves, 666–669
  statistical analysis, 998–999
  television, 1021
  Tokyo Trial, 1032–1033
  written historiography, 449–450
  See also Documentary evidence
Evil, banality of radical, **325–327**,
  839
Evin Prison, 580, 581
Evolution
  biological altruism, 25–26
  social Darwinism and, 969
Der Ewige Jude (film), 415, 827
Exclusion clauses, 876–877
Exclusion of evidence, 324–325
Exclusionism, 921
Excuse
  justification/excuse distinction,
    233
  perpetrators, 793–794
Executions
  Cambodia, 143–144
  Eichmann, Adolf, 281
  European Convention on Human
    Rights, 477
  psychological aspects, 841
  Streicher, Julius, 249
  subsequent Nuremberg Trials,
    774–775
  World War II war criminals, 764–
    765
Executive Outcomes, 687
Exhaustion of local remedies,
  doctrine of, 885
Exhumations, 666–669
Exiles
  Rwandan, 932
  writers, 944
Existence without Life (film), 367
Expert evidence, 323–324
Explanation, **327–330**
  genocide, 821
  investigations and, 575–576
  political theory, 817
  psychology of perpetrators, 838–
    840
  Sierra Leone, violence in, 952–953
Expulsions, 1054
Extermination
  as crime against humanity, 214
  International Criminal Tribunal
    for the Former Yugoslavia
    definition, 560
Extermination centers, **330–334**, *331*
  Khmer Rouge, 614
  killing techniques, 456
  SS involvement in the
    administration of, 995–996
  See also Concentration camps

External bystanders, 137
Extradition, **334–341**
  Argentina's Dirty Warriors, 67
  Barbie, Klaus, 834
  Demjanjuk, John, 240
  Fujimori, Alberto, 800
  national prosecutions, 735, 835–
    836
  Pinochet, Augusto, 169, 487, 737,
    808–809
  states' obligation, 888
  Tal'aat Pash, 490
  torture, 1038–1039
Extraordinary Chambers of
  Cambodia, 866
Extraordinary Commission for the
  Struggle against Counter-
  Revolution and Sabotage. *See*
  Cheka
Eytan, Refael, 935, 937
Ezhov, Nikolai, 1064
Ezrahi, Sidra DeKoven, 354

[F]
Fact-finding missions. *See*
  Investigations
Failure to punish, 909–910
Fair trials, 999
Der Falsche Nero (Feuchtwanger),
  944
Falun Gong, 174
Family
  rights to, 478–479
  Sierra Leone, civil war in, 952
  as victims, 1130–1131
Family camps, 903
Family planning
  government sponsored, 893
  Romania, 917
Famine, **343–350**
  China, 172, 660–661
  Ethiopia, *294*, 295–296, 298
  International Committee of the
    Red Cross, 535
  as massacre, 662
  See also Starvation
Famine, Ukraine, 996, **1055–1061**
Famine Codes, 345–346
Famine Relief and Rehabilitation
  Organization (UFFRO), 296
Fantasies of victims, 845
Far East Commission, 833, 1029,
  1102
Farabundo Martí National Liberation
  Front (FMLN), 282–286
Farben, IG, 98, 101, 389, 776
Fateless (Kertesz), 375
Faurisson, Robert, 244, 246, 587

Ríos Montt, Efraín, 913–914
statistical analysis, 998–999
transitional justice, 1046, 1047
See also Maya
Guatemalan National Revolutionary
Union (URNG), 419–421
Guerilla movements
Argentina, 64
El Salvador, 284–285
Guatemala, 419, 913–914
Namibia, 723
Peru, 799–800
Guernica (Picasso), 87
Gui, Bernard, 154
Guided Democracy, 516–518
Guilt, survivor, 843
Guilt by association, 767
Guissé, El-Hadji, 1095
Gujarat, 508
Gulag, **422–427**, *427*
concentration camps, comparison
with, 333
Lenin, Vladimir, 647, 1063
resistance, 904
Stalin, Joseph, 1066
Gulag Archipelago (Solzhenitsyn),
423, 427
Gumplowicz, Ludwig, 969
Gustloff, Wilhelm, 627
Gutman, Israel, 252
Gutzeit, Kurt, 805
Guzman, Juan, 809
Guzman, Patricio, 357
Gypsies. *See* Romanis

[H]
Haas, Pavel, 710, 712, 714, 718
Habibie, B. J., 274
Habimana, Kantano, 860
Habré, Hissène, 261
Habyarimana, Juvenal, 158, 417, 819,
860, 927–929
Hacker, Melissa, 369
Hadamer euthanasia center, 256
Hadzihansanovic et al., 1013
Hagelin, Dagmar, 67
Hague Appeal for Peace Conference,
430
Hague Convention for the Protection
of Cultural Property in the Event
of Armed Conflict, 312
Hague Conventions, **429–432**
Armenian genocide, 186–187
barbaric weapons ban, 1153
crimes against humanity, 837
denationalization, 242
gasing, prohibition of, 388
Hiroshima and Nagasaki
bombings, 754–755

humanitarian law, 470, 473
International Criminal Court, as
leading to, 541
Martens clause, 210, 391
mercenaries, 684–685
superior responsibility, 1009
war, 1141–1142
war crimes, 1144, 1147
Hague Peace Palace, 541
Haile Sellassie, 292, 295
Haiti
amnesty, 31
humanitarian intervention, 467
Haji Mull, 505
Halabja, 388, *584,* 585
Halevy, Benjamin, 278
Hall of Remembrance at Yad Vashem,
679, 680
Halperin, Michael, 354
Hamas, 91
Hamedian massacres, 70–71, 77
Hamid, Abdul, 811
Hamidiye, 70
Hamit, Abdul, 70–71
Hammarskjold, Dag, 785
Handy, Thomas, 777
Hannibal, 150
Hannover, Nathan, 177
Hansberry, Lorraine, 408
Haq, Fazlul, 116
Hard count victim estimation
method, 616
Harding, Neil, 647
Harel, Isser, 1162
Harkis, 20, **432**
Harlan, Viet, 356
Harm
genocide, 563
incitement, 495–496
terrorism, 1025
Harris, Alice, 619
Harris, Mark Jonathan, 369
Harris, Whitney, 766, 768
Hartunian, Abraham, 678
Hatano, Ribot, 1097
Hate propaganda
freedom of expression, 823
genocide, role in cause of, 825–
827
Streicher, Julius, 1001–1002
Hate speech, **433–436**
banning of, 823–824
Canadian policy, 830
freedom of expression, 829–830
incitement, 497
international law, 830
United States policy, 831

Hauff advertisement, *2*
Hausner, Gideon, 278
Haviv, Ron, 803
HDZ (Croatian Democratic Union),
1051
Headquarter, United Nations, *1070*
Heads of state, prosecution of
Commission on Responsibilities,
185, 187
extradition, 338
Goldstone, Richard, 417
International Criminal Tribunal
for Rwanda, 549, 551–552
International Criminal Tribunal
for the Former Yugoslavia, 556
Heads of state immunity defense,
234, 485–486
Healing process, 879
Heart of Darkness (Conrad), 618
"The Heart of Harlem" (Hughes),
408
Heartfield, John, 944
Hebert, Paul, 776
Heder, Steve, 615
Heesterman, Johannes Cornelis, 501
Heidegger, Martin, 801–802
Heine, Heinrich, 680
Helots, 986–987
Helsinki Declaration, 673–674, 780
Helsinki Final Act, 779–780
Henley, Thomas J., 1178
Hentig, Hans Von, 971
The Hereditarily Ill (film), 367, 368
Hereros, 197, 264–265, **436–438**,
721, 723
Heretics
Cathars, 151–154
Inquisitions, 521–524
Heritage of slavery, 964
Hernández Martínez, Maximiliano,
283283
Herodotus, 470
*Herr Wendriner steht unter der
Diktaur* (Tucholsky), 943–944
Hersey, John, 353
Herszkowicz, Jankiel, 710–711
Hess, Rudolf
gas, 387–388
insanity defense, 236
mass execution, 333
Heuveline, Patrick, 618
Heydrich, Reinhard, **438–439**
extermination centers, 332
Gestapo, 406–408
Göring, Hermann, authority
granted by, 418
Himmler, Heinrich and, 441

Host countries, refugee camp, 872

Host desecration, 42

Hostages, 950

Hostages case, 776, 1010

Hostages (Leonhard), 268

Hotel Terminus: The Life and Times of Klaus Barbie (film), 370

Housing and Property Directorate and Claims Commission, 913

How to Do Things with Words (Austin), 642–643

Howard, John, 103

Hoyt, Michael, 134–135

HREOC (Human Rights and Equal Opportunities Commission), 103, 902

Hu Yao Bang, 1028

Hua Guofeng, 173

Hubayka, Elie, 936, 937

Huber, Max, 532, 537, 1117

Hughes, Langston, 408

Huguenots, **463–465**, *464*

Human Development Index, 952

Human rights, **476–482**
    Africa, 385
    Congo, 619, 620
    Eritrea, 290–291
    Ethiopia, 299–300
    Fujimori government, 800–801
    individuals and companies, 569–570
    internal affairs, 822–823
    restitution, 911
    right to peace, 15
    slavery, 967–968
    state responsibility, 209
    statistical analysis, 998–999
    Uganda, 1054
    United Nations, establishment of the, 1068
    See also United Nations Commission on Human Rights

Human Rights and Equal Opportunities Commission (HREOC), 103, 902

Human Rights Committee
    disappearances, 261–262, 263
    jurisprudence of, 1070
    medical experimentation, 674–675
    minorities, protection of, 695–696

Human Rights Field Operation, 1078

Human Rights First, 750

Human rights law
    development, 475–476
    famine, 349
    London Charter, 655
    medical experimentation, 674–675
    nuclear weapons, 756
    sexual orientation, 463

Human Rights Library, 278

Human rights organizations
    Guatemala, 421
    historiography sources, 448

Human rights treaties
    reparations, 885
    torture, 1036–1037
    United Nations specialized treaties, 1069–1070

Human Rights Watch
    Israel and the Occupied Territories, investigations of, 752
    Kurds, 635, 636
    overview, 750

Human sacrifice, 60, 104–105

Human shields, 1040

Humanitarian assistance
    Ethiopia, 296, 298
    Genocide Convention, 1088
    refugee camps, 872
    Sudan, 1006
    torture victims, 1041
    Ukraine, 1056
    United States policy towards Rwanda, 1115

Humanitarian intervention, **465–469**
    justification, 482
    Kuper, Leo, 631
    Kurds, 1089–1090
    self-defense as justifiable use of force, 14–15
    Srebrenica massacre as a failure of, 989

Humanitarian law, **469–476**
    Helsinki Declaration, preclusion of in the, 780
    principles of, 541
    restitution, 911
    transitional justice, 1045–1047

Humanitarian organizations, 533

Humor. *See* Satire and humor

Hun Sen, 145, 613

Hunchak Party, 76–77

Hundred Flowers Campaign, 660

Hungarian Arrow Cross movement, 182

Hungarian Jews
    Auschwitz, 101
    deportations, 457
    memorials, *679*
    Wallenberg, Raoul, 1137–1139
    Wiesel, Elie, 1159

Hungarians in Romania, 916

Hungary
    forcible transfer, 375
    International Committee of the Red Cross, 537
    statutes of limitations, revocation of, 1000

Huns, 502

Hunt, George T., 146

Huron, 147

Hurst, Cecil, 1101, 1103, 1105

Al-Hussein, Zeid Ra'ad Zeid, 545

Hutu Power, 928

Hutus
    Burundi, 133–136
    denial of Rwandan genocide, 244
    refugee camps, 872
    See also Rwanda

Hutus' Ten Commandments, 861

Huxley, Thomas, 968–969

[I]

IA (International Alert), 288, 631

I Accuse (film), 367

IAEA (International Atomic Energy Agency), 754, 760

"I Believe" (song), 711

Ich klage an (film), 367

ICISS (International Commission on Intervention and State Sovereignty), 468

ICJHC (International Catholic-Jewish Historical Commission), 157–158

ICP (Indochina Communist Party), 608–613

ICRC. *See* International Committee of the Red Cross (ICRC)

ICTR. *See* International Criminal Tribunal for Rwanda (ICTR)

ICTY. *See* International Criminal Tribunal for the Former Yugoslavia (ICTY)

Identification, **483–485**
    group, 821
    Jews, 42, 156, 409, 628, 762, *763*
    religious groups, 883–884
    Rwandan identity cards, 926, 927
    victims, 971–972, 1129–1132

Ideology
    Bolsheviks, 1061–1062
    comparative genocide, 188
    genocidal, 40
    gulag, justification for, 423
    hate propaganda, 826
    Hutu Power, 928
    as motivation for violence, 821
    Native Americans, U.S. dealings with, 740
    pan-Arab, 583
    political, 182
    Sudanese Islamists, 1006
    Talaat, Mehmet, 1019

IDPs (internally displaced persons), 874

Ieyasu, Tokugawa, 596

INPF (Independent National Patriotic Front of Liberia), 651
Inquisitions, **521–524**
  Cathars, 154
  Jews, 43
  witch hunts, 881
Insanity defense, 236–237
Insdorf, Annettte, 363
Insider witnesses, 577–578
Instability, 822
Institute for Historical Review (IHR), 244–246
Institutional responsibility, 914
Institution of International Law, 1144
Insulation and perpetrators, 839–840
Insulza, José Miguel, 169
Insurance claims, 446
Insurrectional movements, 905–906
Intelligence agencies, 575
Intelligentsia, 455
Intent, **524–530**
  births, prevention of, 893
  complicity, 195–196
  Eritrea and Ethiopia violations, 292
  ethnic cleaning/genocide distinction, 302
  forcible transfer, 372–374
  genocide, philosophical aspects of, 802
  group identification, 484
  human rights law, 481
  incitement, 500
  International Criminal Tribunal for Rwanda, 527–528, 554
  International Criminal Tribunal for the Former Yugoslavia, 525–527, 559, 562–563
  investigations and, 576–577
  linguistic genocide, 654
  perpetrators, 790
  prosecution and, 836–837
  residential schools and genocide, 901
  state responsibility and individual responsibility, 909
Intentionalist theory of the Holocaust, 453, 460
Inter-American Convention for the Prevention and Punishment of Torture, 207, 1037
Inter-American Convention on Forced Disappearance of Persons, 263, 1000
Inter-American Court of Human Rights
  collective reparations, 1131–1132
  direct victim representation, 1133
  disappearances, 262
  human rights, 480

reparations, 888
restitution, 912
torture, 1042
victim claims, 1130
Interactionist theory. *See* Labeling theory
Interahamwe, 112–113
Intergovernmental Committee on Refugees, 873
Intergovernmental organizations, 166, 568
Interim Government of National Unity (IGNU), 651
Interior passports, 47
Internal affairs, human rights violations as, 822–823
Internal bystanders, 137
Internal conflicts
  crimes against humanity, 559
  destruction-and-subjugation dynamic, 664
  Geneva Conventions, 393–394
  humanitarian law, 473
  International Committee of the Red Cross, 536
  Lebanon, 936
  mercenaries, 685
  nuclear weapons, 757
  Peru, 799–801
  refugees, 875
  rival claimants and the General Assembly, 1079–1080
  Sierra Leone, 946–953
  Sudan, 1004–1006
  superior responsibility, 1013
  war crimes, 958–959
Internal crimes, 769
Internally displaced persons, 874, 932
International Action against Genocide (Kuper), 631
International aid for refugee camps, 872
International Alert (IA), 288, 631
International armed conflicts
  definition, 34
  humanitarian law, 473
  Special Court for Sierra Leone, lack of jurisdiction of the, 959
International Association of Genocide Scholars, 277
International Atomic Energy Agency (IAEA), 754, 760
International Bill of Human Rights, 1069
International Bill of Rights, 749
International Catholic-Jewish Historical Commission (ICJHC), 157–158

International civil society, 570
International Commission of Jurists (ICJ), 1028
International Commission on Intervention and State Sovereignty (ICISS), 468
International Committee of the Red Cross (ICRC), *470, 472,* **530–539**
  Biafrans, starvation of, 123
  children, protection of, 166
  compound in Monrovia, Liberia, 534
  French treatment of Algerians, 17
  Geneva Conventions, 390–394
  Holocaust, silence regarding the, 139
  incapacitants, 1154
  Liberian massacre, 651
  privilege from having to testify, 324
  Theresienstadt inspection, 714, 718
International Conference on Military Trials, 591
International Conference on the Former Yugoslavia, 128
International Council of the Institute on the Holocaust and Genocide, 631
International Court of Justice, **539–541**
  genocide definition, 396
  human rights law, 480
  humanitarian law, 476
  immunity, 486, 487–488
  intent, 528
  jurisdiction, Genocide Convention recognition of, 216
  nuclear weapons, legality of, 755–761
  state responsibility and individual responsibility, 907–908
  United Nations War Crimes Commission, 1104–1106
  United States, opposition by, 1108–1109
  universal jurisdiction, 335, 1121–1122
International Covenant on Civil and Political Rights
  Commission on Human Rights, 1075
  death penalty and extradition, 338
  disappearances, 261
  domestic remedies for rights violations, 191
  ethnic groups' rights, 305
  free speech, 496–497
  hate speech, 434, 824, 829, 830
  homosexuals, protection of, 463
  human rights, 477–479
  medical experimentation, 674

V1: [1–482]; V2: [483–1016]; V3: [1017–1458]

Iran *continued*
  Saddam Hussein, indictment of, 939
Iraq, **583–586**, *633*
  Abu Ghraib, *478*
  Kurds, 267, 636
  Kuwait, invasion of, 192
  mass graves, *667*
  national laws, 730
  safe zones and no-fly zones, 941
  United States, invasion by, 15, 938–939
  war crimes, 1148
  weapons of mass destruction, 1152
Iraqi Special Tribunal for Crimes Against Humanity, 730, 835, 939
Ireland
  extradition and political offenses, 337
  famine, 344–345
Ireland v. U.K., 1039, 1040
IRO (International Refugee Organization), 873–874, 923–924
Iroquois, 146, 514
Irving, Clifford, 277
Irving, David, libel trial of, 246, **586–588**
Isaacs, Nathaniel, 1182
Isabella: From Auschwitz to Freedom (Leitner), 677
Ishii, Shiro, 598, 671
Islam
  Almohad movement, 24–25
  Armenian massacres, 69–71
  Bosnia and Herzegovina, 125
  Chittagong Hill Tract, peoples of the, 175
  Crusades, 220–223
  India, 506–508
  Iran, 579–582
  Iraq, 583–586
  Izetbegovic, Alija, 588–589
  medieval India, 503–505
  rules of war, 471
  Sudan, 1002–1008
  See also Muslims
Islamic Declaration, 588
Islamic Republic, 581–582
Islamism
  Algeria, 20
  anti-Semitism, 46
  Sudan, 1006
Israel
  collective reparations, 1131
  Commission of Inquiry into the Events at the Refugee Camps in Beirut, 736
  Demjanjuk trial, 240–241, 574–575

Eichmann trial, 834
German reparations, 887
Islamism, 46
Jenin events, 661, 752
memory of the Holocaust, 680
national laws, 730–731
nongovernmental organizations (NGOs), investigations by, 752–753
occupied territories, 534, 752–753
Roosevelt, Eleanor, support of, 924
Sabra and Shatila massacres, 935–937, 1084
state-sponsored assassination, 91
universal jurisdiction cases, 1119
West Germany, compensation from, 191
Wiesel, Elie, 1161
See also Demjanjuk trial; Eichmann trial
Israeli Defense Force (IDF), 935
Israeli Supreme Court, 139
Issarak, 141
Istanbul Charter for European Security, 783
Italy
  Cathars, 151
  Ethiopia, atrocities committed in, 292–295
  Holocaust documentation, 266
  Jews, policy on, 458
  Roman Inquisition, 523–524
  war criminals, 1104
Ittihadists. *See* Young Turks
"Ivan the Terrible." *See* Demjanjuk trial
Ivory Coast, 385
Ivy, Andrew, 673
I Will Bear Witness: A Diary of the Nazi Years (Klemperer), 252
I Will Not Be Sad in This World (film), 359
Izetbegovic, Alija, 127, **588–589**, 1173

[J]
Jaar, Alfredo, 88
al-Jabburi Ta'i, Hashim Ahmad, 585, 586
Jäckel, Eberhard, 1140
Jackson, Andres, 1043
Jackson, Livia, 353
Jackson, Robert, **591–594**, *592*
  aggression as crime against peace, 767–768
  crimes against humanity, 211, 212
  documentary evidence, 577
  documentation of Nazi atrocities, 33

International Military Tribunal (IMT), 766
  Lemkin, Raphael and, 644
  Nuremberg Trials, opening statement at the, 771
  occupied zones, war crimes trials in the, 773
  United Nations War Crimes Commission, 1106
Jacobsen, Maria, 251–252
Jainas, 503
Jallow, Hassan, 549
Jamaica, 1041
Janatha Vimukthi Peramuna (JVP), 990
Janjaweed, 1005
Japan, **594–600**
  Bataan death march, *227, 228, 229*
  China and, 171–172
  denial of genocide, 244
  disabled women, forced sterilization of, 258
  Far Eastern Sub-Commission, 1102
  Fujimori, Alberto, refusal to extradite, 800
  Hiroshima, 442–444, 754–755
  indigenous peoples, 513
  medical experimentation, 671
  Ofuna prison, *1147*
  Rape of Nanking, *595, 597,* 663–664, 1149
  reparations, 885
  See also Tokyo Trial
Japanese American internment, 191
Jaramnus Asa'd, 937
Jarboe, Walter S., 1178
Jaspers, Karl, 326
Java, 519
Javor et al. v. X, 835
al-Jazrawi, Taha Yasin Ramadan, 586
Jazz, 85
JDC (American Jewish Joint Distribution Commission), 1056
Jefferson, Thomas, 740
Jehovah's Witnesses, **600–601**, 710
Jehovah's Witnesses Stand Firm Against Nazi Assault (film), 370
Jelisic case, 321, 525–526, 529–530, 562
Jenin refugee camp, 661, 752
Jenner, Edward, 670
Jersild v. Denmark, 435, 824
Jerusalem, 221
Jescheck, Hans-Heinrich, 822
Jesuits
  Amazon missions, 28
  Canadian indigenous peoples, 146, 147

Krypteia, 986–987
Ku Klux Klan, *433, 495*
Kubra, Najm al-Din, 704
Kuenyehia, Akua, 545
Kujath, Gerhard, 805
Kulaks, **628–630**, 1056–1057
Kulisiewicz, Aleksander, 710
Kulturbund deutscher Juden, 710
Kumar, Radha, 506
Kumaratunga, Chandrika, 993
Kunarac et al., 560–561, 867–868
Kunene, Mazisi, 1182
Kuomintang (KMT), 170–171
Kuper, Leo, **630–632**
  education, influence on, 277
  genocide, broad definition of, 397
  genocide prevention, 1157–1158
  material interest, 821
  total *vs.* partial genocide, 188
Kupreskic case, 559, 561, 562
Kurdish Autonomous Zone, 585
Kurdish genocide, 583–585, *584*
Kurds, **632–637**
  Anfal campaign, 938
  documentation, 267
  gasing of, 388
  UN Council response, 1089–1090
Kuslic, D., 835
Kut, Halil, 74
Kutako, Hosea Komombumbi, 723
Kuwait
  compensation, 192
  Iraq war crimes, 586
  Saddam Hussein, indictment of, 939
  war crimes committed against, 1148
Kuznetsov, Anatoli, 110, 450

[L]
La Cantuta massacre, 800, 801
Labeling theory, 972
Labor camps, **639–642**, *640, 641*
  colonies/settlements/camps distinction, 425
  Lenin, Vladimir, 1063
  Romania, 916–917
  Soviet, 647
  Stalin, Joseph, 996–997
  See also Forced labor
Labor for the Prevention of genetically Diseased Offspring (Germany), 315
Labor strikes, 116
Labrador, *120*
Laframboise, Michael, 1177
Laird, Christa, 354

Lait, Jack, 366
Lake, Tony, 975, 976
Lakota, 1166–1168
Land Claims Court (South Africa), 912
Land issues
  Algeria, 19
  apartheid, 50
  Australian indigenous peoples, 104
  Canadian indigenous peoples, 148–149
  indigenous peoples, 513–514
  Kalimantan, 603–604
  Native Americans, 740, 741, 743–745
  reparations claims, 445
  restitution, 912
Land mines, 474–475, 536
Landau, Moshe, 278
Lang, Berel, 642
Langfus, Anna, 352
Langhoff, Wolfgang, 710
Language, **642–643**
  Bangladesh, 116–117
  ethnicity, 306–307
  incitement, 499–500
  minorities and, 697
  Mugesera's speech, 829
  perpetrators' deception, 230–231
  South Africa, 982
  Sri Lanka, 991
  Tibet, 1026
  Tokyo Trial, 1029
  See also Linguistic genocide
"The Language of War and Peace" (Gay), 643
Lansberg prison, 776
Lansing, Robert, 185, 210
Lanz advertisement, 2
Lanzmann, Claude, 355, 369
Laqueur, Walter, 330
Las Casas, Bartolomé de, 512, 573, 1017, 1018, 1123
The Last Days of the Jerusalem of Lithuania: Chronicles from the Vilna Ghetto and the Camps, 1939-1944 (Kurk), 252
The Last of the Just (Schwarz-Bart), 354
Latin America
  amnesties, 736–737
  Andean Program, 514
  disappearances, 262
  indigenous peoples, 512
  International Committee of the Red Cross, 534–535
  mercenaries, 684
  transitional justice, 1046

Latin American Cartegena Declaration on Refugees, 875–876
Laughlin, Harry, 315, 367
Lauren, Paul Gordon, 1068
Laval, Pierre, 182
Law Against Dangerous Career Criminals (Germany), 890
Law for the Prevention of Genetically Diseased Offspring (Germany), 890
Law for the Prevention of Offspring with Hereditary Diseases (Germany), 255
Law for the Protection of German Blood and Honor, 454, 762, 763, 891
Law for the Protection of the Genetic Health of the German People, 891
Law of National Pacification (Argentina), 737
Law of the Hague, 1141–1142
Law of the sea, 966
The Law of War and Peace (Grotius), 846–847
Law Reports of Trials of War Criminals, 834
Lawrence Geoffrey, 773
Laws of Burgos, 512, 1018
Laws of Manu, 470
Laws of war. *See* International humanitarian law
Lawsuits. *See* Civil litigation
Lawyers, 774
Lawyers Committee for Human Rights, 1135
  overview, 750
  research findings, 753
Leadership Corps of the Nazi Party, 767
League of Nations
  Advisory Committee of Experts on Slavery, 968
  Deskaheh, Chief, request for intervention by, 514
  as first international political organization, 565, 568
  indigenous peoples, 509
  minorities, protection of, 693–694
  refugees, 873
  renunciation of war, 465
  Slavery Convention, 1004
  Temporary Slavery Commission, 967
League of Red Cross Societies, 532
Lean Bear, 942
Lebanese Forces (LF), 935–937
Lebanese Phalangist militia, 872, 935

Mladic, Ratko, **700–702**
  evidence, 322–323
  safe areas, attack on, 1175
  Srebrenica massacre, 988
M'Naghten rules, 236
Mobile brigade, 1156
Mobile gas chambers, 331–332
Moctezuma, *105*
MODEL (Movement for Democracy in Liberia), 652
Model Nuclear Weapons Convention, 759
Modena, Leon, 412
Modernity, 726
Modernization, 579
Modesty, 898
Modi, Narendra, 508
Moffitt, Ronni Karpen, 807
Mogadishu, 11, 973, 1090
Mohammad Shah, 505
Mojahedin, 582
Mok. *See* Choeun, Chhit
Molotov, Vyacheslav, 629, 1060
Momoh, Joseph, 946
Money laundering, 808
Moneylending, 410–412
Mongol conquests, **702–705**, *703*
Mongol empire, 395
Mongolia, 1183
Monroe, Kristen Renwick, 329
Monroe Doctrine, 185
Monrovia, Liberia, *534*
Montesinos, Vladimiro, 800
Montoneros, 64
Montt, Efraín Ríos, 421–422, 731
Moore, James, 741
Moors. *See* Moriscos
"Die Moorsoldaten" (Esser, Langhoff, and Goguel), 710
Moose, George, 973
Moral exclusion and terrorism, 1023–1024
Moral reparations, 1131, 1132–1133
Morality, perpetrators', 840–841
Moreau, Clement, 944
Morel, Edmund Dene, 619
Morely, Bertha, 252
Moreno Ocampo, Luis, 545, 577
Morgenthau, Hans, 765
Morgenthau, Henry, 252, 648, **706–707**, 1111
Moriscos, **707–710**
Morocco, 24–25
Morrison, William, 619

Morton, Rogers, *885*
Moscow Declaration, 1145
Moscow Mechanism, 781–782, 784
Moses, Dirk, 103
Mostar, *662*
Mothers of Plaza de Mayo, *66, 67*
Motivation
  collaboration, 182–183
  discrimination and crimes against humanity, 213
  memoir writing, 677
  perpetrators, 790–794
  physician perpetrators, 804–805
  psychology of perpetrators, 839–840
  Stalin, Joseph, 997, 1066
  terrorists, 1022
  utopian ideology and genocide, 1124–1127
Motley, Constance Baker, 9
Moutet, Maurius, 385
Movement for Democracy in Liberia (MODEL), 652
Mr. Wendriner under the Dictatorship (Tucholsky), 943–945
MRG (Minority Rights Group), 1157–1158
"Mrs. Wernicke" (radio program), 944
Mudejars, 707–709
Mugesera, Leon, 828, 829
Mugesera v. Minister of Citizenship and Immigration, 499–500, 729
Muhammad, 471
Muich Beer Hall uprising, *398*
Muir, Leilani, 316
Mujibur Rahman, 117–118
Mulka, Robert, 389
Mullahs, 581
Multiculturalism, 314
Multidisciplinary courses, 277–278
Multidisciplinary investigations, 575
Multilateralism, 566, 698–699, 975
Multilingualism, 654
Multinational treaties, 1087
Multiple commanders and superior responsibility, 1012
Multiple systems estimation, 998
Mumbai riots, 507–508
Munyeshyaka, Wanceslas, 1120
Murahileen, 1005–1006
Murder, 213–214
Murer, Franz, 1162
Musawi, Abbas, 91

Muscle and nerve regeneration experiments, 672
Musema, Alfred, 554
Musema case, 200, 528, 554
Museum of Civilization, 62
Museums
  architecture, 60–62
  Auschwitz, 101
  memorials, 680
  Museum of Memory (Argentina), 64
  Toul Slen genocide museum, *616*
  transitional justice, 1047
Museveni, Yoweri, 927
Musharraf, Pervez, 119
Music, Armenian Genocide, **714–716**
Music, Holocaust, **710–711**, 711–713, 713–714, 717–719
Music, reconciliation, **716–717**
Muslim League, 115–116, 506–508
Muslims
  Algerian, 19
  anti-Romani sentiment, 921
  Moriscos and, 707–709
  Sudan, 1002–1008
  Utashe killing of, 882
  See also Bosnia and Herzegovina; Croatia; Islam; Kosovo; Yugoslavia, former
Musmanno, Michael, 282, 775
Mussolini, Benito, 182, 295, 532
Mustard gas
  experiments, 671
  Italian use of on Ethiopians, 292–295
  Kurdish genocide, 585
Mutilation, *952, 1054*
Mutually Assured Destruction (MAD) doctrine, 759, 760
My Knees Were Jumping: Remembering the Kindertransports (film), 369
My Lai, 736, 1010, 1148
My Mother's Courage (Tabori), 269
Myanmar, **129–133**, *131,* 346
Myths, 524
Mytilene, 94

[N]
NAACP (National Association for the Advancement of Colored People), 9
Nagasaki, 443–444, 754–755
Nahapet (film), 360–361
Nahimana, Ferdinand, 495, 860, 862
Names, 678–679
Namibia, 436–438, **721–725**, *722*
Namibian Defence Force (NDF), 725

Nanking, 171, *595, 597, 598*, 663–664, 1149

Nansen, Fridtjof, 873

NASAKOM, 517

Nashimana, Ferdinand, 553

Nation building
  Security Council, 1089
  Somalia, 973

Nation of Islam, 45–46

Nation-states
  Kurds, 633–634
  minorities and, 693
  racial groups, 856

National Association for the Advancement of Colored People (NAACP), 9

National Commission of Truth and Reconciliation (Chile), 169

National Commission on the Disappeared, 64, 65, 449, 577, 1049

National Council for Civil Liberties (NCCL), 287

National courts
  immunity, 487
  International Criminal Tribunal for Rwanda and, 549

National Human Rights Commission, 263

National Intelligence Service, Peruvian, 800

National Islamic Front (NIF), 1006

Nationalism, **725–727**
  Afrikaner, 979–980, 981
  anti-Semitism, 44
  Armenian, 72, 80
  Chinese, 170
  Conference on the Human Dimension of the CSCE, 780–781
  Croats, 219
  ethnicity and, 308
  Himmler, Heinrich, 439–441
  India, 506–507
  International Committee of the Red Cross, 531–532
  Romanis, 922
  Slovenia and Croatia, 1171–1172
  Sri Lanka, 989–994
  Talaat, Mehmet, 1019
  utopian ideology, 1124–1127

Nationality
  extradition, 338
  international law, 243, 567

Nationality principle of jurisdiction, 733

National laws, **727–732**
  case law, 529
  compensation, 191
  crimes against humanity as distinct from, 213

German reparations, 887
historical injustices, 445–447
minorities, protection of, 698
Special Court for Sierra Leone, 955–956
superiority of international law over, 1033
torture, 478, 1038
universal jurisdiction, 1120–1121

National League for Democracy (NLD), 131–132

National Liberation Front (FLN), 432

National Plan of Security and Development (Guatemala), 913

National prosecutions, **732–740**, 835–836

National Provisional Ruling Council (Sierra Leone), 947

National Security Council, 974

National Security Strategy Document, 546

National Socialists. *See* Nazis

National sovereignty. *See* Sovereignty

"National Strategy to Combat Weapons of Mass Destruction" (United States), 760

National Unity and Reconciliation Act, 51

National Unity and Reconciliation Commission, 717

National War Crimes Office, 1104, 1106

Native Americans, **740–746**
  colonialism and, 512–513
  destruction-and-subjugation, 664
  famine, 344
  forcible transfer, 375
  Human Rights Committee on Civil and Political Rights, 695–696
  Pequots, 788–790
  racism, 858
  reparations claims, 445
  Sand Creek Massacre, 942
  Trail of Tears, 229, 1043–1045
  United States tribes, 742–743
  Wounded Knee massacre, *741*, 1166–1168
  Yuki, 1177–1178

NATO forces. *See* North Atlantic Treaty Organization (NATO) forces

Natural famines, 344

Nazi and Nazi Collaborators Law (Israel), 730

Nazi Concentration Camps (film), 370

The Nazi Doctors: Medical Killing and the Psychology of Genocide (Lifton), 840–841

The Nazi Doctors and the Nuremberg Code (Annas and Grodin), 319

Nazi Doctors Case. *See* Medical Case

Nazi hunters, 1161–1164

Nazi labor camps, **639–642**, *640, 641*
  See also Concentration camps

Nazim, Mehmet, 72

Nazis
  advertising, 1–2, *2*
  anti-Semitic propaganda, 826–828
  art as propaganda, 85–86
  Auschwitz, 96–101, *97, 98*
  Babi Yar, 109–111
  banned art, 81–82
  compensation, 192
  crimes against humanity, 211
  death marches, 228–229
  deception, 230–231
  defendants, International Military Tribunal, 766–767
  denationalization, 243
  disabled children, killing of, 255–256
  documentary films, 368–370
  documentation, 265–266, 888
  Entartete Musik, 713
  eugenics, 315–316, 366–368
  euthanasia, *254, 256*, 456, 805
  euthanasia program, 318–319
  famine, 346
  forced labor of disabled persons, 256–257
  forcible transfer by, 375
  French national laws, 730
  gas, 387–388, *388*
  gestapo, 405–408, 767
  ghettos, 412–414
  homosexuality, 462
  incitement, 494
  inter-war period, 399–401
  International Committee of the Red Cross, reaction of the, 537–538
  Israeli national laws, 730–731
  Jehovah's Witnesses, persecution of, 600–601
  Jewish resistance, 902–904
  mass graves, 666
  medical experimentation, 256–257, 671–674
  memoirs, 675–676
  Morgenthau's post World War II plan, 706–707
  musicians, persecution of, 711–712
  as nationalist mass movement, 401–402
  Nuremberg Laws, 403, 407, 452, 761–764, 890–891
  photography, 803
  physician perpetrators, *804*, 804–805
  Pius XII, Pope and, 809–811

propaganda films, 355–356, 368–369
prosecution, 833–834
psychology of perpetrators, 840–841
punishment, *848*, 849–850
racism, 859
radio, 859
reproduction, policies affecting, 889–892
satire, 943–944
social Darwinism, 969
Soviet prisoners of war, 984–986
Stalinist/Nazi policies, comparison of, 1065
statutory limitations, 999–1000
stolen art, 83–85, *84*
subsequent Nuremberg Trials, 772–778
U.S. Army war crimes trial at Dachau, 772
utopian ideology, 1125, 1126
victims' deception, 232–233
Wannsee Conference, 455–456, 1140–1141
war crimes, 1145–1148
War Crimes Commission, 1104–1106
women, 792–793
See also Concentration camps; Extermination centers; Holocaust; Nuremberg Trials; SS; Specific individuals
Ndadaye, Melchior, 135–136, 928
Ndayizeye, Domitien, 136
NDF (Namibian Defence Force), 725
Ndiaye, Bacre Waly, 1092
Ne Win, 129, 130
Neconish, Ernest, *885*
Nedic, Milan, 1169
Negative security guarantees, 756
Neier, Aryeh, 750
Neither to Laugh nor to Weep (Hartunian), 678
Nekrasov, Viktor, 110
NEP. *See* New Economic Policy (NEP)
Netherlands
deportations of Jews, 456
hate speech, 435
Holocaust documentation, 266
Neue Synagoge, 450
Neutrality
International Committee of the Red Cross, 532
mercenarism and, 684–685
"Never Say That You Have Reached the Final Road" (Glik), 711
New Agenda Coalition, 759

New Economic Policy (NEP)
famine recovery, 1056
kulaks, 629
Lenin, Vladimir, 647
New facts, 551
New Muslims, 503–504
New Order regime, 603–604
New Testament, 41
New World Order, 1088–1089
New York Agreement, 1155–1156
New York Convention on Special Missions, 485
New Zealand
reparations claims, 445
Treaty of Waitangi, 514
Newfoundland, *120*
Newman, Barnett, 88
News coverage, television, 1020–1021
Newspapers
Kangura, 827, 828–829, 861–862
Der Stürmer, 247–249, *248*, 494, 826–828, 1001–1002
Nexus with war, 768–769, 1082–1083, 1143
Ngeze, Hassan, 57, 500, 553, 861, 862
Ngulinzira, Boniface, 112
Niama, Mulume, 619
Nicaragua
Contra War, *373*
reparations, 912
Nicholas II, 45, 76, 815
Niederland, William, 842
Nietzche, Friedrich, 643
NIF (National Islamic Front), 1006
Nigeria
Biafra and, 121–124
civil war, 121–122, *123*, 533–534
map, *122*
Sierra Leone, peacekeeping forces in, 948–949
Taylor, Charles, asylum of, 951
Night and Fog (film), 363–364, 369
"The Night of the Long Knives," 995
Night (Wiesel), 354, 1159
Nightingale, Florence, 531
Nikolic, Ivan, 738
Nikolic case, 339, 558–559
Nilotic civil war, 1007
Nim, Hu, 611
Nimitz, Chester W., 765
Nineveh, 39
Nishga ruling, 148
Nixon, Richard M., 167
Niyitigeka, Eliezer, 500

Niyonteze, Fulgence, 1120
NKVD
Katyn massacre, 606–608
NLD (National League for Democracy), 131–132
No-fly zones, 585, 940
Nobel Prize
Amnesty International, 288
De Klerk, F. W., 816
Dunant, Henry, 531
International Committee of the Red Cross, 532, 533
Luthuli, Albert, 51
Mandela, Nelson, 659, 816
Menchú, Rigoberta, 421
Sachs, Nelly, 812
Sen, Amartya, 343
Suu Kyi, Aung San, 132
United Nations peacekeeping, 1088
Wiesel, Elie, 1160
Nobunaga, Oda, 595
Nogushi, Hideyo, 670
Nongovernmental organizations (NGOs), **746–754**
accountability, 487
children, protection of, 166
Commission on Human Rights, role in the creation of the, 1074
crimes against humanity, 211
early warnings, 272, 631
indigenous peoples' rights, 514–515
International Criminal Court, 1150
international law, 568–569
investigations, 575
Sub-Commission on Human Rights, UN, 1094–1095
Sudan, 1008
United Nations and, 1070–1071
working groups, 1098
See also Specific groups
Nonintervention, 1080–1081
Nonmilitary use of safe zones, 940–941
Nonproliferation, nuclear, 755, 759–760
Non-Proliferation Treaty (NPT), 756, 759–760
Nonrefoulement, principle of, 874, 878
Nonresponsive bystanders, 137–139
Nonretroactivity, 446–447, 566
Nonskeletal archaeological evidence, 60
Nonstate agents of persecution, 797–798
Nonterritoriality of Romanis, 921

Whitaker report, 1069, 1158
Willaume Report, 18
Representation
 direct victim representation, 1133
 General Assembly, 1079–1080
Representative dance, 225–226
Repression
 controversy concerning political repression, 816
 Gheorghiu-Dej, Gheorghe, 916
 Stalin, Joseph, 996–997, 1064–1067
Reproduction, **889–895**
République de Martyazo, 134
Requiem (Verdi), 712, 714
Rescuers
 documentary films, 369
 group psychology, 329
 perpetrators' deception, 231
 religion, 882
Rescuers, Holocaust, **895–899**
 altruism, 26
 biographies, 125
 Europe, 459
 Wallenberg, Raoul, 1137–1139
Research
 historiography sources, 447–448
 Holocaust causation, 460
 nongovernmental organizations (NGOs), 750–753
Research Committee on Pol Pot's Genocidal Regime, 615
Reservations
 Genocide Convention, 540
 treaties, 566
Reservations to the Genocide Convention case, 335
Resettlement
 Jews, 454
 South Africa, 658
Residential schools, **899–902**
Resistance, **902–904**
 apartheid, 51–52
 Communist Party of Yugoslavia, 1170
 documentary films, 369
 to Japanese colonialism, 597–598
 Jewish, 457
 music, 710
 philosophy, 802
 Sanga people, 619
 South Africa, 982
 West Papua, 1156
 See also Nonviolent resistance
The Resistible Rise of Arturo Ui (Brecht), 944
Resnais, Alain, 363–364, 369
Resolution 688, Security Council, 1089–1090

Resolution 814, Security Council, 1090
Resolution 827, 555
Resolution 955, 547
Resolution 1235, 1071
Resolution 1315, UN, 955
Resolution 1503, 1071, 1095
Resolutions
 effectiveness of, 1086
 United Nations Sub-Commission on Human Rights, 1093–1094
Responsibility
 and altruism, 26–27
 degrees of, 790
 See also State responsibility; Superior responsibility; Individual responsibility
Restitution, **910–913**
 compensation/restitution distinction, 189
 definition, 884
 as remedy, 885–886
Restitutionary justice, 554
Restorative justice, 1024–1025
Restore Hope operation, 11
Retribution, 846, 952–953, 1024–1025
Retroactivity
 Nuremberg Trials, 769
 reparations, 446–447
 Rome Statute, 1150
 statutory limitations, 1000
 subsequent trials at Nuremberg, 774
The Reunion (film), 370
Revanchism, 623
Review proceedings, 551
Revitalization movements, 40
Revolution of 1905, 814–815
Revolution Square, *1062*
Revolutionary County (Burma), 130
Revolutionary Government of National Salvation, 1006
Revolutionary United Front (RUF), 946–952
 amputations, 954
 cease-fire agreement, 950
 diamond mining, 948–949, 951
 mercenaries, 687–688
 mutilations, *952*
 peace process, 947–948
 photography, 803
 stockpiling of weapons, 948
 Taylor, Charles, 651–652, 951, 954
Revolutionary United Party (RUP), 652
Reynolds, Henry, 103

Reza Shah, Mohammad, 579–580
RFP (Rwanda Patriotic Front), 859–860
Rhetoric, 3
Rhodes, Cecil, 979
Rhodesia, 54
Ribeiro, Darcy, 512
Riefenstahl, Leni, 356, *357*, 368
Riggs National Bank, 808
Right to bear arms, 69–70
Right to counsel, 550
Right to die, 318
Right to life, 477–478
Right to privacy, 479
"righteous Among the Nations," 896, 897
Rights of the child, 479
Rijksinstituut voor Oorlogsdocumentatie, 266
Ríos Montt, Efraín, **913–915**
Riot control agents, 1154
Riots, 507
Riruako, Kuaimi, 438
Ritual murder accusations, 42
Rival claimants and the General Assembly, 1079–1080, 1112–1113
Rizvi, 504
Robben Island Guidelines, 1037
Robertson, Geoffrey, 241
Robespierre, Maximilien, 209
Robinson, Jacob, 281
Robinson, Mary, 1097
Robinson, Nehemiah, 822, 892–893
Rock Edict, 502
Rockefeller, Michael, 1155
Röhm purge, 995
Roma. *See* Romanis
Roman, Martin, 712, 714
Romania, **915–919**
 collaboration, 181
 Jews, policy on, 457–458
Roman Inquisition, 523–524
Romanis, *919*, **919–923**
 European Court of Human Rights, protection of by, 696
 motivation for violence toward, 821
 nationalism, 727
 Nuremberg Laws, 762, 763
 racism, 859
Rome, ancient
 Carthage and, 149–151
 Christians, persecution of, 177–179
 homosexuality, 461
 legal system, 564–565

Rome, ancient *continued*
  mercenaries, 684
  rules of war, 471
Rome Conference, 1150
Rome Statute
  aggression, crime of, 15
  amnesty, 35, 36
  apartheid, 53, 203
  attempt to commit genocide, 96
  child soldiers as perpetrators, 165
  children, definition of, 371–372
  conspiracy, 200–201
  crimes against humanity in peace
    or war, 212
  defenses, 233
  disabled persons as protected
    group, 257
  disappearances, 215, 260
  duress defense, 235–236
  "Elements of Crimes," 1037, 1039
  ethnic groups' rights, 305
  extradition, 340
  gender crimes as crimes against
    humanity, 214–215
  human rights law implementation,
    481
  identifiable groups, 275–276
  immunity, 487–488
  impunity, 1078
  incitement, 494, 496
  International Law Commission,
    contribution of the, 571, 572
  international tribunals, influence
    of, 417
  intoxication defense, 237, 238
  jurisdiction and extradition, 335–
    336
  justice, reparative function of, 880
  liberation movements, 291
  London Charter as basis for code
    of offenses, 655
  medical experimentation, 674
  mental disease defense, 237
  military necessity defense, 236
  nuclear weapons, 760
  Nuremberg Trials, influence of
    the, 771
  other inhumane acts as crimes
    against humanity, 215
  persecution, definition of, 795,
    796, 797, 798
  political groups, 816
  principle of complementarity, 487
  prosecution, 835
  punishable acts of crimes against
    humanity, 213
  punishment, 846, 847
  rape and sexual violence, 1097
  reparations, 887, 888
  restitution, 912
  self defense, 235
  sentencing, 850–852
  sexual offenses, 866

  sexual orientation, omission of,
    462
  slavery and apartheid, 3
  soldiers *vs.* citizens, 291–292
  specific intent, 529
  state responsibility and individual
    responsibility, 908–909
  statutory limitations, 1000–1001
  superior orders defense, 234
  systematic rape, 876
  television, 1021
  torture, 1037, 1040
  universal jurisdiction, 1121
  victims' rights, 1133
  Victims' Trust Fund, 751
  violence against women, 1165
  war crimes, 1143, 1149–1150
  See also International Criminal
    Court
Romero, Oscar, 283, *283*, 285
Rondon, Cândido, 29
Rondônia, 30
Roosevelt, Eleanor, 694, *923*, 923–
  924, *1073, 1108*
Roosevelt, Franklin Delano
  Holocaust, awareness of the, 538
  Jewish refugee policy, 628
  post-World War II plan, 707
  war crimes trials, advocation for,
    765
Roschmann, Eduard, 1162
Rosé, Alma Maria, 712
Rose, Michael, 589
Rosenberg, Julius and Ethel, 881
Rosenberg, Martin, 718
Rosewood, **924–925**
Rosner, Henry and Poldek, 712
Ross, John, 1043
Roth, Philip, 352
Rothko, Mark, 88
Round Valley Reservation, 1177–
  1178
Royal Commission on Aboriginal
  Peoples, 900–901
Royal Proclamation of 1763, 147
RPF. *See* Rwandan Patriotic Front
  (RPF)
RPKAD, 519
RSHA. *See* Reich Security Main Office
  (RSHA)
RSS, 507
RTLMC. *See* Radio Television Libre
  Mille Collines (RTLMC)
Rubber industry, 29, 618–720
Ruegger, Paul, 537
RUF. *See* Revolutionary United Front
  (RUF)

Ruhashyankiko, Nicomède, 1096
Rule 61, 322–323
Rule 68, 323
Rules of attribution, 905–906
Rules of Procedure and Evidence
  International Criminal Court,
    544–545
  sentencing, 850
Rules of war
  Hague Conventions, 429–431
  history, 469–472
Rummel, Rudolph, 277, 397
RUP (Revolutionary United Party),
  652
Rupprecht, Philippe, 248
RuSHA (Main Race and Resettlement
  Office), 774, 891
Rushashyankiko, Nicodème, 1069
Russell, Bertrand, 1151
Russia
  anti-Semitism, 44–45
  Armenians, 76–78
  Bolshevik revolution, 1061–1062
  Chechen refugees, 872–873
  concentration camps, 197–198
  Cossacks, 207–209
  Grozny, onslaught against, *624*
  gulag, 422–427, *423*
  Kalmyk massacres, 604
  Kurds, massacres of, 634
  Lenin, Vladimir, 645–647
  October Revolution, 1061
  pogroms, 812–815, *813*
  Russo-Chechen conflict, 160
Russian civil war, 532, 646, 1062–
  1063
Russian prisoners of war, 891
Russian refugees, 874, 1056
Russian Revolution, 78, 604
Russo-Chechen conflict, 160–161
Rutaganda case, 528, 894
Ruzindana case, 527–528
Rwamakuba, André, 553
Rwanda, *214*, **925–933**
  African Crisis Response Initiative,
    11
  artistic representation of genocide,
    88–89
  Bagosora, Théoneste, 111–113
  Belgian national law, 729
  Burundi, similarities to, 133
  Canadian national law, 729
  Catholic Church and, 158
  child soldiers, 165, 793
  children, 164–165, *926*
  Commission on Human Rights
    investigation, 1077–1078
  complicity, 194
  denial of, 244

Gulag deaths, 1066
gulag escapes, 904
gulag victims, 424–425
Holocaust, 459
Human Development Index, 952
indigenous peoples of Central and
    South America, 512
Iranian killings, 582
Kurd displacement, 635
Kurdish killings and
    disappearances, 636
Native American population, 740
Red Terror, 1063
Romanian arrests and deaths, 917
Rwandan genocide, 931
Sabra and Shatila massacres, 936–
    937
Sierra Leone civil war, 946
Soviet prisoners of war, 985–986
Sudanese civil war, 1007
Sudanese slave trade, 1003
Taino, 1017
Tibet, deaths in, 1027
Trail of Tears, 1043–1044, 1045
Uganda, 1053
Yugoslavs killed in World War II,
    1170
Zunghar population, 1184
*Statistics of Democide: Genocide and
Mass Murder Since 1900*
(Rummel), 277
Statutory limitations, **999–1001**
    Commission on Human Rights,
        1075
    crimes against humanity, 212, 215
    European Convention on the
        Non-Application of Statutory
        Limitations, 316–317
    torture, 1038
    war crimes, 1145–1146
    See also Time limits
Steiger, Rod, 363
Der Stellvertreter (Hochhuth), 269
Stereotyping
    anti-Semitic, 43
    group psychology, 329
    media and propaganda, 827–828,
        829
    terrorism, 1023
Sterilization. *See* Forced sterilization
Sterilization Law. *See* Law for the
    Prevention of Genetically Diseased
    Offspring (Germany)
The Sterilization of Leilani Muir
    (film), 316
Sternberg, George, 670
Sterner, Albert, *86*
Stigma, 971–972
*Stigma: Notes on the Management of
    Spoiled Identity* (Goffman), 971

Stimson, Henry, 706–707, 765
Stimson doctrine, 12
Stockholm Convention on
    Conciliation and Arbitration, 698
Stoecker, Adolf, 44
Stojiljkovic, Vlajko, 58
"Stolen Children," 103, 513, 901–902
Stolypin reforms, 629
Stone, John, 788
Stonewall Riots, *461*
Storms, Simmon P., 1177
"Strange Fruit" (song), 9
Stranka demokratske akcije (SDA),
    588
Strasser, Gregor, 401
Strasser, Julio César, 66
Strasser, Valentine, 947
Strategic Minerals Commission, 954
Strauss, Richard, 712
Straw, Jack, 809
Streep, Meryl, 363
Streicher, Julius, **1001–1002**
    anti-Semitism, 45
    crimes against humanity, 216
    editorial cartoons, 85
    incitement, 494
    propaganda, 826–827
    Der Stürmer, 247–249
Stresemann, Gustav, 400
Strict liability and superior
    responsibility, 1010
Stroop, Jurgen, *995*
Structural violence, 308–309
Structuralism. *See* Functionalism
Structure
    International Court of Justice,
        539–540
    International Criminal Tribunal
        for Rwanda, 549–550
    International Criminal Tribunal
        for the Former Yugoslavia, 557
    Special Court for Sierra Leone,
        956
Stuart, James, 1182
Studies
    Sub-Commission on Human
        Rights, 1093, 1096–1098
    United Nations sponsored, 1068–
        1069
*Study of the Problem of Discrimination
    against Indigenous Populations*
    (Cobo), 510–511
Sturmabteilung (SA), 401–403, 627–
    628
Der Stürmer, **247–249**, *248*
    anti-Semitic propaganda, 826–828
    incitement, 494
    Streicher, Julius, 1001–1002

Styron, William, 363
Suavage, Pierre, 369
Sub-Commission on the Prevention
    and Protection of Minorities. *See*
    United Nations Sub-Commission
    on Human Rights
Sub-Saharan Africa, *347*
Subianto, Prabowo, 1157
Subject jurisdiction
    International Criminal Court, 543
    International Criminal Tribunal
        for Rwanda, 548–549
    International Criminal Tribunal
        for the Former Yugoslavia, 556
    Special Court for Sierra Leone,
        958–960
Subjugation and destruction, 663–
    664
Submarine warfare, 765
Subordinates and superior
    responsibility, 1009–1015
Sudan, **1002–1009**, *1003*
    ethnic cleansing, *302*
    religious groups, 883
    Talisman Energy Corporation
        liability, 23
Sudan People's Armed Forces
    (SPAF), 1006
Sudan People's Liberation Army/
    Movement (SPLA/M), 1005–1008
Suffering and torture, 1039
Sufism, 1003–1004
Sugihara, Sempo, 897
Suharto, 273–274, *518*, 1156
Suhrawardy, Husain Shahid, 116
Suicide bombings, 162
Sukarno, 516–518
Sullam, Sara Copia, 412
Summis desiderantes (Innocent VIII),
    881
Summit of Heads of State and
    Government, 779–780
Sumner, William Graham, 968
Sun tzu, 469
Sunnis, 583
Superior orders
    Control Council Law No. 10, 202
    defense of, 234
    Eichmann, Adolf, 279, 280
    International Criminal Tribunal
        for Rwanda, 549
    International Criminal Tribunal
        for the Former Yugoslavia, 556
    London Charter, 655
    Nuremberg Trials, 769–770
    subsequent trials at Nuremberg,
        776

Treaty of Washington. *See* Treaty for the Suppression of the African Slave Trade

Treblinka
construction of, 332
gas chambers, 456
terminology, 330

Tressmann et al., 235

Trial of the Major War Criminals Before the International Military Tribunal, Nuremberg, 14, November 1945-October 1946, 266

Tribal populations. *See* Indigenous peoples

Triffterer, Otto, 893

Trigger, Bruce, 146

Triple Alliance, 104–105

Triumph of the Will (film), 356, 368

Trombley, Stephen, 367

Trotsky, Leon, 197

Truman, Harry S.
Genocide Convention, 1108
Hiroshima bombing, 442–444
Jackson, Robert, appointment of, 591

Trust funds, victim compensation, 751, 888, 889, 1041, 1132

Truth and Reconciliation Commission (Peru), 799, 800, 801, 1042, 1050

Truth and Reconciliation Commission (Sierra Leone), 953, 960, 1050–1051

Truth and Reconciliation Commission (South Africa), *1048*
amnesty, 31, 491
establishment, 51, 983, 1049
Goldstone, Richard, 416
Namibia, 724
victims, 1129
written historiography, 449

Truth commissions, **1047–1051**
amnesty and, 32
Commission for Historical Clarification (Guatemala), 420–421, 913–914, 998–999
Commission on the Truth for El Salvador, 282–285, 381–382, 737, 1050
Commission to Investigate Illegal and Clandestine Security Forces (CICIACS), 422
Mandela, Nelson, 659
National Commission of Truth and Reconciliation (Chile), 169
National Commission on the Disappeared (Argentina), 49, 64, 65, 378–380, 577
Recovery of Historical Memory (REHMI), 420–421

transitional justice, 1046, 1047
Truth and Reconciliation Commission (Peru), 799, 800, 801, 1042
Truth and Reconciliation Commission (Sierra Leone), 953, 960
written historiography, 449
See also Truth and Reconciliation Commission (South Africa)

The Truth Is a Victim in Croatia (film), 356

Tucholsky, Kurt, 943–944

Tudeh Party, 579

Tudjman, Franjo, 127, 219, **1051–1052,** 1171–1172, 1174

Tughluqs, 504

Tum, Rigoberta Menchú, 836

Ibn Tumart, 24

Tunisia, 709

Tuol Sleng Prison, *210,* 266–267

Tupac Amaru Revolutionary Movement, 799

Turkey, *633*
amnesty, 832–833
Commission on Responsibilities, 186–187
Greeks, ethnic cleansing of, 303
India, conquest of, 504
Kurds, 633–634, 634–635
Lotus case, 1117–1118
political theory, 817–818
Treaty of Lausanne, 210
Where Are My People?, response to, 358
See also Armenian genocide; Ottoman Empire; Young Turks

Turkish Military Tribunal, 1019

Turkiyya, 1003

Turkmenistan, 784

Turner, John C., 329

Turnhalle Conference, 724

Turshain, 'Abd Allahi Muhammad, 1004

Turushkas, 504–505

Tusi, Nasir al-Din, 705

Tuskegee syphilis experiment, 671, 893

Tutela Legal, 381

Tutsis
Burundi, 133–136
crimes committed by, 553
group identification, 484, 485
hate propaganda, 827, 828–829
incitement against, 495
See also Rwanda

Tutu, Desmond, 51, 659

Twa, 930

Twagiramungu, Faustin, 928

Typhus experiments, 672

"A Typology of Genocide" (Dadrian), 1123

Tyrer v. U.K., 1040

[U]

UFFRO (Famine Relief and Rehabilitation Organization), 296

Uganda, 927, **1053–1055**

Uganda National Liberation Army, 1054

Uganda People's Congress (UPC), 1054

UHU Glue advertisement, 1

Ukraine
Babi Yar, 109–111
collaboration, 182
Cossacks, 176–177
famine, 346
kulaks, 629–630
mass graves, 666–667
pogroms, 815
Russian refugees in, 1056

Ukraine famine, 996, **1055–1061**
Stalin, Joseph, 1064
testimonies, 252

Ullman, Micha, 680

Ullmann, Viktor, 710, 712, 714, 718

Ulrich Greifelt and Others, 242

Ultrasound, 350

Umar al-Bashir, Hassan, 1002, 1005, 1006

Umkhonto we Sizwe (MK), 51, 658

UNAMIR (UN Assistance Mission for Rwanda), 1091–1092

The Underground (Sobol), 269

Underinclusion, 484–485

Ung, Bunheang, 89

UNIA (Universal Negro Improvement Association), 723

UNICEF. *See* United Nations Children's Fund (UNICEF)

UNIDROIT Convention on Stolen or Illictly Exported Cultural Objects, 312

Union of Soviet Socialist Republics (USSR), **1061–1067**
Armenians, 78–80
Babi Yar, 109–111
banned art, 81
Chechens, 160, *161*
concentration camps, 198
Einsatzgruppen, 281–282
ethnic cleansing, 303
famine, 346
General Assembly intervention, 1082
gulag, 422–427, *427*

United States *continued*
    International Criminal Court,
        objections to the, 545–546
    Iraq, invasion of, 15, *1152*
    Japanese American internment,
        compensation for, 191
    Jewish refugee policy, 626, 628
    landmine use, 475
    Liber Code, 847
    linguistic genocide, 653
    Lipschis, Hans, extradition of, 735
    medical experimentation, 670–671
    mercenaries, *687*
    military tribunal plan, 591–593
    musician immigrants, 711–712
    Native American policies, 740–
        745
    Native American tribes, *742–743*
    nuclear tests, *755, 757*
    nuclear weapons, 756, 759–760
    post-emancipation, 964
    racial policies and the Genocide
        Convention, 893
    racist advertising, 2
    refugee policies, 626, 628, 923–
        924
    reparations claims, 445
    Restore Hope operation, 11
    Rosewood, Florida, 924–925
    Salem witch hunts, 881
    San Francisco conference, 1073–
        1074
    Sand Creek Massacre, 942
    slave trade, *963, 965*
    slavery, *445*
    social Darwinism, 968–969
    Somalia peacekeeping operation,
        786, 973–976, *974, 975,* 1090
    state-sponsored assassination, law
        on, 91–92
    Trail of Tears, 229, 1043–1045
    United Nations, establishment of
        the, 1068
    United Nations War Crimes
        Commission, 1104, 1105
    United States Zone Ordinance No.
        7, 773
    U.S. Army war crimes trial at
        Dachau, 772
    war on terrorism detainees, 536
    Wilhelm II, prosecution of, 185
    Wounded Knee massacre, *741,*
        1166–1168
    Yuki of Northern California,
        1177–1178

*United States Department of Army
    Field Manual,* 243

United States foreign policy, **1107–
1116**

United States Holocaust Memorial
    Council, 1160

*United States of America vs. Karl
    Brandt et al. See* Medical Case

United States v. Greifelt et al., 891–
    892

United States v. Krupp et al., 235

United States v. Ohlendorf et al., 234,
    235, 772, 774–775

United States v. Von Leeb, 234

United States v. Wilhelm von Leeb,
    1009–1010

United States Zone Ordinance No. 7,
    773

Uniting for Peace resolution, 1082,
    1085–1086

Universal Declaration of Human
    Rights, UN
    Commission on Human Rights,
        adoption of the, 1075
    domestic remedies for rights
        violations, 191
    ethnic groups' rights, 305
    General Assembly adoption, 476
    General Assembly agreement on,
        1086
    human rights violations as, 822–
        823
    international law, 569
    minorities, 694
    nationality, 275
    persecution, 797
    reparations, 884
    Roosevelt, Eleanor, 923
    as standard for human rights
        movement, 1069
    torture, freedom from, 1036

Universal jurisdiction, **1116–1123**
    amnesty, 35
    Audiencia Nacional, 808
    Convention on the Prevention and
        Punishment of Genocide, 204
    crimes against humanity, 216
    Eichmann trials, 280
    extradition, 335–336
    humanitarian law, 473
    International Criminal Court, 571
    national prosecutions, 733
    torture, 206, 1038, 1042

Universal Negro Improvement
    Association (UNIA), 723

Universe of obligation, 139

University of Bujumbura, 134

University of Minnesota, Human
    Rights Library, 278

UNPROFOR. *See* United Nations
    Protection Force (UNPROFOR)

UNRRA (United Nations Relief and
    Rehabilitation Administration),
    873

UNTAET (UN Transitional
    Administration in East Timor),
    729

UNTAG (United Nations Transition
    Assistance Group), 724–725

UNTSO (UN Truce Supervision
    Organization), 1088

Uprising (miniseries), 369

Urban II, Pope, 221

URNG (Guatemalan National
    Revolutionary Union), 419–421

Ursu, Gheorghe, 917

Uruguay, 262

*Uruguay: Never Again, and the
    Chilean Truth and Reconciliation
    Commission* (report), 1046

Ustasha, 218–220

Utilitarian genocide, **1123–1124**

Utilitarianism
    Mill, John Stuart, 817
    punishment, 846, 847

Utopian ideology, **1124–1127**

Uwilingiyimana, Agathe, 929

[V]

Vabres, Henri Donnedieu de, 645

Valerian, 178

Van den Berghe, Pierre, 980

Van der Stoel, Max, 783–784

Van Pelt, Robert Jan, 587

Van Riebeek, Jan, 976

Van Wing, R. P., 621

Vance, Cyrus, 1172

Vance-Owen peace plan, 128, 1174

Vande, Vivian, 354

Vansina, Jan, 620–621

Vardapet, Komitas, 715

Varga, Imra, *679*

Varoujan, Daniel, 811

Vasiljevic case, 237

"The Vatican and the Holocaust"
    (International Catholic-Jewish
    Historical Commission), 157–158

Velasquez Rodrigues v. Honduras,
    1038

Venice ghettos, 409–413

Vergès, Jacques, 119

Der Verlassene Raum (Biedermann),
    680

Verneuil, Henri, 360

Versailles Treaty. *See* Treaty of
    Versailles

Verwoerd, Hendrik, 50, 658, 979

Vet, Vorn, 611

Veto power, Security Council, 1086